THE
DOG GROOMER'S
MANUAL

A Definitive Guide to the Science, Practice and Art of Dog Grooming

THE DOG GROOMER'S MANUAL

A Definitive Guide to the Science, Practice and Art of Dog Grooming

Sue Gould MIfL, PGCE, LCGI

THE CROWOOD PRESS

First published in 2014 by
The Crowood Press Ltd
Ramsbury, Marlborough
Wiltshire SN8 2HR

enquiries@crowood.com

www.crowood.com

This impression 2020

British Library Cataloguing-in-Publication Data
A catalogue record for this book is available from the British Library.

ISBN 978 1 84797 590 4

Dedication
To Thelma
For teaching me the skills of my profession; for giving me the desire to learn more and the inspiration to pass on those skills and that knowledge.
Thank you.

Veterinary advisors
Glen Cousquer MRCVS
Ewan Ferguson BVM&S, DVD, MRCVS

Photographs
Glen Cousquer
Sue Gould
Michael Trafford
Simon Fane

Diagrams
Hills Animal Health
Fig. 2.10.2 Budras, McCarthy, Fricke and Richter, *Anatomy of the Dog* (2001), page 5

Frontispiece: Michael Trafford

Typeset by Jean Cussons Typesetting, Diss, Norfolk

Printed and bound in India by Parksons Graphics

Contents

Part 3: The Art of Dog Grooming

Foreword

A freelance lecturer, assessor and consultant, Sue Gould is also director of a busy dog grooming salon and groomers' training school in West Dorset. A qualified teacher and City and Guilds Assessor with over thirty-seven years' combined experience of the grooming industry and related fields, she also holds the Higher Diploma from the British Dog Groomers' Association and is a member of the Guild of Master Groomers. She has worked in grooming salons internationally and ran her own commercial salon for fifteen years before turning towards more academic areas. Her ability has been recognized by the award of a Licentiate of the City and Guilds Institute and the only City and Guilds Medal for Excellence awarded for outstanding performance to a grooming tutor and lecturer in the 200-year history of the Institute. She is passionate about passing on her knowledge and the award of the only City and Guilds Student Medal for Excellence for grooming to one of her students not only bears testimony to her qualities as a teacher but provides a satisfying symmetry to her own achievements. Together, her experience, ability and interest in teaching the science behind what most pet groomers still regard as more of an art, make her uniquely qualified to write what may well prove to be a new benchmark text for her profession.

As a veterinary dermatologist with over twenty years of specialist clinical experience, our respective areas of interest overlap considerably. Although I might just lay claim to having seen more poor-quality coats than Sue, the breadth of her experience of breeds and coat types is unlikely to be matched by many veterinary surgeons.

Invaluable emphasis has been placed on the recognition and understanding of what constitutes 'normal'. Oddly enough, more time is devoted in medical and veterinary schools to teaching this than is devoted to teaching disease as it is only through instilling the knowledge of what is normal that the abnormal can be recognized. Normal can also be a lot more complicated than is usually recognized, for most owners are only truly familiar with their own pets. A professional groomer would have to consider the differences between not only individual animals, but also different areas of the body, grooming and shampooing practices, sexual status, breed, species and even time of year before even considering the impact of health on the coat.

As with any subject that engages people on both an intellectual and emotional level, a wide variety of opinions exist on almost every grooming topic. Unanimity of opinion is rare and this is further complicated by our rapidly advancing understanding of the genetics and mechanisms behind many dermatological disorders, and the appearance of new problems in our pets, such as polyresistant bacterial infections. It's hard to keep up.

The first task, therefore, facing the author has been to separate the evidence from the anecdotes, the science from the dogma, the innovative from the over-optimistic, and then to leaven the mixture with her practical and academic experience. To this end, she has adopted a strongly structured approach which starts by leading the reader through the history of our association with and impact on the development of this popular companion animal. The inclusion of an introduction to the anatomy and physiology of the dog, as well as a guide to undertaking a thorough physical examination before grooming commences, reflects Sue's interest in promoting the science behind the assumptions we tend to make all too easily.

Drawing on her experience of working in the industry, comprehensive advice is provided regarding setting up and running a grooming practice. This acts as a useful check-list for anyone contemplating starting out, as attention is drawn to considerations such as liability insurance and relevant legislation. It is only in the third section of the book that grooming techniques are specifically addressed, by which point the reader should ideally be working from a sound knowledge base in a safe, hygienic and appropriately equipped practice and able to acquire the practical skills described.

This book should provide a valuable reference for anyone interested in or undertaking pet grooming at any level. What is particularly welcome is the emphasis placed on understanding the complexities of the body systems that the groomer will interact with, for along with the ability of a competent and confident groomer to greatly improve the quality of life for an animal, comes the power also to inflict significant harm. Sue does her profession a considerable service by drawing attention to this and sets out a framework for safe, effective practice in a profession that, as yet, remains unregulated.

Ewan Ferguson BVMS DVD MRCVS
RCVS Recognized Specialist in
Veterinary Dermatology

Introduction

This book has been conceived and written to support you faithfully at every stage of your development as a dog groomer, whether you simply aspire to care for your own dogs at home or aim to carve out a career as a professional groomer. Whatever the extent of your ambitions (and they may change with time), this book will provide you with all the information you need to help you become the best groomer that you can be.

It is not a book about traditional styling of dogs; there are other books available to serve that purpose. It is, instead, a book that reaches deep into the field of a speciality subject to give you a comprehensive understanding of everything that the professional groomer and those caring for the grooming requirements of dogs should know in order to do their job well.

There are no hard and fast rules as to how a dog should be styled, any more than there is a specific hairstyle that we are all expected to wear – the choice of style is merely down to the preferences and the requirements of the owner.

It is for you to find meaning in your grooming and this book will help you to work together with your canine subjects and their owners to create an end product that meets the expectations of the owner and the needs of the dog; perhaps most importantly, it will also teach you the safe way(s) to work so that you and the dogs you work with stay safe from injury and protected from illness and disease.

Dog grooming is immensely rewarding. It can prove to be an enormously satisfying experience for the dog-loving home groomer, encouraging the development of strong bonds between owner and pet as they engage in a (usually mutually) pleasurable activity. Grooming can also provide the commercial groomer with a rewarding career and an excellent income. This line of work can be great fun, especially if you enjoy working with dogs.

Whether your intention is to groom your own pets or to develop a career in grooming, the knowledge and principles that inform this practice are the same for everyone; you simply apply and adapt them to your own situation. There are many competent home groomers who become very skilled and go on to work commercially as professional groomers. You may be the next person to decide to go down that route so from here on you are all 'groomers' and this book is for each and every one of you.

According to the Millennium Edition of the Collins English Dictionary, the word 'groom' is defined as 'to rub down, clean and smarten (a horse, dog, etc.)' or 'to train or prepare for a particular task or occupation'. This book will help dog owners, dog grooming students, kennel staff, veterinary nurses and even professional groomers and trainers of dog groomers develop their skills, knowledge, understanding and proficiency in this field. As such, this book fulfils both definitions, for it seeks to groom groomers in the art of dog grooming.

It could be argued that, in the correct sense of the word, a 'groomer' is merely responsible for cleaning and brushing the coat, whereas it is perhaps the job of a stylist to fashion the coat. There is perhaps a certain merit in this argument but the counter-argument is that the role of both groomer and stylist is to care for the skin and the coat of, in this case, the dog. As this may include removing some of the coat in the interests of welfare or lifestyle, we can justifiably refer to everyone working within this field as 'groomers'; after all, the foundations and principles of both roles are the same!

A competent groomer can be the creator of incredible living sculptures, as well as tidy, practical ones. The groomer's raw materials are, of course, the dog and his hair coat. But how are these transformed and how does the groomer go about achieving the desired result? What else does

the groomer need to know and what is required to set up and run a grooming salon? This book aims to answer these questions and will develop your potential and ability as a dog groomer, whether you are just starting out or have been trimming dogs for some time.

Grooming is not, however, something that can be learnt in a hurry, for we are not born with the expertise to be dog groomers. It requires many months of patience, practice and hard work to develop your skills and many hours of study to build up your knowledge and understanding of the subject. The time required depends on you as an individual and varies according to the hours and opportunities you are able to invest in your training and development. This should not put you off, however. Far from it, this simply means that you can look forward to learning and developing throughout your career.

A dog groomer is far more than a trimmer of dogs. Groomers are uniquely positioned to promote the welfare of dogs in their care and, whilst grooming and styling may be fun, the groomer should not overlook or underestimate their responsibility of care for the dog's overall health and, most importantly, for the dog's largest organ: the skin. The more you learn about dogs and their welfare, the more competent you will become in recognizing the signs of illness and disease. The development of this ability can benefit the dog as an individual, but may also contribute significantly to the improved welfare of the canine species.

A well-trained groomer needs a thorough understanding of the dog as a species, allied with a good working knowledge and understanding of canine anatomy, physiology, disease control, parasitology, behaviour, psychology and the many breed-specific problems. In addition to being an art, grooming is a science, based on a systematic approach to understanding and observing the physical appearance, the nature and the behaviour of the dog.

Professional practice is about so much more than the creation of a piece of art and requires the practitioner to have a greater understanding of their wider responsibilities. The lives of many dogs have been saved by a well-informed and attentive groomer who has remained vigilant when dealing with the animals in his or her care. By contrast, there have been many dogs' lives put at risk, or even lost, by a groomer who has neglected or been unaware of their responsibilities.

The regular contact the groomer has with individual dogs (some being seen and worked with as often as every four to six weeks), coupled with the fact that these dogs are physically handled and thoroughly examined throughout each session, invariably means that the groomer will often be the first to notice when something is wrong. This book does not, therefore, shy away from developing the groomer's ability to evaluate the health of the dog and identify problems that would render a dog unfit for grooming or justify seeking veterinary attention and advice.

This book contains photographs of some of the many ailments and diseases that you may encounter and I have no doubt that you will see many more that I have not included. The intention is to show you how to understand and recognize the healthy animal and how to recognize when the dog presented for grooming is unhealthy. Some of the many problems I have included are breed-specific problems that can be attributed to the genetic make-up of a particular dog. Others reflect the onset of age-related illness or disease, whilst there are those that arise from accidental injury. Familiarizing yourself with these examples will, it is hoped, encourage you to continue learning during your career so that you can be an effective link between the owner and the veterinarian.

The information in this book is not in any way a substitute for professional veterinary advice, diagnosis or treatment. Nor is it intended to undermine any veterinary advice or beliefs. Whilst the owner is the primary carer of the dog and is responsible for the dog's day-to-day care, the veterinary surgeon will usually only perform a clinical examination of the dog once a year as part of a yearly health check and vaccination programme. By contrast, the regular physical examination undertaken by groomers provides a unique opportunity for the dog to receive a thorough 'going over'. This can allow the early identification of health problems; these can then be brought to the attention of the owner and vet. It is therefore suggested that the groomer and the veterinary professional can and should develop a good working relationship that is very much in the dog's best interests. To do this successfully, the groomer needs to be well informed and observant whilst never overestimating the extent of his or her responsibilities. Recognizing the signs of disease or a change in health status is the job of the groomer. Diagnosis is the responsibility of the veterinary surgeon.

WHY THIS MANUAL IS DIFFERENT

This manual is different in several ways and seeks to provide the learner and the teacher with a reliable and comprehensive reference source.

(i) Reliability

The dog grooming profession is unregulated and the information available in books, on the various internet websites and from training establishments is not standardized or referenced and is often contradictory. In most cases information and advice is based largely on the views, preferences and opinions of trainers or author(s) who are often self-taught. This is particularly evident within information and advice on styling and the use of tools and equipment; these are, very often, based on fashion or the personal preferences of the individual. The quality of training in any subject is determined by the experience, proficiency, knowledge base and commitment to lifelong learning (and continuing professional development) of the training provider, together with their willingness to subject their practice to critical review. Partiality and inconsistency in information can be very confusing and misleading to any student, but particularly to those who are trying to learn without the support and guidance of an experienced professional.

The biggest problem I have encountered during my very long career (first as an apprentice, then as a commercial groomer and now as a trainer and lecturer in City and Guild courses on dog grooming) is the content of the information available on the internet, circulating in chat forums and written in grooming manuals and articles. Whilst there are several good sources, there are multitudes of others that provide unreliable and inconsistent information that cannot be referenced to a dependable source and where the content is incorrect or misleading. In some cases the information and advice on offer can lead to disastrous results and expensive mistakes, and in a few instances it can even be dangerous or may result in animal neglect or cruelty.

Much of the content 'out there' is therefore unreliable and of poor quality. Sadly, the learner trying to progress without help and guidance will be unaware of this distinction and may struggle to distinguish between the good and the bad. Vacancies for apprenticeships in a professional grooming salon working with qualified supervisors are few and far between. Training providers have limited spaces and fees for complete courses are often out of reach for most. So, for many (perhaps even the majority) of learners, the only option available is to self-teach without help or guidance. Groomers who find themselves having to self-teach need to guard against this risk and actively seek out reliable sources of information and quality support and training.

This book is designed to address this very problem. It draws on my thirty-five years' experience, both as a professional groomer and as a college lecturer. It is not, however, based on my personal opinion(s) and the material has been painstakingly researched and carefully written in collaboration with an experienced veterinary professional. Wherever possible, it has been referenced to sources of reliable information from research journals, papers and books, thus going some way towards standardizing the information required by groomers. Many of the sources of information are freely available to you all for further reading.

It is hoped that this work will also go

some way towards promoting minimum standards within the grooming industry. Raising standards and the promotion of good practice can lead to the professionalization of this line of work. Indeed, if pursued, this could lead to dog groomers becoming increasingly respected for their professionalism.

(ii) Scope, breadth and depth

Another related problem is the lack of breadth and depth in the information provided.

There are many grooming books and websites available but they are limited in their introduction to the profession and the purpose of grooming; they are, instead, generally aimed at the end product – the traditional styling of the dog. The dogs shown are usually very different from the average pet dog. In the majority of cases, styling is often unrealistic for the average pet leading an average lifestyle and living in the average home.

Such books are of little help to the inexperienced groomer when faced with the practical, day-to-day reality of grooming the multitude of pet dogs (of all shapes, sizes, ages and condition) that are brought into salons every day. Each dog is an individual. There are over 400 million of them in the world and there are no two the same – even from the same litter! You cannot know which of these 400 million are going to come knocking at your salon door and, when they do, they won't be anything like the dog in the book.

There are several reasons for this:

◆ the dog is unlikely to be a beautifully coated show dog like the one in the photograph (*show dogs hardly ever find their way into a pet grooming salon because the dog and his coat are far too valuable*);
◆ the dog will not always look like the breed he is supposed to represent (*if you do not know your breeds, this will be even more confusing!*);
◆ the dog may not even be the breed he is purported to be (*accidents do happen!*);
◆ the dog will rarely be in immaculate condition (*which is why they are in your salon – the owner is unable or unwilling to groom the dog*);
◆ the dog probably will not have a correct coat type (*they may have a damaged or incorrect coat for showing, which is why they are lucky enough to be someone's pet*);
◆ very often the owner does not want the dog to be trimmed in the recognized breed haircut (*it may be unsuitable for their lifestyle or they love the breed but do not like the hairstyle*); and
◆ the dog on your grooming table is not a drawing or a model and … he probably will be unwilling to stand still for starters!

Until you know what you are doing and how to do it, it does not matter how hard you try – it is unlikely that you will be able to achieve the picture in the book. For many, this can make the process of learning to groom extremely difficult and very disheartening, particularly if you are trying to teach yourself. But do not lose heart!

As a learner, you do not need another book to show you what a particular breed of dog looks like when it is trimmed because there are plenty already available. What is far more useful to you is a book that advises you on how to develop your skills and use your tools to the point where you can create whatever coat style you, or the owner, desire.

This book will also help you to set up your working environment and to select those tools that best suit your individual requirements. It will then explain how to use them to style any dog into any shape you want, whether the dog is a Cocker Spaniel in elegant show trim or the same dog in a clipped down, pet trim.

A specific set of clippers or a particular comb may suit one person but not another. My observations, as a teacher, have taught me that a vast selection of equipment is needed to suit the needs, preferences and requirements of a group of students. Students are not all the same physically. They arrive at all ages, in all shapes and sizes, and possess different strengths and weaknesses. Some work with their left hand, some with their right; some have physical restrictions and some master the same skills as others but by using a different technique and, sometimes, by using different tools. Some will perfect their skills more quickly than others, some need to discover a learning environment or teaching style that meets and respects their personal learning needs and preferences; even gender can make a difference. My chosen tools are those I have found suit me best and the same will apply to you. The most expensive or the most popular do not always represent the best investment for you personally.

This book explains the differences and options available to you when buying your tools and equipment so that you can buy wisely and appropriately. Having carefully chosen your tools, we discuss and learn how to use them safely. The importance of this last point cannot be overstated as most accidents in the grooming room are caused by misuse of equipment and ignorance of the dangers involved.

WHO WILL BENEFIT FROM READING THIS BOOK?

Anyone and everyone with an interest in grooming their own pets or wanting to be a professional groomer!

The book is aimed at all levels and will appeal to:

◆ dog owners seeking to learn how to groom their own pets;
◆ trainee, student and apprentice groomers;
◆ grooming professionals undertaking further training/continuing professional development; and
◆ teachers and lecturers responsible for teaching animal care and dog grooming.

The reader, regardless of their ambitions, will be encouraged to think carefully and methodically about the requirements of grooming and why they are necessary. Comprehensive background information will be presented to explain why and how we do what we do. Fundamental principles and core skills can then be further developed according to the reader's stage of learning.

Wherever possible, this book has been referenced to documented research and dependable sources of information to provide a responsible and reliable manual for students working towards City and Guilds Professional Groomer status and the British Dog

Groomers (BDGA) Higher Diploma, and students aiming to achieve grooming units as part of National Diploma qualifications in Animal Management and other related subjects, together with other relevant National Vocational Qualifications (NVQs) and Scottish Vocational Qualifications (SVQs). It will be particularly useful for students who do not have access to training courses, part-time students on short courses or those who are unable to complete all of their training under supervision.

This guide could also be used in conjunction with a distance learning course in grooming. It is not, however, a substitute for practical training under qualified supervision. The author recommends that all such students start by attending a practical introductory course at the very least, or gain work experience in a good grooming salon.

HOW TO USE THIS BOOK

This book has been divided into three sections.

Part 1: The Science of Dog Grooming

The first part of this book covers the core scientific units that underpin the subject of dog grooming and provide a factual foundation to sound, well-reasoned practice. I would like to stress at this point that it is not possible to deal comprehensively with each of these subjects, for each has become a scientific discipline in its own right, extending far beyond the realms of this book. This text is, however, designed with the groomer and grooming practice very much in mind and should provide the reader with an appreciation and good working understanding of the dog. You are therefore encouraged to read this section and refer to the further reading list and other sources for more information.

The topics covered in Part 1 are all significant in their own way and will help to develop an awareness of their role in (and relevance to) the health and welfare of the dog. An understanding of the animal you are working with prepares you physically and mentally to handle the dog safely, competently and with confidence, throughout the grooming process. The anatomy of the dog, relevant canine health issues and a description of the pre-grooming assessment are all found in this section, providing essential, practical, useful information for groomers, tutors and dog owners alike.

Disease control and preventive health care is vital in the maintenance of the health and well-being of the dogs in your care and the wider dog population. Recognizing possible clinical signs and understanding the importance of vaccination and biosecurity help the groomer manage the risk posed by infectious as well as zoonotic diseases.

An awareness and understanding of the behaviour and psychology of the dog are also important, and these topics are covered in Chapter 9, Handling and Restraining the Dog, and will help you to read their body language and communicate with your canine subject and them with you, on a level that you both understand. This is essential if you are to develop a better idea of how to keep yourself and others safe and how to recognize signs of stress, anxiety and frustration.

Part 2: The Practice of Dog Grooming

The second part of the book looks in detail at the practice of dog grooming and the fundamentals of the grooming process. Starting with Health and Safety, it also covers legislation, the working environment, salon design and organization, grooming tools and equipment. This section can be read in its entirety or dipped into for specific information, using the contents or index.

The principles of *First Aid* must be understood. Wherever possible, regular training should be undertaken in order to refresh and further develop the skills necessary to allow the groomer to deal with all minor and, indeed, major injuries and thereby save and preserve life. This is an important and much overlooked subject for anyone working with, or owning, an animal. Accidents happen and they are, by their very nature, unplanned and unpredictable. Understanding the extent of your responsibilities and preparing yourself for such eventualities can save time and, occasionally, lives.

Finally, we review the options available when purchasing your equipment. Selecting the right tools and equipment to perform the task is often a difficult and daunting choice for the new groomer as there is such a wide range available. It is important that you understand the choices of equipment that are available to you so that you buy wisely. This section examines those choices and shows you how to use your tools so that you are prepared for the vast array of coat types, coat variations and coat conditions that make up the groomer's work load.

Part 3: The Art of Dog Grooming

This is the fun section!

The art of grooming is about styling or artistry. An artist skilled in the techniques of an art or craft is often called a 'craftsman', and a craftsman who excels in his chosen craft can earn the accolade 'master craftsman'. As you become more experienced and proficient in dog grooming, you learn how to blend science and artistry together. Your talent, hard work and effort may thus, in time, lead you to become a master groomer.

As with all art forms, the raw materials have to be correctly prepared. Your raw materials are the dog and his coat.

This section takes you through a step-by-step guide to help you to become the best that you can be, whatever your level of learning. Preparation, grooming out, bathing and drying procedures are covered in detail. This section also covers clipping, scissoring and styling skills and interpreting the dynamics of trimming styles.

As already stated, this is not a book on traditional grooming styles. It is not based on my views and it does not have a 'this is how you must do it' approach. The end product depends very much on the owner's wishes, the age and condition of the dog and the dog's lifestyle. There is not therefore a 'correct style' for any one dog; departures are possible from traditional pedigree breed styling. What I aim to show you is how to use your tools so you can create your own images or generate a style that meets the requirements of the owner and the dog. Traditional styling as required for City and Guilds exams will, however, be covered.

It is my intention to make good use

of my experience as an instructor to help you to recognize what you personally need to do to develop your skills, knowledge and understanding. I aim to help you to learn and to encourage you to continue learning and investing in yourself, to help you make educated decisions, and to become confident in the knowledge that you have done your best to learn your trade well. Above all, I hope you enjoy the learning experience and find the career that you are embarking upon as rewarding as I have.

And never forget that grooming should be a pleasurable experience for both the dog and the groomer. It is a time when bonding and communication takes place through touch, by feel, through the establishment of mutual trust and respect and by learning to work together. We are privileged that the dog participates and shares in this pleasure.

Other learning aids and features

Photographs are used extensively to provide additional visual information in order to illustrate key learning points. Each image has been carefully chosen to complement the text and carries a caption that provides any necessary or additional explanations. In addition to photographs, you will find the following learning aids and features:

(i) Alert boxes and Note boxes

Alert boxes are highlighted in pink and are used to emphasize key health and safety issues. In some cases they are used to draw attention to a recognized hazard and the need for a risk assessment.

Example:

Note boxes are highlighted in blue and are used to extract from the main text useful information and points that may need special consideration. They are also used as reminders and for checklists.

Example:

> **NOTE**
>
> *To groom your pet at home you need:*
>
> - *plenty of natural light;*
> - *somewhere safe and suitable to groom your pet;*
> - *a table or workbench to stand him on with access to an electric power supply;*
> - *something to bath him in with access to a water supply and drainage;*
> - *dog shampoo and possibly a conditioner;*
> - *towels;*
> - *a hair-dryer;*
> - *grooming equipment for your particular dog;*
> - *either a grooming tunic or old clothing to protect you; and*
> - *a plastic bag or dustbin for the hair.*

(ii) References and further reading

To help you expand your knowledge, references and suggestions for further reading are included at the end of each chapter.

(iii) Breed profiling

Breed profiling is covered in the first part of the book and will be of enormous benefit to you. Not only will profiling give you an in-depth knowledge of the breeds of dog you need to familiarize yourself with, it will also alert you to health issues and problems, temperament issues and anomalies specific to that breed. As a groomer these differences do have a bearing on your work and they also give you the knowledge to advise owners on a suitable breed for their lifestyle and their budget.

(iv) Glossaries

There are two glossaries in this book. The first is a glossary of breed-specific terminology, which is useful when you are learning about breed profiling. It can be found at the end of Chapter 1. The second is a short glossary on veterinary terminology to help you with the descriptive vocabulary used in anatomical and physiological science. It can be found at the end of Chapter 2.

Notes for students using this book for revision

As a student of dog grooming, it is possible that you may be largely self-taught and revising for exams without guidance. Many of you are adults who are possibly embarking on a career change and for some it may be part-time study, juggling around a busy family life. As your school days, with focused learning and few commitments, drift further into the distant past, examinations become more daunting and revision more difficult. This is quite often because, as you progress in years, your life becomes busier and you have more responsibilities. Consequently, your brain has more information to process every day and focusing on a new subject is often difficult.

> **ALERT**
>
> *Dogs are not ornaments. They are intelligent animals, who in many cases have not received correct training or adequate handling by their owners.*
>
> *Every dog being groomed will have a first visit to a groomer or be groomed for the first time by their owner. This can be a daunting or even traumatic experience for the animal, particularly if the dog is several years old when first introduced to the brush and comb. Any traumatic experience can cause a dog to become defensive.*
>
> *Dogs are rarely – if ever – sedated for grooming. Grooming any dog is therefore a risky business and throughout this book there is a strong emphasis on Health and Safety. Learning to respect the dog, your tools and the Health and Safety warnings from this page onward will help you to remain vigilant and to keep you and the dog safe.*

Grooming books may help you to see a style, but you will need to vary your reading to improve your knowledge and understanding of the dog, its mentality and its needs.

Here are a few points to help you study:

1. Start at the beginning and don't skip backwards and forwards through the book. You may miss something and get yourself confused or scare yourself because you don't understand something in its correct context.
2. Do not overload yourself with facts. Pace yourself and read only a few pages at a time. You may need to read the same few pages a second time. Be comfortable with your understanding of the information in those pages before you proceed further. Reading too much will only confuse you and start you worrying.
3. Use a pen or pencil to underline any important words in a sentence. This cuts down the amount of words you need to remember.

   For example: the sentence 'Cleaning is a key factor in ensuring the health and safety of the people and the animals in the grooming environment and promoting the business image to the customers' contains twenty-nine words. Underlining the important words – 'Cleaning is a key factor in ensuring the Health and Safety of the people and the animals in the grooming environment and promoting the business image to the customers' reduces it to fourteen words.

   You will remember this as: *'cleaning ensures Health and Safety of people, animals, the environment and promotes business image'.*

   In a long chapter with a lot of facts or details, highlighting only the bits you need to remember will help you to focus on them.
4. If the context of what you are reading contains lots of facts, rewrite them as bullet points so that you only have a short list to remember.

   For example, under the heading 'Cleaning', the following bullet points could be listed:
   ◆ Health and Safety of people.
   ◆ Health and Safety of dogs.
   ◆ Promotes image.
5. Familiarize yourself with the Glossary early on in your reading and consult it as a matter of habit when you are unclear about the meaning of certain terms. In this way the book will make more sense as you read through it and every time you return to it.

   The 'Glossary of Canine Terms' has generously been made available by the Kennel Club of Great Britain. It is less important in your early stages of learning, but you will become more familiar with these terms as you study your breed profiles. When doing profiles, make sure you understand the terminology for each breed – particularly coat colouring and physical traits.

You then drip feed yourself the information that you need to know and remember as you progress through the breeds.

6. Stop calling it an exam and refer to it as a test! Every moment of your conscious life you are performing tests. If you are asked any question and have to give an answer, someone is testing your knowledge. If someone asks you to do something – no matter how trivial – they are testing your ability. You perform these tests all day, every day without a second thought. Exam is a scary word. Change the word and stop scaring yourself silly!

7. When you start to revise, spend a few moments creating a mental image of your grooming area in your head. Prepare and organize your workspace, ensuring everything is in its place and ready for work. It can be very helpful to visualize the grooming process, picturing yourself working smoothly and confidently through the task.

When you sit your test paper, picture yourself in the same grooming area doing the tasks in the question. The question will be less daunting and your answer more thorough. Conjuring up such positive images is a valuable part of your preparation and helps you to stay focused and confident throughout your test.

8. Remember that Health and Safety is of paramount importance in all situations. Health and Safety issues are assessed in your test(s) and, once you are qualified, continue to influence your practice in many ways. Extract the Health and Safety issues from the text in each chapter and make sure you understand their importance.

9. By learning to profile a particular breed of dog and creating a mental picture of it in your head, you will not only be able to answer questions about the breed, you will also be able to answer questions about the grooming and trimming requirements of that breed. It will help you to identify breed traits in cross-bred dogs and, even without seeing the dog, it will provide you with a clearer picture of what size the dog will be, the type of coat you can expect to be working with and what trimming style will suit the dog. You will also be more aware of any heritable factors that require consideration, including temperament and behavioural issues.

I sincerely hope this book meets and surpasses all your expectations and makes a significant and lasting contribution to canine welfare, the advancement of good grooming practice and the development of the grooming profession.

Part 1
The Science of Dog Grooming

The practice of grooming is informed by a sound and rigorous body of knowledge; this scientific body of knowledge is constantly evolving but can, broadly speaking, be considered reliable. The competent and conscientious groomer needs to be conversant with this body of knowledge in order to play what can be a large and very important role, both in maintaining the health and welfare of the dog, and in educating the owner. It is this knowledge, the so-called science of dog grooming, that is presented over the next five chapters.

During the grooming process, the groomer is able to make a thorough assessment of the dog. This assessment can be particularly and surprisingly thorough, for the grooming process often takes several hours. Furthermore, the groomer can expect to see each dog on a regular basis throughout the dog's life, and he or she will see many transformations as the dog develops from puppyhood to adulthood and through into old age. The structure and physical appearance of the coat will change as the dog ages and the groomer will witness these changes. The groomer may also see other changes, however, and will need to remain attentive, for these could signify the early stages of illness or disease.

Most coat changes are to be expected and are quite normal; others are less obvious and may be abnormal. Some are associated with breed-specific problems that may be present from birth or develop over time, and the groomer needs to be aware of the breeds in which this is likely to occur. The signs of illness and diseases are often very subtle in the early stages of development and, depending on the age and health status of the dog, early effects can be more or less problematic. Disease is mentioned here because the groomer can be expected to encounter signs of disease and therefore can alert the owner and the vet to any such changes early, and also because the groomer has a role to play in the prevention of disease. Bio-security, and protecting others from the spread of illness and disease, is very much a responsibility of the grooming professional.

In many cases the groomer is totally responsible for all of the dog's grooming needs and the dog is therefore dependent on the knowledge of the groomer to identify not only when their health and welfare are being compromised but when medical help is required. Knowing when to refer the dog to a vet for assessment (and knowing when to refuse a dog for grooming) is a responsibility that should not be taken lightly. The groomer must always remain aware of the significance, extent and limitations of their responsibilities and, whilst they are in a position to recognize that things are not 'right', they cannot be expected to be familiar with the wide range of clinical signs of disease. They should, however, feel able to advise that an owner seek veterinary advice where something appears abnormal. Early recognition will assist the veterinary professional to make an early diagnosis and can improve the dog's chances of recovery.

The welfare of the dog as an individual and the survival of the dog as a species depend to a large extent on how we, as their promoters and providers, manage them. The groomer will be responsible for the well-being of possibly thousands of dogs during their career and the expertise of the conscientious professional can have a significant impact, not only on the general health of the dog, but also on disease and parasite control and on breed development. The significance of the groomer's practical experience working with and handling each dog, together with their knowledge of behaviour, physiology (how the body functions) and nutritional needs, can be a real asset to the future of the domestic dog, the owner and the veterinary professional. This experience is not acquired easily and, if you are new to the subject of canine care, it may take several years for you to develop your knowledge base.

Part 1 contains the latest scientific knowledge about the dog, and will help you to acquire a good working understanding of this creature. We need to understand the dog's history and make-up. The following chapters will therefore introduce you to the dog's evolutionary history, anatomy and physiology, and some of the more common diseases and ailments to which dogs can fall victim.

Each of the chapters in Part 1 has a bearing on the work of the groomer. So let's begin by taking a brief look at where dogs came from, how they developed and how they have found their place in modern society.

1 The History of the Dog

A general knowledge of the ancestry of the dog and how he has evolved will help you to keep yourself safe and to work within your limitations. Grooming requires a compromise between dog and groomer. To make that compromise you need to have an understanding of the mentality of the dog, a respect for the work that the dog was bred to perform and an appreciation of how long the breed has been a domestic pet rather than a working companion.

So, why do we need to groom dogs anyway? The short answer is because they can no longer do it for themselves. The long answer is that we, as their custodians and guardians, have over the last few hundred years developed our canine friends to suit our lifestyle(s), tastes, expectations and requirements. Consequently, their current existence and physical appearance means that, in many cases, we have taken away their ability to attend to their own grooming needs. The following chapter explains how this has happened.

1.1 EVOLUTION

The evolution of the dog from his prehistoric ancestors to the domesticated pet that shares our lives and our homes, and now sits curled up on the chair beside you, has taken the dog on a very long journey. Along the way, his appearance has evolved according to the environment, the ecological niche that he has occupied and the selective pressures placed upon dogs at any given point in history.

There are several ways in which the evolution of a species can be traced and mapped out. The existing records for many species, including the dog, are incomplete and we can only speculate about the missing links. There appear to be two problematic questions; the first centres around the identity of the dog's ancestors, the second around how and when the dog came to be domesticated.

The dog's ancestors

It remains unclear whether the dog as we know it today is descended from the wolf or whether it is descended from a very close relative of the wolf. We do know, however, that they both share the same ancestry and that they, along with coyotes, jackals, raccoons and foxes, all evolved over the same period of time.

We also know that, genetically speaking, all dogs, despite their different appearances, are very similar. Up until very recently, if a canine DNA sample was taken for analysis, without prior knowledge of who the donor was, the analyst could have identified the animal as a dog but would have been unable to determine the dog's breed. Recent advances in canine genomic research, however, have established that the range of shape and form seen in the modern domestic dog is due to man's selection of a small number of specific mutant genes (Ratliff, 2012). These genes can now be recognized, opening up the way to precise DNA fingerprinting for dogs.

The dog's family tree stretches back some 30,000 years. The following account highlights some of the key points and findings that have emerged in science's attempt to unravel the origins of the domestic dog. These findings have come to us through studies in a wide range of fields, including palaeontology, archaeology and molecular biology. Whilst fossil remains of the ancestors of the dog are scarce, there have been a number of finds that have allowed palaeontologists to study and piece together the evolution of the dog's prehistoric ancestors.

The first truly terrestrial vertebrates were amniotes and evolved in the late Carboniferous period (approximately 360 million years ago). These animals had developed internal membranes within their eggs; this allowed eggs to be laid on land, rather than in water, as was the case for amphibians. The mammalian lineage became distinct from the reptilian lineage about 320 million years ago. The first true mammals appeared during the early Jurassic period (200 million years ago). There are many gaps in the fossil records of these fish-eating creatures but, around 62 to 50 million years ago (around the time of the dinosaurs), a group of primitive carnivorous mammals called the Miacidae was evolving.

The *Miacoidea* family consisted of a diverse group of mammals, many of whom were small and lived in trees. Fossilized remains show that these mammals had dog-like cutting teeth and were plantigrade, meaning that they walked on the palms or soles of their feet. They were long, slim-bodied creatures and their carnassial teeth indicate that they were predatory animals, who probably looked a little bit like a polecat. It was these creatures that evolved into the carnivores of today.

Miacoidea existed for approximately 32 million years, and over a period of time divided into two families of carnivores: *Viverravidae* and *Miacidae*. This evolutionary process took place gradually during the Palaeocene and late Eocene periods (40 to 60 million years ago). One break-away branch, called *Viveravines*, is known to be the oldest ancestor of the cat. The other group, *Miacidae*, evolved to become the ancestors of all the existing Canid species, such as the wolf, bear, coyote, weasel and raccoon.

Following the Feliform–Caniform split some 42 million years ago, the *Miacidae* gave rise to *Hesperocyon* (meaning 'Western Dog'), the oldest member of the *Canidae* family, dated at approximately 37 million years ago. The remains of this early canine ancestor were discovered in the American states of Wyoming, Nebraska, South Dakota and Colorado, as well as in Western Canada. Interestingly, evidence demonstrates that *Canidae* developed entirely in North America and did not migrate to Europe until much later in their development.

Hesperocyon were digitigrade, which means they walked on their digits (toes), with the long legs and body of a creature built for speed. This indicates that they had moved from their treetop lodgings and become land animals. Remarkably, the Lundehund, a native breed of dog from Norway, is still able to climb trees and rock faces with the aid of several additional toes on each foot.

In due course – about 23 million years ago – *Hesperocyon* developed into *Leptocyon*, thought to be the most recent ancestor of *Canidae*, although there is some controversy over the eventual fate of this mammal. Some accounts say that *Leptocyon* evolved into *Tomarctus*, while others say that *Leptocyon* and *Tomarctus* were breakaway branches of *Hesperocyon*. Regardless, *Tomarctus* gave rise to the dominant group of Canids that developed in North America and were destined to be the primary ancestor of the wolf and the dog.

By the Pleistocene period (about a million to half a million years ago) a variety of larger animals were evolving and we know that they became the foundation stock of wolves, dogs, coyotes, jackals and foxes. It is estimated that the dog, as we know him, probably evolved somewhere around 10,000 years ago and it is generally accepted that the small wolf found on the plains of India is his closest living relative.

The domestication of the dog

Much speculation surrounds the timing, history and circumstances of the dog's domestication.

The oldest authenticated dog skull was found in Belgium and has been dated at almost 30,000BC (Germonpré et al, 2009), which is more than twice as old as the next oldest dog remains, found in Russia and Germany and dated at 14,000 years old. The skeleton of a medium sized Spitz-like dog with a tail that curled over its back was found in Denmark and is estimated to be from 8000BC. Skeletons have also been found in Iraq (6750BC), Jericho (6500BC) and India (3500BC), and historians have numerous accounts from China and India (4,000 years ago), whilst some 3,000 years ago Babylonian civilizations documented the value of their hunting dogs. Whilst Tomarctus may have evolved into the Canidae family in North America, the earliest dogs found there date from 1500BC, suggesting that, rather than develop there, the modern dog found his way back there from Europe.

So why and how did the dog become man's best friend? Evidence for the domestication of the dog has become available through archaeological research but the reasons proposed for it happening are purely speculative. The earliest records point to domestication some 30,000 years ago. More extensive records are available showing that domestication was under way some 7,000 to 12,000 years ago, around the end of the last Ice Age. The first record of a dog buried together with a human dates from 12,000 years ago in Israel (Davis and Valla, 1978). Certainly by the time the Neolithic

hunter reached Northern Europe, he had either domesticated the dog or, more probably, the dog had chosen to become domesticated! Excavations of Stone Age settlements have revealed evidence of humans and Spitz-type dogs, resembling the Husky, living in close proximity. The cat, by contrast, resisted domestication until many thousands of years later.

Dogs, like other canids, are opportunists by nature and some reports suggest that it was the dog's visiting of human settlements to scavenge for food that eventually led to the building of mutual trust between man and dog. This is quite likely as the early dog would have benefited from not having to rely on hunting for his own food; humans, in turn, would have the advantage of an early warning system as the dogs would detect the arrival of unwanted visitors – animal or human. Other theories have been proposed to explain the dog's domestication, including the hand-rearing of orphaned wolf cubs and the natural selection of wolves with a lower/shorter flight distance. In the latter case, it is suggested that the least fearful animals developed a competitive advantage and were encouraged to stay around human living areas. Man's original reasons for encouraging this behaviour are lost in time but may have included the recognition that the wolf could usefully render services such as guarding.

This mutual tolerance and acceptance of each other's presence was

Fig. 1.1.1 Shepherd dogs herding and guarding goats as they drink from a mountain stream in the High Atlas of Morocco. In such areas local people still follow their animals nomadically in search of seasonal grazing, with shepherd and dog spending many months living and working together.

probably the next step along the path towards domestication. Because of the wolf's respect for hierarchical social structures and responsiveness to positive and negative stimuli (reward and punishment), it is easy to understand how the human easily came to dominate this sociable animal. Throughout history there have been countless recordings of working relationships where dogs have been trained to work alongside man (*see* Fig. 1.1.1). It is easy to understand how this happens, but the emotional bond between the dog and the human is far more complex to comprehend.

Dogs are surprisingly like us, which is probably why we get on so well. Dogs like to live in groups but retain their individual personalities, as do we. They work well together in teams and are good at learning their place within a social group, as are we, mostly. They nurture and expect respect from their young, as do we. They learn from each other, play together and seek approval from their peers, as do we. They appreciate close bodily contact, as do we. It is perhaps these attributes that explain why, of all the species that have evolved during man's time on earth, it is the dog that has stayed by our side and moved with us from encampments to mud huts to high-rise buildings. Just like us, the dog is a highly adaptable opportunist and, when his work becomes unfashionable, he can change professions (*see* Fig. 1.1.2).

Over the course of history the dog has developed to suit the environment in which his ally, the human hunter-gatherer, lived and the demands placed upon him by his chosen master.

In the wild, left to his own devices, the early dog would reproduce naturally. The ability to attract a mate, reproduce and successfully raise young is a prerequisite for the survival of one's genes. Competitive advantages can arise in many ways and reflect how well an individual is adapted to its environment. This selection process ensures that genetic variations that confer a disadvantage (or are no advantage) are not encouraged to survive, thereby ensuring that the wild type remains the same. Man, however, has introduced selection pressures that are not natural, as the following account explains.

The domesticated dog's early envi-ronment was a cave, a prehistoric hut or village. In his early days (and even to the present day in some remote areas) the dog would have earned his living by scavenging around the village dumps, thus keeping the encampment clean of waste and vermin. Size mattered: if he was too small, he wouldn't be able to defend himself and he would carry less fat reserves to help him survive leaner times. If he was too large, he would need too much food to sustain him.

The coat type and colour would probably have remained very similar to that of his wild relatives, the Wild Dog we know today. Coat length and density would have been determined by climatic conditions and the environment in which the dog lived, very much as it is in the wild dogs of the present. It would have been a waterproof double coat that would moult and thin out in the warmer weather and be removed by the dog rolling or dragging himself along thorn bushes. In winter it would thicken up again to provide him with protection from the cold. It is unlikely that it was long in length as it would catch and trap him in brambles or undergrowth and hinder him when he needed to fight or flee.

He would probably have had well developed digging skills and the sharpness that we recognize in terriers and vermin hunters. Dogs would hunt to feed themselves and their young, fight to defend themselves, but they were also playful and this may have been what most captured the interest of man.

Whilst it was probably the playful-

Fig. 1.1.2 No longer used extensively for herding sheep, the exceptional trainability of the Border Collie has given rise to new employment. In emergency situations Search and Rescue dogs (SARDA) and their handlers are delivered by helicopter, gaining valuable time in the search for casualties. This also demonstrates the immense trust between the dog and the human.

ness of pups, family groups and indeed all ages that encouraged a friendship to develop between man and dog, it was the dog's survival skills that encouraged man to exploit the dog as a companion. Early man recognized that the dog was an asset. Before the days of the shotgun, hunting would have been difficult and dangerous, and the willingness and ability of the dog to hunt down and kill prey was very useful to man. The attentiveness of the dog made him a good defender and the mutual liking for bodily contact provided both with warmth and comfort.

It wasn't until about 8000BC, several thousand years after Neolithic man began the relationship, that selective breeding for a purpose got under way. This ultimately led to the development of the dog breeds that we see today. And so the skills, natural attributes and desired characteristics of the dog were thus developed. One of the oldest recognized types was the Greyhound, a dog of exceptional speed with very good eyesight. The speed and hunting ability of the Greyhound were widely known and the dog was traded worldwide and bred with many other types to produce other 'sight hounds', such as the Borzoi, Pharaoh Hound and Wolfhound. The Whippet is a recently developed breed but his roots were quite possibly with the Greyhound. The advent of the gun led to shooting becoming a sport, providing a job for slower hunting dogs such as Pointers and Retrievers (*see* Fig. 1.1.3).

The dog's many and various attributes have been appreciated by human societies the world over. In several countries the dog has been given religious significance and it is believed that they accompany their masters into the afterlife. Some dogs were highly prized and presented as gifts, whilst others who showed special traits were traded as commodities.

The many attributes of the dog have ensured his consistent employment, an employment that has taken many forms (*see* Fig. 1.1.4). Throughout history he has served as a guard dog, defending flocks of sheep (*see* Fig. 1.1.5) against wolves or bears, and protecting his family from intruders. He has kept the home free of vermin, served as a hunting companion and has provided several sources of entertainment. He has often been the breadwinner, bringing home the supper – and in some cases he has been the supper.

He has worked hard but life is changing and, as life and society change, the dog, true to his nature, has adapted to these changes (*see* Fig. 1.1.6). During the last few hundred years selective breeding for fashion began in earnest and the dog evolved into the variety of breeds that we see today. Did we recognize that, if we no longer needed him to work for us, we would lose a very dear friend, a comrade and a companion? Perhaps we did. Did we subconsciously decide that the loss would be too great so it was up to us to create a new niche for him? Perhaps we did.

And did the dog mind? Apparently not. Shortened legs, long fluffy coats, pinched up faces and variations in size from miniature to giant haven't deterred him. He has simply changed identity or profession. He learnt how to amuse us by performing tricks, dancing to music, jumping hurdles and running through tunnels, and he adapted to comfy laps, cosy chairs and nestling by the fireside as if he had never known any different. His new role is that of our

Fig. 1.1.3   The invention of the gun meant employment for the slower hunting dogs, and Pointers and Retrievers (Labradors) came into their own.

Fig.1.1.4   Newfoundlands are large, powerfully built and excellent swimmers, and are still employed as Sea Rescue Dogs. This dog has literally just come from swimming in a lake and you can see how his coat has repelled all the water and the dog is already almost dry.

Fig. 1.1.5   Spot the dogs! High in the French Alps and the Pyrenees, the Pyrenean Mountain Dog lives with his flock and protects them from predators. Even today he is widely used and is eminently suited to this role.

Fig. 1.1.6   Search and Rescue Dogs (SARDA) are used by Mountain Rescue teams to help find casualties lost in the hills. In some cases, especially following avalanches, Border Collies can help locate casualties under the snow, demonstrating that herding abilities are just one of the breed's assets.

muse and he's enjoying every minute. That said, we should recognize that this has sometimes come at a cost, for the welfare of certain breeds has not been respected.

So how did we manage to develop so many variations in the dog?

The development of the modern dog

The development of particular physical breed traits is down to growth patterns: at birth, all puppies look very similar and it is only as they grow that they actually develop structural differences. The timing of the growth patterns differs immensely and it is the body's natural programming of this timing that gives each breed its characteristics. If, for example, the timing of the leg growth is slowed dramatically, the dog, at maturity, will have shorter legs than another dog of a different breed at the same age. Similarly, if the growth rate of the nasal bones is accelerated, the dog will mature with a longer foreface. Thus, when nasal bone growth is extended, the dog will have what we describe as a 'good length of foreface', as in the Afghan Hound. If, by contrast, the growth of the nasal bones is slowed dramatically, the dog will have a very much shorter foreface, as in the Pekingese, which, by the time maturity is reached, has not grown any length of nose at all. We selected our dogs and bred them to other dogs with similar traits (and similar growth patterns) and by keeping the puppies with the desired traits to breed on, we selectively bred dogs to suit our requirements and whims.

Where this subject gets really interesting is how this selective breeding – particularly concerning the foreface – changed the setting and the placement of the dog's eyes. This of course affects the dog's view of his environment (see Chapter 2.8) and determines whether he has peripheral vision (meaning his field of sight is more to the side of him) or central vision (meaning he can see straight ahead). The sight hounds actually earned their name through the shape of their noses. The elongation of the nasal bones on the Greyhound pulled the eyes to the front of the skull, helping him to see straight ahead and stare out into the distance as he focuses

for movement. The position of his eyes determines what and where he can see, and this in turn determines the work he can excel at.

Although it is unlikely that early owners of dogs would have known much about the underlying biological mechanisms governing growth and development, they did recognize that some dogs were more useful for some occupations than others and, by continuing to breed the same types of dog with each other, they could produce animals with certain characteristics that met their requirements and suited their needs. Mankind has exploited the dog's generous nature and has moulded and remoulded the dog in response to the expectations of man's practices and desires; it is man therefore who is responsible for the diversity we see within the canine species today.

1.2   THE TAXONOMY AND PHYLOGENY OF THE DOG (SCIENTIFIC NAMING)

Taxonomy is the biological classification of organisms based on phenotype (the organism's appearance and constitution based on both its genes and the environment). This allows organisms to be divided and classified into groups of similar structure and with similar characteristics.

The sequence of events giving rise to the life forms we see around us today is called evolution and can be mapped out to produce an ancestral, or phylogenetic, tree for each species. *Phylogenetics* is a field of biology that studies the evolutionary relationships between different groups of organisms. It classifies organisms according to their evolutionary relationships by analysing their genomes. This modern classification system has been made possible by advances in molecular biology (the study of live molecules) and has confirmed some of the relationships suggested by earlier taxonomic classification systems that relied on physical (phenotypic) characteristics, whilst casting doubt over others.

In essence, two individuals may look like they are related but it is only by analysing their DNA that their common parentage or ancestry can be proved or

disproved. It is best to point out here that there is considerable argument and speculation against the recognized theory of the evolution of the dog.

In the absence of proven evidence, for the purpose of scientific identification the domestic dog is called *Canis lupus familiaris* and the official classification of the dog is as follows:

Kingdom: *Animalia*
The name given to a group of motile multicellular eukaryotic (cells with a nucleus) organisms, meaning that they are made up of collections of nucleated cells that are able to move around, if only at certain life stages. They are also characterized by heterotrophy that means they generally digest food in an internal chamber.

Phylum: *Chordata*
The name given to vertebrate animals and some invertebrate animals that all possess a notochord and a dorsal neural tube at some point in their lives. It is this dorsal neural tube in fish and other vertebrates that develops into the spinal cord.

Subphylum: *Vertebrata*
Vertebrata are chordates with backbones and spinal columns.

Class: *Mammalia*
Mammals are warm-blooded vertebrates that give birth to live young and feed them from mammary glands.

Humans and dogs are both mammals. The whale also comes under the category of mammal for it was once a land animal with legs. Like other mammals, the whale gives birth to live young and nourishes them with food from its milk glands.

Order: *Carnivora*
Carnivores hunt and kill their food. They possess large canine teeth and sharp molars for tearing and eating flesh. They are also characterized by the presence of strong sharp claws with never fewer than four toes on each foot. Dogs, cats, bears, badgers, weasels and seals are all members of this order.

Suborder: *Caniformia*
Caniformia are dog-like carnivores and include the *canidae* (dogs and

foxes), *mephitidae* (skunks and badgers), *mustelidae* (weasels), *procyonidae* (raccoons), *ursidae* (bears) and *pinnipedia* (the superfamily of seals, walruses and sea lions). Most species are simply coloured, and characterized by non-chambered or partially chambered auditory bullae (middle ear) and non-retractable claws. The dog is therefore more closely related to the bear, badger and seal than to the cat!

Family: *Canidae*

Canidae are carnivorous (meat eating) and omnivorous (meat and vegetable eating) animals that include foxes, dingoes, wolves, jackals and coyotes. Canids are all *fissipeds*. This means that they possess separate toes and non-retractile claws. The *canidae* family is divided into tribes including the wolf-like and dog-like members of the caninae tribe and the fox-like members of the vulpinae tribe.

Genus: *Canis*

The *canis* genus contains between seven and ten living species, including dogs, wolves, coyotes and jackals. It does not include foxes. True foxes, including the red fox (*Vulpes vulpes*), are grouped together in the genus *Vulpes*.

Species: *Canis lupus*

Wolves, dingoes and domestic dogs are classified as subspecies of the Eurasian grey wolf and can, in theory, interbreed.

Subspecies: *Canis lupus familiaris*

The canid that our ancestors knew and chose to call 'wolf' is, we believe, the Eurasian grey wolf. Its scientific name is *Canis lupus lupus* to distinguish it from other wolf subspecies, such as the Iranian wolf (*Canis lupus pallipes*), the Arabian wolf (*Canis lupus arabs*) or the Tibetan wolf (*Canis lupus chanco*), which are probably more similar to the variety of wolf that was ancestral to the modern dog (*Canis lupus familiaris*).

References

Bininda-Edmonds, O.R.P. and Gittleman, J.L. (2002). Are pinnipeds functionally different from fissiped carnivores? The importance of phylogenetic comparative analyses. *Evolution*, 54 (3), 1011–23.

Davis, S.J.M. and Valla, F.R. (1978). Evidence for domestication of the dog 12,000 years ago in the Natufian of Israel. *Nature*, 276, 608–10.

Germonpré, M., Sablin, M.V., Stevens, R.E., Hedges, R.E.M., Hofreiter, M., Stiller, M. and Després, V.R. (2009). Fossil dogs and wolves from Palaeolithic sites in Belgium, the Ukraine and Russia: osteometry, ancient DNA and stable isotopes. *Journal of Archaeological Science*, 36 (2), 473–90.

Pemberton, N. (2012). Hounding Holmes: Arthur Conan Doyle, bloodhounds and sleuthing in the late Victorian imagination. *Journal of Victorian Culture*, 17 (4), 454–67.

Ratliff, E. (2012). Mix match morph: How to build a dog. *National Geographic*, 221, (2), 34–53.

Vila, C., Savolainen, P., Maldonado, J.E., Rice, J.E. and Honeycutt, R.L. (1997). Multiple and ancient origins of the domestic dog. *Science*, 276, (5319), 1687–9.

Available from: http://web.archive.org/web/20070926223204/http://www.idir.net/~wolf2dog/wayne1.htm

Wang, X., Tedford, R.H. and Taylor, B.E. (1999). Phylogenetic systematics of the Borophaginae (Carnivora: Canidae). *Bulletin of the American Museum of Natural History*, 243, 1–391.

Suggested further reading

Baratay, E. (2003). *Et l'homme créa l'animal*. Paris: Odile Jacob.

Coppinger, R. and L. (2004). *Dogs*. London, UK: Crosskeys Select Books.

Creel, S. and Creel N.M. (2002). *The African wild dog: behaviour, ecology and conservation*. Princeton, New Jersey, USA: Princeton University Press.

Kemp, T.S. (2005). *The origins and evolution of mammals*. Oxford: Oxford University Press.

Lorenze, K. (1954). *Man meets dog*. Boston, USA: Houghton Mifflin Company.

Wang, X. and Tedford, R.H. (2010). *Dogs, their fossil relatives and evolutionary history*. New York: Columbia University Press.

Wayne. R.K. (1993). *Molecular evolution of the dog family*. London, UK: Zoological Society of London.

1.3 BREED STANDARDIZATION AND THE GROUPING OF BREEDS

It is not really clear when the classification of breeds and varieties was first established, nor when the required standards for each were determined. Records suggest that selective dog breeding began about 2000BC, and by Christian times toy lap dogs – often miniaturized breeds – were becoming popular. About 600BC the Ancient Greeks and the Romans were hunting boar and lions, a line of work for which the swift and relatively light sighthound types were unsuited. It is suggested that man's recognition of the need for a very different type of dog led to the development of a mastiff-type dog, called a Molossus. The Molossus was bred as two different breed lines with different natural traits. One type was used for hunting, the other for guarding livestock against wolves. The bravery of the hunting dogs was tested and vaunted in large public arenas, where they were pitched against other dogs, wolves, gladiators and lions for baiting and fighting. Their descendants became the forebears of many of the stockier breeds we know today, including the Bull Terrier and the Mastiff. The guarding dogs were similar to the Rottweiler and not only did they guard the stock on the hillsides, they escorted the Romans on their march through Europe, herding and safeguarding the animals that would feed the troops en route. When the stock was eaten, there was no need to keep the dogs, so they would often be discarded and left to breed with local populations, contributing to the development of breeds such as the Great Dane.

According to Roman culture, dogs fell into three categories, namely herding dogs, hunting dogs and house dogs. The Romans had thus identified certain desirable traits that characterized the dogs of each category; these were transmitted genetically and could be preserved (and potentially refined) by a selective breeding programme: breeding for type was therefore well under way.

Spaniels are mentioned in Ireland in laws written in AD17 and were divided into two types: land hunting and water hunting. It was the water hunting and retrieving dogs, which included

On the face of it you may well want to argue that it is not necessary for groomers to learn about breed standards because most of the dogs that you will be trimming are pets rather than show dogs so they will be trimmed differently.

Whilst this argument may be plausible, researching breed standards provides you with valuable information so that you can be confident knowing:

i. *What the dog is supposed to look like so you can style it correctly when you are required to do so.*

ii. *The morphological shape of the breed and the problems that it presents, such as long backs and flattened faces.*

iii. *Any breed-specific health issues that you need to look out for.*

iv. *The purpose for which the dog was developed reflects the temperament that you need to deal with.*

v. *The timeline that the breed has been a pet breed rather than a working breed may affect temperament or handling issues.*

vi. *The size of the dog and the weight that you need to manage.*

vii. *The geographical location that the dog was developed to inhabit reflects coat type and density.*

viii. *Geographical relocation reflects the behaviour of the coat.*

ix. *Whether the coat type is likely to be difficult for the owners to manage.*

x. *How long it is going to take you to groom the dog.*

xi. *What you are going to do with the dog, i.e. just bath it or trim and style it.*

xii. *What your options are for grooming and styling the dog, i.e. stripping, clipping or scissoring the coat.*

xiii. *Any risks that you may be exposed to when grooming a particular dog or breed.*

xiv. *How much you should charge the owner for the work involved.*

A Kennel Club Glossary and an illustration of the points of the dog are included at the end of the chapter to help you to understand breed profiles and standards.

Poodles and Portuguese Water Dogs, that were the first breeds to be trimmed. They were developed to have long waterproof coats that would be oiled to keep the dog warmer and waterproof in the water. The thick coats did their job but they were heavy, so the dogs were trimmed in a style resembling a lion: the hair was removed from the rear end and feet of the dog to facilitate swimming, while the front end was left hairy to provide protection to areas such as the throat when the dog faced his prey. Interestingly water hunting dogs have also developed webbed feet and flat foreleg bones so that their legs work better as paddles. The trimming of these breeds for fashion and showing was not, however, developed until much more recently.

Terriers developed much later and were designed to hunt and kill vermin, particularly those types that hide underground. The dogs needed to have a keen, fearless temperament and had to be able to dig quickly. The result was a small dog with a strong neck and jaw and short legs that bowed at the elbow. This, it is suggested, allowed his legs to move freely and rapidly in a rolling mechanical digging action.

In the eighteenth century Buffon separated dogs according to their ear shape, whilst Cuvier chose to do this according to the shape of the skull. By the mid-1800s dogs around the world were being exhibited against one another in competition, whilst national registers were being set up to record and preserve native 'types' or 'breeds'. For the purpose of competitions, dogs were separated into groups, allowing them to compete against others of the same 'type'.

In the world of dogs, a 'group' is defined as a collection of breeds that have certain genetically transmitted characteristics in common, although they do not necessarily look the same. The Corgi and Border Collie, for example, have both inherited genes that make herding instinctive for them; their morphology (form and structure) and appearance are, however, quite different. This common characteristic allows these breeds to be included within the pastoral group (in the UK) or herding group (in the US).

In England, somewhere around the middle of the eighteenth century, the first breed standards, or essential requirements for 'type', were established. The 'showing off' of much-prized specimens began in June 1859 with the first organized dog show attracting sixty entries, at the town hall in Newcastle-upon-Tyne. This coincided with the opening of Stud Books, which recorded not only the names of the dogs and their parentage but also (and most importantly at the time) the dog's prize winnings!

As the popularity of dog showing increased, the English Kennel Club was formed in 1873 to put an end to the confusion caused by large numbers of unidentifiable dogs named 'Bob', 'Spot' and 'Jet'. This allowed 'breed standards' to become formalized as this new central authority was able to establish and maintain an 'official' registration system and stud book.

Today, through selective breeding, we have produced over 400 different pedigree dogs worldwide. There are also many cross-breeds, where the parentage of the pup is the result of either a random mating, or an intentional, increasingly market-driven, crossing of two pedigree breeds to produce the so-called 'designer dog'. Many breeds of dog are still working, performing important and valuable work as guide dogs, rescue dogs, therapy dogs, police dogs, sniffer dogs and bomb detection dogs, as well as undertaking their more traditional roles of shepherding and guarding. Nevertheless, the role of the dog is changing from provider and protector to companion and friend.

Not only do we have dogs of all shapes and sizes, but fashion has encouraged the development of coat variations and, in some cases, even hairless dogs! Slow growth timings, some-

Fig. 1.3.1   *Selective breeding from huge Bloodhounds with dwarfism produced the short-legged Basset Hound, a dog that possesses the same phenomenal scenting skills, helped by large pendulous ears that encase the scent on the ground.*

Fig.1.3.2   *With no chance of pulling a laden sled 200 miles across the frozen Arctic today, instead Lola is preparing for a day at the beauty salon.*

times referred to as dwarfism, have also been exploited. Selective breeding of such mutations in the gene pool of the Bloodhound, for instance, has produced the Basset Hound (*see* Fig. 1.3.1), a shorter-legged version of the larger dog, but still possessing the same phenomenal scenting skills. The Standard Poodle, with his non-moulting coat and excellent hunting and retrieving skills, can now be found miniaturized, small enough, even, to sit in a teacup, his hunting skills redirected to chasing a ball around the family living room. Geographically, the dog is also different. The Saluki of the hot Moroccan desert resembles a Greyhound with very little coat but is very different from the Saluki found in the show rings of America.

Yet, despite thousands of generations of domestication, selective breeding and the countless changes to their physical characteristics and lifestyle, left to his own devices the dog that shares our home today still possesses the instinct to hunt and kill prey that satisfied his ancestor's need for food, sport and stimulation.

Fighting to the death is another matter. As with most other canids, dogs will fight to protect themselves and their young when they feel threatened, but the instinct to survive and hunt another day is so strong that they avoid unnecessary conflict wherever possible. Dog fighting is an artificial, man-made aberration that has thankfully been made illegal in most developed countries.

As groomers we should remember that the dog on the grooming table is there because we have made it impossible for him to look after his own grooming needs; whilst most dogs accept our interference and enjoy the contact, some may not welcome the process. They may even feel threatened and vulnerable – and, if they do, the family pet is more than capable of looking after himself and will do so if this becomes necessary.

Something else in this story that affects us, as groomers, concerns the coat standards set for the various breeds and the recognized or desired presentation for each of them. The style in which the coat is presented is largely determined by fashion but it is often the coat that gives the dog his appeal and influences his image (*see* Fig. 1.3.2). It is perhaps the image that encourages the owner to buy the dog and it is our job to maintain that image.

Breed standardization has often provided the dog with a coat he can no longer groom himself. This has, arguably, given rise to the multi-million pound dog grooming and pet health care industries.

And so now, this begs the question: who is working for whom? As a groomer, you may want to ask yourself that question!

What are breed standards?

Around AD1800 breeders of dogs started to develop a list of requirements for the dogs they were producing for the workplace. By this I mean that certain dogs were needed specifically for certain jobs. Some were required to be brave enough, fast enough and aggressive enough to work in enclosed spaces or underground killing rats, mice, snakes, badgers and other vermin, whilst others needed to have exceptional herding and guarding skills so they could assist herdsmen and live out in remote areas with sheep, cattle and goats. Early breeders recognized that by selectively breeding certain characteristics into their dogs they could not only expect the dog to perform its work well, they could also exhibit their stock so that others would buy their puppies or use their stud dogs.

The rapidly growing sport of exhibiting dogs eventually meant that, in the interests of fairness, all dogs that were acknowledged as a specific breed should look the same. So breed standards were formed and they have remained pretty much the same to this day.

Breed standards serve several purposes. They are the written guidelines that describe the ideal characteristics, appearance and temperament of a pedigree dog; they ensure that the breed has developed to be fit for its purpose and they allow us to recognize dogs as a specific type or kind. Breed standards endeavour to encourage breeders of dogs to preserve the soundness of the breed. Even though many breeds are no longer expected to do the work that they were originally required to do, by following these guidelines breeders are safeguarding some breeds from extinction. Non-breeders of dogs can also relate to the breed standards. They acquire dogs because they recognize and like the image or profile of a breed and its temperament is suitable to fit into the home and their family lifestyle.

Classification of breeds

Once the breed standards were established, it became necessary to divide the dogs into groups, where all the dogs in each group did the same job. This meant that all the dogs in that group, regardless of size, shape or colour, would have the same attributes. They would essentially be good at skills such as hunting, tracking, herding or guarding.

Every country has its own group classifications according to the role that the breeds have in that particular country. Currently the Kennel Club of Great Britain has seven group classifications.

The Hound group

These are dogs that are natural hunters. They generally give the impression of aloofness and are usually good-natured. They vary in shape from the very heavy Bloodhound to the very tall Irish Wolfhound and the very short Dachshund. Coat types vary from the long silken coat of the Afghan Hound to the very fine, short coat of the Whippet. Used for centuries, hounds are divided into two sub-categories:

Sight hounds: these are fast and lithe and can run down their prey once it has been sighted. It includes dogs that are lean, with a good length of leg, such as the Saluki, the Greyhound and the Deerhound.

Scent hounds: with the exception of the Bloodhound, scent hounds generally have shorter legs, making them lower to the ground, and long, heavy, pendulous ears that drag on the ground, encasing the scent. Beagles and Basset Hounds are scent hounds that track above the ground, whereas Dachshunds work underground.

The Terrier group

The word Terrier is derived from the Latin word *terra*, meaning ground, and these dogs were bred to hunt vermin. Varying in size from the large elegant Airedale to the small Norfolk and Norwich Terriers, they are always alert and ready to react to movement. Terriers were bred to live and work outside, going to ground to drive out foxes, snakes and vermin, and in the home they were excellent at keeping rats and mice at bay. Most but not all Terriers have a coarse, harsh topcoat that can be easily cleaned with a good brushing, and that dies and moults out periodically giving the impression that the hair is breaking off at the root. Some groomers refer to this as a 'broken coat'. Other Terriers have a silkier coat that does not moult but will tear and break away easily if the dog become trapped in thorns or bracken whilst working.

The Working group

Most breeds of dog were originally kept to hunt for food and to guard the home. In our society today the need for these skills is limited, but we have harnessed these talents and used them to train dogs to do countless jobs where another pair of hands or another pair of eyes can help us in our lives. This group includes the St Bernard, one of many breeds that have been trained to work as rescue dogs; the Malamute, which will go into harness and drag sleds across the frozen Arctic; and the Newfoundland, an excellent swimmer once used to bring in fishing nets but now often used in sea rescue work. Most members of this group are large, heavily coated breeds that are keen to learn and keen to please their owners.

The Pastoral group

Breeds that work herding and guarding livestock grazing on pastureland make up this group. Although different breeds were developed to cope with different terrains and different sizes of livestock, this group is made up of breeds that demonstrate herding skills. From the short legs and very dense coat of the cattle-herding Corgi to the large corded coat of the sheep-guarding Komondor and the long dense coat of the reindeer-herding Samoyed, this group has a diverse and interesting selection of coat types, breeds and sizes to work with.

The Toy group

This group is made up of dogs that by and large have been bred to join us as companions. Small and often miniaturized, as their name suggests, they have been bred purely for our pleasure, for us to pamper and admire their beauty. Most of these dogs are related to dogs in other groups. The Yorkshire Terrier, for example, is related to the much larger, courageous Skye Terrier, which has excellent guarding skills, whilst the Pomeranian can trace his ancestry back to the sled-hauling dogs of the Arctic. Although much smaller than their ancestors, genetic traits are still often apparent and the little dogs in this group should never be underestimated, as many still have the will and the instinct to do the job that their ancestors were developed to do.

The Utility group

Perhaps surprisingly, this group, with the exception of the Bulldog, is comprised of breeds that are not native to England. The breeds do, however, have roots in either working or guarding roles. Today they are breeds that no longer work but have found their place in our homes as our companions. The Tibetan Spaniel is not needed to guard the Tibetan monasteries and the Chow Chow of China is no longer used for hunting and guarding the home. The Schipperke does not need to guard the barges in the Netherlands and Belgium, and the Poodle is now quite redundant as a retrieving gundog. Within this group there is a vast range of sizes, coat types and personalities which have been preserved for us to enjoy.

The Gundog group

When guns were invented, prey could be killed at a much greater distance and hunting on foot required a dog that would go and fetch the game, to save the hunter having to do all the work. Dogs were developed to help the hunter with his work, to flush out prey from the undergrowth and then to go and fetch it once it had met its demise. This required a dog with a good nose for scenting and an ability to freeze on the spot to locate and point to where the game was under cover. An enthusiasm for running was a necessity and a further skill was required: bringing the game back without eating it! Keen to preserve the traits of these dogs, breed numbers are vast and enthusiastic owners often take part in field trials with their dogs, as well as showing them off in beauty competitions. The group is made up mainly of medium and large dogs, and includes the Vizla from Hungary, the Large Munsterlander from Germany and a variety of Spaniels and Setters from the United Kingdom. Coat types are often silky or smooth and the dogs themselves will often be reserved and obedient.

So how can learning breed standards help the groomer?

The timeline from the days when the role of the dog was entirely functional and unsentimental to the role it plays today is very short and all dogs are still instinctively linked to their past. Knowing what to expect from each breed helps you to work within your limitations and to plan your work. You will also be able to recall a mental image of the breed when you begin your styling, so you will have an idea of how you want your completed work to look.

People acquire dogs because they like what the breed represents, but quite often the dog they choose does not meet the ideal requirements for the breed. When this happens, we, as groomers, are often faced with several challenges:

◆ we may need to modify the coat style to be manageable for the owner whilst ensuring that the dog still represents the breed image;
◆ the dog may not physically look anything like the kind it is supposed to be but the owner would

still like it to represent the breed as closely as possible;

◆ the coat type may not be quite what it is supposed to be so we may need to modify our styling methods so we can still give the dog its correct breed image; and

◆ the temperament of the dog may be an extreme representation of the breed and this may mean that grooming is difficult or almost impossible, so we may have to find alternative methods of getting the job done or perhaps consider using restraints such as muzzles.

Understanding the breed will help you to respect its temperament, and recognizing what it should look like will help you to trim it sympathetically, to make the best of the dog's good points and improve the not-so-good points. Together with plenty of trimming practice, it is the development of these skills that will make you a good groomer and will make you stand out in your work.

It is advisable to familiarize yourself with the Glossary of the terms and phrases used in breed standards, which I have included at the end of this section. It will help you to interpret correct (healthy) from incorrect (unhealthy) when you are health assessing your dogs; for example, a 'Ruby eye' (red in colour) is a cause

> *When learning your breed standards, research the following:*
>
> ◆ *the origins of the breed;*
> ◆ *the physical appearance of the breed and any faults or departures from the guidelines;*
> ◆ *where the breed was developed and what it was used for;*
> ◆ *the coat type;*
> ◆ *alternative styles and trimming methods for the coat type; and*
> ◆ *the history of any medical or inherited conditions affecting the breed.*

for concern in a Labrador Retriever but it is perfectly healthy in a Chihuahua. It will also help you to understand the differences that can apply to such points as coat colours and marking that can vary between breeds. It is very important to establish confidence in your clients and there is no better way to demonstrate knowledge and professionalism than by showing that you are familiar with their chosen breed and the effort that has been put into breeding programmes.

As an example:

◆ a Dalmatian that is white with black spot markings is called a 'black and white';
◆ a Newfoundland that is white with black markings is called a 'landseer';
◆ a Great Dane that is white with black markings is called a 'harlequin'; and
◆ a Pekingese that is white with black markings is called a 'parti-coloured'.

Whilst the differences here are not overly important to you as a groomer, they are very important when you are conversing with a client who may have spent a great deal of money to acquire a particular colour formation on their chosen breed.

Further reading

The Kennel Club's *Illustrated Guide to Breed Standards*. Fourth Edition. 2011. Ebury Publishing.

Useful websites

The Kennel Club of Great Britain: www. the-kennel-club.org.uk
The American Kennel Club: www.akc. org/breeds/index.cfm
The French Kennel Club. Société Centrale Canine: www.scc.asso.fr

---

CAUTION

An understanding of the ancestry of the dog is important because it can help you to avoid accidents.

1. *It has taken over 30,000 years for the dog to evolve but they are relatively new to domestication and many breeds still have very strong hunting and survival instincts. They still know how to protect themselves, particularly if they feel threatened and vulnerable. Keep yourself safe by respecting the breed and the task for which it was bred.*

2. *Breeds of dog bred for hunting vermin, such as terriers, need to be alert and able to respond quickly and deci-sively to movement. These breeds tend to have a less docile temperament and you need to handle them with respect, particularly if you do not know the dog.*

3. *The position of the dog's eyes determines what he can see. Avoid startling the dog and keep yourself safe by approaching and handling the dog within his field of vision. You are more likely to get bitten if you suddenly appear out of a dog's 'blind spot'.*

4. *The task for which the breed was developed and the geographical location in which it was required to work will give you an idea of what type of coat the dog will have, the behaviour of the coat, and how much work it will take to groom the coat. This is particularly important when you are grooming dogs that are bred to live in specific climates. Breeds developed to live in Arctic conditions that are now fashionable in hot climates are a good example: the natural behaviour of the coat will be challenged and you will need to groom the coat accordingly.*

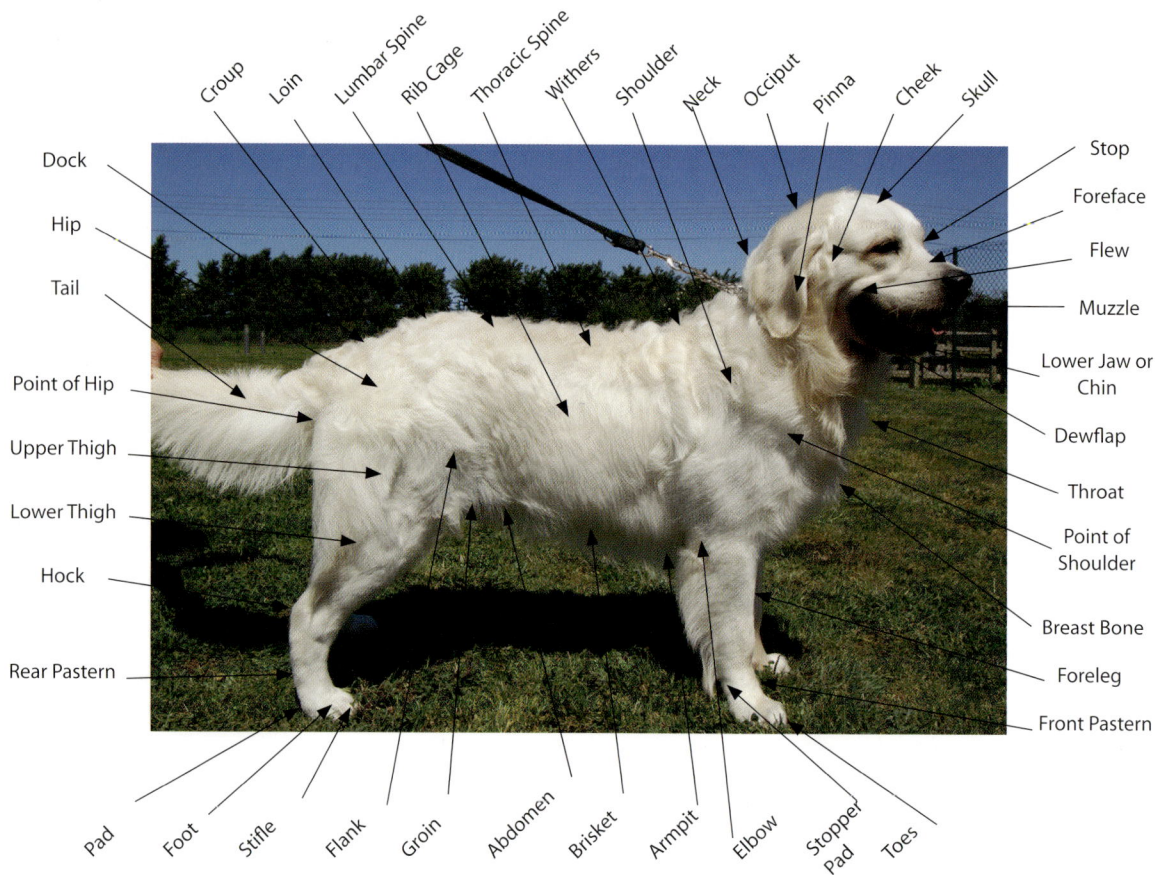

Fig. 1.3.3   *The points of the dog.*

The points of the dog labels: Croup, Loin, Lumbar Spine, Rib Cage, Thoracic Spine, Withers, Shoulder, Neck, Occiput, Pinna, Cheek, Skull, Dock, Hip, Tail, Stop, Foreface, Flew, Muzzle, Point of Hip, Upper Thigh, Lower Thigh, Hock, Lower Jaw or Chin, Dewflap, Throat, Point of Shoulder, Breast Bone, Rear Pastern, Foreleg, Front Pastern, Pad, Foot, Stifle, Flank, Groin, Abdomen, Brisket, Armpit, Elbow, Stopper Pad, Toes.

GLOSSARY OF CANINE TERMS

Copyright © The Kennel Club. Reproduced with their permission.

ABDOMEN   The body cavity between the chest and pelvis.

ACTION   Movement. The way a dog walks, trots or runs.

ALBINO   Lacking in pigmentation, usually with pink eyes.

ANGULATION   The angles formed at a joint by the meeting of bones e.g. shoulder or stifle, when dog is standing erect.

APPLE HEAD   Very domed, rounded skull (e.g. Chihuahua).

APRON   Longer hair below the neck on the chest. Frill.

BACK   Region between withers and root of tail, but in some standards may refer to region between withers and loin.

BADGER COLOUR   A mixture of white/grey/brown and black hairs varying in intensity (e.g. Bloodhound), often occurring in patches about the head and/or body on a basic white background, which is termed badger pied (e.g. Basset Griffon Vendeen).

BALANCE   Consistent whole; symmetrical; typically proportioned as a whole or as regards its separate parts; i.e. balance of head, balance of body, or balance of head and body.

BANDY LEGS   Bowed legs.

BARREL RIBS   Rounded, well-sprung ribs.

BEARD   Thick, long hair on muzzle and under-jaw (e.g. Bearded Collie).

BEAVER   Mixture of white, grey, brown and black hairs (e.g. Pomeranian).

BEEFY   Overweight, over muscled.

BELLY   Underpart of abdomen.

BELTON   Intermingling of coloured and white hairs, as blue belton, lemon, orange or liver belton (e.g. English Setter).

BITCHY   Feminine looking.

BITE   The relative position of the upper and lower front (incisor) teeth when the mouth is closed.

IRREGULAR BITE   Some or all of the incisors have erupted in abnormal fashion.

LEVEL, EVEN, PINCER OR VICE-LIKE BITE   The front teeth meet exactly edge to edge.

OVERSHOT BITE   The upper front teeth overlap and do not touch the lower front teeth when the mouth is closed. Usually a fault.

SCISSOR BITE   The upper front teeth closely overlap the lower teeth and are set square to the jaws.

UNDERSHOT BITE   The lower front teeth project beyond the upper front teeth when the mouth is closed.

REVERSE SCISSOR BITE   The upper incisors close just inside the lower.

BLANKET   Solid colour of coat on back and upper part of sides between neck and tail.

BLAZE   White stripe running up the centre of the face (e.g. Bernese Mountain Dog).

BLENHEIM Rich chestnut markings on a pearly white background (e.g. Cavalier King Charles and King Charles Spaniels).

BLOOM The sheen of a coat in prime condition.

BLOWN When the coat is moulting or casting.

BOBTAIL Naturally tailless dog or a dog with a tail docked very short. Alternative name for the Old English Sheepdog.

BODIED UP Mature, well developed.

BODY Anatomical section between fore- and hindquarters.

BODY LENGTH In some breeds, taken as the distance from point of shoulder to point of buttock; in others, taken from top of withers to set-on of tail.

BONE The thickness, quality and strength of bone as seen in the legs, especially forelegs.

BONE SHAPE Shape of bone in cross-section (forelegs). May be flat (e.g. Gordon Setter), oval (e.g. Pointer) or round (e.g. Australian Cattle Dog).

BOSSY IN SHOULDER Over-development of the shoulder muscles.

BOWED Forelegs curved outward (e.g. Pekingese).

BRACELETS Rings of hair left on the legs of some breeds in show trim (e.g. Poodle).

BREASTBONE Series of bones and cartilages that form the floor of the chest. Also known as the sternum or keel.

BREECHING
1. Hair on outside of thighs (e.g. Chow Chow).
2. Undesirable intermingling of tan amongst black hair on outside of hind legs (e.g. Manchester Terrier).

BREED STANDARD 'Blueprint' of the ideal specimen in each breed, approved by a governing body, e.g. Kennel Club, the FCI and the American Kennel Club. Following agreement at the 1981 World Congress of Kennel Clubs, the Kennel Club changed all its Breed Standards into a standard format to enable easy comparison.

BREED STANDARD (INTERIM) As above for a breed not granted Kennel Club Challenge Certificate Status.

BRINDLE Colour pattern caused by darker hairs forming bands that produce a striped effect on a background of tan, brown or yellow (e.g. Boston Terrier, Boxer, Cairn Terrier, Great Dane).

BRISKET Forepart of body below the chest, between the forelegs.

BROKEN COLOUR Self-colour broken by white or another colour.

BULL NECK Short, thick, heavy neck.

BUTTERFLY NOSE Particoloured nose; dark, spotted with flash colour (e.g. Great Dane (Harlequin), Otterhound).

CHARACTERISTICS Combination of type, appearance, disposition and behaviour.

CHEEK Fleshy part of the head below eyes and above mouth.

CHEEKY Cheeks prominently rounded; thick, protruding.

CHEST The forepart of the body enclosed by the ribs.

CHIPPENDALE FRONT Forelegs out at elbows, pasterns close, and feet turned out.

CHISELLED Clean-cut, showing bone structure of face (e.g. Fox Terrier (Smooth), Spaniel (Cocker)).

CHOPS Jowls or pendulous flesh of the lips and jaw.

CLODDY Thickset, comparatively heavy.

COARSE Lacking refinement.

COAT The hairy outer covering of the skin. Many breeds have two coats: an outer coat and an undercoat. Examples of single-coated breeds are Italian Greyhounds, Maltese and Pointers.

CORDED COAT Narrow or broad twists of felted hair like thick string or ribbon, formed by the intertwining of topcoat and discarded undercoat. Cords should always be distinctly separated from each other, down to the skin (e.g. Hungarian Puli, Komondor).

CURLY COAT A mass of thick tight curls, which traps air, protecting the dog against water and cold (e.g. Retriever (Curly Coated), Spaniel (Irish Water)).

SMOOTH COATED Short, smooth, close-lying hair (e.g. Bull Terrier, Dachshund (Smooth-Haired)).

STAND OFF COAT Long, harsh jacket with hair standing out from the body supported by a shorter, soft, dense undercoat (e.g. Keeshond).

WIRE (BROKEN) COAT Consists of a harsh and often wiry outer jacket with a softer dense undercoat (e.g. German Wirehaired Pointer, Schnauzer).

COBBY Short bodied, compact.

COLLAR Marking around the neck, usually white (e.g. Boston Terrier).

COMPACT Closely put together; not rangy. Neat.

CONDITION Health as shown by the body, coat, general appearance and deportment. Denoting overall fitness.

CONFORMATION The form and structure; physique.

CONICAL HEAD Head that is circular in section and tapers uniformly from skull to nose (e.g. Dachshund).

CONJUNCTIVA Thin membrane lining the inner surface of eyelids and reflected over eyeball.

CORKSCREW TAIL Twisted tail, not straight.

COUPLING The part of the body between the last rib and the start of the hindquarter section; the loin region.

SHORTCOUPLED/CLOSECOUPLED The situation when this distance is short and relatively strong.

LONGCOUPLED The converse to shortcoupled.

OPEN COUPLINGS Long loin and flanks insufficiently well-muscled (e.g. listed as undesirable in the Retriever (Flat Coated)).

COW-HOCKED Hock joints turned or pointed towards each other, causing the feet to turn out.

CRABBING Dog moves with body at an angle to the line of travel.

CRANK TAIL Sharply bent or angled tail (listed as a fault in Bullmastiff).

CREST
1. Upper, arched portion of the neck.
2. Hair starting at stop on head and tapering off down neck (e.g. Chinese Crested Dog).

CROUP (Rump) Part of the back from the front of the pelvis to the root of the tail.

CROWN
1. Highest part of the head.
2. Circular formations of hair at front of ridge, as on the Rhodesian Ridgeback.

CRYPTORCHID Male dog without testicles fully descended into the scrotum.

CULOTTE   Longer hair on the back of the thighs (e.g. Chow Chow, Schipperke).

DAPPLED   Mottled marking of different colours, no one predominant (e.g. Dachshund).

DAYLIGHT   The light showing underneath the body.

DEAD GRASS   Straw to bracken colour (e.g. Retriever (Chesapeake Bay)).

DENTITION   The number and arrangement of teeth. The total number of teeth is forty-two, made up of:

UPPER JAW   Six incisors, two canines (eye teeth), eight premolars and four molars.

LOWER JAW   Six incisors, two canines, eight premolars and six molars.

DEWCLAW   Fifth digit on the inside of pastern. Most breeds do not have rear dewclaws but some breeds require double rear dewclaws (e.g. Briard, Pyrenean Mountain Dog) and the Italian Spinone has single rear dewclaws.

DEWLAP   Loose, pendulous skin under the throat.

DIAMOND   Distinctive shaped marking on a Pug's forehead.

DISH-FACED   When the nasal bone is so formed that the nose is higher at the tip than at the stop; or a slight concavity of the line from the stop to the nose tip (e.g. Pointer).

DOCK   To shorten the tail.

DOGGY   Masculine looking.

DOMED   Evenly rounded in skull (e.g. King Charles Spaniel).

DOWN-FACED   The muzzle inclining downwards in an unbroken outward arch from the top of the skull to the top of the nose (e.g. Bull Terrier).

DOWN ON PASTERN   Weak or faulty pastern set at an exaggerated angle from the vertical.

DRIVE   Powerful thrusting of the hindquarters denoting sound locomotion.

DRY   The skin smooth, neither loose nor wrinkled.

DUDLEY NOSE   Nose lacking in pigment.

EAR   Consists of three parts: the external ear, the middle ear and the inner ear. Standards refer to the outer ear (ear lobe or leather). There are three main types of ear shape:

ERECT   Pricked (e.g. German Shepherd Dog, Pomeranian).

DROP   Pendent, pendulous (e.g. Retrievers; Spaniels, which include Lobular e.g. Spaniels (Cocker) and Spaniels (American Cocker)).

SEMI-DROP   Semi-pricked (e.g. Collies, Fox Terriers).

BAT EAR   Erect ear, rather broad at the base, rounded in outline at the top, and with opening directly to the front (e.g. French Bulldog).

BUTTON EAR   The ear flap folding forward. The tip lying close to the skull so as to cover the opening, and pointing toward the eye.

CROPPING   The cutting or trimming of the ear leather to make it stand erect. No dog with cropped ears is eligible to take part in any Kennel Club licensed activity in the UK.

FILBERT EAR   Rounded-off triangular shape as in a filbert nut (e.g. Bedlington Terrier).

FLYING EARS   Any characteristically drop ears or semi-prick ears that stand or 'fly'.

ROSE EAR   Small drop ear which folds over and back, thus revealing the upper part of the external ear canal (burr) (e.g. Bulldog, Whippet).

ECTROPION   Condition in which the eyelids are turned outwards.

ELBOW   The joint between the upper arm and the forearm.

ELBOWS, OUT AT   Turning out or away from body; not held close.

ELONGATED SKULL   Long, slender, tapering skull.

ENTIRE DOG   Dog with two apparently normal testicles fully descended into the scrotum.

ENTROPION   Condition in which the eyelids are turned inwards, causing irritation.

EQUILATERAL   Equal-sided triangle (e.g. Bichon Frise – Head and Skull clause).

EXPRESSION   The general appearance of all features of the head as viewed from the front.

EYE   All standards include an eye clause, which usually comments on shape, size and eye colour. Shape and size are due to the shape of the area exposed by the eye rims i.e. orbital aperture. (The eyeball is round.) Eye types include:

ALMOND EYES   Aperture basically of oval shape, bluntly pointed at both ends (e.g. English Toy Terrier, Irish Setter (unshelled almond), Akita).

GLOBULAR EYE   Round, slightly prominent, not bulging (e.g. Pug).

GOGGLE EYE   Protruding eye, listed as a fault in the Spaniel (American Cocker).

OVAL EYES   The most common eye shape. Eggshaped aperture (e.g. Saluki, Schnauzer).

ROUND EYES   Eyes set in circular-shaped apertures (e.g. Griffon Bruxellois, Weimaraner).

TRIANGULAR EYES   More angular in contour than oval eyes (e.g. Afghan Hound).

OBLIQUELY SET EYES   Eyes where the outer corners are higher in the skull than the inner corners (e.g. Japanese Spitz).

EYE COLOUR   This is due to the presence of the pigment melanin in the iris. The more melanin, the darker the eye.

CHINA EYE   Both eyes are clear blue.

MERLE EYE   Iris flecked with brown and blue.

WALL EYES   One blue and one brown eye (e.g. Great Dane (Harlequin), Old English Sheepdog).

EYEBROWS   The skin and hair above the eye covering the projecting superciliary ridges.

FALL   Long hair surrounding head (e.g. Lhasa Apso, Yorkshire Terrier).

FALL AWAY   Slope of the croup.

FALLOW   Light reddish or yellowish brown.

FEATHERING   Longer fringe of hair on ears, legs, tail or body.

FEET   These are made up of four separate toes (digits). The toes are joined by a fold of skin termed the web. Feet vary in shape:

CAT (LIKE) FOOT   Short, round, compact foot like that of a cat (e.g. Spaniel (Cocker)).

HARE FOOT   Foot with the two centre toes appreciably longer than the outside toes. The toes should be close together with arching (e.g. Borzoi hindfeet, Tibetan Spaniel).

OVAL (SPOON-SHAPED) FEET Both centre toes are slightly longer than in cat feet (e.g. Pointer, Welsh Corgi (Pembroke)).

WEBBED FEET These have well-developed webs (Newfoundland, Retriever (Chesapeake Bay)).

FLAG Feathering on tail (e.g. English Setter, Gordon Setter).

FLANGE Projecting edge of last rib (e.g. listed as a fault in Basset Hound).

FLANK Fleshy side of the body between the last rib and the front of thigh.

FLAT SIDED Central section of the ribs insufficiently rounded.

FLECKED COLOUR Coat or eye slightly ticked with another colour.

FLEWS Pendulous upper lips – chops (e.g. Bulldog).

FLOATING RIB The last (thirteenth) rib, which is attached only to the spinal column.

FLOCKED Coat of cottonwool texture (e.g. Bolognese).

FLUTING Medium furrow on skull (e.g. Spaniel (English Springer)).

FORECHEST Front part of the chest (e.g. Boxer, Miniature Pinscher).

FOREFACE Head in front of the eyes: nasal bone, nostrils and jaws.

FOREHAND Front part of the dog, including head, neck, shoulders, upper arm, legs and feet.

FOREIGN EXPRESSION Expression not typical of the breed.

FORELEG Front leg from elbow to foot.

FOREQUARTERS Front part of the dog, excluding head and neck.

FOXY EXPRESSION Sharp expression, pointed foreface and upright ears, as in head shape of a fox (e.g. Schipperke).

FRILL Long, soft or silky hair hanging down from throat and chest (e.g. Japanese Chin).

FRINGES Longer hair on ears (e.g. Papillon).

FRONT Forepart of the body as viewed head on.

FRONTAL BONE Skull bone above the eyes.

FROSTING White or grey hairs intermingled with base colour round muzzle (e.g. Belgian Shepherd Dog, Griffon Bruxellois).

FURNISHINGS Longer hair on head, legs and tail of certain breeds.

FURROW Slight indentation on the medium line from stop to occiput (e.g. Bulldog, Hungarian Vizsla).

GAIT The pattern of footsteps at various rates of speed, each pattern distinguished by a particular rhythm and footfall.

AMBLE A relaxed, easy gait in which the legs on either side move in unison or in some breeds almost, but not quite, as a pair. Often seen as the transition movement between the walk and faster gaits (e.g. Bouvier des Flandres).

EXTENDED TROT Trotting gait in which the limbs reach far forward.

FLYING (SUSPENDED) TROT A fast trotting gait in which all four feet are off the ground for a moment during each stride. Because of the long reach, the oncoming hindfeet step beyond the imprint left by the front.

GALLOP Fastest of the dog gaits, has a four-beat rhythm and often an extra period of suspension during which the body is propelled through the air with all four feet off the ground.

HACKNEY ACTION High-stepping front action with exaggerated flexion of the pasterns (e.g. Miniature Pinscher).

PACING Movement where fore- and hind legs on the same side move in parallel. Some breeds typically pace at slow speeds (e.g. Pyrenean Mountain Dog, Spaniel (English Springer)). Many breeds pace slowly as an energy-conserving measure.

ROLLING GAIT Distinctive roll from side to side when moving (e.g. Pekingese, Spaniel (Clumber), Spaniel (Sussex)).

TROT A rhythmic two-beat diagonal gait in which the feet at diagonally opposite ends of the body strike the ground together, i.e. right hind with left front and left hind with right front. Correctly, the hind feet fall immediately behind the front feet.

WALK Gaiting pattern in which three legs are in support of the body at all times, each foot lifting from the ground one at a time in regular sequence.

GAY TAIL The tail carried very high or over the dog's back. Often indicates that the tail carriage is higher than approved in the Breed Standard. Some standards do ask for tails to be carried gaily (e.g. Fox Terrier (Smooth)).

GUARD HAIRS Longer, smoother, stiffer hairs that grow through the undercoat (e.g. Alaskan Malamute).

HALOES Dark pigmentation round or over eyes (e.g. Maltese).

HARD EXPRESSION Harsh, staring expression.

HARLEQUIN Pure white background with irregular patches (black preferred but blue permitted) having the appearance of being torn (e.g. Great Dane).

HAW Third eyelid at the inner corner of the eye; more obvious in certain breeds (e.g. Spaniel (Clumber)).

HEART ROOM Deep and capacious chest.

HEIGHT Vertical measurements from the withers to the ground, usually referred to as shoulder height.

HIND LEG Leg from pelvis to foot.

HINDQUARTERS Rear part of dog from loin.

HOCKS WELL LET DOWN Hocks set low.

HOUND-MARKED Coloration composed of white, black and tan, but sometimes lemon and/or blue. The ground colour, usually white, may be marked with coloured patches on the head, back, legs and tail. The extent and the exact location of such markings, however, differ in breeds and individuals.

IRIS Flat, circular, coloured membrane within the eye. The inner boundary forms the pupil, which adjusts to control the amount of light entering the eye.

ISABELLA A fawn coloration (e.g. Dobermann, Bergamasco).

JAWS The bones forming the framework of the mouth.

JOWLS Flesh of lips and jaws.

KEEL Rounded outline of the lower chest, resembling the keel of a boat (e.g. Bloodhound, Dachshund).

KNEE JOINT Stifle joint.

KNUCKLING OVER Faulty structure of carpal (wrist) joint, allowing it to protrude when dog is standing (e.g. listed as a fault in the Basset Hound).

LANDSEER Black and white colouring (e.g. Newfoundland).

LAYBACK Angle of the shoulder blade, when viewed from the side.

LEATHER See ear (e.g. Foxhound, Poodle, Spaniel (Cocker)).

LEGGY Too long in the leg for correct balance.

LEONINE Looking like a lion (e.g. Chow Chow).

LINTY Soft texture of coat (e.g. Bedlington Terrier) or undercoat (e.g. Dandie Dinmont Terrier).

LION CLIP Style of coat presentation (e.g. Lowchen Little Lion Dog, Poodle).

LIPPY Pendulous lip or lips that do not fit tightly.

LIVER Light to dark shades of brown, always with a liver nose (e.g. Retriever (Curly Coated)), sometimes with a purplish bloom (e.g. Spaniel (Irish Water)). Also known as chocolate (e.g. Retriever (Labrador)).

LOADED SHOULDERS Excess weight in shoulder area.

LOIN Region of the body on either side of vertebral column between the last ribs and hindquarters.

LOW SET
1. Tail set below level of topline.
2. Ears set below line of correct placement for the breed.

LOZENGE MARK Term used for marking on skull of Blenheim King Charles Spaniel and Cavalier King Charles Spaniel, sometimes known as 'Blenheim spot'.

MANE Long, profuse hair on top and sides of neck and chest (e.g. Leonberger, Schipperke, Tibetan Spaniel).

MANTLE Dark-shaded portion of the coat on shoulders, back and sides (e.g. Alaskan Malamute).

MARKINGS Arrangement of coat colour, normally a lighter or darker colour as a contrast to the ground colour.

MASK Dark shading on the foreface (e.g. Boxer).

MEDIAN LINE Line or furrow in the centre of head (e.g. Mastiff, Spaniel (American Cocker)).

MELON PIPS Tan spots above eyes in black, tan and white Basenji.

MERLE Dark colour giving marbled effect within lighter coloured main coat.

MISMARKED Incorrectly marked dog.

MONORCHID A dog that has only one testicle.

MOUTH See Bite.

MOVEMENT See Gait.

MOVING CLOSE When front or hind limbs move close to each other.

MULTUM IN PARVO 'Much in little' (e.g. Pug).

MUZZLE The head in front of the eyes; foreface.

NAPE OF THE NECK Top of the neck adjacent to the base of the skull.

NECK WELL SET ON Good neckline, merging gradually with strong withers, forming a pleasing transition into topline.

OBLIQUE SHOULDERS Shoulders well laid back (e.g. English Setter).

OCCIPITAL PROTUBERANCE A prominently raised occiput characteristic of some breeds (e.g. Irish Setter).

OCCIPUT Upper, back point of skull.

OTTER TAIL Very thick towards base, gradually tapering towards rounded tip, medium length, free from feathering, but clothed thickly all round with short, dense coat, giving a rounded appearance (e.g. Retriever (Labrador)).

OUT AT ELBOW Elbows loose or turning out from the body.

OUT AT SHOULDER Shoulders loosely attached to the body, causing them to jut out, increasing width of front.

OVERREACHING Fault in the trot often caused by more angulation and drive from behind than in front, so the rear feet are forced to step to one side of the forefeet to avoid interference or clipping.

OVERSHOT See Bite.

PADDLING The front feet during movement thrown out sideways in a loose, uncontrolled manner.

PADS Tough, thickened skin on the underside of the feet.

PANTALOONS Longer, thick hair on rear of thighs (e.g. Pyrenean Mountain Dog).

PARTICOLOUR Variegated in patches of two or more colours (e.g. Spaniel (American Cocker)).

PASTERN The part of the foreleg between the wrist and the foot.

PATELLA The kneecap – a small bone at the lower end of the femur that forms part of the stifle joint.

PELVIS Girdle of bones fused together. Each half being composed of the ilium, ischium and pubis; the whole attached to the spine at the sacrum. On the lower sides are the hip-joints.

PENCILLED Type of coat lying in pencils caused by harder hair coming through softer undercoat (e.g. Dandie Dinmont Terrier).

PENCILLING Black lines on the toes (e.g. English Toy Terrier, Gordon Setter).

PEPPER AND SALT Mixture of light and dark hair (e.g. Schnauzer).

PIED Unequally proportioned patches of white and another colour.

> **HARE PIED** More tan than black and white giving a coat resembling the colour of a hare.
>
> **LEMON PIED** Mainly lemon or cream hairs mixed with white or black.
>
> **BADGER PIED** Unequally proportioned patches of black and white, tan and white, mixed together (e.g. Otterhound).

PIGEON-CHEST Chest with a short protruding breastbone.

PIGMENTATION Natural colouring of skin and other tissues.

PIN BONES Upper bony protuberances of pelvis.

PINNING Forefeet pointing in when moving.

PINTO Distinct, dark markings on light background (e.g. Akita).

PLAITING Walking or trotting crossing the front legs.

PLUME Long fringe of hair hanging from the tail (e.g. Papillon).

POINT OF BUTTOCK Rearmost projection of the upper thigh at the point of the ischium.

POINT OF SHOULDER The front of the joint where the upper arm and shoulder blade meet.

POINTS Colour on face, ears, legs and tail; usually white, black or tan (e.g. Cairn Terrier).

POUNDING Gaiting fault resultant of dog's stride being shorter in front than in the rear; forefeet strike the ground hard before the rear stride is expended.

PROFILE   Side view of the whole dog or of the head.

PROUD   Held high, usually head or tail (e.g. Poodle).

PUNISHING   Strong (e.g. Kerry Blue Terrier).

QUALITY   Excellence of type and bearing, giving close adherence to the Breed Standard; the indefinable attribute denoting refinement and nobility. Also, the absence of coarseness, giving strength to a dog and refinement to a bitch without weakness.

QUARTERS   The upper portion of the hindquarters – the pelvic and thigh regions.

QUEEN ANNE FRONT (CHIPPENDALE FRONT)   Forelegs bowed and out at elbows, pasterns close and feet turned out.

RACY   Giving an impression of speed, without loss of substance.

RANGY   Dog of long, thin build, often lacking maturity.

REACH   Distance covered in a forward stride.

REFINED   Elegant.

RIBBED UP   Ribs extended well back.

RIDGE   Streak of hair growing in reverse direction to main coat (e.g. Rhodesian Ridgeback).

RING TAIL   Long tail, all or part of which curves in a circular fashion (e.g. Afghan Hound).

ROACH BACK   Convex curvature of the back towards the loin (e.g. Bulldog).

ROAN   Fine mixture of coloured hairs alternating with white hairs (e.g. Italian Spinone).

RUBY EYE   Iris of dark red colour (e.g. Chihuahua).

RUFF   Dense, harsh hair around neck that frames face (e.g. Keeshond, Norwich Terrier).

SABLE   Commonly used description of coat colour. Definition varies with breed. Black-tipped hairs overlaid on a background of gold, silver, grey, fawn or tan basic coat (e.g. German Shepherd Dog), or each hair shaded with three or more colours (e.g. Pomeranian).

SABRE TAIL   Tail carried in a slightly curved fashion either upwards (e.g. Basset Hound) or downwards (e.g. German Shepherd Dog).

SADDLE
1. Variation in colour over back (e.g. German Shepherd Dog).
2. Area of shorter coat over back (e.g. Afghan Hound).

SCIMITAR TAIL   As sabre tail (e.g. Bloodhound, Gordon Setter).

SCREW TAIL   A naturally short tail twisted in more or less spiral formation.

SECOND THIGH   The part of the hind leg from stifle to hock.

SEDGE GOLD   Red-gold colour (e.g. Retriever (Chesapeake Bay)).

SELF-COLOUR   Whole colour except for lighter shadings.

SESAME   Even overlay of black guard hairs, usually on red coat (e.g. Japanese Shiba Inu).

SET ON
1. Placement of tail on body.
2. Position of ears on skull.

SHAWL   Longer hair around neck and shoulders (e.g. Tibetan Spaniel).

SHELLY   Weakly formed, shallow and narrow in body; lacking substance.

SHORT COUPLED   Short distance between last rib and the beginning of the hindquarters.

SHOULDER HEIGHT   Height of dog's body as measured from withers to ground.

SHOULDER JOINT   Joint between the shoulder blade (scapula) and the upper arm (humerus).

SICKLE HOCKED   Inability to extend the hock joint on the backward drive of the hind leg. Exaggerated narrow angle of hock when standing.

SICKLE TAIL   Carried out and up in a semicircle over the back (e.g. Basset Fauve de Bretagne).

SINGLE TRACKING   All footprints falling on a single line of travel. Many breeds single track at fast pace.

SKULL   Bones of the head. Breed Standards refer to that part from stop to occiput.

SKULLY   Thick and coarse through skull.

SLAB-SIDED   Flat ribs with too little spring from spinal column. 'Herring gutted'.

SLOPING SHOULDER   The shoulder blade set obliquely or 'laid back'.

SNATCHING HOCKS   A gaiting fault indicated by a quick outward snatching of the hock as it passes the supporting leg and twists the rear pastern far in beneath the body. The action causes noticeable rocking in hindquarters.

SNIPEY MUZZLE   Pointed, weak muzzle.

SNOW NOSE   Nose showing loss of pigment resulting in a pink streak on nose in winter (e.g. Siberian Husky).

SOCKS
1. Hair on the feet to pasterns (e.g. Chinese Crested Dog).
2. White colour on feet (e.g. Old English Sheepdog).

SOOTY   Black hairs intermingling with tan or base colour (listed as undesirable in Elkhound standard).

SOUNDNESS   A term particularly applied to movement. The normal state of mental and physical wellbeing.

SPECTACLES   Light shadings around the eyes and dark markings from outer corner of eye to ear (e.g. Keeshond).

SPITZ   Group of breeds that have wedge-shaped heads with prick ears, usually straight and rather harsh outer coats with dense undercoats, moderate turn of stifle and tails usually carried over back.

SPLAYFOOT   Flatfooted with toes spreading.

SPRING OF RIB   Degree of curvature of rib cage.

STEEL BLUE   Body colour of Yorkshire Terrier.

STERN   Tail of a sporting dog or hound.

STIFLE   The joint of the hind leg between the thigh and second thigh, equivalent to the knee.

STILTED   Characteristic gait of Chow Chow due to minimum hind angulation.

STOP   The step up from muzzle to skull; indentation between the eyes where the nasal-bone and skull meet.

STRAIGHT SHOULDER   Insufficient layback of shoulder; upright shoulder.

STRAIGHT STIFLE   Lack of angulation; straight behind.

SUBSTANCE   Correct bone, muscularity and condition.

SWAYBACK Concave curvature of the back line between the withers and the hip bones.

SYMMETRY Overall balance (e.g. Retriever (Golden)).

TAIL SET The position of the tail on the croup.

TEMPERAMENT Mixture of natural qualities and traits that produce character.

TEXTURE OF COAT Quality or feel of coat.

THICK SET Broad and solidly built.

THIGH Hindquarter from hip to stifle.

THROATINESS Excess of loose skin in the throat region.

THUMB MARKS

1. Distinctive black spot in black and tan coloured breeds on pastern (e.g. English Toy Terrier).
2. Distinctive mark on forehead (e.g. Pug).

TICKED Small areas of black flecks, or coloured hairs on a white background.

TIED AT THE ELBOWS Elbows set too close under body, thus restricting movement.

TOPKNOT Long, silky, fluffy or woolly hair on top of head (e.g. Australian Terrier, Bedlington Terrier, Poodle).

TOPLINE Outline from just behind withers to croup.

TRANCE Black line extending from occiput to twist (tail) on a Pug.

TRICOLOUR Coat of three distinct colours.

TUCK UP Upward curve of underline of body (e.g. Hungarian Vizsla).

TURN UP Upturned under-jaw (e.g. Griffon Bruxellois).

TWIST TAIL (e.g. Pug).

TYPE Characteristic qualities distinguishing a breed.

UNDERCOAT Dense, soft coat concealed by longer topcoat.

UNDERLINE The shape found under dog from brisket to flank.

UPPER ARM The foreleg between the shoulder and elbow joints.

UPRIGHT SHOULDER Minimum layback of shoulder.

VARMINTY Game and spirited, usually applied to Terriers.

VEILED COAT Fine, wispy long hair (e.g. Chinese Crested Dog).

WEAVING MOVEMENT Feet crossing over, plaiting when moving.

WEDGINESS Lacking chiselling.

WEEDY Light bone structure, lacking substance.

WELL-LAID SHOULDERS Optimum shoulder angulation.

WELL-SPRUNG RIBS Ribs springing out from spinal column, giving correct shape.

WHEATEN Pale yellow or fawn colour.

WHEEL BACK Back line excessively roached.

WHIP TAIL Relatively long, thin, pointed tail, carried stiffly out in line with back (e.g. Greyhound).

WITHERS Highest point of body immediately behind neck; this is the top of the shoulder blades, the point from which height is measured.

WRINKLE CREASE Furrow or ridge of skin (e.g. Basenji).

WRY MOUTH Lower jaw does not line up with upper jaw, i.e. twisted to one side.

2 Anatomy and Physiology

This section is important because you, the groomer, need to know how the dog is put together, how he functions and how this knowledge and understanding can inform good grooming practice.

The groomer is very often the first person to identify when the dog is developing some form(s) of illness or becoming unstable, either clinically (i.e. in terms of a clinical problem) or mechanically (in terms of a mechanical problem, arising from a biomechanical failure).

A groomer's familiarity with the anatomy and physiology of the dog not only facilitates correct handling, lifting and manoeuvring of limbs and joints, it also allows the groomer to visualize the shape that styling will create.

As a groomer, it is essential that you have a practical working knowledge of the anatomy (structure) and physiology (how it works) of the dog because without this knowledge you will not understand how the dog is put together and functions and you will struggle to understand what makes your actions right or wrong and how you can go about improving your work.

To handle the dog competently you need to be aware of how the joints bend, which way they bend, their range of movement and how you can mishandle and damage them. This helps you to work with dogs without causing them pain or discomfort, or doing any further damage to diseased and injured joints. This knowledge is essential if you are to gain the trust and cooperation of the dogs that you are working with.

Every day, when working, you can expect to encounter a wide range of abnormalities and health problems, including anatomical changes, heritable conditions, skin diseases, parasites, sores, cuts and abrasions. It is essential that you familiarize yourself with these conditions and learn to recognize them in order to then deal with them appropriately. The grooming and health assessment process means that the groomer is very often the first person to identify when the dog is developing some form of illness or abnormality. This ability to recognize a change or an abnormality should always be built on a good understanding of what is normal, both anatomically and physiologically. The groomer's regular hands-on physical and visual examination of the dog allows them to pick up on many changes that are often overlooked by the owner.

We have already identified that the dog is a mammal, which means that, along with all mammals, they have a backbone, are warm-blooded, are covered in hair and suckle their young. Along with most other mammals, dogs are also placental, feeding their unborn puppies through a placenta. Their dentition places them in the Order *Carnivora*, together with cats, wolves and foxes.

Other mammals have certain common features that allow them to be grouped together within different Orders (divisions); thus the goat and the cow are even-toed ungulates because they have two hooves, allowing them to be classed as *Artiodactyla*. Anatomy and physiology are interrelated subjects, relating form with function. All mammals need the same essential organs to survive and on the whole most mammals function in a very similar way (the whale is an obvious exception); as we are also mammals, it should be reasonably easy for you to remember the essentials.

The following pages are intended to provide you with a basic understanding of the anatomy and physiology of the dog. As with all sciences there is a certain amount of terminology to be learnt. This terminology allows the subject to be discussed with everybody understanding what is being referred to; communication is made easier if all concerned are speaking the same language and agree on the meaning of words. A glossary is therefore provided at the end of the chapter to help you.

2.1 THE SKELETON

A good understanding of anatomy, of anatomical differences and of how the bones and joints work is necessary as the grooming process requires you to manoeuvre the dog for access. Some breeds are recognized as potential sufferers of hereditary joint conditions that will affect your work, whilst older patients may have reduced mobility and joint pain. An awareness of the challenges that you will have to deal with will help you complete your work without causing pain, discomfort or damage to the dog.

The skeleton (*see* Fig. 2.1.1) is a light flexible structure that is made up of bones and is designed to support the weight of the body and protect the internal organs. The dog is made up of 319 to 321 bones. Some dogs, such as the German Shepherd Dog, have extra long tails, which accounts for the extra bones.

Bones are formed from cells containing a combination of collagen fibres, a cementing substance and a number of other chemical compounds. The chemical change that occurs during the formation of bone is called ossification. It is a dynamic process with bone being laid down continuously to replace that which is reabsorbed. Bones are thus constantly remodelling themselves, allowing everyday damage to be

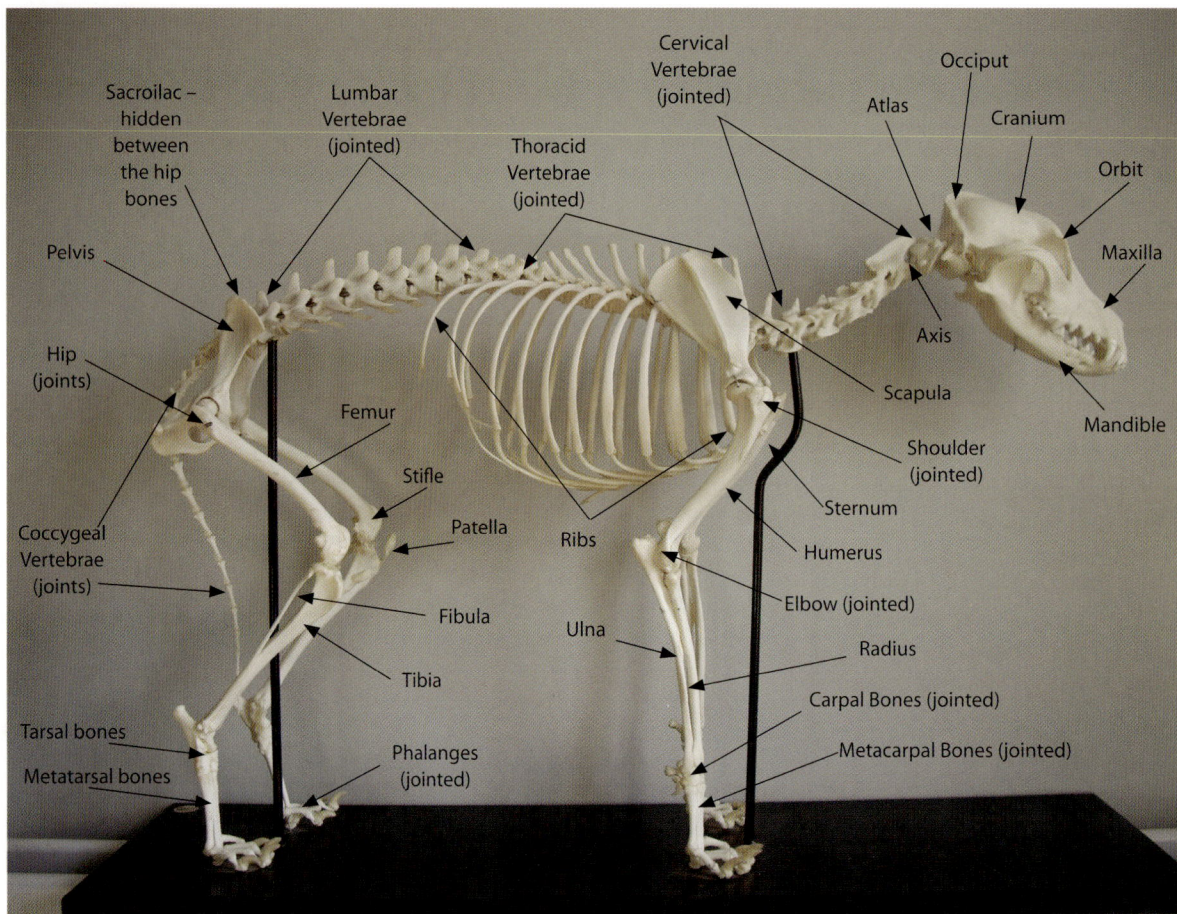

Fig. 2.1.1   The skeleton.

repaired and the body's calcium levels balanced.

In young growing puppies areas of ossification become established within a cartilage model (framework). The primary centre of ossification becomes established in the middle of each bone, with secondary centres establishing themselves at either end. It is the secondary centres of ossification that allow bones to continue growing after birth; these areas are termed growth plates.

Simply put, the developing skeleton begins as cartilage, which gradually transforms into bone by the time the skeleton reaches maturity. Once this has happened, the cartilage begins to break down and eventually disappears. At maturity the cartilaginous models are fully mineralized and the growth plates closed; no further growth is possible following this closure. In young growing puppies the bones are still mineralizing and, although strong, can bend significantly and sometimes

break. When this happens the break is often referred to as a 'greenstick fracture' (because they can bend and break without snapping, like a young branch). Allowing young puppies to jump from heights (grooming tables) or to slip and fall (in the bath) are possibly the most common causes of this type of injury in the grooming room.

The skeleton is basically divided into two sections. There is a straight bit known as the *axial skeleton*, which starts at the head and runs down the length of the spine, taking in the ribcage and finishing at the end of the tail. Then there is the *appendicular skeleton*, which consists of the bits hanging from the axial skeleton – i.e. the legs!

Bones are not designed to bend, of course. The bending is facilitated by joints at key locations that are themselves operated by muscles and tendons. Some bones are straight, like the femur – the long thigh bone running down your upper leg. These act as levers to raise and lower the limbs.

Short bones, such as the carpal (wrist) and tarsal (ankle) bones that bridge the gap between the dog's lower leg and his feet make possible these joints' extensive range of movement (*see* Fig. 2.1.2). Then there are irregular-shaped bones, like the vertebrae of the spinal column and the pelvic bones, which are individually shaped to fit together. And finally, there are flat bones like the patella (knee cap), which are embedded within tendons (*see* Figs 2.1.3 and 2.1.4).

The bones of the skeleton cannot operate themselves. The mobility of the skeleton is made possible by the movement of the bits where the bones meet – the joints – and by the muscles that attach, and transmit forces, to the bones via tendons.

The spine

The spine is made up of thirty-three ring-like bones (vertebrae) linked together to form the spinal column, an

Fig. 2.1.2 Short bones like the carpal bones are used as bridges to fill in the gaps between lots of moving bits.

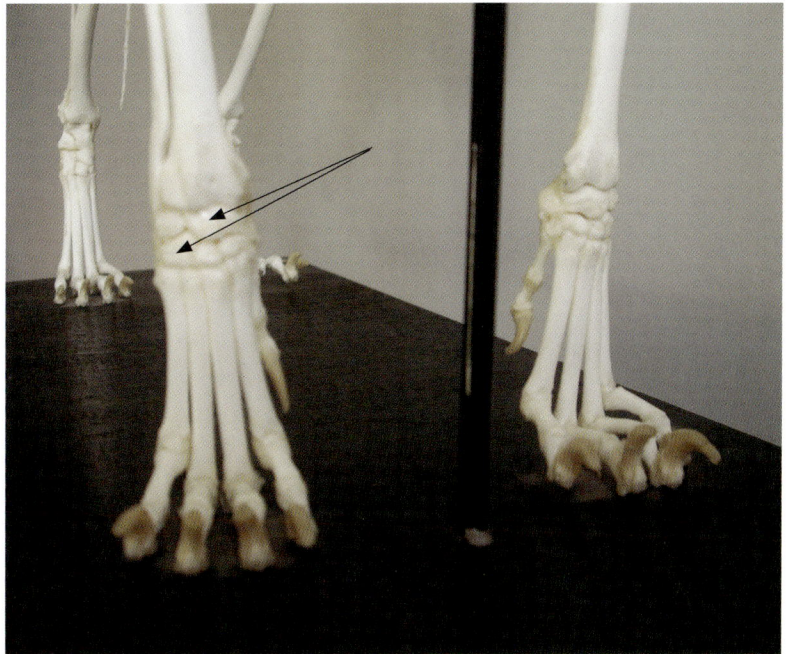

Fig. 2.1.3 The patella or kneecap is embedded within a tendon that stretches with the bending of the knee joint. This tendon normally holds the patella in place within the femoral groove.

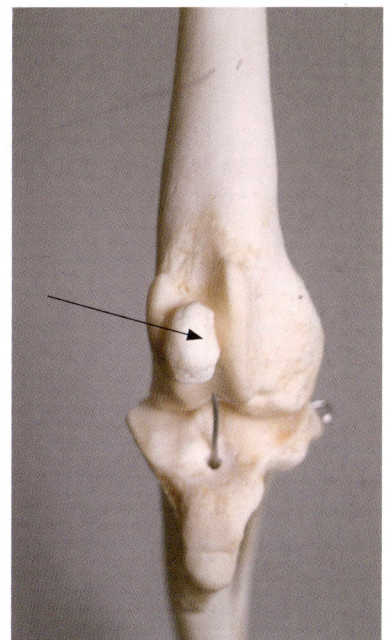

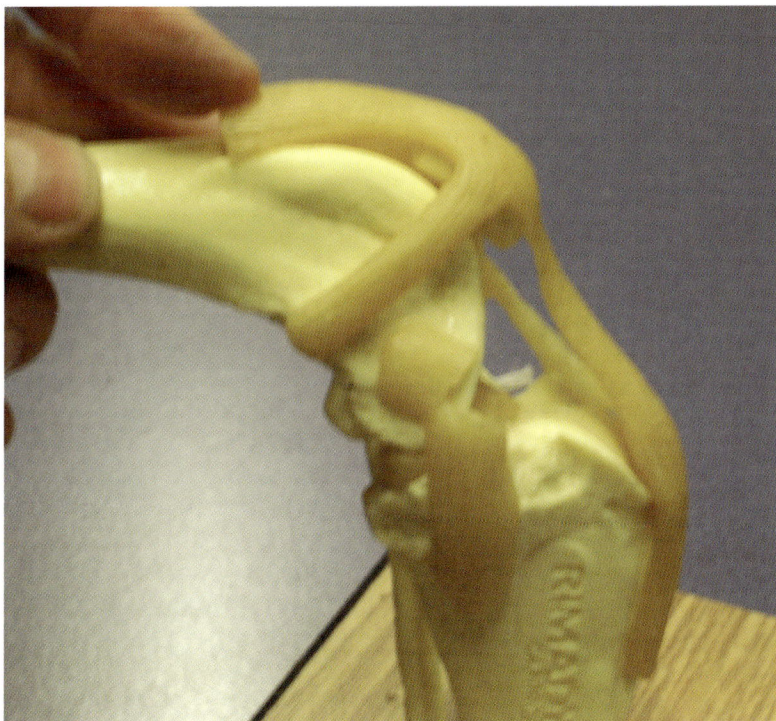

Fig. 2.1.4 Looking at the knee from the front aspect, you can see the patella (arrowed) sitting over the groove in the femur. You can see from this photograph how easily a sideways movement could displace the patella out of the groove and cause injury.

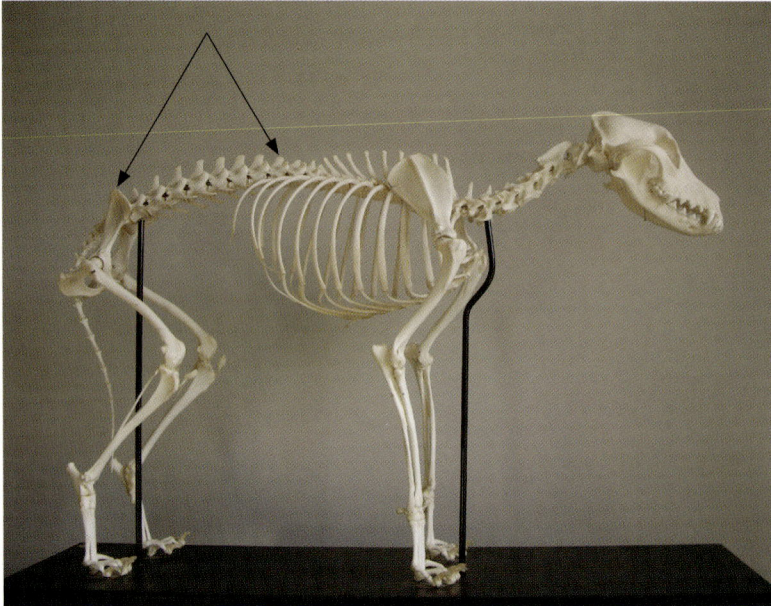

Fig. 2.1.5   The lumbar spine: this is the unsupported bridge that joins the back half of the skeleton to the front half, and is the part that is most vulnerable.

CAUTION: TAKE CARE TO AVOID BACK INJURIES

The lumbar spine is the most vulnerable part of the spine as it is effectively a bridge between the back and front halves of the dog. During pregnancy it supports the entire weight of the puppies and the mother's internal organs. When grooming a pregnant dog, you should not ask her to stand for too long on the grooming table, as this will be uncomfortable for her and may cause back strain. Similarly, you should be careful how you lift her.

The shortening of the legs (a condition known as 'chondrodysplasia' or 'chondrodystrophy') in breeds such as the Dachshund and Basset Hound arises because the cartilage develops and matures abnormally. This translates into a failure of the long bones to grow. This means that the spine is disproportionately elongated relative to the legs; it is therefore out of balance with the legs and subject to considerable strain. The spine (the bridge) is particularly subject to strain when overly loaded or mobilized. This may occur when the dog is balancing on, or loading, either the front two or the back two legs only, as it would be when jumping and landing. Care must therefore be taken to support the entire length of the back in these dogs when lifting and lowering them. For the same reason they should also be discouraged from jumping onto or from the grooming table, or into baths. (See Chapter 9.)

It should also be noted that chondrodystrophoid breeds are particularly vulnerable to disc disease; this should be suspected in these breeds if they appear to develop back pain or lose the ability to use their legs in some way.

---

articulated chain of bones that can flex and extend, whilst providing protection to the spinal cord. Between the vertebral joints are springy shock absorbers; called discs; these cushion movement as the joints flex and extend. The spine is actually a casing to protect the spinal cord (nerve tissue), which runs from the brain through the centre of the vertebral bones, giving rise to pairs of nerves that emerge at regular intervals from the spinal column. These nerves, in turn, travel out to the body tissues and organs.

The spine is divided into five sections. The *cervical spine* starts at the base of the skull and continues to the shoulder, where it becomes the *thoracic spine* – the part that supports the rib cage. After the ribcage it becomes the *lumbar spine* (*see* Fig. 2.1.5), which disappears into the pelvis, where it is known as the *sacrum* (which itself is made up of fused sacral vertebrae). The tail is called the *coccygeal spine*.

The skull and the various head shapes

The bones of the head are collectively known as the skull (*see* Fig. 2.1.6). The skull is made up from a number of bones that are arranged to give the dog's head its shape. Briefly, the skull contains two holes called orbits that house the dog's eyes, two nasal openings that communicate with the nostrils and allow the dog both to breathe and to use his sense of smell, and a hinged bone called the mandible, which forms the lower jaw. As explained in the previous chapter, all puppies, irrespective of their parentage, are born roughly the same shape: with short limbs and flattened faces. The puppy's growth continues immediately after birth and the differences in growth patterns and rates determine the individual characteristics of the breed. Genetically programmed growth patterns and timings affect the shape and the size of the dog, and it is the variety in head shapes that is often most noticeable. Despite the many breeds of dog, we can divide them basically into three head shape groups. These are very different from each other but each contains the same number of bones in their make-up and houses the same number of teeth, plus the usual 'bits', such as the brain and the tongue, which one would expect to find there!

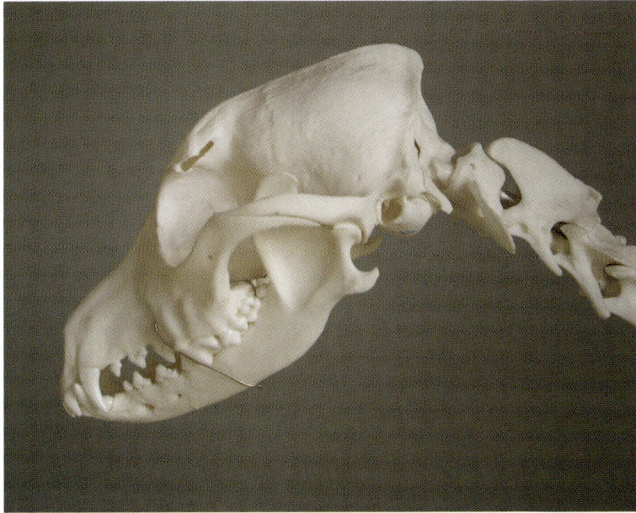

Fig. 2.1.6 The skull is made up of many bones fused together to produce the head's characteristic shape.

Fig. 2.1.7 In the mesaticephalic head shape, the cranium and foreface are approximately the same length.

Dolichocephalic (dolicho – cephalic)

The *dolichocephalic* head is characterized by a long nasal bone, which is much longer than the length of the top of the cranium, and there is no pronounced 'stop' (junction) between the nasal and frontal bones (i.e., they feel smooth/continuous). Examples of dolichocephalic breeds include the Greyhound and Borzoi (see Fig. 2.1.8). The orbits are usually close together, giving the impression of a narrow skull; they are not as deep as in mesaticephalics and the eyes face forward, providing the dog with good forward vision, but not such good peripheral sight. The mandible is long, reaching towards the end of the maxilla, and the top teeth should fit just over the bottom set. Again genetic coding dictates the speed at which the nose grows; in this case, an acceleration, or delayed interruption, in the timing of maxilla growth means it is not unusual to have a top set of teeth extending far beyond the lower set.

Brachycephalic (brachy – cephalic)

The *brachycephalic* head has a grossly shortened nasal bone, which is much shorter than the cranium and this gives these dogs their squashed face (*see* Fig. 2.1.9). In extreme cases the foreface may be absent altogether, as in the Pug or Pekingese. This head shape is the most problematic of the three as the growth of the nasal bones ends

Mesaticephalic (mesati – cephalic)

The *mesaticephalic head* is the most common head shape, in which the length of the nasal bone (which forms part of the nose or foreface of the dog) is roughly equal to the length of the top of the cranium (*see* Fig. 2.1.7). A definite 'stop' can usually be identified where the nose meets the top of the head. The lower jaw (*mandible*) should be long enough to reach the end of the upper jaw (*maxilla*) so that the top teeth just overhang the bottom teeth – as ours do. The bridge of the nose is generally quite wide. The orbits are deep, allowing the eyes to fit well into the head, rather than protruding forwards, away from the skull. The width of the nose prevents the eyes from facing forwards, giving the dog a blind spot immediately in front of him and a slightly off-centre view, with a reasonable peripheral field of vision. This means that the eyes of the dog are not coordinated in what they see as each eye looks slightly

to its respective side of the head. This is an important point to remember and we will come back to this in Chapter 9, when we discuss handling. The beagle is a good example of this head shape.

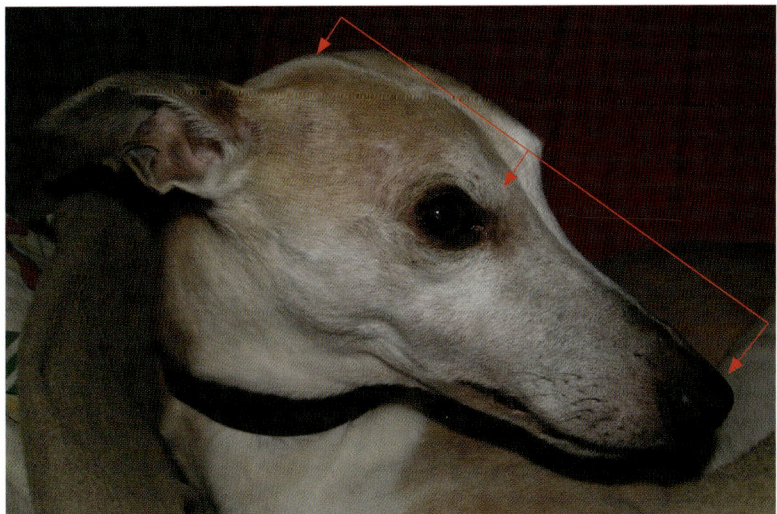

Fig. 2.1.8   In the dolichocephalic head shape, the foreface is considerably longer than the cranium. There is no exaggerated 'stop' or indentation between the eyes where the nose meets the skull.

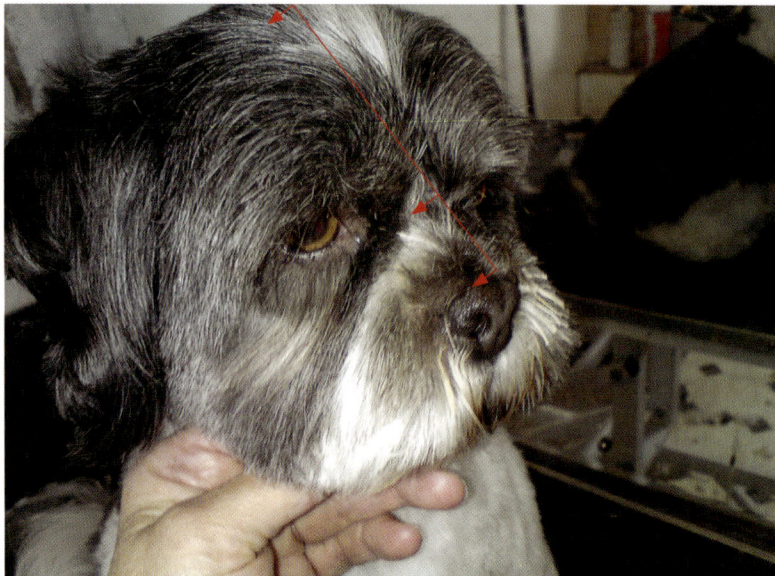

Fig. 2.1.9 In the brachycephalic head, the cranium is much longer than the foreface. This Shih Tzu has a slight length of foreface, whereas a Pekingese, by contrast, has no length at all. In dogs with this head shape, there is a very deep indentation or 'stop' between the eyes.

prematurely and the dog is left with a 'flat face', or sometimes even a concave ('dished') face, where the nostrils are sunken into an indentation. This is the most obvious sign of this developmental disorder and it is worth bearing in mind that the airways of these breeds are often severely deformed, a condition known as 'brachycephalic airway syndrome' (BAS). The deformed airways of these dogs make them particularly vulnerable to heat stress as they are less able to utilize panting as a means of cooling themselves.

The space between the eye sockets is very wide, placing the eyes off-centre. The orbits are shallow, forcing the eyes outwards, and sometimes barely affording them space and protection within the hollow they should occupy. This gives the dog very good peripheral vision but very poor forward vision – sometimes none. More importantly, the eyes are vulnerable to trauma and may even prolapse (see the alert box below and Fig. 2.8.25). The lower mandible in *brachycephalics* is generally very strong and powerful, often exceeding the length of the maxilla and allowing the bottom teeth to extend beyond the upper set. A further problem with *brachycephalics* is the shortening of the hard palate and relative lengthening of the soft palate. This allows the soft palate to vibrate more

on inhalation and can cause breathing difficulties.

CAUTION: GROOMING BRACHYCEPHALIC DOGS

Because the eyes sit shallowly in their sockets, grasping or holding the back of the dog's neck (scruffing), or pulling the coat back from the base of the skull, can cause the eyeball to leave the socket (prolapse). To avoid this risk, you should always brush forwards, towards the head and never grab the back of the neck to restrain the dog.

The shortened hard palate allows the longer soft palate to vibrate excessively when the dog is breathing heavily or panting, impairing oxygen intake and causing the dog breathing difficulties. These dogs should not be put into drying cabinets or any other situation where the oxygen supply is limited.

Excessive panting in these situations can lead to respiratory distress, heat stress and even death.

The limbs

The limb bones of the dog are similar, in many ways, to those of man. The following description of the front (fore) and back (hind) limbs summarizes their anatomy, starting at the top and progressing down to finish at the toes. This structure is then related to the range of movement and function of the limbs.

The forelimb

The front leg starts with the shoulder blade, or scapula, the role of which is to stabilise the limb against the chest wall. There are no bony connections between the scapula and the chest; the forelimb is held in place by muscles (Fig. 2.1.10). The shoulder is connected to the humerus, which is in turn connected to the two bones of the forearm (radius and ulna). The connection between the bones of the forearm and upper arm is called the elbow and it functions as a hinge to allow the limb to fold upwards. The radius and ulna extend down to the carpus, which is the name given to the wrist joint in the dog. The metacarpal area contains five metacarpals, giving rise to five toes (digits). Each toe comprises three phalanges. The dog's first digit is his thumb; it is non-weight bearing, is shortened and gives rise to what we call the dewclaw.

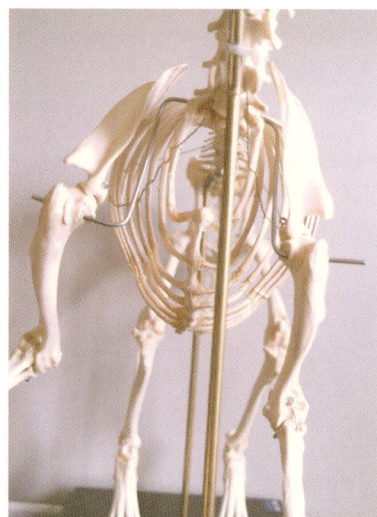

Fig. 2.1.10 The forelimb is held close to the chest wall only by muscles. There are no bony attachments. Here you can see how easily the shoulder can be damaged by pulling the forelimb away from the body with excessive force.

The hind limb

The hind leg starts at the pelvic girdle. The femur attaches to the pelvis at the hip joint, which affords considerable range of movement, in much the same way as the shoulder joint does for the front leg. The femur meets the tibia and fibula at the knee. The tibia and fibula end at the tarsal joint. The calcaneus is particularly prominent in dogs and serves as an attachment for the Achilles tendon. This is the equivalent of the human heel. In the dog, however, neither the heel nor the metatarsals (bones of the foot) rest on the floor. This is because the dog stands on his toes and not on the soles of his feet: that is to say, he is digitigrade rather than plantigrade (*see* Evolution). As with the elbow, it is the knee that provides the hind leg with the ability to flex. The hind leg also possesses five digits; four are in contact with the ground. The other (first) digit is vestigial and, where present, does not usually form a joint with the rest of the leg. Unlike the front dewclaws it is non-functional, as it cannot be used to manipulate things. You will see the extra digit on the hind legs of breeds such as the Briard and Rottweiler (*see* Fig. 2.1.11).

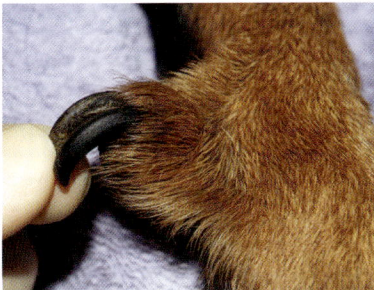

Fig. 2.1.11   A double dewclaw in the hind limb of a Rottweiler.

Joints and their structure

A joint is an articulation formed where two bones meet. Not all joints are freely movable: those in the skull, for example, become fixed after growing has been completed. These are known as fibrous joints.

Others, like the joints between the tibia and fibula, allow only limited movement. These are known as semi-movable synovial joints. The way they fit together and the shape of the cartilage surfaces determine how much they move and which way. Some can move up and down and from side to side, others can only move in one direction: either up and down or side to side. Synovial joints have a small amount of sticky lubricating liquid called synovial fluid in them; this can leak out if the joint is damaged or cut open.

The right and left pubic bones of the pelvis and the right and left mandibles form a symphyseal joint where they come together. This is also known as a cartilaginous joint because it has strong cartilage holding both sides together. Sometimes bone replaces the dense connective tissue in fibrous and cartilaginous joints, causing the joint to fuse, restricting movement and function.

Where bone ends are in contact, connective tissue known as cartilage provides a dense but smooth cushion to ensure that the joint functions smoothly. Layers of fibrous membranes then make up the joint capsule that envelops the joint. The capsule is further covered by more fibres to stabilise and strengthen the joint. These are called ligaments and span the joint from one bone to the other.

The position and angle of the joint contribute to the shape of the skeleton and the way the joints move determines how you can manoeuvre the dog (*see* Fig. 2.1.12).

It is important that you familiarize yourself with the range of movement on a healthy young dog so that you can notice differences when dogs begin to age and their joints become injured or diseased. Any restriction of movement affects how you handle and work around the dog, and you need to adapt your technique to work with the dog, taking into account its capabilities.

Important joints and the problems that may affect them

The hip joint and hip dysplasia

The hip joint on the dog is a ball and socket joint. The round-ended ball at the top of the femur fits into a cup-like cavity, or socket, within the pelvis. This arrangement allows the hip to rotate and the leg to swing and move in several planes. This type of joint therefore provides the upper leg with a wide range of movement (*see* Fig. 2.1.13).

A normal hip joint fits snugly together and provides good stability. In hip dysplasia the socket is shallow and fails to fit snugly around the ball of the hip. This leads to instability and exces-

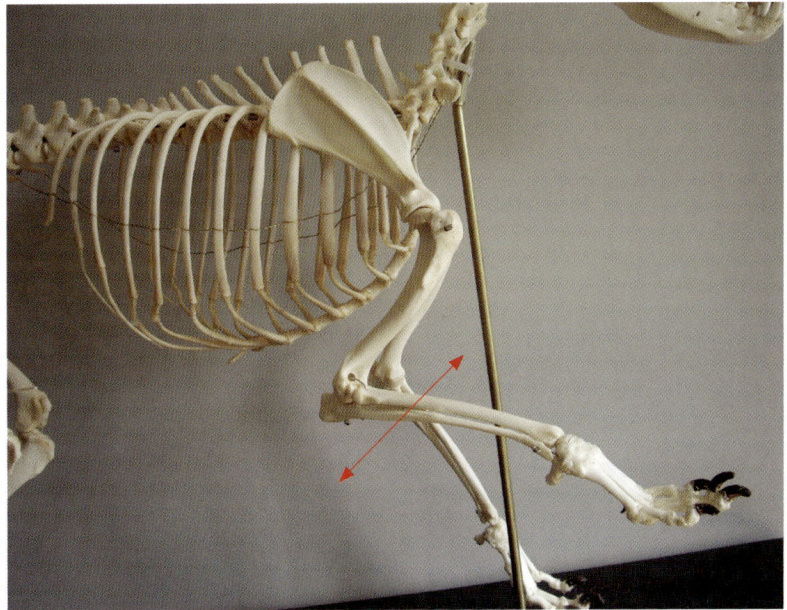

Fig. 2.1.12   The position and angle of the joints determine how the limb moves. With the exception of the hip joint, all the joints on the legs work in lever fashion. This means that they move up and down in one direction only; they do not rotate or bend against the lever action.

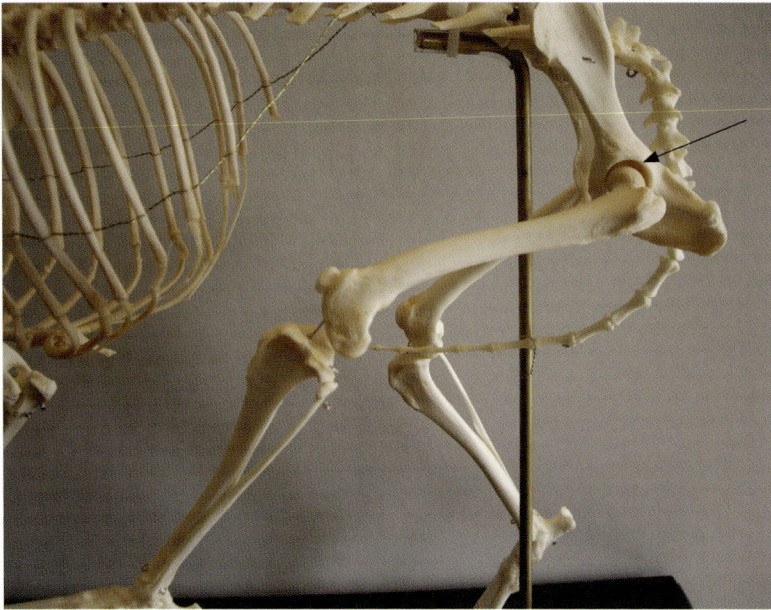

Fig. 2.1.13   A healthy hip joint showing the ball at the end of the femur fitting into the socket within the pelvis.

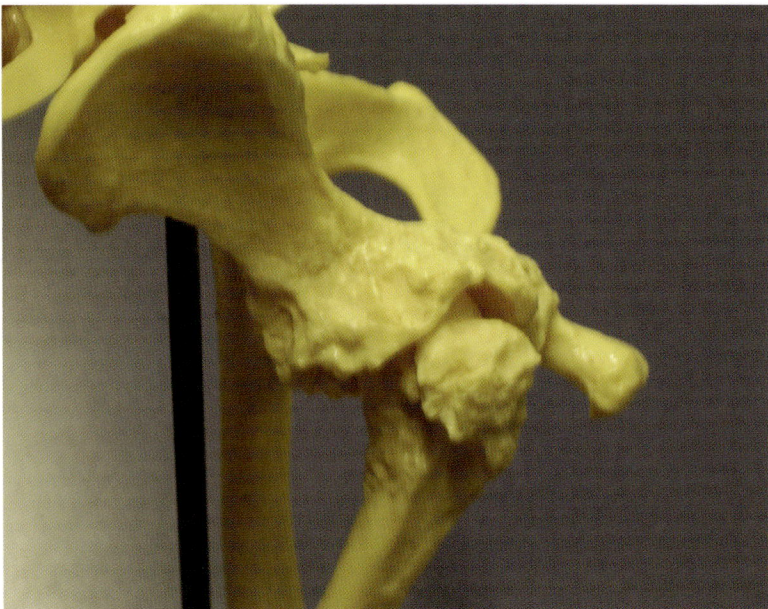

Fig. 2.1.14   Degenerative diseases such as osteoarthritis often affect joints that are unstable. This can be a genetic problem or it can be caused through wear and tear.

sive movement, and can give rise to lameness. In time this can progress to degenerative joint disease, otherwise known as osteoarthritis (*see* Fig. 2.1.14).

Several risk factors play a part in hip dysplasia, although the causes are not fully understood. These factors include:

◆ inherited characteristics;
◆ early, rapid growth and weight gain;
◆ overfeeding; and
◆ a diet too high in protein and too rich in vitamins and minerals.

Signs vary according to the age of the dog. Generally, affected puppies appear 'clumsy' and unstable on their back legs, although with larger breeds this may simply be because of the length of the limbs and lack of coordination. As the puppy grows, he or she may display signs of pain in the hip with lameness and a reluctance to exercise. Several years may pass before the hip in the mature dog becomes arthritic. In severe cases of hip dysplasia surgical intervention may be required.

Elbow dysplasia

Elbow dysplasia loosely describes the abnormal development of the dog's elbow.

The elbow is a high motion (the dog's forward movement depends on it) hinge joint (it opens and closes like a door hinge) made up of complex shapes of bones and cartilage, which fit closely together. Staying with this analogy, elbow dysplasia is a little bit like having a piece of grit or a small stone stuck in a door hinge – it impairs the smooth functioning of the joint in a similar way.

A small abnormality can have large consequences for the function of the joint and once elbow function is affected, so is the forward movement of the dog. This is particularly significant as the animal is more dependent on the elbow joint than it is on any other joint, when moving forwards.

Like hip dysplasia, elbow dysplasia is a multifactorial disease: although most cases have a genetic basis, growth rate, diet and exercise can also influence the development and severity of the disease. Unfortunately, elbow dysplasia is not controlled by a single inherited gene but by the combination of many genes, making it difficult to eradicate from breed lines.

One problem with elbow dysplasia is that not all dogs suffering from the disease are lame and affected dogs can therefore be difficult to spot and identify. If the dog is carrying many of the affected genes it will probably be very lame but, if carrying only a few, the disease may be subclinical (i.e. not detected or obvious clinically). In the latter case, few if any signs are evident. Many dogs suffering from changes associated with osteoarthritis do not show any signs at all until the disease is very advanced. Consequently, they are often bred from early on in life, producing affected, sometimes lame, puppies.

Tests in the United Kingdom have shown that there is a significant increase in elbow dysplasia in many breeds and that the problem appears to be increasingly recognized worldwide, so it is very important that you learn which breeds are vulnerable.

Luxated patella

Luxation is another name for dislocation; in this case, patella luxation refers to a dislocation of the knee cap (patella). A partial dislocation is sometimes called a subluxation.

Dislocations of the knee cap (*see* Fig. 2.1.15) often occur when dogs are racing around and move sharply sideways, causing trauma to the knee joint. They can also arise as the result of inherited or developmental problems that allow the knee cap to slide (or slip) easily out of place.

The patella sits within the patella tendon, which attaches to the large bony tuberosity (the prominent bit) at the top of the tibia. The patella usually sits in a groove on the front surface of the tibia and the femur. In certain toy and miniature breeds of dog a number of deformities can make it easier for the patella to slip out of this groove. These deformities may include an abnormally shallow groove, poor alignment or curvature of the femur and/or tibia. The condition usually becomes apparent in breeds such as the Yorkshire Terrier at four to six months of age.

When the patella becomes dislocated, the contraction of the thigh muscles makes it very difficult for the dog to relax and straighten his leg, forcing him to carry the limb in a strange or unnatural position. Where this arises as the result of a congenital abnormality, without any tearing of supporting tissues, there is unlikely to be any swelling and gentle extension of the leg should allow the patella to slip back into place. Very often affected dogs learn how to perform this themselves and can then be expected to regain full use of the affected limb. When caused by a traumatic injury, the joint is often swollen and very painful, and will be held in an unnatural position. Such cases should always be referred for veterinary attention.

Traumatic patella luxations and recurrent luxations that affect a dog's welfare may require surgical intervention and should be evaluated by a veterinary surgeon.

Ruptured cruciate ligaments in the stifle joint

Whilst on the subject of stifle (knee) injuries, it is probably a good time to mention ruptured cruciate ligaments as groomers are likely to come across these during the course of their careers.

There are two cruciate ligaments that cross each other within the stifle joint. They are termed the anterior and posterior cruciate ligaments (ACL and PCL) and play an important role in maintaining the stability of the joint.

Damage to one or both of these ligaments is a not uncommon injury, especially in older dogs or large overweight dogs. It typically arises following overloading of the limb whilst running at speed.

The joint does not always swell up, the limb does not always appear deformed, and nor is the joint itself always painful. The affected limb will be held semi-flexed and the tips of the toes will be on the ground. The onset of lameness can be sudden following an acute injury. In other, more chronic, cases the signs can be mild and intermittent – sometimes barely noticeable. In some cases, particularly in smaller dogs, the injury is left to heal slowly over a period of months. In larger dogs, however, surgery is often required to stabilize the joint.

It is not unusual for a groomer to be asked to groom a dog that is recovering from cruciate ligament repair surgery. In such cases great care must be taken not to overstrain the joint, particularly if the dog is on pain-relief medication.

Arthritis

Arthritis is a degenerative disease of joints; it is a problem that is often associated with ageing and typically affects load-bearing joints. There are basically two types of arthritis that groomers need to be aware of:

◆ where inflammation of the joints has developed through wear and tear and through age; and
◆ where the disease is secondary to another problem such as hip dysplasia.

In either case the normally smooth cartilage protecting the joint deteriorates and starts to develop defects. Mature cartilage cannot repair itself so, as the problem worsens, the bone beneath the cartilage thickens as a way of protecting itself. Bone spurs commonly build up around the joint.

The new bone spurs, inflammation and other degenerative changes decrease the mobility of the joint, rendering it stiff and painful. A grating sound can sometimes be heard as the bone spurs rub together when the joint is manoeuvred. This noise is referred to as crepitus.

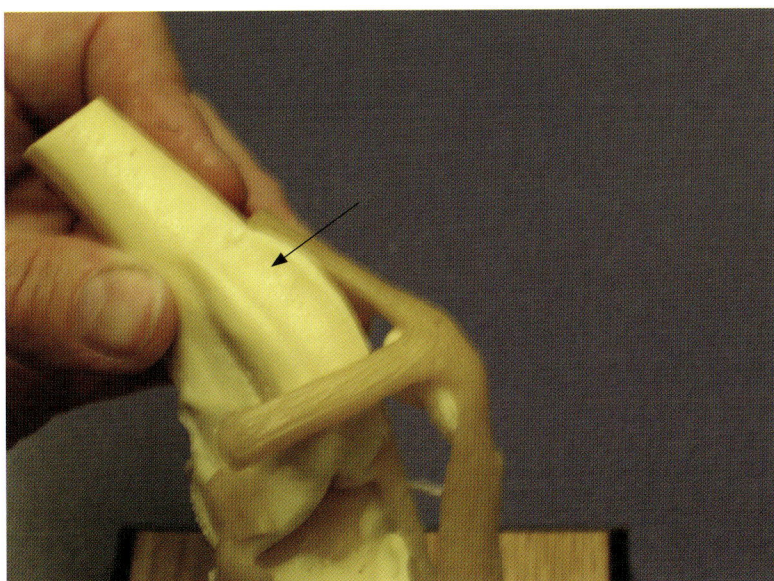

Fig. 2.1.15   A luxated (or dislocated) patella occurs when the patella tendon slips out of its supporting groove in the femur.

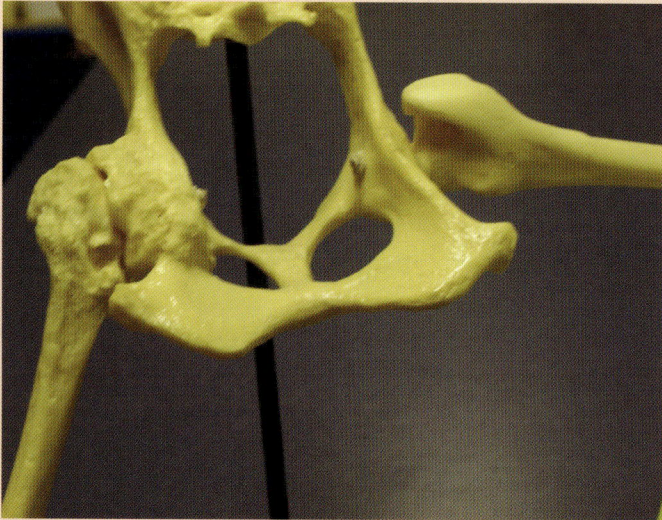

Fig. 2.1.16   *Here you can see how a normal hip can be moved freely, whereas the affected hip is not able to rotate so the leg is only able to move backwards and forwards.*

2.2 THE MUSCLES

The most important point to learn from this section is how the muscles work; this is important because it helps you to understand their effect on the range of movement of each limb, as well as their various roles elsewhere in the body. Working with, rather than against, the muscles, when handling and manoeuvring the dog, help avoids causing the dog discomfort or even injury.

In addition, familiarity with the muscular structure of the dog makes styling the dog easier for you. In a fit, healthy dog, the shape of the dog is defined by the quality and quantity of the musculature. The more coat and body fat a dog carries, the less of the dog's underlying structure will be visible to you. Knowing where the muscles are helps you to make use of them to style the dog into a shape that complements his physique.

There are three types of muscle in the animal body: skeletal muscle, smooth muscle and cardiac (heart) muscle. The first two play a role in the musculoskeletal system and are described here. The cardiac muscle is part of the cardiovascular system and is discussed elsewhere in the book.

Skeletal muscle (*see* Fig. 2.2.1) is by far the largest of these three groups and is what we traditionally think of as 'muscle'. It is the skeletal muscle mass that gives fit, athletic dogs their body shape and definition (see Fig. 2.2.2).

So what do we need to know about muscle structure and function?

Fig. 2.2.1   *The muscles of the forelimb.*

Muscle function

The skeletal muscles perform a number of essential functions: they allow the body to be moved, and provide it with the essential support that allows positions to be held.

Muscles typically work together in pairs, with one muscle producing the opposite movement to its partner muscle; this is often called antagonism.

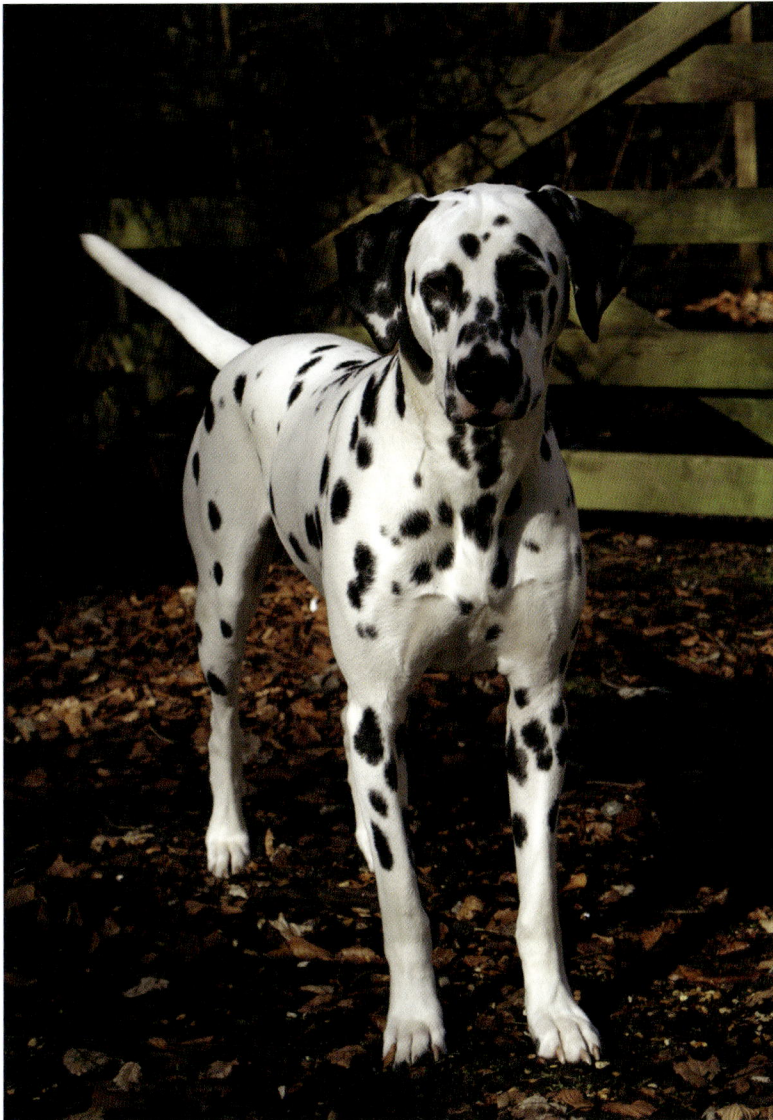

Fig. 2.2.2 It is the skeletal muscle mass that gives the fit dog its body shape.

The biceps and triceps muscles of the upper arm are an example of antagonistic muscles: the biceps causes the elbow to flex, whilst the triceps causes it to extend (*see* Fig. 2.2.1).

Muscles are often described according to the type of movement they perform. Those that are located on the inside bend of a joint and work to decrease the angle of the joint are called flexor muscles. To straighten the joint again, muscles on the outside bend, called extensors, work to increase the angle and open the joint.

Muscle structure

Skeletal muscle is made up of thousands of contractile muscle fibres, which can be induced to contract when stimulated by nerves. The fibres are bound by connective tissue into bundles of long fibres through which run blood vessels and nerves. These nerve fibres originate from the central nervous system and connect with muscle fibres at the neuro-muscular junction. They relay electrical messages from the brain to the muscles and thus allow voluntary control of the muscles.

The muscles themselves can be described in terms of their 'origin', 'insertion' and 'action'. Each muscle attaches to the bony skeleton via a tendon. There are usually two such attachments. The attachment that does not move is usually closest to the body and is referred to as the 'origin'. The attachment on the bone that is moved is referred to as the 'insertion'. Contraction of the muscle linking the origin and insertion produces movement of a particular part of the body relative to another. This is the 'action' of the muscle in question. For example, the biceps brachii muscle of the upper forearm has its origin in two places on the scapula and its insertion on the radius and ulna. Contraction of this muscle causes the elbow to flex.

Tendons are fibrous rope-like structures that relay the force produced by the muscle contraction to the bone it is attached to. As such, they are not contractile.

Smooth muscle

Smooth muscle is found in hollow organs such as the stomach, bladder, intestinal tract, airways and in the walls of blood vessels. Smooth muscle is also to be found attached to the lens within the eye and to the hairs in skin. The pilo-erector muscle, which raises hairs over the body, is therefore a smooth muscle.

Smooth muscle is made up of short spindle-shaped fibres packed together in layers. Smooth muscles produce slow, long-term contractions and are controlled by the autonomic nervous system. This means that these contractions are involuntary and the dog is not aware of them. As such they are well suited to maintaining the tone within blood vessels, controlling the various contractions of the gastro-intestinal tract and mediating a range of thermoregulatory responses. (It is smooth muscle that is responsible for your goosebumps in cold weather and for the increase in blood flow to the skin during warm weather.)

> ### CAUTION: HANDLING THE FORELEGS
>
> *The front legs of the dog are attached to the skeletal frame only by muscle and tendons. There are no bone attachments. When handling the front legs of the dog, you should try to keep the shoulder as close to the dog as possible, because sideways movement away from the body can cause damage to the muscles in the shoulder and in the chest (the inside attachment of the front legs).*

Other useful points

The legs of the dog are kept close to the body by muscles called adductors. When he lifts his leg to urinate, abductors produce the opposite movement, allowing the leg to be lifted away from his body.

Skeletal muscle does not only move the joints and the limbs. For example, the eyeball is moved, the eyelids opened and closed, the ears pricked and the skin twitched, all by skeletal muscles.

Shaking of the muscles (muscle tremor) is common, particularly in Terrier and Hound breeds, and is often perceived as a sign of the dog being cold. Whilst this is possible, it is more likely to be caused by increased stimulation from the nervous system as a result of the dog being in a state of alertness and ready to react, or the dog being in a state of anxiety because he is being restrained from reacting. (Don't forget these breeds are hunters and are always attentive and ready to act.)

A dog that has abnormal or prolonged shaking of the muscles for no apparent reason should be referred to the vet for a check-up because he may have an underlying disease or nerve damage.

2.3 BODY TEMPERATURE AND THERMOREGULATION

> *Left to sort themselves out, dogs are more than adequately equipped to regulate their own body temperature and can warm or cool themselves as necessary.*
>
> *Throughout the grooming process, you expose the dog to a series of temperature changes, particularly during the bathing and drying processes. These processes are of your choosing, not the dog's, and you need to consider their effect on each individual.*
>
> *Under normal circumstances, the dog is able to respond to and cope with these changes. Overheating, however, is perhaps the most common cause of unnatural canine death in the grooming room. Scalding of the skin is also an important risk to the dog's health and well-being.*
>
> *Knowing how the dog controls his body temperature, and the limitations for his doing so, can help you to avoid such problems, thereby keeping him safe, comfortable and stress-free.*

Dogs evolved to cope with temperate climates and can control their body temperature to withstand extreme environmental temperatures better than the cat. Animals residing away from the equator (that is to say, in a temperate climate) also have to adapt to seasonal changes in temperature. In this section we discuss the ways in which a dog adapts to both sudden and seasonal changes in temperature.

The dog is a mammal and therefore an endotherm. This means he is warm-blooded and able to maintain his body temperature independently of the environment by producing heat within his own body. Endotherms generally maintain a body temperature between 35° and 40° C in order to ensure that all metabolic processes, most of which are catalyzed by enzymes, run as efficiently as possible. The dog's core temperature ranges between 37.9° and 39.2°C (100.2° to 102.5°F). A rectal thermometer can be used to measure rectal temperature (*see* First Aid section, Chapter 8). In the healthy dog this gives a figure of around 38.9°C (102°F). As long as the figure falls within the normal range, it is likely to be normal.

Dogs maintain their body temperature within this range using a number of physiological and behavioural techniques; this process is called thermoregulation. The thermoregulating dog is able to conserve and lose heat as and when required.

When cold: the dog increases heat production and takes various steps to reduce heat loss. He can conserve heat by lifting the coat, allowing it to trap a layer of insulating air close to the skin. This is achieved by the contraction of erector pili muscles. In an attempt to reduce heat loss the dog may curl up and tuck his legs in when he lies down, thereby reducing the exposed surface area of the body. About 75 per cent of the energy in muscle contraction is converted into heat so generalized rhythmic contracting of the muscles (shivering) is another method that the dog may use to warm himself up. In the longer term, repeated exposure to cold temperatures leads to the development of a thicker (winter) hair coat.

NOTE: CHECKING THE DOG FOR SYMMETRY

When you examine the dog, before grooming commences, you should check for symmetry. Palpate the muscles, comparing the left side with the right side of the body. There should be no difference between the two sides: that is to say, the dog should feel the same on both sides of his body.

If the dog is healthy and his muscles are performing correctly, his muscle structure will be symmetrical. If, however, he is injured or showing early signs of joint disease or disease of the central nervous system the muscles may not be symmetrical and he should be referred to a vet for a check-up.

Any lack of symmetry will be quite apparent, especially if the dog is recovering from injury, has hip dysplasia, or after surgery such as a cruciate repair.

If you suspect a problem, you can adapt your grooming technique so that no harm or discomfort is caused.

NOTE

The groomer should recognize immediately when a wet dog is cold and begins to shiver to keep warm. This is especially important in older dogs who may be less able to cope with such stresses.

When hot: the dog takes steps to eliminate as much heat as possible. Unlike humans and horses, the dog is unable to sweat and cool himself through evaporative heat loss. Sweat glands are limited to a dog's feet and do not have a role in thermoregulation. Instead, dogs rely heavily on panting to cool themselves down. This allows the surface area provided by the mouth, oropharynx and airways to come into contact with large volumes of rapidly moving air. The air is humidified when it passes over these tissues and this maximises evaporative heat loss.

Dogs commonly demonstrate behavioural changes in response to high environmental temperatures. These may include actively seeking shade and cold surfaces on which to lie.

Interestingly, the groomer may observe instances of apparent 'instantaneous moulting' of the undercoat. This is commonly seen amongst smooth-coated breeds, which appear to be able to shed undercoat as soon as their body temperature is increased. This phenomenon is often noticeable in the grooming room when considerable time has been spent removing moulting undercoat from perhaps a Labrador Retriever or Jack Russell Terrier, so that the coat is totally free of loose undercoat and is ready for bathing. The application of overly warm water, or the hair drier, raises the dog's body temperature and produces more moulting undercoat hair.

The circulatory system can also be used as a means of dissipating heat. Vasodilation allows superficial blood vessels within the skin to dilate (open up). Blood can then course close to the skin surface, allowing heat to radiate from the skin into the air. This may be particularly useful in dogs with large pendulous ears, such as the Bloodhound.

Sweat glands in the dog

There are three types of sweat gland: sebaceous glands, apocrine glands and eccrine glands. Sebaceous and apocrine glands produce complex secretions that waterproof and condition the skin and coat; they are therefore only indirectly involved in thermoregulation. Their structure and function are described in Section 2.10. Eccrine sweat glands produce a secretion that is mostly composed of water. They are therefore ideally suited to thermoregulation as they can dispel large amounts of heat energy through evaporative cooling.

Humans possess some two to three million eccrine sweat glands. These glands are not associated with hair follicles and open up onto the skin all over the human body. They are especially concentrated on the palms, soles of the feet and armpits. Both men and horses rely on these glands to control body temperature during exercise and in hot weather. The dog, like the cat, only has these glands on the pads of the feet. Their role in thermoregulation is therefore very limited. So what are they for? Well, dogs and cats, like us, get sweaty palms (and feet) when stressed. Unlike in humans, however, the moisture produced improves grip and is thought to provide traction to aid in escape.

The dog and the cat have apocrine sweat glands distributed over the entire body surface but they are not effective in thermoregulation. You will learn more about the purpose of apocrine glands when we look at the skin section.

Seasonal coat changes

Dogs are able to change their coats according to the seasonal temperatures. Thus, during the winter months the follicles that give rise to the soft undercoat enter a period of active growth. This is called *anagen*. The extra layer of undercoat is able to trap air close to the body and provides much-needed insulation.

As daylight hours lengthen, a series of hormonal triggers interrupt this hair growth cycle. These same follicles then enter a prolonged resting phase. This period of inactivity is called *telogen*. During telogen hair growth ceases and the old hair is usually shed from the follicle; this allows the coat to thin and makes it easier for dogs to cope with warmer summer weather. The groomer may need to facilitate this moulting process and the transition to a summer coat.

Hair growth cycles are complex and are affected by many different factors. They are discussed further in Section 2.10.

2.4 THE REPRODUCTIVE AND URINARY SYSTEMS

The urinary and reproductive systems share certain parts in common and are often grouped together as the genito-urinary or urogenital system; they are therefore presented together here. This section starts by providing an overview of the urinary system, including the anatomical structures that are shared by the two systems. This is followed by a description of the reproductive system in the dog and bitch, both in health and disease.

Urinary system

The urinary system has a number of functions, including the maintenance of water balance within the body and the elimination of various substances that are surplus to the body's requirements. More specifically, the kidneys eliminate the protein breakdown product urea, produced when the body digests protein. This is made possible by a process of filtration; this process also allows the kidneys to regulate the concentration of water and salts within the body, as well as the pH (acidity/alkalinity) of the blood.

All mammals possess two kidneys, which filter blood continuously and produce a filtrate, called urine, that is then eliminated via the urinary tract. This filtrate is passed via the ureter to the bladder, where it is stored until such time as it can be voided (eliminated) via the urethra. The urinary system thus consists of the kidneys, ureters, bladder and urethra.

In the male dog the excess waste and water produced by the kidneys is dispelled from the bladder into the outside world through a small tube within the penis, called the urethra. The male reproduction system also makes use of the urethra to transport an ejaculate of sperm (from the testes) and prostatic fluid (from the prostate gland).

In the bitch the urinary and reproductive tracts come together within the vagina. The female urethra runs from the bladder to the floor of the vagina and is therefore much shorter than that of the male, which runs from the bladder to the tip of the penis. The vagina runs caudally (towards the tail) and ends at the vulva, which is to be found immediately below the anus.

Reproductive system

The dog reproduces sexually and is therefore characterized by both male and female sexual organs.

The male reproductive system

This consists of the testicles, spermatic cord, vas deferens, prostate gland, urethra and penis (*see* Fig. 2.4.1). Of these, only the penis and testicles are visible. These are commonly referred to as the male genitals. The penis is composed of columns of tissue that become erect when they are engorged (filled) with blood. The gonads of the male dog are called testes (testicles); they are paired and sit side-by-side within a pendulous sac called the scrotum. Scrotal tissue contains a layer of muscle called the cremaster muscle that contracts or relaxes to allow the scrotum to move the testes either closer to, or away from, the body. This allows the temperature within the scrotum to be varied. The testes can thus be kept at a slightly lower temperature than core body temperature, thereby protecting the testes from possible neoplastic (cancerous) changes, whilst favouring sperm production and survival. The testicles should always be checked for lumps, thickenings, pain and swelling as part of your examination. Both testes should be the same size and of the same consistency when examined.

The testes contain many tightly coiled tubes called seminiferous tubules, in which millions of sperm are produced every day. These tubules are lined by germinative cells that are responsible for spermatogenesis (the creation of sperm cells). Once the sperm leave the testes, they pass into a long tube called the epididymis, where they mature and are stored. Each epididymis empties in turn into the vas deferens, which itself empties into the urethra. The prostate gland surrounds the urethra at the level of the urinary bladder. During mating, seminal fluid from the prostate gland is added to the sperm to produce semen; the ejaculate is then propelled along the urethra within the erect penis and into the vulva of the female. Sperm are at various stages of development at different points within the seminiferous tubules; the manufacturing process is therefore continuous and a dog is able to mate at all times during the year and throughout his lifetime.

The dog's penis demonstrates a number of unique characteristics. The body of the penis contains a bone, the os penis. This can be felt within the dog's sheath. This bone provides the penis with support during the early

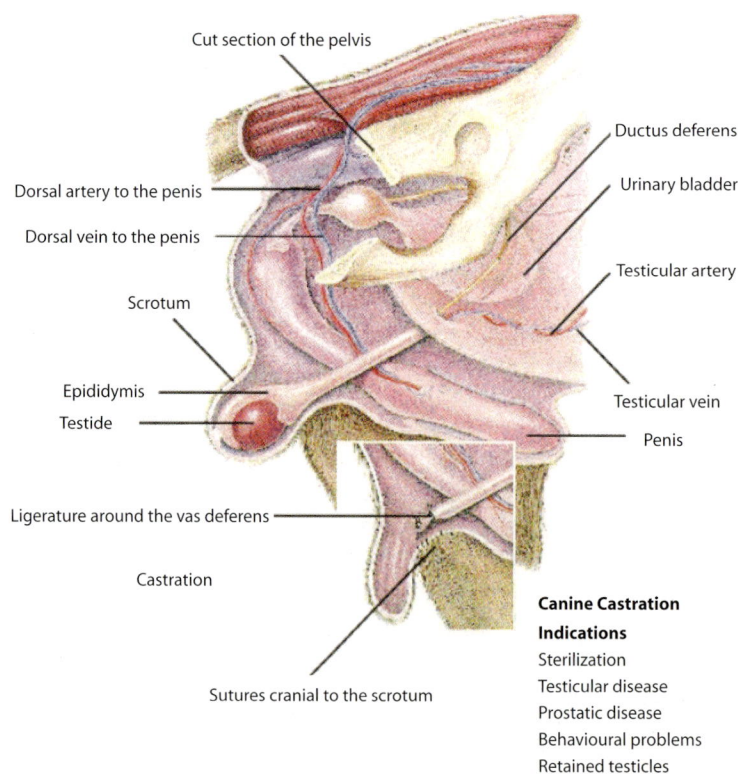

Cut section of the pelvis

Ductus deferens

Dorsal artery to the penis

Urinary bladder

Dorsal vein to the penis

Testicular artery

Scrotum

Epididymis

Testide

Testicular vein

Penis

Ligerature around the vas deferens

Castration

Canine Castration

Indications

Sterilization

Testicular disease

Prostatic disease

Behavioural problems

Retained testicles

Sutures cranial to the scrotum

Fig. 2.4.1 The male reproductive organs and what happens when the dog is sterilized or 'castrated'.

stages of mating. At the base of the penis is an area of tissue called the bulbis glandis, which becomes engorged (swollen) during mating and locks the penis inside the bitch's vulva. The dog and bitch thus become 'tied'. The tie can last between five and eighty minutes and is normal. Tied dogs should never be forcibly separated as this can cause damage to the tissues involved. They should, quite simply, be left alone until they break away from each other.

It is not uncommon to see male dogs with an engorged penis who are unable to replace their penis within the sheath (prepuce) that usually provides it with protection. This condition is known as *paraphimosis (see* Fig. 2.4.2) and is commonly seen in young dogs when they get excited. You can expect to see this when entire young male dogs visit you for grooming, especially if they meet or smell a bitch in heat. Great care must be taken to prevent the exposed penile tissues (glans) from becoming traumatized. Where possible cold water and/or cold compresses can be used to reduce the swelling *(see* Fig. 2.4.3) at the base of the penis. The dog should be prevented from licking the exposed tissue and removed to somewhere calm, away from other dogs. If the penis fails to retract inside the sheath, veterinary advice should be sought. In some long-haired breeds, long or curly hair at the tip of the penis can interfere with the free movement of the glans. These hairs can be trimmed back from the sheath opening. They should not, however, be clipped as this can cause irritation to the sensitive skin.

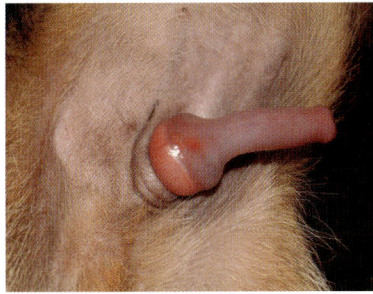

Fig. 2.4.3   *The engorged tissues of the Bulbis glandis of the penis are clearly preventing the penis sliding back into the prepuce. It is this swelling that is largely responsible for the 'tie' during mating.*

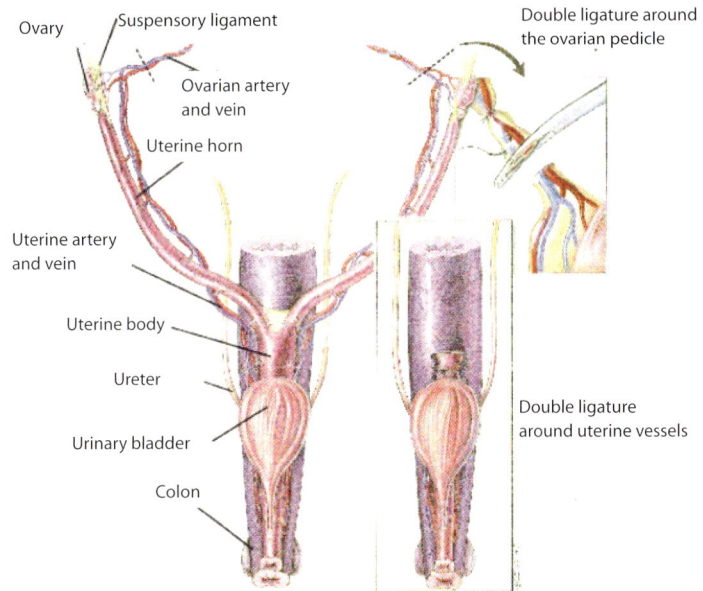

Fig. 2.4.4   *The female reproductive organs and what happens when the bitch is sterilized or 'spayed'.*

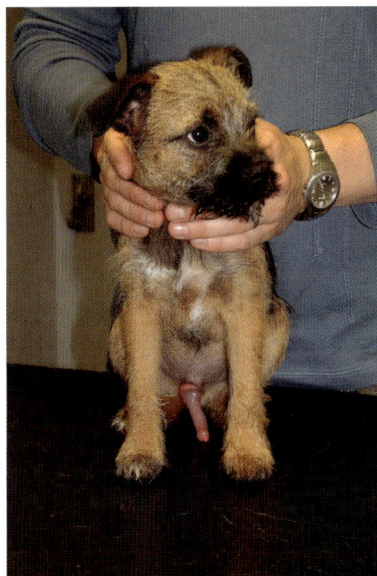

Fig. 2.4.2   *Paraphimosis in a young male Border Terrier.*

The female reproductive system

Unlike the dog, the bitch is only available for breeding once or twice throughout the year. It is generally believed tha bitches have two oestrus cycles each year but this is not strictly true, as some bitches do not maintain a regular cycle; some breeds, such as the Basenji, have adapted to only have one cycle per year to coincide with annual environmental seasons.

The bitch's reproductive system consists of the ovaries, oviducts, uterus, vagina and vulva *(see* Fig. 2.4.4). The bitch has two ovaries sitting behind the kidneys within the abdominal cavity. The ovaries are responsible for the production of the female gametes (sex cells), which are called ova (eggs). Following ovulation, the ova pass from the ovary into the oviduct, which connects each ovary to its corresponding uterine horn. The two uterine horns merge to form a common uterine body, which runs down to the cervix. The cervix is an oval-shaped musculo-fibrous structure that controls the communication between the uterus and the vagina. The thick muscular walls of the cervix can relax to open and allow sperm to enter during mating, as well as to permit the expulsion of puppies at birth. The highly expandable vagina sits entirely within the pelvic canal and extends from the cervix to the vulva, which is effectively the outside entrance *(see* Fig. 2.4.5).

The female is only receptive to the male at certain times, during oestrus. At this time the bitch is commonly described as 'on heat' or 'in season'. Oestrus generally coincides with the release of ova from the ovaries (ovulation) and can occur at any time of year *(see* Figs 2.4.6 and 2.4.7).

There are four stages to the female oestrus (breeding) cycle and they generally start when the bitch reaches puberty, between six and twelve

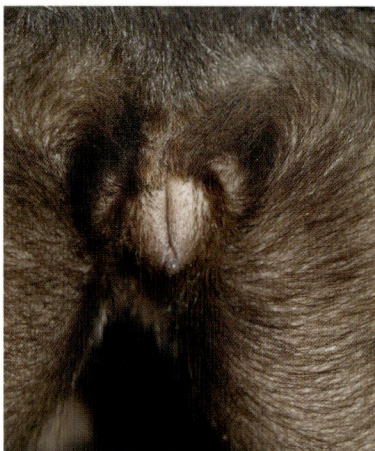

Fig. 2.4.5   Vulva of the bitch out of season (i.e. during anoestrus). During this time the reproductive system is quiescent or resting. The vulva is not obviously swollen and any secretions are minimal or absent.

Fig. 2.4.6   The swollen vulva and bloody discharge of the same bitch in season. The thinning hair on the medial and caudal aspects of the thighs is normal in sighthound and sighthound crosses.

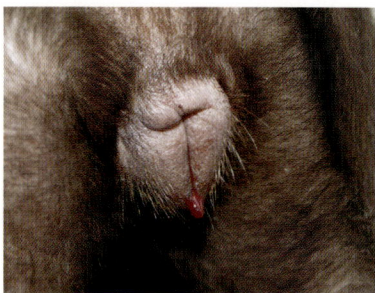

Fig. 2.4.7   Close-up of the swollen vulva. This bitch is in pre-oestrus. This phase lasts approximately nine days and is characterized by swelling of the vulva and a bloody discharge. Its precedes oestrus, at which point the vulval swelling reduces and the bitch will accept the dog.

months of age. Certain dogs, particularly of the larger breeds, may not attain puberty until they are in their second year, sometimes leaving this as late as twenty months. There is therefore considerable individual variation between bitches.

The dog's oestrus cycle is precisely that: a cycle. We will describe it starting with pro-oestrus and follow it chronologically through oestrus, dioestrus and anoestrus (PR-O-DI-ANA may help you remember this sequence).

Pro-oestrus is the stage when the follicles in the ovaries begin to develop in preparation for ovulation. In doing so, they release the hormone oestrogen, which prepares the uterus, vagina and vulva for mating and pregnancy. The vulva swells and there is a bloody vulval discharge. Pro-oestrus generally lasts about nine days, with a range of six to eleven days. Towards the end of this period the female becomes more tolerant of the male.

The next stage is *oestrus*. It is characterized by a decline in circulating oestrogen levels and an increase in progesterone levels. This period also lasts for about nine days and is the time when the bitch will accept the dog. The hormonal changes – and specifically the drop in oestrogen – result in the pituitary gland releasing follicle stimulating hormone (FSH) and luteinizing hormone (LH). Ovulation occurs 24–72 hours after the LH surge. The number of eggs released by the ovaries as a result of this hormonal stimulus can vary according to the age and breed of the bitch. The ova then take two to three days to mature, at which point they can be fertilized by a spermatozoon. This usually takes place in the lower part of the oviduct.

Technically, oestrus corresponds with the first day that the bitch will stand for the male. Pheromones within the vulval discharge make the bitch highly attractive to male dogs. The vulval discharge loses its bloody character and becomes light pink or straw coloured.

The progesterone-dominated *dioestrus* follows oestrus and lasts for approximately sixty days, regardless of whether or not the bitch has been mated. The *corpora lutea* ('yellow bodies') formed within the ovaries following ovulation continue to produce progesterone throughout dioestrus, regardless of whether the bitch is pregnant or not. In the latter case, the bitch may show varying signs of 'pseudo-pregnancy' or 'false pregnancy'.

During *dioestrus* a number of physical changes are apparent: the vulva gradually reduces in size and the vulval discharge disappears within a few days of the end of oestrus. Towards the end of dioestrus, some bitches may demonstrate development of the mammary tissue and start lactating. Parturition marks the end of pregnancy and signals the transition from dioestrus to the next stage.

A bitch that has given birth to puppies (whelped) thus enters a period of sexual inactivity called *anoestrus*. The timing of this transition from dioestrus to anoestrus is similar in the non-pregnant bitch. The duration of this phase varies markedly between females, with a range of two to ten months reported. It is this variability in the length of anoestrus that gives rise to the variation in length of the oestrus cycle between bitches. During this stage there should not be any vulval discharge.

The glands of the body, including the thyroid and adrenal glands, together with the gonads, are all under the control of the hypothalamus and pituitary glands. These form part of the mammalian brain and are sensitive to a range of complex homoeostatic feedback mechanisms, as well as to environmental and internal stimuli. As mentioned earlier, the pituitary gland produces a number of hormones that can act upon the ovarian tissues. In addition to FSH and LH, the pituitary gland also produces prolactin, which stimulates lactation.

Reproductive disorders and related problems

As mentioned above, the entire male dog can develop testicular problems. The testicles should always therefore be checked for abnormalities. Certain testicular tumours can produce hormones and have an effect on the skin and hair coat. Sertoli cell tumours, for example, can produce female oestrogens; these feminizing hormones typically result in mammary gland enlargement and localized hair loss/thinning. Where abnormalities are detected, the dog should always be referred to a vet.

Entire bitches can develop a number of disorders, including mammary tumours and disorders of the uterus. Any lumps or swellings within the mammary tissue should be brought to the attention of the owner. Dogs can develop benign and malignant mammary tumours and these are always best investigated by a vet. Entire bitches frequently develop infections of the uterus. This is called a *pyometra*.

Pyometra (*see* Fig. 2.4.8) occurs during the *dioestrus* phase of a bitch's oestrus cycle. That is to say, it develops when the bitch's uterine tissues are exposed to progesterone for a long period. This hormone stimulates the lining of the uterus to produce 'uterine milk', which then accumulates within the endometrial glands. These glands dilate and the wall of the uterus is thickened. This is called cystic endometrial hyperplasia and is a precursor to pyometra. The uterine milk is an irritant, as well as an excellent culture medium for bacteria. Usually cystic endometrial hyperplasia regresses during the second half of dioestrus but, with time and increasing numbers of non-pregnant oestrus cycles, it may fail to do so in certain areas of the uterus. A uterine infection can then easily take hold. Whilst gestation has a protective effect on the endometrium, bitches that remain entire and are not bred remain at risk of this condition. It may also be provoked by the administration of synthetic progestogens (progestins), which were historically used to treat skin conditions and prevent a bitch from coming into season.

The condition can manifest itself in two ways: either as an open *pyometra* or as a closed *pyometra*. In the first case, the cervix is open and the uterus is able to drain through the vagina and vulva to the outside. A thick bloody or purulent discharge may be seen and the bitch may be seen to make repeated attempts to clean her vulva. In closed pyometra, as the name suggests, the cervix remains closed and prevents the uterus from draining. The uterus can then become filled with fluid.

Affected dogs can become very ill and may even die. Bacterial toxins can be absorbed and cause the bitch to become toxic. Associated clinical signs include increased thirst, nausea, vomiting, pyrexia and loss of appetite. This is a very serious condition that is typically seen approximately two weeks after the end of a bitch's season. Urgent veterinary referral is essential where this condition is suspected.

Before finishing with reproductive problems and disorders, it is worth mentioning the effect of reproductive hormones on temperament and the pros and cons of sterilization.

Temperament

The reproductive hormones demonstrate a wide range of actions and can have a bearing on the behaviour and temperament of the dog. Testosterone, produced by the testes, is responsible for male characteristics in dogs and can have an influence on behaviour, whilst oestrogen and progesterone in the female can have similar effects. The relationship between hormonal state and behaviour is a complex one and can be difficult to unravel. Aggression, anxiety, mood swings and other unusual behaviours may be seen. Dogs that are usually placid and unthreatening can behave very differently when in the presence of bitches ready for mating. Perhaps most significantly, a dog smelling a bitch in heat can escape and run off to find her. This can be highly embarrassing if the dog is in your care.

Sterilization

Sterilization, or neutering, involves the removal of gonads. In dogs this is termed castration, in bitches *ovariohysterectomy*, or 'spaying'. It is recommended as a means of avoiding unwanted pregnancies and reducing the urge of dogs and bitches to roam. It also reduces the risk posed by a number of diseases of the reproductive tract, including testicular cancer, pyometra and mammary cancer. The removal of the gonads can, however, sometimes result in changes to the physical condition of the dog and of the hair coat.

Sterilization reduces circulating testosterone levels in male dogs, and in female dogs terminates the oestrus cycle for good. This may improve, or otherwise change, the temperament in both the dog and the bitch and inhibits the desire to roam. In ageing bitches spaying may give rise to oestrogen responsive urinary incontinence, particularly when she is relaxed or sleeping.

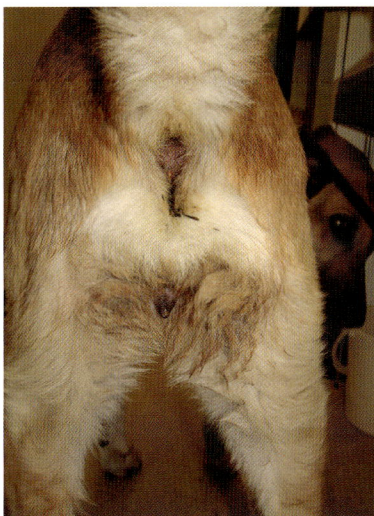

Fig. 2.4.8 Heavy vulval discharge in an entire German Shepherd bitch two weeks after her season. The discharge is discoloured and is consistent with a pyometra. Urgent veterinary referral is advised.

> ### CAUTION: BITCHES IN SEASON
>
> *A bitch in season should be watched at all times. All entire male dogs think they have the right to breed whenever the opportunity presents itself. It is patently unfair to expect a dog to behave rationally when he is in the presence of a bitch ready for mating. So be careful and don't get bitten!*
>
> *Both testes on the male dog should be the same size and should have the same consistency when examined. Neither the dog nor the bitch should have any sign of discharge. The only exceptions to this are when the bitch is in pro-oestrus and oestrus and during the fortnight following whelping.*
>
> *Bitches are often brought in for bathing and freshening up soon after the end of their 'season'. Be sure to assess them thoroughly for signs of pyometra (whatever their age) and advise the owner to seek veterinary advice immediately if you suspect a problem.*

Suggested Further Reading

Cooper, B., Mullineaux, L. and Turner, L. (1994). *BSAVA textbook of veterinary nursing* (formerly *Jones's Animal Nursing*), 5th edition. Cheltenham: BSAVA.

Evans, J.M. and White, K. (2004). *Book of the bitch. A complete guide to understanding and caring for bitches*. Dorking Surrey: Interpet Publishing.

Reece, W.O. (1997). *Physiology of domestic animals*, 2nd edition. Baltimore: Lippincott Williams & Wilkins.

Turner, T. (2004). *Veterinary notes for dog owners*. London: Popular Dogs Publishing Ltd.

2.5 THE DIGESTIVE SYSTEM

There are three parts of the digestive system that may benefit from intervention by a knowledgeable groomer: the health and the condition of the dog's teeth; the health and condition of the mouth and gums; and the health and condition of the anal sacs.

It is part of the groomer's responsibilities to check the dog's teeth and mouth thoroughly for signs of damage or disease and to promote good dental hygiene. Early recognition of disease or damage by a knowledgeable groomer may prevent sickness, ill health or even death if the condition is referred to a vet and treated promptly. At the other end of the digestive tract, care and hygiene of the anal sacs can help to prevent infection, disease – and immense discomfort!

It is therefore necessary that groomers should be familiar with what is 'correct' and 'healthy' and can recognize when veterinary intervention is required.

The digestive system of the dog is devoted entirely to physically and chemically breaking down food and processing it, so that nutrients can be absorbed from the intestines and circulated around the body. Food molecules that have been ingested by the dog are generally too complex to be absorbed in their natural state, so digestion pro-

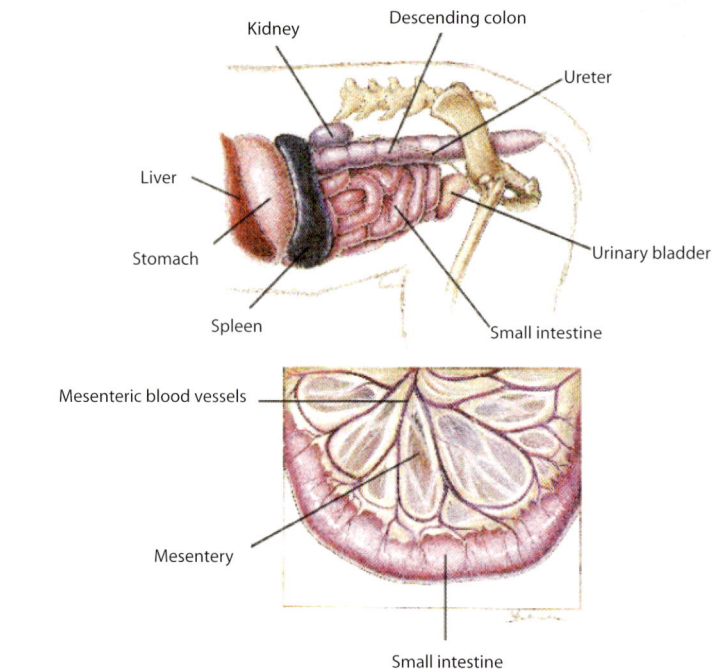

Fig. 2.5.1   The digestive system.

vides simpler molecules that can be taken up and used by the cells. Any residue or waste from the food is then solidified and eliminated from the body in the form of faeces.

The digestive system is essentially a long tube that starts at the mouth and ends at the anus (*see* Fig. 2.5.1). Along with the associated organs that contribute to its tasks, the digestive system can be divided into three functional sections dealing with ingestion, digestion and elimination respectively. The following discussion works through them in order.

The mouth

The oral cavity (mouth) of the dog has a large entrance that opens into a sizeable cavity that can be sealed closed by the lips. The inside of the cavity is lined with a moist, fleshy covering, or mucous membrane. These membranes, along with the skin on the gums, are generally pink (*see* Fig. 2.5.2) in colour but can sometimes be black or a combination of black and pink (*see* Fig. 2.5.3). The mucous membranes should never be pale, white or grey in colour and should always be warm to the touch. (*See* pre-grooming health check section.) The upper jaw of the mouth (*maxilla*) is static and does not move, whereas the hinged lower jaw (*mandible*) moves up

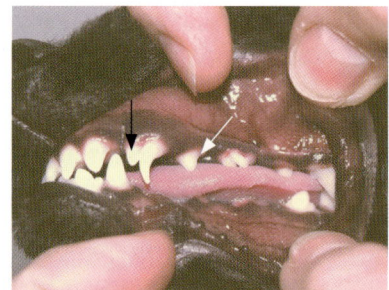

Fig. 2.5.2   The pink quality of the oral mucous membranes is evident in this young poodle's mouth. Note the pinkness immediately above the teeth (white arrow): this is a small band of unpigmented gum. The emerging adult upper left canine (black arrow) can also be seen in front of a retained deciduous canine.

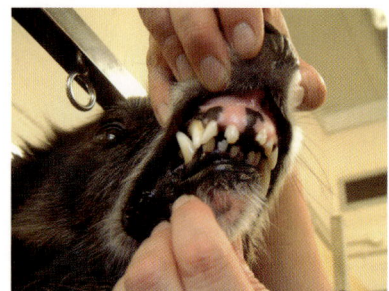

Fig. 2.5.3   The dentition on this dog is very poor. The length of the maxilla has exceeded the length of the mandible to form an 'overshot jaw' or 'parrot mouth'. The black and pink pigmented gums are, however, healthy.

and down and has limited side-to-side movement.

The oral cavity houses the teeth, the tongue and the ducts for the salivary glands.

The teeth

The teeth of the dog are designed to tear at flesh and nibble flesh off bones. They differ somewhat from ours as we are better able to chew from side to side and grind food into small morsels before swallowing.

The centre of the tooth is called the 'pulp' and contains a mass of nerves and blood vessels. The pulp is held together in connective tissue and is encased in a protective covering called dentine that resembles bone but is much harder. The adult teeth are held fast in cavities within the jaw by one or more large (*see* Fig. 2.5.4) roots, which are protected by a cement covering that is softer than the dentine. The visible part of the tooth is called the crown and its dentine construction is protected by an outer layer of extremely hard tissue called enamel.

The adult dog has forty-two teeth made up of four different types (*see* Fig. 2.5.5). Starting at the front of the mouth, on both jaws there are six small pillar-shaped, single-rooted teeth called *incisors*; these are the grasping (nibbling) teeth. Working backwards, the next two taller conical teeth (one on each side) are called *canine* teeth and these also have only one root. These are the teeth that hold and tear at flesh. Behind the canines, on each side, are four *premolars*, the last of which is enormous and is called a 'carnassial tooth'. Behind the premolars are two *molars* (three on the bottom jaw). The carnassial teeth (Premolar 4 on the upper jaw and Molar 1 on the lower jaw) are the largest teeth on the upper and lower arcade respectively. These are shearing teeth and are used for cutting, with the dog often turning his head to one side so that he can use these teeth. Premolars and molars are used for crushing flesh and other food materials before swallowing.

The carnassial tooth of the upper jaw (Premolar 4) is the largest tooth in the dog's mouth and is the only tooth to have three roots. The other molars and premolars have two or, in some cases, one root.

Puppies are born without teeth; they begin to develop their first set of disposable deciduous teeth (*puppy* or *milk teeth*) at around three to four weeks of age. All of the puppy teeth should have erupted (emerged from the gum) and be fully functional by two months of age. Puppy dentition is made up of twenty-eight teeth, with each side of each jaw comprising three incisors, one canine and three pre-molars. Puppies lose these deciduous teeth at about five months of age, when they are replaced by permanent adult teeth (Fig. 2.5.6).

In the young dog the teeth should be white (*see* Fig. 2.5.7) and the breath should not be offensive. As the dog ages, the teeth may start to darken to a yellow colour (*see* Fig. 2.5.8) and, usually in response to a soft food diet, bacterial film on the teeth can become mineralized by the calcium in saliva and form *calculus* (tartar). If not removed, the calculus can cause the gums to become inflamed (*gingivitis*); further progression may result in the gums receding, exposing the roots of the tooth. Once this happens, the tooth develops an infection that is very difficult to contain and may spread along the gums to other teeth. This progression can be slowed down by regular cleaning and regular check-ups with a veterinary surgeon.

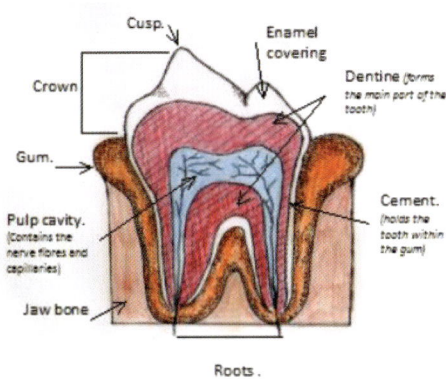

Fig. 2.5.4   Cross-section of the tooth.

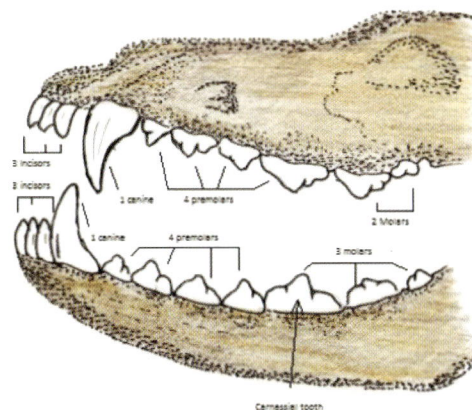

Fig. 2.5.6   The smaller tooth is a rootless deciduous upper canine tooth from a Miniature Poodle puppy, the larger one an upper canine tooth from an adult Miniature Poodle. The black arrows to the left of the red line show the length and size of the root. The part to the right of the red line is the part that is visible when you look into a dog's mouth.

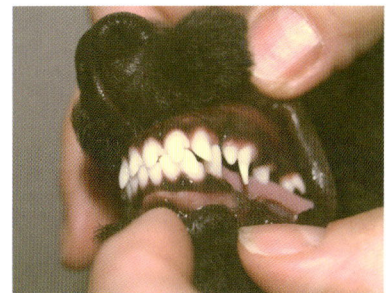

Fig.2.5.7   White puppy teeth in a young Miniature Poodle.

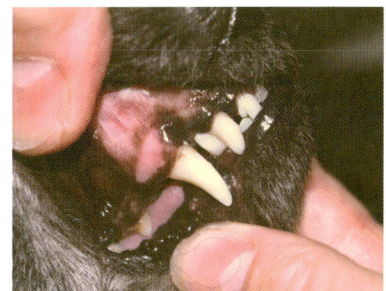

Fig. 2.5.5   Cross-section of dentition for the adult dog.

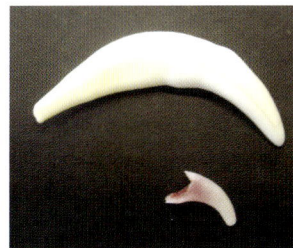

Fig.2.5.8   Off-white (yellowing) adult teeth in a ten-year-old Miniature Poodle.

To function properly the teeth need to be aligned correctly. This is called 'the bite'. There are three correct bites: the 'scissor', the 'level' and the 'reverse scissor'.

The *scissor bite* (see Fig. 2.5.9) is the configuration found in most humans. The teeth of the maxilla (top jaw) sit slightly forward and overlap the teeth of the mandible (lower jaw). This is the most common bite in dogs and is the correct bite for all mesaticephalic (nose equal in length to that of the cranium) and dolichocephalic (cranium longer than the nose) breeds. The bite becomes incorrect when the maxilla exceeds the length of the mandible to produce a gap between the two sets of teeth, so that they do not make contact when the mouth closes. This condition

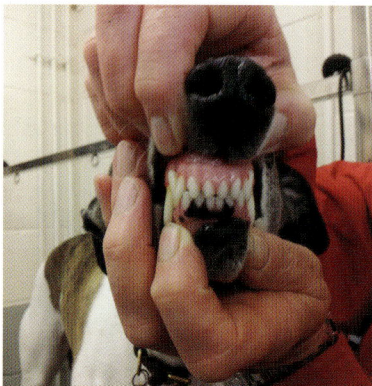

Fig. 2.5.9   *A very good example of a scissor bite.*

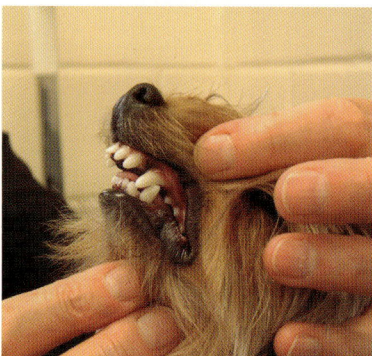

Fig.2.5.10   *Another example of an overshot jaw. Here the maxilla has extended to leave a wide gap between the two sets of teeth.*

is termed 'overshot' or 'parrot mouthed' (see Fig. 2.5.10).

The *level bite* (see Fig. 2.5.11) is where the top set of teeth sits immediately above, and rests directly on top of, the bottom set. This is the correct bite for brachycephalic (nose shorter than the

head) breeds, but is incorrect for mesaticephalic and dolichocephalic breeds, or if the maxilla overlaps to either the left or the right of the mandibula. This last deformity is termed a 'wry' or 'twisted' mouth (see Fig. 2.5.12).

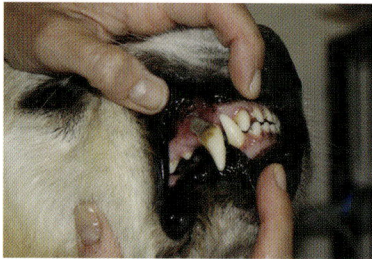

Fig. 2.5.11   *This Golden Retriever is demonstrating a level bite, where the top set of incisors sit on top of the bottom set. This bite would be correct on a brachycephalic head, such as that of a Shih Tzu, but it is considered an incorrect bite for this breed.*

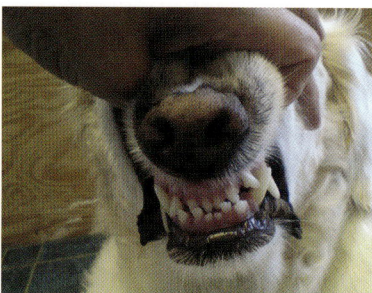

Fig. 2.5.12   *The mandible on this Golden Retriever is slightly longer than the maxilla, and both the upper and lower canines on the right are leaning outwards. This has caused the mandible to twist to the right and is termed a 'wry' mouth. The canine teeth on the left are straight, preventing the mouth from twisting to the left.*

The *reverse scissor* bite (see Fig. 2.5.13) occurs when the lower set of teeth sits slightly forward of the top set, giving the impression of a stronger, more prominent, mandible. This bite is correct for extreme brachycephalic breeds where there is very little – if any – length of foreface. The bite becomes incorrect when the mandible exceeds the maxilla to the extent that a large gap appears between the two sets of teeth, so that there is no contact between the two sets as the mouth closes. This condition is termed 'undershot' (see Fig. 2.5.14).

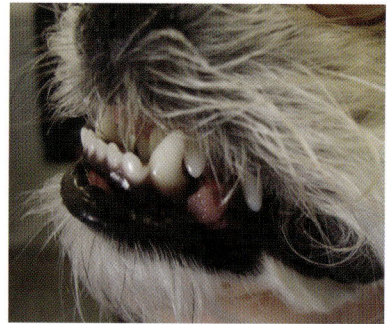

Fig. 2.5.13   *The reverse scissor bite of a Llasa Apso. On this dog the top teeth are crooked and incorrectly fall backwards into the mouth on the side nearest the camera, but you can see how the lower teeth should fit just in front of the top teeth.*

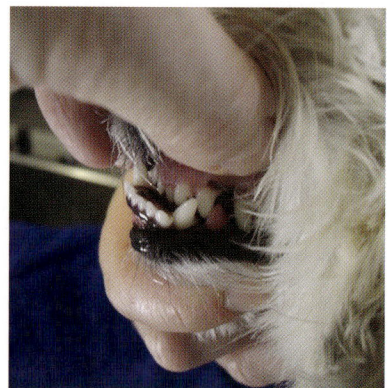

Fig. 2.5.14   *The bite becomes incorrect when the mandible exceeds the maxilla to the extent that the two sets of teeth do not touch each other.*

The tongue

A mass of multi-directional muscles covered in mucous membrane make up the tongue. This muscle lies on the floor of the mouth and is attached to the lower jaw bones on either side and suspended – along with the larynx – from the hyoid apparatus in the throat. The tongue should be warm to the touch and, although it is generally pink in colour, can be black, dark blue or a combination of black and pink (see Fig. 2.5.15). It should never feel cold or clammy or be pale grey in colour. (See pre-grooming health check section.) The surface of the tongue is covered in small protrusions called papillae, and it is these that make the tongue rough to the touch. This roughness not only helps to control the food in the mouth, it also helps the dog with grooming himself.

Some of the papillae contain special nerve endings called taste buds, which, along with the nerve fibres within the mucous membrane, convey messages to the brain about the taste and texture of anything taken into the mouth. The dog's sense of taste is confined to the tongue, the palate and the epiglottis; the sense of flavour that humans experience is a result of the combination of smell and taste, and it is safe to assume that this is also the case with the dog. Humans have about 9,000 taste buds but the dog has only around 1,700. It therefore appears that the dog's sense of taste is less well developed than that of the human, although, like us, his most abundant taste buds are those that respond to sugars. Along with most other animals, the dog can discriminate by taste between substances that in their natural state are harmful and those that aren't.

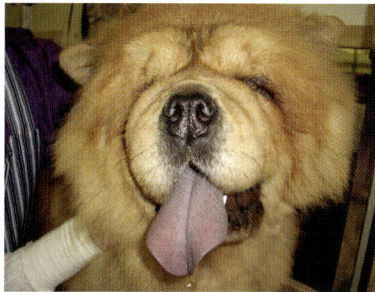

Fig.2.5.15   *It is quite normal for the tongue and the mucous membranes within the mouth of the Chow Chow to be blue in colour. Here you can clearly see that the blue pigment has a pink undertone but in some cases the blue pigment is a lot darker, almost black.*

Salivary glands

Saliva is a watery fluid that is present in the mouth to keep it moist and to aid the digestion of food.

There are many sets of salivary glands sited around the head, the largest of which – the parotid, zygomatic, sublingual and mandibula – have several ducts opening into the mouth. The parotid glands are located in front of the ear and have a duct that opens inside the cheek by the molars. The sublingual gland is located deep inside the floor of the mouth, along with the mandibular gland, near the back of the jaw bone; these have ducts that open into the small swelling that can be seen underneath the tongue. The zygomatic gland lies close to the eyeball within the eye socket (orbit) and has ducts that open into the palate.

When a dog begins to eat, the smell of the food stimulates the production of saliva. Saliva is about 99 per cent water and acts to soften the food by adding moisture, so that swallowing is made easier. Saliva also contains the digestive enzyme amylase, which helps to break down the starch and sugar in the food.

Saliva also has a role to play in heat regulation by providing the water that is evaporated during panting.

> ### CAUTION
>
> *The healthy mouth should be moist and warm at all times. The gums and the mucosa are usually pink in colour but they can be black or dark blue. They should not be grey in colour, nor should the mucosa feel cold or clammy.*
>
> *The gums should be free of growths and, when pressed with the finger, they should return to their normal colour within a few seconds.*
>
> *There should not be any signs of receding gums.*
>
> *The teeth should be white and clean in the young dog but may darken as the dog ages.*
>
> *The retention of deciduous teeth in the puppy beyond seven months of age, particularly in smaller breeds, can cause misalignment of the adult teeth and can lead to dental disease.*
>
> *Adult teeth should be checked for damage, wear and calculus.*
>
> *Any abnormalities within the mouth, or offensive-smelling breath, should be referred to a vet for investigation.*

The oesophagus

Long gone are the days when the dog hunted for his supper: his food is now commercially prepared, or cooked at home and provided for him. He therefore no longer has to tear and chew at it. There is very little stimulation other than smell to aid mechanical pre-digestion, so once moistened, the tongue pushes the food (which is generally in large lumps) into the oesophagus. Swallowing then triggers relaxation in the muscles of the oesophagus to allow food to pass on its way down to the stomach.

The *oesophagus* is a long straight pipe, or tube, leading to the stomach. As the food continues to arrive, involuntary strong muscular contractions (*peristalsis*) work in a downward wave to push the food through the thoracic cavity, past the diaphragm and through a circular muscle known as the 'cardiac sphincter', which works as a valve to open and close the entrance to the stomach.

When the muscular contractions work in a reverse or upward movement (*anti-peristalsis*) the cardiac sphincter opens to allow partially broken-down food to be ejected from the stomach. This expulsion is produced by the contracting stomach muscles pushing up against the diaphragm, forcing the stomach contents back up through the oesophagus and through the mouth. This is called vomiting.

> ### CAUTION: PREVENTING DAMAGE TO THE THROAT
>
> *The oesophagus lies in the throat alongside the trachea, which takes oxygen to the lungs. Both can be easily bruised or damaged by neck restraints that are too tight or badly fitted. This may result in the dog not being able to breathe or in painful bruising that may prevent the dog from eating or drinking.*
>
> *Whilst it is natural for the dog to pull against or bear down on a neck restraint (they often do this whilst walking on a collar and lead), you should make sure that neck restraints are correctly fitted and can be loosened easily if necessary. When restraining a dog on the grooming table, you should use a belly restraint, so that he is less likely to put all of his weight into the neck restraint.*

The stomach

It is quite interesting to note that a small dog's digestive tract represents about 7 per cent of the total body weight, whereas it represents only 3 per cent of the body weight of large dogs. This may explain, if only in part, why large dogs are more susceptible to digestive problems.

The stomach, which lies on the left side of the dog, slightly beyond the ribcage, is made up of longitudinal, circular and oblique layers of smooth muscle. It resembles a deflated elastic ball that can expand to fill almost half of the abdominal cavity when the dog eats. Due to the dog's predominantly meat-based diet, and the fact that food generally arrives at the stomach in chunks, a significant number of mechanical and chemical changes are required before the proteins, lipids and glucides that make up the food can be broken down sufficiently to be absorbed.

Glands within the mucous membrane of the stomach produce gastric juices – a combination of hydrochloric acid and several enzymes – which split the proteins and lipids. Mucus is also produced to line the stomach and protect it against the acids.

Amylase, an enzyme in saliva, will already have started to break down some carbohydrates. Protein digestion is initiated by the enzyme pepsin, which is activated by the stomach acid.

The food and gastric juices are mixed by the muscular movement of the stomach wall, which further facilitates digestion. By the time the particles have broken down sufficiently to leave the stomach the food is in a semi-fluid state called 'chyme' (pronounced kime). The exit from the stomach into the next phase of digestion, the small intestine, is through another circular muscle called the 'pyloric sphincter'. This muscle stops the chyme from returning to the stomach.

The small intestine

The intestines are separated into two parts: the small intestine and the large intestine. The small intestine is so called because it is narrower in circumference than the large intestine, although it is longer in length. Its job is to continue with the digestion and absorption process.

The small intestine is a long muscular tube that contains many glands. It is divided into three parts: the duodenum, jejunum and ileum. The first section, the duodenum, is fixed in the upper part of the abdomen but the second and third sections lie freely in large loops within the abdominal cavity. The inside wall of the intestine is lined with microscopic, finger-like projections called *villi*, which increase the surface area for absorption. Food comes into contact with the villi as it is passed very slowly through each section by muscular, peristaltic waves. Unlike the strong muscular contractions that allow large chunks of food to travel very quickly from the mouth to the stomach, the contractions within the small intestines are much slower and the peristaltic waves ripple along the tube in small sections, rather than from one end to the other in a continuous movement. This serves to mix the food and move it along the tube for short distances at a time, ensuring that there is adequate time for the contents to be broken down further and the nutrients absorbed fully.

Throughout this process glands within the intestine walls continue to add digestive juices. These include pancreatic juice from the pancreatic ducts, containing the enzymes amylase, trypsin and lipase to digest proteins, starch and fats, and bile from the liver. Bile contains essential salts for breaking down fats into even smaller modules, allowing the lipase to work more efficiently. The high level of bicarbonate in these juices is required to neutralize the stomach acid and produce an alkaline environment, which allows the enzymes present to do their job effectively. Once broken down by the juices the food is absorbed by the small intestine and passed through its walls into the bloodstream and the lymphatic vessels.

The majority of the liquid that has been added to the food is also absorbed by the villi but the material passing onto the next stage is still in a liquid state as it leaves the small intestine through a muscular valve called the ileocaecal valve, into the large intestine for the third stage of processing.

The large intestine

The large intestine is divided into three sections: the caecum, colon and rectum.

When the food waste leaves the small intestine, through the ileocaecal valve, it passes into the caecum; this is a relatively short, blunt-ended tube extending away from the main section of intestine, like a cul-de-sac. The main section of the large intestine is called the colon and it continues caudally, towards the anus, passing through the pelvic canal, where it becomes the rectum.

Movement through the large intestine is even slower than through the small intestine. No more digestion or absorption of food takes place here but the absorption of water and fluids continues so that the final waste product has a semi-solid consistency as it enters the concluding stages of elimination. The waste products are passed intermittently from the colon into the rectum in the form of faeces.

The last section of the digestive tract, the rectum (or 'anal canal'), is a very short piece of tube that is made up of, and held closed by, circular sphincter muscles. As the walls of the rectum stretch to accommodate the faeces, nerve endings within the rectal walls are triggered to relax the anal sphincter muscles, allowing the waste to pass through into the canal. Final elimination does not take place until the dog feels the time and place are appropriate; then, the lifting of his tail relaxes the external part of the sphincter and controlled evacuation of faeces in the form of stools is performed. This is called *defecation*.

Disorders of the digestive system

The digestive system is complex and can be affected by many factors, such as the dog's lifestyle or his mental attitude, as well as by parasite burdens and more sinister diseases. Whilst it is often possible for you to detect that the digestive system is compromised (i.e. not functioning normally), the eventual diagnosis will almost certainly require an extensive and thorough examination by the dog's vet.

There are some common signs that you will see. Most of these concern the dog's weight, others affect the formation of faeces and some may affect the coat and skin quality. It is very easy to make a wild guess and assume that there is an obvious explanation to these problems but it is rarely that simple.

Body weight changes

The *underweight* dog may have a worm problem but weight loss can also be caused by malabsorption; both explanations are often accompanied by a dry coat with a scurfy skin. The 'fussy feeder' may also present underweight but the reason why the dog is not eating needs to be addressed and it may not be as simple as the dog not liking his food. In all underweight dogs the health and condition of the teeth should be considered as potential causes of the weight loss. Persistent weight loss should always be investigated by the dog's vet.

The *overweight* dog could be the result of over-eating or under-exercising but weight gain may also be an indication of disease. Some breeds, such as the Cavalier King Charles Spaniel, are prone to obesity, which may be caused by an inherited heart condition; others, like the Dalmatian, are prone to weight increase from an inherited liver disorder.

Vomiting and diarrhoea

Vomiting can be a natural reaction in the dog. It can often be caused by over-eating or needing to empty the stomach contents in a hurry, perhaps in an escape situation. It may also be caused by stress, illness or disease. Alternatively, it may be caused by swallowing something poisonous and/or irritant, such as shampoo, or something that can't be digested like the stuffing from soft toys. In other cases vomiting can be a sign of *gastritis* (inflammation of the stomach).

You should always monitor the frequency and amount of vomiting. Persistent vomiting leads to dehydration; if this is the case, veterinary attention should always be sought.

Loose faeces (*diarrhoea*) should also not be left unmonitored as, again, this can result in dehydration. As with vomiting, diarrhoea can be caused by

> ## CAUTION
>
> *In the grooming salon you will see dogs on a regular basis. You can therefore monitor them for signs of weight loss or weight gain. You can also keep tabs on, and record the frequency of, parasite control.*
>
> *Learn which breeds are subject to obesity through an inherited disease and those breeds that are predisposed to malabsorption so that you know what signs to look out for and can alert the owner to a potential problem. If the affected dog is not in one of the above categories, it may be appropriate to discuss and recommend a diet or lifestyle change, or parasite control.*
>
> *In the otherwise healthy dog, vomiting and diarrhoea may be the result of stress from travelling to the grooming room or from the actual grooming process. If these signs existed prior to the visit, if the dog is unwell or the problem continues after the dog has left the salon, veterinary advice should be sought.*
>
> *The digestive system is complex. Don't ever assume that you know what the signs you detect relate to. Veterinary advice is certainly needed before a diagnosis can be made.*
>
> *See Chapter 8, First Aid and Emergency Care, for further information on vomiting and diarrhoea.*

a stress reaction but it can also be a sign of illness or disease. In a stressful situation it is normal for a dog to have diarrhoea but if the problem continues after the dog has been removed from that situation, veterinary advice should be sought.

The anal sacs

Although these glandular structures are not strictly part of the digestive system as they don't have any function or part in the processing of food, they are mentioned within this section because they share part of the same apparatus – the anus. They will, however, be discussed more fully in the skin section.

Anal sacs (popularly called 'anal glands') (*see* Fig. 2.5.16) are two small pouches situated either side of and slightly below the anus, roughly at about 4–5 and 7–8 o'clock. A small tube or duct passes from each sac to open at the anus.

Anal sacs vary in size from pea- to walnut-sized, depending on the size of the dog. They contain a secretion from numerous glands within their walls, which is used to scent mark. Some of this secretion is used in inter-canine communication and is deposited when the dog passes faeces to make a stool. The rest is stored within the sacs for later use.

The storing of the fluid can often

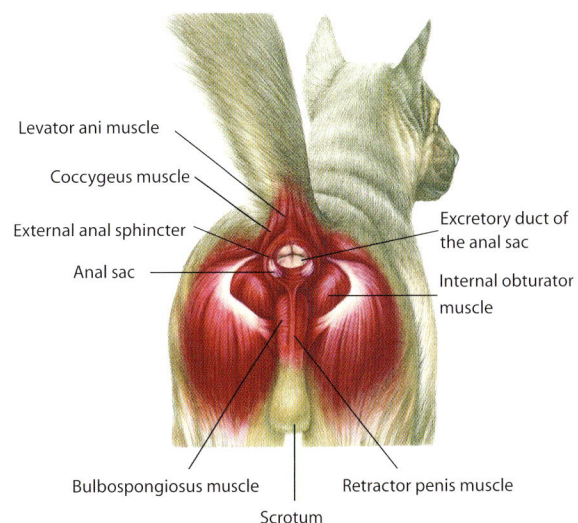

Fig. 2.5.16
Perineal anatomy. and the position of the anal sacs.

Levator ani muscle
Coccygeus muscle
External anal sphincter
Anal sac
Excretory duct of the anal sac
Internal obturator muscle
Bulbospongiosus muscle
Retractor penis muscle
Scrotum

be problematic because, if the ducts become blocked, the secretion accumulates and the pouches become distended. As the pouches fill, the dog experiences discomfort and sometimes pain. When this happens the dog may be seen rubbing his bottom along the floor (scooting), or licking or biting at the anus in an attempt to relieve the irritation.

Impacted anal sacs

If the ducts remain blocked the contents of the sacs can dry out and solidify, causing what is termed an impaction. This is very painful for the dog and can result in the lining of the pouches tearing and causing an abscess. In such cases veterinary treatment is needed. Care must be taken when examining a dog with impacted anal sacs as he will be in a lot of pain and even the most docile of animals may need to be muzzled for your own safety.

ALERT: ANAL SAC DISEASE

The anal sacs are located at about 4 and 8 on the clock face, slightly below the anus. Although the sacs vary in size according to the size of the dog, they should not feel distended when examined. Slight finger pressure on either side of the sacs should empty the pouches of their contents. It is normal for the liquid contents to have an offensive smell that may linger; the colour can vary from brown to pale fawn. If the contents appear thick and dry, contain signs of blood or are difficult to remove, advise the owner to consult a vet.

Check the anal sacs for signs of impaction, infection or abscessation, and, particularly in older male dogs, check for signs of tumours. Where any such abnormalities are identified, advise the owner to take their dog to the vet.

2.6 THE CARDIOVASCULAR SYSTEM

The cardiovascular system itself has minimal impact on the day-to-day work of the groomer. Heart conditions, however, are not uncommon and are not necessarily an age-related problem. Sooner or later you will be asked to groom a dog with a heart problem. You therefore need to understand how to work with dogs that have been diagnosed with heart disease and will need to take steps to identify these dogs on admission.

With this in mind, it is useful for the groomer to have some understanding of how the cardiovascular system works. You need to be able to recognize when a dog is struggling (not coping/stressed) and when this stress level is putting the dog at risk. This section explains what is happening when a dog is under stress and why some dogs, particularly those with a heart problem, struggle to cope (because of the extra demands placed on the heart in a stressful situation). These 'at risk' individuals need to be identified so that you can adapt your work and proceed at a pace they can cope with.

Another concern that does affect groomers is loss of blood from accidental injuries involving sharp cutting tools. This is a particular worry with dogs that have a blood clotting disorder. You therefore need to remain alert to this possibility and know how to take appropriate precautions and deal with any resulting problems.

The cardiovascular system is the name given to the heart and the network of blood vessels (arteries, veins and capillaries) that transport the blood around the body.

Blood is pumped from the heart around the body via the arterial system (i.e. within arteries), and returns to the heart via the venous system (i.e. within veins – see Fig. 2.6.1. for the position of the inlet veins and outlet arteries). The arterial system carries oxygenated blood and nutrients to nourish the muscles and vital organs, whereas the venous system removes waste products from the tissues for disposal and carries deoxygenated blood back to the heart. The two systems are linked by a network of tiny blood vessels called capillaries, whose thin, permeable walls allow the exchange of oxygen, nutrients and waste products – such as carbon dioxide – between the blood and tissue cells.

The heart has a left and right side, each with two chambers (see Fig. 2.6.2). The left side of the heart receives oxygenated blood directly from the lungs, which it then pumps via the aorta to all parts of the body (including the brain, liver, kidneys and muscles). This is also known as systemic circulation. Blood returning from these organs is low in oxygen and high in carbon dioxide; it enters the right side of the heart and is then pumped via the pulmonary artery to the lungs for reoxygenation. The pulmonary artery is thus the only artery to carry deoxygenated blood. After visiting the lungs, however, the blood becomes rich in oxygen and has got rid of the carbon dioxide that it was carrying. It is this oxygenated blood that then returns to the left side of the heart via the pulmonary vein (see Fig. 2.6.2). The entire process takes about a minute. Without this supply of oxygen, all the cells in the body would quickly die.

Arteries have thick walls to cope with the high pressure produced by the heart pumping blood into them. By contrast the venous system is a low pressure system and the walls of the veins are generally thinner.

The heart needs a generous supply of oxygen, which is carried by a generous supply of blood. The heart muscle therefore has its own separate network of blood vessels called the coronary system.

The heart would continue to pump at the same rate of beats per minute continuously if it were not for the influence of the autonomic nervous system. This is the part of the nervous system that is not under conscious control but reacts, instead, to a range of stimuli from within the body. The autonomic nervous system slows down the rate of the heart beat during periods of rest or sleep and rapidly speeds it up again in response to exercise or stress. It thereby responds accurately to demand.

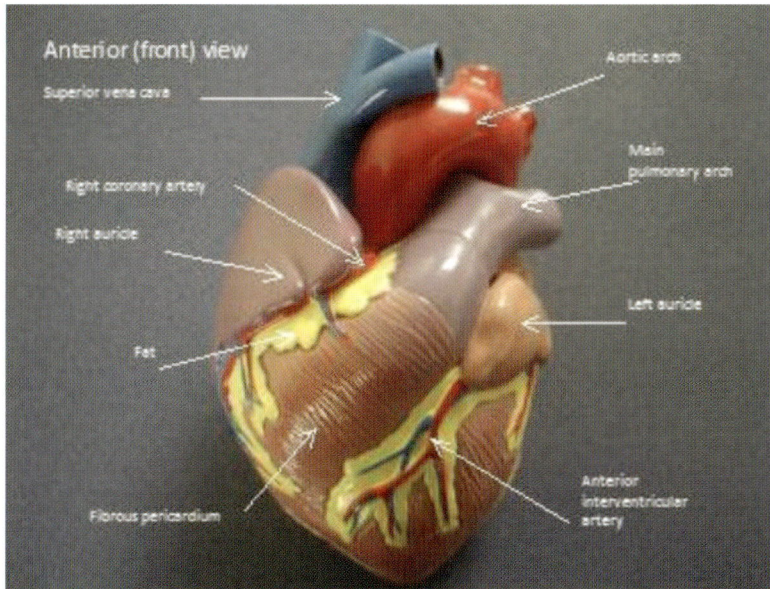

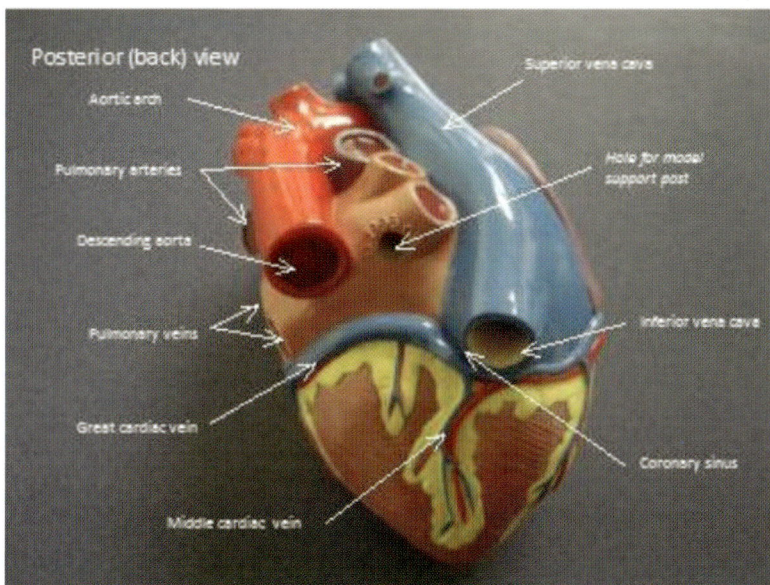

The rhythmic heart beat and the pressure of the blood flow can be felt in the arteries nearest to the skin surface. We call this the 'pulse', and in the dog the rhythm may vary considerably depending on the size of the dog. Very large dogs have a resting pulse rate of approximately 80 beats per minute, whereas toy dogs can have a rate as high as 120 beats per minute.

Maintaining the blood pressure is essential to keeping the body nourished with the oxygen and nutrients vital for its survival. If the pressure – and consequently the blood flow rate – is reduced, waste accumulates and tissues may become starved of oxygen. Without oxygen, the heart may falter or it could stop altogether, and the cells of other vital organs will soon die.

A drop in blood pressure produces a condition known as 'shock'. A wide range of causes can result in 'shock': these can be psychological and reversible, as in fainting. They can also be due to more serious problems, such as heart failure and the resulting reduction in blood pressure and circulating blood volume. Heavy bleeding (blood loss) is another common cause of a reduction in blood volume and may also give rise to 'shock'. These conditions are discussed further in the first aid section.

Grooming dogs with heart failure

Heart failure is a progressive condition in which the performance of the 'pump'

ABOVE: *Fig. 2.6.1 The heart (anterior and posterior views).*

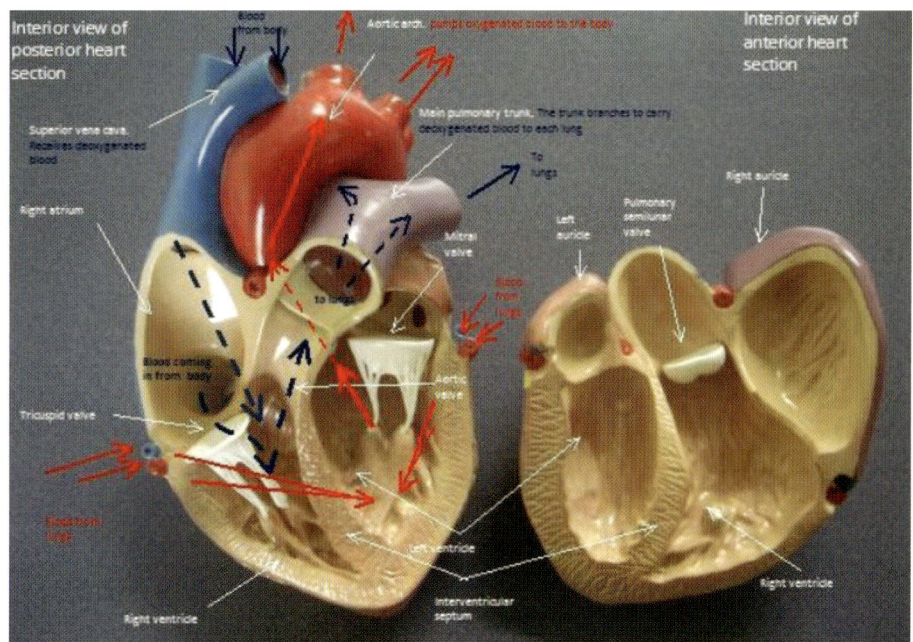

RIGHT: *Fig. 2.6.2 The heart (left and right chambers).*

gradually deteriorates. Dogs with heart failure can live surprisingly fulfilled lives until their hearts finally pack up. It is quite likely that, sooner or later, you will be asked to bath and trim these patients; you should undertake this work cautiously but in the knowledge that you can make a valuable contribution to the dog's welfare.

The heart of a dog that has been diagnosed with heart failure is less able to deal with increased demands for oxygen than a normal, healthy heart. Consequently, you must pay careful attention to how these dogs are coping with the grooming process. This is always easier if you know the dog and have groomed him before. If, however, you are grooming the dog for the first time, you should check with the owner how the dog usually copes with grooming. If in doubt, it may be advisable to ask to speak with the dog's vet.

When grooming a dog with heart problems, you should monitor their gum colour regularly; this should be done throughout their stay with you. If the gums become paler and the dog starts panting, stop what you are doing. If the dog recovers quickly, this is a good sign. If he fails to recover quickly, veterinary advice should be sought immediately.

Learning which breeds are vulnerable to heart disease will forewarn you of potential problems. Careful monitoring of dogs for signs of stress throughout the grooming process also helps to reduce the risk of serious problems in dogs with heart failure.

Grooming dogs with clotting disorders

Haemophilia is an inherited condition that manifests itself as poor clotting of the blood. It can represent a serious health problem as a small skin wound, a cut or even bruising can result in significant blood loss. Most owners will, providing they know, tell you if their dog is haemophiliac. Some, however, will not and others simply do not know!

The condition is passed on through a recessive sex-linked gene. All males carrying the gene develop the condition, whereas females carrying the gene can either be affected (if homozygous, i.e. if they are carrying two copies of the gene) or be carriers. It follows then that the gene is recessive because it may not manifest itself in the carrier female but is likely to be passed on to her puppies (with the disease appearing in male dogs further down the line). Another name for canine haemophilia is von Willebrand's Disease. Haemophilia A arises as a result of a failure in the production of clotting factor VIII, whereas Haemophilia B is due to a deficiency in clotting factor IX.

This condition has been recorded in some twenty-five breeds of dog, including the German Shepherd, Doberman, Siberian Husky and many others. White German Shepherd Dogs appear to be particularly affected. The prevalence of this condition varies from area to area depending on local genetics. It would therefore be sensible to find out what breeds are affected in your own area.

A nose bleed or a cut nail quick in these dogs can easily result in an unstoppable bleed that will need veterinary intervention. Such problems are always best avoided and it therefore pays to identify these individuals and treat them with great care. It may be worth having a specific question

---

ALERT

The heart beat should always maintain a regular rhythm. Learn to detect the dog's pulse and how to monitor it.

Monitor all dogs throughout the grooming process and frequently rest dogs that are anxious or become stressed, irrespective of their age.

Take particular care with those dogs known to be suffering from heart failure.

Rapid blood loss can result in shock and ultimately death. Don't rely on the dog's owner telling you that their dog suffers from a blood clotting disorder. Ask the question and consider requesting this information on your admission form.

Accidents can happen, so learn which breeds are predisposed to haemophilia, especially those bred in your area. Keep client records up to date, particularly the telephone number of the dog's vet.

---

on your admission form asking if the dog suffers from haemophilia. Where such dogs are identified, you may, for example, wish to adopt a conservative approach to trimming their nails or may even choose to file them.

Dealing with emergencies is discussed in the First Aid section.

Suggested further reading

Gough, A. and Thomas, A. (2010). *Breed predispositions to disease in dogs and cats*. 2nd edition. London: Wiley Blackwell.

2.7 THE RESPIRATORY SYSTEM

The respiratory system (see Fig. 2.7.1) is generally given little consideration by owners and groomers, partly because you cannot see what is going on within it, but also because changes to the dog's breathing are often, in the early stages, very subtle and easily overlooked.

Respiration is a process, or function, that keeps the dog alive by allowing oxygen to enter the body and carbon dioxide to be removed from it. The morphology of the dog and certain grooming practices can be detrimental to respiration. It is therefore important that groomers have an understanding of what happens when the dog breathes and how efficient breathing can become impaired. By remaining alert to these dangers, you are better able to safeguard each dog's health whilst they are in your care.

Several factors influence the efficiency of respiration:

The length of the dog's nose and the shape of his head can affect the amount of air (and therefore oxygen) the dog can inhale;

The shape of the nostrils can also influence air intake; and

If the dog becomes stressed, air intake and oxygen uptake can both be affected.

If the oxygen uptake (into the blood) is reduced or inhibited, the dog cannot breathe effectively and may die.

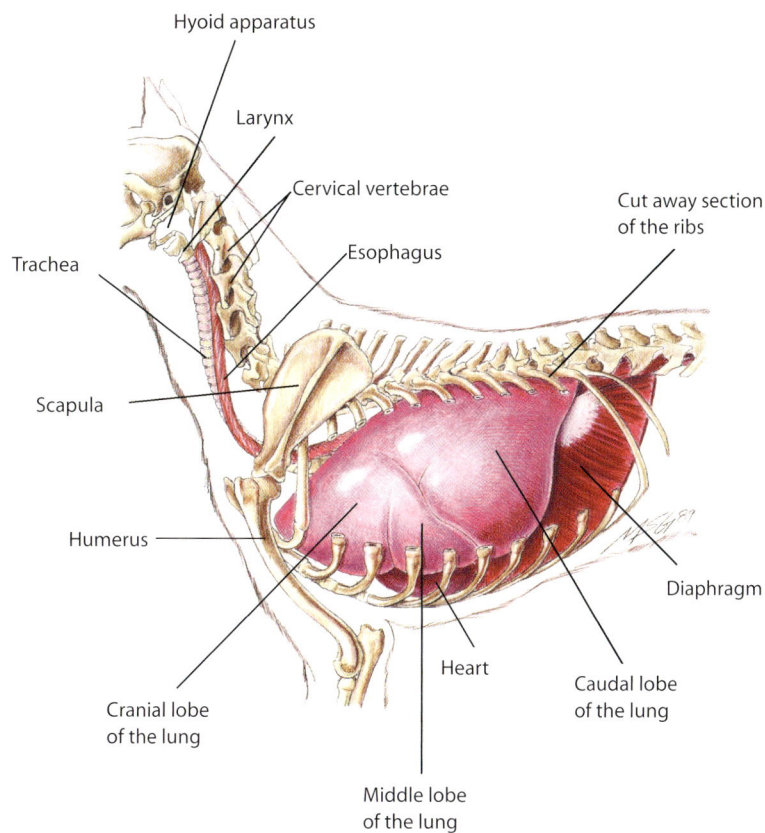

Labels (clockwise):
- Hyoid apparatus
- Larynx
- Cervical vertebrae
- Esophagus
- Cut away section of the ribs
- Diaphragm
- Caudal lobe of the lung
- Middle lobe of the lung
- Heart
- Cranial lobe of the lung
- Humerus
- Scapula
- Trachea

Fig. 2.7.1   The respiratory tract.

(extension) of the skin that becomes hairless to form the nose, extending into the inside of the nostril cavity, where it becomes mucous membrane. The cartilaginous structure of the nostrils provides them with strength and rigidity, allowing them to be maintained open, whilst enabling them to be flared when an increase in the size of the nasal opening is required. This allows air to move freely through the nasal opening during both inhalation and exhalation.

The *nasal cavities* begin just behind the nostrils, inside the bridge of the nose. Mucous membranes extending back from the nostrils form chambers, which are supported by delicate, scroll-like bones that turn in on themselves to form cones, called turbinates, and the passageways of the nasal sinuses. The mucous membranes covering the turbinates provide a large surface area and possess a rich blood supply that efficiently filters, warms and humidifies inhaled air.

Respiration is the exchange of gases between the environment and living structures. Oxygen from the environment is essential for chemical reactions to take place within the body. In mammals oxygen is carried by the blood to all cells within the body, where it is used in a process known as 'internal' or 'tissue respiration'. Once the cells have processed the oxygen, the by-product, carbon dioxide, is exhaled into the environment. The exchange of gases is called 'external respiration'.

The respiratory system is divided into two parts: the 'upper respiratory tract' and the 'lower respiratory tract'.

The upper respiratory tract

This part starts with the nostrils and continues internally with the nasal cavities, the pharynx, the larynx and the trachea. The mouth is used as an additional airway for panting (and during resuscitation) but it is not part of the actual respiratory system.

The nostrils are a continuation

CAUTION: CHECK THE DOG'S NOSTRILS

Not all dogs have open nostrils. Brachycephalics, such as Pekingese, Pugs and Bulldogs, often have very narrow nostrils that are misshapen as a result of bad breeding, or pinched closed through malfunction of the nostril muscles.

Fig. 2.7.2   Brachycephalics, such as Pugs, can have breathing difficulties.

These dogs cannot breathe normally and have a reduced oxygen intake. They should not therefore be dried in drying cabinets as this can expose them to heat stress, which in turn can exacerbate their existing breathing difficulties.

The mucous membranes covering the turbinates, furthest away from the nostrils and closest to the brain, are involved in smell detection and the communication of sensory scent information to the brain. Glands within the mucous membranes secrete mucus, which traps particles and microbes in the air; this mucus can then be passed into the throat to be swallowed.

After leaving the nasal cavities, air passes through to the *pharynx* at the back of the mouth. The pharynx is shared with the digestive system; these two systems, however, have different entrances separated by a muscular membrane called the soft palate. The dorsal (upper) entrance over the soft palate is the nasal part and the ventral (lower) entrance is the oral part. The oral entrance can be used as an additional airway in times of respiratory distress or panting. The dorsal region of the nasal part of the pharynx also has openings to the Eustachian tubes of the ear.

The wall of the pharynx is muscular and its lining is continuous with that of all the other tubular structures that enter or leave it, including the larynx and the oesophagus.

Situated in the floor of the pharynx, the *larynx* is a complex mechanism of cartilage, muscles, fibrous tissues and mucous membranes whose purpose is to stop anything other than air passing through to the next stage of the respiratory system. If water, or food, touches the densely innervated tissues around

the larynx, a protective 'gag reflex' is elicited and the larynx closes immediately.

The larynx is attached to the skull by the hyoid bone and sits midway between the mandibles. The larynx is also home to four other cartilages: the thyroid, cricoid and arytenoid cartilages, together with that of the epiglottis. These are moved by strong muscles that allow the larynx to open during breathing and close when swallowing.

The larynx also controls the flow of air and, because it also houses the vocal chords, which vibrate as air passes across them, it contributes to sound production (vocalization).

Next comes the *trachea*. This is a long tube kept permanently open by forty C-shaped, incomplete cartilaginous rings. It lies on the ventral aspect of the neck with the rounded part of the 'C' cartilage sitting ventrally, towards the dog's throat; the open part lies dorsally. The cartilages are connected to the tracheal tube by fibrous tissues and smooth muscles known as tracheal muscle. Tracheal muscle can relax and contract to regulate airflow and can also prevent the trachea over-dilating when the dog coughs.

The lower respiratory tract

Beyond the trachea, the system becomes the lower respiratory tract. The windpipe branches into two sets of tubes called *bronchi* and thereby enters the lungs. The bronchi continually branch and resemble branching trees (hence their name) and, just like

a branching tree, they start off large and decrease in size (cross-section) to become *bronchioles*.

The larger tubes possess a cartilaginous structure but the small bronchioles do not; they are all lined with mucous membranes. These tubes, their blood vessels and connective tissue form the lung tissue, which is enveloped by the pulmonary pleura, together making up the lungs. Each of the bronchioles (now called respiratory bronchioles) branches into several alveolar ducts, which in turn end in an alveolar sac. The alveolar sacs consist of a large number of pulmonary alveoli, surrounded by a rich supply of capillaries. It is here, at the end of the respiratory tree, that gaseous exchange takes place between alveolar air and the blood flowing within the thin-walled capillaries. Oxygen diffuses across a thin layer of tissue and into the bloodstream, where it dissolves and is then bound by haemoglobin. At the same time carbon dioxide moves out of solution and leaves the blood to enter the alveolar airspace, to be exhaled and removed from the body.

The two gases – oxygen and carbon dioxide – are therefore always travelling in opposite directions. This process, whereby fresh air and venous blood are brought into close contact, ensures the constant replenishment of oxygen in the blood and the elimination of carbon dioxide.

Most of the oxygen is bound to an iron-rich molecule called haemoglobin, which is contained within the red blood cells. This acts as a store of oxygen, allowing it to be transported around the body and released where it is most needed.

The lungs fill nearly all the chest cavity and consequently the size of the lungs depends on the size of the cavity. The right lung is larger than the left and they are divided into lobes. Both lungs have a cranial lobe, a cardiac lobe and a diaphragmatic lobe, whilst the right lung has an extra one, the accessory lobe, which sits between the two lungs. The lungs are richly supplied with blood vessels that allow the exchange of gases over a large surface area. The lungs are separated from the chest wall by the pleurae which define the pleural cavity; these paired membranes transmit forces to the lung when the chest is expanded during inspiration, thereby causing the lungs to inflate.

Breathing

Breathing is achieved by expanding and contracting the size of the thorax (chest). The muscles of the chest wall (and sometimes the diaphragm) contract to enlarge the space within the chest cavity. This draws air in through the airways during inspiration, much as it is drawn into a set of bellows when the handles are moved apart. When these muscles are relaxed, the chest wall falls, decreasing the size of the thoracic cavity, and producing an 'out breath', or exhalation. This movement is usually passive but can be forced if necessary.

Breathing is controlled by the autonomic nervous system and is an unconscious process; it only becomes consciously driven when there is forced breathing, such as a sigh.

The normal breathing rate for a dog depends on his size, but lies between ten and thirty breaths per minute. The age of the dog, his state of health and mental state (excitability or lethargy) all have a bearing on the respiratory rate. Whereas normal breathing has a regular rhythm and the volume of gas intake is consistent, dogs can increase the frequency and volume of their breathing by panting.

CAUTION: PANTING

A dog often pants in an effort to cool himself down after exertion. This is normal and allows a greater volume of cold air to enter the mouth and upper airways, where it comes into contact with a series of mucous membranes. Water is lost from these membranes, resulting in 'evaporative heat loss'. Note, though, that panting can also be an indication of overheating, stress and anxiety.

When a dog pants, he requires more oxygen because of the increase in muscle activity. The extra effort involved in panting causes his heart to beat faster and the body to heat up more quickly. If the underlying cause/problem (e.g. hot conditions) is not addressed, the dog's ability to thermoregulate may be exceeded, leading to heat stroke. Any dog affected in this way should be removed from the heat source, cooled down, calmed as quickly as possible and monitored for heat stroke.

A significant amount of moisture can also be lost as water evaporates from the mouth and airways. The dog therefore needs to replace these fluid losses and water should be made available.

NOTE: BRACHYCEPHALIC AIRWAY SYNDROME

This condition – also known as Brachycephalic Obstructive Airway Syndrome (BOAS) – occurs in all brachycephalic breeds. It consists of a complex collection of airway abnormalities that are present from birth. It is a particular problem in the Pekingese and is thought to affect all members of this breed.

The abnormalities occur because, whilst the bones of the upper jaw and nose are shortened, the associated soft tissues are not. Instead, they are disproportionately lengthy relative to the size of the dog's head. The excess soft tissue takes up a lot of room and literally obstructs the airways.

Possible abnormalities include:

◆ *stenotic nares (narrow nostrils);*
◆ *overlong soft palate;*
◆ *tracheal hypoplasia (narrow windpipe); and*
◆ *laryngeal hypoplasia (narrow larynx).*

All of these abnormalities disrupt the normal flow of air and make it difficult for the affected dog to breathe properly. The increased effort required to breathe often sucks the excessively long soft palate into the larynx, causing further breathing difficulty and distress.

BOAS is associated with snoring, noisy breathing and respiratory distress. Affected dogs literally struggle to breathe and do not cope well with exercise and stress. Their sleep is perpetually disturbed, and they are prone to heat stress.

2.8 THE EYE AND VISION

Unless a dog is born blind, or with a genetic problem that affects vision, it can be assumed that most puppies will develop good eyesight. The maturing puppy uses this sense throughout his development as a means of exploration, navigation and protection. Being able to see goes a long way in building the puppy's confidence. As dogs age, however, their eyesight usually deteriorates and this can affect their confidence; some individuals become disorientated and their temperament can change.

The groomer therefore needs to be more considerate and sensitive to the dog's vulnerability when eyesight fails or eye problems become apparent. An understanding of the eye, and the crucial role played by this sense in a dog's life, will help you to empathize with (and understand) the changes the dog is experiencing. This is not only of benefit to the dog, but will also help keep you safe.

This section will also help you to recognize and remain vigilant to other problems with the eye that you may encounter during your work.

The eyeball is a complex globe-shaped structure that is specially adapted to receive and respond to light and visual stimuli (*see* Figs 2.8.1, 2.8.2 and 2.8.3). All mammals possess a pair of eyes, each of which sits within a deep, and therefore protective, bony hollow in the skull called the orbit. Although the eyes appear to be separate, because they lie either side of, and are divided by, the bridge of the nose, the nerves from each eye (optic nerves) converge and meet on the floor of the brain cavity so that the eyes move and work together.

A group of eye muscles (*ocular muscles*) are attached at one end to the eyeball and at the other end to the skull at the back of the orbit. These muscles allow the eye to move freely (left, right, up and down), whilst remaining within the confines of the orbit. Within the

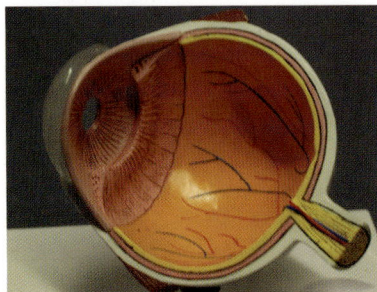

Fig. 2.8.1   The eye.

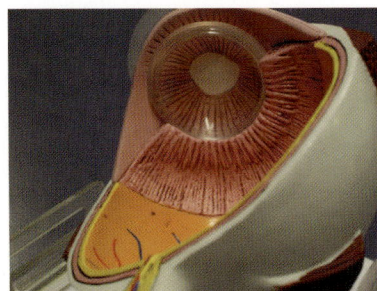

Fig. 2.8.2   A healthy lens cortex in place.

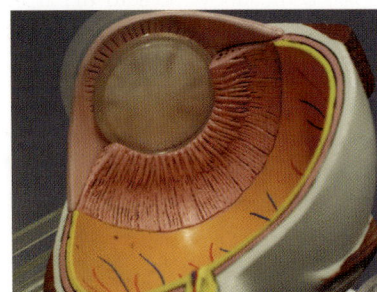

Fig. 2.8.3   The lens with a mature cataract.

orbit, the eyeball rests on a layer of fat (*periorbital fat*), which protects it from bruising. The exposed area at the front of the eye is protected by the upper and lower eyelids.

There are three main layers in the eye. The outer layer is made up of a fibrous tunic or shell called the *sclera*. At the front of the eye this outer layer is transparent, and is called the *cornea*. The middle layer of the eye is called the *uvea* and is made up of the choroid, iris, lens and ciliary body. The innermost layer is called the *retina*; it lines the back of the eye and contains the light receptors that are responsible for converting an image into an electrical signal, which is then relayed to the brain via the optic nerve.

The eye can also be divided into two anatomically distinct compartments that are separated by the lens. The compartment in front of the lens contains a liquid called *aqueous humour* and the other, behind the lens, contains a gelatinous substance called *vitreous humour*. The function of both the aqueous and vitreous humours is to provide nutrients for the structures within the eye and preserve the eye's shape. The compartment in front of the eye is further divided into two chambers by the *iris*. The outer chamber is known as the anterior chamber and extends from the iris forwards to the cornea; the space between the iris and the lens is behind the iris and is therefore known as the posterior chamber.

The inner surface of the upper and lower eyelids is covered and protected by a fine membrane called the *conjunctiva* (*see* Fig. 2.8.4). This membrane also covers both sides of the third eyelid. The conjunctiva attaches to the sclera at the limbus.

The *sclera* forms the outer covering of the eyeball. It is the white bit that is clearly visible when looking at the eye; it consists of dense fibrous connective tissue and elastic fibres and covers 5/6ths of the total eyeball surface. Its main function is to protect the delicate internal structures, whilst also helping to maintain the shape of the eye. In the centre of the sclera is an oval transparent disc called the cornea, which makes up the final 1/6th of the eye's outer covering. The junction between the sclera and the cornea is called the limbus.

The cornea bulges slightly forwards

from the front of the eye, away from the orbit. This is the first part of the eye to be hit by light and is curved so that it can receive the maximum number of incoming rays. Together with the lens, the cornea refracts light and helps to focus the light rays on to the retina at the back of the eye.

The *uvea* is a layer of membrane that is firmly attached to the inside of the sclera at the back of the eye where the optic nerve exits. Elsewhere it is less well attached.

The *choroid* is the vascular layer of the eye that lies between the sclera and the retina. It is a pigmented membrane full of blood vessels supplying nutrition to the retina and other structures within the eye. Its function is to reflect light back to the photoreceptor cells of the retina, increasing the eye's ability to see under low levels of light and thereby improving night vision. The choroid membrane projects forwards from the back of the eye and, within it, at the centre front, behind the cornea and in front of the lens, lies the beautifully coloured iris.

The *iris* (*see* Fig. 2.8.5) often appears to take up the whole of the visible portion of the dog's eye. It is in fact a circular disc of smooth muscles, with pigmented cells interspaced between them, and with an opening in the centre, called the pupil. The function of the iris is to regulate the amount of light entering the eye, for when the pupil dilates, more light enters the eye. It possesses both dilator and constrictor muscles, allowing the pupil to contract and expand according to the strength of the light and other factors such as the dog's psychological state (whether he is calm, anxious, fearful, etc.). In the dog the pigmented colour of the cells in the iris varies depending on the breed; although generally brown or almost black, the iris can be light amber-coloured or even blue, if the coat colouring is merle or blue.

The *ciliary body* is a thickened layer of muscle from which the lens is suspended. It sits towards the centre front of the eye. This muscle forms a circular support controlling the thickness and the shape of the lens, which is suspended in a capsule behind the iris. Around the lens perimeter are ligaments attached to the ciliary muscle. These ligaments transmit the forces exerted by the

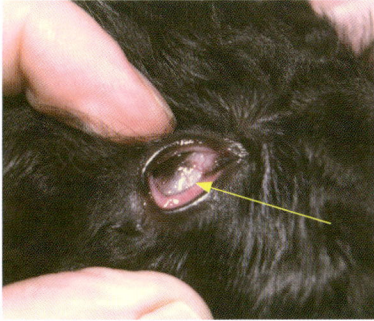

Fig. 2.8.4   Here the conjunctiva lining the outer surface of the third eyelid and the inside of the lower eyelid are examined. They are both healthy and demonstrate a light pink coloration.

Fig. 2.8.5   The iris is the pigmented part that gives the eye its colour. It often appears solid in colour but it is actually made up of a blending of colours.

action of the ciliary muscles, causing it to change shape; this allows objects to be brought into focus.

The *lens* is similar to a lens in a camera, the main difference being that it can change its surface shape and thereby vary its refractive powers; a camera lens, by contrast, has a fixed shape. It also differs in this respect from the cornea. The lens is made up of layers of crystalline and elastic fibres arranged a little bit like the layers of an onion.

The *retina* is the innermost layer of the eye. It is, in fact, a complex structure with several layers of neurons sitting above the light-sensitive photoreceptor cells. Light therefore has to travel through these outer layers before it is able to stimulate the sensory cells. These photoreceptor cells are named according to their shape: the *cones* are sensitive to bright light, providing colour vision, and the *rods* are sensitive to low light levels but not to colour. Thus the rods provide dogs with both black and white and night vision. In the dog

the photoreceptor cells are made up of 95 per cent rods and 5 per cent cones, meaning that the dog has very poor, if any, colour vision but excellent night vision. Dogs are thus able to see well in varying degrees of light and shade.

To form an image, light rays pass through the cornea and through the pupil at the centre of the iris. Constriction and dilation of the pupil are controlled by the autonomic nervous system according to the amount and intensity of the light. This is called pupillary light reflex (PLR). The rays of light then strike the lens, which alters its shape so that the rays are converged into a point on the retina. Photoreceptor cells (rods and cones) send electrical nerve impulses along the nerve fibres that converge at the optic nerve head (optic disc) and thence along the optic nerve to the brain. The image formed on the retina is upside down but the brain processes the information and interprets it the right way up.

Whilst the orbit protects the majority of the eyeball, the front of the eye needs to act as a window on the world, rendering it vulnerable to injury. Windows, after all, can easily be broken and are therefore often protected by shutters; they also need to be kept clean. In much the same way the surface of the eye must be kept moist and bathed regularly if it is to stay clean. This role is performed by the *lacrimal system*, whilst the eyelids act as a rapid-response shuttering system that can be closed 'in the blink of an eye'.

The lacrimal system consists of glands that secrete a clear saline fluid that we call 'tears'. This lubricating liquid provides a means whereby the eye can be kept moist and free of dust, dirt, pollen and other foreign material. The lacrimal gland lies towards the back of the orbit; the salty fluid it secretes flows down through several small ducts within the upper eyelid onto the conjunctiva. A second gland, called the 'nictitating gland', further contributes to tear production; it is located at the base of the third eyelid.

As they move across the eye the tears lubricate the eyelids and bathe the space between the eyelids and the eye. Tears also contain a number of additional ingredients, including antibodies and cellular components, which can protect the eye against infection.

The action of the eyelids sweeping across the eye helps ensure the eye is kept clean and lubricated. The fluid drains into a duct in the inside corner of the lower eyelid to be expelled through a small tube in the nose (*nasolacrimal duct*). It is this tear production that gives a dog his wet nose!

The eyelids can close to cover the eye completely. Whilst the upper eyelid is more mobile than the lower one, their movement is coordinated when the blink reflex is provoked. The outer surface of both eyelids is further protected by a covering of fur. The inside surfaces of the eyelids are lined by conjunctival (mucous) membranes, which should be moist and pink. Whilst the dog is awake, the eyelids move constantly across the eyeball, moving the tear film to clean and moisten the surface of the cornea. Along the edges of the eyelid grow strong, well-defined hairs resembling eyelashes. These help to protect the eye from dust and dirt and will also signal the eyelids to close for protection if they are touched.

The third eyelid is a plate of cartilage and smooth muscle covered on both sides by mucous membrane. It can be seen projecting from the inside corner of the eye. The third eyelid is supplied with glandular and lymphoid tissue to further protect against infection.

Range of vision

The positioning of the dog's eyes determines where he can actually see. With sight hounds (*see* Figs 2.8.6 and 2.8.7) and other breeds of dog that use their eyes to detect their prey, the eyes are set fairly close together to enable them to see and focus forwards. This, however, means that their peripheral vision is not brilliant. According to the breed, as the skull gets wider and the nose gets shorter, the eyes are placed further apart and slightly more to the sides of the skull (see Fig. 2.8.8). These dogs have poorer central binocular vision but better peripheral vision. In the case of some of the brachycephalic breeds, such as the Pug, the Shih Tzu and the Cavalier King Charles Spaniel, the eyes are so far apart that the dogs have little binocular vision but extremely good peripheral vision (*see* Fig. 2.8.9).

The way you approach these dogs affects their confidence. In the case of

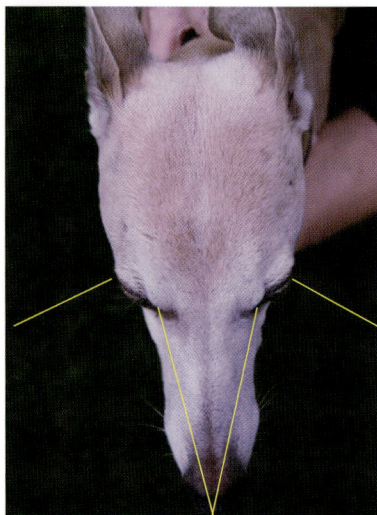

Fig. 2.8.6 *Sighthounds such as whippets have a narrow bridge to the nose that set the eyes close together facing forwards. This gives the dog very good forward focus (which he needs to home in on his prey) but not very good peripheral vision – he cannot see a lot to the side. The two lines drawn from each eye illustrate the approximate field of vision for each eye.*

Fig. 2.8.7 *Viewed from this angle, it is not possible to see the Whippet's eye, illustrating the extensive blind spot behind the typical dolichocephalic head.*

Fig. 2.8.8 *As the skull gets wider and the nose gets shorter, the eyes are placed further apart and slightly more to the sides of the skull. These dogs have poorer central binocular vision but better peripheral vision.*

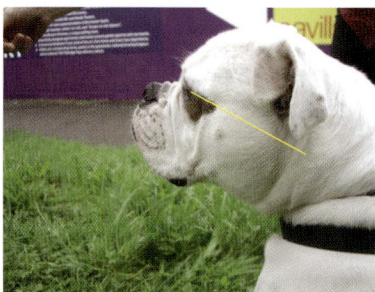

Fig. 2.8.9 *This picture shows how far the dog can see behind him.*

the brachycephalic dog, you may startle him if you approach from the centre front because he may not see you coming. The same applies to approaching a sight hound from behind. You should therefore always approach a dog from within their line of vision to avoid startling them.

Diseases and disorders of the eye

It is a sad fact that there are many diseases affecting the eyes of the modern dog. Some are inherited and avoidable; others are acquired diseases that the dog can develop. Regardless of the number and variety of conditions, they are all characterized by a small number of clinical signs that you should learn to recognize.

The signs you may see include soreness, discomfort or pain; these are easily recognized and fairly obvious. Loss of sight, especially if it is progressive and partial, may not be so easy to notice in the early stages. You should also learn to distinguish normal tear production from an abnormal ocular discharge.

Inherited eye disease is specific to certain breeds and breed lines, although one should not assume that it is confined to pedigree dogs. The current trend of crossing breeds for fashion may not take into account the heritable problems within the breeds being crossed. You may therefore see these eye problems (along with many others) cropping up in crossed breeds (so called 'designer dogs') like the Cockapoo and Labradoodle, and even sometimes in mongrels. These diseases often remain undetected for several years before clinical signs are observed.

Sadly, treatment is often not possible and is rarely successful.

Acquired eye disease is usually the result of an infection or accident. In many cases modern medicine can be very effective and treatment is possible if the problem is detected in its early stages.

Whilst you should never assume that you know how to interpret clinical signs, and should always leave the diagnosing of an ocular condition to the vet, it is very helpful for you to have some awareness and understanding of common eye conditions. Some of these are listed below, together with the signs to look out for. The sooner you detect a problem, the more chance there is of treating it, and in all cases you must advise the owner to seek veterinary advice as soon as possible.

Blue eyes

Blue eyes in some breeds of dog, such as the Husky, Malamute (see Fig. 2.8.10), Corgi, Shetland Sheepdog and Collies, are normal and should not be a cause for concern. This coloration is also associated with some merle coat colouring: affected dogs typically have either blue or blue mottled eyes; in such cases it is the iris that appears blue in colour. This is a heritable condition. There are also occasions when the iris in one or both eyes may be pigmented with broken blue or white markings. This is called a 'wall eye' and is sometimes seen in blue roan-coloured dogs, such as Cocker Spaniels (see Fig. 2.8.11) and English Setters.

A smoky blue coloration to the cornea is not normal, however, and may be associated with a number of conditions, including the highly infectious disease called Canine Viral Hepatitis. The 'blue eye' clinical sign usually appears

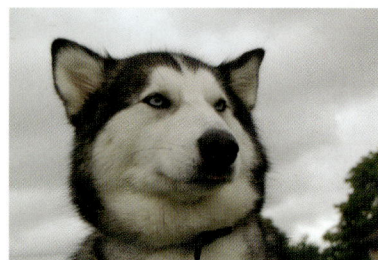

Fig. 2.8.10 *In some breeds, such as the Malamute, blue eyes are quite normal.*

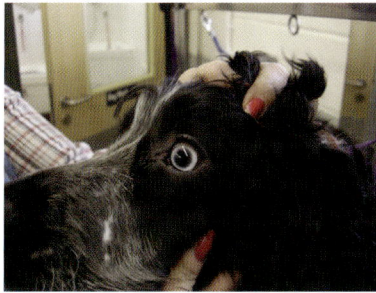

Fig. 2.8.11   This blue roan English Cocker Spaniel has a good example of a 'wall eye' (an unpigmented area), which is quite common with this coloured coat.

Fig. 2.8.13   This photograph shows you what the eye would see through this type of cataract. The dog is only able to see through the centre of the lens and the image is distorted.

Fig. 2.8.16   This is what a dog would see through a posterior subcapsular cataract. This type of cataract is particularly affected by light and is the most common.

a week or two after the onset of the disease, so you are unlikely to see the dog in your salon (see Infectious Diseases). Other conditions that cause the cornea to become swollen (including uveitis, glaucoma, keratoconjunctivitis sicca and corneal ulceration) can also give rise to a blue coloration. Where this coloration is present and associated with squinting, redness, photophobia (avoidance of bright lights) and pain, the dog should immediately be referred to a vet.

Cataract

A cataract is essentially an opacity of the lens (see Figs 2.8.12 to 2.8.17). The resulting loss of transparency results in the centre of the eye developing a cloudy appearance. This condition must be differentiated from nuclear sclerosis, which arises as the lens ages and hardens. The majority of cataracts are inherited and can appear at any time of life. Cataracts can also be caused by diabetes and in some cases poisoning, so they should always be checked out.

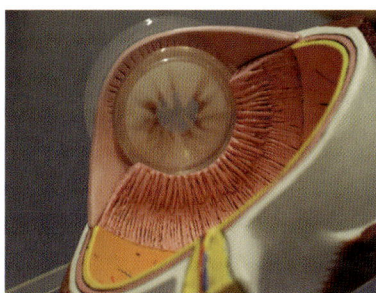

Fig. 2.8.14   As cataracts mature, the dog gradually has less vision. If this happens over a period of time, the dog can learn to adapt but sometimes, as in the case of cataracts associated with diabetes, the blindness can come on quite suddenly and can cause the dog to become confused, anxious and disorientated.

Fig. 2.8.17   A closer look through the same lens. A dog with this type of cataract has a blind spot in the centre of the eye and his vision is badly affected but not lost completely. An affected dog has an awareness of things approaching him but the distorted images may confuse him and this can affect his temperament.

Conjunctivitis

Conjunctivitis (see Fig. 2.8.18) is an inflammation of the conjunctiva. It is often caused by dust, sand or debris, as well as hair and other contaminants. It can also be caused by bacterial and/ or viral infections. The first signs of

ABOVE AND BELOW: Fig. 2.8.15 a and b   These photographs clearly show how a mature cataract has affected the dog's vision. Other than light reflection he cannot see anything through the affected lens.

Fig. 2.8.12   Looking outwards from the inside of the eye, this 'spoke-formation' on the lens replicates a cortical cataract.

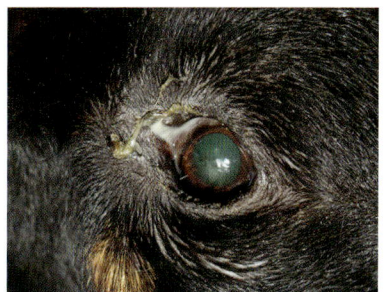

Fig. 2.8.18   Conjunctivitis is inflammation of the conjunctiva. It is often caused by a contaminant entering the eye (dust, sand, hair, etc.). The eye linings swell and become sore, with green or yellow pus being visible in the corners of the eye.

conjunctivitis are redness and some-times swelling to the eye linings, togeth-er with a substantial amount of tears. The dog may try to keep his eye closed. As the infection progresses, yellow or green pus is often visible in the corners of the eye. In some dogs immune-mediated destruction of the lacrimal tissue can lead to a deficiency in tear production. This 'dry eye' problem is usually associated with conjunctivitis and a thick, ocular dis-charge.

Dry eye (Keratoconjunctivitis sicca)

Keratoconjunctivitis sicca (KCS) is a com-mon disease characterized by a chronic inflammation of the lacrimal glands, cornea and conjunctiva (*see* Fig. 2.8.19). It is a condition in which the lacrimal glands fail to function; the resultant qualitative and quantitative deficien-cies in tear production leave the eye surface dull and rough. The mucosa will be sore, the eye is often painful and there is often a mucoid ocular discharge with debris sticking to the eyeball. Repeated corneal damage can eventually lead to blindness. In many cases this condition is associated with other skin disorders and many affected dogs also present with seborrhoea (a scaling disorder of the skin) and atopy. It is therefore thought that most cases of KCS in dogs are due to an auto-immune disorder. In some studies the vast majority of Cocker Spaniels with KCS also had seborrhoea. Similarly this eye condition may be strongly associ-ated with atopy in Lhasa Apsos and Shih Tzus.

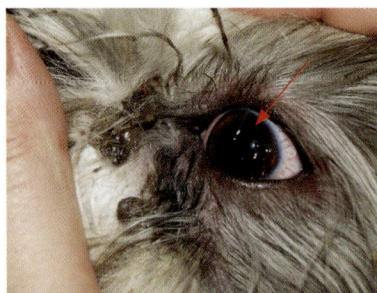

Fig. 2.8.19   Keratoconjunctivitis is a common condition often referred to as 'dry eye'. It is characterized by chronic inflammation of the lacrimal glands (tear glands), and very often the eye is not lubricated, leaving dirt and debris attached to the dry eyeball.

Distichiasis and ectopic cilia

Canine eyelids can sometimes grow abnormal hairs. A *distichia* is an eye-lash growing from an abnormal part of the eyelid. They usually grow from the opening of the meibomian glands, which are situated on the inner margin of the eye and produce lubricants for the eye. These hairs, for there are usual-ly several, follow the duct of the gland, which causes the hair to be directed towards the eye. As a result they do not curl away from the eye like a nor-mal eyelash, but instead curl towards it. When they come into contact with the cornea, they can cause consider-able discomfort and even damage. This problem may be relatively insignificant if the hairs are very fine, but bristly hairs can cause a great deal more irritation.

This inherited disease is often seen in Yorkshire Terriers, Shih Tzus, Cocker Spaniels and Pekingese. Surgery is usu-ally required to remove the hair roots of the offending lashes and has a lower risk of recurrence than cryoepilation or plucking. In the latter case the hairs invariably grow back again.

An *ectopic cilia* is a special type of dis-tichia. The abnormally located hair folli-cle is not situated on the eyelid margin but instead lies on the inner aspect of the eyelid. The hair that emerges from this follicle grows directly towards the eye and can cause considerable irrita-tion to the surface of the cornea. It is typically seen growing from the mid-dle of the upper eyelid. Affected breeds include the Golden Retriever and the Shih Tzu.

Ectropion

This is an inherited condition in which the eyelids roll outwards or droop to expose the conjunctiva and the third eyelid (*see* Fig. 2.8.20). The mucous membranes become very sore and the conjunctiva can become infected (*see* Conjunctivitis), often as a result of dust and dirt collecting within the hanging lower eyelid. Commonly seen in Bas-set Hounds and Cocker Spaniels, the condition can often be rectified with surgery but will, of course, reappear in any offspring of the dog. Although pri-marily inherited, dogs that are over-weight and develop extra heavy jowls can also suffer from ectropion.

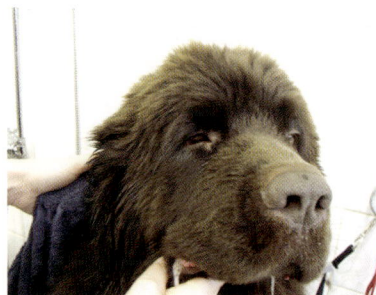

Fig. 2.8.20   Ectropion is where the lower eyelid rolls away from the eye, leaving the mucosa exposed and vulnerable to infection. This condition is commonly found in dogs that are heavily jowled or have long hanging ears. When grooming these dogs you must take care not to get hair and dirt into the lower eyelid.

Entropion

In this inherited condition the eyelids turn inwards, forcing the eyelashes and haired skin against the eye, caus-ing considerable discomfort and even blindness. It is very common in brach-ycephalic breeds and breeds with a lot of facial wrinkles, such as the Chow Chow (*see* Fig. 2.8.21). The mucous membranes of the eye are very red and the eye waters profusely, often mak-ing the face very wet as the drainage ducts in the lower eyelids struggle to cope with the volume of increased tear production.

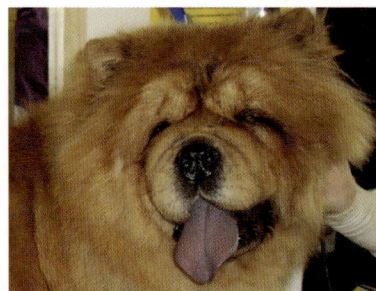

Fig. 2.8.21   The Chow Chow is an example of a breed that suffers with entropion. Here the excessive skin folds above the eye and on the face cause the eyelids to roll inwards towards the eye, causing the eyelashes (and sometimes the facial hair) to rub against the eyeball.

Glaucoma

Glaucoma is a condition where the fluid content within the eye builds up above normal limits, causing the eyeball to swell and bulge (*see* Fig. 2.8.22). Its cause can be hereditary but it can also be the result of another eye disease. Glaucoma is a very painful condition and the dog may be blinded because of the pressure on the optic nerve. This is a medical emergency and, if the eye is to be saved, requires immediate referral to a vet.

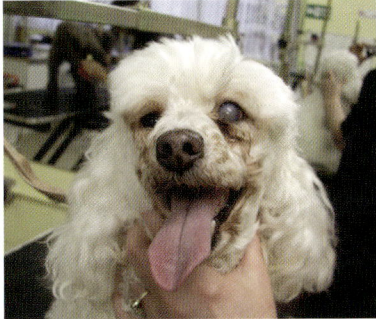

Fig. 2.8.22   Glaucoma is a painful condition that causes the eyeball to become enlarged, putting pressure on the optic nerve. This condition needs urgent veterinary attention if the eye is to be saved and the dog's vision preserved.

Progressive retinal atrophy (PRA)

This inherited disease of the retina is often known as 'night blindness' because the affected dog is unable to see properly in poor light (*see* Fig. 2.8.23). The blood vessels in the retina

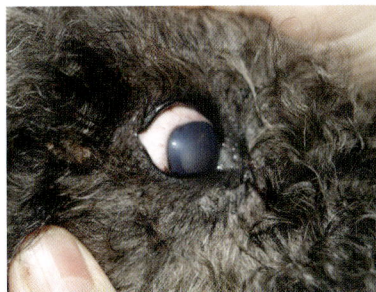

Fig. 2.8.23   This Poodle is affected by a condition called Progressive Retinal Atrophy (PRA). It is a congenital disease that affects many breeds, and affected dogs can lose their sight at an early age. The disease is passed by a recessive gene, which means that it can appear after two or three generations. Sadly the crossing of breeds for fashion does not take this into account and many affected dogs are now passing the gene on through unregulated breeding programmes. Early blindness and the process of going blind can cause all sorts of behavioural and temperament problems, so as a groomer you would be wise to learn which breeds are affected.

progressively waste away and, in an effort to retain vision, the pupil dilates widely, giving the dog a startled expression. The reflection from the back of the dog's eye may also appear brighter and both eyes are usually affected simultaneously. The dog will progressively lose his sight as treatment can only delay the onset of blindness. Affected dogs should not be bred from and breeders of affected breeds have a moral responsibility to ensure that their dogs are DNA tested to ensure that they are not carriers of the disease.

Ocular ulcers

An ulcer of the cornea arises where the corneal surface has been damaged and/or eroded. This may occur through blunt trauma (e.g. a knock or a blow) or repeated micro-trauma. Corneal ulcers should be suspected where a dog has started squinting and is reluctant to open the affected eye. There may also be increased tear production and a bluish coloration to the cornea. Ulcers are very common in brachycephalic breeds because the eyeball is large, exposed and vulnerable to injury (*see* Fig. 2.8.24). This painful condition represents an emergency and veterinary referral is recommended.

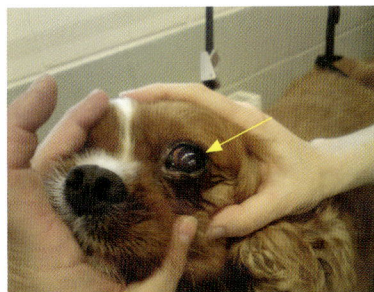

Fig. 2.8.24   Ulcers are very common in brachycephalic breeds because the eyeball is large, exposed and vulnerable to injury. The ulcer (arrow) will cause the cornea to become dull and lose its transparency. If you look carefully, you can see that the sclera, which is usually white, has become red and inflamed, and tear production has increased.

Prolapse of the eye

This is a condition where the eyeball is displaced from the socket as a result of trauma (*see* Fig. 2.8.25). In some breeds with very shallow eye sockets and pro-

tuberant eyes (particularly brachycephalics such as the Pug and Shih Tzu), it may even be caused by pulling the skin on the back of the neck backwards away from the head. This can cause the eyes to prolapse out from between the eyelids. In longer-nosed dogs the eye socket is usually deeper and more force would be needed to cause the eye to prolapse. When the eye has prolapsed, it slips down from the orbit and hangs suspended by the mucous membranes. Veterinary help must be sought immediately if the eye is to be saved.

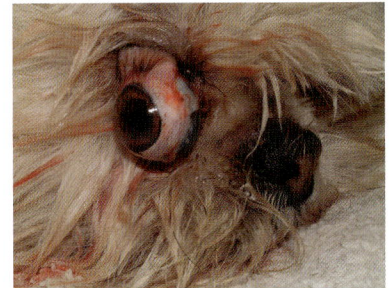

Fig. 2.8.25   This dog has a prolapsed eye caused by being shaken by another dog. The accident did not happen in a grooming room but it illustrates what can happen if a brachycephalic breed is groomed without care. The eye sockets on these breeds are shallow and the eyeball is large. Pulling the hair backwards from the top of the head when you are grooming could cause this to happen.

Examining the eye

Before beginning the grooming process, take a good look at the dog's eyes. In the young dog they should be bright, alert and clear, whilst the periocular tissues around the eye should be clean and dry. The conjunctival mucosa should be pink, the eye surface moist and the eye free of any discharge (*see* Fig. 3.1.6). In the older dog you may see signs of cloudiness in the centre of the eye and the mucosa may appear more red than pink. The eye, however, should always be moist.

Any discharge, excessive watering, bulging, swelling, redness or signs of pain and discomfort should be viewed as abnormal and investigated by a vet as soon as possible.

The First Aid section of this book explains how to clean the eye and what to do if you have an accident involving the eye, or find a foreign body there.

SUMMARY

The eye is a complex structure that can be easily damaged.

There are many heritable and acquired diseases that can affect the eye. An ocular problem may be characterized by one or a number of the following clinical signs:

- *soreness, pain or discomfort, manifested by avoidance of bright light, rubbing and reluctance to open the eye;*
- *redness, swelling and inflammation of the ocular tissues, with or without an ocular discharge;*
- *increased tear production, resulting in tear overflow and a wet eye; and*
- *loss or partial loss of sight.*

Learn which breeds are affected by heritable eye diseases so that you can identify suggestive signs of the disease and advise the owner to see their vet.

Always approach the dog within his line of vision. Take a note of where the eyes are situated and which way they are looking – this is not always straight ahead. You are then less likely to startle the dog and get bitten. If the dog's vision is impaired, ensure that you talk to him as you approach so that he is not startled.

Carefully examine the dog's eyes before you start grooming. They give a good indication of the health status of the dog and can alert you to the possible onset of disease. The eyes should appear bright, clear and free of discharge in the young dog. In the older dog there may be signs of cloudiness. Any abnormalities should be investigated by the dog's vet as soon as possible.

Shampoo and hair clippings can cause irritation and infection so take care to protect the eyes during the bathing and grooming process.

Eye conditions should never be overlooked or neglected. Sometimes prompt action can save the dog's sight.

It should also be noted that clipping around the face can lead to hair being deposited on the surface of the cornea and conjunctiva. Care should be taken to avoid this wherever possible. Where such contamination has arisen, the eye should be irrigated with an eyewash, or plenty of water, to remove any offending hairs.

2.9 THE EAR, HEARING AND BALANCE

Look around you at all the different breeds of dogs you see and you will be amazed at the variety of ear types they have. The canine ear comes in a wide range of sizes and shapes but each gives expression and character to the dog's face and all of them provide us with vital clues as to what the dog is thinking and feeling. Our ability to understand our canine friends is very much dependent on our ability to interpret their body language and understand how they interact with the world. We therefore need to develop our understanding of the dog's hearing

One of the responsibilities of the groomer is to look after the health and hygiene of the dog's ear. The ears can often give cause for concern, for several reasons:

- *they are prone to infection;*
- *they are prone to injury; and*
- *they provide excellent accommodation, both internally and externally, for visiting mites and other parasites.*

The ears play a key role in canine communication and you need to understand how they are used and how to interpret the messages they communicate.

The ears are also very important from an aesthetic point of view: fashion plays its part and ears are included in the hairstyle of the dog. Groomers therefore need to know about ears! This chapter is intended to help you understand all you need to know about ears, how they work and how to work with them.

apparatus, as well as the significance of ear movements and position.

The ear of the dog is more than just an organ for collecting and processing sound waves and relaying them to the brain; the ear also plays important roles in balance and communication. This section focuses on the ear's role in hearing and balance.

The ear itself is divided into three sections: the external (outer) ear, the middle ear and the internal (inner) ear. Sound waves are collected by the funnel-like external ear (*pinna*), and channelled down through a tube to the middle ear for transmission to the inner ear. There they are transformed into electrical signals, which are passed along the auditory nerve to the brain. It is a fairly simple set-up and it works quite well as long as external maintenance checks are carried out *regularly*. This, of course, is where you come in!

Structure

Fig. 2.9.1   The structure of the ear.

Pinna

The pinna (*see* Fig. 2.9.2) is the bit that we can see easily, that pricks up, flops down or curls to resemble a rose bud. It is made of cartilage and is covered on both sides with skin. The pinna does not carry any fat to keep it warm so the outside of the pinna and about two-thirds of the inside are covered with fur.

Fig. 2.9.2   The pinna is the part of the ear that pricks up, flops down (as here) or can curl to resemble a rosebud.

the cartilage around the base of the pinna is the only part that can move. The pinna on these dogs lies close to the sides of the head and the temperature inside the ear canal is much warmer.

Fig. 2.9.6   'Bella' the Basset Hound is a scent hound, and she uses her very heavy long ears to encapsulate scent on the ground when she is hunting. The weight of these ears prevents ventilation to the ear canal, which can make the environment within the ear unhealthy.

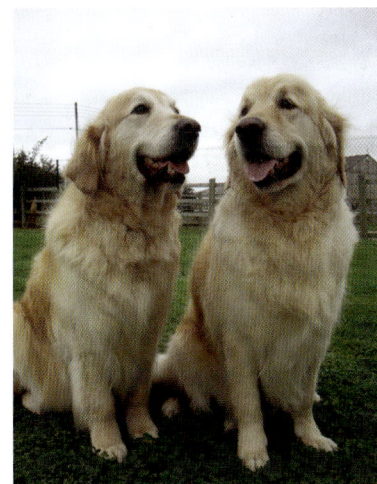

Pricked eared (*see* Figs 2.9.3 and 2.9.4) and semi-pricked eared dogs (*see* Fig. 2.9.5) have small muscles for moving the erect pinna to locate the direction of sound and focus the dog's 'antennae' in the same way that a satellite dish rotates to capture the best signal. Movement of the erect ear can also open up the external auditory *meatus*. This refers to the opening to the ear canal and the canal itself (meatus is Latin for opening or canal), both of which must be kept clear if the canal is to remain well aerated. Movement of air into the canal reduces the temperature within the canal and helps to keep the ear dry.

Fig. 2.9.4   'Lester' the West Highland White Terrier also has pricked ears, but they are much smaller. The ear is protected whilst the dog works by the hair in front of the entrance to the ear canal, but the ear can still ventilate.

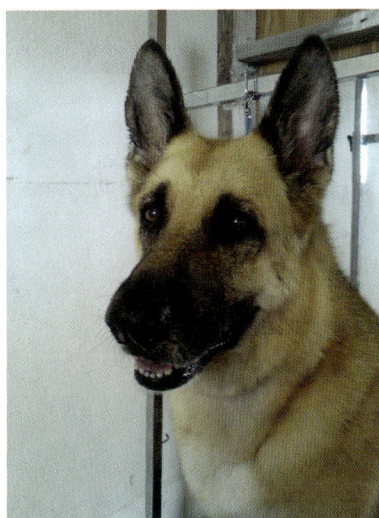

Fig. 2.9.7   Jake and Finn illustrate a less extreme dropped ear shape. Their ears are shorter and less heavy but are still sufficient to protect the entrance to the ear whilst hunting and retrieving. The cartilage at the base of the ears can lift the pinna enough to allow air to cool and dry the ear canal.

Fig. 2.9.5   'Lily' the Wire Fox Terrier has semi-pricked ears. Terriers need keen hearing as they work close to or under the ground. The semi-pricked ear channels sound and gives protection to the ear canal when the dog is working.

Fig. 2.9.3   'Zena' the German Shepherd has pricked ears. Cartilage at the base of the ear moves the erect ear to pick up sounds and direct the dog's attention. This shape of ear has the advantage of being well ventilated, since the entrance of the ear canal is free of any obstructions.

Dogs with dropped ears (*see* Figs 2.9.6 and 2.9.7) still possess and use the small muscles for movement but, because the weight of the pinna makes it impossible for the ear to stand erect,

The 'rose' ear (*see* Fig. 2.9.8) is a pinna that starts off erect at the cartilage and then, almost immediately, rolls or folds backwards, leaving the entrance to the ear canal exposed and the pinna tucked neatly against the head. This ear type is often seen on hounds that run at great speeds. The folding is thought to protect the delicate pinna from bruising and wind damage as the dog accelerates.

Fig. 2.9.8 'Wally' the Whippet has ears that roll backwards to form a curl. This is termed a 'rose' ear. Whippets can reach great speeds when hunting and the curl of the ear protects the pinna from bruising and damage from the wind, excessive movement and other potential hazards.

Auditory meatus (ear canal)

The cavity inside the pinna narrows to a tube or canal shape that runs inside the head. This part of the external apparatus is called the *auditory meatus* or auditory canal. If you look into the ear, you can see the beginning of the canal. Made of cartilage and lined with modified skin, the auditory meatus acts as a funnel for sound waves. There are two parts to it: the first part is the vertical canal, which drops down from the pinna and then turns through 90 degrees to become the second part, the horizontal canal. At this point the canal straightens and continues to meet the ear drum, where it terminates, closes and attaches firmly to the temporal bone. The lining of the canal contains two types of glands which together produce wax (*cerumen*), an essential secretion that protects the structure from moisture and may help with the removal of foreign bodies that have found their way in.

Tympanic membrane (ear drum)

The *tympanum*, *tympanic* or *temporal membrane* is the deepest and final part of the meatus. It is a relatively fragile and easily damaged membrane guarding the opening to the *tympanic cavity*.

It is stretched tight across this opening and divides the external ear from the middle ear. As sound waves reach the end of the meatus, they cause this tight membrane to vibrate like a drum skin, hence the descriptive term 'ear drum'.

The *middle ear* is a large bubble of very fine bone enclosing an air-filled cavity, known as the *tympanic bulla*. Near the entrance to this chamber lies a chain of three little bones – the *auditory ossicles* – which span the middle ear.

These three bones are the hammer (*malleus*), anvil (*incus*) and stirrup (*stapes*). They are the smallest bones in the body and articulate with each other. They are attached to the tympanic membrane (ear drum) by the largest of the three bones, the malleus. The function of these tiny bones is to convert sound waves to vibrations or movements. The malleus picks up the vibrations of the sound waves from the temporal membrane and transmits them to the second ossicle, which in turn transmits them to the third ossicle, which transmits them, finally, to the internal ear.

Eustachian tube

The Eustachian or auditory tube is located at the lowest part of the middle ear and opens into the throat. Its function is to regulate and balance the pressure on both sides of the tympanic membrane so that this delicate membrane does not rupture or get damaged when environmental pressure increases. Air from the pharynx can enter these tubes to ventilate and cool the middle ear.

The internal ear

The internal or inner ear is by far the most complicated part of the ear and is responsible for balance and the production of auditory signals. Anatomically, the inner ear consists of a complex arrangement of membrane-lined, fluid-filled sacs and channels floating within a cavity called the *bony labyrinth*. The internal ear can be divided into two main sections, that responsible for hearing (which can be further divided into the *vestibule* and the *semicircular canals*) and the *cochlea*, which is responsible for balance.

The *vestibule* occupies a central

location and is a chamber with several openings. Laterally, the oval window communicates with the middle ear via the stapes. Below and a little behind the oval window is the round window, which communicates with the cochlea.

The *semicircular canals* are concerned with maintaining balance. The membranous labyrinth has three tubular hoops called *semicircular ducts*; these sit neatly into the bony labyrinth of the semicircular canals. The membranous labyrinth floats in a fluid called perilymph and is itself filled with a fluid called endolymph. The two fluids do not intermingle but their movement is responsible for maintaining balance. Any infection, or altered quantities, in either of these two fluids can affect the balance of the dog.

The *cochlea* is so called because it looks like a snail's shell. Within the cochlea are three small tubes placed side-by-side. In the central tube is an apparatus called the *Organ of Corti*, which is where the vibrations picked up by the tympanic membrane finally get turned into nerve impulses and are sent to the brain. This process is called 'transduction' and is mediated by sensory hairs within the Organ of Corti that respond to the movement of fluid over them. Sound transmitted across the middle ear by the ossicles thus arrives at the oval window, passes across the vestibule to the round window and produces a wave of fluid within the cochlea. This wave stimulates the sensory hairs, causing them to bend and produce an electrical impulse. Fortunately, you do not have to worry about grooming these hairs! You should, however, be conscious that clipper vibration against the base of the skull will pass across the middle ear and be picked up by these hairs. Dogs can therefore react both to clipper noise and vibration.

The ear in health and disease

As with any sensitive apparatus or machinery, the ear benefits from regular checks and maintenance if it is to remain healthy and perform its functions well. The following section therefore discusses the healthy ear and the various factors that can predispose to, and result in, ear disease. The importance of identifying ear problems early and the signs you need to look for in order to distinguish the healthy from the unhealthy ear are also discussed.

The healthy ear

The inner aspect of the healthy ear should be a light pink colour with little or no associated discharge or smell (*see* Fig. 2.9.9). There should be no redness, swelling or thickening of the skin, weeping or strong smells and the ear should be free from discharge and non-painful. You should learn to recognize these signs and look for them as part of your examination.

Fig. 2.9.9   The healthy ear should be light pink in colour, and there should be no redness, discharge or offensive smells.

The diseased ear

Ear problems may be either acute (in which case they have appeared relatively suddenly) or chronic. Chronic ear diseases are those which recur, have been left untreated or have failed to respond to treatment. In such cases there are usually associated inflammatory changes to the external ear (*see* Fig. 2.9.10).

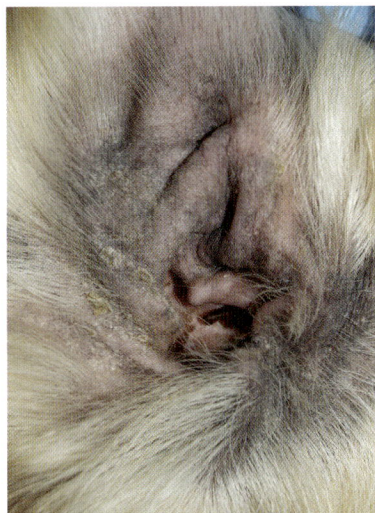

Foreign material finding its way into the ear canal can cause discomfort, leading the dog to scratch his ears and/or shake his head. In some cases the dog may be able to eliminate water and other foreign materials. Where such materials are not eliminated, the problem can progress rapidly, resulting in an ear infection.

Ear infections are characterized by pain and inflammation. The pinna itself may feel hot to the touch and may be pinker (or indeed redder) than normal (*see* Fig. 2.9.11). Inflammation within the ear canal can lead to increased turnover of skin cells and the production of significant amounts of discharge, which may be visible and have a strong smell. In some cases a thick, purulent discharge may be seen. Any tissue damage is likely to be painful, and both examination and palpation of the ear may be resented. Behavioural changes may be seen and can include scratching, head-shaking and rubbing. In severe cases the dog may become depressed and systemically unwell; this is especially likely if the infection crosses the ear drum into the middle ear.

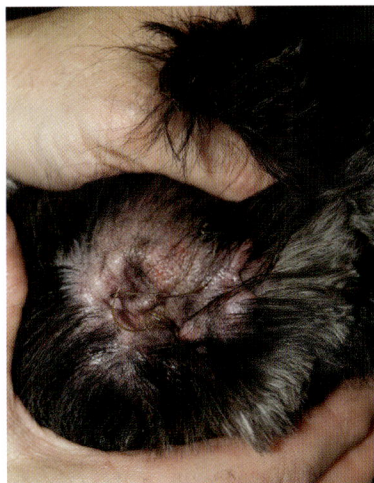

Fig. 2.9.11   The opening to the ear canal of this Shih Tzu is obscured. The skin of the pinna is thickened and inflamed, so much so that in one or two places it is reddened. The ear was warm and painful to the touch. Some brown discoloration of the hair emerging from the ear canal is evident. These signs are all consistent with an ear infection and the owner of this dog was advised to seek veterinary attention.

Fig. 2.9 10   The diseased ear can show signs of chronic inflammatory changes. In this case the skin is thickened and hyper-pigmented and there is evidence of a build-up of scale.

Causes of ear disease

In many ear infections a contributing cause is the design of the ear. Ears that are poorly designed and therefore difficult to maintain are predisposed to ear infections. Consider the position and design of the ear. What do you think a well-designed ear should look like?

Good air flow is required for a healthy ear. This performs the task of drying and cooling the ear canal in much the same way that we use a towel to dry between our toes after a bath. Failure to do so can lead to the skin macerating and a bacterial and/or yeast overgrowth and infection.

Fluids or moisture entering the ear, or wax and sebum produced within the ear, accumulate at the base of the ear canal, which happens to be the lowest part of the structure. It doesn't take a lot of working out to realize that water does not run uphill of its own accord! This is why dogs need to shake their heads when they get water in their ears. Where the fluid is prevented from escaping, it soon warms up within the confined space of the ear canal. The resulting environment is both warm and moist and favours the development of infections.

Nature has therefore provided the ear with a ventilation system. For this to work, however, air needs to reach the opening to the ear canal and circulate within it, thereby allowing air in to dry everything out. At this point you should be able to list a handful of factors that reduce the efficiency of this process:

◆ dropped ears;
◆ narrow (stenotic) ear canals; and
◆ hair build-up within the ear canal.

Breeds such as Cocker Spaniels and Labrador Retrievers have dropped ears, which do not ventilate well. This can be a significant contributing factor in predisposing a dog to ear disease. In certain dogs the ear canal may be abnormally narrow. This may be an inherited problem but more commonly it is an acquired problem, resulting from inflammatory thickening and scarring of the ear canal after repeated ear infections (*see* Fig. 2.9.12). Certain breeds have particularly hairy ear canals, giving rise to the problem of hair accumulation. The skin lining the ear canal in these breeds possesses large numbers of hair follicles that grow hair for protection. In the longer-haired breeds the hair within the ear also grows long, so it can soon fill the space within the canal, impairing the ear's natural cleaning process and restricting air movement. And it gets worse. The thicker and woollier the coat of the dog, the thicker and woollier the hair within the ear canal. Cocker Spaniels have been shown to possess large numbers of compound hair follicles throughout the length of the external ear canal, resulting in a greater hair density. Whilst the presence of hair in the ear canal may be significant, it should not be assumed that hair growth equals disease; it is one of a number of factors that can predispose to disease, thus making disease more likely when other factors are thrown in.

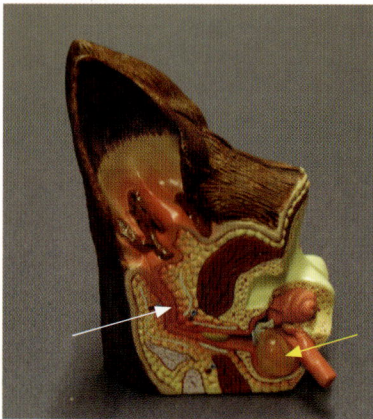

Fig. 2.9.12   This model illustrates what happens when the wall of the ear canal becomes inflamed and thickened (white arrow). The ear canal becomes blocked and infection has burst through the ear drum and entered the tympanic bulla (yellow arrow). There is therefore both an otitis externa *and an* otitis media.

Other factors that predispose to ear disorders are unrelated to the anatomy of the ear and are, in fact, quite diverse. The ear canal is part of the largest organ of the body, the skin, and as such may be affected by the various disorders that affect the skin. Allergic conditions can therefore affect the ears and may be the root cause of recurring ear infections. These are discussed further below, together with some of the more common ear problems.

The grooming process can itself trig-

ger ear problems and the professional groomer should do everything possible to avoid causing damage to the ear. The three main grooming-related problems relate to water getting into the ear canals during washing, overly vigorous ear plucking and using dirty equipment.

It is essential that care be taken not to introduce soap and water into the ear canal. Where this has occurred, the ear should be carefully dried and allowed to ventilate. When ear plucking, the skin should not be traumatized. Ear plucking should always be a gentle process, with small numbers of hairs being removed at a time. Different pieces of equipment should be used for each ear to prevent cross-contamination and all equipment should be thoroughly washed and sterilized after use.

Common ear problems

The following list describes some of the diseases and disorders that affect the ear. Some have signs that you can learn to identify and some you may be able to help prevent, but in all cases, as soon as you suspect something is wrong, the dog should be seen by a vet for a thorough investigation.

Aural haematoma

A large 'blister' forms within the pinna of the dog and will be both visible and palpable as a smooth swelling of variable size. It is always located on the concave (inner) aspect of the pinna (*see* Fig. 2.9.13). A haematoma is simply another word for bruise or bruising, and reflects the fact that there has been bleeding into the tissues. The fluid in an aural haematoma (a haematoma of the ear) is more akin to seroma fluid than blood, however, reflecting the fact that this is an inflammatory process.

The cause of aural haematoma is not known. In some cases the haematoma may have arisen through continuous and repeated shaking of the dog's head, resulting in trauma to the ear. In the vast majority of cases, however, there is no obvious cause and it is now thought that the haematoma arises as the result of an immunological process that attacks and damages the cartilage of the pinna.

The appearance of a smooth swell-

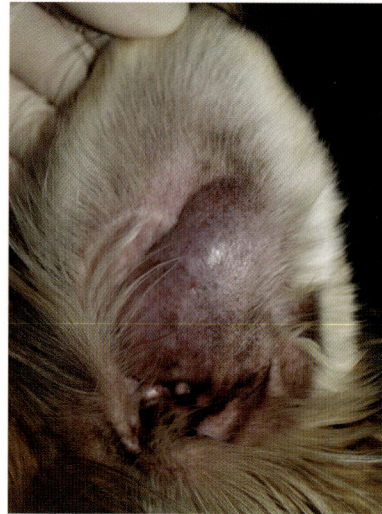

Fig. 2.9.13   The large smooth swelling on the inner aspect of this dog's pinna is typical of the appearance of an aural haematoma. The swelling bulges out from the cartilage, and it is filled with as much as 10–20ml of serosanguinous fluid.

ing within the pinna is suggestive of an aural haematoma and affected dogs should always be referred to a vet for treatment of the haematoma and investigation of any underlying causes.

Otitis externa

Otitis is a general term used to describe inflammation or infection of the ear. Otitis externa is therefore an inflammation or infection of the outer (external) part of the ear (*see* Fig. 2.9.11). The causes of otitis externa are not always apparent, but the condition is very common. Certain breeds, such as Cocker Spaniels, Poodles and German Shepherds, are predisposed to the disease but in many cases the condition is connected to an underlying disease or skin condition.

> LEAVE THE EAR ALONE! YOU MUST NOT INTERFERE WITH THIS CONDITION AS YOU ARE LIKELY ONLY TO MAKE MATTERS WORSE. THE DOG SHOULD BE REFERRED TO THE VET AS SOON AS POSSIBLE SO THAT THE UNDERLYING CAUSE CAN BE ESTABLISHED AND TREATMENT INSTITUTED QUICKLY.

On examination, the skin on the pinna is found to be very sore and inflamed and may appear thickened and ulcerated. You may also see what appear to be lumps of dried skin or crusting, and there may or may not be a discharge. The dog will often be in a lot of pain and discomfort.

Otitis media

Infection or inflammation of the middle ear is known as otitis media. It too is a common condition; it often goes unrecognized, however, and is potentially much more serious. Otitis media almost invariably accompanies otitis externa and results from the extension of an infection of the outer ear across the tympanic membrane into the middle ear (see Fig. 2.9.12). As such, the clinical signs are usually those of otitis externa and this in part explains why many cases of otitis media go unrecognized. Rupture of the tympanic membrane may occur secondarily to a severe infection within the external auditory meatus but may also occur as a result of trauma. Invasion of the middle ear with bacteria gives rise to a deep-seated infection that can be hard to eliminate. In a small number of cases neurological signs may be seen, including head tilt, loss of balance (ataxia), nystagmus (where the eyes move from side to side) and other problems.

All forms of ear infection are potentially serious and the owner should always be advised to seek veterinary advice as soon as possible.

Otitis interna

Inflammation or infection of the inner ear is known as otitis interna. It usually arises as a result of extension of an otitis media. Associated clinical signs include head tilt, loss of balance, circling, nausea and vomiting. Acquired deafness may also develop. The vet can advise the owner about treatment and management.

Whilst you are not expected to be able to distinguish inflammation of the inner ear from inflammation of the middle or outer ear, it is important to appreciate that an infection of the outer ear can progress to the deeper structures with serious implications for the dog's welfare. Early veterinary diagnosis and treatment of an ear infection is therefore always advisable.

Otodectes cynotis

Otodectes cynotis are large mites (0.3mm × 0.4mm) that live predominantly in the ear canals of dogs and cats. Commonly called ear mites, they are the size of a pin-head and white in colour (see Parasitology Section). They are just about visible to the naked eye but are more easily seen using some form of magnification. They dislike the light and prefer to live on the skin surface deep down in the ear canal, where they feed on tissue fluid and debris. A small number of mites can cause intense irritation, leading the dog to scratch at the ear, which in turn causes further inflammation and skin trauma. It is thought that the dog is irritated by the saliva of the mite as well as mechanically by the mite itself. The main features of ear mite infections are otic pruritus (itchy ears) and the presence of dry lumps of dark brown crumbly cerumen (wax).

The mite's life cycle is three weeks on the host but they can live longer in the environment. They can also live in the hair and skin surrounding the ear.

Ear mites are more commonly seen in younger animals, which acquire the infection from their mothers. Mites are thus transmitted by contact with an infected host. The potential for transmission of this parasite means that you have a responsibility to observe good hygiene practice within the grooming room in order to minimize the risk of transmission. Materials used to clean ears should be disposed of carefully and all equipment cleaned and disinfected between dogs. These mites are potentially zoonotic – they can therefore be passed on to you. You should advise the owner to take the dog to the vet where medication and a cleaning routine can be prescribed.

Ticks

Ticks may be found in and around the ear. They may be mistaken for foreign bodies and warts (see Parasitology Section). They are easily identified and removed.

Harvest mites

Harvest mites are the larvae of Neotrombicula autumnalis. The larval form of this mite is orange in colour and causes intense pruritus (itchiness) when feeding (see Fig. 2.9.14). It may be found in and around the ear, particularly in the deep folds of skin covering the cartilage.

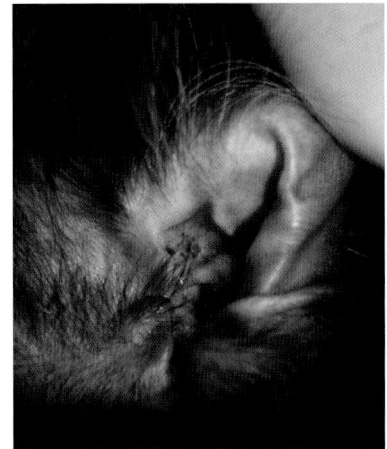

Fig. 2.9.14   The larvae of the harvest mite are orange in colour and can cause intense irritation when feeding. They are particularly active during the late summer and early autumn and show a predilection for the recesses of the ear.

Alopecia

Alopecia is a condition characterized by hair loss. It can be an inherited or acquired problem. It is an inherited problem specifically affecting the ears in some breeds, like the Smooth Coated Dachshund and the Chinese Crested, and you must learn to recognize this characteristic. Where, by contrast, it presents in breeds that are characterized by a hairy pinna, it is probably abnormal. In such cases it may be due to scratching or some other underlying disease process and should be investigated.

There are many reasons why a dog may start to lose hair from their ears (and indeed other parts of their bodies). Common causes include parasitism, ringworm, sebaceous adenitis and a host of other problems. Parasites affecting the pinna include the burrowing mite Sarcoptes scabiei, which is both zoonotic and transmissible to other dogs. It can only be diagnosed by skin scraping and/or blood testing. You are therefore unlikely to see burrowing mites, whereas *Otodectes* mites are surface mites and may be seen with the aid of magnification. Until a vet has had the chance to examine the dog and determine the cause of any problem, you should treat the dog as potentially infectious. Maintain hygiene precautions and refer the dog to the vet.

Excessive hair

Excessive hair in the ear canal is very common and, in itself, is not a problem (see Fig. 2.9.15). However, it can predispose to problems and should be removed without damaging the sensitive skin within the ear canal. The ear canals should be checked for hair every time the dog is groomed and the hair should be removed where necessary (see Chapter 18). Failure to remove the hair can hinder ventilation and promote an environment suitable for yeast and bacterial growth. Woolly coated and long-haired dogs are the most likely to have the problem but new groomers need to remember that it is not a 'one-off job'. Once removed, the hair grows back!

Fig. 2.9.15   Hair build-up in and around the ear of a Standard Poodle. The associated skin appears healthy and there is only a small build-up of wax darkening the hair emerging from the external auditory meatus.

Foreign objects

Probably the most common foreign body found in the ear canal of dogs is the grass seed (see Fig. 2.9.16). During the summer months, when grasses have matured and seeded, many dogs pick up grass seeds in their coats. These seeds are able to travel down the ear canal and can even penetrate into tis-

sues. The most problematic seeds are barbed; that is to say, they have bristles extending caudally that make it difficult for the seed to move in any direction other than forwards. Retrograde movement is difficult if not impossible, and this is probably why these seeds migrate so easily along the ear canal and into any tissue that they penetrate. Affected dogs may shake their

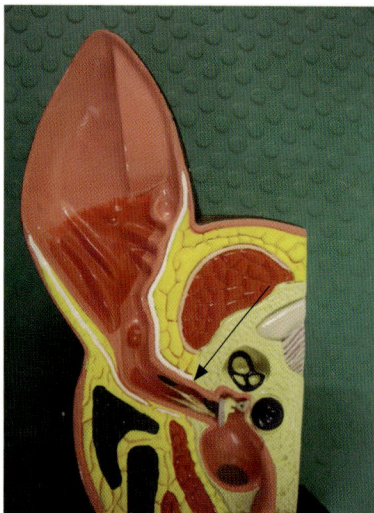

Fig. 2.9.16   In this model a grass seed can be seen resting against the ear drum at the bottom of the horizontal ear canal. The backward-pointing barbs make removal of grass seeds extremely difficult.

heads frantically. Unfortunately these seeds can be very difficult to detect and an otoscopic examination is often required. If you are able to see the seed and remove it early, do so before it disappears down the ear canal. If, however, the seed has descended too far into the ear, the dog should be referred to a vet. During the summer months it is often safest to refer dogs with sudden onset ear discomfort to the vet so that any grass seeds can be identified and removed early before they are able to penetrate the ear drum. Spaniels and Golden Retrievers appear to be most commonly affected by this problem. Owners should be advised to avoid walking these dogs through long grass at certain times of year. The inside of the ear can be kept clipped clean (see Fig. 2.9.17) to reduce the chances of a grass seed being picked up and to allow owners to inspect the ear after every walk.

Swimmer's ear

In the same way that humans can pick up ear infections after going swimming, dogs can too. It is therefore important that a dog's ears be dried out and carefully monitored after swimming. Similarly, be very careful when bathing the

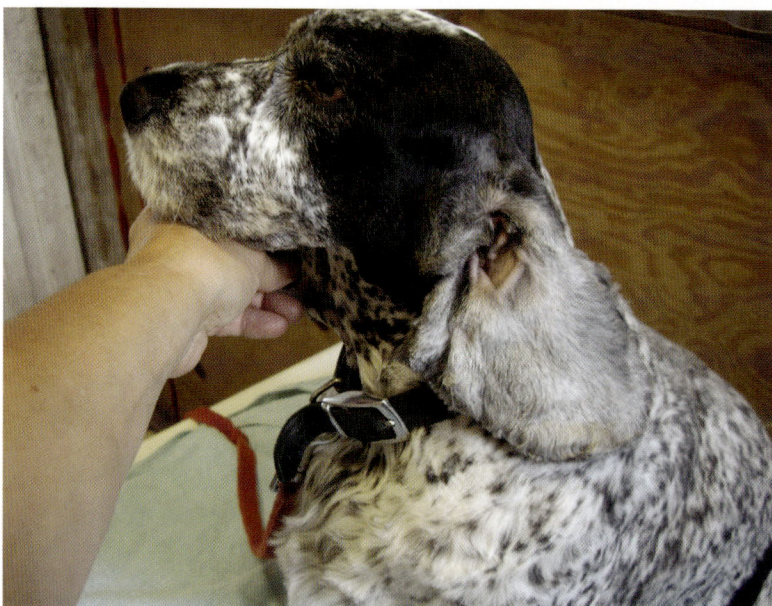

Fig. 2.9.17   During the summer months especially it is a good idea to keep the hair clipped from the inside of pinna in dogs such as this English Cocker Spaniel. This helps the ear to ventilate and stay dry, and is particularly recommended in dogs that are prone to otitis. Clipping the ear can also reduce the amount of grass seeds these dogs pick up, and makes is less likely for a grass seed to find its way into the ear canal. Where grass seeds do attach to the coat, they are also more readily spotted and removed.

dog not to get water into the dog's ear canal. Remember it cannot drain out again. Any such water will be difficult to clear and will add to the moisture in the canal environment, whilst any soap or detergent can irritate the sensitive skin lining and this may lead to *otitis externa*.

It is sometimes difficult to avoid getting water in the ears, particularly in dogs with long ear furnishings that need a good wash or with dogs that refuse to stand still in the bath. The bathing section offers ideas on how to prevent it from happening.

If you do get water in the ear, dry it out as best as you can with cotton wool and tell the owner, who can monitor the dog for signs of irritation or infection.

All in all, the ear can be quite troublesome! I hope this section has given you a clearer idea of how the ear functions in health and disease, and convinced you that the dog's ears will benefit from regular maintenance checks and cleaning.

Ear cleaning is covered in Chapter 18 and you are advised to keep referring back to these two sections as you meet more ears and your understanding of them develops.

2.10 THE SKIN, SKIN DISEASE AND SKIN DISORDERS

> *The skin supports the hair coat and is perhaps the most important and interesting part of the dog to you, the groomer. You will be touching, inspecting, working with and advising on the skin and hair coat on a daily basis, throughout your working life. A good working understanding of skin anatomy and physiology is therefore essential.*

The skin, you may be surprised to learn, is an organ and is actually the largest organ of the body. It fulfils a number of very important roles. Table 1 summarizes the main functions of the skin, with an explanation of the mechanism(s) by which the skin fulfils these functions.

Table 1   The main functions of the skin.

Function	Mechanism
Protection	The skin forms a complex barrier between the body and the environment and provides the body with a defence against pathogenic organisms and damage.
Insulation	The hair coat traps an insulating layer of air close to the skin. Fat deposits under the skin provide additional insulation.
Thermoregulation	Blood vessels within the skin can be dilated (widened) and constricted (narrowed) to release and conserve heat as required. The hair coat can be raised to trap a thicker layer of air against the skin. In some mammals sweating can result in significant evaporative heat loss, which is a very efficient means of cooling the body.
Water regulation	The skin provides a waterproof barrier that keeps water both in and out.
Storage and synthesis	The skin synthesizes a number of compounds including lipids and Vitamin D.
Sensation	The skin contains a number of receptors that respond to stimuli (temperature, pressure, pain, etc.) and relay this information via nerves to the central nervous system.
Excretion	The skin is able to serve as an organ of excretion, allowing the body to rid itself of chemicals in sweat. Salts and small amounts of ammonia and urea can, for example, be excreted through the sweat glands. Certain chemicals may also be eliminated from the body within the sloughed skin cells and hair.

2.10.1 Anatomy and function of the skin

Canine skin is similar to that of other mammals. It can range in colour from almost white through to pink, brown, blue or black, and it can also be two-tone, pink with black patches for example (*see* Fig. 2.10.1). It possesses two layers: the *epidermis* and the underlying *dermis* (*see* Fig. 2.10.2). The dermis lies on top of the *hypodermis*, or *subcutis*, a subcutaneous (under the skin) layer of fat cells, blood vessels and other tissues that support the overlying skin.

The following account provides a description of the epidermis, dermis, hypodermis and epidermal appendages (hair, nails, claws and glands).

Epidermis

The superficial skin layer – that which can be seen and touched – is called the epidermis and consists of several distinct layers. The upper layer is dead and is called the *stratum corneum*. It sits on top of four living layers that grow from a basal layer, the *stratum germinativum*.

The *stratum corneum* is a horny layer of skin consisting of between thirty-five and fifty-one layers of flattened keratinized cells that have no nucleus. Its average thickness is 13.3µm (this equates to 0.0133mm), although the thickness varies at different places on the body. The surface of this layer is itself covered by an amorphous film of lipid and aqueous constituents. These mainly contain fatty acids and waxes but also include various proteins and antibodies (immunoglobulins). Together with the lipid barrier, these constitute the skin's first line of defence.

The living epidermis is approximately 10µm thick (this equates to 0.010mm). The deepest layer is called the *stratum germinativum* and it is made up of cells that divide continuously to replace the more superficial cells, which are progressively shed from the skin surface. The total turnover time for this process is about three weeks. The cells of the stratum germinativum are columnar/cuboidal in shape, and very different from the flattened squames (dead/squamous epithelial cells) of the stratum corneum.

Fig. 2.10.1 *The pigment of skin can range from almost white through to pink, brown, blue and black. In some cases it can be pigmented in two colours, as can be seen on the pads of this black and white Springer Spaniel.*

Common integument

Legend:
a Intrapapillary capillary loop
b Apocrine sweat gland
c Elastic fiber
d Collagenic fiber
e Unilocular adipocyte
f Dermal root sheath
g Epithelial root sheath
h Hair papilla

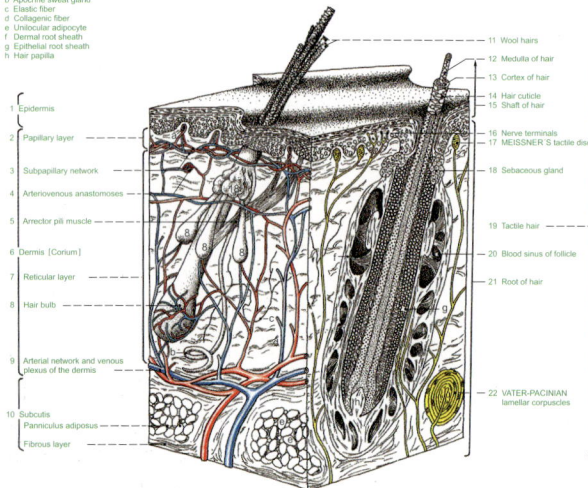

1 Epidermis
2 Papillary layer
3 Subpapillary network
4 Arteriovenous anastomoses
5 Arrector pili muscle
6 Dermis [Corium]
7 Reticular layer
8 Hair bulb
9 Arterial network and venous plexus of the dermis
10 Subcutis
Panniculus adiposus
Fibrous layer

11 Wool hairs
12 Medulla of hair
13 Cortex of hair
14 Hair cuticle
15 Shaft of hair
16 Nerve terminals
17 MEISSNER'S tactile disc
18 Sebaceous gland
19 Tactile hair
20 Blood sinus of follicle
21 Root of hair
22 VATER-PACINIAN lamellar corpuscles

Epidermis

Epidermis of digital pad   Epidermis of wall of claw

23 Stratum corneum
24 Stratum lucidum
25 Stratum granulosum
26 Spinous layer
27 Stratum germinativum

Fig. 2.10.2 *The dog's skin. (Diagram courtesy of Budras, McCarthy, Fricke and Richter)*

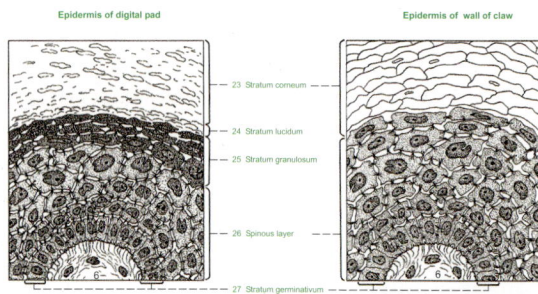

BELOW: Fig. 2.10.3 The dead skin cells (dander or squames) among the hairs on this table have been removed from the coat during grooming.

As the cells produced by the stratum germinativum move upwards, their columnar/cuboidal shape becomes progressively flattened until they resemble the typical drawn-out squame. As they move upwards, they produce more and more keratin, lose their nucleus and undergo a programmed cell death. This process of maturation leads to the shedding of skin cells at the skin surface; if progressing normally, this loss of cells should not be visible to the eye.

Dermis

The *dermis* lies between the epidermis and hypodermis. It is generally thickest in areas of dense hairy skin and thinnest where there is least hair. The dermis consists of a matrix of connective tissue fibres, of which collagen is by far the most important. These fibres are arranged in bundles, together with single elastic fibres, and provide support around blood vessels, hair follicles, skin glands and other structures found within the dermis. These various components are all held in a mass of amorphous ground substance consisting mainly of hyaluronic acid and chondroitin sulphates.

The synthesis of both collagen and amorphous ground substance is affected by hormones. Cortisol and oestrogen reduce its production and cause thinning of the skin, whilst androgens (such as testosterone) increase their formation. This is the basis for the thinning of skin in dogs with hyperadrenocorticism and the reason why gloves should be worn when applying topical steroids to a dog's skin.

The dermis contains a number of cellular components, including mast cells, histiocytes and fibroblasts. Mast cells are inflammatory cells (cells of the immune system) that, when stimulated, degranulate to release histamine, heparin and other chemicals. They play an important role in wound healing and protecting the body against pathogens. They can also cause problems, however, and it is their release of histamine that is responsible for the various signs associated with an allergic reaction (hives, redness, swelling and urticaria). Histiocytes are also known as macrophages and are inflammatory cells with the ability to gobble up bacteria and other foreign material.

Hypodermis

The hypodermis supports and cushions the overlying tissues. It consists of a loose network of connective tissue and a network of elastic fibres, fat cells, blood vessels and nerves. The fat deposits laid down in this layer help to insulate and cushion the body.

Epidermal appendages

Epidermal appendages include glands, claws (nails) and hair. Hair is covered in Section 2.10.2 below.

[i] The glands associated with canine skin are of several types: *sebaceous glands, eccrine sweat glands, apocrine glands* and *anal sacs.*

Sebaceous glands are microscopic glands found within the skin; they are responsible for the production of an oily secretion called sebum that lubricates the skin and hair of mammals. Sebaceous glands are associated with all hair follicles and are therefore typically found in hairy skin. They are also to be found at other sites where they are not associated with hair follicles: these include the external auditory meatus, prepuce, vulva and perianal tissues.

Each gland consists of a collection of large, foamy, lipid-filled cells that are continually produced and ultimately burst to release their contents. The gland opens and empties via a short duct into the lumen of the upper hair follicle. Sebaceous secretions are composed mainly of essential fatty acids (EFAs), cholesterol and waxes. On leaving the hair follicle, the sebum, having coated the hair(s), is further spread over the adjacent skin. The lipids and waxes in the sebum aid in keeping the skin and hair hydrated. It is the sebum that provides a shiny lustre to the hairs.

Dogs possess a particularly high concentration of these glands on the dorsal (upper) part of the first third of the tail. This grouping of glands is very well developed and is associated with apocrine glands in what is called the tail *gland area.*

The secretion of sebum from these glands does not appear to be under direct neurological control. It is thought that these glands respond instead to hormonal stimuli. Testosterone can cause these glands to increase in size (hypertrophy), whereas oestrogen and cortisol cause them to regress.

Apocrine glands are also associated with the hair follicles and empty via a duct to the hair follicle lumen close to the skin surface. In humans, these glands are associated with certain haired parts of the body, including the armpit as well as the perineal, mammary and genital areas. Some large breeds, including the German Shepherd Dog and Labrador Retriever, can demonstrate visible sweating from these glands in their axillae (armpits), groin and along the ventral abdomen.

The *apocrine glands* produce a sweat that is rich in proteins. These include immunoglobulins, which play an important role in the protective barrier film that coats the skin surface. Apocrine sweat also contains lipids and steroids and is usually odourless. That said, certain components can be processed by bacteria, resulting in the release of certain smells. It is also thought that apocrine sweat contains pheromones, which allow dogs to communicate with other dogs.

The apocrine sebaceous glands are able to respond to a range of stimuli, including the dog's emotional state. Secretion is stimulated in response to various cues, including fear, stress, anxiety and sexual arousal. It is therefore possible that dogs can pick up on pheromonal clues that may identify another dog's (or indeed a human's) emotional state.

Eccrine sweat glands are the major sweat glands of the human body and play an important role in thermoregulation. In dogs, however, they are only to be found on the pads of the feet. They produce a clear odourless secretion composed mainly of water and salt (NaCl).

The glands are located deep in the dermis and communicate with the skin surface via a long excretory duct that opens on the epithelium of the foot. It is these glands that are responsible for the sweaty paw marks that you may see on a dark work surface when a dog becomes stressed.

Anal sacs are specialized apocrine glands that are used to scent mark. They can be expressed at the time of defecation and can also be voided when stressed or frightened. As such, the secretion can function as an olfactory cue communicating alarm; this ability is particularly well developed in mustelids (badgers, skunks, ferrets, etc.) and cats, as well as in dogs.

The anal sacs are located between the internal and external anal sphincters and open via a duct that is itself lined by sebaceous glands. The material produced by the anal glands is therefore a combination of sebaceous and apocrine secretions.

There are two anal sacs, positioned at approximately 4 and 8 o'clock, and they can be palpated (felt) by running a finger over the skin close to the external anal sphincter (*see* Fig. 18.3.1 in Chapter 18). The anal sacs have a neck and a fundus (the sack part); it is the fundus that is lined by apocrine glands.

The *anal sacs* are to be distinguished from the *anal glands* and *circumanal glands* that are modified sebaceous glands located at the mucocutaneous junction where the skin and mucosa of the anus meet.

The anal sacs produce a viscous oily material that is thought to play a role in olfactory communication. The nature and character of this secretion is complex and highly variable. The character and consistency of the material produced by the apocrine glands within the fundus of the anal sac is affected by a range of factors. This can, in turn, affect the consistency of the contents of the anal sacs themselves. The normal healthy dog will usually have no difficulty expressing their anal sacs. In some cases, however, the anal sacs can become impacted, inflamed and/or infected (*see* Fig. 2.10.4). These three changes characterize anal sac disease and can cause the affected dog to 'scoot' (drag his bottom against the ground), lick and chew the affected area. Anal sac disease is discussed further under the skin diseases section.

[ii] *Nails* or claws are specialized skin appendages made from tough keratin, organized to produce a horn-like material similar to that found in human nails, although very different in shape. The canine claw is conical in shape and surrounds a process (outgrowth) that is attached to the third phalanx. This process is enveloped in sensitive tissues and is popularly known as the 'quick'. The claw grows continuously

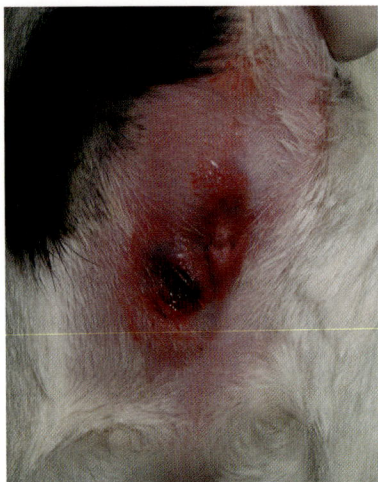

Fig. 2.10.4   An ulcerated cavity on the left of the anus where the anal sac has ruptured.

from a number of different germinative regions.

The shape of the foot and the terrain over which the dog is exercised have a bearing on the shape and length of the nail. Hare-footed dogs, such as the Greyhound, naturally have long nails that grow along the ground, whereas a dog with 'knuckled up' or 'cat-shaped' feet, such as the Pomeranian, has short nails that grow towards the ground. Skin disease may also affect the shape and condition of the nail and its growth (*see* Fig. 2.10.5).

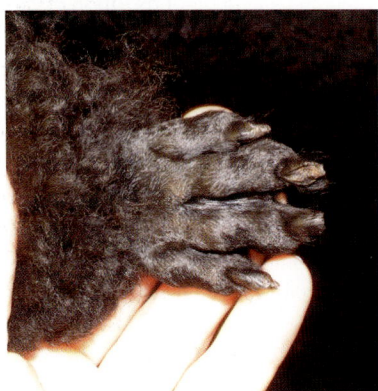

Fig. 2.10.5   The nail is made up of hardened keratin. Very often, if a dog has a skin problem the nails will also be affected. However, a nail bed infection can also cause dystrophic nails and abnormal nail growth.

2.10.2 The hair coat

The hair coat provides the dog with protection against the elements, physi-

cal trauma, cold, ultraviolet light, heat and noxious chemicals. Natural wear and tear on the hair results in the ends becoming roughened and damaged. The hair coat is replaced as part of the normal process of hair growth. There is therefore a turnover of hairs in much the same way that skin cells are continuously replaced.

Hair is a filament made of the structural protein keratin, and it is this unusual protein that accounts for the many properties of hair fibres. Keratins are made up of long chains (polymers) of amino acids that can be coiled into helical structures and further twisted into supra-helical structures that can be further coiled again. The end result is a coiled fibre with considerable strength. The keratin fibres are bound together by regular intra-chain hydrogen bonding and disulphide chemical bonds. These are very strong and difficult to break apart. It is these bonds that largely account for hair's resistance to environmental damage. The greater resistance of the keratin found in claws, compared to that found in hair, is largely due to the greater number of disulphide bonds between the keratin chains.

A cross-sectional view of a hair reveals three distinct layers. The outer layer consists of several layers of thin, flat cells that overlap each other; this layer is called the *cuticle*. The overlapping structure allows these cells to slide over each other and accommodate any swelling of the hair. The hair is further protected by a thin, water-repellent lipid coating. The next layer is called the *cortex* and contains the bundles of keratin fibres that extend like rods up the length of the hair. The cortex contains melanin, a pigment that colours the hair, with the precise colour varying according to the density, distribution and type of melanin granules at any given point. The innermost layer is called the *medulla* and is a relatively disorganized and empty layer at the hair's centre.

Each hair emerges from a hair follicle. The portion of hair above the level of the epidermis is called the *hair shaft*, that lying within the follicle is called the *hair root*. There are a number of different sorts of hair follicle and these give rise to different sorts of hairs and therefore of hair shafts – the part you

can see and will be trimming, sculpting, working with and caring for. The hair follicle of dogs with straight hair tends to be straight, whereas that of dogs with curly hair is itself curly! The hair follicle can give rise to a number of different sorts of hairs seen on any given dog; an even greater diversity of hair type is seen between dogs. The following three types of hair can be distinguished:

- *Guard hairs* are the longest and coarsest hairs in a dog's coat. They form the topcoat and protect the skin and undercoat from the elements. They are not generally present at birth and only start growing from around twelve weeks of age.
- *Secondary hairs* are much finer and usually make up the undercoat. Multiple secondary hairs can grow from the same follicle as a guard hair. Only secondary hairs tend to grow from the hair follicles during a puppy's first three months of life. Dogs do not therefore lose their puppy coat but acquire an adult coat that is better able to protect them.
- *Sensory hairs* are tactile hairs: sensory structures that provide the central nervous system with information. These hairs are present over much of the face and include the long whiskery supraorbital (above the eye), zygomatic, buccal, superior and inferior labial (upper and lower lip), mental and intermandibular hairs. The superior labial hairs are the hairs we usually call whiskers. Each of these hairs grows from a follicle that is surrounded by a blood sinus supplied by abundant nerve fibre terminals that respond to movement. These can be particularly useful to a dog when he is moving around in the dark or in other situations where there is a need to rely on the sensation of touch.

Genetic changes have influenced the ratio of guard hairs to secondary hairs. This has resulted in the wide variation in coat types that we see today, and that are significant in breed standards. Inherited hair length, texture and density have played an important role in the survival of the dog as, throughout his history, he has been faced with both environmental and occupational challenges.

Hair growth

The dog's hair follicle, or *pilosebaceous* unit, is unusual in that it develops a number of hairs, which all emerge from a common opening, together with the secretions from the sebaceous and apocrine glands discharging into the hair follicle lumen. This arrangement is described as a compound hair follicle and gives rise to a single guard hair together with a variable number of finer secondary hairs. Variations in the number of secondary hairs and guard hairs are seen between different breeds of dog (*see* Figs 2.10.6a–c).

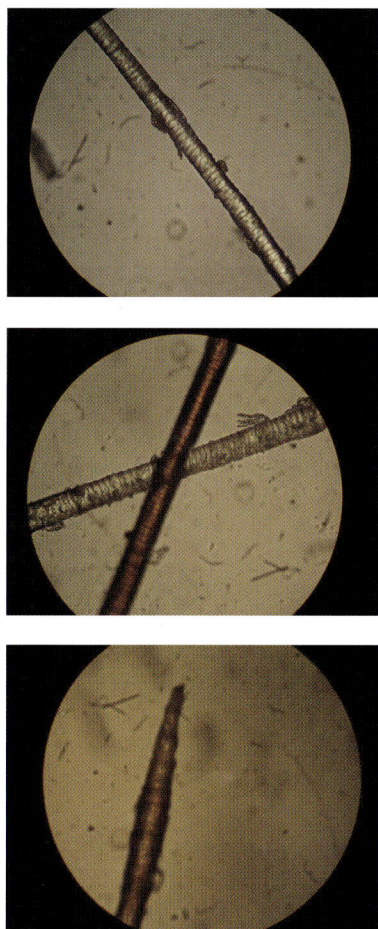

Fig. 2.10.6a–c   These are hairs from a Springer Spaniel. The first picture shows the cuticle: the overlapping flat cells that make up the outer casing of the hair shaft. The centre picture shows a strong shiny dark guard hair and a weaker dull undercoat hair, whilst the third picture shows the tip of the guard hair.

Each and every hair grows from a papilla located at the foot of each hair follicle. During the active phase of hair growth the germinal bulb of the hair is attached to this papilla.

Hair growth is not continuous but follows a cycle. The hair growth cycle has three key phases: anagen, catagen and telogen. Fortunately, these names are ordered alphabetically and spell the word 'ACT', which may help you to remember them.

> ### ACT: THE THREE PHASES OF HAIR GROWTH
>
> *Anagen: when the hair forms and moves upwards (grows).*
>
> *Catagen: when the hair base starts to degenerate and die.*
>
> *Telogen: the hair follicle rests and moulting may occur.*

The period of active growth when the hair is actually formed and moves upwards, along the hair follicle, to emerge at the skin surface is called *anagen*. Any remaining retained old hair(s) are pushed out by the growing hair (groomers refer to these as 'dead' or 'moulting' hairs). This phase lasts approximately six to eight weeks but can be longer in some breeds. Long-coated dogs tend to have a longer anagen phase, although the precise duration varies according to the area of the body.

The next phase corresponds with a cessation of hair growth. Degenerative changes at the base of the hair follicle break down the hair's attachment(s) with the papilla. This phase is called *catagen*. During the third and final phase, there is no activity within the follicle; this is effectively a resting phase during which the old hair may be shed. The length of this *telogen* phase can be highly variable.

Each hair follicle possesses its own rhythm of activity; individual hair follicles can therefore be at different stages of the hair growth cycle. Guard hairs tend to cycle continuously and maintain their density throughout the year; in doing so they demonstrate a relatively short *telogen* phase. Second-ary down hairs (undercoat), by contrast, tend to demonstrate a prolonged resting (*telogen*) phase during which they do not grow.

During the winter months most guard hairs and approximately 50 per cent of the secondary follicles are in telogen. Follicular activity then picks up again in the spring, leading to the 'spring moult'. Retained winter coats may be seen during this time if and when the secondary hairs of the undercoat undergo a prolonged telogen phase and there is failure to shed hair(s) from the resting hair follicles. Generally speaking, hair growth is maximal in spring and early autumn, which is why active hair shedding is usually seen in those seasons.

Many neural, hormonal, chemical and other factors (including photoperiod, nutrition, ambient temperature, health status and genetics) can influence the hair growth cycle. The mechanisms of hair growth control are therefore complex and still far from being fully understood. Debility and systemic disease affect the hair growth cycle, as can localized trauma (even if minor), inflammation and infection. Variations in the secretion or availability of hormones may also profoundly influence hair follicle activity, both generally and regionally. The mechanisms by which these effects are mediated are complex and can involve the stimulation of various receptors, including growth factor receptors, on the hair follicles. Other effects may be mediated via changes in blood supply or nerve control. These mechanisms have evolved over a long period of time to allow mammals to respond to environmental and other changes. These essentially reflect different requirements for heat regulation and camouflage, as well as for sexual and social communication.

References and further reading

Van Duijkeren, E. (1995). Disease conditions of canine anal sacs. *Journal of Small Animal Practice*, 36 (1), 12–16.

Scott, D.W., Miller, W.H. and Griffin, C.E. (2001). *Muller and Kirk's small animal dermatology*, 6th edition. Philadelphia: W.B. Saunders.

Thomsett, L.R. (1986). Structure of canine skin. *British Veterinary Journal*, 142, 116–23.

2.10.3 Canine skin diseases and disorders

This section builds on the reader's understanding of the healthy canine skin and hair coat, in order to develop the ability to recognize when the skin and/or hair is 'not right'. The role(s) and responsibilities of the groomer are discussed first in order to clearly define the limits of their responsibilities. An overview of skin disease in the dog is then provided, followed by a discussion of the main presenting signs. Finally, notes are provided on a number of common skin diseases in order to develop a deeper understanding of these conditions.

Skin disease and the dog groomer

Groomers spend their professional

> **CAUTION: THE GROOMER'S ROLE AND RESPONSIBILITIES**
>
> *This section is not intended to be a substitute for obtaining veterinary advice or care. Quite the reverse: it should improve your ability to recognize a problem, bring it to an owner's attention and induce them to seek veterinary advice.*
>
> *Many skin diseases look similar and without diagnostic testing it is often difficult to diagnose a particular skin disease and institute an appropriate treatment plan. This is the role of the vet.*
>
> *The purpose of this chapter is to help you understand the causes and presenting signs of some of the more common skin diseases so that you can recognize when something is wrong. You can then refer the dog for a veterinary examination. If a problem is confirmed, the dog will be prescribed treatment to resolve the problem. In this way you can play an active part in the prevention and management of skin disease.*
>
> *Remember the 3 'R's: Recognize, Refer and Resolve. Do nothing else unless you are instructed (preferably in writing) to do so by the dog's vet.*

careers working closely with the skin and hair coat of dogs. It is therefore only natural for them to develop a feel for healthy skin and hair and an ability to recognize when it is unhealthy (*see* Fig. 2.10.7). In the same way that you would expect your hairdresser to warn you about a suspicious change in your hair, or the skin of your scalp, and recommend that you get it checked out by your doctor, the groomer also has a responsibility to draw the dog owner's attention to any abnormalities or problems affecting their dog's skin or hair coat.

As a groomer, you have a responsibility for the care of the dog's skin. During your work you access the skin on every part of the dog, particularly those areas that no one else usually sees, and you will soon learn to recognize when it is not in good health (*see* Figs 2.10.8 and 2.10.9). The conscientious groomer in possession of this information has a duty to advise that the dog be seen by a vet.

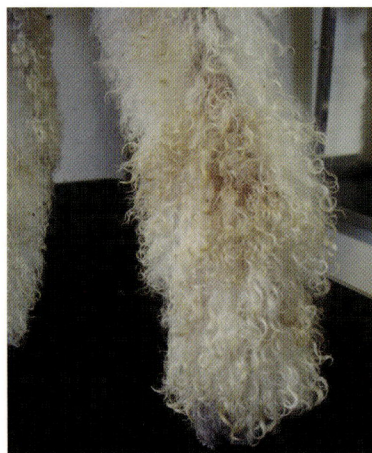

Fig. 2.10.7   During your health assessment of the dog before grooming begins, any discoloured areas of coat should alert you to an underlying skin problem. This white coat clearly shows discoloration where the dog has been licking at his hock, and you can just see the inflamed skin showing through the coat.

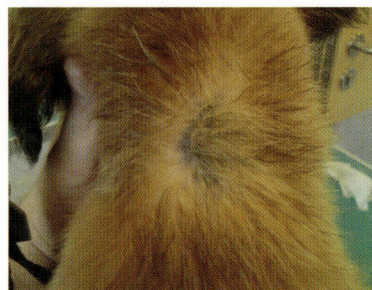

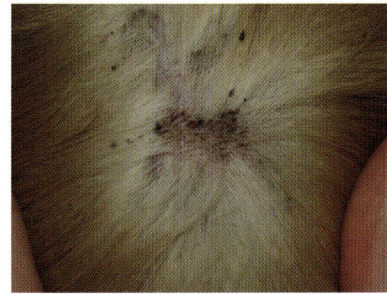

Fig. 2.10.9   Epidermal collarette on the inside leg of a Golden Retriever. This breed is vulnerable to this type of skin disorder, which can become extensive. A prescription shampoo can manage the problem and prevent it from becoming worse.

You are responsible for:

◆ giving the skin and coat a thorough physical examination;
◆ recognizing when something is wrong;
◆ determining whether it is appropriate to continue grooming the dog;
◆ monitoring and caring for existing skin or coat conditions;
◆ protecting the skin from trauma whilst grooming out (*see* Chapter 11);
◆ cleaning the skin properly (*see* Chapter 12);
◆ protecting the skin from harsh chemicals (*see* Chapter 12);
◆ protecting the skin from drying out (*see* Chapter 13);
◆ protecting the skin from injury from sharp tools; and
◆ alerting the owner to a potential problem and advising they consult their vet as soon as possible.

A commercial groomer sees several dogs a week with some form of skin disorder. Many of these are pre-existing conditions that you need some understanding of in order to undertake your job. In other cases you may be the first to notice a problem. In such cases your alertness to, and awareness of, any

Fig. 2.10.8   This Border Terrier has had an adverse skin reaction to a topical flea treatment. The black patch shows where the skin has changed colour (hyper-pigmented) and there is evidence of hair loss.

abnormality results in it being brought promptly to the owner's attention. You can then encourage them to seek veterinary advice. I can confidently say that the lives of many dogs have been saved or extended by vigilant groomers alerting owners to the early stages of skin disease and skin changes so that help could be sought in good time (*see* Fig. 2.10.10).

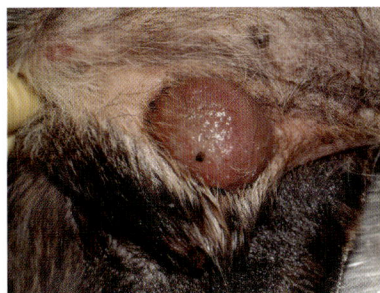

Fig. 2.10.10   This very angry looking mass appeared suddenly and was growing very fast on the prepuce of this dog. Closer examination showed that there was also some bruising to the area (arrow). In this case the mass was a mast cell tumour. These tumours are among the most serious (often fatal) skin masses, so early diagnosis is essential if the dog is to have a chance of survival.

In practice, skin problems may only become apparent during the grooming process itself, as the skin is often easier to visualize when the coat is wet. There are, however, some clues that help you identify such problems during the pre-grooming assessment. These include coat discoloration, isolated matting, breed predisposition and signs of chewing.

Skin disorders and disease

In order to develop your ability to recognize when a dog's hair coat and skin are unhealthy, you need to become familiar with what is normal for any given dog. This can vary according to their breed, their age and a host of other influences. The healthy skin and hair coat were described in the previous section; this section provides an overview of the various causes of skin diseases and the clinical signs associated with them. It is helpful to familiarize yourself with the vocabulary that allows you to describe what

Table 2   Classification system for different causes of skin disease.

Aetiology/Cause		Definition/Explanation	Examples
V	Vascular	Involving the blood to the skin.	Frostbite; avascular necrosis*.
I	Infectious/ Inflammatory	(i) Caused by an infectious agent; (ii) Arising through an inflammatory reaction.	Pyoderma (bacterial infection); dermatophytosis (ringworm infection); flea infestation; mite infestation.
T	Trauma	Arising through trauma to the skin.	Skin tears and other injuries; self-trauma.
A	Auto-immune/Immune mediated	(i) Arising as a result of damage inflicted by the body's immune system against itself; (ii) Immune mediated.	(i) Pemphigus**; (ii) Allergic skin disease; atopy; adverse food reaction; flea allergic dermatitis.
M	Metabolic/Endocrine	(i) Metabolic disorders describe disease processes in which cell metabolism is disturbed. (ii) Endocrine disorders are mediated by hormonal disturbances and can cause metabolic disease.	(i) Metabolic epidermal necrosis (previously called Hepatocutaneous syndrome); (ii) Hypothyroidism; hyperadrenocorticism (Cushing's disease); diabetes mellitus.
I	Idiopathic/Iatrogenic***	(i) Of unknown cause (idiopathic). (ii) Caused by the groomer/vet (iatrogenic).	(i) Sebaceous adenitis; (ii) Clipper rash; drug reaction (although perhaps best described as immune mediated).
N	Neoplasti	Arising through the development of cancerous cells.	Tumours.
C	Congenital	An inherited condition present at birth or developing after birth.	Follicular dysplasia; colour dilution alopecia.
D	Degenerative/ Developmental	Some skin changes can arise through degenerative (ageing/wear and tear) or developmental (growing) processes.	Thinning skin in old dogs; acquired skin fragility syndrome; paraneoplastic skin diseases (appearing as the result of cancer).
E	Environmental	Arising as a result of some environmental influence.	Dry air/heat (natural or artificial)/ice and snow. Dry air can cause the skin to dry out. Heat can cause skin burns or blistering. Ice and snow can cause ice burn to exposed skin.

Notes:

* *Avascular necrosis* is where living cells or tissues die through loss of, or damage to, their blood supply.

** *Pemphigus* is an auto-immune condition giving rise to ulcers and crusting on the lips and nose (typically at the mucocutaneous junction).

*** Strictly speaking, *iatrogenic* refers to a problem caused by a doctor; it is also used to describe disease caused by vets, and it is probably not unreasonable to include groomers here, too.

is wrong with a dog's skin. These terms are used to describe common presenting signs of skin disease and are discussed further below.

The skin is an intricate and complex structure that provides a mechanical and chemical protective barrier between the dog and his environment. As such, it can be affected by both external and internal influences and disease processes. It is all too easy to overlook the fact that abnormalities of the skin and hair coat may be a reflection of a secondary rather than a primary problem. That this is so should make sense when one considers that the skin and hair coat are affected by the general health of the dog.

Skin diseases can have many causes, and the following account attempts to provide the reader with an overview of the subject. In doing so, the different forms of disease are classified according to their underlying pathological cause(s). The reader should note, however, that the cause will often only become apparent following a thorough veterinary dermatological investigation.

Table 2 summarizes the causes of skin disease in this way, using the VITAMIN CDE mnemonic. Many such mnemonics are used by human and veterinary clinicians to classify diseases according to the underlying cause. But no classification system is perfect and it should be noted that there may be some overlap between causes: flea allergic dermatitis, for example, has both an infectious (flea) and an immune (allergic response) cause. The main thing to conclude from this table is just how many different causes of skin disease there are and how difficult it can be to investigate and unravel them. Part of the reason for this difficulty is that the skin can only behave and respond to a disease process in a limited number of ways. It is these reactions that are grossly apparent to the owner and groomer. Whilst Table 2 provides a useful summary of the various causes of skin disease, the groomer is more likely to understand a skin disease classification system that is based on the main presenting sign(s). Table 3 therefore summarizes skin diseases according to presenting signs.

Table 3 Common presenting signs of skin disease that may be seen by the groomer, and some of their common underlying causes.

Presenting sign	Explanation and signs	Common causes
Alopecia	Hair loss, hair shedding, baldness.	(i) Scratching; (ii) Moulting; (iii) Hormonal disorder.
Pruritus	Excessive itchiness and scratching.	(i) Fleas; (ii) Other ectoparasites; (iii) Bacterial skin infections; (iv) Allergic skin disease; (v) Food allergies; (vi) Contact irritants.
Dermatitis	Inflammation of the skin. Signs: reddening, itchiness, scaling, lesions, sores, skin thickening, increased pigmentation.	(i) Fleas; (ii) Other ectoparasites; (iii) Bacterial skin infections; (iv) Allergic skin disease; (v) Food allergies; (vi) Contact irritants.
Lumps and bumps	Various swellings in the skin. Signs: lumps may be of varying size, hard, soft, smooth, ulcerated, fast or slow growing.	(i) Tumours; (ii) Warts; (iii) Cysts; (iv) Engorged ticks.
Seborrhoea	A scaling disorder of the skin. A build-up of scale (scurf dandruff/dead skin cells) may be seen.	(i) Primary seborrhoea; (ii) Allergic skin disease; (iii) Endocrinopathy; (iv) Neoplastic skin disease; (v) Parasitic skin disease.

Common presenting signs of canine skin disease

The following pages describe some of the more common presentations and problems that you can expect to see and that may benefit from your help. In order to help you develop a framework for thinking about these conditions, they have been categorized under five headings: Alopecia, Pruritus, Dermatitis, Lumps and Bumps and Seborrhoea.

[i] Alopecia

Alopecia is the term used to describe complete hair loss, whereas hypotrichosis is the term for the presence of less hair than normal (hair thinning). These terms do not refer to a specific hair-loss-related disease, as both alopecia and hypotrichosis are signs arising from an underlying skin disease or disorder. Therefore they are more correctly used to refer to any form of hair loss where there was formerly hair growth. The word 'alopecia' can be traced back to the Greek word alopekia, which itself derives from the word alopek, meaning 'Fox'. Alopekia is the Greek name for fox mange.

Alopecia can be localized or generalized, symmetrical or asymmetrical, and can affect different parts of the body (*see* Figs 2.10.11 to 2.10.14). It can have many causes, including hormonal problems, stress and parasitism, as well as genetics, to mention a few. In humans alone there are several hundred diseases where alopecia is a primary symptom. Alopecia should never be taken lightly and where you notice hair loss, you should check the skin for obvious causes such as parasite infestation (*see* Fig. 2.10.15) and consider any biosecurity risk! Your examination should allow you to establish whether it is safe and appropriate to continue grooming the animal. In many cases it is perfectly acceptable for you to con-

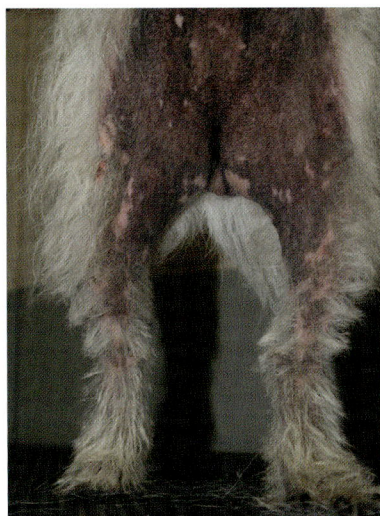

Fig. 2.10.11   This picture shows extensive hair loss. The skin is red and inflamed and there is evidence of skin thickening and hyper-pigmentation.

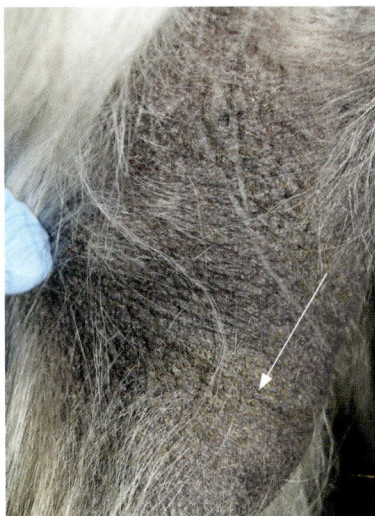

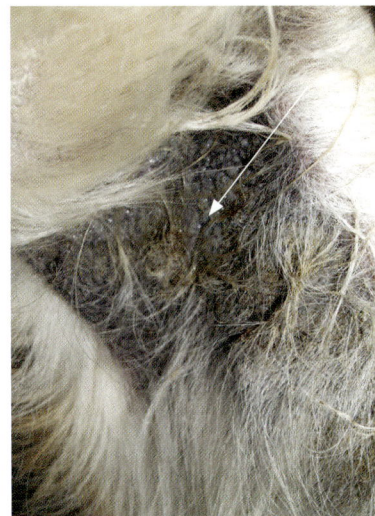

Fig. 2.10.12a–b

Alopecia, skin thickening and hyper-pigmentation may be seen following chronic inflammation. Note the excessive scale build-up on the skin surface (arrows).

Fig. 2.10.13   Alopecia in a young Jack Russell Terrier. In this case the skin is not hyper-pigmented but is two-coloured, as is the dog's coat.

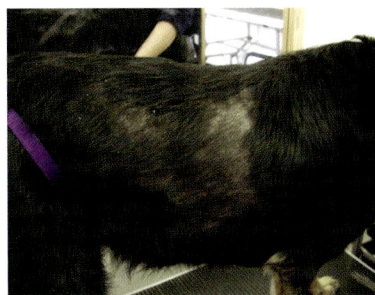

Fig. 2.10.14   Symmetrical alopecia on a German Shepherd cross – the hair loss was the same on the other side.

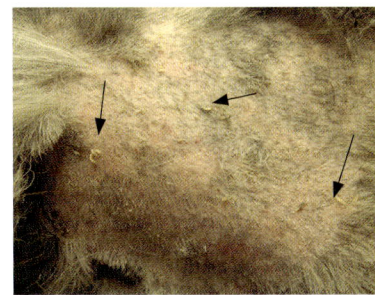

Fig. 2.10.15   When a skin problem is evident, always check carefully for parasites. This dog has a first stage maggot infection.

tinue working on the dog. The following list of hair loss conditions details some of the cases that need not necessarily be a cause for concern within the salon environment.

Moulting

Hair loss through moulting is a common occurrence in dogs and is particularly pronounced in those that moult heavily. It may occur seasonally but is also seen in bitches after whelping. In some cases dogs can moult to the extent that they exhibit large areas of almost bald patches of coat that are quite normal. The coat will return to its former glory as the dog comes back 'into coat'.

Selective breeding

In some breeds, such as the Chinese Crested, Mexican Hairless and American Hairless Terrier, selective breeding has deliberately produced a dog with an ectodermal defect, predisposing them to either ultra fine hair growth or, in some cases, no hair growth at all. The skin of these breeds is often prone to bacterial infection (especially of the hair follicles), blackhead formation and hair foreign body granulomas.

> *You should check the skin for signs of parasite infestation, changes in pigmentation, skin thickening, lesions or sores just to be certain. If the skin is clear (i.e. healthy) then it is probably safe to continue grooming as usual.*

These dogs are also vulnerable to sunburn and seborrhoea. When presented with such a dog, you should check to see if the skin is healthy. If it appears unhealthy, you should consult with the dog's vet before continuing. Learn the various breed profiles so you are familiar with breeds that are intended to be hairless.

Follicular dysplasias

Follicular dysplasias are a collection of relatively common inherited disorders of the hair follicle. They are particularly common in Dobermans (blue and fawn coloured), Rottweilers, Siberian Huskies, Malamutes, Chesapeake Bay Retrievers, Portuguese Water Dogs and Labrador Retrievers. A seasonal form of the condition is not uncommonly seen in Boxers and English Bulldog breeds, as well as in Airedale Terriers and Schnauzers. This condition is popularly called 'seasonal flank alopecia' or 'canine recurrent flank alopecia'; it can start as early as one to two years of age and progresses slowly over time. Hair loss is seen in various locations but most symmetrically on the trunk and flank areas, ventral neck or caudal thighs.

The condition is more common north of 45° latitude (the 45th parallel). The 45th parallel is an imaginary line circling the earth 45° north of the Equator and marking the halfway point between the Equator and the North Pole; it passes through Bordeaux in France and more or less follows the border between the US and Canada. This finding suggests a link between the condition and changing photoperiod (light exposure).

Colour dilution alopecia is the name given to a follicular dysplasia seen in certain breeds bearing the coat colour genotype dd, which renders black genotypes blue and liver genotypes beige or fawn. This syndrome is best known in Dobermanns but is also reported in colour dilute Dachshunds, Italian Greyhounds, Whippets and Yorkshire Terriers. In blue coats clumping of black pigments is seen within the hair shafts; this causes weakening of the shafts. Affected hairs break easily and are readily lost. In fawn coats a similar pathology occurs with brown pigments clumping in the hair shaft. A similar condition known as 'black hair follicular dysplasia' has been reported in a range of dogs, including Chihuahuas, Terriers, Bearded Collies, Border Collies, Basset Hounds, Beagles and American Cocker Spaniels. In this condition hairs in black areas break off, whereas hairs in unpigmented white areas appear completely normal.

Pattern baldness

This is a fairly common skin condition consisting of a delayed hair-loss reaction in dogs that are born with normal coats. Hair loss can be seen as early as six months of age and continues into adulthood. It tends to appear in breeds predisposed to hypotrichosis and is commonly seen in Whippets, Greyhounds, Dachshunds, Boston Terriers and Chihuahuas. It can be quite striking but is generally cosmetic in nature. Hair loss in front of the ears, on the ventral neck, chest, head and caudal thighs is often described; hair loss over the back would be unusual. A number of different types of pattern baldness have been described. In Dachshunds and other breeds hair loss is seen around the temples, the ventral neck, chest, abdomen and back of thighs. In male Dachshunds, especially, hair loss over the pinna may be seen. Saddle alopecia may be seen in American Water Spaniels and Portuguese Water Dogs.

Pattern baldness is a congenital hypotrichosis and it is recommended that affected dogs should not be used for breeding. Although largely a cosmetic problem, the exposed skin is vulnerable and can be harmed by environmental factors (sun, cold, shampoos, etc). This can lead to localized skin changes, including hyperpigmentation.

A groomer familiar with breed-specific abnormalities should be able to recognize this complaint. If, on examining the skin, you find it is clear and there is no sign of scratching or skin trauma, it is safe to continue grooming. If in doubt, consult a veterinary surgeon.

Alopecia X

This poorly understood condition is seen in Pomeranians and a number of other breeds, including the Samoyed, Chow Chow, Siberian Husky and Alaskan Malamute. It was first described in the early 1980s at the University of Tennessee in America. Affected dogs were generally young adults and those tested were found to have abnormal sex hormone results. Typical presenting signs include marked hair loss on the trunk, ventral neck and caudal thighs. The condition was originally termed a growth-hormone or castration-responsive dermatitis, but as yet the cause – and an effective treatment – remains elusive. New theories on the condition are focusing on genetics and hair follicle receptors.

Initially, a loss of guard hairs (with retention of the undercoat) in the frictional areas, around the neck, caudomedial thighs (i.e. the inside and back of the thigh) and tail, is seen. Gradually, all hair is lost in those regions and eventually the guard hairs over the trunk are also lost, giving the remaining coat a puppy-like appearance. Over time (several months to years) the undercoat becomes thin. In some cases hyperpigmentation of the exposed skin and/or colour changes in the remaining hair coat may be seen.

Post-clipping alopecia

Some breeds of dog appear predisposed to hair loss after clipping. This problem most commonly affects the trunk or limbs of plush-coated Nordic breeds with guard hairs and thick undercoats, including the Siberian Husky, Alaskan Malamute, Samoyed, Keeshound and Chow Chow, as well as the Labrador Retriever and German Shepherd Dog. Areas of alopecia are typically seen several months after clipping and may show hyperpigmentation. It has been suggested that this may arise through localized vasoconstriction (constriction of the blood vessels) at the site of clipping and a halt in the hair growth cycle. It has been suggested that these breeds normally have a hair growth cycle with a prolonged telogen phase, which may have developed as an adaptation to cold climates to allow dogs to avoid shedding and regrowing their coats. The geographic region in which these dogs live may also play a role in this condition.

Post-clipping alopecia is also seen with other conditions, including hypothyroidism, Cushing's disease and Alopecia X. Veterinary investigations will be required to rule these conditions out. In the case of post-clipping alopecia, new hair growth can be expected in six to twelve months.

If, by contrast, the hair loss is a new process that is not related to the dog's breed or associated with other signs, or if the dog appears unwell, or, indeed, if you are simply unsure about the dog, veterinary advice should always be sought.

In summary, if a dog presented for grooming appears to be suffering from alopecia, you should examine it carefully and only proceed with grooming if the skin appears healthy. Dogs with obvious signs of skin disease should be referred to a vet. If in doubt, seek veterinary advice

[ii] Pruritus

Pruritus is the term used to describe an itchiness of the skin; an itchy dog is described as 'pruritic'. Along with hair loss, itching is probably one of the two commonest signs you can expect to see in a dog with skin disease. It can arise from a number of causes including ectoparasitism and bacterial skin infections.

Pruritus rapidly leads to skin trauma through repeated scratching and chewing. If the underlying cause of the itchiness is not identified and eliminated, it can soon lead to secondary infections, which will require treatment. The itchy dog may already have been treated for fleas by the owner. Given that fleas are one of the most common causes of pruritus this is not unreasonable but it may be unsuccessful if both the dog and his environment have not been treated or if the condition has been allowed to progress too far and a secondary infection has taken hold. Where flea treatment has not resolved the problem, veterinary attention should be sought (*see* Fig. 2.10.16).

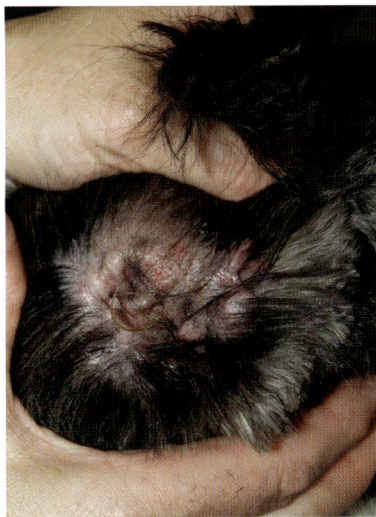

Fig. 2.10.16   A moist dermatitis on the inside of the pinna.

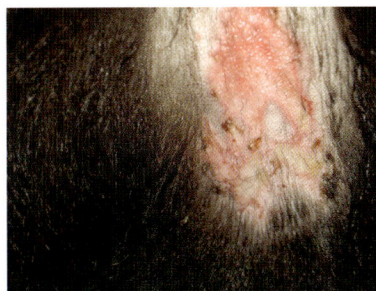

Fig. 2.10.17   A 'hot-spot' above the tail. Note the very sore red skin and the moisture emitting from the wound.

[iii] Dermatitis

Dermatitis is a term loosely used to describe inflammation of the skin; as such, it is a broad all-encompassing term. A dog's skin can become inflamed for many different reasons. Common causes of dermatitis include parasites, allergies, chemical irritants, diet and environmental factors (such as sunlight and wet environments), to name just a few. It is important that the groomer is able to recognize when skin is inflamed and can advise the owner to seek veterinary advice promptly.

Inflamed skin can show any of the following signs:

◆ redness (*see* Fig. 2.10.16);
◆ weeping/oozing from broken skin (*see* Fig. 2.10.17);
◆ itchiness/discomfort;
◆ pustules (white heads containing pus) and papules (raised red spots);
◆ hair loss (*see* Figs 2.10.11, 2.10.13 and 2.10.14); and
◆ signs of scratching/self trauma (*see* Fig. 2.10.17).

Once affected dogs have been referred to a vet and a diagnosis made, it is likely that the groomer will see these dogs again; the groomer therefore needs to have some understanding of any underlying problem and how it is best managed. This allows the grooming regimen to be adapted to the condition. It is sensible to ask the owner and their vet if there are any specific recommendations to be followed (e.g., products to use/avoid, frequency of bathing, etc.).

[iv] Lumps and bumps

In the course of grooming a dog, especially in view of the prolonged physical contact with him, it is not uncommon to find various lumps and bumps on the dog. Some of these may be innocuous, others much more serious. All should be noted in your records and brought to the attention of the owner and, ultimately, the vet.

In some cases a lump may pose you a particular problem, as is the case with warts and skin tags (*see* Figs 2.10.18a–b); these are easily caught by the clippers (and/or scissors) and bleed readily. Your pre-grooming examination should identify their presence and lead you to take greater care when clipping

the area. Another lump to look out for is the aural haematoma (*see* Section 2.9, and Fig. 2.10.19), particularly in dogs with dropped pinna. In other cases a lump may be found to be an engorged or recently attached tick. Prompt and proficient removal of these ticks is recommended (see Chapter 18).

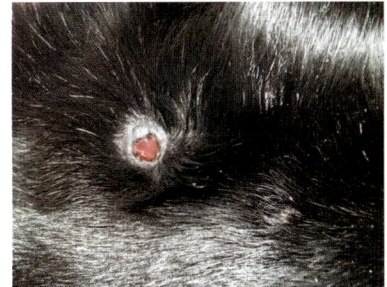

ABOVE AND BELOW: Fig. 2.10.18a–b   Warts are often not considered to be anything to worry about but they should be monitored and watched for signs of ulceration (left), or if they are in areas where they are likely to be rubbed and damaged. It is always best to get warts checked out by a vet because some tumours resemble warts in appearance.

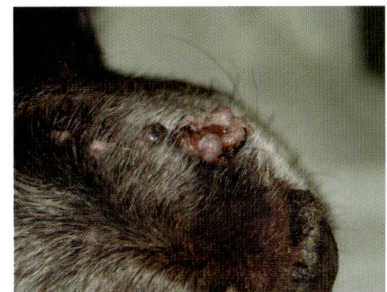

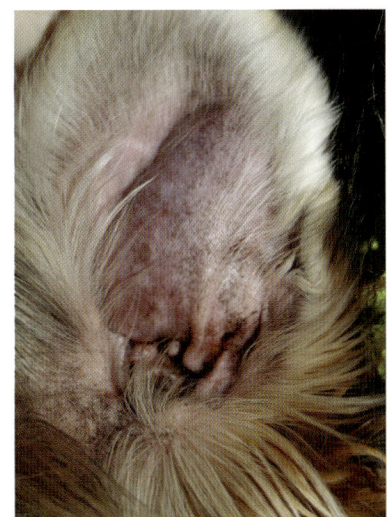

Fig. 2.10.19   An aural haematoma is not considered to be a skin problem but it is caused by damage (often bruising) to the skin and the underlying tissues.

A lump may also prove to be a tumour or neoplasm (*see* Fig. 2.10.20). A tumour is a swelling or mass of tissue formed by a new growth of cells, normally independent of the surrounding structures. Tumours may also be caused by neoplasms and these can be broadly separated into three categories:

◆ a benign neoplasm is localized, non-infiltrative and, because it is surrounded by a capsule, easy to excise (remove);

◆ a neoplasm of intermediate malignancy is locally infiltrative and difficult to excise, but does not metastasize (spread to other tissues); and

◆ a malignant neoplasm is infiltrative and has metastatic potential (can spread).

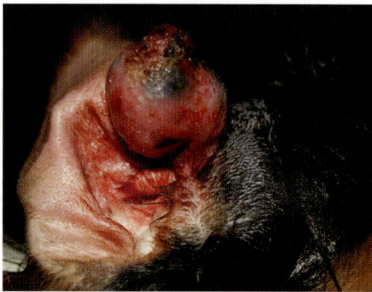

Fig. 2.10.20   A fast-growing cell mass at the opening of the auditory meatus on a Cocker Spaniel. The mass was malignant and had grown to this size in a week.

The variability in presentation can make distinguishing neoplasms from inflammatory disease, and benign neoplasms from malignant ones, difficult. In order to establish a definitive diagnosis histopathology is often required. Veterinary referral is therefore always the best option.

[v] Seborrhoea

Seborrhoea is a keratinization defect of the skin that results either in a derangement of sebum production or of skin cell production. Either may become excessive, causing the skin and hair coat to become either oily and greasy or excessively dry with lots of dandruff.

The groomer can expect to see two types of seborrhoea in the dog:

(a) *Seborrhoea sicca* is the dry form of seborrhoea and is characterized by an overproduction of skin cells. This results in large numbers of skin cells being shed, which gives rise to dandruff. This can, in turn, lead to itchiness of the skin and to the dog nibbling and scratching excessively. This can lead to further trauma and secondary infections. The coat of affected animals looks dull and contains a lot of dandruff.

(b) *Seborrhoea oleosa* is the oily form of seborrhoea and is characterized by an overproduction of sebum. The coat and skin become very greasy and this can give rise to an unpleasant odour.

Secondary infections are common in seborrhoeic dogs as the changes to the skin provide ideal conditions for bacterial and yeast infections.

Seborrhoea can be a primary disease or may be secondary to some other disease process. Primary seborrhoea is an inherited condition and is seen more commonly in American Cocker Spaniels, English Springer Spaniels, Basset Hounds, West Highland White Terriers, Dachshunds, Labrador Retrievers and German Shepherd Dogs.

Most seborrhoeic dogs have excessive skin or sebum production as a result of an underlying skin disease. The most common underlying diseases are skin allergies and endocrinopathies. A dog suffering from seborrhoea could have any one of a number of conditions, some of which are potentially contagious. Veterinary referral is recommended to allow a full investigation to be undertaken.

2.10.4 Some common skin problems in dogs

Atopic Dermatitis

Atopic skin disease occurs in dogs suffering from atopy. Atopy is a genetic predisposition to develop hypersensitivity to environmental allergens. Where a dog is exposed to such allergens, and develops an inflammatory and pruritic skin disease as a result, atopic skin disease is said to exist. A precise definition has yet to be agreed upon; perhaps the best working definition has been proposed by the International Task Force on Canine Atopic Disease (ITFCAD):

NOTE: SEBORRHOEA

Seborrhoeic dogs often have a dull flaky coat, with patches of dead flaky skin cells and crusts. More often than not the arrival of the dog is preceded by a strong musty odour. The skin abnormalities make bacterial and yeast infections more probable and very often these dogs have an increase in cerumen (ear wax), giving rise to ear infections (*see* Fig. 2.10.21).

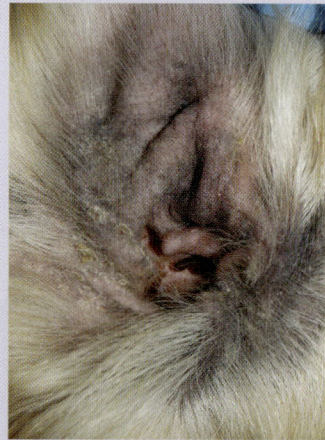

Fig. 2.10.21   A close look at the ear of this dog shows hyper-pigmentation on the inside of the pinna and surrounding the entrance to the ear. There is wax within the auditory meatus and lichenification of the skin is also evident.

If the ears of the dog are infected, they are likely to be very sore and very painful. It is therefore best not to try to clean inside the ear canal and to make sure that the pinna (inside and out) are dried carefully and thoroughly so that the skin does not remain wet. The owner should be advised to seek veterinary advice for the infection.

◆ *Canine atopic dermatitis*: a genetically predisposed inflammatory and pruritic allergic skin disease with characteristic clinical features associated with IgE antibodies most commonly directed against environmental allergens.

◆ *Canine atopic-like dermatitis*: an inflammatory and pruritic skin disease with clinical features identical to those seen in canine atopic dermatitis, in which an IgE response to environmental or other allergens cannot be documented.

(Source: Halliwell, R. (2006). Revised nomenclature for veterinary allergy. *Veterinary Immunology and Immunopathology* 114, 207–8.)

Atopic dermatitis is one of the most common skin diseases in dogs, affecting 10–15 per cent of the canine population.

Common environmental allergens causing atopic dermatitis include house dust mites, pollens, mould spores and occasionally foods. Unfortunately, many dogs have multiple allergies and may even suffer from a combination of atopic dermatitis and other hypersensitivities, most notably flea allergy. Some of the breeds most commonly affected include West Highland White Terriers (and some other Terriers), Boxers, Labrador Retrievers and German Shepherd Dogs.

The condition usually appears between six months and three years of age, and affected dogs may demonstrate intense itching and redness of the skin. The disease may be seasonal, especially where pollens are involved. Clinical signs wax and wane as a function of the dog's exposure to allergens, the presence of secondary infections and other allergic diseases.

Where a dog is suffering recurrent skin problems, an underlying atopic dermatitis may be present but this can only be confirmed following veterinary investigation. Affected dogs will benefit from such investigation and the development of a detailed management plan to allow this lifelong condition to be managed. This typically involves a multimodal approach involving the use of immunosuppressants (such as cyclosporine and steroids), allergen avoidance programmes, desensitization (using specially prepared vaccines, the composition of which is based on the results of allergy testing). Where appropriate, secondary bacterial infections will need to be controlled. Treatment may also include the reinforcement of the skin's lipid barrier using topical preparations or essential fatty acid supplements.

Groomers who regularly see an atopic dog should consult with the dog's owner and veterinary surgeon to ensure the optimal management of this potentially distressing condition, thereby keeping the dog healthy and comfortable.

Contact dermatitis

Contact dermatitis begins when the skin surface comes into contact with, and reacts to, a particular substance that is either an allergen or an irritant. Contact dermatitis can be divided into two subcategories: allergic contact dermatitis and irritant contact dermatitis.

Allergic contact dermatitis is rare, relative to irritant contact dermatitis. It arises when the skin (and/or the body) becomes sensitive to a substance. Further contact with that substance will then trigger a reaction. The immune system reacts abnormally to the allergen and produces an exaggerated inflammatory response that is damaging to the tissues. Symptoms can appear instantaneously but may take as long as several days to develop and the skin will become sore and inflamed. This causes itchiness, encouraging the dog to scratch and rub in an attempt to relieve the irritation. Over time, the trauma that this causes to the skin will result in sores and lesions appearing. Once the skin has erupted into sores and lesions, a secondary bacterial infection is a strong possibility.

Irritant contact dermatitis occurs when, as the name suggests, the skin comes into contact with a substance that damages the skin tissues directly. Such substances include detergents, some plants and even, in some cases, hard or chalky water. It can occur after multiple exposures to weak irritants or it may be the result of a single exposure. Clinical signs can appear instantaneously or they may take up to 48 hours to develop. In all cases the skin will be damaged and becomes sore, red and inflamed at the point of contact.

Contact dermatitis is very painful and often leads to extensive self-mutilation and secondary infections. It can be made worse by:

◆ friction;

◆ exposure to chemicals; and
◆ heat and cold.

Any dog that is presented to you with signs of soreness, irritation or self-mutilation should be referred to a vet as soon as possible without being groomed. If these signs have appeared after you have bathed the dog, it may be the chemicals you have used that are causing the hypersensitivity, even if you have not seen the dog for several weeks. The dog will require extensive testing before a diagnosis of the cause can be made, however, as there are many possible causes to rule out. Once the cause has been established, you will need to play your part in the continued care and monitoring of the condition with regular bathing and coat maintenance.

Flea allergic dermatitis

Flea allergic dermatitis or 'flea bite hypersensitivity' is a very common, intensely itchy skin disease caused by hypersensitivity to flea saliva. Dogs with flea allergy dermatitis may display intense pruritus despite only a few fleas being present, so much so that you may struggle to find any sign of them and may be unable to demonstrate their presence to the owner!

This condition can affect dogs of any type or age with signs first presenting between ten months and five years of age. The typical area affected is around the tail base, the top and back half of the dog, as well as the flanks and inner thighs.

If confirmed by a veterinary surgeon, a concerted treatment programme for the dog and his home environment will be required to break the flea's life cycle.

Food allergy

Food allergy is better termed an 'adverse food reaction', as the evidence for a true hypersensitivity is vanishingly small in the dog, with opinions as to its true incidence varying between 1–2 per cent and 15 per cent amongst the veterinary profession. Where a true food allergy exists, it is commonly known as 'canine food hypersensitivity'. It typically presents as a non-seasonal pruritic condition. It is caused by a hypersensitive reaction to dietary proteins (and sometimes carbohydrates) and can occur in dogs of any breed and age.

It is seen in 10–20 per cent of dogs with atopic dermatitis. It may be associated with gastro-intestinal signs and is often associated with ear infections. Veterinary investigations of pruritic dogs often involve a dietary exclusion trial. If this confirms a food allergy, the condition can then be managed with a hyposensitivity diet.

If you are grooming a dog with canine food hypersensitivity you should ensure that you only feed it the diet provided by its owner and prescribed by its vet. Additionally, you should ensure that it does not have any opportunity to steal food when kennelled as this may trigger a skin flare-up. Treats should never be given to a dog during or after grooming without the owner's permission.

Sebaceous adenitis

Sebaceous adenitis is a condition of the sebaceous gland. In the early stages of the disease the gland becomes inflamed and as the disease progresses the gland is totally destroyed.

This perplexing disorder is inherited as an autosomal recessive trait in the Standard Poodle, although the precise mechanism of inheritance is unclear. It is also seen in the Vizsla, Samoyed (*see* Fig. 2.10.22) and Akita, but can be seen in almost any breed. It is usually noticed in young dogs between one and five years of age. It can appear differently in different breeds. Typically affected Standard Poodles have dry skin and areas of hair loss over the top of the head, neck and back. More severely affected dogs can present with thickened skin, extensive areas of hair loss and a musty smell. Similar signs are seen in the Samoyed and Akita. In the Vizsla, however, a moth-eaten appearance is seen, together with mild scaling, affecting the head, ears and trunk.

Sebaceous adenitis usually starts to develop on the head and presents itself as an excessive amount of loose scales on the skin surface with clumps of what resembles dandruff around the hair roots. The coat becomes brittle and sparse (alopecia) and often has a rusty tint to it. The skin has a musty odour that persists even after bathing. Gener-

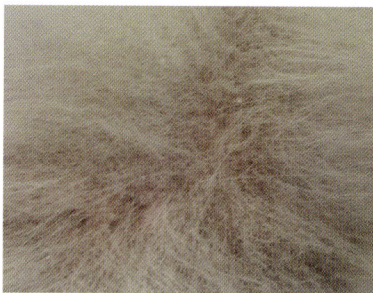

Fig. 2.10.22   Sebaceous adenitis in a Samoyed. Note the thinning coat, the orange/pink tinge to the skin and the excessive amount of skin scales (dander) within the coat.

ally the skin is not itchy unless there is a secondary infection; affected dogs are not usually therefore in any discomfort. Learning which breeds are predisposed to the disease ensures that you remain vigilant when working with these dogs. As soon as you suspect a problem, you can alert the owner to it and encourage them to have it looked at.

Whilst the condition is mainly of cosmetic concern, it can be complicated by secondary infections. Once confirmed by a veterinary surgeon, it will require long-term management with anti-seborrhoeic shampoos. When washing affected dogs, you will find a large deposit of dead skin (dander) coming away from the skin surface; wearing a face-mask is recommended.

> **CAUTION: RINSE THE DOG WELL**
>
> *Be absolutely certain to rinse the dog well (see Chapter 12), particularly if you are using a non-prescription shampoo. Residue left in the coat will cause irritation and the resulting scratching may well cause further problems and lead to a secondary infection.*

Ectoparasite infestation

This subject is largely covered in the section on parasites (see Chapter 4), but the damage they inflict on the skin is significant and warrants a mention here. The problems caused by parasites range from mild irritation to severe allergic reactions, but also include a number of serious illnesses that can be transmitted by parasites.

Mites and parasites are often a significant trigger and cause of dermatitis. Irritation and possibly an allergic reaction to a single flea on a flea-allergic dog will give the dog reason to scratch and rub himself in an attempt to alleviate the annoyance. This in turn can lead to skin trauma with sores and lesions then becoming secondarily infected, thereby compounding the problem. Once the surface of the skin is broken, the skin and the dog are vulnerable to invasion by bacteria. This additional source of irritation can seriously aggravate the problem and requires prompt recognition and treatment in order to avoid more serious consequences.

All parasite infestations should be referred for treatment as soon as possible and, because parasites can spread easily, a thorough clean-up is necessary within the grooming room.

Bacterial infections

Bacterial infections of the skin are called pyodermas. They can be classified as surface infections, superficial pyodermas or deep pyodermas. The infection may occur as a primary disease process or, more commonly, as a secondary disease. In the latter case bacteria living on the skin surface take advantage of damage to the skin's natural defences, arising from self-trauma, allergic skin disease or some other disorder.

Bacterial skin disease is usually intensely itchy. Hot spots (also known as wet eczema), for example, can produce an intensely inflamed, red, painful and exudative (oozing) lesion (*see* Fig. 2.10.17), despite only being a superficial infection.

Lesions may be focal or generalized. Examples of localized infections include skin-fold pyoderma, interdigital pyoderma (*see* Fig. 2.10.23) and otitis externa. Superficial pyodermas typically involve the hair follicle and superficial layers of the skin. Where such infections spread into the deeper tissues, *furuncles* (boils) are produced. This can then progress to a more widespread tissue infection, or cellulitis.

All bacterial skin infections benefit from topical and/or systemic therapy and should be referred to a veterinary surgeon for assessment and treatment.

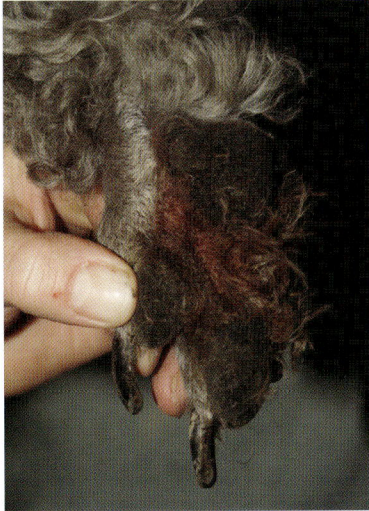

Fig. 2.10.23   Interdigital pyoderma in a Standard Poodle. A moist dermatitis is evident here, with the skin being damp and reddened. Checking carefully between the pads often reveals evidence of this problem, particularly in winter when the feet are subjected to wet weather, salt and grit used to de-ice walkways.

Fungal infections

Yeast dermatitis is a common fungal skin overgrowth. Strictly speaking, it is not an infection as the yeast organism involved is a skin commensal, i.e. a normal inhabitant of the skin. The yeast species involved is *Malassezia pachydermatitis* and the condition is generally limited to the outer layers of the skin, hair and claws. The condition is also known as 'Malassezia-associated dermatitis' and is common in dogs of any age or breed. It is more common, however, in the following breeds: West Highland White Terriers, Basset Hounds, Dachshunds, Cocker Spaniels, German Shepherd Dogs, English Setters and Shih Tzus.

This type of dermatitis most frequently occurs secondarily to other underlying diseases and factors that allow the yeast to grow. Severe disease may then result from an inflammatory/hypersensitivity reaction to yeast allergens or to metabolites produced by the yeast (*see* Figs 2.10.11 and 2.10.12a–b).

Dermatophytosis is an infection of keratinized tissues (skin, hair and claws) by one of three genera of fungi (*Trichophyton*, *Microsporum* and *Epidermophyton*). These dermatophyte fungi only grow in keratinized tissue and the infection does not progress beyond living tissue. The inflammation triggers the development of host immunity, inhibiting the further spread of infection; this process may take several weeks, however, during which time the disease may have spread. In most healthy adult hosts dermatophyte infections are self-limiting, but they can cause serious problems in colonies, breeding establishments and hospitals, where young and immuno-compromised individuals may develop severe forms of the disease.

Acral lick granuloma

This type of inflammatory reaction is very common and usually results from a dog's persistent licking of a specific part of his body (*see* Fig. 2.10.24). There are a number of reasons, medical and psychological, why a dog might do this and a vet should be consulted to investigate the underlying cause.

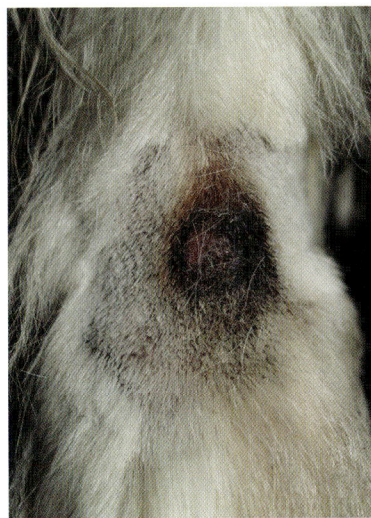

Fig. 2.10.24   Acral lick granuloma is the result of a dog licking himself continuously on the same spot. There are a number of medical and physiological reasons why a dog might do this and a vet should be consulted.

Hypothyroidism

Hypothyroidism is the commonest endocrine (hormonal) disorder seen in dogs. It is thought to arise in most dogs following the immune-mediated destruction of the thyroid gland. This results in a deficiency in the production of thyroid hormone. It appears to be more common in certain breeds, including Boxers, Dachshunds, Dobermanns, Golden Retrievers, Miniature Schnauzers and Poodles.

It is characterized by a gradual onset of lethargy and depression, together with weight gain. The hair coat may be slow to regrow after clipping. Skin changes may be seen, including hyperpigmentation, scaling, bilaterally symmetrical hair loss and puffiness of the skin. Pruritus is generally absent, unless there is a secondary bacterial infection. Given this wide range of clinical signs, hypothyroidism may go unsuspected in many dogs and requires laboratory testing before it can be confirmed.

Medical treatment involves thyroid hormone supplementation.

Hyperadrenocorticism (Cushing's syndrome)

Cushing's syndrome arises when the adrenal gland produces an excess of adrenal hormones. Any breed can be affected, although Toy and Miniature Poodles, Boxers, Dachshunds and Terriers are commonly affected.

A range of clinical signs may be seen, including increased thirst and hunger. A bilateral symmetrical alopecia is commonly seen (*see* Fig. 2.10.25), together with an increase in skin pigmentation, thinning of the skin (especially on the belly) and calcification within the skin (especially on the back, gluteal area and inguinal region (i.e. buttocks and groin)). Blackheads are not uncommonly seen and dogs are vulnerable to recurrent secondary bacterial infections.

Fig. 2.10.25   A pot belly and symmetrical alopecia are both very obvious signs that this little dog is unwell. Yorkshire Terriers are frequent visitors to the grooming room and the groomer should have noticed changes to the skin colour and thickness long before the dog reached this stage of its illness.

Laboratory testing is required to confirm the disease. Medical treatment is possible and involves the administration of a drug to suppress the adrenal gland and the excessive amounts of hormone it produces.

References and further reading

Cerundolo, R. (1999). Symmetrical alopecia in the dog. *In Practice, 21,* 350–9.

Cerundolo, R. (2009). Canine alopecia X. *Companion Animal,* 14, 47–52.

Coward, P.S. (2010). A clinician's approach to canine alopecia. *Companion Animal,* 15, 35–41.

Favrot, C. (2009). Clinical signs and diagnosis of canine atopic dermatitis. *European Journal of Companion Animal Practice,* 19 (3), 219–22.

Gross, T.L., Ihrke, P.J., Walder, E.J., Affolter, V.K (eds). (2008). Dysplastic diseases of the adnexa, in *Skin diseases of the dog and cat: Clinical and histopathologic diagnosis,* 2nd edition. Oxford, UK: Blackwell Science Ltd.

Hill, P. (2007). Treatment of canine atopic dermatitis: balancing the three factors. *In Practice,* 29, 566–73.

Mecklenberg, L., Linek, M. and Tobin, D.J. (2009). *Hairloss disorders in domestic animals.* Oxford, UK: Wiley Blackwell.

2.11 HAIR AND COAT TYPES

The hair or coat type might seem a strange inclusion within the anatomy and physiology chapter. It is, however, an important secondary feature of the dog's natural body covering, the skin. It is, furthermore, of particular interest to the dog groomer and deserves a special section all to itself.

Coat types have been selected for, both by man and by natural selection. Chapter 1 explained how man has altered the dog's coat for aesthetic reasons and how the end result is often very different from what nature would have chosen for the dog – so much so that the dog has struggled to maintain it. Similarly, we are currently guilty of removing dogs from the geographical location in which they have evolved and lived over thousands of years and of keeping them in alien environments to which they are unsuited. We should not be surprised that the Siberian Husky struggles to cope with and adapt to life in a centrally heated apartment block. Such factors can have a serious impact on the health of the skin and hair coat and therefore on the welfare of the dog. They also affect the behaviour, quality, quantity, density and type of coat that you will be working with. This, in turn, has implications for how you manage and maintain the dog's coat.

Coat type is therefore very important to you and your work. Groomers are often heard discussing coat type, referring to those grooming methods used on a specific coat type and talking about the handling and treatment of a coat type. Brushes and combs are purchased for exclusive use on a coat type, whilst drying and styling practices are adapted to suit coat types.

So what exactly does coat type mean and why does it have such an influence on the way in which groomers work? The following section explains how a groomer identifies coat type and how it affects the decisions we make when we are presented with a dog for grooming.

I must stress that the definitions used in this chapter are for the purpose of grooming only. Each and every breed standard specifies the 'correct coat' for any given breed. The terminology that has evolved to support these descriptions is a reflection of this classification system and the 'standards' and 'types' humans have created. Groomers simplify this by classifying dogs into a few groups according to how we prepare and handle their coats.

Originally, it is most likely that the dog had a smooth/sleek coat like his closest ancestor, the grey wolf, or the wild dogs still living free in remote wilderness areas (*see* Figs 2.11.1 and 2.11.2). Over the last few hundred years man has tinkered with the design of the dog through selective breeding and in doing so we have, usually intentionally but sometimes unwittingly, changed his coat. Mutant genes within the genetic make-up

Fig. 2.11.1   *Left to their own devices, wild dogs like these, found on the sunny slopes of Mount Etna in temperate Sicily, have a smooth coat.*

Fig. 2.11.2   A slightly longer and denser coat, similar to that of the Dingo, develops in colder or more changeable climates. (Photo: Michael Trafford)

of individual dogs have suddenly appeared and altered coats from the smooth/sleek appearance. We have often exploited these dogs by selectively breeding from them, thereby preserving the mutant variants and producing the variety of coat types that we see, appreciate and have to groom today.

Section 2.10 described how all but a few breeds of dog have two basic types of hair that make up their coat: an undercoat that is designed to keep the dog warm and a topcoat that provides protection from the elements. This means that most dogs are 'double'-coated. The undercoat is always soft and downy, although it does vary in length and density, but, because of our interference, the weatherproof topcoat is either:

◆ short and smooth (as it was originally), e.g. the Labrador Retriever;
◆ short and curly, with or without furnishings (mutated), e.g. the Airedale Terrier;

◆ long and curly, with or without furnishings (mutated), e.g. the Poodle (*see* Fig. 2.11.3); or
◆ long and straight, with or without furnishings (mutated), e.g. the Bearded Collie.

The list of possible permutations is short but, in reality, when it comes to grooming the dog, the combinations vary greatly and they are complicated by factors such as:

◆ coat texture, which can range from very soft to very harsh;
◆ coat density, which is determined by the amount of undercoat the dog has;
◆ coat behaviour, i.e. whether it moults or not;
◆ the environment in which the dog lives; and
◆ the age, health and condition of the dog.

So, when deciding how to groom a coat, groomers sort the coat variations into groups (coat types) according to how the coat is best handled and managed. This helps us select our tools and choose appropriate grooming techniques. In practice, we divide all dogs into five coat types or groups: 'smooth coat', 'wire coat', 'silk coat', 'double coat' and 'wool coat', with a subgroup, the 'corded coat'. (*See* Groomer's guide to coat types, Table 4.)

In other words, when grooming dogs we separate the many different coats that we see into groups, according to whether they demonstrate similar characteristics of coat texture, length, density and behaviour. This categorization into named groups applies to all dogs, whether they be pedigree dogs, crossed breeds (dogs that are the result of crossing two recognized breeds) or non-pedigree dogs (mongrels). To give an example, a coat that is short, sits close to the body and does not have any added coat length anywhere at all would be a 'smooth coat'. All dogs with this 'type' of coat, whether pedigree or non-pedigree, would be groomed using the same tools and grooming procedures.

The *smooth coat* appears sleek and shiny and sits close (smoothly) to the dog's body. It can range from very short with a fine undercoat, as on the Dalma-

Fig. 2.11.3   The wool coat of the Poodle has been deliberately fashioned by breeding dogs carrying a mutant gene that produces a sparse but long coarse topcoat and a profuse long-growing undercoat.

tian (*see* Fig. 2.11.4), to the longer length (2–3cm) and denser undercoat of the Labrador Retriever (*see* Fig. 2.11.5). In both cases the coat sheds (moults) readily and heavily according to the dog's body temperature. Although this coat is generally considered to be the easiest to look after, it requires regular (almost daily) grooming if the dog lives indoors – especially if the owner is house-proud! The relentless shedding of this coat means that the coat is continuously being replaced with new hair growth. Debris within the coat often comes away with the moult, helping to keep the dog clean – and the floor hairy! This is, perhaps, the most common coat type and, particularly with non-pedigree dogs, the coat is almost always short and sleek (providing no mutant genes have been inherited) and does not need styling or scissoring unless the owner requests this. Sometimes an owner will clip a smooth coat in an effort to stop the shedding; this is counterproductive as coat regrowth will be more rapid and hairs will still shed.

The *wire coat* has a short undercoat (*see* Fig. 2.11.6) covered by a crisp (coarse/harsh), often curly, topcoat that grows to a maximum length before it dies and falls out. The wire coat often has longer length hairs on the legs, tail and undercarriage and on the foreface. Generally recognized as the texture of the Terrier coat, it is sometimes referred to as a 'broken coat' because it gives the impression that it breaks away from the roots. The harshness of the coat makes it difficult for mud and dirt to stick to

Fig. 2.11.5   Also a smooth coat, the Labrador Retriever by contrast has a longer topcoat and a very dense undercoat.

the coat hairs when these dogs are working and it is therefore considered to be self-cleaning. Dead, faded coat detaches easily from the hair follicles and can be stripped or plucked out by the groomer (*see* Fig. 2.11.7) to leave strong, shiny new hairs that will grow into a vibrantly coloured new coat. The coat growing cycle will then be repeated.

Alternatively, the coat can be styled and shaped before the coat dies by using clippers and styling tools (*see* Fig. 2.11.8). The undercoat will still shed but it will generally need to be removed by combing and brushing. Apart from Terriers, this type of coat is commonly seen on non-pedigree dogs that have Terriers in their ancestry, and

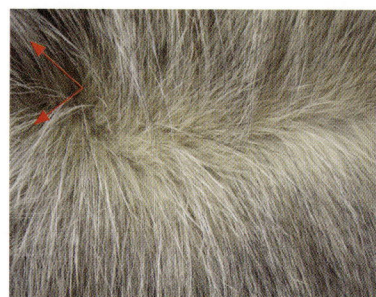

Fig. 2.11.6   The coat on this Cairn Terrier is categorized as a wire coat because the topcoat is coarse and harsh to the touch. The red arrows show the topcoat hairs that have reached maximum length and are at the stage where they can easily be plucked by hand out of the coat. The white arrow indicates the soft undercoat hairs that remain once the topcoat is removed.

in crossed breeds such as the Lurcher (Greyhounds or Whippets crossed with another breed).

The *silk coat* is generally long and flowing and is soft and silky to the touch, not unlike the feel of long human hair. This most tender of coats requires as much care as we give our own hair, and great care is needed to avoid damaging it or pulling it out. We therefore handle it as if it were silk! Similar to the wool coat, the silk coat also gives the impression that it is a single coat, as very often the skin is visible through the hair, but this again is not the case (*see* Fig. 2.11.9).

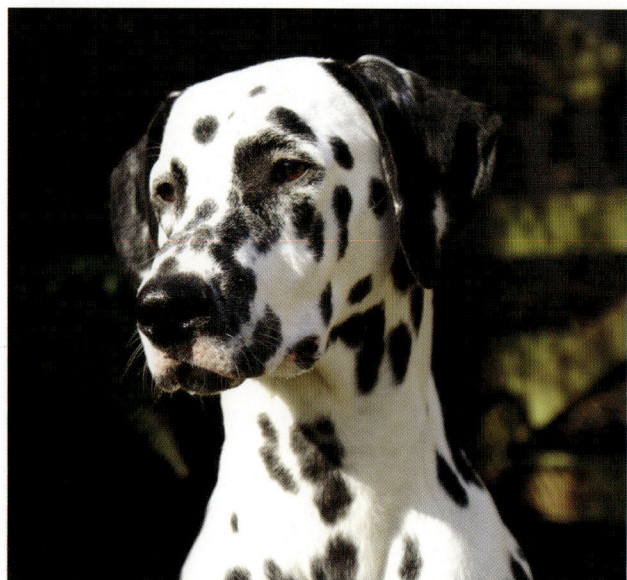

Fig. 2.11.4   The Dalmatian (smooth coat) has a very short topcoat with a fine undercoat.

Consider the Afghan Hound as a representative example; this breed has an extremely long coat on most of the body, but short, very shiny, waterproof hairs on the face. If you separate the body hair and take a closer look, you will see these short hairs continue over the entire body, hidden underneath the very long, paler-coloured coat that, in texture, is light and soft, resembling the undercoat of other dogs. This is because it is undercoat and, like all undercoats, it is fragile and will fall out or break easily. The Afghan Hound lives in a climate where he needs a coat to keep him warm in the sub-zero night-time temperatures of the high mountains of Afghanistan. At the same time, however, he also needs to be able to keep cool during the tremendously hot daytime temperatures. His under-coat, the one that keeps him warm, has grown to a tremendous length to help keep his body temperature up during

Fig. 2.11.7   Dolly and Maud demonstrate the wire coat before and after hand plucking.

Fig. 2.11.8 Traditionally the wire coat is plucked out by hand, but with practice the groomer can achieve a very nice effect using modern grooming methods and equipment.

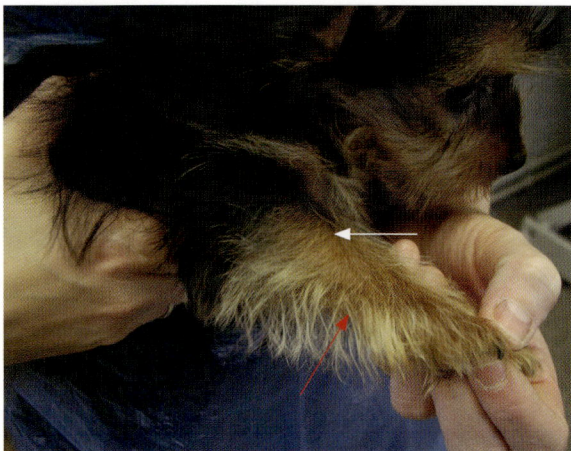

Fig..2.11.9 This Yorkshire Terrier puppy is just three months old. His silk coat has a lot of growing to do but here you can clearly see both his short undercoat (white arrow) and his growing topcoat (red arrow).

the coat and allows us to present it, fully groomed, falling like strands of silken thread from the dog's body. Another breed with a long coat, similar to that of the Afghan Hound, is the Yorkshire Terrier. His coat is not reversed but this breed does have a very short undercoat close to the skin, which you can see if you look at the tips of the ears on a show dog. Here, the hair will have been stripped or pulled out to reveal the colour (and indeed evidence) of the second coat. Notice that the hair on the tips of the ears is dull and soft in comparison to the long body hair; this is because it is undercoat hair.

Other breeds in the silk coat category may not have coats as long as those of the Afghan Hound and the Yorkshire Terrier. Spaniels (*see* Fig. 2.11.11), Setters and Borzois, along with many other dogs, have a coat that grows to a good length, is silky in texture and has a minimum of undercoat. These coats have longer hair on certain parts of the body; this can reach great lengths if the coat is handled with care and carefully groomed to prevent damage. Hand-stripping random or out-of-place long hairs from the body coat will preserve the silky texture and enhance the

the night; the length of the coat allows it to move freely in the slightest breeze during the heat of the day, helping the dog to keep cool. Waterproofing is still needed so the coat of the Afghan is reversed, with the waterproof coat closest to the skin. The short, body-hugging waterproof hairs prevent frost and water from seeping down through the long hairs to the skin, so at skin level he remains dry and warm. If the Afghan Hound's coat was reversed, so that the temperature regulating coat was the shorter of the two, it is possible that the dog would struggle to cope with the massive range between nighttime and daytime temperatures.

For the show ring the long hair covering the spine of the Afghan Hound is stripped or pulled out into a shape called a 'saddle', which reveals the glossy waterproof coat beneath. If the stripping were to be continued over the entire dog, he would resemble his close relative, the Saluki Hound (*see* Fig. 2.11.10).

The Afghan coat is classed as a silk coat because we use tools and a technique that does not damage or remove

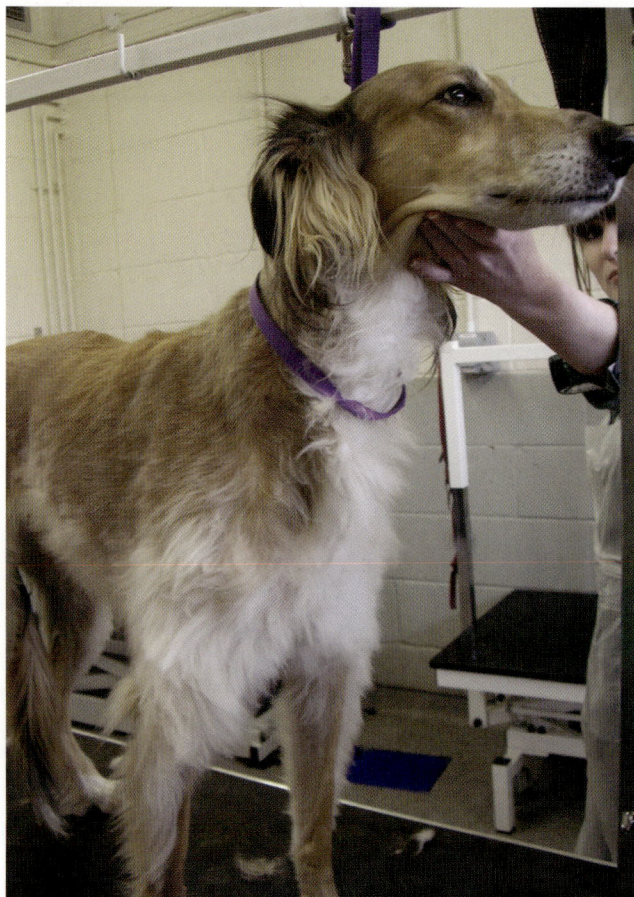

Fig. 2.11.10 This Saluki has an excess of undercoat hair growing longer than the topcoat. If the undercoat continues to grow in this way, the dog's coat would resemble that of the Afghan Hound. In this instance, Maddie's undercoat hair was pulled out to reinstate her shiny silky textured topcoat.

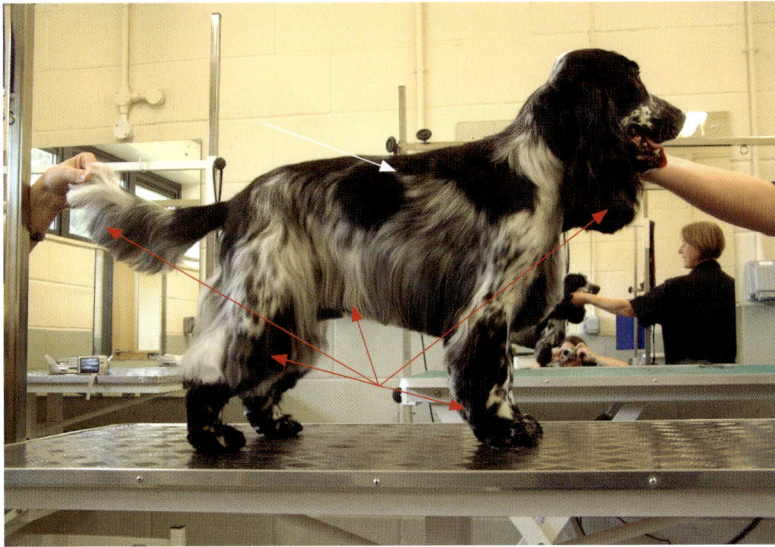

Fig. 2.11.11   The English Cocker Spaniel also has a coat that is classified as a silk coat. On this dog you can see the body coat (white arrow) is shorter than the feathering on his legs, undercarriage, ears and tail (red arrows), where the individual topcoat hairs grow long, sleek and silky in texture.

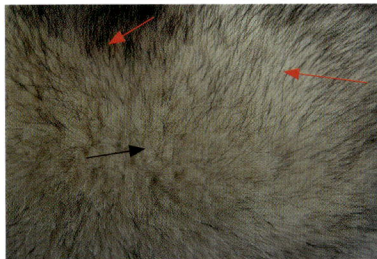

Fig. 2.11.12   The double coat of this Alaskan Malamute shows the density of the undercoat (black arrow) with the sparsely distributed topcoat hairs (red arrows) showing through. Note how the two coats are of similar length, as the environment in which this dog evolved called for a coat that would minimize the accumulation of snow and frost rather than waterproofing the coat against the rain.

shape of the dog, whilst ensuring the coat continues to function effectively. Alternatively, the coat can be clipped or scissored into place. Care should be taken, however, not to cut into the undercoat with your clipper blades as this will expose the undercoat and make the coat appear dull in colour. It will also increase coat density because both the undercoat and the topcoat will be the same length. In practice, this prevents the coat from moving freely and does little to help cool the dog.

Silk coats do not shed in any significant quantity but the tenderness of the hairs means that they break and come away from the body easily. The length of the hair allows the coat to knot up

Fig. 2.11.13   The very dense but short double coat of the Japanese Akita. (Photo: Michael Trafford)

easily and, as with the wool coat, it needs regular bathing to prevent a build-up of dirt and debris in the coat.

The double coat is very obviously what it claims to be. Look into the coat and you will see two very different types of hair. The differences in the density and the length of the double coat hairs can be a little confusing when you are learning to recognize coat type.

Some coats, like that of the Rough Collie, are long, with a fairly thick undercoat that can be separated with your fingers, allowing you to see through to the skin without too much difficulty. The Rough Collie was bred as a herding dog to live and work on the hills and mountainsides of Scotland and northern England. The average nighttime temperature on Ben Nevis (Scotland's highest mountain) hovers around minus 3 degrees C, whilst average daytime temperatures can be as high as 19 degrees C. The Rough Collie's coat reflects this: he has a very thick undercoat to keep him warm but it is long enough to move with the breeze so that he can cool down when the day warms up. The undercoat moults out when the summer arrives and is replaced by a thinner undercoat – just enough to cope with the chilly nights. This, in turn, is shed in the autumn to be renewed again, much denser this time, in preparation for the winter weather.

Other double coats, like that of the Alaskan Malamute (*see* Fig. 2.11.12), will be very short, incredibly dense and difficult to part to show the underlying skin. This coat has evolved to protect the dog from the elements and is perfectly suited to this breed's natural environment. The Malamute was developed to live alongside the people of the Arctic and he often lives outside. His coat must offer protection against temperatures that regularly drop to minus 45–50 degrees C. These temperatures would be even lower if wind-chill were factored in: it is therefore important that the coat does not move, or open up, with the force of the wind. The undercoat is almost the same length as the topcoat and the two coats are packed tightly together. The Arctic summer causes some shedding of the coat, which is replaced in time for winter. It is usual for Arctic breeds to shed their coats only once a year, and in some cases it occurs every other year.

This is a reflection of the harsh climate that the dog has had to adapt to, for survival.

The Japanese Akita Inu (*see* Fig. 2.11.13) has a very dense undercoat that tends to be shorter than that of the Malamute. The Chow Chow has a similarly short coat, or a long coat, with longer hair on the legs, tail and rear end. Shetland Sheepdogs and Rough Collies (*see* Fig. 2.11.14), in contrast, have a much longer topcoat than either of those breeds and a less dense (more open) undercoat, through which the skin is easily exposed.

The common link between all these breeds – and the many other breeds with a double coat – is that when they moult they shed their undercoats (*see* Fig. 2.11.15), leaving the topcoat in place. The soft, downy undercoat comes away from the body and, if not removed, will stay trapped within the topcoat, causing an accumulation of loose hairs that collect together to form a dense layer of dead hair, somewhere between the skin and the top of the coat. We call this accumulation *wadding* and it will often include dense knots and tight tangles, which need to be removed by intensive grooming. If a double coat is clipped, the coat will appear dull because of the emergence of the undercoat and, once again, because the two coats are of the same length, coat density will increase until

the coat regrows. The coat will need to complete a growth cycle before it can be restored to its former glory; it can therefore take several months for this new coat to grow.

The *wool coat* is often considered to be a single coat because the two coats are difficult to separate and tell apart. Its woolly appearance derives from the fact that the coat is made up predominantly of dense, continuously growing

Fig. 2.11.15   Double coats moult profusely, with the old undercoat shedding to make way for new undercoat growth. The timespan between moults depends on the breed and the environment in which the dog lives.

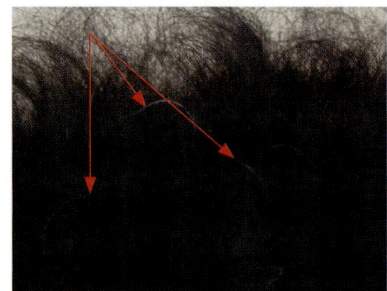

Fig. 2.11.16   The wool coat is made up predominantly of dense undercoat with sparsely distributed, coarser topcoat hairs. On this dog the topcoat hairs are white and you can just see them showing through the density of the woolly undercoat.

undercoat with sparse but coarse topcoat hairs; these are very much in the minority. To see this for yourself, have a close look at the coat of an adult Poodle (*see* Fig. 2.11.16). Once correctly dried, and before it is trimmed, you can see the sparse, coarse hairs making their appearance above the denseness of the woolly undercoat. Apricot-coloured coats show this well because the topcoat hairs are brightly coloured.

Unlike other coats that have a greater number of guard hairs, this coat does not shed and fall out, but it does die and, in doing so, it packs itself close to the dog's body, interspersed with the new, replacement hairs. This is the

Fig. 2.11.14   Also double-coated, the once very popular Shetland Sheepdog and the larger Rough Collie have much longer length coats. The coat has a more open topcoat that can be separated easily to see the very dense undercoat. (Photo: Michael Trafford)

reason why the wool coat is perhaps the most difficult to look after. Once the coat is dead, it will hold on to dirt and debris more easily. It will also tangle and become matted with knots very quickly; these will need to be removed with tools specially designed to cut through the matting and split the knots.

And it is not only the dead coat that will cause these problems, as dirt, mud and grime are all readily attracted to the density and softness of the wool coat. Daily brushing is essential and usually the coat will need bathing at least once a fortnight. The wool coat can be fun to work with, however, as, once stretched, clipped and scissored, the volume of the 'two' coats is maximized and the coat will support the shapes and sculptures into which it can be fashioned. Such sculptured coats can be seen on the Poodle and the Bichon Frisé (*see* Fig. 2.11.17). It is also a fast-growing coat because it grows at the speed of undercoat; fashions can therefore be changed (and any mistakes will grow out) very quickly. Wool coats generally need trimming every four to six weeks to keep them manageable and presentable (*see* Fig. 2.11.18).

Scissoring or clipping the coat will reduce the length of the hair but increase the density, so clipping the coat shorter in the summer does not necessarily mean that the dog will be cooler. The wool coat does have an advantage in that when it gets damp it separates into curly cords, revealing the skin of the dog, which helps keep him cool. Where the coat fails to sepa-

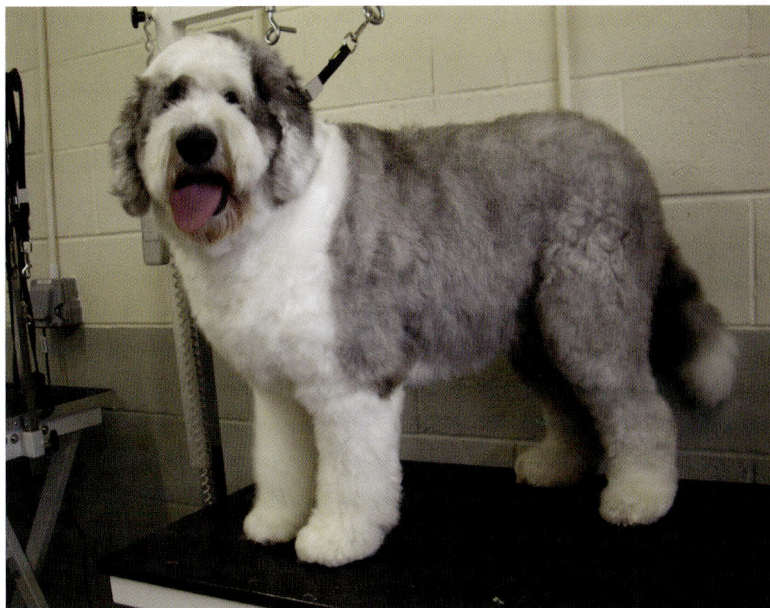

Fig. 2.11.18   The woolly coat of the Old English Sheepdog is often clipped or scissored to a manageable length to aid grooming. This coat has been bathed and dried straight so that it can be scissored to a shorter length.

rate, or is left unclipped, the dog may be vulnerable to overheating. If the coat is allowed to grow very long, it must be kept clean, knot- and tangle-free so that it can move freely in the breeze and when the dog moves, thereby helping the coat to ventilate and cool the dog.

The *corded coat* is a subcategory of the wool coat. It is not truly a different coat type but it does behave differently. The corded coat is a very curly, woolly coat that grows in lots of different directions (*see* Fig. 2.11.19) and to a great length, twisting itself into long cords as it does so (*see* Figs 2.11.20 and

2.11.21). The coat is very dense but the cords are easy to separate to reveal the skin beneath. The corded coat does not require any brushing or combing but does need the individual cords to be tidied with a special tool (a hook, resembling a crochet hook) so that they fall as individual locks. Corded coats are generally seen on the Hungarian Puli, the Komondor and the Bergamasco, all of which are sheep-herding breeds that live on mountain pastures and rely on their coats not only for warmth but also as camouflage and protection from wolves. Bedlington Terrier and Poodle coats both cord easily and, if you take a look at the coat of either breed, particularly if the coat is either damp or

Fig. 2.11.17 When correctly prepared, the density and volume of the wool coat provides an excellent 'raw' material for the groomer to sculpt into a variety of shapes and styles. (Photo: Michael Trafford)

Fig. 2.11.19   Clipped down to the skin, the coat of this standard poodle illustrates the many directions in which the hair grows. This particular formation of wool coat is prone to twisting and curling as it grows, forming cords.

Fig. 2.11.20   *This picture clearly shows the coat of a Standard Poodle naturally forming into cords.*

Fig. 2.11.21   *In some other breeds, such as the Puli and the Komondor, the cords are wider and dense. (Photo: Michael Trafford)*

has dried naturally, you will see how the coat naturally falls into very curly strands, which, if encouraged, will form tight cords.

There is no doubt that it can be confusing when you begin learning which coat falls into which category, but learning the breed standards is a good starting point. The development and history of the breed will tell you where the breed originated from and the dog's intended role. This usually provides enough information to determine the coat type, the tools required for grooming and how to use them on the coat in question. There are occasions when a pedigree dog will not have the type of coat that you expect it to have; in such cases it should be groomed according to the category in which the coat texture falls.

Non-pedigree dogs may or may not have coats similar to those of their parents; the texture of their coats will, however, still allow them to be grouped into one of the five categories.

Poor coats and changes in coat quality

As mentioned above, a dog may not always have the expected coat type or texture for the breed. Where this occurs, the dog must be groomed according to the category that his coat falls into. For example, a Lhasa Apso should have a long, straight, heavy, shining coat, but if one is presented with a woolly, dull and very dense coat, then he should be groomed according to the techniques and tools used on woolly coats.

Certain factors have a bearing on how a coat may deviate from the rec-ommended/recognized breed coat structure. These include breeding, clipping, neutering and health problems.

Breeding

A reputable and responsible pedigree dog breeder will carefully select the parentage of puppies, ensuring they do their best to meet their obligation to preserve the breed (one of these being coat quality, both 'type' and texture). Not all breeders do this conscientiously and deviations from the breed prerequisites (standards) do occur.

Sometimes, despite a great deal of thought going into a breeding programme, a poor quality or undesirable coat results. The coat may revert to the 'type' of an ancestral breed, one that contributed to the development of a 'new' breed. An example of this is the Border Terrier (wire coat). The Border Terrier originated from a cross between the Dandie Dinmont Terrier (which proudly sports a soft silky coat on the top of his head and has a coarse, wiry body coat), the Bedlington Terrier (which boasts a soft woolly coat) and the Lakeland Terrier (which also possesses a coarse coat). This combination has produced a dog with a sleek body coat that is protected by a harsh (wire-textured) topcoat. Occasionally you will find a Border Terrier with a soft, silky coat, particularly on the top of the head; this is more than likely a 'throwback' to the soft coat of his Dandie Dinmont ancestors. When this happens, the coat (not the dog or his breed) is regrouped from 'wire coat' to 'wool coat' and is groomed in the manner of the wool coat.

In the crossed breed (a first generation cross between two pedigree dogs), the puppies can take on the coat type of either parent, if they are of different textures; alternatively, the coat can be a mixture between the two.

For example, the Labradoodle is a cross between the (short-coated) Labrador Retriever and the (woolly coated) Standard Poodle. The puppies can take the coat of:

◆ The Poodle, which is long, soft to the touch and non-moulting. The density is, however, increased by the coat of the Labrador, which is itself short but very dense. This combination can result in a very thick, long coat that will not moult, will need constant grooming and will knot very easily.
◆ The Labrador, which is generally short, sleek and dense. The Poodle's contribution adds length, together with a softer, woollier texture that may or may not moult. If non-moulting, the coat will knot easily.

◆ Both parents. In this case the pup has a short Labrador coat with just the coarse guard hairs from the Poodle coat. This results in a coarse, harsh topcoat that can be stripped or pulled out regularly as it reaches its maximum length and dies, leaving the dog with a smooth Labrador-type of coat. Once pulled out, the coat will start to grow again.

The crossed breed takes the predominant coat type of the many dogs in his make-up and generally his coat will sit quite easily within one of the grooming categories. You will, however, find that there are instances where the dog will most definitely have two different types or textures of coat; indeed, these may appear in different locations across the body. Two-coloured dogs may thus show one coat type associated with areas of one coloration and another coat type associated with areas of the other colour.

Clipping

The phenomenon of 'coat reversal' is not exclusive to the Afghan Hound, although it is possibly the only breed where the undercoat grows to such lengths. Coat reversal is often seen in other breeds, particularly silk-coated dogs that have been clipped.

Clipping has an effect on the texture, colour and quality of a coat, especially when a coat is clipped down to a depth where the clipper blade cuts into the undercoat. The undercoat is paler and of a different texture from the topcoat. Thus, if the topcoat is removed, the dog's coat will be the colour and texture of his undercoat – paler, softer and dull! We also know that the undercoat is fast growing and that it keeps the dog warm so, once the weather-resistant topcoat has been removed, the undercoat responds by thickening and lengthening quite rapidly, in order to keep the dog warm. Once a coat has been clipped to the length of the undercoat, if you look closely you will be able to see the guard hairs sparsely dispersed amongst the dense undercoat hairs. They will be a different colour and a different texture, so are easily identified (*see* Fig. 2.11.22).

The undercoat grows much faster than the topcoat so very often the sparser topcoat hairs will be lost within the density of the undercoat; they do not have the opportunity to grow back to their natural length and therefore return the coat to its natural colour and texture. The fast-growing undercoat will become more dense and longer, until the dog is clipped again. Eventually, the coat always appear woolly textured and dull.

All is not lost, however! The coat grows and renews itself from the inside out and the clippers only cut what is on the outside. Leaving the coat until it has completed a full growth cycle and is ready to moult (which can take up to a year) allows the groomer to remove the undercoat and – hey presto! – all else being well, the coat should regain its natural colour and texture (see Hand-stripping). It is worth mentioning here that the coat can look pretty awful and very unruly whilst you are waiting for it to moult out, but it is worth the wait.

Neutering

Neutering can sometimes appear to alter the quality of the coat but this is quite unusual. What generally happens is that neutering slows down the dog's metabolism and he or she will gain weight. An overweight dog is less active so it is quite possible that the undercoat of the dog thickens to keep the dog warm, rather than the dog doing this himself through exercise.

Another reason for the coat changing after neutering may be related to the natural development of the dog and his coat. Somewhere between the ages of seven and eighteen months (depending on the breed), the coat changes as the softer textured and vibrantly coloured puppy coat is replaced by the adult coat. This is generally coarser in texture and often slightly paler in colour. It is during this period that most dogs are neutered so any change in the coat is coincidental and probably unrelated to neutering.

As the dog ages, the coat will become paler, with grey hairs also making an appearance; coat change in an older, neutered dog can also be accounted for by the natural ageing process (*see* Fig. 2.11.23).

Health problems

Changes in the dog's health can also have an effect on the coat. For example, anaesthetics occasionally leave the coat dry and brittle for a period of time; these changes have to wait until the completion of a moult before they disappear. Some medicines and a range of chemical compounds in the environment also have the potential to alter coat texture and density. Such chemicals need to be cleared from the body before they cease to have an effect on hair quality. This may take time and you will have to wait for the damaged hair

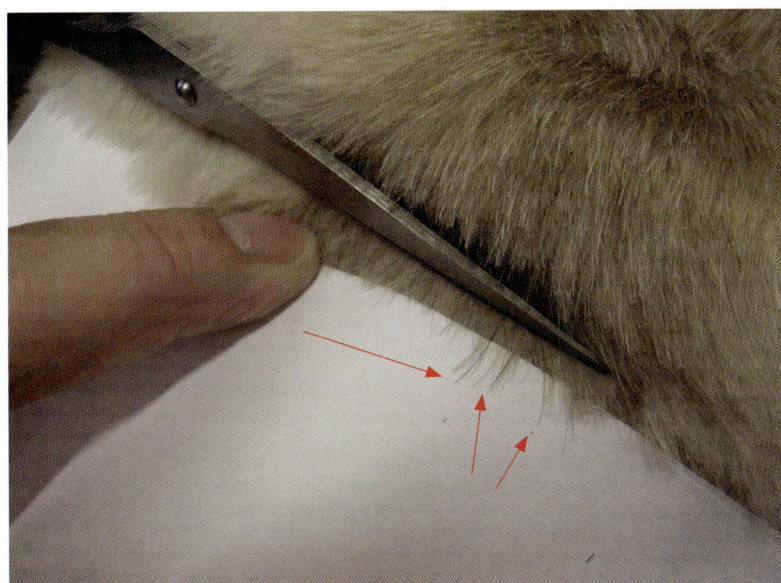

Fig. 2.11 22   Guard hairs showing through the clipped undercoat of a Shih Tzu.

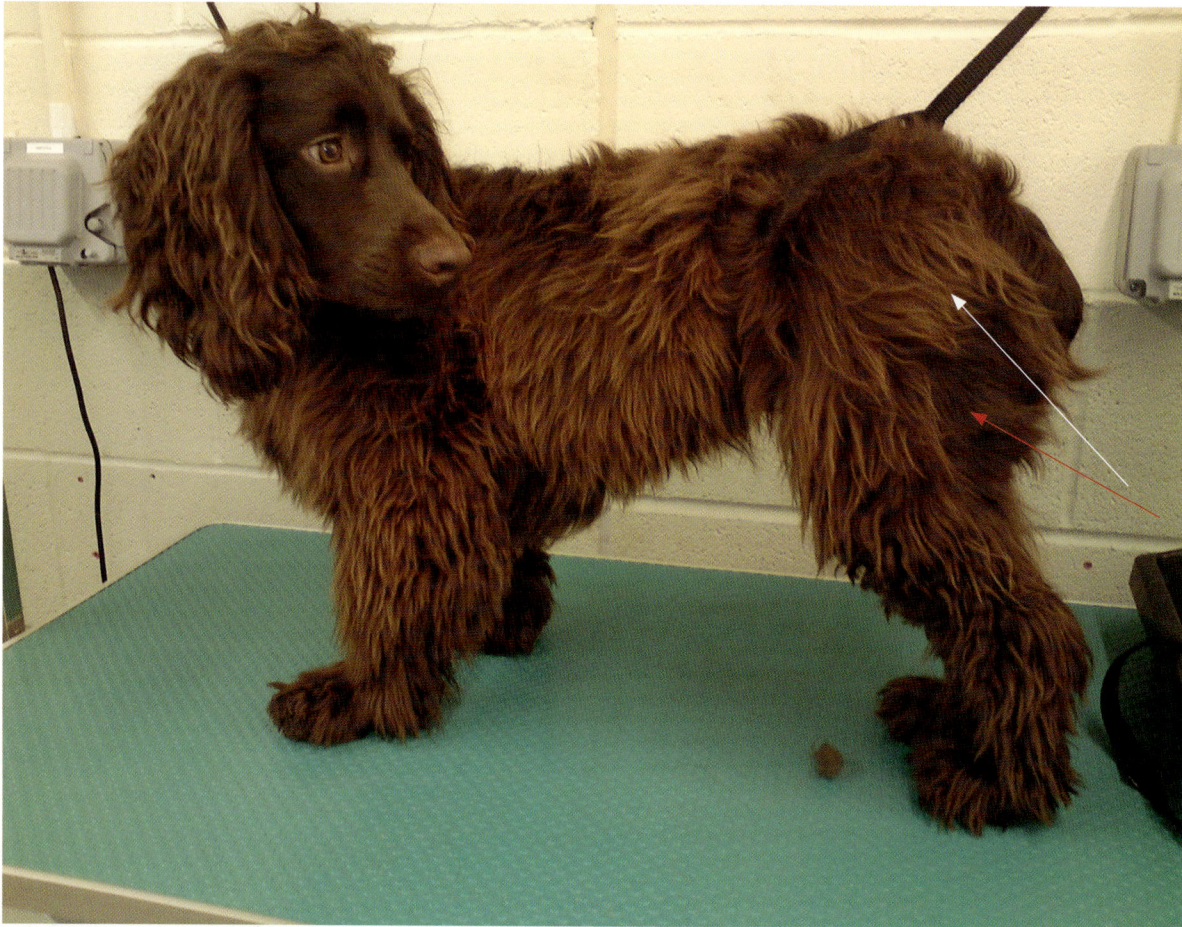

Fig. 2.11 23   *This puppy was neutered at ten months old and his puppy coat has died but remains in situ. The adult silk coat (red arrow) has been smothered by an excess of undercoat. This has produced a woolly texture, but the coat should still be treated as a silk coat and can be restored by hand plucking the errant undercoat (white arrow), or the coat can be clipped.*

coat to be shed and replaced. In the intervening period, the coat should be groomed in accordance with its texture.

An example of this is the coarse wire coat that is usually hand-plucked/ stripped. It may become unusually soft for a while. In such a case it would be advisable to avoid plucking and to clip or scissor the coat instead. This will avoid traumatizing and bruising the skin by pulling on the hair. Any underlying problem should be investigated and addressed by the dog's vet. The priority is getting the dog well again; the coat can be sorted out again another day!

A short description of veterinary terminology

Allergic: Adjective describing a process that occurs as a result of an allergy (e.g. an allergic reaction).

Allergy: An abnormal reaction to a previously encountered substance (allergen) resulting from an exaggerated or excessive immunological reaction. The interaction between the allergen and the immune system sets off a series of responses that are designed to protect the body but are actually excessive and unhelpful (e.g. itching, sneezing).

Anaphylaxis: An extreme allergic reaction that can result in swelling around the airways and airway blockage.

Anatomy: The scientific study of the structure of the body.

Arterial: Adjective describing the blood supply system that delivers oxygenated blood from the heart to the tissues of the body in vessels called arteries.

Ataxia: A lack, or loss, of muscular coordination, resulting in collapsing and stumbling.

Atopy: A genetically predisposed, itchy, inflammatory, allergic skin disease associated with IgE antibodies that are, most commonly, directed against environmental allergens.

Bacteria: A tiny, microscopic, single-cell micro-organism.

Benign: Relatively harmless, the opposite of malignant.

Binocular: Seeing with both eyes. The information from both eyes is perceived by the brain as a single image and provides the individual with greater depth perception.

Brachycephalic: Having a head that is nearly as broad from side to side as it is long, from front to back.

Capillaries: Minute blood vessels connecting the arterial blood system with the venous blood system. They form an intricate network throughout the body and ensure that a range of essential substances are exchanged between the blood and the tissues.

Cardiac: Adjective: relating to the heart.

Carpus: Wrist joint.

Caudal: Of, at or near the tail (e.g. closer to the tail than to the head).

Caudomedial: Towards the rear (tail) and on the inside rather than the outside.

Chondrodysplasia: An abnormal growth of cartilage that results in dwarfism. This is typically a genetic condition characterized by shortening of the legs.

Cranial Towards the head. The opposite of caudal.

Cryo-epilation: Use of a cryo-probe to destroy hair follicles by the application of very low temperatures.

Digit: Finger or toe.

Disease: Illness or health disorder.

Distal: Anatomically located away from the point of reference (e.g. distal to the elbow = below the elbow.)

Dolichocephalic: Having a narrow, long head.

Dorsal: Close to, or near, the back or upper part of an anatomical structure.

Dysplasia: An abnormality of development.

Epithelium: The cellular covering of internal and external body surfaces.

Forelimb: Front leg.

Genotype: The genetic constitution of an organism.

Hypersensitivity: An excessive sensitivity to a foreign agent, such as an allergen. May also be used to describe an exaggerated emotional reaction.

Hyposensitivity: A lower than normal sensitivity to a foreign agent, such as an allergen.

Hypotrichosis: A less than normal amount of hair.

Immune system: The body's defensive system that protects against disease.

Immunization: Vaccinations that stimulate the immune system to produce antibodies to provide protection (immunity) against a particular infectious disease.

Infectious: Catching, spreading, transmissible. Typically used to describe a disease that can be passed from one individual to another.

Inflammation: A protective tissue response to injury or tissue damage. It serves to destroy, dilute or wall off both the cause of the injury and any damaged tissues and is characterized by pain, heat, redness and swelling.

Malignant: Threatening to life. Can also mean, in the case of tumours, that they are likely to spread/invade/metastasize.

Mesaticephalic: A skull with the nasal cavity and cranium of equal length.

Metacarpals: Any of the five long bones that form the metacarpus (equivalent to our palm) and articulate with the bones of the distal row of the carpus (wrist) and with the five proximal phalanges of the toes in the front legs (forelimb).

Metatarsals: The equivalent bones in the foot, extending between the tarsus (ankle) and the proximal phalanges of the toes.

Neoplasm: An abnormal new growth of tissue that grows by cell division and proceeds more rapidly than normal.

Neoplastic: The adjective used to describe a neoplasm.

Nystagmus: A rhythmic, to-and-fro movement of the eyes that is generally involuntary and can be both normal (as when watching the countryside go by from a train) or abnormal (due to disease).

Ophthalmic: Adjective: relating to the eyes.

Osteoarthritis: A progressive degenerative inflammatory condition of the joints that is characterized by loss of cartilage and the deposition of bony spurs around the joint.

Palmar: Towards the palm (the lower part of the front foot).

Palpable: That can be felt/detected by palpation (e.g. is the pulse palpable?).

Pathogenic: Capable of causing disease.

Peripheral: Away from the centre (e.g. the peripheral circulation is that furthest from the heart).

Peristalsis: An involuntary contractile movement of smooth muscle in tubular structures such as the intestinal tract that allows material to be mixed and moved. (Adjective: peristaltic.)

Phenotype: The observable physical (or biochemical) characteristics of an organism, as determined both by the individual's genetic make-up (genotype) and environmental influences.

Physiology: The scientific study of the normal function of living organisms.

Plantar: Towards the sole (the lower part of the hind foot).

Prolapsed: A slipping down, or displacement, of a part of the body from its normal position.

Pruritus: Itchiness. (Adjective: 'pruritic'.)

Pulmonary: Adjective: relating to the lungs (e.g. the pulmonary circulation).

Pyrexia: A fever in which the body temperature is abnormally raised.

Spermatogenesis: The production of sperm within the testes.

Squame: A flattened epithelial cell, typical of the skin.

Subcutaneous: Adjective meaning below the skin.

Vasodilation: An opening up/widening of the blood vessels allowing blood to enter (perfuse) a particular tissue.

Venous: Adjective relating to the veins. The venous circulation is made up of the veins that return blood from the tissues to the heart.

Ventral: Opposite of dorsal, meaning towards the belly (ventrum).

Virus: A micro-organism that is so small that it cannot be seen by the light microscope. Typically it lacks independent metabolism and is reliant on a living host cell to multiply.

Yeast: A unicellular fungus that reproduces by budding.

Table 4 The groomer's rough guide to popular coat types.

w = wire, wl = wool, d = double, sk = silk, sth = smooth, cd = corded

Breed		Breed		Breed	
Affenpinscher	w	Chesapeake Bay	w	Japanese Chin	sk
Afghan	sk	Chihuahua	sk	Japanese Sheba Inu	d
Airedale	w	Chinese Crested		Japanese Spitz	d
Akita	d	Chow Chow	d	Keeshond	d
Alaskan Malamute	d	Clumber Spaniel		Kerry Blue Terrier	sk
Am. Cocker Spaniel	sk	Cocker Spaniel	sk	King Charles	sk
Anatolian Shepherd	sth	Coton de Tulear	w	Labrador	w
Australian Cattle Dog	d	Dachshund wire	w	Lakeland Terrier	w
Australian Silky Terrier	sk	Dachshund smooth	sth	Leonberger	d
Australian Terrier	w	Dachshund silk	sk	Lhasa Apso	sk
Basenji	sth	Dalmatian	sth	Lowchen	sk
Basset Bleu	sth	Dandie Dinmont	sk	Maltese Terrier	sk
Basset Fauve	w	Deerhound	w	Maremma	d
Basset Griffon Vendeen	w	Dobermann	sth	Min. Schnauzer	w
Basset Hound	sth	Elkhound	d	Newfoundland	d
Beagle	sth	English Setter	sk	Old English Sheepdog	wl
Bearded Collie	sk	English Springer	sk	Pekingese	d
Beauceron	sth	Eskimo Dog	d	Pomeranian	d
Bedlington Terrier	wl	Flat Coated Retriever	sk	Poodle	wl
Belgian Shepherd Dog (Groenendael/Tervueren/Malinois) Belgian Shepherd Dog (Laekenois) wire-coated	d	Fox Terrier (smooth coat)	sth	Pyrenean Mountain Dog	
Bergamasco	cd	Fox Terrier (wire coat)	w	Rough Collie	sk
Bernese Mountain	d	German Pointer LH	sth	Russian Black Terrier	sk
Bichon Frise	wl	German Pointer SH	sk	Saluki	sk
Black and Tan Terrier	sth	German Pointer WH	w	Samoyed	d
Bolognese	sk	German Shepherd Dog	d	Schipperke	d
Border Collie	d	Giant Schnauzer	w	Scot. Deerhound	w
Border Terrier	w	Glen of Imaal	sk	Scottish Terrier	w
Borzoi	sk	Golden Retriever	sk	Sealyham Terrier	d
Boston Terrier	sth	Gordon Setter	sk	Shetland Sheepdog	sk
Bouvier	sk	Havanese	sk	Shih Tzu	sk
Boxer	sth	Hungarian Kuvasz	d	Siberian Husky	d
Briard	sk	Hungarian Puli	cd	Skye Terrier	sk
Brittany	sk	Hungarian Vizsla (smooth)	sth	Soft Coated Wheaten Terrier	sk
Bull Terrier	sth	Hungarian Vizsla (wire)	w	Tibetan Spaniel	w
Bulldog	sth	Irish Setter	sk	Tibetan Terrier	sk
Bullmastiff	sth	Irish Terrier	w	Welsh Corgi	d
Cairn Terrier	w	Irish Water Spaniel	wl	Welsh Terrier	w
Cavalier KC Spaniel	sk	Irish Wolfhound	w	West Highland W. Terrier	w
Cesky Terrier	sk	Italian Spinone	w	Yorkshire Terrier	sk

*Note: All spaniels and setters are silk coated unless otherwise listed.

3 The Pre-grooming Health Assessment

The health assessment constitutes a crucial part of your work for it allows you to establish that the dog is in a fit state to be groomed. The flip side of this is that it also means that you need to recognize those dogs that have something 'abnormal' going on. In doing so, you can contribute to their health and well-being by referring them to a vet for early investigation, diagnosis and treatment.

The various sections on the anatomy and physiology of the dog should have given you an understanding of how the healthy dog is put together and functions. With time, experience and practice, your knowledge and understanding will grow and you will become increasingly proficient in recognizing the healthy from the unhealthy, the normal from the abnormal.

But what is 'healthy' and what is 'normal'? First of all, 'healthy' and 'normal' do not mean the same thing. A dog that is termed 'healthy' enough to be groomed is well enough to undergo the process without suffering pain or deterioration in his health. Recognizing what is termed 'healthy' should come to you fairly quickly. The more dogs you handle, examine and assess, the easier this becomes.

Because a dog is in good health, it does not necessarily mean that what you are seeing is 'normal'. 'Normal' for one dog (for the individual) is not necessarily 'normal' for another. The concept of 'normal' for an individual can also change with time. Similarly, 'normal' for one breed may not be 'normal' for another.

To give you an example, you will have learnt in Chapter 2 to recognize the shape of the hind leg of a healthy dog and will have discovered how the knee joint bends. When you next lay your hands on a Chow Chow, pay special attention to his back legs: these are very straight with only the slightest bend; if anything, they bend slightly forwards so the feet are usually placed cranial to (in front of) the hip. For the healthy Chow Chow this is 'normal'. Incidentally, dogs of this breed walk with their feet skimming the ground rather than clearing it. This motion is 'normal' for a Chow Chow but would not be normal for a Golden Retriever.

It is only fair to point out here (and emphasize) that it may take many years of observation before you can answer the question: 'What is normal?' Your health assessment should therefore focus on what is 'healthy' and what is 'unhealthy'. If in doubt, you should, if possible, consult with a more senior colleague or a veterinary professional. In certain cases veterinary referral will be indicated.

You are encouraged to revisit and reread Chapter 2 every now and again, and should most certainly spend as much time as you can learning about the various breeds and their anomalies. In this way you are more likely to develop your observational skills and become proficient in health assessing the dogs you see.

Increasing familiarity with individual dogs and knowledge of the many canine breeds will help the groomer develop a heightened awareness of the healthy dog, both as a breed and as individuals.

The health assessment needs to be thorough so do not try to cut corners or miss bits out! Take your time and go through each stage meticulously, particularly if you do not have a supervisor or someone who can advise you and double-check your work.

A health assessment is also, to some extent, a risk assessment. It serves several purposes:

◆ to keep the grooming environment safe;
◆ to keep you and anyone working with you safe from the spread of zoonotic diseases;
◆ to keep other dogs in the grooming room safe from the spread of disease;
◆ to monitor and update records of existing disease;
◆ to identify any obvious signs of new illness or disease;
◆ to evaluate any increased risks of grooming a dog with an existing health concern;
◆ to evaluate any increased risks of grooming a dog with age-related problems; and
◆ to give you an idea of the dog's pre-grooming stress level so that this can be monitored throughout the grooming process.

When presented with a dog for grooming, you should ask yourself the following four questions:

1. Is the dog healthy enough to be groomed?
2. Will grooming have any adverse affects on existing health problems?
3. Are there any risks to other dogs, yourself or anyone else?
4. Should the dog you are looking at be referred to a vet?

Having asked yourself these questions

and assessed the dog, you should have enough information to decide whether the dog is fit to be groomed. In most cases this is a very straightforward decision, although it is always surprising how many things are discovered during the grooming process that owners have been blissfully unaware of. If you find yourself presented with a dog that you have doubts about, you should express your concerns to the owner, who then can consult their own vet for advice.

The infectious diseases section in Chapter 5 provides further information about the diseases that can be transmitted from one dog to another. It is worth pointing out here, however, that the risks posed by these diseases can be reduced by a number of simple measures. It is recommended that you:

◆ make sure all dogs, including your own, are kept up to date with vaccinations. Details can be recorded on the customer record card;
◆ make sure all dogs have been treated for parasites and keep a record of any details (e.g. date and product used); and
◆ send an introductory pack to new clients, explaining your policies on biosecurity, together with a 'customer record card' for the recording of existing health conditions and preventative health measures, for them to bring to their first appointment.

3.1 CHECK-LIST FOR A 'HEALTHY' HEALTH CHECK

Make full use of your senses when carrying out a health check: use your eyes to look, your ears to listen, your hands to feel and your nose to smell.

First impressions

The dog should appear bright, alert and responsive to verbal and visual stimulation (*see* Fig. 3.1.1). He should, ideally, be approachable and willing to make contact with you and he should have free movement of all limbs. The dog should be standing squarely on his legs and his neck should appear comfortable and relaxed, with free movement of the head.

CAUTION: NEVER BE TEMPTED TO DIAGNOSE

Diagnosing a condition is the job of the veterinarian. Misleading an owner with an incorrect identification or judgement of a condition has potentially serious consequences. It can not only cause misery and heartache for the dog's family, it may also leave you open to legal action by the owner or the dog's vet. It could also create/lead to mistrust or bad publicity for your business, affecting both existing and potential clients' confidence in you. As you become more experienced and recognize the seriousness of some of the problems you see, it is acceptable to stress the urgency of veterinary diagnosis and treatment in some cases.

Your job is to:

◆ *observe;*
◆ *report findings to the owner; and*
◆ *record all your findings for future reference.*

And nothing more!

Fig. 3.1.1   This Samoyed is fourteen years old and has just arrived for grooming. She has not yet had a health assessment but first impressions are that she walked in comfortably, is bright, alert and standing firmly on all four legs.

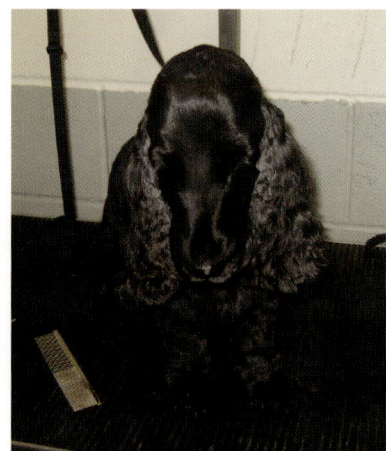

Fig. 3.1.2   This Cocker Spaniel appeared subdued and depressed, but was not obviously unwell. The owner was able to confirm that he had been behaving like this since losing his companion. Depression must be distinguished from lethargy, which is generally more serious as it may be associated with an underlying health problem.

Look out for:

◆ *lethargy, indicating illness (see Fig. 3.1.2);*
◆ *lack of response, indicating possible deafness or blindness;*
◆ *difficulty standing on all four limbs;*
◆ *standing with the neck extended;*
◆ *signs of lameness; and*
◆ *signs of anxiety, aggression or unsociable behaviour (see Fig. 3.1.3).*

Fig. 3.1.3   This dog is not aggressive to the point where he cannot be handled but he does clearly show a degree of unsociable behaviour. The general impression on his face is hard and businesslike, instead of being soft and yielding.

Start with the dog facing you to check his head, eyes and nose

The head should be held straight and should be able to turn comfortably from side to side and move both up and down. The muscles of the cheeks and on the top of the head should be firm and symmetrical. The dog should be willing to have his head examined.

> **Look out for:**
>
> ◆ *tilting of the head;*
> ◆ *lack of symmetry on the top of the head or the cheeks (see Fig. 3.1.4);*
> ◆ *restricted movement at the atlas/axis junction (the first intercervical joint, located immediately behind the head); and*
> ◆ *signs of pain or discomfort around the ear or mouth region.*

The eyes (*see* Figs 3.1.5 to 3.1.9) should be fully open, clear and bright, with a shiny, barely visible, white sclera. The conjunctival membranes, covering the inner linings of the eyelids, should be pink and the third eyelid barely visible. The eye colour (iris pigmentation) can range from almost black to light brown; in some breeds blue is acceptable. The pupils should be the same size as each other.

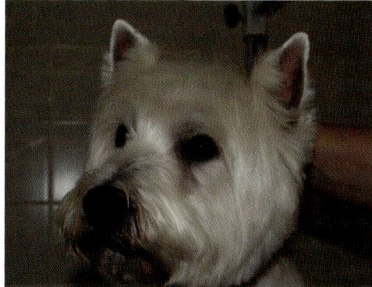

Fig. 3.1.5   A clean healthy eye in a West Highland White Terrier. The eye is clear and bright and the dog has an alert expression.

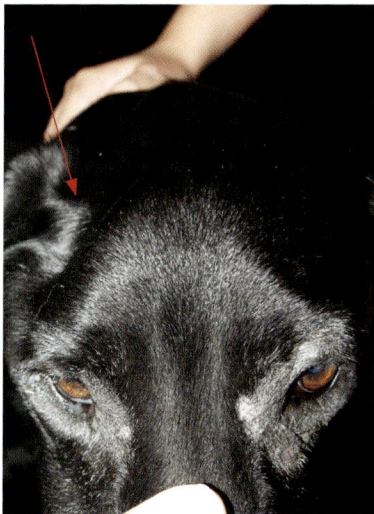

Fig. 3.1.4   This dog has quite pronounced wastage of the temporal muscle. The condition is obvious at this stage but careful examination of the head should reveal any lack of symmetry long before this amount of damage is evident. It is more difficult to feel the shape of the dog through a heavy coat so get used to using both hands simultaneously. In the case of the head, face the dog and start with your hands flat on the head with your thumbs touching each other at the centre line. Slide your hands away from each other towards the ears and think about what you are feeling, rather than trying to see what you are feeling. A dense coat can mask anything that you are trying to see.

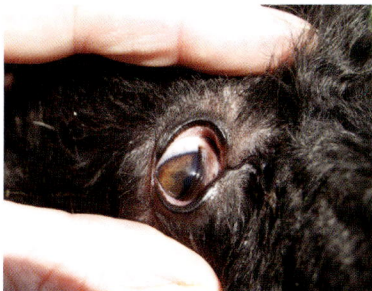

Fig. 3.1.6   The sclera and conjunctiva are viewed by raising the upper eyelid as demonstrated.

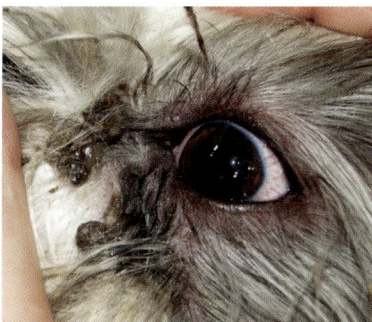

Fig. 3.1.7   Ocular discharge inside and below the left eye of a Shih Tzu. However, the eye is bright, there is no squinting or obvious sign of discomfort, and the blood vessels of the sclera are visible. This discharge may be abnormal for this dog so veterinary advice should be sought, but the dog can be groomed.

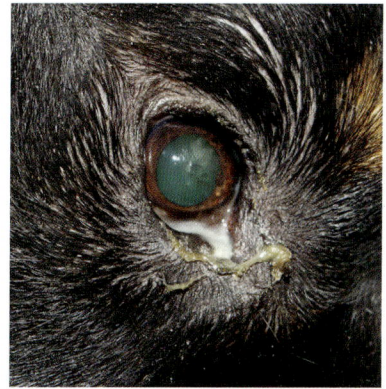

Fig. 3.1.8   This milky white discharge is abnormal. The eye appears sunken and the dog was lethargic and unwell. This dog was not admitted for grooming but was sent for immediate veterinary attention.

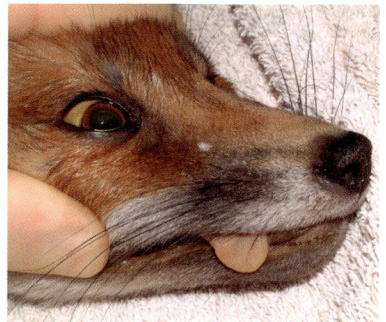

Fig. 3.1.9   The sclera of this fox cub has taken on a yellow tinge. This is called 'jaundice' and clearly reflects an underlying problem. Any dog presenting with this discoloration to the eyes or mucous membranes should not be groomed and should see a vet as soon as possible. [Note: this photograph was not taken in a grooming room.]

> **Look out for:**
>
> ◆ *redness;*
> ◆ *soreness;*
> ◆ *cloudiness;*
> ◆ *pain or discomfort;*
> ◆ *discharge;*
> ◆ *weeping;*
> ◆ *foreign bodies;*
> ◆ *differences in the size of the pupils; and*
> ◆ *squinting (this may be more obvious in bright light)*

The nose (*see* Figs 3.1.10 to 3.1.13) should be cold. It should have good open nostrils and be moist but not necessarily wet, with clear skin that may be black or brown in colour.

Fig. 3.1.10 The general impression of the nose should be that it is moist and cold. The skin is not necessarily black but it should be unbroken and without signs of injury.

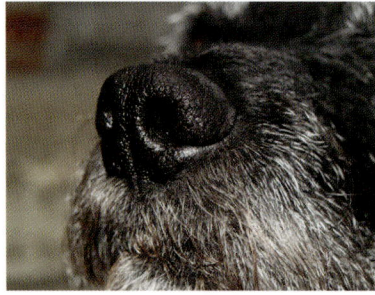

Fig. 3.1.11 The nostrils should be open and without signs of discharge. The skin on this nose is showing some pink pigment.

Fig. 3.1.12 The colour of the nose is often affected by the coat colour. Brown (liver-coloured) dogs often have a liver nose, whereas brown and white dogs often have a brown and pink nose.

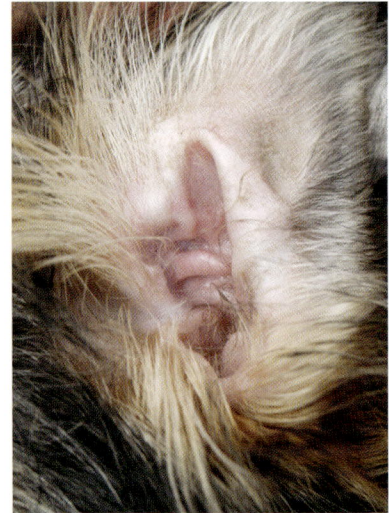

Fig. 3.1.13 Harry's nose is a good example of a healthy terrier's nose. The nose is moist and free of any discharge.

Look out for:

◆ **warm skin;**
◆ **dry or crusty skin;**
◆ **discharges (including bleeding);**
◆ **lumps or sores; and**
◆ **pink patches, redness or evidence of sunburn.**

Turn the dog sideways to check the ears and the mouth

The ears (*see* Figs 3.1.14a-b to 3.1.18) should be examined using all your senses. The inside of the ear should be dull pink and should not smell. Listen carefully for sounds that may indicate the presence of liquid within the ear canal. The pinna should be of an even thickness when felt, and visually the skin on both sides should appear to be an even colour.

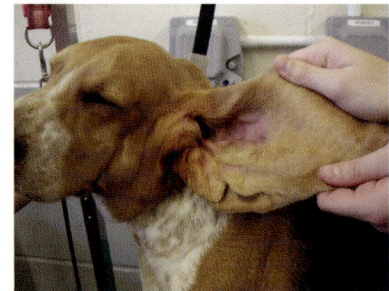

Fig. 3.1.15 This Tibetan Terrier had a strong smell coming from her ears. Closer inspection revealed an increased amount of liquid wax within the ear canal, some of which had dried hard. The ear was cleaned and the dog sent to the vet for treatment.

ABOVE AND BELOW: Fig. 3.1.14a–b Here we can see two very different ears, both of which are healthy. The photo above shows the ears of a terrier cross, with long hair accumulating at the entrance to the ear canal. The pinna is small and folds down so it is essential to remove this hair. The photo below shows the very impressive ear of a Basset Hound. This dog does not have any hair accumulation but the weight of the ear prevents the ear canal from cooling when the pinna hangs down. The skin inside both these ears is a healthy pink and there is no sign of wax or discharge.

Fig. 3.1.16 Some dogs, such as this Miniature Poodle, have an excessive amount of hair growing inside the ear canal which must be removed by plucking. This ear was otherwise healthy.

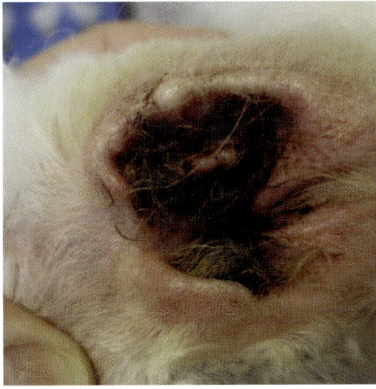

Fig. 3.1.17   The ear of this Bichon Frisé is in an unhealthy state and will benefit from being cleaned and having the hair removed before seeing the vet for treatment.

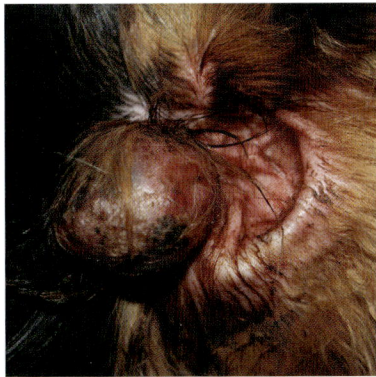

Fig. 3.1.18   An ulcerated mass was attached to the entrance of the ear canal of this Spaniel. It bled readily when scratched and had grown quickly. A trip to the vet was advised.

Look out for:

♦ **redness;**
♦ **sore skin;**
♦ **inflammation;**
♦ **pain or discomfort;**
♦ **hair in the ear canal;**
♦ **excess wax;**
♦ **foreign bodies;**
♦ **discharge or offensive smells;**
♦ **discoloured hair around the ear entrance;**
♦ **swellings within the pinna;**
♦ **head shaking; and**
♦ **signs of scratching.**

The mouth (*see* Figs 3.1.19 to 3.1.26) should be warm, have pink or pigmented (pink and/or black) tongue and mucosa. The mouth should be moist and may show a moderate amount of salivation. The breath should not be offensive in youngsters but, as the dog ages, it may deteriorate and develop an odour.

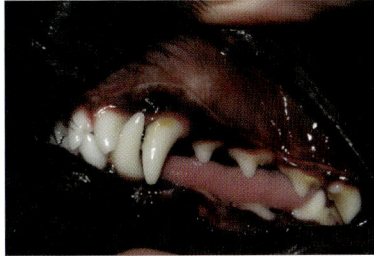

ABOVE AND BELOW: *Fig. 3.1.19a–b   These photos illustrate the extremes you may find when asses-sing mouth condition. The young adult dog above has a full set of healthy white teeth, but is already starting to show signs of calculus build-up that needs to be removed. The old dog below has badly neglected teeth that are in urgent need of professional dentistry. Dirty teeth are associated with many diseases, including heart disease, and owners should be encouraged to have their dog's teeth cleaned and scaled professionally at least once a year. Any problems that you see within the mouth need to be looked at by a vet.*

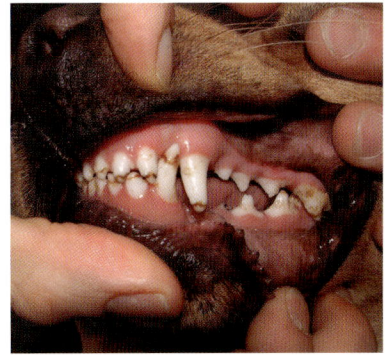

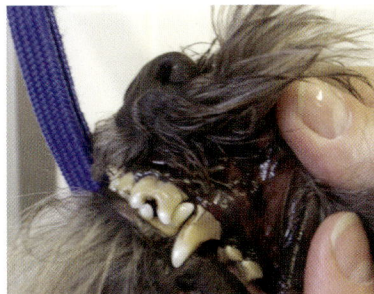

Fig. 3.1.20   Gingival hyperplasia developing in a West Highland Terrier. Gum overgrowth can spread to the extent that it may reach along the length of the tooth or, in an extreme case, encompass the whole tooth, making eating difficult.

Fig. 3.1.21   The marks on this adult dog's teeth are the result of the dog having had distemper as the teeth were developing. Note the healthy pink gums.

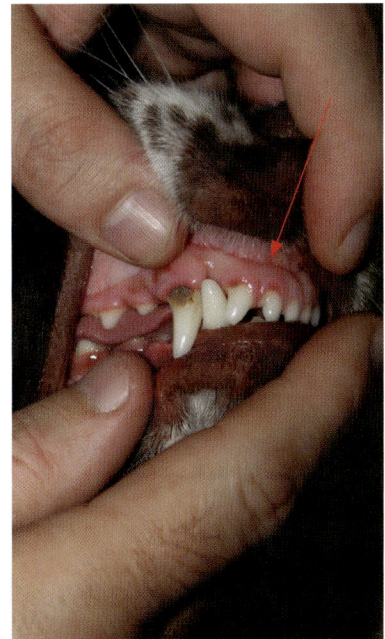

ABOVE AND BELOW: *Fig. 3.1.22a–b   The subtle reddening of the gum (above) is evidence of gingivitis associated with tartar build-up. This is more marked on the adjacent canine tooth. If it is left untreated, the tooth will eventually look like the tooth in the photograph below. A good dental examination is essential and dental hygiene should be promoted at all times.*

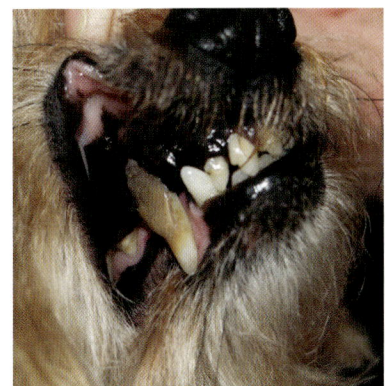

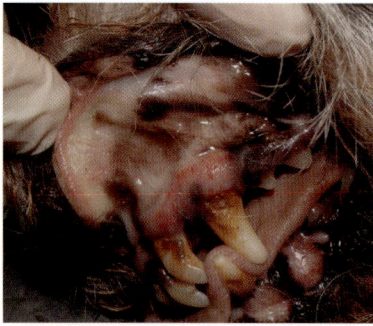

Fig. 3.1.23 *The gums of this dog are very pale, the mucosa of the upper lip is almost white and there are some little haemorrhages over the gums above the upper canine. This dog also appeared unwell and was referred straight to the vet. Note also the heavy build-up of calculus on the incisors and canines.*

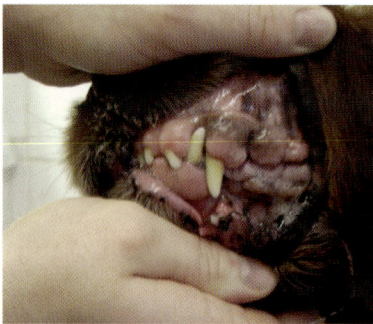

Fig. 3.1.24 *Other changes in the mouth may be impossible to diagnose without a biopsy. Prompt veterinary investigation and diagnosis can allow cancerous changes to be identified and treated early.*

The gums should be rosy pink, or pigmented, and should not bleed when touched. The capillary refill time (CRT) can be evaluated by pressing on the gums with your finger. This empties the capillaries of blood, causing the gum to go pale; on releasing the pressure, the blood flows back into the capillaries, returning them to their normal colour. The time taken for the colour to return should be no slower than one to two seconds.

Teeth should have a correct bite for the breed. There should be only one set of teeth and they should be clean and in good condition (white in a young dog, staining towards yellow in the older dog). Pay special attention to the developing bite of young puppies (*see* Figs 3.1.25a-b, 3.1.26a-b and 3.1.27a-b). Many dental problems can be rectified if the condition is recognized and treated at an early age.

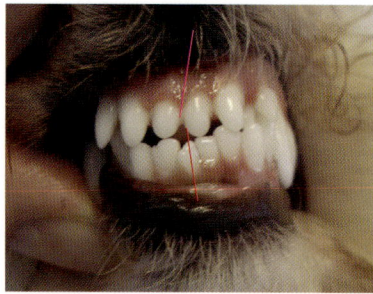

ABOVE AND BELOW: *Fig. 3.1.25a–b* This six-month-old puppy is developing a twisted (wry) mouth. This means that the bottom set of teeth are not centred with the top set. The photo above shows the bottom jaw shifting very subtly to the right. The second picture shows how the bottom canine tooth on the left is opening to the outside of the top canine, whereas on the opposite side of the mouth the canines are touching (the tips meet) when the mouth is open.

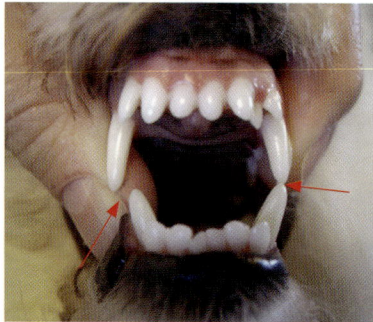

Fig. 3.1.26a–b *The photograph above shows how the right side of the mouth is crowded and there appear to be only five incisors in the top jaw. The second photo shows two retained deciduous teeth (arrowed). To the left a deciduous incisor is preventing the adult incisor developing in its rightful place; to the right a deciduous canine is pushing the adult canine forwards and providing a site for food to accumulate in.*

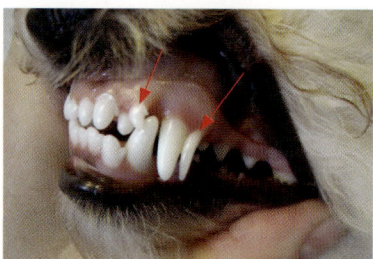

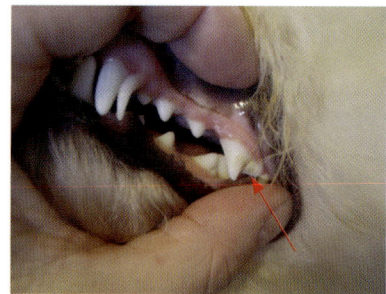

ABOVE AND BELOW: *Fig. 3.27a–b* It is important that the mouths of puppies are very carefully examined. If you look closely at the molars in both photographs you will see that, even at this young age, the teeth are starting to become discoloured. This may be because the dog is not eating properly. Whatever the reason, this little dog is going to need his teeth for many years to come, and if he sees a vet now the mouth may be able to be straightened and his teeth may be saved.

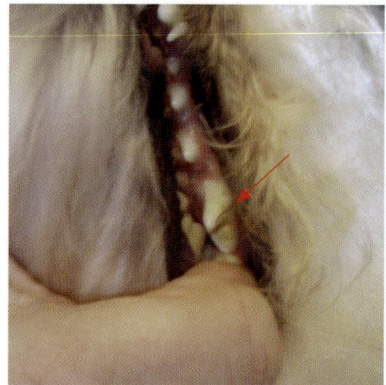

Look out for:

- **grey or pale tongue or mucosa, indicating shock or anaemia;**
- **yellowing of the mucosa, indicating jaundice;**
- **poor (slow) capillary refill;**
- **lumps on the gums or membranes;**
- **redness (+/- bleeding) along the gum line;**
- **retained teeth;**
- **incorrect bite;**
- **plaque or calculus on the teeth;**
- **broken or loose teeth;**
- **offensive breath (halitosis); and**
- **excessive salivation or dribbling.**

With the dog facing you, start with your hands on the shoulders (Fig. 3.1.28) and run your hands simultaneously down the front legs (Fig. 3.1.29). Turn the dog away from you. Starting at the back of the neck, check the length of the dog's body. Use both hands simultaneously, with one working opposite the other.

The body, including the legs (*see* Figs 3.1.30 to 3.1.34), should be carefully examined. Listen for noiseless, regular breathing and few or no gastric sounds. The body should be symmetrical and free of lumps and bumps. The skeleton should move freely and be covered with sufficient weight: the ribs and vertebral processes should be palpable (felt by gentle touch) but not

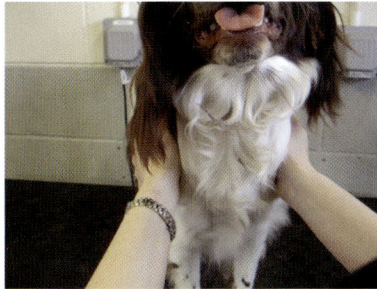

Fig. 3.1.28   With the dog facing you, start at the shoulder.

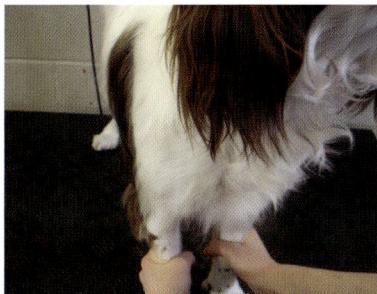

Fig. 3.1.29   Look for symmetry and work down the front legs to the feet.

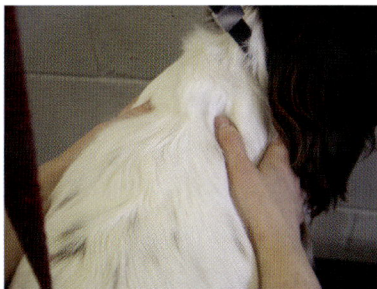

Fig. 3.1.30   Turn the dog away from you. You are looking for looseness or tightness in the shoulder.

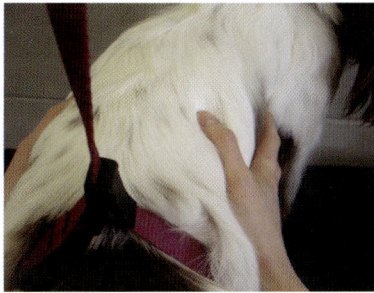

Fig. 3.1.31   Slide both hand simultaneously over the ribs and check the heart rhythm.

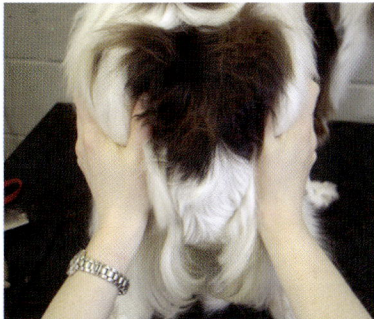

Fig. 3.1.32   Feel both hips at the same time and check for stability in the joints.

Fig. 3.1.33   Wrap your hands around the muscles to check for symmetry then work towards both back feet.

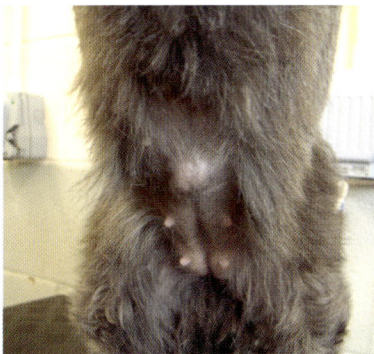

Fig. 3.1.34   An umbilical hernia.

clearly visible. If they cannot be easily palpated, this indicates the presence of a covering of subcutaneous fat and the dog may well be overweight.

Muscle tone in the young dog should be firm, but in the older dog may be softer; it should, however, always be symmetrical. The dog should be comfortable with being handled. Placing the fingers of your left hand over the heart region will allow you to detect the heart beat.

> **Look out for:**
>
> ◆ **noisy breathing (including coughing);**
> ◆ **difficulty breathing (increased effort);**
> ◆ **lack of symmetry;**
> ◆ **lumps;**
> ◆ **cysts;**
> ◆ **warts;**
> ◆ **tumours;**
> ◆ **hernias;**
> ◆ **stiff joints;**
> ◆ **restricted mobility;**
> ◆ **poor muscle tone/loss of muscle mass;**
> ◆ **obese and overweight dogs;**
> ◆ **underweight dogs;**
> ◆ **pain or discomfort;**
> ◆ **noisy gastric sounds;**
> ◆ **bloated stomach/ abdominal distension;**
> ◆ **reluctance to be handled; and**
> ◆ **over-sensitivity when touched.**

The coat (*see* Figs 3.1.35 to 3.1.39) should be even, buoyant and dense. It should be shiny, odourless and free from parasites. Cyclic moulting is normal but it should be evenly distributed over the entire coat. The coat of some smooth-coated dogs may not be as dense as in other breeds and there may be areas where the coat is very fine. This is particularly noticeable on breeds such as the Whippet (legs and undercarriage) and is not a cause for concern. The ears of all breeds should have a covering of hair, although in some cases this may also be very fine.

Fig. 3.1.35   Check the coat thoroughly. Make sure that you separate the coat so that you can see the skin, and gently pull on the undercoat to test if the dog is about to moult.

Fig. 3.1.36   The condition of the coat should give you an idea of how much grooming the owner is able to do between grooms and how much time you are going to need to do your job.

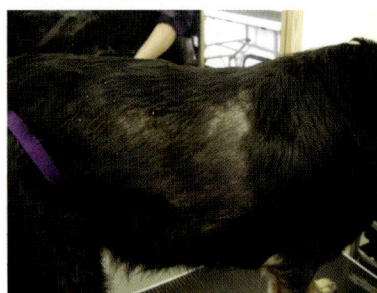

Fig. 3.1.37   Uneven coat density may indicate the presence of parasites that are making the dog scratch. It could be that the dog is trying to remove moulting or dead coat, or it may indicate a skin condition.

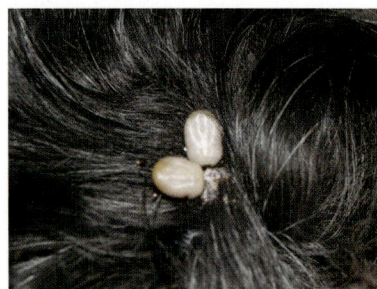

Fig. 3.1.38   Check the coat for parasites. These ticks are easy to see on a black dog; flea dirt would of course be more difficult to detect.

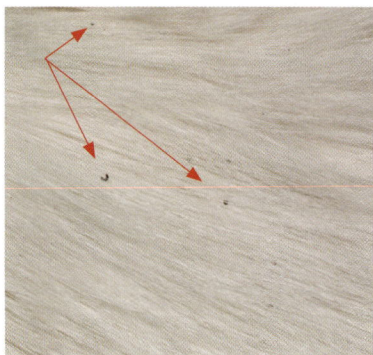

Fig. 3.1.39   Flea dirt on a white coat.

Look out for:

- ◆ **dullness (coat lacking in lustre);**
- ◆ **greasiness;**
- ◆ **unpleasant odours;**
- ◆ **evidence of parasites;**
- ◆ **hair loss (alopecia);**
- ◆ **symmetrical thinning patches or uneven moulting;**
- ◆ **excessive matting or wadding; and**
- ◆ **evidence of scratching at, or chewing out, the coat.**

The skin can be pink or pigmented, and should be warm to the touch and even in thickness. It should be supple, and clear from signs of growths (*see* Figs 3.1.40 to 3.1.46), lumps or tumours, trauma, infection, bad odours and itchiness (pruritus). Dogs should, generally speaking, always be comfortable having their skin touched.

Fig. 3.1.40   Clear healthy skin.

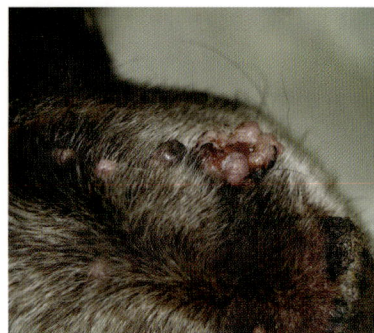

Fig. 3.1.41   Warts are commonplace. Cluster warts like this one are systemic and the dog is likely to have many of them over his body. They are a nuisance rather than a health problem because they bleed easily when traumatized.

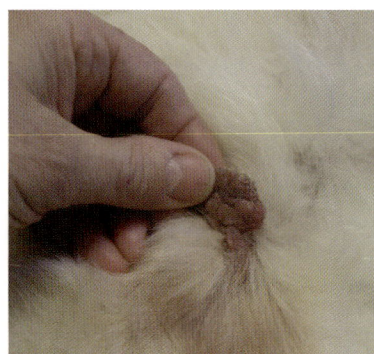

Fig. 3.1.42   This type of wart is less common. It hangs from the skin by a beck or cord, and can reach quite a size. Although it is often mistaken for a tumour, it is quite harmless, but because they hang down, care must be taken when working around them with sharp tools.

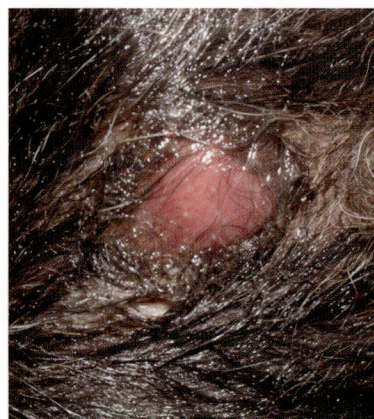

Fig. 3.1.43   This mass is a tumour and the dog should not be groomed without the vet's knowledge. Mast cell tumours are nasty and aggressive and should be disturbed as little as possible.. The sooner they are diagnosed by the vet the better.

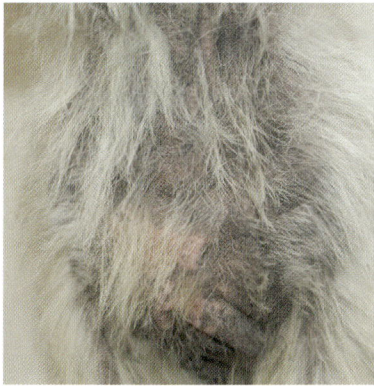

Fig. 3.1.44 Malassezia dermatitis is commonly seen in West Highland Terriers. Hyperpigmentation of the skin is evident and the dog has alopecia. The condition is not contagious and the dog can be groomed. However, the condition does need to be managed by a vet, who can advise you on grooming and skin care.

Look out for:

- thickened patches of rough skin;
- abnormal pigmentation and changes in pigmentation;
- lick granulomas;
- redness;
- inflammation (redness, heat, pain, etc.);
- spots (papules or pustules, the latter being filled with pus and indicative of a bacterial infection (pyoderma));
- lumps, swellings or tumours in (or on) the skin;
- abscesses with or without evidence of foreign bodies;
- scaling and crusting;
- itchiness (pruritus), as demonstrated by an exaggerated scratch reflex when the skin is touched and/or rubbed;
- excessive grease/oil;
- excessive dander (dandruff);
- unpleasant odour(s);
- sunburn;
- scalds and burns; and
- hotspots.

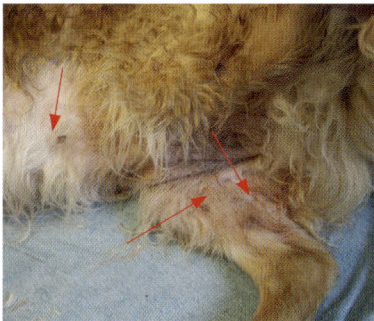

Fig. 3.1.45 This Golden Retriever has been licking her groin and undercarriage. The coat is saliva-stained and the licking has caused knotting. Close inspection shows a bacterial dermatitis and pustules. This is common in the breed, but the dog should still be sent to the vet for a positive diagnosis and treatment.

The anus and anal sacs should be inspected as part of the health examination. The anus should be neatly closed and the skin rosy pink in colour. The anal sacs should not be evident (*see* Fig. 3.1.47) and there should not be any signs of swelling (*see* Fig 3.1.48), pain, discomfort, redness, discharge or trauma (*see* Figs 3.1.49 and 3.1.50).

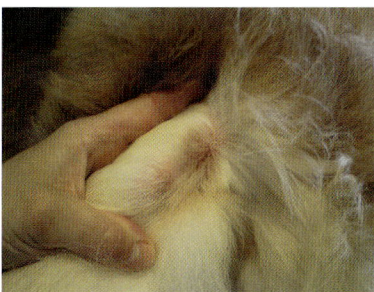

Fig. 3.1.47 A healthy bottom. The rectum is clean and there is no sign of swelling around the area of the anal sacs (arrows).

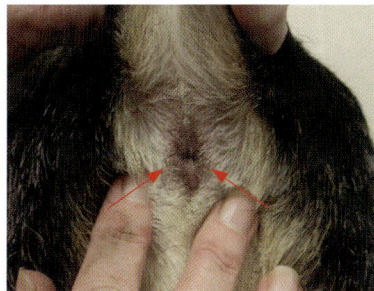

Fig. 3.1.49 An anal sac abscess to the left of the rectum. The abscess is discharging pus and a little blood. If care is taken, this dog could be bathed. A trip to the vet, however, is essential.

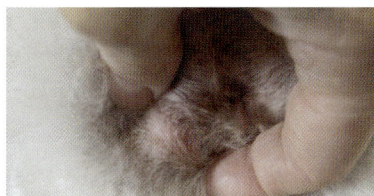

Fig. 3.1.46 Epidermal collarettes at the base of the tail on a Golden Retriever. These are signs of a skin infection.

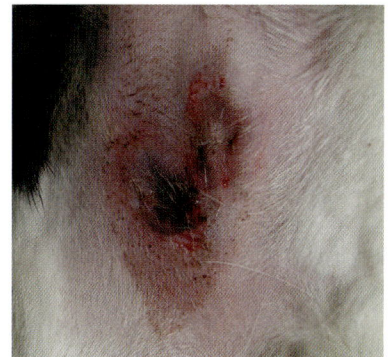

Fig. 3.1.48 Here you can see a swelling of the anal sac that could not be expressed. This may indicate an impaction or a developing abscess, and needs to be seen by a vet.

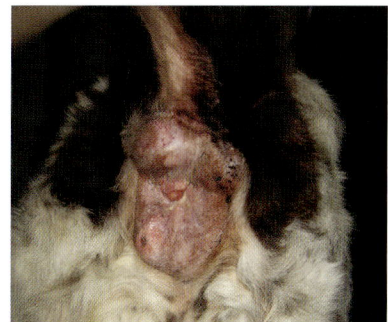

Fig. 3.1.50 This poor chap has a combination of at least two anal sac abscesses and several tumours. The condition is very painful but not infectious or contagious so he can be groomed. Veterinary treatment was needed for the abscesses and to make a positive diagnosis of the tumours.

In the coatless breeds it is normal for the skin to appear slightly dry but it should still be supple and not have a strong odour. It can range in colour from very pale pink to blue black and it may also be pigmented.

Look out for:

- skin tumours on or around the anus;
- swelling of the anal sacs;
- abscesses;
- signs of self-mutilation (rubbing);
- unpleasant odour;
- skin trauma;
- discharge from either the anus or the anal sacs; and
- signs of faeces, diarrhoea or tapeworm segments on the surrounding skin and hair.

The genitals: entire males should have both testicles descended and they should be even in size (*see* Figs 3.1.51 to 3.1.55). Depending on the ambient temperature, they may be pulled close to the body or be hanging away from the body. The skin over the testicles should feel thick and robust and may or may not be pigmented. Discharge from the penis can be normal but there should not be an offensive smell and the glans should be a healthy pink colour. The skin surrounding the penis – the prepuce – should be even in thickness and free from lesions or sores.

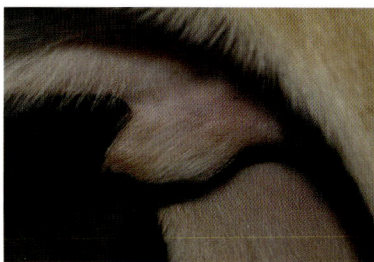

Fig. 3.1.51   The sheath should be free of sores, swellings and any offensive smelling discharge.

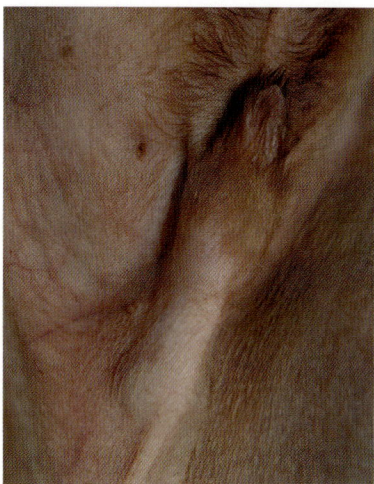

Fig. 3.1.52   There should be evidence of moisture within the prepuce and the membranes should be a healthy pink colour.

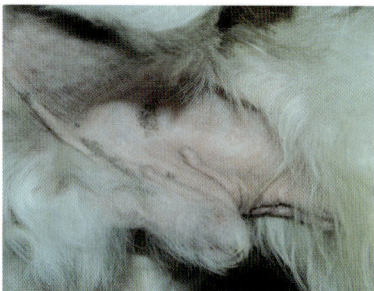

Fig. 3.1.53   This dog is showing signs of papular eruptions in the groin.

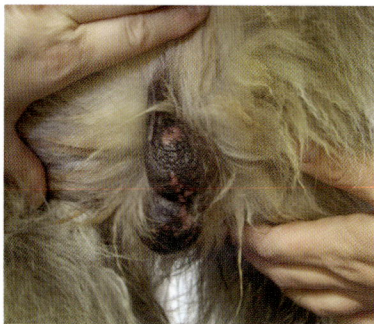

Fig. 3.1.54   Testicles should be equal in shape and size.

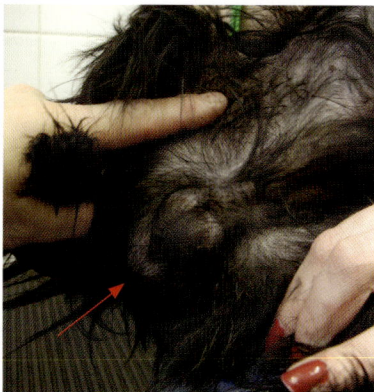

Fig. 3.1.55   This dog was referred to a vet to check the swelling behind the testicles.

Look out for:

In males:
- ◆ *entire males with retained or undescended testes;*
- ◆ *swellings or enlarged testes;*
- ◆ *lumps;*
- ◆ *shrivelling of either testicle;*
- ◆ *ulceration of the skin on the testes;*
- ◆ *excessive or offensive-smelling discharge from the penis;*
- ◆ *thickened skin or sores on the prepuce; and*
- ◆ *paraphimosis.*

Young male dogs may not have both testicles fully descended until five or six months of age and it would not be unusual for testicles to descend one at a time. By six months of age, however, they should both be in place.

In all bitches:
- ◆ *offensive odours;*
- ◆ *any abnormal shape or swelling of the vulva;*
- ◆ *redness of the vaginal membranes;*
- ◆ *frequent or constant urination; and*
- ◆ *discoloration of the hair surrounding the vulva, suggesting excessive licking.*

In unspayed bitches, with or without oestrus:
- ◆ *discharge when not in oestrus;*
- ◆ *swelling and soreness in the abdomen, with or without a vaginal discharge (suspect possibility of pyometra); and*
- ◆ *signs of enlarged vaginal tissues extending out from within the vagina (possible polyp or prolapse).*

All bitches, including neutered (spayed) bitches, should have a neat vulva tucked fairly close to the body (*see* Figs 3.1.56 and 3.1.57. There should not be any sign of discharge or offensive odours. The internal membranes will be a healthy rosy pink colour. Unneutered bitches in oestrus will have an enlarged vulva with reddened membranes. There may or may not be evidence of coloured discharge and, although there will be an odour, it should not be offensive.

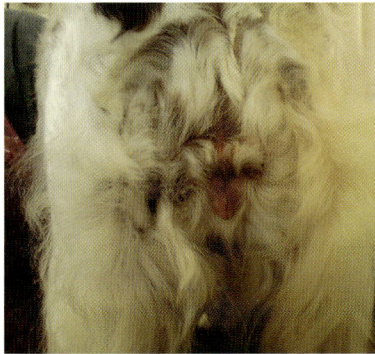

Fig. 3.1.56   This is a normal presentation for an ageing bitch, whether it is has been neutered (spayed) or not. The skin surrounding the vulva is often soft and feels 'fatty' to the touch, with very little firmness of underlying muscle.

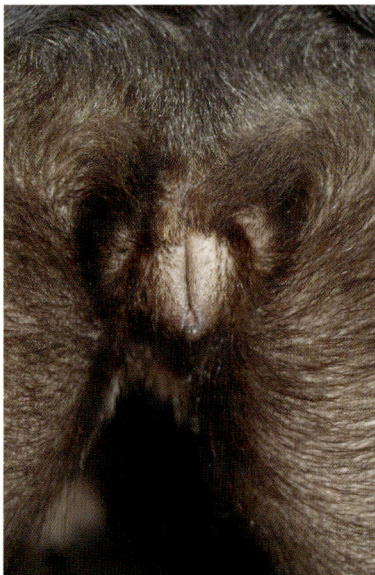

Fig. 3.1.57   Normal presentation for a young bitch, whether neutered or not. The skin surrounding the vulva is much firmer. In all cases the visible mucous membranes inside the vulva should be a healthy pink colour and should appear moist.

The tail (*see* Figs 3.1.58 to 3.1.60) should be free of any lumps or swellings.

Straight tails should not have any unexplained bends that could signify a break. The joints of the tail should bend easily from side to side and up and down with a little persuasion.

Corkscrew tails should be examined for skin infection between the curls and at the dock (the point where the tail sits on/meets the back). The joints of

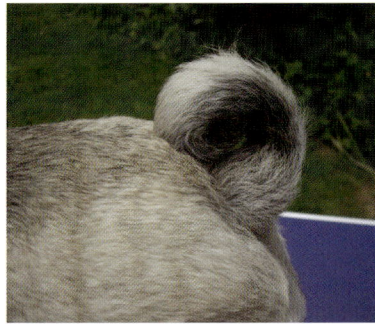

Fig. 3.1.58   Corkscrew tails are particularly prone to dermatitis within the coils.

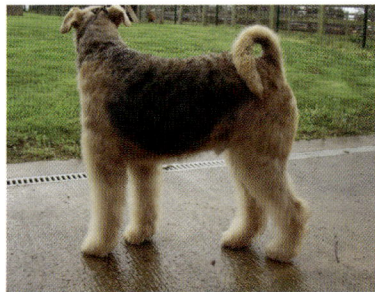

Fig. 3.1.59   Many breeds that were once docked are now sporting full-length tails. Take particular notice when assessing larger dogs that live in the house because there is more likelihood of the tail being knocked against doors or furniture and damaged.

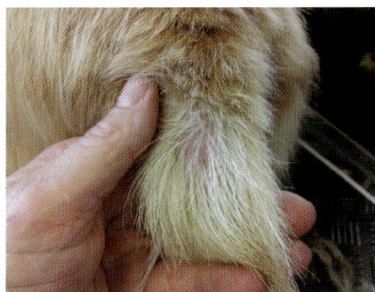

Fig. 3.1.60   It is quite common to see a balding patch of hair near the tail root. This is thought to be caused by a group of sebaceous glands that respond to hormonal stimuli and is not a cause for concern.

the corkscrew tail will have very little, if any, sideways or up-and-down movement.

Curled tails should be examined at the dock for signs of skin infection. The joints along the entire length should be able to bend easily from side-to-side and up and down.

The collection of sebaceous glands on the top of the tail, about a third of the length from the base, can become enlarged. This condition is called 'tail gland hyperplasia'. The glands appear raised and will give the impression of a swollen lump. This may be associated with hair loss over the affected area or a change in hair colour and/or texture. Some dogs will chew at this area of the tail, causing skin damage.

> **Look out for:**
>
> ♦ **unexplained lumps;**
> ♦ **unexplained bends/kinks;**
> ♦ **restricted movement;**
> ♦ **pain;**
> ♦ **tail gland hyperplasia;**
> ♦ **sore skin;**
> ♦ **bald patches;**
> ♦ **evidence of scratching or rubbing;**
> ♦ **evidence of parasites; and**
> ♦ **foul smells, particularly in heavily furnished tails.**

The feet and nails (*see* Figs 3.1.61 to 3.1.72b) need to be examined by picking them up and handling them.

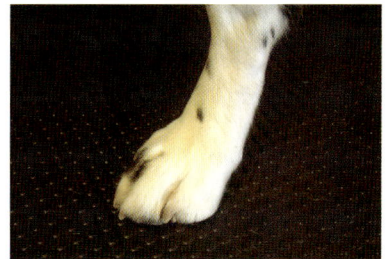

Fig. 3.1.61   Healthy feet are incredibly important. The shape of the foot depends on the breed. These feet belong to a Springer Spaniel: the feet are well padded below and the toes are tight and bent to direct the nails towards the ground, where they wear down naturally. These feet are in good condition. The short untrimmed nails indicate the dog is able to move correctly. This dog can therefore be said to be 'sound in movement'.

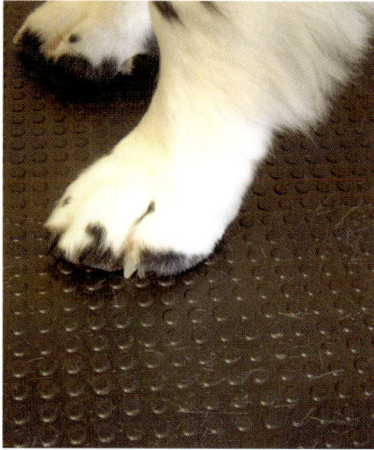

ABOVE AND BELOW: Fig. 3.1.62a-b   The feet on the Bedlington Terrier and on the Whippet are, by contrast, long and stretch along the ground (hare feet). The nails on these breeds grow forwards and do not wear down in the same way as the Springer's nails. These nails will naturally be longer.

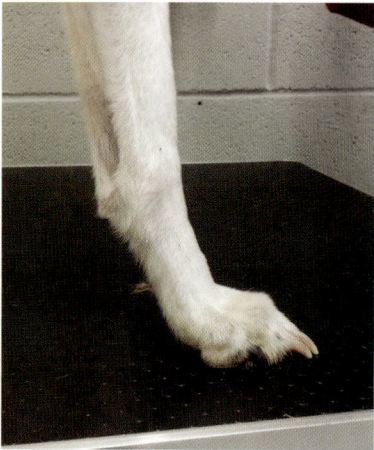

Fig. 3.1.64   The hair between these pads is knotted and needs to be removed. Such knots can cause bruising to the tissues between the pads.

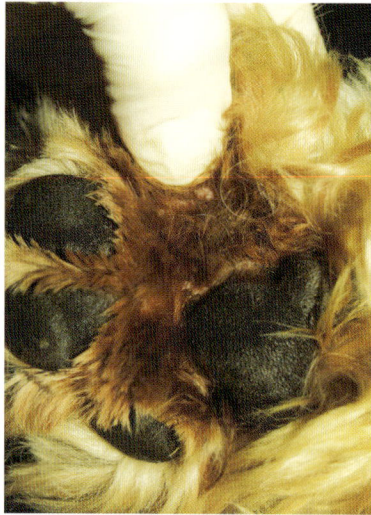

Fig. 3.1.66   Check that the dewclaws are not curling into the pad.

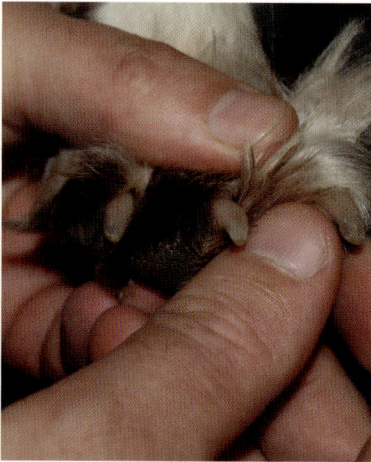

Fig. 3.1.67   Look for signs of the nail breaking down. This may be an indication of a nail infection.

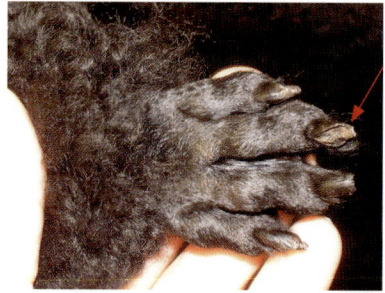

ABOVE AND BELOW: Fig. 3.1.65a-b   Check all the nails individually and remember to check for dewclaws on both front and back legs. Some breeds have two or more dewclaws on the hind legs.

Fig. 3.1.68   These nails are clearly in need of cutting. The length of the nail alters the way the dog uses its feet and this can have an impact on the elbow and shoulder position.

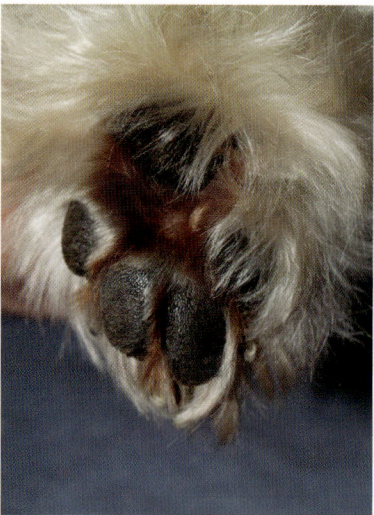

Fig. 3.1.63   Check between the pads. There should be a little hair to protect the skin but there should be no knots, broken skin or signs of skin infection.

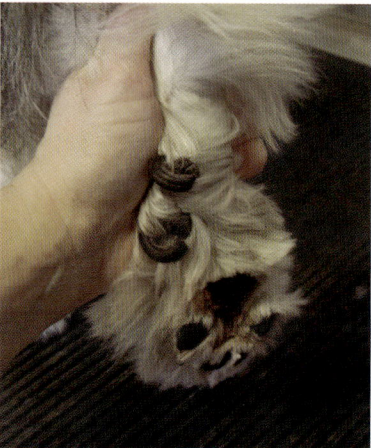

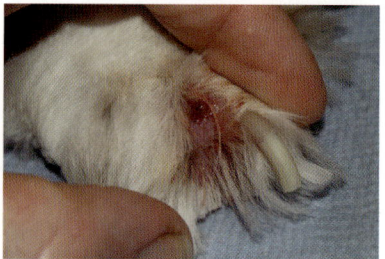

Fig. 3.1.69   An inter-digital cyst between the toes of a Cavalier King Charles Spaniel. Some breeds are more prone to these than others; they are painful and need to be looked out for. When removed, they often recur somewhere else, so keep looking!

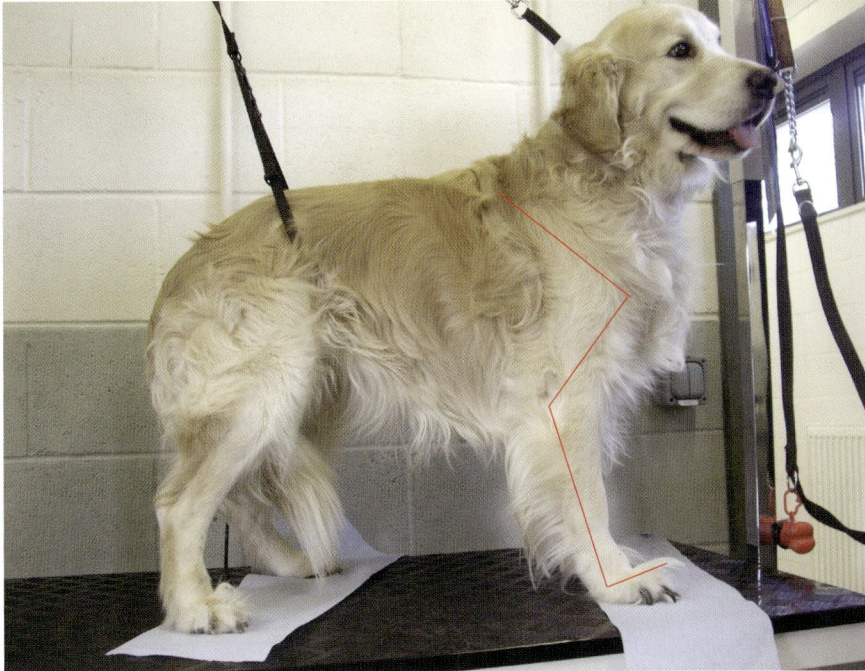

Fig. 3.1.70 This dog has very long nails that have altered the position (carriage) of its feet. You can see how the back part of the foot is lower than the front, meaning that the dog's weight distribution over its feet has changed. Walking is affected, but the nails are unlikely to wear and will become increasingly long. The angle of the feet also alters the angles of the elbow and the shoulder.

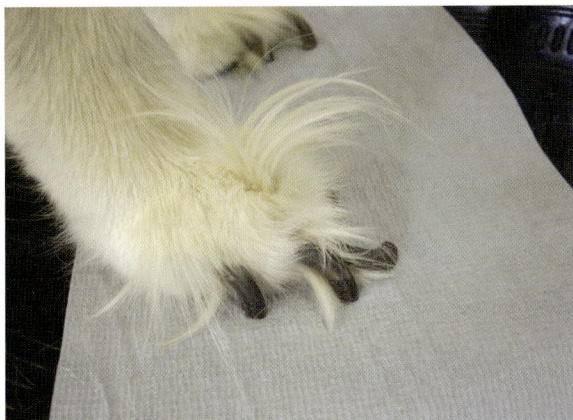

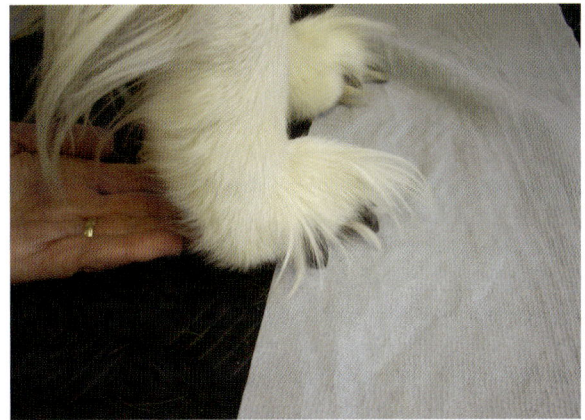

Fig. 3.1.71a–b   Here you can see the length and deformity of the nail before cutting (a) and how the foot position improves following nail clipping (b).

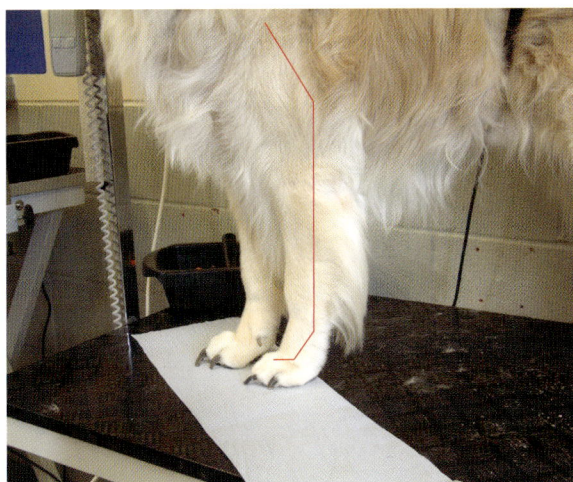

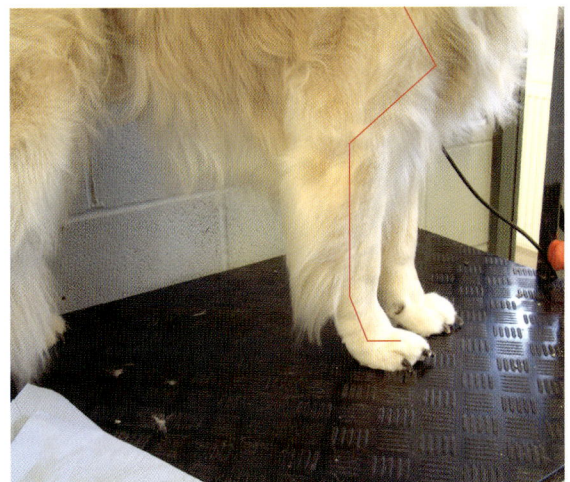

Fig. 3.1.72a–b   More nail care is needed, but even after this initial cutting the dog was able to stand better on its feet. The angle of the foot has changed so the nails can wear down better during exercise. The elbow and shoulder angles have also improved, thereby reducing the risk of unnecessary strain being placed on these joints.

Fig. 3.1.73 Alert and bright-eyed, this Labrador looks healthy and first impressions would suggest that he is in good condition and able to be admitted into the salon for grooming.

> **Look out for:**
>
> *Feet:*
> ◆ *cuts and lesions between the pads of the feet and between the toes;*
> ◆ *bruising caused by hard debris and knots in long interdigital hair;*
> ◆ *interdigital cysts;*
> ◆ *signs of self-mutilation;*
> ◆ *signs of harvest mites; and*
> ◆ *soreness or discomfort, particularly in the winter time when salt (used to keep roads and walkways free of ice) can cause 'salt burn' between the pads.*
>
> *Nails:*
> ◆ *brittleness;*
> ◆ *roughness or flaking of the nail surface;*
> ◆ *dullness;*
> ◆ *discoloration, swelling and heat at the nail bed, indicating an infection;*
> ◆ *uneven wear in a young dog, indicating lameness, restricted muscle action or a skeletal injury/deformity;*
> ◆ *uneven wear in an old dog, indicating restricted muscle function or skeletal disease (arthritis);*
> ◆ *excessively long nails;*
> ◆ *uneven growth in length or density; and*
> ◆ *pain and/or reluctance to have a foot lifted and examined, indicating a possible torn nail (or similar injury).*

The skin on the pads should be thick, robust and supple. Between the pads the skin should be pink or pigmented. The nails should be shiny, smooth and strong, and evenly worn (showing even signs of wear). They may be white, brown, black or any combination of these three colours.

The shape of the foot will, to an extent, have a bearing on the length of the nail. A short rounded foot, such as you would find on a Cocker Spaniel, will have short nails because the nail is pointing towards the ground and is worn down as the foot rolls in movement. The 'hare' foot of the whippet, by contrast, has long toes which lengthen the foot. These nails grow forward along the ground and will be naturally longer in length.

Remember:

If you find something that should not be there, advise the owner and encourage them to seek veterinary advice. Record your findings and the course of action you have recommended to the owner.

4 Parasites, Parasitism and Parasite Control

Parasites can be a consider-able nuisance both on and inside the dog. Dog groom-ers encounter parasites on a regular basis and must learn to recognize and deal with many of them. More often than not, you will be the first to identify that a dog is parasitized and you need to be able to advise the owner of the nature and significance of the problem.

This chapter provides an overview of common canine parasites, their signifi-cance to dogs and their owners, as well as to society and, of course, to you the groomer. After reading this chapter you will have acquired a better understand-ing of parasites and their life cycles. Armed with this knowledge, you will be able to take effective measures to ensure that your premises and equip-ment are kept free of parasites. You should also be able to identify the signs that a parasite problem is taking hold and know when to advise the owner to seek veterinary advice.

The chapter starts with a definition of parasitism, and then looks at the many different sorts of parasite that can affect dogs, detailing their signifi-cance, their typical appearance and the problems they cause. Once we have covered all the different types of parasite you can expect to see in the dog (and some that you will only see the evidence of), we will consider how they can best be controlled.

4.1 DEFINITIONS

A *parasite* is an organism that lives in or on another organism of a different species, otherwise known as the host. In doing so, the parasite is dependent on the host's body for nourishment.

Parasitism is the relationship in which a parasite lives off its host, sometimes causing the host damage. The para-site obtains food and/or shelter from the host but contributes nothing to its host's welfare. Some parasites live on the host, whereas others live and feed inside the host (*see* Fig. 4.1.1). This allows us to distinguish between *ectoparasites* (external ones) and *endoparasites* (internal ones).

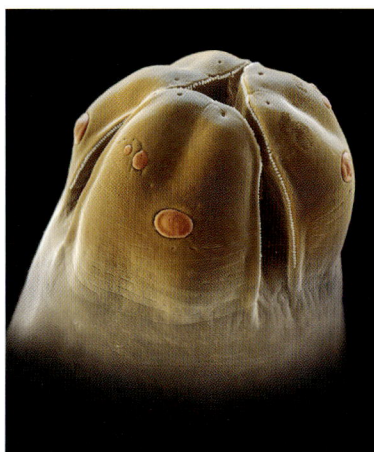

Fig. 4.1.1 The head of a roundworm. Note the number of small teeth that attach the worm to the lining of the host's intestines for feeding. (Courtesy of Bayer Animal Healthcare)

A *definitive host* is the organism that the adult parasite parasitizes, lives and reproduces in or on. The parasite can thus complete its life cycle in or on the definitive host. A *paratenic host* is an organism that the parasite can take advantage of and live in, without it being necessary for the completion of the parasite's life cycle. An *intermediate host* is an organism that serves as the host for one or more of the larval stages of a parasite and allows some develop-mental stages to be completed. The larvae can then go on to infect the definitive host. The intermediate host

is required for the parasite to complete its life cycle.

Endoparasites

The two main groups of endoparasites we need to concern ourselves with are helminths and protozoa. Helminths are a group of worm-like parasites that include tapeworms (*cestodes*), round-worms (*nematodes*) and flukes (*trema-todes*). They are invertebrate multicellu-lar organisms with variably elongated bodies. Some are flattened (tapeworms and flukes), others are round bodied (roundworms) (*see* Fig. 4.1.2). They all develop through egg, larval and adult stages. With few exceptions, the eggs of flukes, tapeworms and roundworms are passed in the excretions and secre-tions of the host, allowing them to leave the body of the host and infect either an intermediate host or another host of the same species (the definitive host).

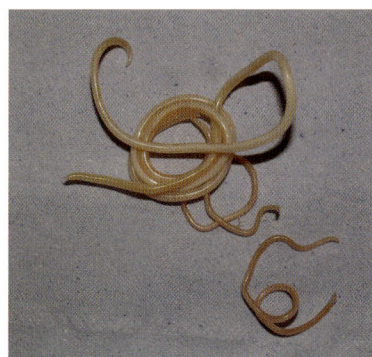

Fig. 4.1.2 These roundworms are probably Toxocara canis. *Adult worms can measure from 9 to 18cm in length!*

An understanding of the life cycle of each parasite is essential if we are to understand how parasitic diseases are transmitted and how they can best be controlled. The life cycle of some of the common tapeworms and roundworms infecting dogs will now be described to illustrate the important points.

Roundworms

Toxocara canis

This is probably the best known nematode in dogs. It is a member of the *ascarid* family and is renowned for its potential as a zoonotic disease and for its prenatal transmission from bitch to pup. Activation of a dormant (latent) infection during pregnancy results in the bitch passing on this infection to her pups via the placenta. In some cases transmission through her milk is also possible. Most puppies therefore run the risk of infection unless the mother has been wormed during her pregnancy.

The infection is especially common in young puppies. Mild infections may pass unnoticed; heavy infestations by contrast will result in a range of signs and clinical problems. Affected puppies may demonstrate poor growth and a pot-belly. In some cases intestinal obstructions, vomiting (*see* Fig. 4.1.3) and even intussusception ('telescoping', where the intestine is drawn up into itself) may occur. In such cases the puppy will appear sore and unwell, and the suspected internal complications can be confirmed by veterinary investigation. Pneumonia may also occur secondary to the damage caused by larvae migrating through the lungs. This may be associated with coughing. From a grooming point of view, a noteworthy sign associated with infection is that of a thin and/or dull coat.

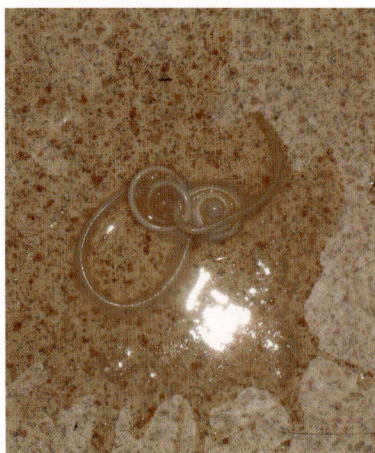

Fig. 4.1.3   Roundworms vomited up by a young puppy with a heavy worm burden.

Puppies and adult dogs can also become infected by the ingestion of eggs from the environment. Contamination of the environment by infected dogs plays a significant role in perpetuating the problem. Eggs within the environment have been shown to remain infectious for as long as five years and reinfection therefore occurs relatively easily. Ingested eggs hatch to release larvae that cross the wall of the gut and migrate through the body tissues. This is called *somatic migration* (migration through the body) and results in the larvae being deposited within body tissues. These larvae are said to be 'dormant' but, should an infected bitch become pregnant, the larvae become reactivated and migrate back to the uterus to infect the foetuses.

Toxocara canis is a serious zoonotic disease that can cause serious health problems in man, including damage to eyesight (*see* Chapter 5).

The prenatal infection of puppies and the subsequent release of large numbers of *Toxocara* eggs into the environment by the bitch necessitates a well thought through worming plan. Bitches should be wormed with a preparation licensed for use during pregnancy and at the prescribed dose rate. Standard dose rates have been shown not to prevent transmission to puppies; your veterinary surgeon will be able to advise on the available licensed products and dose rate to be used.

A puppy acquiring an infection in the uterus (*in utero*) will generally have fully developed worms in its intestines by two to three weeks of age. It is therefore recommended that pups be wormed at two weeks of age and then regularly every two to four weeks until they are three months old. This repeated worming will kill off any newly acquired infections in the vulnerable pups. Between three and six months of age monthly worming is advised as these young dogs are still vulnerable to infection. Thereafter worming every three months is recommended by the British Small Animal Veterinary Association (BSAVA). A policy statement and advice sheet can be viewed on their website (see Further Reading).

Toxascaris leonina

Another member of the *ascarid* family

that also parasitizes dogs, *Toxascaris leonina* differs from *Toxocara canis* in that it is not transferred *in utero* or through the bitch's milk. Instead it is acquired following the ingestion of embryonated (containing a developing embryo) eggs or through the ingestion of a rodent or other paratenic host.

Adult *Toxascaris* worms live within the gastro-intestinal tract. The life cycle of *Toxascaris leonina* starts with the laying of eggs by the adult worm and their passage from the body in the faeces. These eggs become infective after three to six days in the environment and are typically ingested by a foraging rodent. On hatching, the larvae migrate through the tissues of the rodent. The definitive host, usually a dog, fox or cat, can then become infected following the ingestion of the infected rodent.

Clinical signs associated with *Toxascaris* infestations are relatively uncommon in the dog. They include vomiting, diarrhoea, a pot-bellied appearance, loss of appetite and a thinning, dull hair coat.

Hookworm

Hookworm is a collective term used to describe a number of roundworm species with a characteristic bending of the head where it joins the body. Hookworms are generally smaller than members of the *ascarid* family, described above, and are less likely to cause obstructions or tissue damage. They do, however, possess well developed mouths and can cause significant damage to the lining of the gut when feeding. The most significant risk associated with hookworm infestations is therefore blood and protein loss, resulting in anaemia.

Hookworms are significant zoonoses in human mothers and their babies in tropical and subtropical countries. Their presence often goes undetected and it is the chronic and insidious nature of hookworm infections that makes them so dangerous. A similar problem can be seen in dogs. The two species of hookworms found in British dogs are *Uncinaria stenocephala* and *Ancylostoma caninum*.

The life cycle of hookworms is relatively simple: eggs are passed in faeces, develop into third-stage larvae and are then ingested by a dog. Contaminated areas can carry a heavy burden of larvae, which are easily ingested by an investigative dog. The larvae can also penetrate the skin and produce a localized dermatitis. This issue should be borne in mind when designing kennelling and exercise areas, which will need to be kept free of infection and decontaminated regularly.

Trichuris vulpis

This is the scientific name given to the whipworm. This parasitic roundworm lives in the large intestine and embeds its mouthparts in, and feeds from, the intestinal mucosa. Heavy infestations can result in bloody diarrhoea.

Lungworm

Lungworms, as the name suggests, reside within the lungs of the dog (*see* Fig. 4.1.4). A number of different lungworms are known to affect dogs. Two are described here.

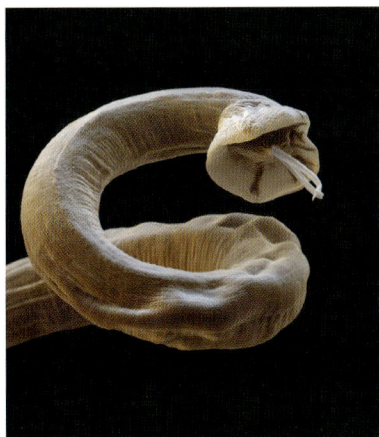

Fig. 4.1.4   The mouthparts of a lungworm. (Courtesy of Bayer Animal Healthcare)

Oslerus osleri, also known as *Filaroides osleri,* has a direct life cycle, which means that the parasite cycles from dog to dog with no involvement of an intermediate or paratenic host. Adult female worms live within the lungs and produce thin-shelled eggs, which mature within the lung tissue. Eggs and larvae can be coughed up at any time and are often passed to other dogs, and especially puppies, in the saliva. Infection is also possible through the ingestion of infected stomach contents or faeces. Puppies thus typically contract

lungworm from their mother, with the severity of the clinical signs depending on the amount of eggs ingested. Infestation may be inapparent or may be associated with coughing as the nodules formed around the adult worms within the trachea and bronchi of the lungs become enlarged.

Angiostrongylus vasorum has been variously described as both a heartworm and a lungworm as it lives within the pulmonary artery and the right ventricle of the heart (*see* Fig. 4.1.5). The definitive hosts of this nematode worm are the dog and fox, as well as a number of other carnivores, including the European badger. In most parts of the world wild foxes serve as the reservoir host and therefore as an infection reservoir for domestic dogs. The adult worms produce eggs that become lodged in the smaller arteries, allowing the larvae to migrate into the airways; these are coughed up, swallowed and passed in the faeces. The larvae then infect intermediate hosts, which can be one of a large number of slugs and snails, which a dog must eat for the disease to be acquired. Infestation is associated with the presence of adult worms within the pulmonary blood vessels and larvae within the airways. Clinical signs include coughing, breathing difficulties, exercise intolerance and blood clotting disorders.

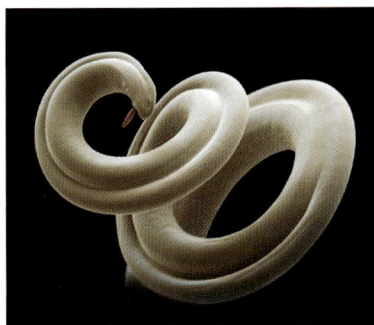

Fig. 4.1.5   Angiostrongylus vasorum is described as a heartworm and a lungworm as it lives within both the pulmonary artery and the right ventricle of the heart. (Courtesy of Bayer Animal Healthcare)

Other roundworms known to infect dogs around the world include *Filaroides hirthi* (in the US), *Crenosoma vulpis* (a fox lungworm), *Dirofilaria immitis* (heartworm) and various *capillaria* species.

Tapeworms

Tapeworms (more properly known as cestodes) have a flattened, ribbon-like appearance. They are segmented and it is these segments, known as proglottids, that can break off and be passed in the faeces. All segments, except those of *Echinococcus*, are visible to the naked eye and may be seen on the perianal tissue (around the anus) or within the faeces (*see* Figs 4.1.6 and 4.1.7).

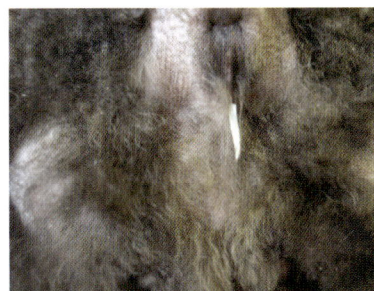

Fig. 4.1.6   A fresh tapeworm segment containing thousands of eggs being passed into the environment.

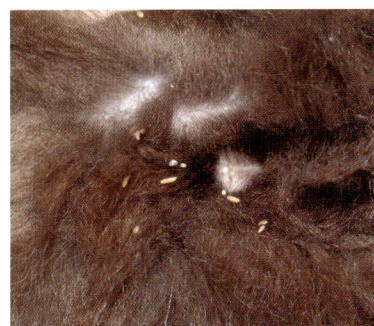

Fig. 4.1.7   Tapeworm segments, or 'proglottids', in the fur surrounding the anus. These segments have not made it to the ground where they remain moist and telescopic; instead they are caught in the dog's coat and are drying out to resemble grains of rice. Closer inspection may also identify some flea dirt (arrowed).

Tapeworms generally do not cause a significant clinical problem to the definitive host. They live within the dog's gastro-intestinal tract and may cause some irritation around the anus, associated with the presence of the proglottids. Each tapeworm species requires the involvement of a specific intermediate host to complete its life cycle and clinical signs are associated with these infections.

There are three families of tapeworm

commonly found parasitizing the domestic dog: *Taenia* species, *Dipylidium* and *Echinococcus* species.

Taenia species

These are acquired by the dog following the ingestion of infected raw or undercooked meat. Species of note include *Taenia serialis* and *Taenia pisiformis*, which have rabbits as their intermediate hosts, and *Taenia ovis*, *Taenia hydatigena* and *Taenia multiceps*, which use sheep as their intermediate hosts.

Dipylidium caninum

These tapeworms are carried and spread by fleas, as well as by lice. These ectoparasites become infected when their larval stages ingest *Dipylidium* eggs or segments in the environment. The parasite then develops within the flea and infects the dog following ingestion of the flea during grooming.

Echinococcus species

These tapeworms are tiny, measuring as little as 3–7mm. There are two main species of note: *Echinococcus granulosus* and *Echinococcus multilocularis*.

Echinococcus granulosus subspecies *granulosus* cycles between dogs and sheep, whereas the *equinus* subspecies cycles between dogs and horses. In the intermediate hosts this tapeworm produces hydatid cysts that are infectious to the dog if eaten. These tapeworms are particularly prevalent in parts of south Wales and western Scotland, where dogs have historically had access to sheep carcases.

Echinococcus multilocularis is fortunately not present in the UK, although it is prevalent in continental Europe, where it is present in the fox, dog and cat populations. The cysts formed in intermediate hosts are particularly invasive, can be difficult to treat and may even be life-threatening. Requirements to treat dogs and cats for tapeworms when entering the UK from the continent are designed to preserve the UK's disease-free status with regard to this particular zoonosis.

Having dealt with the helminths, we can say a few quick words about protozoal parasites in the dog. Protozoa are a diverse group of single-cellular organisms, many equipped with motile flagella that can be used to provide movement. Many protozoa are parasitic and have been responsible for a number of the most important diseases to affect mankind, including, of course, malaria. Malaria is an example of a protozoan disease living in the blood. There are a number of other such diseases, including Babesia, the cause of Babesiosis. Some protozoal parasites live within the digestive tract and include *giardia*, *coccidia* and *cryptosporidia*.

Ectoparasites

Ectoparasites are of particular interest and importance to the dog groomer because they live on the skin and/or within the hair coat. Many of these parasites cause visible and significant damage to the skin and hair, the very organ that you are working to keep clean and healthy. Certain ectoparasites can also represent a health risk to the groomer, as well as to other dogs. The groomer can expect to be confronted with these parasites on a regular basis and needs to be able to recognize the signs of a parasitic skin problem. Early recognition of a problem and prompt referral to a veterinary surgeon can lead to early diagnosis and elimination of a problem.

Ectoparasites are organisms that live on the skin, or outgrowths of the skin, of a host species for various periods of time. Their parasitic relationship with the host animal can be damaging, especially if the parasite is present in large numbers. The damage relates to the feeding habits of the parasite and the host resources that are used in the process. There is considerable variation and diversity amongst ectoparasites. Some are species-specific, others are less fussy. Lice, for example, have evolved species preferences, whereas ticks are more opportunistic. Some parasites spend most of their time on the host, others leave the host once they have finished feeding.

A wide range of different external parasites have been found living on dogs. These are generally all invertebrates, with most falling within the phylum *Arthropoda*, which groups together insects along with arachnids and crustaceae. In order to preserve this distinction, the insect parasites of the dog are presented here first, followed by the arachnid parasites.

Insect parasites

The insect parasites of the dog include fleas, flies and lice. Insects are characterized by the presence of a chitinous exoskeleton, a three-part body (head, thorax and abdomen) and the possession of three pairs of legs, compound eyes and antennae.

Fleas

Fleas are wingless insects possessing specially developed mouth parts that allow them to pierce the skin of their host and suck its blood (*see* Fig. 4.1.8). Their legs are long and their last pair of legs is particularly well developed, allowing them to jump as high as 18cm and as far as 33cm! This is very impressive for an insect that only measures between 1.5 and 3.3mm long! Their tough exoskeletons provide them with considerable protection and they can be surprisingly difficult to squash. This isn't helped by the fact that their bodies are laterally compressed (flattened on the sides), an adaptation that allows them to move easily through the hair coat.

Fig. 4.1.8 Flea dirt is easy to spot in a white coat. A flea can produce 0.77mg of flea poo per day! A spiral of poo is produced from the flea's anus within ten minutes of feeding. The faeces passed by the female flea vary in shape (spherules and coils are both produced). The latter are particularly rich in protein (11 per cent) and are thought to provide the larvae with nourishment during their development.

Fleas demonstrate a four-stage life cycle, consisting of egg, larva, pupa and adult. The adult female flea is only able to lay eggs after a blood meal. After

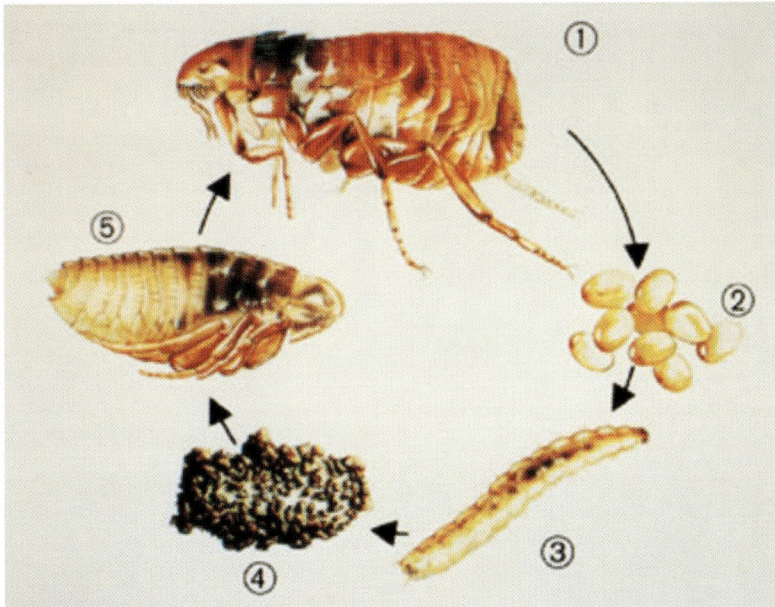

The life cycle of the Flea (Photo: Bayer Animal Health)

1   The adult 'fed' flea – The adult flea becomes a 'fed' flea after its first meal on the host. After feeding, the female adult flea lays about forty to fifty eggs daily on her host. The flea's lifespan varies but can be as long as four to six weeks. During this time between 300 and 800 eggs may be laid. Adult fleas account for only approximately 1 per cent of the total flea population.

2   Eggs – Eggs and flea dirt are non-sticky and fall from the host into the environment. The eggs measure 0.5mm long and incubate best in high humidity environments. In the grooming salon, bathing rooms and drying cages are likely to provide an ideal environment. Eggs hatch within one-and-a-half to six days.

3   Larvae – At any given time, as much as 75 per cent of the flea population is in the larval stage. When the eggs hatch into larvae, there is plenty of food available to them in the form of flea dirt. The larvae then proceed to have three moults: 1st, 2nd and 3rd stage instars. This takes between six and sixty-three days. The 3rd stage instar larvae are capable of spinning a cocoon and pupating. Larvae are often killed off by an assortment of environmental factors and it is possible that as few as 8 per cent make it to pupation. If the environment is suitable, it can take as little as six to nine days from larval stage to pupal stage. Once secure inside their cocoon, they are nearly indestructible but die in temperatures exceeding 95 degrees C. The sticky cocoon easily attaches itself to fibres, such as carpets and curtains, for safety and can often be found in shaded parts of the environment out of direct sunlight.

4   Pupae – The pupae can remain dormant within the safety of the cocoon for as long as a year or more. Development into the adult flea can take as little as seven to ten days and is stimulated by the detection of vibrations within the environment. This is what stimulates the appearance of fleas when a family returns from a holiday to their empty home or move into an empty house. Inside the cocoon, the pupa is able to detect noise vibrations and it waits patiently until a host is detected, whereupon it develops into an 'unfed' flea and emerges from the cocoon.

5   Unfed fleas – Once hatched and 'on board' the host, the 'unfed' flea eagerly feeds and becomes a 'fed' flea, ready to reproduce and continue the cycle afresh. The complete lifecycle of the flea lasts for some thirty to seventy-five days, depending on the prevailing environmental conditions.

on dogs is, surprisingly, the cat flea (*Ctenocephalides felis*). This diminutive insect is probably the most significant ectoparasite in dogs and cats across the world and is responsible for a number of diseases.

Ctenocephalides felis (*C. felis*) has benefited enormously from the domestication of the dog and the cat (*see* Fig. 4.1.10). In bringing these two companion animals into our living spaces we have also provided the cat flea with a perfect environment for year-round breeding. In the wild state, the cold winter months would have killed off a large proportion of flea eggs and larvae in the environment, but these can now happily overwinter in the modern, centrally heated home.

Adult cat fleas locate their hosts by visual and thermal cues. The modified

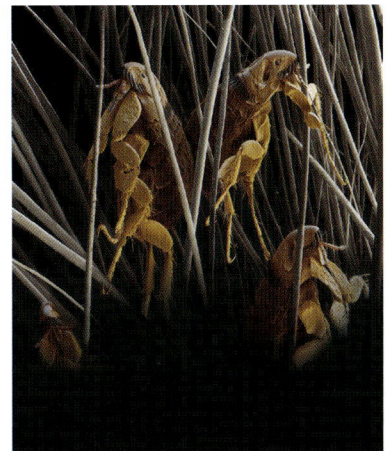

Fig. 4.1.10   The cat flea has benefited enormously from the domestication of the dog and cat. It produces a large number of eggs and larvae in our homes that happily overwinter in a centrally heated environment. (Courtesy of Bayer Animal Healthcare)

feeding, she lays her eggs on the host; these, once dry, can fall from the hair coat and will therefore contaminate the resting, sheltering and living areas of the host. Approximately 60 per cent of eggs drop from the hair coat within two hours of being laid (Rust & Dryden, 1997). Some species of flea only stay on their host long enough to feed, whilst others spend their entire lives on the host.

The most common flea found compound eye of the flea is able to recognize the movement of an object across a background of light and the flea jumps towards a moving shadow. Once on the host, the flea initiates feeding; mating will then usually occur within eight to twenty-four hours and egg laying within twenty-four to thirty-two hours.

When host grooming is restricted, female fleas can lay as many as forty or fifty eggs per day. Up to 85 per cent of females remain on the host for fifty days, and many will stay on for more than a hundred days, although egg production declines at this point. A single adult flea can produce some 1,500 eggs during its first month on the host!

Egg hatching is very much dependent on environmental conditions, in particular the temperature and relative humidity. It has been shown that at 16–27 degrees C some 70 per cent of eggs will hatch when the relative humidity is greater than 50 per cent. This is why moist warm environments are perfect for flea development. The time required for eggs to hatch can be as little as one and a half days at 33 degrees C, dropping to six days at 13 degrees C. From this, it should be apparent that a flea infestation can develop exponentially in a very short space of time. Practically speaking, you can have a flea infestation on your premises within a matter of weeks: with one flea laying fifty eggs within thirty-six hours of entering your grooming salon, and 70 per cent (i.e. thirty-five) of these hatching within two days given the right conditions!

The larvae that hatch from these eggs feed on the protein-rich faeces passed by the adult fleas; where no faeces are available, larvae can demonstrate cannibalism and eat other larvae. Larvae do not generally move more than 15cm from where they hatched, although they tend to migrate away from light and gravitate downwards. In the home environment they therefore typically move to the base of carpets and under floorboards, where they pupate and eventually emerge as adult fleas. The full cycle from egg to adult flea can take as little as fifteen days to complete, but can also take much longer depending on the environmental conditions.

The adult flea, feeding on the dog, can cause intense irritation. This is partly because they introduce saliva into the skin, which contains a number of proteins that can be intensely allergenic. An antibody response is directed at these proteins, resulting in an allergic reaction. Many dogs and cats can thus develop a hypersensitivity to flea antigens, commonly known as flea allergic dermatitis (FAD) (*see* Fig. 4.1.11).

Whilst the cat flea is the most common flea found parasitizing dogs, a number of other species can also be found on dogs, including the dog flea

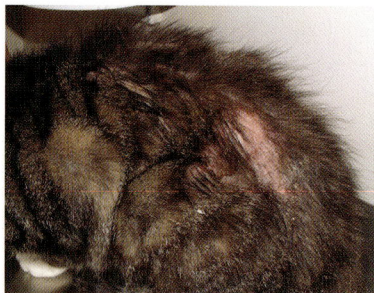

Fig. 4.1.11   Flea allergic dermatitis in a cat. A similar allergic dermatitis may be seen in dogs. Note the hair loss and scaling. The coat is wet in places from over-grooming. This allergic condition arises when an animal reacts to proteins within the flea's saliva. It is intensely itchy (pruritic) and causes excessive grooming (sometimes to the point of extensive self-trauma).

(*Ctenocephalides canis*), as well as a number of rabbit and rodent fleas. In the New World the mammalian (or 'false human') flea, *Pulex simulans*, also parasitizes dogs. These fleas require fairly specialist knowledge and equipment to tell apart. Significantly though, the presence of fleas is demonstrated, quite simply, by identifying flea dirt within the coat. This is far more reliable than searching for fleas as the adult flea that has produced the faeces may well have been and gone, particularly if the dog has been grooming itself vigorously. The identification of flea dirt is discussed further under identification, prevention and treatment of flea infestations (*below*).

Lice

Lice infestations on cats and dogs are relatively rare, and most commonly associated with an unhygienic living environment or sickness and debilitation (*see* Fig. 4.1.12). Sick and debilitated animals may struggle, or be either disinclined or unable, to groom themselves. Host grooming (self-grooming by the host animal) is an important cause of mortality for both lice and fleas, therefore any reduction in a dog's grooming allows these parasites to build up within the hair coat. It is therefore possible that you may find yourself presented with a dog that appears to the owner to be in need of a groom. If you detect lice within the dog's hair

coat, you should suspect an underlying problem and advise the owner to seek veterinary advice.

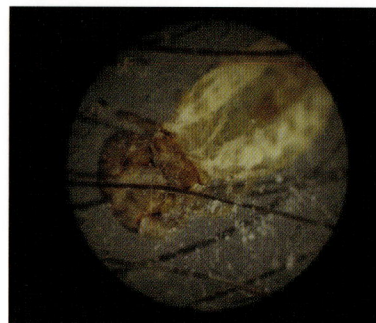

Fig. 4.1.12   A louse taken from a working spaniel that lives out and is bedded down on straw. An underlying health problem and/or poor husbandry and living conditions should be suspected.

Lice can be divided into those that chew or bite and those that suck. Lice are generally very host-specific and some are even site-specific, preferring a particular part of the body. Two chewing (biting) lice and one sucking louse have been reported on dogs. The common chewing louse, *Trichodectes canis*, is found worldwide, whereas *Heterodoxus spiniger* is found only as a parasite of dogs in Australia, where it is thought to have evolved from a marsupial louse that switched to feeding off dingos. The dog sucking louse is called *Linognathus setosus*. It is relatively uncommon and is found primarily on the head, neck and shoulder areas, as well as under the collar, in long-haired breeds.

Chewing lice possess mouth parts that allow them to scrape and chew at the skin and hair. Chewing at the skin can cause significant irritation, and the secretions produced by the skin are then ingested by the louse. Sucking lice, by contrast, possess mouth parts that can penetrate the skin, allowing the louse to feed off blood. Thus sucking lice can transmit certain diseases. Perhaps the best known example of this was the transmission of trench fever and louse-borne typhus amongst First World War soldiers by the human body louse (*Pediculus h. humanus*). Fortunately, no significant diseases are transmitted by the sucking lice of dogs. *Trichodectes canis*, however, has been incriminated in the transmission of the *Dipylidium* tapeworm.

Flies

The reader may be surprised to see flies included here as an ectoparasite of dogs. It is hoped that means you have never seen maggots on a dog (*see* Fig. 4.1.13). Nevertheless, the larvae of flies and the adults themselves can be a significant parasite problem in dogs.

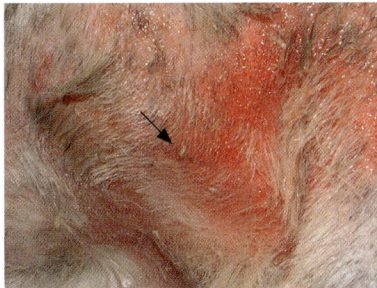

Fig. 4.1.13   *This thirteen-year-old arthritic rough collie was targeted by greenbottles (*Lucilia sericata*). The eggs hatched into maggots, which proceeded to attack the skin around the rump and tail area with their digestive enzymes, causing extensive enzymatic burns. Fortunately, they had not eaten their way through the skin.*

Flies are insects of the order *Diptera*, which literally means 'two-winged'. It is a large order, grouping together mosquitoes, midges and many others. Their significance to the health and welfare of both man and animal alike should not be underestimated, for members of this order are responsible for the transmission of many infectious diseases, including malaria, yellow fever, Leishmaniasis and dengue fever. In the UK, at present, flies are only really responsible for the mechanical transmission of bacterial diseases such as *E. coli*. You should bear this in mind next time you sit down for a coffee break and see a fly wander back in from the kennel room and land on your coffee mug. You can probably guess where his feet have been recently!

Flies can also transmit diseases from one animal to another. These infectious diseases are typically picked up by a blood-sucking fly, such as a mosquito, and subsequently passed on to another animal when the fly feeds again. Fortunately, few if any such diseases occur in the UK. The situation in other countries is different, however. British dogs visiting the continent, and especially the Mediterranean basin, may be attacked by the sand fly (*Phlebotomus papatasi*), which transmits Leishmaniasis.

Flies demonstrate similar life cycles to the flea. Where the larvae of fleas simply eat flea poo and each other, the larvae of some flies are able to attack living flesh. Fly larvae are commonly called maggots. Those of the greenbottle (*Lucilia sericata*) and a small number of other species can literally attack living flesh, digesting it with powerful enzymes. This condition is called fly strike and is occasionally seen in dogs, especially if they soil themselves or are otherwise unable to keep themselves clean. The ammonia smell released from a coat soiled with urine or faeces attracts female flies to lay eggs; these can rapidly hatch and moult into increasingly aggressive and voracious larvae. As a groomer, this is something you need to be able to recognize as maggot infestations can inflict considerable tissue damage and, in rabbits, are the cause of a particularly severe disease that is often fatal.

Your responsibility as a groomer is to clean the coat and eliminate any contamination that may prove attractive to flies. You should also alert owners to the possibility that their pet may develop fly strike and encourage them to seek veterinary advice. This is especially important if coat soiling is not a one-off and is likely to recur. A few words of advice from the groomer can spare rabbits considerable suffering, as this species can succumb to fly strike within a matter of days (*see* Fig. 4.1.14).

In the dog, fly strike is likely to be seen in small, heavily coated breeds like the Pekingese that are prone to soiling themselves and dirtying their long dense coats. It may also be seen in breeds with heavy hair growth around the rectal area, such as Rough Collies and long-coated German Shepherd Dogs. The law restricting the docking of tails means that some very heavily coated breeds, like the Old English Sheepdog, may be more prone to fly strike if they are kept in full coat.

Arachnid (spider-like) parasites

These include mites and ticks (see next section). Mites are generally much smaller than ticks and will often be

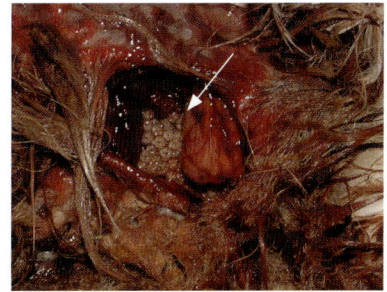

Fig. 4.1.14   *Severe fly strike in a rabbit. Sadly these mature maggots had invaded through the skin and into the underlying tissues. The rabbit was literally being eaten alive and had to be euthanased. The pocket (arrowed) can be seen to be packed full of third-stage maggots. You may be asked to groom long-haired rabbits or a rabbit with a 'sticky bum' (poo stuck to its bottom) or soiled fur. Such rabbits are very vulnerable to fly strike. This can also happen to long-haired dogs such as Pekingese and Old English Sheepdogs, and is a serious welfare issue that you must make the owners aware of.*

invisible to the naked eye, requiring a microscope to visualize and identify them. Adult mites and ticks possess four pairs of legs and are therefore typical arachnids; their larvae, however, possess only three pairs.

The mites commonly found as parasites on dogs can be divided into two groups: surface mites and burrowing mites. Surface mites live on the skin and cause a localized irritation. Three species will be discussed here: *Otodectes cynotis*, *Cheyletiella yasguri* and *Neotrombicula autumnalis*. Burrowing mites live within the skin of the dog and include *Sarcoptes scabiei* and *Demodex canis*.

Otodectes cynotis

This parasite is associated with ear disease in a number of mammalian species, including cats, dogs and ferrets. It is a large and highly active white mite that can just about be seen by the naked eye crawling around within the ear of an infected animal (*see* Fig. 4.1.15). The mechanical irritation caused by these mites is thought to provoke increased secretions from the ceruminal glands, resulting in a build-up of waxy debris within the ear canal. Affected animals will often demonstrate considerable discomfort and may scratch their ears persistently. In extreme cases hearing may be impaired. The entire life cycle of this mite takes place within the ear and adult mites can only survive off the host for between ten and twenty days.

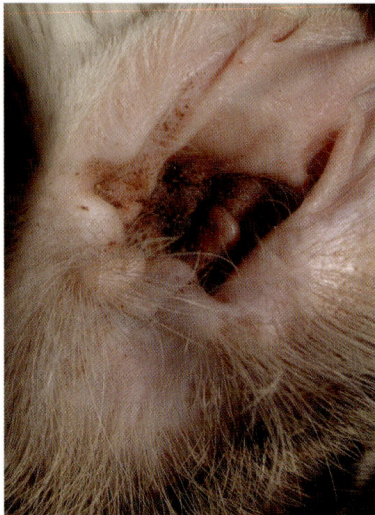

Fig. 4.1.15   Heavy ear mite infestation in a cat's ear. The mite involved is a surface mite called Otodectes cynotis. The female mite is larger than the male and can measure 0.5 × 0.3mm. The mite is white in colour and can often be seen moving. A thick dark build-up of waxy debris usually accompanies this condition, which is often referred to as 'Otodectic mange'.

Otodectes cynotis is highly contagious and can spread through a group or colony very quickly. Young puppies and kittens can pick up ear mites from their mothers and other animals with which they have close contact. Mechanical transmission via equipment (e.g. forceps) introduced into the ear of an infected animal is also possible.

Treatment using either a mineral or plant oil (e.g. olive oil), together with a licensed preparation prescribed by a veterinary surgeon, should aim to eliminate all mites in order to minimize the risk of reinfestation. Treatment for a minimum of twenty-one days is therefore advised. Concurrent use of a 'spot on' preparation licensed for the treatment of this parasite will ensure that any mites that have migrated onto the hair coat are also eliminated.

Cheyletiella yasguri

This is the name given to the Cheyletiella mite found in dogs. These sur-

face-feeding mites are responsible for a scurfy condition popularly known as 'walking dandruff'. The adult mite is some 0.385mm long and just about visible to the naked eye. The entire life cycle takes place on the host and lasts twenty-one days. In most cases this condition arises in individuals that are not grooming themselves. It results in skin irritation, scratching, a high turnover of skin cells and a build-up of dandruff in the coat. The mite can also be passed onto humans, where it can cause skin irritations and lesions.

Neotrombicula autumnalis

This mite is commonly known as the harvest mite, aoutat, chigger or berry bug. It is unusual in that most of its life cycle takes place away from the host. In fact, it is only the larval stages that are parasitic to mammals. The remainder of the life cycle is completed in the environment with the nymphal and adult stages feeding on insect and vegetable matter.

The larvae feed for between two and ten days, using their mouth parts to inject lytic enzymes into the upper layers of the skin and to ingest the digested cells. This causes an intense itchy reaction in affected animals (and, indeed, people) that can lead to self-trauma. This condition is often called 'autumnal erythema' and, as the popular name of the mite suggests, it is associated with harvest time, typically occurring during the summer months. Dogs, cats and rabbits become infected if living in or visiting suitable habitats.

In dogs the mites may typically be found between the toes or around the face, but can also appear in the armpits and groin. They are visible as bright orangey-red specks.

Sarcoptes scabiei

This burrowing mite causes sarcoptic mange. It is a highly contagious, potentially zoonotic, mite that is found worldwide. Different subspecies occur in different mammals. That found in the dog is described as *sarcoptes scabiei var. canis*, that in the fox *sarcoptes scabiei var. vulpes*. These two variants are readily transmitted between dogs and foxes (*see* Fig. 4.1.16).

The mite lives within burrows exca-

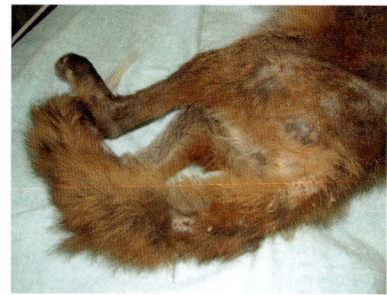

Fig. 4.1.16   Sarcoptic mange in a fox. This parasitic condition is popularly known as 'fox mange' and can be passed on to dogs that come into contact with objects in the garden, or when out walking, that the intensely itchy fox has rubbed itself against. [Note: this photograph was not taken in a grooming salon.]

vated in the skin. These burrows can be a centimetre or more in length but never extend beyond the stratum corneum. Female mites lay eggs within these burrows. The eggs hatch and undergo a sequence of moults, maturing into adults over the space of ten to thirteen days. This sarcoptic mite has four stages to its life cycle: egg, larva, nymph and adult. The larvae that emerge from the eggs find their way onto the skin and create new burrows for themselves in which they moult. These burrows are called moulting pouches.

The adult female mite measures between 0.3mm and 0.45mm in length. Males are smaller and will actively burrow into the mating pouch of the female to mate with her. Following mating, the female emerges onto the skin and then digs herself a deep serpentine burrow in which she will spend the remaining month or two of her life laying eggs.

Transmission is thought to occur primarily by the transmission of impregnated females, although larvae and nymphs that may also be found on the skin surface are likely to be involved. The likelihood of transmission is probably increased by itchy dogs rubbing up against objects and depositing females in the environment. Direct and indirect transmission is therefore to be expected.

The intensely pruritic reaction seen in many dogs and foxes, as well as in other affected mammals, is thought to be due to a hypersensitive reaction to mite antigens and, in particular, to the faeces passed by the mite. An acute infection results in raised erythematous lesions, papules, seborrhoea and hair loss. These signs may be masked by the hair coat and overlooked, although there is every chance that they may be noticed during the grooming process. In chronic cases the infestation causes more widespread skin lesions: typically hyperkeratosis, crusting and scaling, skin thickening and extensive areas of hair loss may be seen.

Demodex canis

This is the only other burrowing mite to be found in dogs. The demodex mites are follicle mites, so called because they reside within the close confines of the hair follicle and its associated glands.

Demodex mites are extremely small and elongated. It is likely that most dogs carry small numbers of this mite at some point in their lives and remain completely free of any associated signs. In some dogs, however, the mite takes hold and the infestation becomes established and may even become generalized. This may occur for a number of reasons, including immunosuppression, malnutrition and stress.

This condition can appear in juvenile and adult dogs. In juveniles it is associated with certain breeds, including Boxers, Bull Mastiffs, German Shepherd Dogs, Beagles, Dalmatians and Dobermanns, although any breed can be affected. The juvenile onset condition is thought to have a strong familial link. By contrast, the adult onset condition is more likely to be associated with some sort of suppression of the immune system.

Clinical signs of this condition are associated with secondary bacterial infections of the affected hair follicles. Signs therefore include papules, pustules and furunculosis (boils). The feet, face, ears, back, elbows and hocks may all be affected. The condition can be hard to diagnose and may require multiple and repeated samples to be taken in order to demonstrate the presence of the mites.

The *demodex canis* mite is not thought to be a significant zoonotic threat.

Ticks

Ticks are the other arachnid parasites occurring as ectoparasites on dogs. Ticks are bigger than mites and are very apparent to the groomer if present on the dog. You are likely to see them regularly on dogs in the grooming room and should be aware of their significance and the various problems they can cause.

Ticks do not have wings and cannot jump. They travel on their host or by crawling up plants or along the ground. They possess special hooks on their legs that allow them to attach to passing animals when they brush up against vegetation. Ticks have eight legs, although the larval stage has only six. Ticks vary in colour but are typically reddish, brown, grey or black, depending on the species. The size of the tick also varies with the species, age and sex of the tick. The biggest factor influencing size, however, is feeding. The ticks you are most likely to see are those that have taken in a blood meal and become engorged (*see* Fig. 4.1.17). An unfed female tick can measure 3mm in diameter but can increase in size to 11mm when engorged!

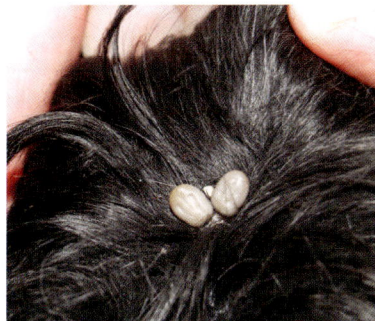

Fig. 4.1.17   Engorged ticks. These ticks have fed and are full of a blood meal.

Ticks can be divided into two families: hard ticks (*Ixodidae*) and soft ticks (*Argasidae*). Hard ticks are so called because they possess a tough dorsal scutum or shield behind the head. This covers the entire dorsal surface of the male tick but only a third of the female's. Most of the commonly reported ticks found on dogs are soft ticks and will be described here.

The tick life cycle has four stages: egg, larva, nymph and adult. The larva that hatches from the egg possesses only three pairs of legs. It needs to feed before it can moult and therefore goes searching for a host (*see* Fig. 4.1.18). Once fed, it moults into a nymph, which again must feed before it can moult into the adult. Female ticks mate, have an enormous blood meal, lay thousands of eggs and then die. In most cases the tick (whether it be larva, nymph or adult) falls off the host after feeding. The next blood meal will therefore usually be on a different host; ticks therefore generally have three-host life cycles.

Ticks are blood-sucking external

Fig. 4.1.18   Wandering ticks may be found within the hair coat if they have yet to start feeding. This is a larval tick as it has three pairs of legs rather than four.

parasites of vertebrate animals (mammals, birds and reptiles) and are very well suited to the transmission of a wide range of nasty diseases. Larval ticks can become infected with a disease either through feeding off an infected host or because their mother passed on the disease through her ovaries. Ticks are thus able to pass on an incredibly wide range of bacterial, viral and protozoal diseases; these include Lyme disease (otherwise known as Lyme borreliosis), Ehrlichiosis and the blood parasite babesia. The good news is that ticks take as long as two days to firmly fix their mouthparts into a host and start feeding (*see* Fig. 4.1.19). Early removal of ticks, before they have had a chance to introduce material from their salivary glands, is therefore strongly recommended. In the case of Lyme disease, it has been demonstrated experimentally that Ixodid ticks must be attached for more than two days in order to transmit the disease.

When removing ticks, it is essential that the mouth parts are not left behind as these can be contaminated with bacteria and provoke a foreign body reaction. The body of the tick must not be squeezed either, since this can introduce material from within the tick into the host. Tick removal is described in Chapter 18.

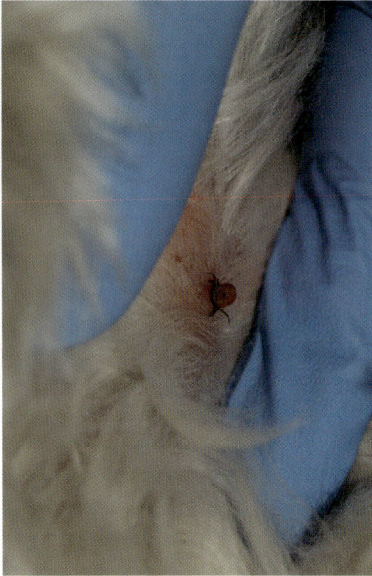

Fig. 4.1.19 *Small firm lumps detected on the skin surface may be ticks. The hair should be parted or wetted down to allow the lump to be examined. Close examination will reveal the presence of legs that may be moving if it is a tick.*

Ixodes ricinus is the scientific name given to the sheep tick. It is also variously known as the deer tick, wood tick and castor bean tick, and is the commonest tick in northern Europe. It has been identified as an important vector of Lyme disease. It has a three-host life cycle, which typically takes two to three years to complete, although under harsh conditions it can take as long as six years. The larvae tend to feed on small insectivores, such as hedgehogs and rodents, as well as rabbits, birds and other animals. The nymphs tend to feed on larger mammals, including deer, sheep, dogs and man! Peak activity is seen between the months of March to June and August to November. Its preferred habitat includes woodlands, heaths, forests and scrubland.

Ixodes hexagonus is popularly known as the hedgehog tick, but it is often found on other large mammals, including cats, dogs, foxes and badgers.

Ixodes canisuga is popularly known as the dog tick or fox tick. It is found across the UK and tolerates dry conditions, which may explain why it can be found in kennels.

Dermacentor reticulatus is known as the ornate cow tick or marsh tick. It is a grassland and pasture tick that is also found in woodlands. It is prevalent in south-west England and Wales and

is found on many different wild and domestic mammals, including dogs and cats.

Rhipicephalus sanguineus is also known as the brown dog tick or kennel tick. It too is often found in kennels and other sheltered spaces. It is prevalent in southern England and commonly found on dogs, foxes and cats.

It should be noted that this list is far from exhaustive and that species distributions evolve over time and can be expected to change with global warming.

Before finishing with ectoparasites, we need to mention one last group: fungal parasites. These are not members of the Animal Kingdom but instead are fungi.

Fungal parasites

Fungal parasites causing disease, or 'mycoses', on dogs can be described according to the site of infection.

Superficial mycoses grow on the surface of the body or on the hair shaft. They do not invade living tissue and usually provoke no clinical signs. An example of a superficial mycoses is the yeast *Malassezia*. *Malassezia globosa* is associated with the formation of dandruff in man. The fungus requires fat to grow, which is why it is most commonly found in areas with many sebaceous glands, such as the face and scalp. When the fungus grows too rapidly, it produces a lipid breakdown product called oleic acid; this penetrates the stratum corneum, provoking an inflammatory response that results in erratic cleavage (random breaking up) of the skin cells, dandruff formation and itchiness of the scalp.

In dogs the main *Malassezia* species implicated in skin problems is *Malassezia pachydermatitis*. This yeast is an opportunistic pathogen that can secondarily infect skin. It is likely to take advantage of situations in which there is excessive sebum production, moisture build-up and disruption of the skin's normal defences. Proliferation of this yeast can induce both inflammation and pruritus (itching). *Malassezia pachydermatitis* has also been shown to trigger a hypersensitivity reaction. Atopic dogs can react excessively to yeast proteins resulting in a *Malassezia* dermatitis.

Cutaneous mycoses group together a number of fungi found in the outermost layers of dead skin. Although these organisms do not invade living tissue, they produce a number of enzymes and metabolites that provoke a localized inflammatory response, typically seen as a reddening within the skin. These fungal organisms are collectively known as dermatophytes and give rise to a condition called dermatophytosis or, more commonly, 'ringworm' (*see* Figs 4.1.20 and 4.1.21). Cutaneous mycoses are caused by *Microsporum*, *Trichophyton* and *Epider-*

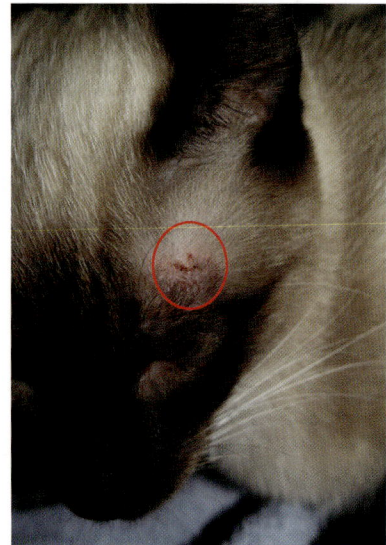

Fig. 4.1.20 *A ringworm lesion above the eye of a Siamese-cross cat. Note the scaling, crusting and associated hair loss. The lesion spreads outwards from a central point and often, but not necessarily, forms a perfect circle. It is difficult to see these lesions in a long-coated dog and they may not become apparent until the coat is completely separated during the course of the grooming process.*

Fig. 4.1.21 *Typical ringworm lesions on the ear of a young guinea pig. Note the hair loss, scaling and crusting. In the home environment ringworm can readily spread to other animals, children and people.*

mophyton fungi. Athlete's foot in man is caused by a *Trichophyton* fungus.

Ringworm infections in dogs are commonly caused by *Microsporum canis* or *Trichophyton mentagrophytes*, although a number of other fungal species, including *Microsporum persicolor* and *Microsporum gypseum*, can be involved. Ringworm is most commonly seen in young dogs (under a year old) but may also be seen in older immuno-compromised dogs. Many individuals will show no signs of infection. The hair follicle is typically affected and this gives rise to circular lesions ('rings') as the infection spreads outwards from the infected area. These lesions are characterized by hair loss and scaling may be seen. They are often not itchy. Diagnosis is usually confirmed by the testing of samples taken during a veterinary dermatological examination.

Ringworm transmission usually occurs through direct contact with infected animals or mechanically, through contact with infected equipment. Infected hairs or scale deposited on work surfaces, or on grooming equipment, are often implicated. Other sources can include animal bedding or other items from within the infected animal's environment. Some animals may act as asymptomatic carriers, giving no sign that they are contaminated. It should be apparent from this that strict hygiene in the grooming room is essential if you are to avoid transmitting this infection to other animals – including your own!

Subcutaneous and *systemic mycoses* are invasive fungal organisms that can penetrate into the deeper layers of skin and, in the case of systemic mycoses, may invade the rest of the body. These may be encountered in certain parts of the world, such as the southern United

Table 5 Significance of canine endoparasites.

Parasite		Significance
Nematodes		
	Toxocara canis	Heavy infestations may be seen in puppies and can cause vomiting, poor growth, a dull coat, intestinal blockages and intussusceptions. Zoonotic infections possible with the risk of worm migration in the body (visceral larvae migrans).
	Toxascaris leonina	Vomiting and a pot-belly may be seen in puppies, although less often associated with clinical signs.
	Uncinaria stenocephala	Chronic infections can result in anaemia and protein loss.
	Trichuris vulpis	Heavy infestations can result in bloody diarrhoea.
	Oslerus osleri	Lungworm that can cause coughing in dogs and lead to pneumonia.
	Angiostrongylus vasorum	Parasitic roundworm that lives in the pulmonary artery and can cause coughing, poor exercise tolerance and clotting disorders.
Tapeworms		
	Dipylidium caninum	Transmitted by the cat flea and the dog louse (*Trichodectes canis*).
	Taenia serialis	Can cause disease in the intermediate host (rabbit) and result in the condemnation of meat.
	Taenia multiceps	Can cause disease in sheep grazing on pastures contaminated by infected dog faeces. Can also result in the condemnation of meat.
	Echinococcus granulosus	Ingested by livestock on contaminated pasture. Results in hydatid cysts in the intermediate host. Can result in a disease of the central nervous system (called gid) if the cyst presses on the brain.
	Echinococcus multilocularis	Produces highly invasive cysts in intermediate host (including man) that can be very difficult to treat. Controlled by the Pet Passport Scheme. A serious zoonotic disease.
Protozoa		
	Babesia canis	Red blood cell parasite that can cause considerable blood loss leading to anaemia.
	Giardia lamblia	Causes intestinal damage and diarrhoea.

Table 6   Significance of canine ectoparasites.

Parasite		Significance
Insect		
Flea	*Ctenocephalides felis*	
Lice	*Trichodectes canis*	
Lice	*Linognathus setosus*	
Flies	*Lucilia sericata*	The larvae of the 'greenbottle' can attack tissues and cause fly strike, especially in rabbits.
Flies	*Phlebotomus papatasi*	The sand fly is the vector of the Leishmania parasite responsible for Leishmaniasis.
Arachnids		
Mites	*Otodectes cynotis*	Ear mite causes otodectic mange, a severe ear irritation in cats and dogs.
Mites	*Cheyletiella yasguri*	A surface mite that causes skin irritation and 'walking' dandruff in dogs. Can bite humans.
Mites	*Neotrombicula autumnalis*	A seasonal, intensely itchy, condition caused by the larval stage of this mite. Humans and other animals may also be affected.
Mites	*Sarcoptes scabiei*	A burrowing mite that causes sarcoptic mange. Highly contagious between dogs and foxes. Causes intense pruritus and can be very debilitating. Potentially zoonotic.
Mites	*Demodex canis*	A follicle mite living within the skin that can give rise to folliculitis and deeper skin infections in some dogs if secondarily infected.
Ticks	*Ixodes ricinus*	Sheep or deer tick. Very common and can transmit a number of diseases, including Lyme borreliosis.
Ticks	*Ixodes canisuga*	Dog tick. May often be found in kennels. May also transmit diseases.
Fungi		
	Malassezia pachydermatitis	Superficial skin infections and malassezia dermatitis in atopic dogs.
	Microsporum canis	One of a number of dermatophytes causing ringworm. Contagious and potentially zoonotic.
	Trichophyton mentagrophytes	Another cause of ringworm. Contagious and potentially zoonotic.

States, but are rarely seen in northern Europe.

4.2 TREATMENT AND PREVENTION OF PARASITES

You now have an understanding of the various endoparasites and ectoparasites commonly encountered in dogs. Many of these are contagious, many can cause significant disease, and quite a number are zoonotic and can therefore be transmitted to humans.

Transmission of these diseases requires the host to ingest or come into contact with infectious material. In the case of endoparasites, these are usually acquired following the ingestion of eggs or infected tissues containing encysted parasites. In the case of ectoparasites the host must usually come into physical contact with another infected animal or pick up the infection from some part of the environment that has, itself, been contaminated by an infected animal.

This section will draw on the preceding descriptions of these parasites to highlight the practical implications for the groomer. In particular, the groomer should be able to:

◆ protect themselves and their staff from zoonotic parasites;
◆ keep their premises free from parasites;
◆ keep their equipment free from parasites; and
◆ identify parasitized animals.

Each of these aspects will now be discussed in more detail.

Protecting yourself and your staff

You should remain alert to the risk of acquiring a zoonotic infection when working with dogs and cats. Whilst the subject of zoonotic disease will be discussed in more depth in Chapter 5, it is appropriate here to draw the reader's attention to certain important zoonotic parasites.

Toxocara canis

◆ Toxocara eggs need to be ingested for you to become infected with Toxocara canis. Whilst the main risk is from faecal material, you should also be aware that toxocara eggs are often found in the hair coat. In untreated dogs, cats and foxes, the amount of eggs in the perianal fur can be of the order of one to four eggs per gramme of hair.

◆ Always practise high standards of hygiene to ensure that this risk is minimized. Ideally, this means not eating and drinking in the grooming room.

◆ Food should be stored, prepared and eaten in a dedicated clean area (e.g. a staff room or office).

◆ Regular hand washing and disinfection should be practised. This is essential before eating and drinking, and hand washing facilities should be available for this purpose.

◆ Additionally, you should clean as you go along and not allow hair to build up. Ideally, this means depositing hair directly into a bin so that it is less likely to drift around in the air and enter your mouth.

◆ Extra care should be taken around dogs that are likely to be shedding eggs. Pregnant bitches, young puppies and stray dogs should all be viewed as potential risks. It may be appropriate to wear gloves when handling such animals and, at the very least, hands should be washed thoroughly after work.

◆ It is good practice to check a dog's worming history on admission, at the same time as you check their vaccination history.

Ectoparasitic zoonoses including sarcoptic mange and ringworm

◆ Signs of skin disease consistent with such diseases should be identified on admission or, failing that, as part of the pre-grooming check. This then allows you the time to return the dog to the owner, so they can have the problem evaluated by a vet. In particular you should look for signs of itching, hair loss, broken skin and scaling. Where such problems are identified, the dog should not be accepted for grooming and the owner encouraged to seek veterinary advice.

◆ If you, or a member of your staff, has broken skin you may be vulnerable to skin infections, including ringworm. You are encouraged to ensure that your skin condition is managed appropriately and the skin's defences fully restored. Whilst it is compromised, you should consider wearing gloves and protecting any areas of broken skin with dressings and creams if appropriate.

◆ If you or a member of your staff develops a skin lesion, you should seek medical advice. If you have knowingly come into contact with a mite-infested, flea-infested or ringworm-affected animal, you should share this knowledge with your doctor.

Protecting your premises

◆ The animals you work with can deposit infectious material(s) within your premises. You need to be aware of the various ways in which this can happen and how you can address this problem.

◆ Nematode eggs can contaminate the floors, kennelling areas and exercise areas. Where the surfaces are easily cleaned and disinfected, this is not too much of a problem. Grassy areas, by contrast, can be harder to clean and decontaminate. If using a grassy area, you could insist on a policy of only allowing dogs that have been wormed within the last three months to access the area. All faeces should be collected and disposed off promptly. Grass should be mown during the summer in order to allow the sun's

rays (heat and UV) to eliminate as many eggs as possible.

◆ Flea eggs and larvae are likely to be introduced into your premises on an ongoing basis. Again, you should insist that dogs and cats have been treated for parasites before attending your salon. This emphasizes to the owner how seriously and responsibly you take the prevention of such problems.

◆ The floor surfaces in your premises should be solid, easily cleaned and disinfected. This will make it harder for flea eggs and larvae to hide away in the depths of a rug, or under rubber matting or floorboards.

◆ All hair should be swept up and disposed of regularly through the day. Bins and vacuum cleaners should be regularly emptied and treated for parasites.

◆ A flea collar can be placed inside your vacuum cleaner to ensure that adult fleas and larvae entering the cleaner are killed.

◆ You should also ensure that you treat your premises once yearly with a product that is licensed to eliminate flea eggs as well as larvae and adult fleas. Many products on the market do not deal with eggs. You should therefore check that the product you are using contains an insect growth regulator, such as pyriproxyfen or methoprene. These essentially prevent eggs and larvae from maturing into adult fleas. As such, they ensure that eggs deposited in the environment cannot develop into fleas, thereby reinfesting both the premises and visiting animals. Regular treatments with an adult insecticide can also be used at the end of each day; the frequency will depend on the longevity of the ingredients used. Such treatments will not eliminate eggs, however, and you will be relying on the regular use of an adult insecticide to kill any larvae or adult fleas as they develop from the egg.

◆ If you are kennelling dogs within your salon until they can be groomed and then collected by their owners, you should have a cleaning regimen that ensures that each kennel is thoroughly cleaned between uses. A suitable veterinary disinfectant should always be used. In choosing a product, you should always check what it has been tested and approved for. In particular you want to establish to what extent it is bactericidal, virucidal, fungicidal and sporicidal (see Chapter 5). Cleaning should always be conducted before disinfection, especially if there is a significant amount of material to be removed. Disinfection of a surface is always more efficient if that surface is clean.

Protecting your equipment

◆ All grooming equipment should be cleaned and disinfected between animals. The cleaning process should ensure that all gross (obvious) contamination is removed and the equipment can then be disinfected in order to eliminate fungal spores, parasite eggs and bacteria. Alternatively, a succession of kits (one per dog) can be used and these then all cleaned at a convenient time during the day.

Identifying infected animals

As part of your admission procedure, you should ask owners if their dog (cat or rabbit) has any of the following: skin lesions (sores, scabs, etc.), scaling, hair loss, itchiness or other skin-related problems.

Where a problem is identified, the animal should not be admitted and the owner should be encouraged to seek veterinary advice. It is helpful if you follow up on the animal to establish what was found by the vet and when it would be safe for the animal to be booked back in for grooming. This allows you to learn from the experience, demonstrates your concern and professionalism, and provides you with a chance to book the animal back in. This can appear pedantic to some owners, in the same way that insistence on a kennel cough vaccine by boarding kennels can be seen as 'over the top' by owners who fail to understand the importance of such measures. The frustration and cost of checking and dealing with a problem is always preferable to dealing with an outbreak of mange or ringworm and the damage such an outbreak can do to your reputation!

If the owner has not signalled a skin problem, you should then double check that there are no signs of unhealthy skin. This should form part of your pre-grooming health check. Where skin lesions, itchiness, scaling or other skin problems are identified, you should isolate the animal in a kennel and contact the owners to discuss your findings. The decision to proceed with the grooming process should not be taken lightly. If you are convinced that it is justified and you can do so safely (if, for example, you have no other animals in that day or you are visiting the animal at home), you should minimize

> ### CAUTION: AVOID CONTAMINATION OF YOUR PREMISES AND EQUIPMENT WHENEVER POSSIBLE
>
> *Animals with skin lesions should not be admitted for grooming and their owners should be advised to see a vet.*
>
> *Implement a strict cleaning regimen in your salon. Kennels, tables (including frames) and equipment should be cleaned between dogs.*
>
> *Practise good hand hygiene: wash your hands regularly throughout the day and always before eating and drinking.*
>
> *Remember that Toxocara canis eggs can be found in the hair coat. Clean up as you go, depositing all hair into a suitable bin.*
>
> *Treat your premises once a year with a flea product containing an insect growth regulator. This will ensure that eggs cannot develop into larvae and adult fleas.*

contamination as far as possible and ensure that your working area and all equipment are cleaned and disinfected.

Further reading

Case, L.P. (2005). *The dog, its behaviour, nutrition and health*. Oxford, UK: Blackwell Publishing, pp. 301–34.
Lane, D.R. and Cooper, B. (2003). *Veterinary nursing*. 3rd edition. London, UK: Butterworth Heinemann, pp. 375–400.

References

Cousquer, G.O. (2006). Veterinary Care of a Giant Lop Rabbit with Severe Fly Strike. *World Wide Wounds*, February 2006. Available from: www.world-widewounds.com
Cousquer, G.O. (2006). Veterinary Care of Rabbits with Fly Strike. *In Practice*, 28, 342–9.
Fisher, M. (2001). Endoparasites in the dog and cat. 1. Helminths. *In Practice*, 23, 462–71.
Fisher, M. (2002). Endoparasites in the dog and cat. 2. Protozoa. *In Practice*, 24, 146–53.
Mullen, G.R. and Durden, L.A. (2009). *Medical and veterinary entomology*. 2nd edition. Burlington, USA: Academic Press.
Roddie, G., Stafford, P., Holland, C. and Wolfe, A. (2008). Contamination of dog hair with eggs of Toxocara canis. *Veterinary Parasitology*, 152, 82–93.
Rust, M.K. and Dryden, M.W. (1997). The biology, ecology and management of the cat flea. *Annual Review of Entomology*, 42, 451–73.

Useful websites

The British Small Animal Veterinary Association (BSAVA) website provides a policy statement and advice sheet on worming:
www.bsava.com/Advice/PolicyStatements/AnthelminticsinDogs/tabid/167/Default.aspx

The Feline Advisory Board (FAB) website provides excellent information sheets, including one on flea control in the cat and another on ringworm:
www.fabcats.org/owners/fleas/info.html

The Rabbit Welfare Association website provides excellent leaflets on a wide range of rabbit health issues. The leaflet on fly strike is particularly useful.
www.rabbitwelfare.co.uk/resources/index.php?section=leaflets.html

The Canine Vector Borne Disease (CVBD) website is an excellent resource on diseases transmitted by various vectors such as ticks, fleas and sand flies:
www.cvbd.org/3041.0.html

5 Infectious and Zoonotic Diseases of the Dog

This chapter provides a broad overview of the various disease threats that the dog and dog groomer may encounter and how the risks associated with these diseases can best be managed. It is a very important chapter because it will help you to appreciate how important disease control is to protect you, your staff and the dogs that you are working with.

In contemplating how we can best understand and relate to the immune system and its role in keeping us safe from disease (which is a complicated enough subject at the best of times!), it may be helpful to imagine yourself as a general (you), leading an army (your immune system) to defend your country (your body) against attack. The general needs to understand the threats he faces so that he can organize and maintain his army in a state of preparedness. Thus when an enemy attacks, his army is fully prepared to repel the invaders.

In the same way, you need to understand how we and our immune systems can maintain a state of preparedness to protect ourselves from the threat of disease and illness. The focus throughout this chapter is on disease threats to the dog and the dog groomer.

To start with, a description of the mammalian immune system is presented and developed. This system constitutes our main defensive line against a wide range of organisms that have the ability to attack and damage our bodies in some way. This subject is quite involved and the reader may prefer to jump straight to the section on infectious diseases before coming back to the subject of how the immune system is able to protect us.

5.1 THE IMMUNE SYSTEM

The immune system consists of the body's 'armed forces', a network of defensive cells and other key components that provide protection against invasion. It must monitor all the borders and remain alert, watchful and primed to act, if it is to identify and effectively repel any threat. It is therefore present throughout the body and interacts with all the other body systems. As such, it provides a series of lines of defence against attack. The defence system and the weaponry it has at its disposal are highly developed, for they have evolved over time to keep us safe. The organization of these defences will be described below. The use of such weaponry is not without disadvantages, however, and there are many disease processes of the immune system that arise from the inappropriate deployment and use of the body's 'armed forces'. These immunological diseases are the equivalent of what we might think of as 'civilian casualties': killed or injured by friendly fire. Allergic reactions to pollen or flea saliva, together with immune attacks on the body's own tissues, are all examples of immune-mediated disease.

The immune system has two types of 'army': the innate and the adaptive immune systems. In the same way that a country has sea and land defences, so the body has innate and adaptive immunity. Sticking with the military analogy, these two immune systems can be viewed as a first line of defence (innate immunity) guarding the coast, backed up by a supporting second line of defence (adaptive immunity) patrolling the interior, which collects information, monitors the situation and deploys targeted responses where needed.

Innate immunity is charged with policing the mucocutaneous surfaces of the body, including the skin, the gastro-intestinal tract, the urogenital tract and the upper airways. These each represent a barrier or 'border' that a disease must cross if it wishes to enter the body. These borders therefore have their own 'border guards'.

The innate immune system possesses a number of important defences:

◆ the structure of the barriers themselves;
◆ the movement and behaviour of the barriers;
◆ the secretions coating the barriers;
◆ the natural microflora living on the barriers; and
◆ the cellular components of the barrier's defensive team.

The building blocks of the skin, oral and respiratory mucosa represent a physical barrier that is able to keep many substances and organisms safely outside the body. The skin, as discussed in Chapter 2.10, is a highly specialized and resistant multilayered keratinized shield. The mucosal tissues that line the airways, urogenital and digestive tract are, by contrast, not keratinized, and in many cases are only a single cell thick. They are therefore reliant on other defence systems (including movement, behaviour and secretions) to protect them. The peristaltic movement of the digestive tract is one such mechanism. In many cases the development of vomiting and diarrhoea magnifies these movements in order to eliminate potentially dangerous food material rapidly from the body. The surfaces of these barriers experience a regular turnover of cells that further protects them, representing a means of eliminating materials on the surface and 'changing the guard', thereby refreshing the defences.

These barrier surfaces possess a number of glandular structures that produce a wide range of products and chemicals that further contribute to the defensive wall. Mucus secretion within the urogenital and gastro-intestinal tracts and airways provides a sticky layer that can trap organisms such as bacteria and prevent them from reaching the mucosa. The fine, hair-like extensions of the mucosa of the trachea (windpipe) waft continuously and move the mucosa up the trachea to the back of the throat where it can either be swallowed or spat out. This is an example of a movement working together with a secretion to protect a mucosal surface. The secretions produced by the body and deployed on various barrier surfaces are highly complex. They include the sebum produced by the sebaceous glands of the skin, as well as tears and saliva. They have been shown to contain a wide range of enzymes and other proteins that can attack bacteria, viruses and other potential pathogens. These include lysozymes, proteases, iron sequestering (capturing) proteins and antimicrobial peptides.

The naturally occurring flora (microbes) within the digestive tract, as well as on the skin and other surfaces, provides powerful competitive exclusion to potential pathogens. These 'good bacteria' will usually overwhelm any pathogens ('bad bacteria') but can become impaired following a course of antibiotics or a period of stress. It is for this reason that fungal infections, such as thrush (a candida overgrowth), can take hold following a course of antibiotics.

The cellular components of the innate immune response include phagocytic cells that can gobble up potential pathogens. These are generally white blood cells and include neutrophils, mast cells, macrophages and a type of lymphocyte called the natural killer (NK) cell. These contribute to the inflammatory response to a disease threat. If you think back to the last time you had a cut, a scratch or a splinter, the inflammatory response around the wound was characterized by swelling, heat and redness, with the area becoming painful to the touch. This all arises following an outburst of frantic messages that produce a series of emergency responses. The blood vessels are instructed to allow certain white blood cells to enter the tissues and very quickly the attack point is brimming with reinforcements and equipment (otherwise known as white blood cells, accompanied by inflammatory proteins and other chemicals). It is this reaction that causes your injury to swell up, become red and throb!

These various components of the innate immune response work together to protect the body and mount an effective first line of defence. Their importance has frequently been overlooked, with research attention being focused on the high-tech advanced defensive weaponry of the *adaptive immune response*. This tendency to underestimate innate immunity has now been reversed and it is recognized as a key player in the body's defences.

Adaptive immunity is that part of the immune response that is activated by the innate immune system via an antigen presenting cell (APC). These are specialist cells that are able to communicate effectively with a special group of white blood cells responsible for the adaptive immune response. In military terms, the APCs are front-line soldiers (or agents) who collect, process and present information, communicating this information to a special command centre. The antigen presenting cell that has gobbled up (phagocytosed) a bacterium can digest it with enzymes, chopping it up into smaller pieces that it then displays on its cell surface. These small pieces can bind antibodies and are called antigens. Consequently this cell is known as an antigen presenting cell. These cells travel to draining lymph nodes (the command centre), where they interact with cells of the adaptive immune response. The lymphocytes within the lymph node and elsewhere within the body express an enormous range of receptor specificities enabling them to recognize any antigen that may be presented.

Stimulation of the adaptive immune response in this way leads to a number of different responses amongst the lymphocyte cells within the draining lymph nodes. Some of these responses lead to the production of antibodies, others to a variety of cell-mediated responses. These mechanisms are incredibly complicated and will not be discussed further here other than to emphasize how sophisticated the mammalian immune system has become.

In summary, the innate and adaptive immune responses provide the mammal with a number of different lines of defence against disease threats. The two responses are distinctly different but can work closely together. Whereas in evolutionary terms the innate system is an older, more primitive system, the adaptive immune system represents a highly evolved defence mechanism that allows the immune system to recognize and remember specific pathogens and produce a protective immune response to them. In particular, it allows the body to mount increasingly stronger attacks against the pathogen each time it is encountered. In this sense it is truly adaptive because it allows the body to prepare itself for future threats. This is, in many ways, the basis of immunity.

> ### NOTE
>
> *Innate immunity is often described as* **non-specific immunity** *because it can be directed at a wide range of threats. Adaptive immunity, by contrast, recognizes and homes in on individual threats and is therefore often described as* **specific immunity.**

5.2 INFECTIOUS DISEASE

Now that you have a better understanding of the defensive measures the immune system can call upon, we must switch our attention to the enemy. We now need to address the following three questions:

1. What threats do we have to protect ourselves against?

2. What are their preferred strategies of attack?
3. What can we do to prepare ourselves for an eventual attack?

In answering these three questions, we need to consider the many different types of infectious disease (threats) affecting dogs and man, the routes and mechanisms of transmission (attack strategies) and how we can prepare ourselves so that we are not taken by surprise.

This subject requires us to introduce a certain amount of vocabulary. The following definitions may be helpful.

Definitions

An *infectious disease* is one that can spread from one animal to another and results in clinical signs of illness in the affected animal. These signs reflect an abnormality of structure or function and will differ depending on the disease pathology (the damage caused to the tissues affected by the disease). Infectious diseases are also described as contagious or *transmissible*. Some infectious diseases of the dog can be transmitted to humans; these are termed *zoonoses*.

An *infectious agent* is an entity that is able to invade our bodies, make us ill and therefore provoke an infectious disease. Such agents are also called pathogens and they come in many different shapes and sizes. Some are single cell organisms, others are multi-cellular. There are also infectious agents that lack the complexity of a cell and are much simpler in structure.

A *microbe* is a microscopic organism. Single-cell organisms, for example, can only be seen using imaging techniques such as the light microscope. Some microbes are 'friendly' and do not usually cause disease; others tend to cause disease and are therefore termed pathogenic microbes.

An *infection* is a condition in which a pathogen has invaded the host and overwhelmed the host's defences. An infection can be localized, as in the case of an abscess, or generalized, in which case it has spread through the body.

Transmission of these various infectious agents takes place by means of one or a number of *transmission routes*. It is these routes that allow pathogenic microbes to leave an infected individual and be passed to a healthy individual. Infectious organisms can be found in a wide range of bodily excretions, tissues and products. Table 7 provides examples of common transmission routes.

Transmission can be either *direct* or *indirect*. Direct transmission involves animal to animal, animal to human or human to human contact, while in indirect transmission the contact is mediated by a third object that could be an object or surface (e.g. grooming tools,

tables, towels, blankets, water bowls or contaminated food and water).

Infectious diseases

Infectious diseases are caused by infectious agents. In many cases these agents are microscopic and it is for this reason that the cause of many such diseases eluded scientists and doctors for so long. Researchers had to develop special techniques, technologies and theories in order to discover and study these 'invisible' diseases. It is precisely because these diseases are so hard to see that we can underestimate them. A detailed understanding of disease processes allows us to take sensible precautions in seeking to prevent disease in ourselves and in our animals.

Multi-cellular pathogens and single-cell pathogens are relatively easy to see and could be demonstrated using the light microscope. The sarcoptic mite, for example, is an arachnid parasite and very much a multi-cellular organism. It is best demonstrated by taking skin scrapings and examining these microscopically. Other multi-cellular pathogens include *Toxocara canis* and *Otodectes cynotis* (*see* Parasites section). These are macroscopic multi-cellular organisms that can cause infectious disease under certain conditions and are easily seen with the eye, although they too are best identified under the microscope.

Single-celled pathogens tend to be either yeasts, bacteria or protozoa. Some of the common single-cell pathogens causing disease in man and

Table 7   Transmission routes and examples of diseases that are passed via these routes.

Means of transmission	Example(s)
Urine	Leptospirosis
Blood	HIV
Saliva	Rabies
Skin debris/skin contact	Sarcoptic mange
Aerosol – sneeze	Common cold and influenza (flu).
Aerosol – urine droplets	Leptospirosis
Faeces	E. coli, Giardia and Toxoplasmosis
Food (meat)	Tapeworm and Toxoplasmosis
Semen	Canine Brucellosis
Pus	Tuberculosis

dog are listed in Table 8. Viruses, by contrast, are not single-celled. They are much simpler structures, smaller in size, invisible under the light microscope and best demonstrated using electron microscopy. They can only replicate (multiply) by hijacking the cellular mechanisms of a living cell. Some of the common viral diseases of man and dog are listed in Table 9. In addition to the viral diseases, there is another type of pathogenic material that has not been mentioned: these are the prion proteins, which are thought to cause transmissible spongiform encephalopathies (e.g. BSE).

Bacteria

Bacteria are single-celled organisms that have no nucleus and are generally large enough to be seen under the light microscope. They are classified in their own kingdom. Their size and shape vary considerably and are used to help classify bacteria. Most bacteria are either spherical (*cocci*) or rod-shaped (*bacilli*). Large numbers of bacteria exist within the gut and on the skin. Most of these are readily dealt with by the body and some are even helpful, producing B vitamins in the gut and undertaking a range of other functions. Some of these bacteria can take advantage of tissue damage and give rise to an infection. These are opportunists and the infection is described as an opportunist infection. Others are pathogenic and cause disease if contracted; they include the bacteria that cause diseases such as anthrax, cholera and bubonic plague in man and leptospirosis in dogs.

Fungi

Fungi are distinct from the plant and animal kingdoms, although fungi used to be classified as plants because they are generally immobile and share similarities in terms of their shape, structure and habitat. There are a number of key differences, however. Perhaps most significantly, fungi have to externally digest their food source before absorbing it. Unlike plants, fungi do not possess chloroplasts and cannot therefore undertake photosynthesis. Additionally, the cell wall of a fungus contains chitin, whereas that of a plant contains cellulose.

The fungi kingdom contains a diverse collection of organisms ranging from mushrooms and moulds to single-celled yeasts. Many fungi are parasites on plants and animals, and in many cases they can give rise to disease. Humans and animals suffering with an immunodeficiency are particularly vulnerable to infections such as aspergillosis, which can be fatal if untreated. Many other fungi grow on the hair, nails and skin, where they can cause localized infections such as ringworm and athlete's foot.

Reproduction of fungi can be either sexual or asexual. In both cases spores are produced and these are released to allow the fungus to spread.

Viruses

Viruses are tiny infectious agents that can only replicate inside the cells of

Table 8   Important bacterial and protozoal diseases of man and dog. These are all single-celled organisms.

Group	Organism	Disease	Species affected
Bacterium			
	Clostridium tetanii	Tetanus	Man (and horse); dogs are rarely affected
	Clostridium perfringens		Can cause food poisoning in man and dogs
	Clostridium difficile		Can cause diarrhoea in man and dogs
	Leptospira	Leptospirosis	Causes a range of conditions in man, dogs and other animals
	Bordetella Bronchiseptica	Bordetellosis/Kennel Cough	Causes tracheobronchitis in dogs but rarely affects man
	Bordetella pertussis	Whooping Cough	Causes tracheobronchitis in man
	Mycobacterium tuberculosis	Tuberculosis	A chronic disease that attacks the lungs in man
	Borrelia burgdorferi	Lyme Disease	Tick-borne disease that can affect both man and dogs
	Staphylococcus aureus	MRSA	Methicillin-resistant staphylococcus aureus is a bacterium that lives on the skin and nostrils of humans, dogs and cats and can cause a range of infections
	Staphylococcus intermedius	Pyoderma	This staphylococcal bacterium lives on the skin of the dog and can cause secondary skin infections
Protozoa			
	Toxoplasma gondii	Toxoplasmosis	Man and dogs
	Giardia lamblia	Giardiasis	Man and dogs
	Leishmania donovani	Leishmaniasis	Man and dogs
	Babesia canis	Babesiosis	Dogs
	Plasmodium falciparum	Malaria	Man

Table 9   Common viral diseases.

Viral Disease		Species affected
Virus	Common Disease Name(s)	
Lyssavirus	Rabies	Man and Dogs
Parvovirus	Canine Parvovirus	Dogs
Coronavirus	Canine Coronavirus	Dogs
Morbilliviruses	Canine Distemper Measles	Dogs Man
Adenovirus	Infectious Canine Hepatitis	Dogs
Herpesvirus	Canine Herpesvirus Chickenpox Herpes Simplex	Dogs Man Cause of cold sores in Man
Orthomyxoviruses	Canine Influenza Human Influenza (flu)	Man and Dogs
Rhinoviruses and Coronaviruses	Common Cold	Man
Paramyxovirus	Mumps	Man

other organisms. They are able to 'hijack' these cells and use the internal organs of the cell to replicate and produce more virus.

Each viral particle is composed of two or three parts: the genetic material (encoded on molecules of either DNA or RNA), a protein coat that protects this genetic material, and in some cases a protective coat of lipids. This lipid envelope is derived from the host cell membrane and may contain viral proteins that allow the virus to bind to other cells and thereby allow the virus to infect the target cell. The viral particle is not therefore a cell, but something much simpler that can parasitize animal and human cells.

In many cases the cycle of viral infection and replication causes minimal damage to the host. Where there is extensive cell (and therefore tissue) damage, however, a viral infection can cause disease.

Protozoa

Protozoa are nucleated single-celled organisms that are usually motile. As such, they are members of the animal kingdom. They are just about visible to the naked eye: the largest protozoa can measure as much as 1mm but most are between 10 and 52μm (0.01 to 0.052mm). The proliferating form is known as a trophozoite; this can encyst, resulting in the formation of cysts that

can survive both in the environment and within tissues. The ingestion of cysts, either from the environment or following the ingestion of infected meat containing cysts, can lead to infection.

Examples of diseases caused by protozoa include toxoplasmosis, giardiasis, amoebiasis and malaria.

Infectious Diseases of Dogs

There are a number of important infectious diseases in dogs. Their importance stems from the fact that they are highly contagious (and therefore spread easily) and can cause severe, if not fatal, disease.

Dogs in the UK and Europe are likely to be vaccinated against canine distemper, leptospirosis, canine hepatitis, canine parvovirus and canine parainfluenza. Vaccination will be discussed further towards the end of this chapter. Vaccination is also possible against three other infectious diseases: kennel cough, rabies and babesiosis. Each of these diseases will now be discussed further:

Canine Distemper

This is a highly infectious viral disease of dogs that can cause mild symptoms in some individuals whilst proving fatal in others. It is caused by a large virus related to the morbillivirus that causes measles in man. It is spread by the inha-

lation of aerosol droplets during close dog to dog contact. The virus does not survive easily in the environment and can be killed by most household disinfectants.

The interval between infection and the disease appearing (the incubation period) varies between three days and three weeks. During this time the virus travels first to the lymphoid tissue of the upper and lower airways and then on to other lymphoid organs. Nervous, lymphoid and epithelial tissues are also targeted and during periods of active viral replication dogs can demonstrate a high temperature.

Clinical signs of distemper are various and include:

◆ *Fever*
◆ *Loss of appetite*
◆ *Discharge from the nose and eyes*
◆ *Coughing*
◆ *Laboured breathing*
◆ *Diarrhoea and vomiting*
◆ *Lack of coordination*
◆ *Tremors and seizures*
◆ *Hardening of the nose and footpads ('hard pad')*

Where there has been severe damage to the respiratory tissues, secondary infections such as pneumonia are common.

Distemper is, fortunately, now only seen in areas where there are significant numbers of unvaccinated dogs. Dogs less than one year of age are most commonly affected, although unvaccinated and immune-compromised dogs are also at risk.

Canine Parvovirus (CPV)

This is another highly infectious viral disease of dogs that is still relatively common in unvaccinated dogs. It is a small but extremely hardy virus that can survive for long periods (months or even years) in the environment. This is significant because it means that an infected dog can not only infect other dogs directly, but also contaminate its environment, leading to indirect transmission days, weeks or months after the infected dog has gone. Shoes, clothing and a range of other items and surfaces can carry the disease. Any affected dog should be refused entry to your salon and should be referred to a vet for treatment, where it can be placed in isolation and barrier nursed.

Canine parvovirus is resistant to many disinfectants and it is essential that products used to disinfect veterinary surgeries, dog kennels and grooming parlours be independently tested and approved for the control of this disease (see Chapter 7). The most effective disinfectants against CPV are based on halogen compounds (chlorine and iodine), aldehydes and sodium hydroxide. Bleach and formaldehyde-based chemicals are therefore to be recommended. It should be noted, however, that the presence of animal protein interferes with the activity of the two most commonly used disinfectants and it is therefore recommended that all surfaces be cleaned before disinfection.

There are several different types of Canine Parvovirus. CPV-2 causes the most severe disease and this can present in two forms: an intestinal disease and a cardiac disease. The cardiac form is less common and is usually acquired by foetuses before birth or during the first eight weeks of life. Vaccination of breeding bitches has resulted in this form of the disease becoming increasingly rare. The intestinal form is acquired following the ingestion of viral particles, either from contaminated surfaces, soil or faeces. Incubation is usually between four and seven days and the virus replicates in the lymphoid tissue of the throat before spreading through the body via the bloodstream. It attacks dividing cells in the lymph nodes, bone marrow and intestinal tract. This attack results in the destruction of white blood cells in the lymph nodes and of certain dividing cells in the intestines. The damage to the intestinal tract can be very severe and can allow bacteria within the gut to enter the bloodstream. Such secondary bacterial infections are often life-threatening.

The disease is worse where concurrent infections and parasitism are present. It is also thought to be particularly severe in certain breeds of dog, including Rottweilers and other black and tan coloured dogs.

CLINICAL SIGNS OF CANINE PARVOVIRUS

The intestinal form of CPV infection is characterized by:

- *Severe lethargy*
- *Vomiting*
- *Fever (up to 41 degrees C)*
- *Bloody diarrhoea (see Fig. 7.1.6a)*
- *Dehydration*
- *Shock*
- *Collapse and death*

Canine viral hepatitis

This is a viral disease that causes an acute liver infection in dogs and other canids. It can affect the liver, kidneys, eyes and lungs of the dog. It is transmitted by direct contact with infected urine, saliva and faeces. It usually enters the body via the oral and nasal passages and then multiplies in the tonsils before spreading via the lymphatic system and bloodstream to the liver and kidneys. Replicated viral particles are shed from the kidneys into the urine and also appear in the faeces.

This viral hepatitis is caused by a canine adenovirus (CAV1) that is relatively hardy and can survive for months in the environment. It can therefore survive on bedding, feeding bowls and other contaminated surfaces. Furthermore, infected animals can continue shedding the virus for several months after recovery.

Clinical signs of canine viral hepatitis include:

- *Loss of appetite*
- *Fever*
- *Conjunctivitis*
- *Coughing*
- *Abdominal pain*
- *Vomiting and diarrhoea*

Signs of liver disease, including jaundice and vomiting, may be seen. Oedema (fluid accumulation) of the cornea may be seen following infection, giving the eye a characteristic blue appearance. This may persist but usually resolves over time

---

Leptospirosis

Leptospirosis is a contagious and often fatal bacterial disease that can affect various mammals, including man and dogs. There are two common forms of this disease: *Leptospirosis icterohaemorrhagiae* and *Leptospirosis canicola*.

L. icterohaemorrhagiae is also known as Weil's disease and is transmitted by infected rats (and other rodents), which are the main carriers for this disease. Transmission to dogs arises following contact with infected urine or contaminated water. It may therefore be associated with drinking from, or swimming in, water that rats have access to. The symptoms vary in severity. In some cases they may be mild and non-specific, including lethargy and depression. In others they may be severe, in which case jaundice, liver damage and even death may result. *L. canicola* is primarily carried by dogs. This form of leptospirosis attacks the kidneys and again can vary in severity. In the severe form it can result in kidney failure and death.

Following ingestion of the bacterium, it enters the bloodstream via the mucous membranes and spreads to the liver, kidneys and spleen. The bacteria are then excreted back into the environment in the animal's urine. This can continue for some time after recovery and represents a significant threat. The bacterium is easily destroyed by sunlight, disinfectants and extremes of temperature.

> **Clinical signs of leptospirosis include:**
>
> ◆ **Fever**
> ◆ **Shivering and muscle pain**
> ◆ **Jaundice**
> ◆ **Vomiting and diarrhoea**
> ◆ **Dehydration**
> ◆ **Collapse**
> ◆ **Shock**

Parainfluenza

This is a viral disease that is incriminated in the Kennel Cough syndrome. It is highly contagious and readily shed in respiratory secretions. Whilst infection with this virus is usually self-limiting, it can cause an unpleasant tracheo-bronchitis, which has the potential to progress to bronchopneumonia.

> **Clinical signs of parainfluenza infection include:**
>
> ◆ **Sore throat**
> ◆ **Hoarseness**
> ◆ **Inappetence**
> ◆ **Weight loss**
> ◆ **Lethargy**

Bordetella bronchiseptica

This is an infectious bacterial disease affecting dogs, cats, rabbits, pigs and a number of other mammals. It is the commonest cause of kennel cough in dogs. The *Bordetella* bacterium is present in respiratory secretions from infected dogs and can readily contaminate surfaces such as kennel floors, grooming tables, weighing scales and pavements. It is a relatively hardy organism and can survive in the environment, which aids in its transmission.

Outbreaks may be seen when large numbers of unvaccinated dogs are housed together. Such outbreaks typically occur in kennels but can just as easily arise in grooming parlours and veterinary practices.

The nasal and tracheal inflammation that accompanies this condition typically lasts for up to two weeks, sometimes longer. During this time viral shedding is to be expected but this can continue for up to four months after the infection.

> **Clinical signs of Bordetella bronchiseptica *infection include:***
>
> ◆ **Coughing**
> ◆ **Sneezing**
> ◆ **Fever**
> ◆ **Nasal discharge**
> ◆ **Respiratory distress**
> ◆ **Inappetence**
> ◆ **Weight loss**

Rabies

Rabies is a particularly unpleasant viral disease of dogs that is transmitted via the saliva of an infected animal. It is caused by a lyssavirus and is a member of the rhabdovirus family that also includes European Bat Lyssavirus (EBL). Lyssaviruses are characterized by an extremely broad host spectrum, which makes them particularly dangerous. They can affect a wide range of mammals, insects and plants. In the case of rabies, the disease can infect all mammals and horses, man, cattle, dogs and cats can all therefore be affected.

Following an infected bite (or lick), the virus rapidly invades the local nerves and then ascends within the nerves to invade the central nervous system. The incubation period typically varies between nine days and over a year. During the incubation period the virus is moving from the site of initial entry to the spinal cord and brain. There is then further spread of the virus to other organs and, in particular, the salivary glands. This allows the virus to be secreted in high concentrations within the saliva.

There are usually three phases to infection. The initial preclinical phase lasts about two to three days and is characterized by local irritation at the site of injury. There may be fever, mild behavioural changes, dilation of the pupils and a slowing of eye reflexes. The second phase is the excitable phase and may be characterized by irritability, aggression, loss of coordination, disorientation, seizures, increased salivation and fear or avoidance of light. The third phase is often described as the dumb phase. It is characterized by paralysis, excessive salivation, breathing difficulties, respiratory failure and death.

The rabies virus is relatively fragile and can only survive for short periods of time within the environment. It is destroyed by most disinfectants, soap, heat and light. It is even suggested that the virus is no longer infective once the saliva it is in is allowed to dry.

> **Clinical signs of rabies:**
>
> **First stage:**
> ◆ **Possible fever**
> ◆ **Mild behaviour changes**
> ◆ **Dilation of the pupils**
> ◆ **Slow eye reflexes**
>
> **Second stage:**
> ◆ **Irritability**
> ◆ **Aggression**
> ◆ **Loss of coordination**
> ◆ **Disorientation**
> ◆ **Seizures**
> ◆ **Increased salivation**
> ◆ **Fear of light**
>
> **Third stage:**
> ◆ **Paralysis**
> ◆ **Excess salivation**
> ◆ **Breathing difficulties**
> ◆ **Respiratory failure**
> ◆ **Death**

Babesiosis

This is a protozoal parasite of the red blood cells of dogs. It is transmitted by biting ticks and is common in parts of continental Europe, where it is mainly caused by *Babesia canis canis*. It is likely to become more frequently diagnosed in the UK as large numbers of British dogs with no immunity to the condition visit France and other parts of continental Europe.

The parasite multiplies in the red blood cells and can result in the destruction of large numbers of these cells. A wide range of signs are seen, typically a pronounced anaemia that may be associated with lethargy, collapse, blood in the urine, jaundice, fever, and raised heart and respiratory rates. Other signs may include coughing, vomiting, diarrhoea and lameness. These signs are very varied and hard for the owner to interpret. Urine containing large amounts of haemoglobin can be dark yellow, brown or red. Mucous membranes can be very pale or even yellow. These signs can appear between two and thirty days after the infected tick has fed. Urgent veterinary attention should always be sought as deterioration is rapid, especially in naïve dogs that have no protective immunity.

Clinical signs of babesiosis can be many and varied and may include:

- ◆ *Anaemia*
- ◆ *Lethargy*
- ◆ *Blood in urine*
- ◆ *Jaundice*
- ◆ *Fever*
- ◆ *Raised heart and respiratory rates*
- ◆ *Vomiting and diarrhoea*
- ◆ *Coughing*
- ◆ *Lameness*
- ◆ *Collapse*

5.3 VACCINATION

All of the infectious diseases of dogs described above can be prevented through the judicious use of an appropriate vaccination programme. Effective vaccines will stimulate the production of antibodies that destroy the pathogen prior to its entry into cells, and elicit cytotoxic T-cells that can destroy host cells that the pathogen has infected. Together these responses protect against disease.

In the UK and in other countries of the developed world dogs are vaccinated against distemper, hepatitis, parvovirus, parainfluenza (DHPPi) and leptospirosis (L). It is universally recommended that puppies be vaccinated as the maternal antibodies from their mother are wearing off. This usually coincides with the second month of life. Two vaccinations are recommended at this age as maternal antibodies may still be present at eight weeks of age and may interfere with the vaccine. A second vaccination is therefore provided two to four weeks after the first.

Puppies are said to possess passive immunity in the first two months of life. This is acquired from the bitch via the colostrum (the antibody-rich milk produced in late pregnancy and fed to the new-born). A well immunized healthy bitch will be able to pass antibodies to her newborn pups in this milk. These antibodies have a limited lifespan and will be lost progressively from the pup's blood between three and twelve weeks of age. It is at this point that vaccination needs to step in and provide *active immunity*.

Active immunity can also arise following natural infection but is dependent on the animal recovering from the disease. The idea of vaccination is to stimulate antibody production and cellular immunity without the immunized individual becoming unwell. The vaccines therefore contain preparations of the disease that have been treated in some way in order to reduce their ability to cause disease. Some of these vaccines are live organisms, others are killed or inactivated, whilst a small number simply contain certain proteins from the pathogen.

Vaccination stimulates the immune system and gives rise to adaptive immunity. This is often described as *acquired active immunity*. This means that the immune system is primed to produce protective antibodies that are specific to the disease threat. These antibodies play a key role in allowing the body to respond to and fight off an infection. Reinfection with the same pathogen reactivates the mechanisms laid down during the initial exposure and allows the body to rapidly deal with and eliminate the pathogen without any signs of disease.

The body's adaptive immunity, or acquired immunity, may be short-lived or it can give rise to long-term protection. Once the infection has been cleared, some of the B-lymphocytes that were responsible for antibody production become memory B-cells. Similarly the T-lymphocyte responsible for cellular immunity is also able to persist as memory T-cells. In some cases, this protection is long-lasting, but in others it offers only a temporary safeguard. The best leptospirosis vaccines only produce short-lived protection against this disease. Annual vaccination is therefore strongly recommended. Protection against distemper, hepatitis and parvovirus is longer-lasting, and currently a number of canine vaccines are licensed for use every three years from the second annual vaccination.

Vaccination against the kennel cough complex of diseases is required by all good kennels prior to admission of any dog. The same should be viewed as best practice in grooming salons. The vaccine stimulates local antibody production within the airways and it is these antibodies that protect the dog against disease. In order to produce this antibody protection, an annual intranasal vaccine containing both *bordetella bronchiseptica* and parainfluenza is used. You should therefore be checking that this vaccine has been administered within the last twelve months to all dogs admitted to your grooming salon.

5.4 ZOONOTIC DISEASES

It is appropriate here to discuss those infectious diseases of dogs that can be transmitted to humans. This subject is discussed further under the hygiene,

---

NOTE

Vaccination is just one part of a preventative health plan: good standards of hygiene are also required and are essential if premises are to be kept free of contamination from infectious material(s).

Your cleaning regimen should be planned to minimize the risk of infection. With this in mind, you are encouraged to read the section on cleaning (Section 7.2) and to pay particular attention to the importance of disinfection protocols in protecting dogs from parvovirus, kennel cough and other infectious diseases that can persist in the environment.

Table 10 Zoonotic diseases that a groomer may encounter.

Zoonotic Disease	Significance	Transmission	Prevention	Vaccination	Diagnosis and Treatment
Bordetellosis	Respiratory infections may be seen in immuno-compromised people but are rare otherwise	◆ Respiratory secretions ◆ Inhalation of aerosolized droplets	◆ Vaccination of dogs ◆ Identify and exclude affected dogs ◆ Clean all surfaces with approved cleaning agent	Not necessary/None available	Seek medical advice and treatment if immuno-compromised and suffering from respiratory infection
Giardiasis	Diarrhoea and weight loss	◆ Faecal contamination of food and water resulting in ingestion of cysts	◆ Good kennel hygiene ◆ Hand washing ◆ Good food hygiene	Not available	Seek medical advice if suffering from diarrhoea. Faecal analysis will confirm infection
Leptospirosis	Flu-like symptoms; liver damage; kidney failure; meningitis	◆ Contact with infected urine when contaminated water comes into contact with cuts/muscous membranes or as an aerosol	◆ Annual vaccination of dogs ◆ Exclusion of rats, mice and other wildlife ◆ Protect water supply ◆ Good hand and food hygiene	Not available for humans	Seek medical advice if suffering from flu-like symptoms. Advise your doctor that leptospirosis should be included in the differential diagnosis list
Rabies	Almost invariably fatal if post exposure prophylactic treatment is not obtained	◆ Contact with infected saliva ◆ Bites from infected dogs and other animals	◆ Vaccination of dogs ◆ Identify and exclude affected dogs ◆ Avoid being bitten ◆ Protect all cuts	Country specific; vaccination advisable if working in a country where rabies has not yet been eradicated	If working in a country where rabies is a potential danger, seek immediate medical advice and treatment
Ringworm	Skin disease causing localized skin irritation; most often affects children and immuno-compromised adults	◆ Contact with an infected individual, carrier or contaminated equipment	◆ Regular disinfection of equipment and working surfaces ◆ Protect broken skin ◆ Identify and exclude affected dogs	Not necessary/none available; natural immunity will develop in most adults	Seek medical advice if you develop dry, itchy, reddened skin or other sores
Sarcoptic mange	Burrowing mite that can parasitize humans; causes an intensively itchy dermatitis	◆ Direct or indirect contact with an infected animal or human	◆ Identify and exclude affected dogs ◆ Wear protective gloves	None available	Seek medical advice if you develop a skin irritation. Deep skin scrapes are diagnostic
Toxocariasis	Larval migration can lead to tissue damage; ocular larva migrans can lead to blindness	◆ Ingestion of infective eggs from the faeces, hair coat or environment following faecal contamination	◆ Ensure all dogs are wormed regularly ◆ Good hand and food hygiene	None available	Seek medical advice to discuss a preventative worming plan
Toxoplasmosis	Acute disease can result in flu-like symptoms; infection during pregnancy can be dangerous for the foetus	◆ Ingestion of cysts in raw or undercooked meat ◆ Ingestion may also occur if hands are contaminated during gardening or when handling cat faeces	◆ Good hand and food hygiene essential	No vaccine is available but exposure before pregnancy is protective.	Seek medical advice if pregnant

health and safety section but is so important that it is also covered here. In doing so, we hope to build on, and develop, your understanding of infectious diseases.

Your overriding priority will be to ensure that zoonotic diseases are not contracted by you or your staff. With this in mind, we need to focus on the mechanisms of transmission of these pathogens so that you can institute simple measures to keep everybody safe.

Of the list of infectious diseases discussed above, how many do you think are zoonoses? Which ones are they?

It is hoped that you will have at least two diseases on your list: leptospirosis and rabies. You may also have included bordetella. It is possible that you may have jotted down one or two of the other zoonotic diseases carried by dogs and cats, including toxocara, toxoplasmosis and sarcoptic mange, as these were listed in Tables 5 and 6 and discussed elsewhere in this text.

This section focuses on leptospirosis and rabies in order to explore how a detailed understanding of their transmission can allow us to minimize any risks.

Leptospirosis

Transmission may occur via:

i) contact with infected urine;
ii) urine aerosol;
iii) water contaminated with infected urine;
iv) infected rats and other rodents;
v) infected dogs; or
vi) bites from an infected animal.

Quantifying the risk for dog groomers working with dogs in a grooming environment requires you to consider each of these transmission routes.

You are likely to come into contact with urine when cleaning out kennels and removing soiled bedding. You should therefore wear disposable gloves for this and take great care not to stir up any urine and create an aerosol which you may inhale.

Urine aerosols can also be created when urine splatters on a hard surface. Infected dairy cows urinating in the milking parlour can pass leptospirosis

to farmers in this way. You should not be exposing yourself to urine aerosols as long as you take care when cleaning kennels. By checking that all dogs visiting your parlour have been vaccinated against leptospirosis within the last year you are also reducing the chances of an affected individual entering your grooming parlour.

Clearly, if you have rats urinating in your water tank there is potential for you to drink or breathe in contaminated water. This risk may be increased if you create an aerosol when showering dogs. Water tanks should ideally be sealed to prevent rats urinating or falling into them. Sick or potentially infected dogs should not be admitted to the grooming parlour. Stray unvaccinated dogs should also be excluded until they have been health-checked by a vet and vaccinated. If bitten by a dog you should always seek medical advice. If you fall ill and consult your doctor you should explain the nature of your work so that they can consider leptospirosis and other zoonotic conditions, and do not overlook these as potential diagnoses.

By following these simple steps you reduce the chances of your being exposed to this infectious disease. Finally, by providing your doctor with information about your possible exposure to this disease, you ensure that it is diagnosed and treated early.

Rabies

Transmission may occur via either the saliva of an infected animal, or dog bites. Fortunately, the UK and much of Europe are now free of rabies and the chances of you being exposed to this disease are very small. You may, however, find yourself working in a country where it is still prevalent. In such cases you should seek medical advice about vaccinating yourself and your staff, explaining that dog bites are an occupational hazard. You should also consider adopting a policy of only grooming vaccinated dogs.

If you are bitten by a dog in an area where rabies is present, seek immediate medical advice and treatment. In many cases the dog will be placed under observation and subject to regular veterinary checks.

The steps outlined above allow you to put in place appropriate defence measures that are proportionate to the threat. Returning to the military analogy used at the start of this chapter, you can use your understanding of the enemy to work out an appropriate set of precautions that eliminate the threat or allow you to respond quickly and efficiently should it attack.

Other Zoonoses

Table 10 provides a summary of the zoonotic diseases you may encounter, their potential significance for you and the measures you can take to:

i) eliminate or minimize the chances of encountering the disease;
ii) eliminate or minimize the risk of transmission;
iii) prepare your immune system to counter the disease; and
iv) ensure early diagnosis and treatment.

References and further reading

Hirsh, D.C., Maclachlan, N.J. and Walker, R.L. (2004). *Veterinary Microbiology*. 2nd Edition. Oxford, UK: Blackwell Publishing.

McGaving, D. (2008). Inactivation of canine parvovirus by disinfectants and heat. *Journal of Small Animal Practice*, 28 (6), 523–35.

Moriello, K.A. (2003). Zoonotic skin diseases of dogs and cats. *Animal Health Research Reviews*, 4 (2), 157–68.

Schoeman, J. and Leisewitz, A. (2006). Disease risks for the travelling pet: Babesiosis. *In Practice*, 28, 384–90.

Woolfrey, B.F. and Moody, J.A. (1991). Human infections associated with Bordetella bronchiseptica. *Clinical Microbiology Reviews*, 4 (3), 243–55.

Useful Website

The following website is provided by Intervet Schering Plough and provides useful information on infectious diseases of dogs and cats and the use of vaccination in the fight against these diseases.

www.future-of-vaccination.co.uk

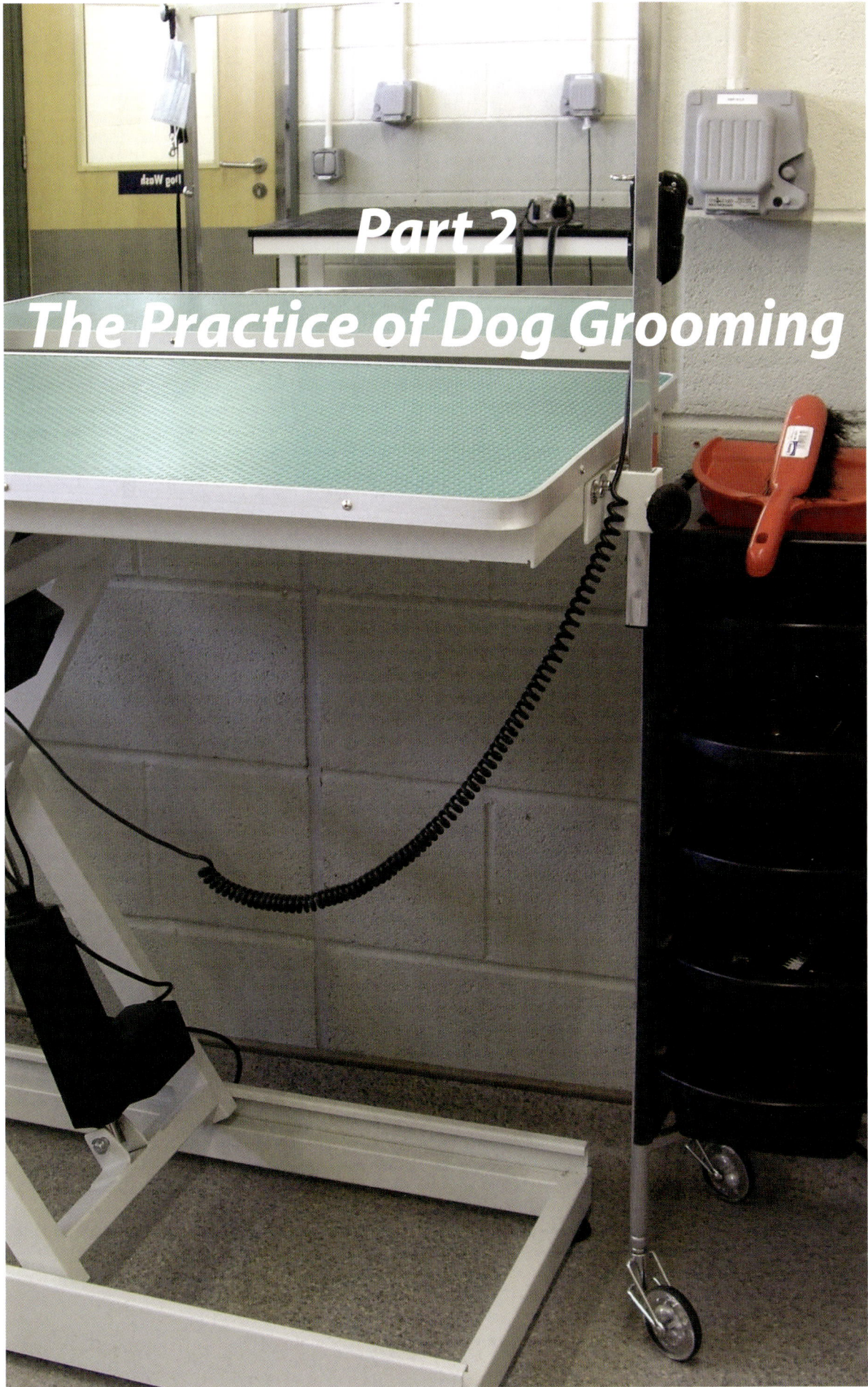

Part 2
The Practice of Dog Grooming

After studying the science that underpins and informs the work of the dog groomer, it is now time to look at the practical realities of grooming. There are many questions to consider here, including:

◆ Where are you going to do your grooming?

◆ Will you set aside a dedicated space within your own home?

◆ Or are you planning to 'set up shop' elsewhere?

◆ If you plan to open a salon and practise commercially, from purpose-designed premises, how do you do this?

◆ What are the many considerations you need to think about during the planning and design stages?

◆ How will your business function, be run and develop?

This section will help to guide you through the fundamentals of selecting and designing a suitable working environment. It will also help you investigate the legal requirements with which you must comply and advise you on how to select and purchase your tools and equipment.

The section starts with the planning and design of the working environment (Chapter 6) and then discusses the importance of salon hygiene, Health and Safety issues, risk assessment and your responsibilities to the environment (Chapter 7).

Working with animals is a medium-risk to high-risk vocation; you therefore need to be aware of your responsibilities and your limitations when required to administer first line treatment in the event of illness, accident or injury. Chapter 8 therefore provides advice on both human and animal First Aid.

Moving gradually closer to the grooming chapters, we then discuss the handling and restraint of dogs. This very practical subject is critically important to the groomer and plays an essential role in keeping you, the dog and anyone else in the grooming salon safe from harm or injury.

Finally, this section takes an in-depth look at the wide range of grooming tools and equipment available to you and how they are used. The discussion of the differing feel and handling action of each tool will enable the reader to make educated choices when selecting equipment that will suit both their needs and physical abilities.

Part 2 is designed as a section that can be read in its entirety or dipped into for specific information. It will be of particular value to those preparing for examinations or having to learn without guidance.

Please note that all information regarding Business Law is current in the United Kingdom at the time of writing. Laws differ between countries, however, and are subject to change and amendment. If grooming commercially and/or employing staff, you should periodically review the relevant legislation. This can be undertaken using the website addresses provided by the relevant authorities within your country of work, or by contacting them directly. Suitable sources are suggested within the text.

Fig. 6.0   Grooming your own dog can be immensely rewarding and the garden on a warm spring day is the ideal place to do it. Just remember that even at this time of the year the sun can be intense and the dog will get warm very quickly so give him plenty of rest breaks to drink and cool off or provide some sort of shelter to shade your table.

6 Setting up Practice and Creating your Workspace

Whether you plan to groom your pet within your own home, or to establish and build a business and groom other people's pets, an organized workspace will make the job a lot easier and more enjoyable. This chapter will help you to think about your grooming environment and help you to make judicious choices and good decisions when designing your workspace.

Your workspace must meet your personal requirements and be appropriate for the work you plan to undertake. It has to be comfortable for you to work in and it has to be able to accommodate the amount of work you want to do. Above all, it has to provide a safe environment for all concerned.

All work involving animals or the handling of animals comes with risks; this is especially true of dog grooming. Careful thought and forward planning, when setting up your working area, can help minimize the risk of injuries and enable you to organize yourself so that you can work safely and efficiently. There is more detailed information on risks and risk assessing in the Health and Safety section of Chapter 7.

Careful planning can also save you time and money: get it right first time and you will not need to expend valuable resources altering and rebuilding to accommodate a growing business. You will also minimize damage to existing facilities, the repair of which can be costly.

Most dog owners enjoy grooming their pet(s) at home and many, if not most, commercial groomers have developed their passion for grooming from similar humble beginnings. With this in mind, this chapter starts by focusing on the home groomer looking to groom their own pet(s), and then moves on to look at the setting up of a commercial salon.

6.1 GROOMING YOUR DOG AT HOME

Grooming your own dog should be a pleasure for you both. To ensure this is the case, and remains that way, you should identify a suitable area for grooming within your home environment, one that will cause as little disruption as possible to the running of the household and will be easy to clean.

If it takes you longer to clean up your home after grooming your dog than it does to actually groom him, the job will become a chore and you will soon become dissatisfied.

Make sure that your chosen area is available whenever you need it so that you can use the same space every time you groom your dog. He will soon learn to recognize it as the place where he must co-operate whilst you do what you have to do, and that way the task becomes a lot easier for both of you.

So, where are you going to groom your pet?

Your choice of grooming area will be limited by the facilities available to you.

Grooming dogs can be a messy business, particularly if they moult profuse-ly or need a lot of trimming. If possible, make use of a garage, shed or outbuilding where dog hair will be easy to clean up and will not contaminate your living area. Alternatively, in the absence of a suitable outbuilding, a utility room or conservatory could be used, as could a patio or a concreted yard, providing you can erect a portable table. In wet weather a gazebo could usefully keep you and the dog dry, whilst in the heat of the summer it could afford you both shelter and shade from the sun.

You would not be the first person, nor the last, to groom their dog in the spare room, or even the lounge, but remember that carpeted areas are a haven for fleas! Hair collects in the carpet fibres and may be difficult to vacuum clean. In time the carpet will develop a smell and may even need to be replaced. Covering the carpet with a dust sheet is one option, but ensure that it does not make the floor slippery under your feet if it moves on the carpet surface below, or trip you up should you need to move quickly.

The kitchen should be the last resort. When hair is being removed from the dog, small hair particles – particularly light, fluffy undercoat hairs – readily become airborne and will settle on surfaces such as cupboard tops, work surfaces, cooker tops and shelving, finding even the smallest grease spots to attach to. Food is easily contaminated and even closed fridges and cupboards will attract hair particles and other airborne pollutants, once the doors are opened. And remember that the use of a hair-dryer will disperse hair easily and ensure it gets everywhere!

Make use of dust sheets

For easy cleaning and safety, your

chosen workplace needs to be as clutter-free as possible. If you are working within the home, consider using dust sheets to cover surfaces and furniture; these can be affordably purchased from DIY stores. It may seem a lot of unnecessary preparation, but if you have a moulting dog, or one that needs a lot of trimming, it will be well worth the effort.

If you are working in a garage or outbuilding, it is not quite as important to use dust sheets, although over time hair will accumulate in corners and crevices and can become a haven for fleas. Plastic dust sheets can be shaken outside and material dust sheets vacuum cleaned and washed.

Something to stand the dog on

Your work area should be big enough to accommodate a grooming table, or something similar for your dog to stand on. If you are not using a height-adjustable table, make sure that your table (or workbench) is the right height for you to work at and that it is not so wide that your dog is able to move out of reach.

To prevent your dog from trying to jump off the table, you will need to find some way to restrain him, either by a tethering ring fitted to the wall, or via a removable 'holding arm' that attaches to the table (or workbench) and can be taken down when not in use.

Electricity

An electricity supply for clippers and a hair-dryer will be needed. If you are working inside your home, or in an outbuilding, a standard wall socket is perfectly safe and will supply the correct voltage for your equipment. If you are working outside, however, you will need to make sure that sockets are weatherproof and any extension leads comply with regulations for outdoor use.

Where are you going to bath your pet?

If you are lucky enough to be able to use an outbuilding, you may wish to purchase a portable bath rather than use the family bathroom. You will need

---

CAUTION WHEN MAKING USE OF HOUSEHOLD TABLES AND WORKTOPS

Try to find a work surface that allows you to stand in a natural upright position with your dog at a height where you can easily reach and groom him. The height and width of your worktop will depend on the size of your dog. Use a rubber bath-mat to provide a non-slip surface for your dog, where appropriate.

You should not:

1. *Lean forwards over a table that is so wide the dog can move to the back of the table out of your reach. This can strain your back and bring your face within reach of your dog's teeth.*
2. *Overstretch yourself upwards to reach the dog's back or head. This position will put you off balance yourself whilst working, leaving you vulnerable to falling backwards if your dog pushes towards you.*
3. *Lean over your dog on a table that is too low. This will put strain on your back because you are in a half-bent position; you will be off balance and your face vulnerable should the dog try to bite you.*

CAUTION: HANDLING AND RESTRAINING THE DOG

Read through Chapter 9 'Handling and Restraint' to make sure that you know how to secure your dog safely.

CAUTION: WATER AND ELECTRICITY

WATER AND ELECTRICITY SHOULD NEVER BE MIXED!

Remember that your dog will shake when wet and the resulting spray will be dispersed over a large area. If you are bathing in a kitchen or utility room, check that sockets are not vulnerable and consider using safety 'socket protectors' to prevent water entering any exposed pin holes.

Think twice about using an extension lead to provide you with electricity in the bathroom; it is not recommended that you dry your dog in the bathroom with an electrical appliance. If drying your dog in the bathroom really is the only option, make sure that the lead and socket are suitable for outdoor use and will therefore be better insulated against condensation.

CAUTION: DRYING YOUR DOG

Drying your dog on your own with a hand-held dryer can be difficult and frustrating, particularly when you need to use both hands to hold him and brush his coat. You may benefit from investing in an adjustable hair-dryer holder that can be attached to your table and will hold the drier for you.

Do not under any circumstances consider making an enclosed space (a cage, for instance) to dry your dog with a working hair-dryer directed at the cage and/or the dog. This is an incredibly dangerous practice that could very easily cost the life of your pet in a few moments. Your dog needs to be able to move away from the heat as soon as it becomes uncomfortable and you need to monitor the drying very closely. If a dog is prevented from moving away from heat, this can lead to burns and, in extreme cases, life-threatening injuries and heat stroke.

to sort out some form of plumbing and drainage. This arrangement will, however, save a lot of mess and cleaning (and even redecoration!) of your home, particularly if your pet is large and has to walk through the house whilst wet. The other point to consider is how wet the bathroom may become when a large dog shakes or scrambles to get out of the bath. Investing in plumbing for the garage (or a Hydrobath®) may be worth considering, although this is an expensive option!

Smaller pets can be bathed in utility room sinks, or baby baths placed inside the family bath. Shower hoses are handy for wetting and rinsing, but if you do not have one a couple of buckets of warm water and a plastic jug will get the job done. It is unlikely that you will find bathing your dog in a floor level bath very comfortable. If using one, you should take care not to injure yourself and consider using a back support.

Light

Good light is very important and you need as much natural light as possible. Electric light, in any form, can put strain on your eyes and will cast shadows on the dog's coat. The shadow effect can make it difficult to see dark-coated breeds clearly; likewise, the brightness of an electric light can reflect off white coats, causing an effect similar to 'snow blindness' – the coat will appear as a solid white mass, making it difficult to see the dog and distinguish trimming lines precisely. If you have to rely on electric lighting, try to have the light behind you so that it lights up the dog

---

CAUTION! MAKE SURE THAT YOU HAVE ADEQUATE LIGHTING

Solid black and solid white dogs are particularly difficult to see in either inadequate or very bright light. Using sharp tools and equipment that can hurt the dog when you cannot see him is clearly a dangerous practice, so do not do it!

---

in front of you. A light fitting directly above your work area will cast unwelcome shadows, whilst a light fitting in front of you will cause glare resulting in eyestrain and 'blind spots' in your vision.

Your grooming equipment

Keep your grooming equipment handy. It needs to be within an arm's length of where you are working so that you can keep one hand on your dog at all times, whilst reaching with the other hand for your equipment. You may find it makes sense (and is easier) to keep them in a tool box; these can be purchased from a grooming supplier or a DIY store. Such boxes protect tools and keep them clean; they are often robust enough to be put on the floor, if you need your work table clear at any time, and are easily stored away. Alternatively, tools can be kept in a plastic box, a grooming bag or a tack box. The important point is to have them readily accessible when you are working and to store them in a container that can be easily cleaned.

Check-list: to groom your pet at home you need:

- *plenty of natural light;*
- *somewhere safe and suitable to groom your pet;*
- *a table (or workbench) to stand him on, with access to an electric power supply;*
- *something to bath him in, with access to a water supply and drainage;*
- *towels;*
- *a hair-dryer;*
- *grooming equipment for your particular dog;*
- *either a grooming tunic or old clothing, to protect you and your clothes;*
- *a plastic bag or dustbin for the hair;*
- *dust sheets to protect furniture, carpets, etc.; and*
- *cleaning equipment.*

6.2 COMMERCIAL GROOMING

We live in a litigious society so, before you start looking at suitable locations and properties for your commercial grooming business, you should make yourself aware of the many legal requirements and responsibilities that running a small business involves. This will help you decide on the type and size of business you would like to have and whether you are prepared for the responsibilities that becoming an employer entails.

The legislation relevant to the commercial groomer covers a number of areas, providing protection to the environment, to civil society and to employees when working within the workplace.

Planning permission

Whichever country you live in, it is likely that your local government will have policies in place to regulate the demand for housing, industry and commerce; these recognize the need to protect the environment against irresponsible developments. When a planning permission application is considered, such influences as noise, increased traffic and increased demand on electricity, water and drainage are all taken into consideration.

Even if you plan to work from your own property you should apply for planning permission. If you plan to build your premises, you need to abide by planning and building regulations relevant to your country. In the United Kingdom permission can be sought retrospectively; however, if permission has not been sought, has been refused or your development involves a breach of planning regulations, your local council may take enforcement action against you and ask you to remove or close the premises.

Outdoor signage

Erecting a sign outside your business may require permission from both your local council or governing body, who will advise you on the size of the sign and the lettering, and the land owner (who may be the local council or highways authority).

Change of use

You may not need to apply for 'change of use' for a commercial property if the previous business was of the same (or similar) nature to your intended business. If, however, the previous business was a 'take-away', for instance, you may not be able to use the property for animal-related work without 'change of use' permission.

A full explanation of those Acts of Parliament currently relevant to businesses in the United Kingdom is freely available for public viewing on the government website: www.legislation.gov.uk.

Aspects of this subject are discussed in more detail in the Health and Safety section of Chapter 7. The following list provides an overview of key business legislation; not all of these Acts will necessarily apply to you. You should, however, familiarize yourself with those laws relating to business practice in your country of residence and work.

Laws concerned with business

Health and Safety at Work Act 1974

This law protects everyone in the workplace, including employers, employees, visitors and anyone else on the property. Each place of work needs to be assessed by the employer and a written Health and Safety policy must be made available if there are five or more employees.

Management of Health and Safety at Work Regulations 1992

These regulations require employers to assess the risks to Health and Safety of all employees (even if there is only one) and anyone else who may be affected by the activities of these employees, in order to identify preventative and protective measures. The employer is also responsible for setting up emergency procedures and for providing information and training.

Health and Safety (Display Screen Equipment) Regulations 1992

Implementing the European Directive 90/270/EEC, this regulation enforces the minimum Health and Safety requirements for working with display screen equipment (VDUs), such as computer screens and televisions. Employers must carry out a risk assessment on all computer workstations and analyse the Health and Safety risks to which operators are exposed. Employers must reduce these risks to a minimum.

Provision and Use of Work Equipment Regulations 1992

This law emphasizes the employer's duty of care to employees when selecting equipment for use in the workplace. Employers must provide adequate training, information and instructions and they must ensure that the equipment is safe and suitable for use. The law also requires the employer to protect the employee from dangerous parts and occurrences with adequate signage, warnings and isolation from power switches.

Manual Handling Operations Regulations 1992

Implementing the European Directive 90/269/EEC, this law places a duty of care on employers to avoid hazardous handling as far as is reasonably practical. There is a further requirement that risk assessments are written down, closely monitored and revised as necessary to prevent injury.

Environmental Protection Act 1990

All business operators have a duty of care to ensure that all waste arising from their activities is disposed of without harm to human health or the environment. The law requires that all waste be disposed of by a registered carrier to the appropriate authorized disposal facility. If you wish to dispose of your own waste by incineration, or similar means, you may require a waste management licence.

Controlled Waste Regulations 1992

This covers what is known as clinical waste. Clinical waste includes animal tissue, blood, urine and excreta, used dressings such as plasters, bandages and used cotton wool. The safe disposal of syringes and hypodermic needles is also covered by this law.

The Control of Substances Hazardous to Health Regulations 2002

This law governs the control of substances that are used in industry and are deemed hazardous to health. Employers are required to perform risk assessments for all chemical-based products and to provide appropriate storage facilities and appropriate training to ensure the risks are appropriately managed. The HSE provides an up-to-date guide that defines 'harmful substances' and provides advice on how they can be used safely: www.hse.gov.uk/pubns/indg136.pdf.

This law further requires that employers control the exposure of employees to chemicals and that employees are also protected from exposure to zoonosis (diseases transmitted from animal to human). Employers are required to complete written risk assessments and to provide information, training and suitable advice on risks and precautions including, in some instances, vaccination as a preventative control.

Electricity at Work Regulations 1989

It is a requirement that electrical equipment and wiring is sound, properly installed and properly maintained. Both employers and employees are responsible for the safe usage of all electrical equipment.

Fire Precautions Act 1971

This act ensures that fire escapes are operational at all times, firefighting equipment is serviced and maintained as required and that all employees are aware of (and trained in) evacuation procedures. It is recommended that plans and details of the premises are logged with the local police and that advice is sought from the local Fire Protection Officer regarding appropriate firefighting equipment, its situation and training in its use.

Staff should be trained in evacuation procedures, including policies for the protection and removal of dogs. Notices displaying the evacuation procedure and the collection (muster) point should be prominently displayed, and fire escapes should be conspicuously and appropriately signposted/marked.

Employer's Liability (Compulsory Insurance) Act 1969

Employers must take out insurance against claims made by employees for injuries and illness acquired within the workplace. It is a requirement that an up-to-date certificate be displayed at all times.

Business Names Act 1985

The name and address of the owner of the business must be displayed in a prominent position inside the premises.

The Offices and Shops Act 1963

This Act deals with opening hours, hours of work, lighting, ventilation, temperature control, cleanliness and the safe operation of machinery in the workplace.

Consumer Transactions (Restriction on Statements) Order 1973

This law prevents shop owners from displaying any signage or notices that appear to deny/affect consumer rights.

Weights and Measures Act 1985

This law covers the weight stamping or liquid measure/volume markings of products that are either packed by the manufacturers or repacked by retailers. The Act covers both metric and imperial measurements.

Sale and Supply of Goods Act 1994; General Product Safety Regulations 1994; Unfair Terms in Consumer Contracts Regulations 1994

These three Acts cover the rights of the retailer and the consumer against defective goods and the conditions attached to cash refunds, credit notes and replacements.

Laws concerning animals

Protection of Animals Acts 1911–1964 (amended 2001)

These acts make it an offence for anyone (including owners, groomers and grooming staff) to cause or permit any unnecessary suffering or neglect to domestic or captive animals. Penalties include fines and a ban on keeping animals. Subsequent court orders can permit the removal, sale or destruction of the animals involved.

The Pet Animals Act 1951

This law protects animals sold in pet shops. A licence to sell pets must be applied for and is granted once the licensing authority is satisfied that the animal accommodation is clean and that appropriate food and water is supplied. Conditions may be attached to the licence and the authorities may inspect the property from time to time.

Animals Act 1971

Under this act, keepers (including pet-shop owners) of dangerous animals are liable for any damage that they cause. Species not commonly domesticated in England are classified as 'dangerous animals'. Fully grown animals with characteristics that require them to be restrained to prevent damage are also classified as 'dangerous animals'. Keepers of domestic animals are not liable unless they were aware of the animal's ability to cause harm.

The Control of Dogs Order 1992 (S1901)

It is the law that all dogs, whilst in a public place, must wear a collar bearing the name and address of the owner. A 'public place' is anywhere that the public has access to, including streets, walkways, rights of way and common parts of buildings that are accessible by the public.

Dangerous Dogs Act 1991

This act makes it an offence for anyone to have in their possession, or custody, a dog belonging to certain breeds (or types) of dog that are bred for fighting purposes. It makes provisions for other breeds or types of dog which present a serious danger to the public, and it makes a further provision for keeping these dogs under control.

Veterinary Surgeons Act 1966

Clinical treatment, surgical treatment, diagnostic testing and the diagnosing of disease and injuries can only be performed by a registered veterinary practitioner or a registered veterinary surgeon.

Veterinary Medicines Regulations 2005

These regulations impose control over the production, sale and use of medicines. The regulations created four categories of medicine, shown in Table 11.

Further information on the legal categories of veterinary medicines is available from the website of the National Organisation for Animal Health (NOAH): www.noahcompendium.co.uk/Compendium/Overview.

Welfare of Animals During Transport Order 1997

This order makes those in charge of the movement of animals responsible for their welfare and outlines the care that must be provided during that time. This includes the provision of water, food, ventilation, rest and suitable space within the carrying containers.

The Animal Boarding Establishment Act 1963

This act defines a boarding establishment as any premises that provides temporary accommodation for other people's dogs and/or cats. The local council is responsible for providing a licence, which will take into account location, suitability of accommodation, quantity of animals being housed, exercise facilities, ventilation, lighting, temperature, noise control, waste disposal, storage and disease control, amongst other factors. This law also applies to day-care boarding establishments.

To learn more about these acts visit:
www.defra.gov.uk
www.scotland.gov.uk

To learn more about the regulations

Table 11 The four categories of medicine.

Category	Definition	Prescriber or supplier
POM–V	Prescription only medicine – for veterinary use	Prescribed by veterinarians and requires the animal to have been assessed and under the care of a vet. Supplied by veterinarians and pharmacists.
POM–VPS	Prescription only medicine – for veterinary use.	Prescribed and supplied by any registered qualified person (RQP), including veterinarians, veterinary pharmacists and suitably qualified persons.
NFA–VPS	For veterinary use in non-food animals.	Can be supplied by a RQP (including veterinarians, veterinary pharmacists and suitably qualified persons) without a prescription.
AVM–GSL	Authorized veterinary medicine.	No legal restrictions although a responsible approach is expected.

involving animal medicines and for training contact:

Animal Medicines Training Regulatory Authority (AMTRA)

Gable Court, Parsons Hill, Hollesley, Woodbridge, Suffolk, IP12 3RB

Tel: 44(0)1394 411010

Email: info@amtra.org uk

Data Protection Act 1998

This Act protects the rights of a person to privacy and sets out the requirements for handling personal and sensitive data. Personal data is information that identifies living individuals, including their name, where they live, their post code and contactable telephone number. Sensitive data is information that identifies racial or ethnic origin, health conditions and any other information about an individual's beliefs or lifestyle.

Under the Act, any organization that holds personal information must notify the Information Commissioner's Office and state who is responsible for the security of the information being stored.

Further information on the up-to-date version of this Act can be obtained from:

www.legislation.gov.uk/ukpga/1998/29/contents.

The Information Commissioner's Office (ICO) website is another useful source of current information: www.ico.gov.uk.

Insurance

If you are home grooming, you may not need to purchase additional insurances but you would be wise to ask advice from your home insurance company if you intend to fit water, drainage or electricity in an area that has not previously been supplied with these, particularly if you are renting your home.

If you are grooming commercially (i.e. charging for your services), whether from your own home or from business premises, you will need insurance cover.

Property insurance

Depending on where you choose to work, it may be necessary to insure the property. In most instances a rented property will be insured by the owner but it is wise to check on this. If you are working commercially from your garage or outbuilding, this may be covered on your home insurance but you must notify your insurance company as they need to know that at least part of your property is being used for com-

mercial reasons; this may affect your premium.

Contents insurance

This is not a legal requirement but it makes sense to have proper contents cover. Animals are unpredictable and your expensive equipment can be easily damaged by an over-excited dog, or a large dog being manoeuvred within a small workspace.

Public liability

This is a legal requirement. You will have owners and visitors attending your salon and you must have adequate insurance cover in the event of an accident.

Employer's liability insurance

You will not need this if you are working on your own, but as soon as you employ your first member of staff, regardless of their status, this becomes a legal requirement.

Car insurance

If you intend to offer a collection and delivery service for your clients, your car/vehicle may need to be reclassified as a commercial vehicle rather than as a vehicle for personal/domestic use only. It is very important to check this and make any necessary changes because, if you have an accident whilst you have a client's dog in transit, you may not be insured if your vehicle is wrongly classified on the policy. Some, but not all, companies may increase the premium for changing the use of your vehicle, so shop around.

Mobile groomers need commercial vehicle insurance for cars, vans and trailers.

Insurance packages

It is possible to buy a groomer's insurance package that will provide adequate cover for you and your business, so look around to see what is available. These packages usually include 'Public and Employer's Liability', 'Material Damages' and 'Business Interruption' insurance. The latter may prove invaluable if you are working alone and were to get hurt. Packages are also likely to include 'Professional Indemnity' and 'Personal Accident' insurance.

In the United Kingdom the following websites may prove helpful:

◆ www.cliverton.co.uk
◆ www.petbusiness.co.uk
◆ www.simplybusiness.co.uk/dog_groomer_business_insurance
◆ www.eandl.co.uk/pet/groomer insurance

Taxes

In the United Kingdom, as soon as you start trading you must inform:

◆ HM Revenue and Customs (HMRC);
◆ Your local Income Tax Office; and
◆ Your local Social Security Office.

HMRC will advise you on how to complete tax forms, which taxes you have to pay and when you have to pay them. They can also provide you with an information pack to help you start your new business. Included in the pack will be information about self-assessment for tax, taxing profits and calculation tables (*see* Fig. 6.2.1).

You must also notify the Tax Office if you plan to recruit an employee. They will send you a 'new employer's starter pack' that contains all the relevant forms, calculation tables and advice about filling in forms.

Unless your business is registered as a limited company (which means that you are an employee of the company), you will need to register as self-employed with your local Social Security Office.

6.3 SETTING UP A COMMERCIAL GROOMING ESTABLISHMENT

If you want to make a career of grooming, you need to decide what sort of business you want to run and how you want to run it. Here you have two choices:

◆ *You could set up a salon and work in situ; or*
◆ *You could become a mobile groomer.*

You also need to be clear from the beginning about how big you would like your business to be. If you don't know where you are going, you will never get there! So, start by thinking about:

◆ *How much grooming do you want to do?*
◆ *Do you plan to expand and grow your business?*
◆ *Where would you like to locate your business?*

The next section looks at setting up a grooming salon.

6.3.1 The commercial grooming salon

Based in premises that are designed for the purpose of grooming many dogs, your location could be a shop in the high street, a unit on a trading estate or an area attached to another business such as a veterinary surgery, pet shop or garden centre. It could even be a converted garage (*see* Fig. 6.3.1) or out-building attached to your home.

Fig. 6.3.1 *A garage has been utilized to make this grooming area. The bath has been made from breeze-blocks and fibreglassed over. The groomer works alone so the ramp is a useful addition to help with large dogs. Kitchen units provide a hand washing sink and useful cupboard space, and the floor has been painted with washable garage floor paint.*

NOTE: A BUSINESS WON'T BUILD ITSELF OVERNIGHT

It will take many months, maybe years, for your clientele to grow. View this as a positive thing (an opportunity) and make good use of the time.

When you first start grooming, you will be slow in your work. You need time to perfect your skills and to become 'grooming fit'. As you build muscles in the right places and your confidence grows, you will be able to work faster and take on the extra work as it arrives. If your business were to grow too quickly, before you have learned and practised your new trade, you are in danger of making mistakes and producing poor-quality work. You are also more likely to hurt yourself and have accidents.

Look out for grooming seminars, visit dog shows and attend short courses that will help you gain confidence and knowledge.

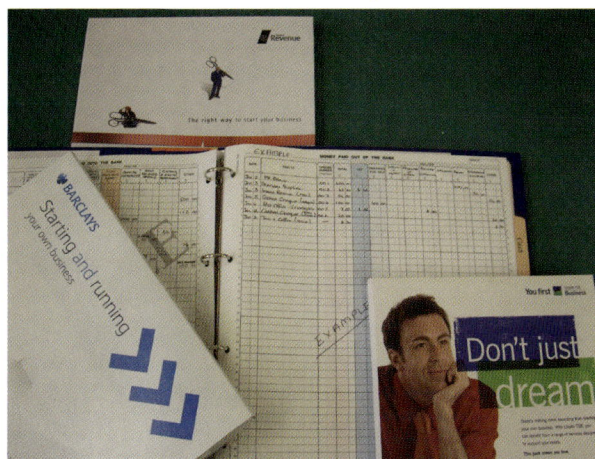

Fig. 6.2.1 *In the United Kingdom you can get help and advice on how to get your business started from your bank and from the Inland Revenue.*

One significant advantage of setting up your own salon is that you can tailor it specifically to your needs and requirements. Your work area will become familiar and comfortable to work in, and it will always be ready for you to work in. These are all essential elements if you want to build a business, particularly as a visibly functioning business is a good way to attract passing trade to generate more income without the expense of advertising.

One disadvantage is that commercial premises can be expensive to buy or rent; another is that, should your business outgrow the premises, it may necessitate relocating. This may come at a cost if you have to move to less accessible premises.

Think ahead, plan ahead!

Try not to restrict your thinking to the position that you are in now because your situation and circumstances will change. Start by thinking about where you want your business to be in five years' time and plan your salon accordingly.

Careful consideration of the following questions can help you prepare for the growth of your business, without having to make too many changes along the way; this will help keep your costs to a minimum.

Do you want to buy or rent your premises?

This will usually depend on the availability of funds, followed closely by the type and location of properties available to you. The advantages to renting or leasing a property are that you do not have the worry of a long-term financial commitment and that any structural repairs are likely to be the responsibility of the landlord. The landlord will also be responsible for property insurance and property taxes. The disadvantages are that you may be restricted in how you can alter the interior; additionally, most leases are fixed term and not necessarily available for a subsequent term. This can have an effect on the value of your business should you decide to sell it and, equally importantly, if the lease is not renewable at the end of its term, you have to move.

The main advantage of buying your premises is that you are in control. With the appropriate planning permission, you can make alterations and, because you own the property, you will benefit from the added value. The building is an asset that adds to the value of your business, should you decide to

sell. The disadvantages are that you are responsible for the maintenance and upkeep of the property, for property insurance and both owner and occupier taxes.

What size premises are you looking for?

If you are planning for growth, your premises must be able eventually to accommodate enough workstations for however many staff (and possible students) you intend to have working there at any given time. Moving a business is costly and may mean losing part of your client base; it may, however, give you the opportunity to generate new clients and many bonded clients will travel a surprisingly long way to continue using your services.

What type of premises do you require to accommodate your business?

Do you want premises that will be used for grooming and/or training only? Do you intend having a retail area or an area for an ancillary business such as 'doggy day-care' facilities? Consider the needs of your local community and whether you can make up any shortfalls by providing a much-needed service.

Where would you like to be located?

You have many options here. You may decide that you want a stand-alone business that will only be a grooming salon, or you may decide that you would like to be attached to another business such as a pet shop, a veterinary surgery or a garden centre. The type of business you want to run will have a bearing on the ideal location.

A high street shop may not be the best place to site a grooming business if you wish to have a 'doggy day-care' centre attached, although your client catchment area would be good. This type of business may be better located on a trading estate, where there would be more exercise space and dog-walking opportunities, with noise pollution from barking dogs posing less of a problem. The grooming salon part of the business may be disadvantaged, however, through lack of passing trade.

You therefore need to think carefully about your options.

How many dogs do you plan to groom daily?

You need to decide whether you intend working full-time or part-time. The hours that you work will have a bearing on your income, which may affect how much rent you can afford, how many dogs you plan to have in the building at any one time and the space required to house them.

Do you need approval from a local authority to run your salon?

Check this out before you start. Business legislation is likely to differ between countries and may still apply to you, even if you are working from home.

In the United Kingdom local councils may have different legislation relating to setting up a business, whether from home or from commercial premises. A phone call to your local council, or a visit to their website, will advise you on how to go about gaining permission to operate. You may also need to ask permission from your landlord if you are renting the property. You do not want to find yourself in the situation of having spent a lot of money setting up your salon only to be told that you cannot operate from the premises.

What type of building should you look for?

The type of building can impact on the comfort of your working facilities and your business's potential for growth. Your choice of building similarly depends on the type of business you are planning to run. In all cases you need the following facilities.

Natural lighting

As much natural lighting as possible is needed, though preferably not from south-facing windows that will allow full sunlight in. This will produce a glaring light in the room and cause eyestrain. It will also make the facilities unbearably hot during the summer months

Good ventilation

Good ventilation is essential to your health and to ensure that the facilities can be thoroughly dried. Blasting and drying wet dogs, in particular, will leave a lot of moisture in the atmosphere; the resulting high humidity levels need to be managed. Ventilation can be provided by windows that are easily opened, or by an air extraction system that allows the air in the room to be changed constantly.

Good access

Your grooming salon should be easy and safe to access. New dogs, in particular, may not be keen to come into the grooming room, so good access is essential to prevent accidents to the dog or the owner. The same consideration applies to very large dogs or boisterous dogs. Older dogs with reduced mobility, together with disabled dogs and disabled owners, will all benefit from easy, uninterrupted access. The opportunity to park as close as possible to the salon is essential and dedicated parking spaces should be designated for this purpose.

Security

Good security is essential for two principal reasons: firstly, to prevent dogs getting out should they break loose, and secondly, to stop unwanted visitors getting in. Ideally, you need two doors (or a door and a high half-door, which could be part of a built-in reception desk) between the dogs and the outside world. You also need to think about how to secure all possible break-in/break-out points. These include windows, roof lights and shared entrances. Wire cages are recommended over any windows that open to the outside.

Health and safety issues

Consider how you are going to make the premises safe not only for yourself and the dogs that you are working with, but also for any person visiting the premises. Such factors include:

◆ Marking the edge of steps (or stairs) with yellow and black tape.
◆ Marking any low overhead fittings

or cupboards so that they are more visible and less of a hazard.

◆ Identifying narrow entrances that do not allow easy access.
◆ Ensuring storage areas are secure – especially the COSHH cupboard.
◆ Ensuring display stands are positioned safely.
◆ Optimizing each groomer's workspace to ensure they are able to work safely.
◆ Allowing uninterrupted space to safely manoeuvre dogs within the building.
◆ Providing clear information, including salon policies on vaccination and parasite control.
◆ Ensuring appropriate vessels are available for waste disposal.

Exercise areas

Where are you going to exercise any visiting dogs? How are you going to secure the area and keep it clean?

Drains

Is the property on mains drainage or a septic tank? Do you need permission to expel waste water into the drainage system? Some mini sewage/foul waste treatment plants can be severely damaged by chemicals found in shampoos and cleaning agents. Check that the treatment plant can safely process your grooming by-products.

Power supply

Check that your salon's power supply meets the requirements of your work (both current and future), and is compatible with your tools and equipment.

◆ Does it have sufficient power points? If not, how difficult would it be to fit extra ones?
◆ If the power supply is shared, how is the bill divided?
◆ Is the voltage sufficient for heavy-duty equipment, such as drying cabinets and powerful hair-dryers?
◆ Are you able to set up further grooming stations if they are required?

Passing trade

Is there any opportunity to increase

business from passing trade? If not, are you able to put up an advertising board close by to advertise your business and encourage passing trade?

Noise

Dogs will bark and blasters can be very noisy. Is this likely to upset neighbours or adjoining businesses?

Extra traffic

Is there likely to be a significant increase in traffic flow to the area? Particularly if you are going to work from home, you need to consider whether and how this will affect your neighbours. Increased traffic is the single most common reason for neighbours objecting to you running a business from home; it is also quite probably the most likely cause for your local government authority declining permission for your salon.

How are you going to finance the setting-up of your business?

If you require financial assistance to set up and run your business, you may need to produce a business plan and projection before applying to your bank/lender. Contact your bank for details and a small business information pack that will help you to put a plan together. You may be able to apply for a local government loan so it is worth researching relevant websites for more information.

How much of the work can you do yourself or will you need to employ builders?

If possible, make use of your own skills and enlist the help of family and friends for any conversion work to your premises. Builders do not come cheaply, they are also in business to earn a living, so talk to your family and friends to see if anyone can help you. Any electrical fitting or plumbing may have to be carried out by qualified tradesmen to comply with local government requirements, legislation, tenancy agreements and insurance clauses.

What resources do you already have available?

Consider your home premises. Could a garage or outbuilding be converted to provide suitable accommodation? If so, be sure to obtain any necessary planning permission before you start any alterations and, if the conversion is costly, make sure that the premises really are able to support the business that you want to run and will allow you to earn a living and pay back the conversion costs.

You may already have some grooming tools and equipment. If not, you will need the funding to purchase at least the basic equipment that will get you up and running. In a commercial business this means that you have to be able to trim all dogs (i.e., a wide range of types and breeds). You would do well to carefully plan your purchases by shopping around for second-hand tables, driers and other costly items, whilst always ensuring that these are safe and legal. Beware of buying second-hand clipper blades and scissors; this is often a false economy because they may look in good condition but you really cannot tell how much work they have done or how they have been looked after.

How soon do you need your salon to be ready and open?

Plan a specific timescale and aim to keep to it. Having invested time in your training and money in the conversion of a property and purchase of equipment, you need to start earning as soon as you can.

Fitting out your salon interior

When you fit out your salon you need to consider the following points.

The floor surface

This should be of a non-permeable, non-slip material that can be easily washed down and disinfected, without perishing. Hospital-grade linoleum (*see* Fig. 6.3.2) or non-slip tiles (*see* Fig. 6.3.3) are ideal if funds permit. Alternatively, a concrete floor painted with garage floor paint is a cheaper, although less ideal, option.

Fig. 6.3.2   Ideally, in a commercial grooming salon the flooring should be continued up the sides of the walls so there are no gaps between the floor and the walls. This stops fleas and hair collecting between the two surfaces and prevents wash water seeping under the flooring.

Fig. 6.3.3   The bathing area in this commercial grooming salon is functional and very easy to keep clean. The room is fitted with an extractor system to refresh the air supply, windows provide adequate ventilation and the radiator dries the room. The walls are tiled to a height that minimizes water damage to the property, and the non-slip tiled floor provides a safe surface to work on when it is wet.

The wall surfaces

The walls should be non-permeable and fully washable. Tiles are preferable; alternatively, plastic-coated boarding will work as long as the joins are correctly sealed. If you are using a garage, garage floor paint over the concrete blocks will enable them to be washed and disinfected with a power hose. Concrete blocks will need deep cleaning regularly as their uneven texture allows hair particles to collect and can provide accommodation for parasites and bacteria (*see* Fig. 6.3.4).

Insulation

Insulation is helpful if you need to keep noise to a minimum. If your salon is below living accommodation, insulated ceiling tiles will help to reduce the noise level, as will insulating any dividing walls.

Heating

You will need heating for the winter time. If there is no heating system in the premises, your best option is likely

Fig. 6.3.4   Painted walls are a good idea but make sure that the paint fills all the texture holes. Here you can see where texture holes have not been filled. These little crevices make excellent accommodation for parasites and collect dust and hair particles that will provide an environment for the growth of micro-organisms.

Fig. 6.3.5 *Sealed unit radiators provide safe heating without the worry of hair getting onto heating elements. Fitted to the wall, they cannot be knocked over.*

to be the purchase of electric wall-mounted radiators (*see* Fig. 6.3.5). These closed units offer a number of advantages: they have no motorized parts to go wrong, and they are wall mounted and cannot therefore be knocked over. This arrangement also eliminates any need for cables to be trailed across the floor, thereby eliminating a potential trip hazard from the grooming room.

and ventilation to dry the room out at the end of the day.

Electric plug points and fuse box

Each workstation should have adequate electric sockets for your equipment. A double socket is usually sufficient, placed within reach of the workstation, high enough that it is out of range of dogs lifting their leg to scent mark, but not so high that cables hang down onto tables. In the bathing and drying area the sockets should have safety covers. The fuse box should be easily accessible in case of emergencies.

Fig. 6.3.6 *This station is equipped for either a left- or a right-handed groomer. The area has plenty of natural light which is reflected back on to the dog from the wall mirror. When fitting wall mirrors, it is a good idea to fit them on a piece of board so that they are cushioned from rough walls and are less likely to break whilst you are cleaning them.*

Ventilation

If you do not have windows that can open to air the room, an extractor fan can be fitted to maintain the quality of room air (*see* Chapter 7). It is important to keep changing the air in the room.

The facilities will also become very damp because of the bathing and drying process, so you need both heating

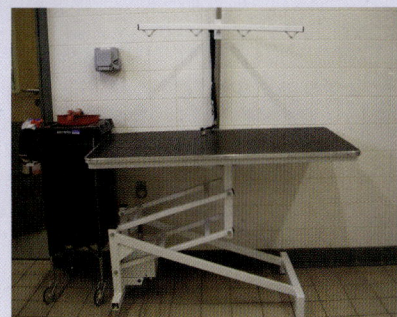

Fig. 6.3.7 *This drying station has been set up for a left-handed groomer. The plug socket is on the left, so cables do not need to cross either the table or the groomer when electrical equipment is in use. The table is close to the bath, so a hydraulic table has been chosen instead of an electric table and the plug socket has a protective cover.*

Water heating system/tank

If possible, a wall-fitted electric shower unit that warms the water to within a fixed temperature range is ideal. This is cost-effective because you are then only heating the water as you use it. Alternatively, a holding tank with an immersion heater is an option. This can be expensive, however, because as you draw off the pre-heated hot water from the supply, the tank then refills with cold water, which needs to be heated. It is also possible to run out of hot water if you are bathing lots of dogs one after the other.

Lighting

Natural light needs to be supplemented by artificial lighting. 'Daylight' strip lights are recommended but bear in mind that energy-saving lighting needs time for the bulbs to warm before you get the full benefit of them. If you are going to use mirrors on the walls behind your grooming tables, be careful where you fit strip lights: they can cause a reflective glare on the glass and will create 'blind' spots, not to mention causing eyestrain.

The ideal position for lighting is slightly behind where the groomer will be standing so that it throws the light onto the part of the dog that you are looking at. Alternatively, fit ceiling lights one on either side of where the groomer is standing; this should ensure light is always focused on the part of the dog that is being worked on. The height of the ceiling will also have a bearing on whether reflections are produced; you may therefore have to play around with temporary fittings before you finalize the positions.

Windows ideally also need to be behind the groomer so that they throw light onto the dog on the grooming table, where it is most needed – right in front of you! You will not gain any benefit from windows lighting up the wrong side of the dog: the bit facing you will be in the dark and against the light.

Animal security

Cages, holding pens or wall tie-up rings are required to keep the dogs in your care safe from other dogs and

> **NOTE: THE SUN SHINING DIRECTLY INTO THE ROOM WILL HAVE BOTH ADVANTAGES AND DISADVANTAGES**
>
> ◆ *Advantages: it will warm the room and give plenty of natural light to work with.*
> ◆ *Disadvantages: it will reflect off mirrors, causing glare, and it may make the room too hot for the comfort and safety of the dogs (and possibly the groomers).*
>
> *You may therefore need to consider fitting blinds.*

secured, so they do not escape from the property (*see* Chapter 9). You will also need at least two doors (or a door and a half-door) to prevent escape should a dog break loose when a visitor to the salon opens the front door.

Staff safety

A reception desk can serve as a good deterrent to any unwelcome visitors (including people wandering in without an appointment when the front desk is unmanned). The reception desk should be high enough that dogs cannot jump over the top. The cash register and telephone should be out of reach (and sight) of the general public. You may also want to fit an emergency alarm under the reception desk if you are working alone. This will enable you to call for assistance if you are threatened by an unwanted visitor, or if you have been badly hurt by a dog and need help.

Toilet facilities

It is helpful to have toilet facilities within the premises because you will not be able to leave the salon (and any dogs you are working on) unattended whilst you take a break – unless you remove the dog from the table to the safety of a holding cage or tie-up ring and lock up the salon.

Secure area for personal effects

Think about where your personal effects can be safely stored whilst you are working.

Most premises will be able to accommodate all of these requirements without too many alterations and without spending too much money. This list is by no means exhaustive and not all of the items are necessary for the operation of your business. These are, however, the facilities you should consider having to make your salon a healthy, safe, well-organized and efficient place to work from.

A grooming salon with a retail area

Some groomers like to provide a selection of shampoos, collars, leads and other accessories to complement their business, so their salons accommodate a retail area in which to display items such as these. This can generate extra income and the groomer can encourage clients to buy the correct equipment/products to help keep their pets groomed between appointments. Offering grooming sessions to teach owners how to use the basic tools that you sell can also generate additional income.

The disadvantages are that stock on the shelf is 'dead' money and it is very tempting to over-stock. You need to manage your stock well, particularly if you are selling products such as dog food that have a sell-by date. Another disadvantage is that grooming salons have quite a lot of dust and hair floating around. Any stock on the shelves will be more appealing to the consumer if it is clean and fresh-looking, so it will need to be kept clean and dusted. It should be displayed away from the grooming area, in another room, or within a cabinet in the reception area.

This may mean renting or buying a larger unit or shop than you need for your grooming work, which can be costly; you therefore need to weigh up your expected sales profit against any extra costs.

Buying an existing business

You may find yourself in a position to buy an existing business. There are several points to consider here, as well as the advantages and disadvantages of taking on an established 'going concern'.

CAUTION: GET LEGAL ADVICE

Get a solicitor to help you with the legal process and an accountant to thoroughly check the business accounts. Investing in professional advice will give a much clearer idea what you are taking on and could well be worth every penny!

The main advantage of this option is that you can take over and start earning immediately and will soon begin recouping your expenditure.

The main disadvantage is that, although the purchase price may include an element of 'goodwill' (in the shape of an existing clientele), there is absolutely no guarantee that they will come to you. You should therefore be very wary of paying large sums of money for the client base because at the end of the day the client makes his own choice on where to spend his money.

Check:

- The length of any existing lease and whether there are any problems renewing or extending it;
- any restrictions on the lease and the get-out-clause;
- the accounts very carefully and seek the advice of an accountant;
- the credibility of the business with suppliers;
- that all equipment is in good repair and in good working order; and
- the lease on any 'company' vehicles.

WARNING: CHECK THAT THE SELLER IS DEFINITELY GIVING UP OR MOVING OUT OF THE AREA

To protect your investment, make it a clause in the purchase agreement that the seller does not continue to work in the industry, either for themselves or for any other company or person, for a given period of time, within a given radius of your premises.

BASIC ESSENTIALS CHECK-LIST

The reception area:

- Telephone
- Diaries/appointment books
- Recording system
- Desk and chair(s)
- Seating (for clients)
- Cash register (till) or cash-box
- Credit card facilities
- Stationery, including business cards and promotional materials

The holding/kennel area:

- Kennel range, multi-cage unit or collapsible cages
- Tie-up rings
- Bedding
- Newspapers to line the base of cages
- Animal waste bin
- Name tags for kennels

The bathing area:

- Bath
- Water heating system/shower unit, shower hose and shower head
- Bath mats
- COSHH cupboard
- Cleaning equipment cupboard
- Washing machine
- Tumble drier

The grooming area:

- Tables (hydraulic, electric or static) – ideally one per person
- Restraints and 'H' frames (on tables)
- Driers (hair drier, blaster or a combination)
- Equipment trolley (one per person)
- Grooming tools

Extras:

- Grooming uniform (one per person and spares)
- Towels and/or high absorbency cloths
- Shampoo
- Conditioners
- Coat dressings
- Stock
- Pictures or paintings
- Pot plants
- Seating
- Tea- and coffee-making facilities
- Poo bags
- Dustbins and waste bins
- Spare leads
- Muzzles
- Leather gauntlets
- A tie-up chain for dogs that chew!

If possible, spend some time at the premises both working with the seller, and meeting and observing the clientele. This gives you the opportunity to see what you are taking on; it also gives the clients an opportunity to meet you. This can be time well spent and can make the transition of ownership smoother and more pleasant.

Mobile grooming

Mobile groomers provide a service for clients who either cannot bring their dog to you, or prefer to have their dog groomed at home. There are many clients who either cannot drive, have limited access to public transport or have a dog that does not travel well. There is often therefore a need for this service, which can be provided either as a home visit or using a mobile grooming vehicle.

Mobile grooming vehicles

These are usually purpose-equipped high-top vans that are fitted with a bath, a grooming table and everything else that the groomer needs to provide a grooming service, all within the vehicle. Such vehicles may be either purchased, adapted and equipped by the groomer, or purchased as a ready-to-go facility, often as a franchise (contract) vehicle.

The advantage of a grooming vehicle is that you do not have the running costs and perhaps the ties (and commitments) of a shop lease or mortgage. There are no building repairs, adaptations or decorating to consider and you will not have to move premises if the business expands.

Disadvantages include the need to purchase a potentially expensive vehicle, together with the cost of the conversion. If you do not own and convert the vehicle yourself, you may have the cost of a franchise agreement to consider. Running costs can be high and are not limited to fuel: other costs include vehicle insurance, road tax, servicing, Ministry of Transport testing (MOT) and any other legislation relevant to your country of work. This is in addition to the cost of your 'Public Liability' and 'Groomer's Liability' insurances. Valuable time can be lost travelling between clients, especially in heavy traffic. Simply maintaining, repairing and running the vehicle may be costly. Ice and snow in the winter may make driving difficult so you may struggle to keep appointments and may lose income.

Parking for the vehicle is another consideration, both at home and at the client's house. Another disadvantage is that you can only have one groomer working within the vehicle because of space restraints. Work can therefore be lonely and there is little room to expand the business without buying another vehicle and employing another groomer.

Home grooming visits

Another option to consider is having a portable table and equipment that can be set up in the home of the client.

The advantages here are that the groomer can usually fit all necessary equipment in a standard estate car, so a special vehicle is not needed. All electricity costs, water costs, towel washing and deep cleaning of the area used are the owner's responsibility. Business expansion is possible if another groomer is employed to make home visits in the same way.

The disadvantages are that dogs may be more difficult to handle in the presence of their owners, lighting can sometimes be poor, facilities cramped and baths or showers positioned too low for safety or comfort. The risk of injury and strains (particularly back strains) to the groomer are particularly significant in the home of the client because this is, invariably, a 'make-do' environment.

Mobile groomers undertaking home visits need to limit the amount of grooming equipment they carry with them, for obvious reasons. Tools and equipment will be packed and unpacked frequently as you travel around; if you decide to work in this way, you would do well to invest in a suitable carrying case to protect them. There are some very compact toolboxes available from grooming suppliers and DIY stores; these are sturdy and roomy, and provide adequate protection for valuable equipment during transportation.

You also need to make sure that tools and equipment do not get left behind when you are packing up to leave as it may be some time before you are back in the area again to collect it.

> ### CAUTION: TWO VERY IMPORTANT POINTS TO CONSIDER CONCERNING YOUR DRIVING LICENCE
>
> 1. *If you are buying a vehicle to convert into a mobile grooming salon, check (before you buy) that there are no restrictions that may prevent you from driving it. You may not be permitted to drive vehicles of a certain size or that fall into certain categories.*
> 2. *It takes a lot of time and effort to build up a business and a mobile grooming business will depend on you (and your employees and partners) maintaining a valid driving licence. If you lose your licence and cannot continue to travel for your work, you may have to give up or sell your business and lose your living. If you are forced to sell, you will only receive what someone is prepared to pay for it and this may represent a significant loss.*

6.4 RECEPTION AND ADMINISTRATIVE DUTIES

Before you offer your services to the public, get your administration requirements planned and organized, and think about your responsibilities for

> *The reception area sets the tone of your business. It typically provides the client with their first impression of your salon and the standard of professionalism you are offering. It is where you meet and greet clients (and their dogs) and welcome them into your working world. It is also where business is transacted. With this in mind, it should always be equipped with a few pens, a least one pencil and an eraser.*
>
> *It does not have to be a large area but must be orderly, functional, clean, tidy and free of empty coffee cups, providing a reassuring impression of organization and professionalism.*

receiving clients and their dogs into your salon. Advance planning gives you the opportunity to receive customers in a professional and confident manner, demonstrating to them that they are respected individuals, that you value their patronage and that their pet will receive the very best care and attention whilst in your charge.

Start by drawing up and drafting your practice (salon) policies; these should be clearly displayed in your reception area. These can include:

◆ your hours of business;
◆ your policy on vaccination and parasite control;
◆ your policy on cancellations;
◆ the services that you offer;
◆ a 'prices from' list; and
◆ your preferred method(s) of payment.

Record keeping

Whether you prefer to keep all records and transactions in paper form or electronic form is entirely up to you. There are advantages and disadvantages to both.

Keeping your records in files and books is a perfectly acceptable way to record all the details that you need at your disposal. They are easily accessible, easily understood and for a small business they are cost-effective. The disadvantage of paper records is that they take up a lot of room, they can get lost, they become untidy after lots of alterations, they need to be locked away for security and they must be replenished regularly.

Computer-generated records take up less room and require less storage space. Specialized groomer's programmes are easy to use and access; they allow comprehensive records to be maintained, along with appointment diaries, appointment histories, health records, business projections and finances, all collated in one small storage vessel. The disadvantages are that, in the event of a power cut, you will not be able to access your records; the computer software can become damaged or corrupted and, as an electrical appliance, your computer may not take kindly to the damp environment of a grooming room.

Whatever your choice, you must keep your records secure and up to date.

The diary

Your diary should always be available for bookings and re-bookings. Your bookings provide your income so it is vitally important that you take control of how and when you book dogs in for grooming. You need to organize regular appointments so that you can manage the grooming requirements and influence your income. If your diary is unavailable, you risk losing clients:

◆ New clients may feel that you are uninterested in their patronage;
◆ existing clients may forget to call back to book their next appointment;
◆ when (if) they do call back, you may be too busy and they may take their patronage elsewhere; and
◆ grooming routines may be interrupted and will result in too long a gap between trims, causing problems with coat condition, extra work for you and less income.

An available diary therefore demonstrates commitment.

Try to make it your policy not to cancel appointments once they have been made unless it is unavoidable. It may be a convenience to you to do so but it can be an inconvenience to your client and it gives the impression that you are inconsiderate.

Have your diary marked out with your working timetable for at least three months in advance; this allows you to re-book dogs that need to return on a twelve-week cycle. By August of each year you should have invested in a diary for the following year – and wasted no time marking it out ready for use.

Make sure that you cross out times and dates when you are not working, including annual holidays and public holidays.

The telephone

Answering the telephone requires a certain amount of skill, training and practice. You and your business will often be judged by the manner in which you answer the call. Never forget that the person on the end of the phone cannot see you. What you say – and how you say it – will form the basis of their appraisal and judgement of you.

An *answer-phone service* is essential to your business because you will not always be able to take calls personally and your telephone is your main link to the outside world. So:

◆ set it to answer after four rings (which gives you time to answer it in three);
◆ rehearse your answering message several times before you record it, so that you sound confident and fluent;
◆ smile whilst you record your message;
◆ give the name of your business in the message (including your name is nice and welcoming but not essential);
◆ ask the caller to speak clearly, leave their name and telephone number and the reason for their call;
◆ include a ring-back time in your message and stick to it (for instance, before the close of business that evening, or tomorrow morning); and
◆ remember to change the message if you are closing for holidays, etc.

It is possible to purchase headsets so that you can talk on the phone whilst you are working. These are favoured by many, but consider the point about being distracted and inattentive before investing in one. The caller will know if you are not committed to the call and it may impact on your work. Experiment with a friend and experience it yourself.

Greeting the client face to face

The rules for meeting the client in person are just as important as the way you answer the phone, only now the client can read your body language and see your face. So:

◆ Always tidy yourself before receiving a client;
◆ smile and look pleased to receive them;
◆ greet both the owner and their dog;

A few hints on answering the telephone:

- *Never let it ring more than three times before you pick it up to answer.*
- *Always take a deep breath, release it and smile before you pick up. This will take any stress from your voice and you will sound friendlier and more welcoming.*
- *Practise how you are going to introduce yourself. A blunt 'Hello' is not good enough! Try something like 'Good morning, this is (name of business), you are speaking to (your name). How may I help you?'*
- *Stop doing everything else and concentrate on the call. The caller will sense if you are preoccupied and may lose interest in you and your business.*
- *If the caller is an existing client, always sound pleased to hear from them. If the client is a new customer, try to sound welcoming and professional.*
- *Remember to use the client's name and the dog's name.*
- *Make acknowledging sounds whilst the client is talking.*
- *Answer the client by paraphrasing (repeating back) to them their instructions. This demonstrates that you have listened carefully and respectfully and have understood them.*
- *Remember the Data Protection Act and do not repeat any sensitive information in the presence of another client.*
- *Always confirm the appointment day, date and time by repeating them back to the client.*
- *Never hurry the client, remain polite and calm at all times.*
- *Always speak clearly and give precise instructions.*
- *When you say goodbye, wait until the client puts down their phone before you replace your receiver.*

- speak confidently, clearly and precisely;
- with existing clients that are well known to you, always ask after their pet's health and the health of their family;
- with new clients do not push for personal information – wait until it has been volunteered;
- do not invade personal space;
- make sure that both you and the client are in agreement over the service(s) you are to perform/carry out;
- inform the client of any differences in the services (or any protocols) that may have changed since their last visit;
- double-check record card details; and
- never joke or get too familiar with a client as this breaks down the professional distance.

Business and/or appointment cards

These should always be available, even if the client insists on writing their next appointment in their diary. Writing the appointment details on a card allows you to check that the date and time of the appointment are correctly recorded; this can help prevent dogs turning up on the wrong day. Another good reason for handing out appointment cards is that the client will always have your details available to pass on to friends and family. You may even want to advertise on the back of cards and make clients aware of any offers you are running.

Customer records and data protection

It is imperative that you keep details of the animals in your care and update these records after every visit. You therefore need to have some way of managing this, either by keeping a paper record card in a box file or by recording the information in a book or as an electronic record on a computer.

Note that customer details – wherever and however recorded – are private and are covered by the Data Protection Act 1998 (*see* Section 6.2.3). Your customer records (including your salon diary) contain information that is covered by this Act; this also applies to any information that you retain on employees.

The cash register and recording transactions

When you begin trading, you should advise HM Revenue and Customs (HMRC) of this. It may be many years before you reach the tax threshold, but the powers that be prefer to be kept informed of these things! You can apply for a free business information pack that will advise you on everything you need to know about keeping the information the tax officer will require and when he will require it (*see* Taxes).

You need to keep records of all your financial transactions, including copies of receipts for funds received and invoices/receipts for your expenditures.

Payments can be received in several ways. Cash payments are straightforward transactions using legal tender. With cheque payments, be aware that your bank may charge you a transaction fee for banking cheques. Make sure that the client has a valid cheque guarantee card, bearing the correct signature, and that the cheque is properly completed (if appropriate) with:

- The name of the payee
- The date
- The amount in figures
- The amount in words
- A signature

For *credit or debit card payments* you may need to purchase a card reader, although it may be possible to hire readers from some credit card companies. There is usually a bank charge for using this service. You will also need to purchase paper receipt rolls for the machine. Further information is available from the following websites:

www.chipandpinsolutions.com
www.cardsave.net/Small businesses

WARNING!

There are many card reader rental service providers, so shop around for the best and most efficient service. Read both the small print and get-out clauses.

For owners of dogs that are on a regular grooming programme, paying by *direct debit* is an option. The money is automatically transferred into your bank on an agreed date, usually at no extra charge.

Primarily set up for small businesses selling their goods online, Paypal is a reliable, safe, electronic payment service that allows you to take payment via your business website, or even via your mobile phone. It is quick, easy and free to set up and there are no monthly charges. For further and up-to-date information on this service visit: www.paypal-business.co.uk.

A few tips on salon notice-boards and client notices

♦ *Any 'sensitive' subject can often be accepted more readily if the client reads it in notice/poster form. In this form it is available for all to see and is not directed at any one person.*

♦ *Make all notices clear, with a precise message.*

♦ *They can be amusing but they must be polite.*

♦ *They should appeal to all clients.*

♦ *They must be displayed at a height that allows all clients to read them.*

♦ *They must not demonstrate racist language, be prejudicial or offensive in any way.*

♦ *Think twice about using fancy writing or slang words. Not everyone will be able to read or understand the message.*

♦ *Company protocols and/or policies should be signed and dated.*

Table 12   A sample client record card.

Name of client	Name of dog
Address: Home telephone no.: Work no.: Mobile no.:	Breed: DoB: Sex: Neutered: Y/N Colour: Microchip no.: Distinguishing marks:
Veterinary surgery Telephone no: Emergency no:	In the event of an emergency, if my own vet is unobtainable, or too far away, I give permission for treatment to be given by the veterinarian used by your company. Signed: _____ Date:
Vaccination due date: Vaccination card checked: Y/N	Flea treatment: Date due: Worm treatment: Date due:
Health issues	Medication
Grooming requirements:	

date	groomer	cost	date	groomer	cost

7 The Working Environment: Health and Safety, Hygiene and Environmental Protection

The title of this chapter may have put you off already; indeed, it may appear tedious to some readers and frightening to others. But fear not! You will find it surprisingly interesting, relevant and useful, and it is essential reading!

This chapter aims to cover three key aspects of the salon environment, namely Health and Safety issues, salon hygiene and, last but not least, our responsibilities towards the environment. Health and Safety is discussed in a practical and constructive manner, the aim being to make this subject a positive contribution to your working environment rather than some onerous set of hard-to-understand regulations to attend to. A grooming salon should be a clean, safe, healthy and pleasant place to work, so hygiene issues and the importance of a well-planned cleaning regimen will be addressed. Finally, your attention will be drawn to the environmental footprint of your business and suggestions provided that will help you in formulating your own environmental policy.

If you are grooming your own dog at home, your responsibilities are unlikely to extend beyond those you owe to yourself, your dog, members of your household and the environment. In order to meet these responsibilities, however, you need to develop your awareness and understanding of the potential problems you may encounter or may cause. By contrast, this chapter is vitally important if you are, or plan to be, a commercial groomer, for it deals with your responsibilities towards all who enter the salon environment, whether they be staff, clients, visitors, dogs or indeed you. Your actions can impact on the health and welfare of all those you have dealings with, as well as affecting the wider environment beyond your door.

We are all affected by, and responsible for, these issues; the information in this chapter may help you to avoid problems such as the loss of your career and income through poor health, as well as the loss of business through the spreading of disease, bad publicity and litigation.

If you are not working in the United Kingdom, you should check government websites for all legislation (and advice) relevant to these subjects.

7.1 HEALTH AND SAFETY

The subject of Health and Safety is an enormous and growing one, and cannot be covered comprehensively here. Where complex issues are touched upon, links to useful, reliable websites have been included to allow you to research further information from reputable sources. This will not only answer all your questions, but also enable you to keep up to date with relevant legislation as changes are made after the publication of this book.

Health and Safety issues are often the butt of jokes and derisory comments in the media and amongst the general public. This is unfortunate and ill-advised, for it deflects attention from the core objective of Health and Safety policy, which should always be to keep everybody safe at all times and ensure that risks are managed and accidents prevented wherever possible. It is not about taking disproportionate measures and preventing people from doing their jobs. It is about practical and sensible risk evaluation and management. This is achieved by looking at each and every activity, evaluating it, identifying who and what is at risk and determining appropriate control measures (precautions) to keep everybody safe. These then need to be implemented and enforced.

Most of us continuously evaluate the risks to ourselves and others throughout our everyday lives. We monitor the traffic before we cross the road; we agree to wear seatbelts and comply with speed limits for road safety; we prevent small children from hurting themselves with hot water, irons and open fires; and we calculate the consequences of simple things like climbing ladders that could topple if unstable or poorly secured. And yet, when this is brought to our attention and we are lawfully required to evaluate hazards and risks, we often view it as a tiresome, unnecessary task. Health and Safety evaluation is, however, a legal obligation and is essential to the development of reliable protocols and procedures that ensure the protection and security of everyone in your workplace.

Perhaps most importantly, it is also something that we can all, as individuals, take ownership of. In doing so, we are empowered to take responsibility for our own safety and that of the people our actions can affect. This requires us to develop a set of skills that allow dynamic risk assessments in particular to be undertaken.

HEALTH AND SAFETY DEFINITIONS AND TERMINOLOGY

HSE (Health and Safety Executive) *The HSE is a national independent watchdog for work-related health, safety and illness. The HSE is an independent regulator, whose role is to protect the public and reduce work-related deaths and serious injury across the workplaces of Great Britain.*

RIDDOR (Reporting of Injuries, Diseases and Dangerous Occurrences Regulations) *The RIDDOR 1995 Act places legal obligations on employers, self-employed persons and those in charge of work premises to report work-related deaths, major injuries, work-related diseases and dangerous occurrences (near-miss accidents) in the work place.*

HASAW (Health And Safety At Work) *The Health and Safety at Work Act 1974 is legislation covering occupational Health and Safety in the United Kingdom, which is enforced by the HSE.*

COSHH (Control Of Substances Hazardous to Health) *COSHH is the law that requires employers to control all substances, whether in liquid, solid or powder form, that are hazardous to humans or animals. The law is enforced by the HSE.*

SOPs (Standard Operating Procedures) *A SOP is a set of written instructions that documents a routine or repetitive activity that should be carried out and respected within an organization.*

PPE (Personal Protective Equipment) *Personal protective clothing is subject to the PPE at Work Regulations 1992, which covers all protective equipment in the workplace including, masks, gloves, clothing, footwear, hearing protection, etc. It is enforced by the HSE.*

Health and Safety Policy *This is a workplace policy intended to prevent people 'being harmed by work or becoming ill, by taking the right precautions and providing a satisfactory working environment' (HSE 2003).*

Hazard *A situation, circumstance or event that can result in an unexpected or undesirable consequence. A hazard can also be described as something that has the potential to cause physical or mental harm.*

Risk *Risk is the likelihood of the hazard's potential being realized. It can also be defined as the likelihood and severity of harm.*

Risk Assessment *The identification and assessment of hazards. It is the determination of a quantitative or qualitative risk, relative to a given situation, specific threat or hazard.*

PAT (Portable Appliance Testing) *Annual testing of all portable electrical appliances that must be undertaken and recorded by a qualified electrician.*

7.1.1 Health and Safety Law

This section deals with current (at the time of writing) Health and Safety legislation in the United Kingdom. These regulations and recommendations are concerned with human welfare, animal welfare and legislation, as discussed in Chapter 6. There are many Health and Safety risks in the workplace and there are a number of different pieces of legislation corresponding to these risks.

These risks and the relevant legislation covering each of them are summarized in Table 13.

Some of the more important pieces of legislation are the Health and Safety at Work Act 1974; the Control of Substances Hazardous to Health Regulations 2002; the Personal Protective Equipment at Work Regulations 1992; and the Reporting of Injuries, Diseases and Dangerous Occurrences Regulations 1995. Knowledge of these laws is very important so the following sections look at them individually in more detail.

7.1.2 The Health and Safety at Work Act

Health and Safety in the workplace is covered by an Act of Parliament the Health and Safety at Work Act 1974, which is also known as HASAWA 1974. It is enforced by the Health and Safety Executive (HSE).

HASAWA 1974 specifies the duties and responsibilities of employers and employees as well as other individuals in the workplace, and protects the health, safety and welfare of persons within the workplace. If you are employed, your employer has a legal duty to protect you and to keep you informed about Health and Safety matters. Within the workplace, all employees also have a responsibility to their employers as well as to themselves and their work colleagues. General duties also exist that are undefined under the Act; they include the requirement that all self-employed persons ensure that their undertakings do not expose other persons (non-employees) to risks to their health and safety.

An employer's duties include:

- ensuring, as far as is reasonably practical, the health, safety and welfare of employees within the workplace;
- making the workplace safe and without risk to health;
- keeping dust, fumes, contaminants and noise under control;
- ensuring that all machinery is safe for use and standard operating procedures (SOPs) are in place to ensure such machinery is used safely (*see* Fig. 7.1.1);
- ensuring systems are in place for the safe movement, storage and usage of articles and substances;
- providing clear instructions on how to use chemicals (*see* Fig. 7.1.2);
- providing adequate signage (*see* Fig. 7.1.3);
- ensuring that all staff and volunteers are given information, instruction, supervision and training necessary for the protection of health and safety. This includes, for example, training in the use of fire

extinguishers and evacuation procedures in the event of a fire;

◆ providing, free of charge, any protective clothing or equipment specifically required by Health and Safety law;

◆ keeping and maintaining an accident book for the recording of all accidents and dangerous occurrences within the workplace;

◆ reporting certain injuries, diseases and dangerous occurrences to the enforcing authority;

◆ providing adequate First Aid facilities; and

◆ providing adequate firefighting equipment (*see* Fig. 7.1.4).

Fig. 7.1.1   An employer is responsible for ensuring that all staff and volunteers are given the information, instruction, supervision and training necessary for the protection of health and safety. This includes checking equipment before and after use.

Fig. 7.1.2   Employers are responsible for providing clear instructions on how to use chemicals. The dilution rates for these chemicals are on the bottles but to safeguard against the labels becoming soiled and unreadable, the instructions are also on the wall for all to see.

If there are five or more employees, the employer must, by law, draw up a Health and Safety policy statement, which includes the Health and Safety arrangements that are in force. The statement and any revisions to it must be brought to the attention of all staff.

Fig. 7.1.3   Adequate signage should be provided and used whenever there is a risk of injury. Signs such as the one illustrated are placed either in the doorway to prevent entry or in front of a spillage.

Fig. 7.1.4   The grooming room should be equipped with both CO2 and water fire extinguishers. CO2 is used in the event of electrical fires arising from tumble driers or other pieces of electrical equipment overheating. Instruction and training should be provided on the use of the equipment and fire drills should be practised. A fire alarm should also be fitted.

Other duties are included but these vary between workplaces according to the type of work undertaken. In the grooming establishment these duties will include:

◆ taking adequate precautions to prevent exposure to dusts, moulds, chemicals and contaminants;

◆ maintaining an acceptable workroom temperature;

◆ providing a work space that is not overcrowded and that is well ventilated and lit;

◆ providing clean washing and toilet areas and a supply of drinking water;

◆ ensuring that employees do not have to lift, carry or move any load (including dogs) that is likely to injure them (there are no legal weight restrictions);

◆ providing supervision for employees, particularly the new, young and inexperienced;

◆ providing suitable breathing, eye, ear and skin protection, and limiting exposure to substances and environments that may damage health; and

◆ ensuring that all electrical equipment is safe, maintained according to the manufacturer's instructions and complies with legal requirements, e.g. Portable Appliance Testing (*see* Fig. 7.1.5).

Fig. 7.1.5   This plug is from a hand-held hairdryer and clearly shows that the live wire was not correctly wired into the terminal, causing the wire to catch fire. The cables on hair-dryers and clippers are often stressed during a day's work and cable connections and plugs need to be regularly checked. PAT testing annually to check the condition and fittings of portable electrical appliances is a legal requirement if you employ staff.

Employees also have their legal duties. Their responsibilities include:

◆ taking reasonable care of their own health and safety and that of others who may be affected by their actions;

Table 13   Key areas for inclusion in your Health and Safety Policy and the relevant legislation.

Risk	Further Details	Relevant legislation
Accidents at work	First aid provision. Accident reporting. Bites, scratches and scissor injuries are discussed further under the First Aid section.	Health and Safety (First Aid) Regulations 1981
Injuries, diseases	Certain injuries, diseases and dangerous occurrences must be reported to the the enforcing authority. Zoonoses are discussed further under Health and Disease.	Reporting of Injuries, Diseases and Dangerous Occurrences Regulations 1995 (RIDDOR)
Slips, trips and falls	It is especially important to keep hair swept up and deposited straight into a bin and to use warning signs after washing floors.	
Fire	Fire precautions. Fire equipment. Fire drill.	Regulatory Reform (Fire and Safety) Order 2005. Information on fire exits, fire extinguishers and alarms is available from local fire authorities.
Chemicals and substances that may be hazardous to health	All chemicals used in the workplace should be risk assessed and clear instructions provided regarding their use and the measures to be taken if a problem arises (e.g. if the product is ingested or splashes into someone's eye).	Control of Substances Hazardous to Health Regulations 2002 (COSHH) (as amended). Chemicals (Hazard Information and Packaging for Supply) Regulations 2002 (as amended)
Air quality	The enclosed workplace should be ventilated by a sufficient quantity of fresh or purified air, so that the air breathed does not pose a risk to airways.	Workplace (Health, Safety and Welfare) Regulations 1992
Noise	Barking in kennels can potentially damage hearing.	Control of Noise at Work Regulations 2005
Electricity	Electrical appliances and water can prove a deadly combination. Sockets should have covers (see Fig. 7.1.6). All electrical appliances require annual PAT testing by a qualified electrician.	Electricity at Work Regulations 1989
Manual handling (see handling and restraint section for further information)	Especially important if working with large dogs and lifting them in and out of baths, or on and off tables.	Manual Handling Operations Regulations (1992)
Escaping dogs	Risk to the public (bites, road traffic accidents, etc).	

NOTE

The HSE produces a number of publications that the reader may find interesting and useful. The HSE books catalogue can be accessed online from the HSE website: www.hse.gov.uk/pubns.

Useful titles include **An Introduction to Health and Safety** *and* **The Essentials of Health and Safety at Work.** *These can be ordered online from www.hsebooks.co.uk or from HSE Books, PO Box 1999, Sudbury, Suffolk, C010 2WA. Tel: 01787 881 165.*

Many of the titles are available free as downloads, so check the HSE website. A further reading list is provided at the end of this section.

Fig. 7.1.6 *Water and electricity do not mix so plug sockets should be protected by a waterproof cover to prevent the risk of fire. For those of you just grooming your own pets at home, make sure that all plug sockets within the vicinity of your grooming and bathing space either have a child-proof plug protector or a plug in them to stop water penetration.*

♦ co-operating with their employer and following all instructions and standard operating procedures (SOPs);

♦ not interfering with or misusing equipment provided for their health and welfare;

♦ reporting all damaged equipment to their supervisor; and

♦ reporting all injuries and dangerous occurrences to their supervisor.

7.1.3 The Control of Substances Hazardous to Health (COSHH) Regulations 2002

As a groomer, your work will bring you into contact with a number of chemical products. It is essential that you know what these products contain, the risks posed by the ingredients and how the product should be used safely, so that any risk to your health is managed appropriately (*see* Fig. 7.1.7).

All manufacturers are required to

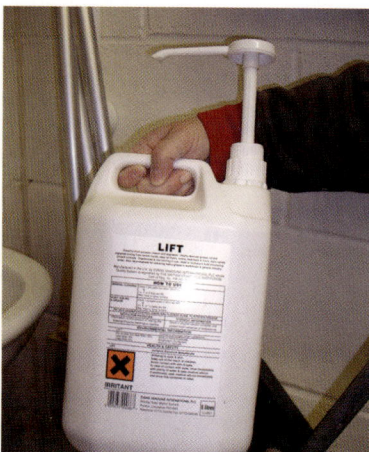

Fig. 7.1.7 *Read the labels on all products carefully. They advise you on how to use the product safely, whether or not you need to protect yourself and what to do if you use the product incorrectly. A COSHH sheet should be held on the premises for all products that you may be exposed to. This product carries a warning that it can irritate your skin.*

CAUTION

1. **Canine grooming products may have been tested thoroughly before being marketed. This does not mean, however, that they are safe for everyone to use. Reactions to perfumes, detergents and other ingredients are common and caution should always be exercised when ordering and trying out a new product. Container labels are relatively small and provide limited information (see Fig. 7.1.8) so always ask for the COSHH data sheet.**

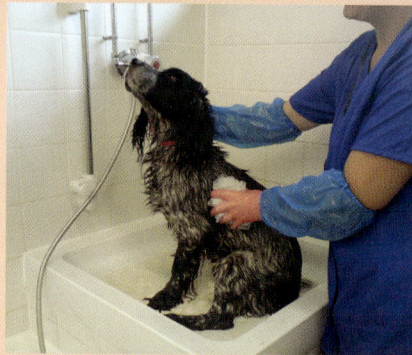

Fig. 7.1.8 *Animal shampoos have to be thoroughly tested before they are marketed but this does not mean that they are safe for everyone. Gloves and arm protectors (Personal Protective Clothing – PPE) are being used to safeguard this groomer's skin whilst bathing a dog.*

2. **Natural ingredients are often viewed as harmless and safe to use. This can give rise to an alarming degree of complacency. Henna can cause dermatitis and asthma, whilst citrus oils and tea tree oil can cause severe skin irritations. A COSHH data sheet should always be requested. At the very least groomers are advised to read and keep labels from bottles in case they (or a dog) suffers an adverse reaction.**

3. **You may be asked to use an unfamiliar product by an owner or veterinary surgeon. Such requests should always be made in advance and full details of the product, including a COSHH data sheet, supplied. The groomer should allow themselves the time to read up on the product before consenting to use it. By doing so, they ensure that they do not unwittingly expose themselves to a prescription drug or unpleasant chemical and are fully aware of the precautions they should take when using such products.**

---

provide you with a COSHH data sheet for their products. You should ensure that you have a data sheet for each and every substance used on your premises. Staff should know where the data sheets are kept and should be familiar with the data sheets, have read and understood them, and should comply with any recommendations made for using the product.

The COSHH data sheets indicate which products should be stored securely (i,.e. in a locked cupboard), which products contain toxic chemicals and irritants, and what to do in the event of exposure or ingestion. The data sheets also provide an indication of the shelf-life of the product and what sort of protective equipment should be worn when using the product.

A free leaflet entitled 'COSHH Essentials' is available from the HSE website (see Further Reading at the end of this section).

7.1.4 The Personal Protective Equipment at Work Regulations (1992)

The regulations require PPE such as gloves, eye protection and high-visibility clothing to be supplied and used at work wherever there are risks to workers' health and safety that cannot be adequately controlled in other ways.

PPE must be provided free of charge by the employer to the employee, although at the termination of a contract the employee is responsible for returning non-disposable PPE to the employer.

The PPE at Work Regulations (1992) specify that PPE:

◆ must be properly assessed before use to ensure its suitability for the work to be done;
◆ must provide adequate protection to the user;
◆ must be maintained and stored properly (e.g. in a clean cupboard or locker);
◆ must be supplied with instructions on how to use it safely; and
◆ must be used/worn correctly by employees when required.

The use of PPE should be viewed as a last resort after other control measures for dealing with the hazard have been considered and declared unsatisfactory. Training in the use of PPE should be provided and employers should ensure that everyone using PPE is aware of why it is required and the consequences of not using it. It is important that users wear it at all times when they are exposed to the risk, and exemptions should not be made even for the shortest of jobs. Regular checks should be made on the condition of non-disposable PPE and supplies of disposable PPE should not be allowed to run out.

It is important to remember that disposable PPE should be discarded after use. Your local authority will be able to advise on the safe disposal of used PPE.

All non-disposable PPE should be washed and maintained according to the manufacturer's instructions. Table 14 provides a list of protective equipment that may be indicated in the grooming room. Not all of this equipment is covered by the PPE regulations, as the regulations do not apply to hearing protection or to respiratory protective equipment – these are covered by other regulations.

Table 14   Personal Protective Equipment (PPE) in the grooming room.

Protective equipment	Indications and recommendations
Grooming tunics and trousers	Hair-resistant nylon clothing that does not attract hair or allow hair to penetrate through to your skin. For maximum safety the body should be covered from the neck to the ankle, with sleeves reaching the elbow. Fast drying if the groomer gets wet bathing the dog.
Disposable gloves	Latex, vinyl or nitryl disposable gloves that provide hands with protection from over-washing, wetting, over-exposure to cleaning and shampoo chemicals and other contaminants. Especially indicated when performing oral examinations and cleaning ears. Some individuals may have an allergy to latex and/or powder and should use alternative materials. A choice of gloves should always be provided.
Gauntlets	Strong leather gloves that may be used when restraining dogs who appear aggressive or likely to bite.
Face masks	Protect the user from breathing in airborne hair particles, micro-organisms, dust and dander. Sometimes difficult to get used to but essential when grooming out and blasting. (FFP2 valved respirator or similar is recommended.)
Protective glasses/safety glasses	Provide eye protection from hair particles, airborne dander, aerosols, sprays and even bouncy dogs.
Aprons	Disposable aprons can be used when washing dogs to keep the user dry and therefore minimize exposure to shampoo chemicals through wet clothing or when cleaning the salon. Non-disposable PVC aprons are more environmentally friendly but require regular washing.
Oversleeves	Either disposable plastic or waterproof nylon sleeves that are elasticated at both ends to stay in place, covering the arm from wrist to elbow. Used to prevent exposure to chemicals when bathing dogs and cleaning the environment.
Footwear	Non-slip, enclosed-foot, firmly fastened footwear should be worn when working in the grooming room. Some chemicals in cleaning products can penetrate leather easily. Consider wearing wellington boots when cleaning large areas such as exercise areas to protect feet and lower legs from chemical splashes.
Back supports	Not a legal requirement but recommended to prevent strain to the lower lumbar region during heavy work or long periods of standing.
Hearing protectors	A safeguard to protect the hearing of groomers from excessively noisy dogs, blasters and hair-dryers, particularly in a multi-groomer environment.

7.1.5 The Reporting of Injuries, Diseases and Dangerous Occurrences Regulations (RIDDOR) 1995

A few facts about gloves from HSE form S101.

- *Incorrect selection or misuse of disposable gloves can lead to skin diseases such as dermatitis.*
- *Do not assume that everyone can use the same type of glove. Latex and powder may result in an allergic reaction in some persons.*
- *Chemicals can seep through knitted cuffs on gloves, exposing the skin to a concentration of chemicals.*
- *Gloves can also keep materials against the skin if allowed to enter via the cuff.*
- *No glove is tested to give more than eight hours' protection against chemical permeation. Wear and tear, stretching and abrasion are not included in any testing.*
- *Gloves cannot be maintained. They nearly always become contaminated inside once they have been put on or during use. This contamination will continue working through the glove when it is not in use. Single-use gloves possibly therefore offer better protection.*
- *Gloves should be wiped dry before you take them off, otherwise you expose your skin to the chemicals as you remove them, defeating the object of wearing them.*
- *If you are using powdered gloves, you should wash your hands after you have taken them off.*

Accidents, by their very nature, are not planned and can happen in even the best-run health and safety-conscious establishments. All accidents, whether serious or minor, together with near-misses (where someone has just avoided being hurt) need to be recorded in the accident book and such incidents monitored. In some cases reports should be made to the relevant authority. This includes acts of violence towards a member of staff and the diagnosis of certain diseases. There are several reasons for this:

- To safeguard you in the event of litigation.
- To help you manage your business more effectively.
- Because it is a legal requirement to report some accidents to the relevant legal authority. By doing so you help to provide essential information that will contribute towards further protective legislation for accidents within the grooming (and other) workplaces.
- Reporting violence to yourself or an employee will help with further legislation to protect those (particularly lone workers) who are vulnerable to assault in the workplace.

RIDDOR place a legal duty of responsibility on:

- employers;
- self-employed persons; and
- people in control of work premises.

This includes everyone working either in commercial premises or in adapted commercial work areas in the home. Under the regulations a responsible person is required to notify the enforcing authority of an incident, accident, injury or disease as soon as possible after it occurs (or within ten days).

Groomers should report incidents to the local Health and Safety Executive (HSE) by telephoning a report through to the Incident Contact Centre, a one-stop reporting service for work-related health and safety incidents within the UK. They will be asked a few questions and their report will be passed to the relevant enforcing authority. They will then be provided with a copy of their report for filing, thus meeting the RIDDOR requirements to keep records of all reportable incidents.

What must be reported:

- deaths;
- major injuries;
- over three-day injuries where a person has been unable to resume work duties for more than three consecutive days;
- injuries to members of the public who are not on the premises for work, where they are taken from the scene of the accident to hospital;
- some work-related diseases (a free up-to-date guide is available from the HSE website). Such diseases include Bursitis, Carpal Tunnel Syndrome, Dermatitis, Hand and Arm Vibration Syndrome and Occupational Asthma); and
- dangerous occurrences which do not result in injury but could have done.

The Accident Book

Under Social Security law anyone making a claim for Industrial Injury Benefit in the UK must have proof that the injury is work-related. Employers are therefore required to keep a record of accidents for this purpose. As a result an 'Accident Book' or some equivalent means of recording accidents is needed. The main function of the Accident Book is to maintain records of minor injuries, a requirement imposed by the Social Security (Claims and Payments) Regulations 1979.

Your report in the accident book should contain the following information:

- the full name, address and occupation of the injured person;
- the date and time of the accident or incident;
- the place where the accident or incident took place;
- the cause and nature of the injury, or potential injury; and
- the name, address and occupation of any witnesses, or the person notifying you, if this is not the injured person.

At the time of writing, a new publication entitled *HSE Accident Book (B1510)* has been made available to comply with Data Protection requirements. Accident books preceding December 2003 will no longer be acceptable as the enclosed data does not comply with the current Data Protection Act.

The accident book must be retained

for at least three years after the date of the last entry.

The new Accident Book (ISBN 0717626032) is available from HSE Books, PO Box 1999, Sudbury, Suffolk, CO10 2WA. Alternatively, it is available from the HSE website: www.hsebooks.co.uk.

7.1.6 Developing a 'Health and Safety Plan' for the grooming salon

The Health and Safety Executive produces a booklet on Health and Safety for small businesses that provides a good overview of the subject and will guide you through the creation of a Health and Safety policy statement (HSE, 2003). The following list of recommendations will help the groomer and salon manager develop an effective Health and Safety plan:

◆ Obtain copies of all Health and Safety legislation relevant to your business (HSE, 2003).

◆ Consider any 'Industry Standards' as well as those in similar industries (e.g. hairdressing and veterinary practice) and compare these with the situation in your own business.

◆ Ensure appropriate risk assessments are undertaken, by a competent person, for all areas of your business and that these are reviewed regularly.

◆ Develop a written set of standard operating procedures (SOPs) that address all Health and Safety issues identified during the risk assessment (*see* Fig. 7.1.9).

◆ Review all SOPs and salon safety policies on a regular basis and after any accident or near-miss.

◆ Ensure that staff inductions and training cover all areas of Health and Safety policy, including the fire and evacuation drill. Specific training should be provided on fire prevention and how to respond in the event of a fire.

◆ Ensure adequate supervision is provided for new and inexperienced staff.

◆ Ensure that employees can report any safety concerns they may have.

◆ Ensure that adequate insurance cover is held at all times. This should include employer's and public liability cover.

◆ Ensure that up-to-date COSHH data sheets are held (and are readily available) for all chemical products used in the salon (this includes shampoos, grooming sprays, antiparasitic treatments, topical skin treatments and clipper oils and sprays as well as cleaning products) and that all staff are familiar with this information and any risks they may incur in using the product.

◆ Ensure that appropriate protective clothing and equipment are provided and that staff understand when and how to use them (Table 14).

◆ Ensure that all risk areas are provided with adequate signage (*see* Fig. 7.1.10).

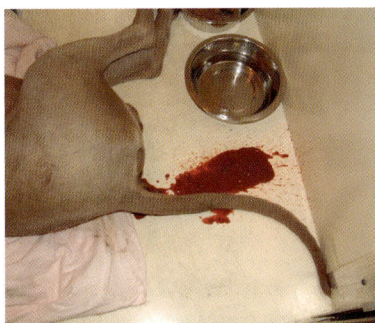

Fig. 7.1.9   It is not unusual for dogs to defecate whilst in your care. A standard operating procedure (SOP) to address all the health and safety issues identified during such an occurrence should be in place, including the correct use of PPE, disposal of bedding, deep cleaning the area, isolation, recording of the incident, the chemicals used to clean up and the persons exposed to the incident.

Tables 15 and 16 list some of the main hazards that a groomer is likely to identify when conducting a salon risk assessment. This list is intended to provide you with a check-list and starting point when you set about developing your own Health and Safety policy. Some of the areas listed in Table 15 may not be immediately obvious as threats to the health and safety of staff. This is particularly true of dangers that are more insidious in nature and build up over time. Thus the threat posed by a fire or an aggressive dog is very obvi-

Fig. 7.1.10   Ensure that all risk areas are adequately signed. Signs on gates and entrances help to prevent dogs escaping by warning the public to take precautions.

ous, whereas that posed by poor air quality is less so and may only become apparent over time. It is therefore important that a thorough risk assessment be carried out so that all risks are carefully evaluated and addressed.

The following examples will highlight two of the common risks a groomer may be exposed to, how they can be assessed and what measures can be taken to manage the problem.

Example 1: Air quality in the grooming room

Groomers may be exposed to a warm, high humidity and dusty environment for long periods during the day. These conditions can adversely affect the health of the skin, eyes, nose, throat and lungs.

The Canadian Centre for Occupational Health and Safety (CCOHS) describes indoor air quality problems as those occurring in buildings where chemical or biological contaminants build up to levels that can adversely affect some occupants (CCOHS, 2008). In the short term symptoms may include headache, nausea, flu-like symptoms, dry, itchy or runny eyes, stuffy or runny nose, dizziness, respiratory problems and chest tightness. In the long term exposure to polluted air can result in serious and permanent damage to one's health. A number of conditions arising from exposure to indoor air pollution have been identified and include Multiple Chemical Sensitivity (MCS), Tight Building Syndrome (TBS) and Building-Related Illness (BRI), as well as chemically induced hypersensitivity and occupational asthma.

In the UK employers have a duty to consider air quality issues. According to Regulation 6 of the Management of Health, Safety and Welfare Regulations (1992), 'effective and suitable provision shall be made to ensure that every enclosed workspace is ventilated by a sufficient quantity of fresh or purified air'.

An employer's legal duty arises under Section 2 of the Health and Safety at Work Act 1974 and requires them to do all they can to provide a safe system of work and a safe working environment. Employers may have to conduct a risk assessment, either under Regulation 6 of the Control of Substances Hazardous to Health Regulations (1995), if the polluting substance(s) is used in the workplace or results from a manufacturing process; or under Regulation 3 of the Management of Health and Safety at Work Regulations (1992). The latter places a duty on the employer to make a risk assessment if the substance arises from some other source.

Careful consideration must therefore be given to the subject of air quality and indoor air pollution. So where do we start? As with any aspect of the risk assessment process, definitions need to be provided, and the key hazards and their significance identified. Appropriate precautionary measures then need to be instituted. These are described below and summarized in Table 15.

Definitions

Air quality: The 'quality' of air reflects its purity. Pure (high-quality) air should be free from contamination. Air quality can also be defined in terms of the requirements of one or more living organisms. Thus, as air quality deteriorates, an increasingly large percentage of the population will experience adverse health effects.

Dust and hair particles: Dust can be defined as particulate matter in the air. As such, this material has the potential to enter our mouths and noses (*see* Fig. 7.1.11) and can gain access to our

digestive and respiratory tracts. Dust can be classified as inhalable or respirable, depending on the size of the particle and the depth to which it can penetrate our airways. Inhalable dust tends to get trapped in the saliva of our mouths and mucus of our airways. As such, it is unlikely to reach the lung tissues and is coughed up and/or swallowed. Respirable dust, by contrast, is fine enough ($2-10\mu m$) to pass down into the unciliated airways of the lungs (those that are not protected by cilia and mucus).

Fig. 7.1.11   Fine particles of hair and dead skin cells (dander) are a health hazard and can cause breathing problems and occupational asthma.

Ventilation: This is the process of changing or replacing air in any space in order to preserve its quality. Ventilation allows the control of air temperature, the replenishment of oxygen and the removal of carbon dioxide. It also allows the removal of moisture, odours, vapours, smoke, dust, airborne bacteria and other pathogens. It also promotes the circulation of air within a building to prevent it stagnating.

Allergic airway disease: The body's immune system can react to certain sensitizing substances, resulting in an inflammatory condition. Where the airways are affected, this is termed allergic airway disease. This response can take time to develop and there is usually a gap between exposure and the development of symptoms.

Asthma: Asthma is a condition in which the airways leading to the lungs become narrowed, resulting in reduced air flow and poor ventilation. It arises when the lining of the small airways of the lungs become inflamed and the smooth muscle within the airways goes into spasm. This produces a range of symptoms, including shortness of

breath, chest tightening, wheezing and coughing.

Irritants: Airway dysfunction can also be produced by irritants without the involvement of the immune system. Such materials are often vapours (e.g. ammonia) and may be given off by disinfectant products. They cause an irritation that produces an immediate protective response (muscle spasm, chest tightening, etc).

Hazards

All forms of air pollution that can provoke allergic airway disease, act as an irritant or otherwise affect the health of staff should be viewed as a hazard. These include mould spores (*see* Fig. 7.1.12), animal proteins, dust, fumes from chemical agents, oil mist, aerosols, ozone, carbon monoxide fumes and electrostatic discharges (Table 15). The significance and severity of this problem is difficult to quantify as working conditions vary considerably, as do the sensitivity and susceptibility of any given individual.

Fig. 7.1.12   Mould grows underneath bathmats and around bath seals. Mats should be disinfected daily on both sides and disposed of once the rubber starts to deteriorate. A broad spectrum disinfectant or bleach can be used to clean the seals around the bath, which should also be replaced as soon as they start to deteriorate.

The British Occupational Health Research Foundation quotes HSE figures for occupational asthma in the UK of 1,500–3,000 cases per year. This increases to 7,000 when work-aggravated cases of pre-existing asthma are taken into account.

A number of trades are recognized as being at particular risk. These include workers who are exposed to animal fur (*see* Fig. 7.1.13), dander, dried urine and saliva dust. These materials contain animal proteins that the body's immune system can react to. Laboratory animal workers and pigeon fanciers have been identified as high-risk groups but all those working in animal care are potentially at risk.

Fig. 7.1.13   Hair is a hazard. It should not be allowed to accumulate on the floor, where it can spread parasites and disease. It also puts the groomer at risk of slipping, and the movement of the hair around your feet will put hair and dust particles into the air.

Safety measures

Ventilation can be either dilution ventilation or exhaust ventilation. *Dilution ventilation* ensures that the pollution is dispersed by being evenly distributed throughout the workplace (e.g. fans mixing up the air and moving air around within a room). *Local exhaust ventilation* (LEV) ensures pollution is removed at its point of generation. This can be achieved by the strategic positioning of suitable extraction systems in problem areas, which should capture specific airborne contaminants before they are spread into the environment. This is suitable for water vapour control. *General exhaust ventilation* (GEV) ensures that the air in the workplace is replaced with pure air. Three complete changes of air per hour is the European standard according to the *Guidelines for Ventilation Requirements in Buildings* published in 1992 by the Commission of the European Communities.

Management of dust should be prioritized so that the amount of particulate matter in the air is kept to a minimum. This can be done by disposing of hair regularly and systematically into a bin or bin bag. The workstation has to be organized in order to make this easy.

Care should also be taken not to disturb or raise dust unnecessarily when placing hair and other waste products in the bin, closing bin bags, emptying bins or emptying the vacuum cleaner. Where bin bags are being closed, the hair should be damped down before carefully sealing the bag; failure to do so can release large amounts of dust into the air.

Vacuum cleaners should be fitted with High Efficiency Particulate Air (HEPA) filters to ensure that respirable dust particles are collected. Filters must be renewed regularly to remain effective. Check that your vacuum cleaner meets these standards as most vacuum cleaners only remove inhalable dust particles.

Use of an air ionizer can help reduce the amount of material in the air by attaching an electrostatic charge to the particles that makes them more attractive to room surfaces, such that they fall to the ground.

Protecting airways is easily done by using a suitable face-mask. The face-mask (*see* Fig. 7.1.14) should filter out particles down to 1μm at the least. Higher-specification face-masks or respirators can provide higher levels of protection and often eliminate aerosolized droplets as small as 0.1μm. Comfort is likely to prove a very important consideration with this sort of equipment, especially if it has to be worn for long periods of time.

By taking all reasonable measures to prevent exposure to sensitizing aller-

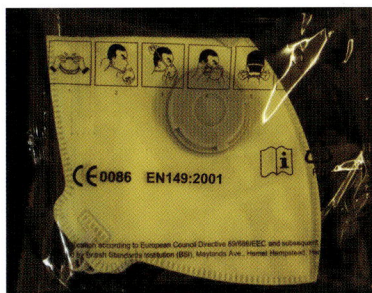

Fig. 7.1.14   Protect your airways at all costs. You may think that it is unnecessary but failure to do so can result in the loss of your career and permanent health problems. Pictured is a disposable mask with a ventilator that allows the wearer to breathe in filtered air. Washable grooming masks are also available from grooming suppliers.

gens, the risk can be managed. Working practices should, however, be regularly reviewed to ensure that all staff, especially those predisposed to complacency, adhere to standard operating procedures. Spot inspections may identify areas of mould growth that have not been addressed (for example, on the underside of bath mats (*see* Fig. 7.1.12), between tiles and around tap bases), unacceptable levels of humidity in the wash room and excessive levels of dust in the grooming room (usually above eye level).

Example 2: Hand care in the grooming room

Groomers use their hands constantly in their work and are exposed to all sorts of chemicals, materials and environments as well as the occasional bite or scratch. Prolonged and/or frequent contact with water, shampoos, hot air, sprays, potions and lotions can all cause damage to your hands. It is therefore essential that the groomer knows how to protect and look after their hands, if they are to avoid problems.

Definitions

Dermatitis: An inflammatory condition or irritation of the skin is referred to as a *dermatitis*. It is also popularly known as 'eczema'. There are many subclassifications of dermatitis depending on the underlying cause.

Contact dermatitis: Exposure of the skin to allergens (substances provoking an allergic reaction), irritants or light (photocontact) can result in a skin reaction known as *contact dermatitis*.

Atopic dermatitis: The skin of individuals suffering from *atopic dermatitis* reacts abnormally and readily to a range of irritants, food and environmental allergens. It is characterized by the development of red, flaky and very itchy skin. It is an inherited condition and is not contagious. It is a condition that typically develops in childhood and can persist into adulthood. It is also common in dogs.

Work-related dermatitis: Dermatitis arising through exposure to certain substances or conditions at work is termed

Table 15 Airway pollution hazards and control measures.

Airway pollution hazard	Significance	Control measures
Animal hair (especially if coated in saliva) Animal dander (skin cells) Animal urine	Contain animal proteins that can sensitize in contact individuals and lead to the development of allergic airway disease.	Can be reduced through regular washing. Wear protective face-mask or respirator. Place all hair immediately and systematically into a bin bag. Ensure vacuum cleaner is equipped with a HEPA filter and that this is changed regularly.
House dust mite	Found in soft furnishings. One of the main allergens causing allergic airway disease in the home environment.	Eliminate soft furnishings from the grooming room. Ensure floors are carpet free.
Mould	Inhaled mould spores are a common allergen that can provoke allergic airway disease. Mould can grow under carpets and behind wallpaper so may not be visible.	Mould should not be allowed to grow on surfaces within the grooming salon. It can be prevented by ensuring humidity levels are minimized and all surfaces dry out completely at the end of each day. Mould can be removed where it does occur with suitable cleaning products.
Chemical fumes	Fumes from solvents, glutaraldehyde and ammonia are potent irritants and are likely to cause airway spasm.	Consider switching to other products. Only use in well-ventilated areas using an appropriate respirator.
Aerosols	Produced when bathing dogs, using aerosol cans or spraying liquid cleaning agents.	Use aerosols sparingly and in well-ventilated areas. Ensure disinfectant spray bottles are set to produce a jet rather than a mist.

work-related dermatitis. Employees exposed to chemical agents and wet work, where the hands become wet repeatedly and for prolonged periods during the working day, are particularly prone to this type of dermatitis. Other agents include biological factors (e.g. bacteria and fungi, etc.), physical factors (e.g. drying, vibration or radiation) and mechanical factors (e.g. abrasions).

Groomers' hands are exposed to a range of hazards. These can be divided into four groups:

◆ those that cause irritation to the skin leading to irritant contact dermatitis;
◆ those that sensitize the skin causing allergic contact dermatitis;
◆ those that cause other forms of skin disease such as changes in pigmentation and skin cancer; and
◆ those that cause other effects such as drying, scratches, burns and other abrasions.

Many of these hazards are difficult to avoid. Each, however, needs to be identified and considered in order to determine how best to manage the risks (Table 16).

The incidence of work-related dermatitis amongst groomers is unknown. What is clear, however, is that groomers are an 'at risk group' as they regularly come into contact with hazardous substances such as shampoos, detergents and cleaning products, and have their hands in water for about two hours a day, possibly more for apprentices. Work-related dermatitis can cause considerable pain and discomfort. It has also resulted in people having to take time off work or even change jobs, and has resulted in millions of pounds being paid to victims in compensation. It therefore needs to be taken very seriously, whether you are an employer or an employee.

Safety measures

◆ List all substances used in the salon and ensure COSHH sheets are held for each substance. Identify all those that carry irritant or corrosive signs.
◆ Where irritant or corrosive substances are used, see if an alternative substance can be found. If they must be used (e.g. for cleaning), ensure that staff have adequate

training in the usage of the product, that they understand the instructions on the container and that the necessary protective clothing is available.
◆ The HSE **Skin Checks for Dermatitis** poster should be displayed in the grooming room. It is available from:
www.hse.gov.uk/skin/posters/skindermatitis.pdf.
◆ Staff can be issued with the HSE leaflet 'It's in your hands' on preventing work-related dermatitis, available on line from: www.hse.gov.uk/skin/emply/gloves.htm.
◆ Monitoring of hand and skin problems will help identify any potential problems. Staff should report if they are suffering any of the following symptoms: redness or swelling hands/fingers, itching and cracking of the skin, blisters, flaking/scaling of the skin. Where these symptoms recur or clearly improve when away from the grooming environment, this raises the suspicion of a work-related dermatitis.
◆ Reduce exposure of all staff to hazardous substances and wet working conditions (including clothing). This may be through careful

selection of grooming products (selecting those that are less harmful/kindest to hands), reducing the frequency of bathing dogs per person or insisting that gloves and arm protectors are used, and minimizing the time hands are working under driers by removing as much water from the coat as possible before drying.

◆ Provide adequate personal protective equipment (PPE) for staff as individuals, together with the training required for each piece of equipment. The selection of gloves, masks and clothing is surprisingly complex and you will benefit from consultation with staff and suppliers as well as with the manufacturers of the equipment.

◆ Provide hand-care products that help to maintain the skin in good condition and reinforce its natural protective function. Pre-work creams, skin cleansers and after-work creams all have a role to play. *Pre-work creams* are used to provide a semi-resistant barrier when gloves are not needed. *Skin cleansers* are intended to remove contamination from the skin and should not be unnecessarily powerful. *After-work creams* are typically moisturizing products that restore the skin's moisture content. They should be used after washing hands and at the end of the working day.

References and further information

CCOHS (2008). *Indoor air quality: A Health and Safety Guide*, 3rd edition. Hamilton, Canada: Canadian Centre for Occupational Health and Safety

Health and Safety Executive (1994). *Preventing asthma at work: how to control respiratory sensitizers.*

Health and Safety Executive (2003). *An Introduction to Health and Safety: Health and Safety in Small Businesses.*

Table 16 Hand care hazards and control measures.

Hazard	Mechanism of damage	Control measure
Floor cleaning products Detergents	May be corrosive or irritant.	Follow COSHH data sheet and manufacturer's guidelines. Wear appropriate PPE.
Soaps and hand cleaning products	Floor cleaning products. Detergents.	Ensure soaps used are as mild as possible and pH neutral Ensure after-work moisturizer is available to rehydrate the skin after washing.
Shampoos	May be drying and/or irritant.	Careful selection of products will ensure that they are not excessively drying or irritant. Exposure to shampoos should be reduced. Protective gloves can be worn whilst washing.
Water	Prolonged and repeated exposure to water will dry the skin by exposing the skin to increased evaporative losses. Warm water increases evaporative losses. Hard water can also contribute to the problem. Lime, magnesium and iron salts deposited on the skin cause a mechanical irritation. Hard water is less able to dissolve soaps and shampoos. This means that such products are more concentrated in the water and are harder to remove from hair coats and skin (yours and the dog's).	Minimize your exposure to water. Wear gloves and arm protectors. Use cooler water. Use a water-softening device in order to remove the limescale from the water. Apply a barrier cream/emollient to your hands after washing and after work to lock in the water and minimize evaporative losses.
Gloves	Some gloves may themselves cause skin irritations and reactions. Gloves do not provide adequate protection if washing water enters via the cuff.	When selecting protective gloves, the choice should be based on the work, the wearer and the environment they work in. Latex and powdered gloves should be avoided.
Scratches and bites	Can represent an infection risk.	Appropriate handling. Some protection is offered by gloves.

Note: the potency of chemicals, time spent in water and under dry heat can also have an effect on the health of the dog's skin, which may react adversely to them, leading, ultimately, to the development of skin inflammation, otherwise known as dermatitis.

Health and Safety measures can appear onerous to those who just want to get on with their work. By contrast, they can also prove life-saving to those who find themselves in harm's way. They are not meant to make work difficult; their true value lies in making work safe. This is not possible without undertaking a risk assessment and deciding how working practices can be modified to minimize the risks. Fortunately, much of the data collection and evaluation has been undertaken by organizations such as the HSE. Such organizations should therefore be viewed as our allies in tackling work-related injuries. An essential part of this work involves ensuring that the key information is made available to employers and employees so that safe working practices can be promoted.

Available online from: www.hse.gov.uk/pubns/indg259.pdf.

Health and Safety Executive (2008). *A guide to the reporting of injuries, diseases and dangerous occurrences regulations 1995*. 3rd edition.

Available online from: www.hse.gov.uk/pubns/priced/l73.pdf.

WCB (2005). *Indoor air quality: A guide for building owners, managers and occupants*. British Columbia, Canada: Worker's Compensation Board.

Available online from: www.work-safebc.com/publications/health_and_safety/by_topic/assets/pdf/indoor_air_bk89.pdf

Weese, J.S., Peregrine, A.S. and Armstrong, J. (2002). Occupational health and safety in small animal veterinary practice. Part I Nonparasitic zoonotic diseases. *Canadian Veterinary Journal*, 43 (8), 631–6.

Weese, J.S., Peregrine, A.S. and Armstrong, J. (2002). Occupational health and safety in small animal veterinary practice. Part II Parasitic zoonotic diseases. *Canadian Veterinary Journal*, 43 (10), 799–802.

Websites

www.hse.gov.uk/index.htm.

Website of the UK government's Health and Safety Executive.

www.hse.gov.uk/legislation/hswa.htm.

Provides information on the Health and Safety at Work Act 1974 and a link to the UK legislation website.

www.hse.gov.uk/fireandexplosion/workplace.htm.

Provides details on workplace fire safety, together with useful links.

www.communities.gov.uk/fire/fire-safety/firesafetylaw.

Provides details on fire safety law and guidance documents for businesses.

www.bohrf.org.uk/downloads/asthwork.pdf.

Website of the British Occupational Health Research Foundation, providing a free download of 'Occupational Asthma: a guide for employers, workers and their representatives.

www.coshhessentials.org.uk.

Provides a free internet version of COSHH essentials: Easy steps to control chemicals.

www.barbicide.co.uk/index.htm.

Provides details and COSHH data

sheets on products such as Barbicide and Clippercide.

7.2 HYGIENE

The grooming salon should be a clean, safe and healthy place to work. We have already considered how it can be made safe but why, how and to what extent should it be kept clean?

Salon hygiene standards will need to be established and respected if your premises are to remain clean and presentable. Clearly this is necessary if your premises are to impress clients and be pleasant to work in. Perhaps most importantly, however, high standards of hygiene are required as a control measure for a wide range of disease threats, both human and canine.

This section summarizes the main points that you must consider in drawing up a cleaning regimen before providing the reader with a description of how to go about cleaning and disinfecting the grooming environment.

Salon hygiene and cleaning regimens

A busy salon will be visited by a large number of dogs, creating the possibility of disease transmission. Whilst the subject of infectious diseases is discussed elsewhere (*see* Chapter 5), and a strong emphasis placed on ensuring that dogs visiting the salon are both vaccinated and healthy, there is also a need to ensure that the grooming environment and equipment are not themselves contaminated. This is important if they are not to serve as sources of infection to visiting dogs.

Contamination with fungal spores, bacteria and viral particles is, by its very nature, microscopic and therefore invisible. Contamination has to be assumed, and both cleaning and disinfection therefore have to be undertaken as part of a regular routine.

At this point it is important to distinguish between cleaning and disinfection. *Cleaning* is the process whereby hair, dirt, grease and other contaminants are removed from a surface or piece of equipment. *Disinfection (dis – infection)* makes use of a disinfectant to destroy micro-organisms living on a non-living surface. Disinfectants are

different from *antibiotics* (that destroy bacteria within the body) and *antiseptics* (that are applied to a living surface such as the skin).

Disinfection cannot be assumed to kill all micro-organisms for there are some that are especially resistant (e.g. certain bacterial spores). The complete destruction of all micro-organisms relies on extreme chemical and/or physical processes and is termed *sterilization*.

Sterilization is required for the preparation of surgical equipment and the cleaning of operating theatres, where concerns over wound infections and the infection of immuno-compromised patients dictate the highest possible standards. It is less important in low-risk environments, such as the grooming room, where a different level of cleanliness is acceptable. The grooming room therefore needs to be cleaned and disinfected rather than sterilized; this ensures that the common disease threats are minimized and, it is hoped, eliminated. Grooming equipment, however, benefits from sterilization to help protect each dog from cross-contamination from another animal (*see* Fig. 7.2.1).

Within a busy grooming room, spot cleaning must be done many times throughout the day. This is where baths, tables and equipment are cleaned and disinfected between dogs (*see* Fig. 7.2.2). It needs to be done with as little disruption to dogs and colleagues as possible, and with pre-prepared solutions. At the end of the day, when the dogs have gone home and it is safe to do so, a complete clean should be implemented.

When planning and organizing your working environment (*see* Chapter 6), ease of cleaning should be high on your list of priorities. Cleaning equip-

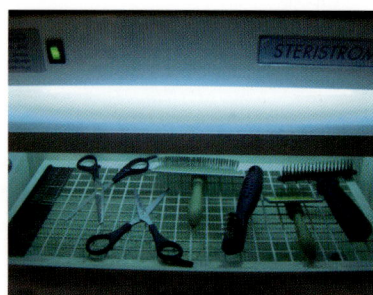

Fig. 7.2.1 A UV sterilizer supports your cleaning regime. Sterilize all tools after they have been washed to remove grease and dirt.

Fig. 7.2.2   A quick wipe over a grooved table top is not sufficient because the deeper grooves may not be treated. Care must be taken to ensure that cleaning disinfectants reach between the grooves. Groomers should know the dilution rate of the disinfectant, how long the ingredients remain active once they have been diluted and what PPE to use.

NOTE

Cleaning is necessary before disinfection in order to remove organic material such as grease and sebum that can get in the way and therefore reduce the efficiency of the disinfection process. The presence of proteins interferes with the two most frequently recommended CPV disinfectants – sodium-hypochlorite and formaldehyde (McGaving, 1987).

---

ment should always be accessible and ready for use.

When formulating your cleaning routine, the following things need to be considered.

Surfaces and equipment to be cleaned:

◆ Table tops and frames
◆ Baths, towels, body scrubs and sponges
◆ Cages, kennels and bedding
◆ Grooming tools, scissors and clipper blades
◆ Muzzles and restraining equipment
◆ Mirrors
◆ Walls
◆ Floors
◆ Exercise areas
◆ Reception, office and communal areas
◆ Cleaning equipment, including mop heads, vacuum cleaners, brooms, dustpan and brushes
◆ Washing machines and tumble driers

Cleaning products and disinfectants:

◆ All cleaning products should have clear labels and should be used at all times according to the manufacturer's instructions.
◆ Ensure all cleaning products are safe to use and do not pose a danger to the health of humans or animals.
◆ Cleaning products should remove all contamination (such as grease and hair) from surfaces and equipment prior to disinfection.
◆ Disinfection is less efficient if surfaces are coated in dirt and grime.
◆ Disinfectants should ideally be approved for veterinary use and should destroy the common canine pathogens, including canine parvovirus (CPV), parainfluenza virus (kennel cough), leptospirosis and Trichophyton mentagrophytes (ringworm) – *see* Table 17.
◆ Halogen compounds (i.e. those that contain chlorine or iodine), aldehydes and sodium hydroxide (i.e. caustic soda) were found by McGaving (1987) to be the most acceptable CPV disinfectants.
◆ Rycroft and McLay (1999) found that hypochlorite (bleach), benzalkonium chloride and glutaraldehyde-based disinfectants were the most effective of twelve agents tested against the fungus Microsporum canis. Phenolics, anionic detergents and alcohol were found to be inadequate.
◆ Many products claim good fungicidal activity based on tests on Trichophyton mentagrophytes. It is unclear if they are effective against all ringworm organisms, however, so check data sheets or contact the manufacturer if you are in doubt.
◆ The products used should not damage or degrade work surfaces and equipment.
◆ Anti-parasite treatments of the environment may also be indicated in order to deal with any flea eggs or larvae deposited in the environment. The manufacturer's instructions should always be followed; this is likely to mean spraying the grooming room last thing at night so that no staff or dogs are exposed to the product.

Frequency of cleaning:

◆ Equipment including muzzles, table ties, grooming out and de-matting tools, clipper blades, scissors and tool trays should be washed and/or cleaned and disinfected between dogs.
◆ Baths, body scrubs and sponges should be cleaned and disinfected between dogs.
◆ Tables should be cleaned and disinfected between dogs.
◆ Don't forget mirrors. They should also be sprayed and cleaned at the end of the day, or before if they become soiled.
◆ Floors and walls should be spot cleaned and disinfected after soiling has occurred and washed thoroughly once a day (at the end of the day).
◆ All kennels and cages used should be cleaned and disinfected, and the bedding changed, between dogs.

CAUTION

If a sick animal has entered the grooming salon, or has become sick whilst in your care, they may have contaminated the environment, so do not hesitate to institute an unplanned cleaning session!

Method of cleaning and disinfection of the grooming environment:

◆ The area to be cleaned should be free from clutter, making it easier to clean. Cleaning should not interfere with other groomers or dogs. Make a note of drying times for disinfectants and sterilizing times for equipment so that you can be sure to allow the treatment times to be completed.
◆ Cleaning the environment should be done from top to bottom and then from back to front.
◆ Hair should be swept from the table with a dustpan and brush

and placed directly into the bins, or swept from the floor carefully into a pile with a broom, without raising any dust; the area should then be vacuumed. It is a good idea to attach a bag to the side of the table to put the hair into whilst you are working.

◆ The table – including the frame – should be washed over with a general cleaner to remove grease, etc., sprayed with a suitable disinfectant, wiped over with a cloth (to spread the disinfectant evenly and ensure the whole surface is disinfected) and left to dry.

◆ Mirrors can be cleaned with a suitable glass cleaner once a day or as needed, and once a week washed with a general cleaner, spray disinfected and then cleaned with a glass cleaner.

◆ Bath mats need to be removed, washed with a cleaning agent, dried to remove excess water and sprayed with disinfectant. The bath and the surrounding walls should be washed down with a cleaning agent, wiped to remove excess water and then sprayed with disinfectant. The bath also needs to be washed down with a cleaning agent, wiped with a cloth to remove excess water and then sprayed with a suitable disinfectant. At the end of the day bleach can be put into the drain to clean the sump and the plumbing. Sponges and body scrubs can be washed in the washing machine.

◆ The washing machine should be used for grooming room laundry only to prevent the spread of bacteria and micro-organisms. A standard 40° wash is not sufficient to kill pathogens so it is wise to put the machine on a boil wash every few days or after washing heavily contaminated bedding (*see* Fig. 7.2.3).

◆ Floors should be swept and vacuumed to remove all hair and debris and then washed with a mop. The mop head should be agitated in the cleaning/disinfectant solution and wrung out before proceeding to clean the floor. Wash from the back of the room and work towards the door.

◆ The recommended concentration and contact time for the disinfect-

Fig. 7.2.3   A separate washing machine should be used for dog towels and bedding to prevent the spread of disease. A standard 40 degree wash with washing powder does not kill bacteria and micro-organisms so it is wise to put the machine on an empty boil wash every few days.

Fig. 7.2.4   Hair clogged into the wheels of stand dryers and grooming trolleys are a potential breeding ground for parasites and bacteria. It also reduces the mobility of the wheels and may cause the dryer or trolley to tip over rather than wheel away if it is pushed out of the way by a groomer in an emergency.

ant you are using should be established and adhered to. This means leaving the disinfectant in contact with the surfaces to be disinfected for a set amount of time (often 15–30 minutes).

◆ Wheels and castors on trolleys, stand dryers and cages should have the hair removed on a regular if not daily basis. Hair clogged into wheels is a potential breeding ground for parasites and bacteria. The mobility of the wheels is also compromised and may cause the dryer or trolley to fall over if it has

to be pushed aside in a hurry. With a dryer, this may present a fire risk, whilst with a trolley the contents could spill and cause a hazard, not to mention damaging your equipment (*see* Fig. 7.2.4).

◆ Kennels and cages should be cleaned between each dog. The bedding should be removed and put to wash unless it is soiled, in which case it should be put to soak in disinfectant before washing. The area should be swept, or vacuumed, to remove hair particles and debris and then washed with a suitable cleaning agent. Once dry, the area should be sprayed or washed with disinfectant and left to dry.

◆ Tumble driers should have lint removed from the filter after every use (*see* Fig. 7.2.5). Lint and moisture are the products of the drying process and are pulled from the dryer by a motorized fan. The build-up of lint will reduce the efficiency of the machine and can cause overheating; this represents a significant fire risk.

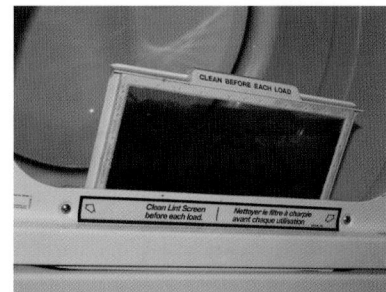

Fig. 7.2.5   Tumble driers should have the lint removed from the filter after every use. Lint and moisture are by-products of the drying process and are pulled from the dryer by a motorized fan. The build-up of lint reduces the efficiency of the dryer and can cause overheating. This may result in a significant fire risk.

◆ Exercise areas should be cleared of faeces straight away and urine posts hosed down. Concrete areas should be hosed down and scrubbed with disinfectant daily. Grass and sand areas are less easily cleaned but can still benefit from being hosed down daily. Grass should be kept mown to eliminate shady areas and ensure the sun's rays are not prevented from reaching the ground (UV is an effective natural disinfectant).

◆ Communal areas, such as the reception area, will need to be dusted or vacuumed daily to remove hair particles that travel in the atmosphere and settle. Floors will need to be washed and disinfected daily and may need spot cleaning. If soft furnishings, such as material-covered chairs and cushions, are used in staff or communal areas, they should be regularly cleaned and treated with a suitable antiparasitic treatment according to the product recommendations (once a year may be sufficient for long-lasting preparations).

◆ Kitchens should be kept clean and tidy at all times, with cups and dishes washed after use. Tea towels should be changed daily and washed separately from the dog towels and bedding (i.e. in a different machine). Work surfaces and floors should be washed down daily. Toilets should be equipped with a sanitizing pump hand wash and paper hand towels and should be cleaned on a daily basis.

◆ Office areas should be dusted or vacuumed daily to remove hair particles from keyboards and surfaces. Disinfectant wipes are useful for wiping down telephones, desks and electrical equipment. Floors should be washed daily.

Cleaning and disinfecting, or sterilizing, equipment:

See Chapter 10 for the requirements of individual pieces of grooming equipment.

Fig. 7.2.6   Chemicals for storing and washing clipper blades are tested for safety but this does not mean that everyone is safe. Wash your hands thoroughly if your skin has been exposed to blade wash and consider wearing gloves.

Fig. 7.2.7a-b   These pictures illustrate the accumulation of hair and grease in the filter of a hand held dryer. The build-up of hair will reduce the air flow to the dryer, which in turn can then overheat and catch fire. It is important to keep filters clear at all times.

◆ Equipment should be cleaned first and then disinfected or sterilized.

◆ Cleaning techniques should be appropriate to the equipment and ensure that all contamination is removed. Blades, for example, should be soaked in a cleaning solution (*see* Fig. 7.2.6). Before the blade is used again, it can be left on absorbent paper to dry and then sprayed with a spray disinfectant.

◆ Scissors can be wiped with a blade wash solution, dried and then sprayed with a disinfectant before being put into a UV sterilizer.

◆ The recommended concentration and contact time for the disinfectant you are using should be known and respected.

◆ Disinfectant solutions should be changed according to the manufacturer's instructions or sooner if contamination is heavy.

◆ Ensure all equipment is included in the cleaning programme. Items that may be overlooked include nail clippers, hair driers, bins, table legs and table casters/wheels, water bowls and washing machines.

◆ Hair should be removed from the filters of hair driers (*see* Fig. 7.2.7a-b) on a regular basis.

◆ Hair-dryer filters may need to be removed for washing.

◆ Tumble dryers will need to have the lint removed.

◆ Sterilization, if required, can be undertaken via a number of methods, including chemical, heat, steam and ultra-violet (UV) light.

Cleaning equipment:

◆ Dedicated cleaning equipment should be readily available for use and should include a sweeping brush (*see* Fig. 7.2.8), mop and bucket, rubber scraper, vacuum cleaner, cleaning sponges or cloths for the worktop and toothbrushes for cleaning clipper blades.

◆ Mop heads should be washed regularly (daily or weekly) in the washing machine at more than 40°C.

◆ Cleaning sponges and cloths can be put through the washing machine at the end of the day.

◆ Also at the end of the day dustpans can be washed over with a suitable cleaning agent and then sprayed with disinfectant, whilst brooms, brushes and the brush on the end of the vacuum can have the hair removed with an OLD slicker; they can then be washed in soapy water before being dipped into floor-cleaning disinfectant.

◆ All other cleaning equipment should be cleaned and disinfected regularly.

◆ Vacuum cleaners should be emptied every day and the collection cylinder wiped out and sprayed with disinfectant, providing there are no electrical parts visible. Vacuum cleaner bags should be taken out as soon as they are full, or at the end of the week, whichever is soonest and should not be allowed to overfill.

◆ The inclusion of a flea collar within the vacuum cleaner bag can avoid the build-up of such parasites within this piece of equipment.

◆ Once or twice a week the washing machine can be put on an empty boil wash with added soap powder or a suitable cleaning product. Cleaning the drum is especially important if the machine is going to be out of action for any length of time such as annual holiday periods.

Fig. 7.2.8   Floor cleaning equipment, including sweeping brush, mop, scraper and broad spectrum disinfectant. This equipment should itself be kept clean and regularly disinfected.

CAUTION: CHOOSING A DISINFECTANT

The characteristics of a good disinfectant include:

- ◆ *broad spectrum of activity*
- ◆ *rapid onset of action (fast acting)*
- ◆ *long-lasting activity (residual effect)*
- ◆ *non-destructive to the surfaces and materials to which they are applied*
- ◆ *should not have an offensive odour*
- ◆ *should not stain surfaces*
- ◆ *should not be palatable (it should be foul-tasting).*

The disinfectant used in the grooming room needs to be active against parvovirus. The disinfectant used on clippers and grooming equipment (see Table 17) should be active against ringworm and fungal spores.

References and further information

Bağcigil, A.F., İkiz, S., Özgür, N.Y. and Ilgaz, A. (2010). Recovery of dermatophytes in pet grooming tools from veterinary clinics and pet grooming salons. *Journal of Small Animal Practice,* 51 (1), 39–42.

Dallas, S., Jones, M. and Mullineaux, E. (2007). Managing clinical environments, equipment and materials. In: *BSAVA Manual of Practical Veterinary Nur¿ ̈lineaux and M. Jones. Cheltenham: BSAVA.

Eterpi, M., McDonnell, G. and Thomas, V. (2009). Disinfection efficacy against parvoviruses compared with reference viruses. *Journal of Hospital Infection,* 73 (1), 64–70.

Heit, M.C. and Riviere, J.E. (2001). Antiseptics and disinfectants. In: *Veterinary pharmacology and therapeutics,* 8th edition, ed. H.R. Adams. Iowa, USA: Blackwell Publishing, pp. 783–95.

Marchetti, V., Mancianti, G. and Luchetti, E. (2006). Evaluation of fungicidal efficacy of benzalkonium chloride (Steramina G.u.v.) and Virkon-S against *Microsporum canis* for environmental disinfection. *Veterinary Research Communications,* 30 (3), 255–61.

McGaving, D. (1987). Inactivation of canine parvovirus by disinfectants and heat. *Journal of Small Animal Practice,* 28 (6), 523–35.

WASTE DISPOSAL

Your local authority will be able to advise on waste disposal regulations. You should establish that any cleaning products or disinfectants you propose to use can be disposed of via the main drains. You should also determine how best to collect and dispose of dog hair, and how dog faeces and urine-soiled newspaper are to be treated. Where private companies are used for waste collection, you should establish whether they have any rules that should be followed regarding the waste your salon generates.

The London Evening Standard, on 29 June 2011, reported that a barber from Islington in London was fined £60 (with the threat of prison if he failed to pay the fine) for putting hair into a BLACK plastic bag rather than the required GREY plastic bag.

Rycroft, A.N. and McLay, C. (1991). Disinfectants in the control of small animal ringworm due to *Microsporum canis. Veterinary Record,* 129, 239–41.

7.3 MINIMIZING YOUR ENVIRONMENTAL FOOTPRINT

It is to our great shame as a species that, in becoming civilized, we have lost touch with nature, and have been largely unaware of the damage that our inconsiderate exploitation of the world's resources has caused to the planet that supports us. The word *civilized* is derived from the Latin *civitas,* meaning city. The word implies a reclamation from a savage state, a refinement or enlightenment, and it is indeed tempting to believe that a move to the cities and a consumer economy is an improvement on the 'savage state', for it has brought man material comforts and technological advances. It has, however, not been without cost, for there are now fewer of us who see the natural world as a beautiful extension of ourselves and appreciate that we are a small part of an infinitely complex living system. In the same way that we are naturally concerned for our own health, and that of our families, communities and societies because we recognize their importance to us, we should be concerned for the natural world that supports us. The health of that system is something we should therefore care strongly about.

The menace of climate change and environmental degradation needs to be faced up to by all sectors of society. Each and every one of us has a responsibility, and indeed a duty, to care for the world around us. We need to ensure that we do as much as we possibly can to reduce the impact of our activities on the environment.

Businesses (and householders) are increasingly motivated to reduce their carbon footprint, for in doing so they can present themselves as eco-friendly whilst achieving significant reductions in their fuel bills. One might argue that it is sad that businesses are choosing to act now for public relations and financial reasons rather than out of concern for the environment. It is not unreasonable, however, to view these different motivating forces as catalysts

Table 17 Disinfectants classified according to the type of active ingredient. The activity against bacteria, viruses and fungi and against bacterial and fungal spores is indicated by Y (active), P (partly active) and N (inactive).

Disinfectant Type	Bactericidal	Virucidal	Parvovirus	Fungicidal	Sporicidal	Remarks	Examples
Alcohols	Y	P	N	P	N	Mainly used as an antiseptic. Commonly used as a rapid-acting antiseptic for disinfecting hands. Non-corrosive but can be flammable. No action against spores or non-enveloped viruses.	i) Ethanol ii) Isopropanol (e.g. surgical spirit)
Aldehyde	Y	Y	Y	Y	Y	Aldehydes are reducing agents. They are partly inactivated by organic matter and have slight residual activity. They have a broad range of activity but are extremely irritating and should not be used in the presence of animals.	i) Formaldehyde ii) Glutaraldehyde
Oxidizing agents	Y	Y	Y	Y	Y	Bleach can be irritating to tissues and is inactivated by the presence of organic matter. Bleach is, however, effective against fungal spores. Iodophores are only partially effective against spores. Retain activity even in the presence of organic matter. Iodine and iodophores are commonly used on skin. Hydrogen peroxide releases oxygen and is used to disinfect water and instruments. Peroxide compounds are fast acting and have a wide range of activity. Powder is irritating to eyes and airways.	i) Halogen-containing compounds: – Sodium hypochlorite (NaOCl, = bleach) (e.g. Milton) – Iodophores (e.g. povidone iodine) ii) Peroxides: – Hydrogen peroxide – Benzoyl peroxide – Potassium permanganate – Potassium peroxymonosulphate (e.g. Virkon)
Phenolics	Y	P	N	Y	N	Good activity in the presence of organic matter. Active against enveloped but not non-enveloped viruses. Toxic to cats.	i) Phenol (e.g. Jeyes and Clippercide). ii) Chloroxylenol (e.g. Dettol) iii) Thymol
Quarternary ammonium compounds	Y	P	N	Y	N	Active against enveloped but not non-enveloped viruses. Non-corrosive and low toxicity. Deactivated by extremely hard water.	i) Benzalkonium chloride (e.g. Trigene, Vetaclean)
Biguanide polymer polyaminopropyl biguanide	Y	P	N	Y	N	Commonly used as a skin disinfectant. Non-toxic. Wide germicidal activity but ineffective against some important pathogens.	i) Chlorhexidine (e.g. Hibiscrub, Nolvasan)

for change and welcome them whole-heartedly.

High oil prices, coinciding with the global economic down-turn, present us with a fantastic opportunity to 'go green'. Some larger industries are already taking the lead and have started gearing up for a low-carbon or carbon-free economy. Other sectors have been a lot slower. Many small businesses do not have the resources to action a vast environmental plan, but every little helps. This section is intended to provide you with a range of ideas and suggestions, together with lists of potential sources of further information and advice, so that you can set about developing your own eco-plan.

Starting point: the eco-audit

Within our grooming rooms and homes we would do well to conduct an ecological audit and review the impact our activities have on the environment. Where finances permit, this can be done using one of a number of auditing companies and may well be a good starting point. Do not despair if finances are tight, for you can tackle this issue yourself by taking a critical look at your working practices and, in particular, the resources you use up and the waste you are responsible for producing. Ongoing audits can and should be conducted regularly either by yourself if you work alone or, in a larger business, by members of staff, perhaps by means of a

Table 18 A list of some of the popular disinfectants currently used in UK veterinary practices and grooming salons.

Disinfectant	Active Ingredients	Manufacturer	Comments
Barbicide	Dimethyl benzyl ammonium chloride (5.12%) and Isopropyl alcohol (13%)	Blueco Brands Corp. (Renscene Ltd)	Tested against HIV, hepatitis, ringworm. Solution needs to be changed daily.
Clippercide	O-Phenylphenol (0.41%) and Isopropyl alcohol (45.6%)	Blueco Brands Corp. (Renscene Ltd)	Tested against various germs including Pseudomonas aeruginosa, Salmonella enterolitica and Trichophyton mentagrophytes.
F10	Quarternary ammonium compounds and biguanides (5.8%)	F10 Biocare (Meadows Animal Healthcare)	Broad-spectrum bactericidal, virucidal and fungicidal disinfectant suitable for use in high-risk areas.
Formula H	Benzalkonium chloride Glutaraldehyde (0.6% w/v)	Petlife International	Broad-spectrum disinfectant.
Milton (sterilizing fluid and tablets)	Sodium hypochlorite (2%) and salt (16%)	Milton	Sterilizes in 15 minutes and shows a broad spectrum of activity.
Sanivet	Quarternary ammonium compound	Alstoe Animal Health Ltd	Economical disinfectant for low-risk area disease control.
Trigene	Halogenated tertiary amine	Medichem International	DEFRA-approved broad-spectrum disinfectant available in a number of preparations. Compatible with a range of\ materials.
Vetcide	Benzalkonium chloride Glutaraldehyde	Millpledge Veterinary	General disinfectant. Almost odour-free.
Vetaclean Parvo	Quarternary ammonium compound	Animalcare	Versatile disinfectant with broad-spectrum activity against viruses, bacteria and fungi.
Vetasept Chlorhexidine	Chlorhexidine (0.5%)	Animalcare	Skin disinfectant and hand sanitizer.
Virkon.	Peroxygen compounds	Alstoe Animal health Ltd	Broad-spectrum disinfectant.

rotating eco-committee whose role it is to monitor and report on the business's energy usage and environmental impact. Involvement of all members of staff in this way can encourage them to explore and understand these issues and take responsibility for their own as well as their employer's environmental impact.

Three areas have been chosen to focus on here: energy usage, waste management and transport policy.

Energy usage

If you want to give all your hard-earned pennies to your energy supplier, that is up to you but grooming businesses, like any other business trying to make money, should be monitoring the amount spent on utility bills. With spiralling gas and electricity costs, it is even more important to keep track

of such costs and ensure that energy usage is not wasteful. This can be difficult to achieve in a busy salon environment. The first step is to raise awareness of energy wastage with your staff. The energy usage of the salon can be monitored and converted into meaningful units; for some of us this will be in money terms, for others units of carbon dioxide. The total energy usage of the business can be monitored using a unit such as the 'OWL', whereas the energy usage of specific appliances can be monitored using an appliance such as the 'Kill-a-Watt'. The former raises the awareness of staff and management to the energy usage of the salon at different times of day and during different situations, whilst the latter provides information on the energy usage of individual appliances in different modes of use and, of course, in stand-by. It would not be difficult

to monitor all stationary electrical appliances and establish their daily and weekly energy usage. This information can then be taken into account when determining how they can be used more efficiently and how they compare to other models on the market when they come to be replaced. This is particularly important when training a new member of staff joining your team.

The amount of energy used by appliances in stand-by mode is alarming. Once staff and management are more aware of such issues, plans can be formulated to improve the salon's energy efficiency. Some of these will require all members of staff to work together to reduce energy wastage. This can be further helped by the judicious use of posters and stickers (available from the Carbon Trust) to encourage people to 'TURN THINGS OFF'.

Switch the sterilizer off when it is not in use, turn lights out in empty rooms and switch the computer, radio and kettle off at the end of the day rather than leaving them on stand-by. Question whether the air conditioning is necessary or could a window be made safe to open?

Salons can also review where they source their energy from. Many energy suppliers allow you to choose to use energy derived entirely from renewables. Such energy may be more expensive in financial terms but is less costly to the environment.

CAUTION

Salon design and construction (even little ones and garage conversions) should prioritize environmental considerations as much as possible. Failure to take energy efficiency into account during the design process could mean that not only is your carbon footprint more than it need be, it is also costing you more in energy bills for the privilege.

Within the UK, buildings are responsible for almost 50 per cent of energy consumption and carbon emissions, and a little over half of this is produced by commercial properties and public buildings. The Communities and Local Government website provides details on the new legislation and guidelines seeking to reduce energy consumption. As of October 2008 all buildings (homes, commercial and public) that are being built, rented or sold require an Energy Performance Certificate (EPC). From January 2009 inspections for air conditioning systems were introduced and it may be only a matter of time before local governments insist that even small home-run businesses meet these requirements. These initiatives aim to improve dramatically the energy efficiency of our buildings and are described in more detail on the website:

www.communities.gov.uk/planningandbuilding/theenvironment/energyperformance

Heating and hot water systems account for some 60 per cent of carbon dioxide emissions in a gas-heated home or building. The Energy Saving Trust recommends that old boilers be replaced with high-efficiency condensing boilers that recover as much as possible of the waste heat lost through the flue of a normal (non-condensing) boiler. The best high-efficiency condensing boilers convert more than 90 per cent of their fuel into heat, compared to 78 per cent for conventional types. In addition, the installation of heating controls such as a programmer, room thermostats and thermostatic radiator valves will allow greater control of energy usage. The thermostat should generally always be set to the lowest comfortable temperature in order to save energy.

NOTE: TRACKING YOUR ENVIRONMENTAL FOOTPRINT

In the grooming room the thermostat for the bath water can be set as low as 40 degrees C (see Chapter 12). The use of hot water systems, hair driers, washing machines and tumble driers should all be reviewed. Water heating systems may best be operated on a timer and use made of the thermostat to specify the maximum temperature. A Hydrobath® that recycles water is worth considering.

Effective use of high-absorbency towels can minimize the amount of hair drying required per dog. Additionally, their use has the added benefit of reducing the exposure of the dog's skin to artificial heat.

Modern building design should seek to reduce energy expenditure on heating and lighting. Heat exchange systems are now commonplace on the continent and allow water for heating to be warmed as it is pumped through the ground, before then being circulated through the walls. Architectural plans should ensure that heat loss is minimized, whilst windows are designed so that natural lighting is used to maximum effect. In the UK this system is still very expensive but it is something to consider in the future.

Energy usage – some things to think about

Consider using energy from renewable sources, so-called green energy. This may cost a little more but will be seen as evidence of a salon's green credentials.

Identify where energy savings can be made:

◆ Nominate a person to be responsible for turning off lights and non-essential appliances at night.
◆ Fit movement sensors and timers to turn lights on and off in little-used areas.
◆ Switch off the display screen of server PCs when not in use.
◆ Ensure that power-saving features are activated on all computers.

Train/encourage staff to be economical in the way they use energy:

◆ Do not leave water running unnecessarily when bathing dogs.
◆ Make better use of high-absorbency towels to reduce drying time.
◆ Boil only the water you need: i.e. fill your cup and pour measured amounts into the kettle.
◆ Turn the lights off if you are the last person to leave the room.
◆ Turn off appliances when not in use and do not leave appliances on stand-by.
◆ Employee awareness posters are available from the Carbon Trust and cover key issues such as lighting, heating, refrigeration, computers, photocopiers and air conditioning. www.carbontrust.co.uk/energy/startsaving/staffawarenessposters.htm.

Assess all electrical appliances:

◆ How often are they used (hrs/day or hrs/week)?
◆ How much energy do they use (kWh)?
◆ How much energy do they use when on stand-by?
◆ How do they compare with other products?
◆ When are they due to be replaced?

The energy usage of products can be measured both during use and when they are on stand-by using an appliance such as the Kill-a-Watt. This informs users of energy usage and wastage, and promotes a more informed and less wasteful salon. www.reuk.co.uk/Buy-UK-Power-Meter.htm.

Consider investing in an energy monitor to provide feedback on the total energy usage and expenditure of a business or home. The OWL electricity meter attaches to the electricity supply and relays a wireless readout to the monitor that is then converted from kWh to £s. This is then also converted to carbon dioxide emission readings. The monitor also provides a reading of the temperature and humidity levels of the premises. www.ethical superstore.com/products/2-save-energy/owl-wireless-energy-monitor

Assess the efficiency of heating and hot water systems. A government guide for businesses can be downloaded and used to cut the costs and environmental impact of heating premises and water. www.communities.gov.uk/publications/planningandbuilding/businessguide.

Consider employing an energy consultant to conduct an energy saver review and develop an energy plan. The Carbon Trust, for example, provides a range of services including a small- and medium-sized business toolkit. www.carbontrust.co.uk/solution/sme/toolkit.htm.

A REAL EXAMPLE OF RUNNING COSTS

The following is an example of running costs that cannot be avoided in a grooming room. They can, however, be reduced with a little bit of thought and effort, thus benefiting the environment and your pocket. Such considerations are worth reflecting on when planning the purchase of new equipment: consider the running costs of a product rather than the attractive purchase price or its trendy looks. There are many products out there, all claiming to do a better job, faster and more efficiently than the next, but the true running costs are seldom explained fully. Spare a little time to research your purchase and ask those awkward questions.

Calculating the cost of drying a dog

Do you know how to calculate the cost of drying the dogs that you bath? In order to calculate the running costs of any given piece of electrical equipment, you need to know:

◆ *the power rating (in Watts);*
◆ *the amount of time the equipment is being used for; and*
◆ *the cost per unit of electricity.*

You can then do the following calculations:

The rating in Watts/1000 x the time in minutes/60 = the amount of electricity used in kW/h

The amount of electricity used (kW/h) x cost per unit = the total cost

Therefore, assuming that drying takes 15 minutes, and using a unit cost of 14.31 pence per unit with VAT at 5 per cent, the cost will vary depending on the power rating of the equipment used:

i) **Using a 1875 Watt hand dryer for 15 minutes:**
   1875/1000 x 15/60 x 14.31 = £0.06
ii) **Using a 2600 Watt stand dryer for 15 minutes:**
   2600/1000 x 15/60 x 14.31 = £0.09
iii) **Using a 4225 Watt drying cabinet for 15 minutes:**
   4225/1000 x 15/60 x 14.31 = £0.15

Interest-free loans for replacing and upgrading equipment may be available from the Carbon Trust. www.carbontrust.co.uk/energy/taking action/loans.htm.

If you cannot find the energy usage information when you are buying a product, the circumference of the cable on electrical equipment is a good indication as to how much electricity it uses. The more electricity it uses, the thicker the cable it will need to carry it (an electric cooker cable is a good example).

If all of this seems too much effort and you don't feel that the environment is your responsibility, take a look at how much of your hard-earned income is being paid out to your energy supplier. Saving energy will benefit everyone – except your energy supplier!

Waste Management

It is important that we are conscious of the amount of waste we are actually responsible for producing. We should also remind ourselves of where that waste goes and the impact it has on the environment. It is too easy to live in a bubble, isolated from and ignorant of the true consequences of our actions. If you believe in waste reduction because it is right, then you are more likely to do something about it and take an active approach to reducing, reusing and recycling. There are many good reasons for tackling the amount of waste we generate and with a little forethought the process can be facilitated within the workplace. Much of the waste we produce could be reduced. Table 19 provides some ideas on waste management.

The humble battery is an example of something potentially toxic that many of us use and throw away with little consideration for the environment. Switching to rechargeable batteries makes a significant difference instantly. The EC Directive on Batteries and Accumulators (2006/66/EC) was published on 26 September 2006 and is now in force in the UK. It aims to minimize the impact of batteries on the environment and encourage the recovery of the materials they contain. Since February 2010 shops selling more than 32kg of batteries a year must provide battery recycling collection facilities in-store. You therefore have the option to use rechargeable batteries or to recycle any disposable batteries you choose to buy. The legislation previously referred to will ultimately force us to change but we really should be changing of our own free will because it is the right thing to do.

◆ According to DEFRA, UK households alone produced 30.5 million tonnes of waste in 2003/4. Only 17 per cent of this was collected for recycling, compared to a figure approaching 50 per cent for some of our EU neighbours.

◆ Some 70 per cent less energy is required to produce recycled paper than to produce it from raw materials. Recycled paper produces 73 per cent less air pollution than if it were made from raw materials.

◆ It takes twenty-four trees to make one tonne of newspaper.

◆ Recycling just one plastic bottle provides enough energy to power a 60-Watt lightbulb for six hours.

◆ Glass is 100 per cent recyclable and can be used again and again. If thrown away and allowed to enter landfill, it will never decompose.

◆ It takes just twenty-five 2-litre plastic drinks bottles to make one adult-size fleece jacket.

◆ Plastic bottles are made from oil, a fossil fuel that will one day run out.

◆ Making one aluminium drink can from raw materials uses the same amount of energy that it takes to recycle twenty.

Recycling facilities now exist for organic matter, aluminium foil, food and drink cans, plastics, plastic bags, glass, textiles, small electrical appliances and many other items. There are many good websites providing information both on this subject and on the availability of local recycling facilities. The Recycle More website provides comprehensive details on what materials can be recycled, including a number of downloadable posters. One such poster explains how the different types of plastics can be identified by the stamps they carry. Plastics made from polyethylene terepthalate (PET), high-density polyethylene (HDPE) and polyvinyl chloride (PVC) can all be recycled. A poster in the reception area would bring this to the attention of both staff and clients.

By identifying where certain waste is generated, recycling bins can be strategically placed within the home or workplace. Recycling facilities could be available in the kennel, kitchens and staff rooms, whilst paper recycling bins should be present in the office (*see* Fig. 7.3.1).

Fig. 7.3.1   *Recycling bins can be provided to encourage the sorting of rubbish and the collection of those materials that can be recycled.*

So what can be done to reduce waste?

There are lots of small changes that we can make, both individually and collectively, that will significantly reduce our waste production (*see* Fig. 7.3.2). The following are just a few suggestions:

◆ Embrace, whenever possible, the three R's: Reduce, Reuse, Recycle.

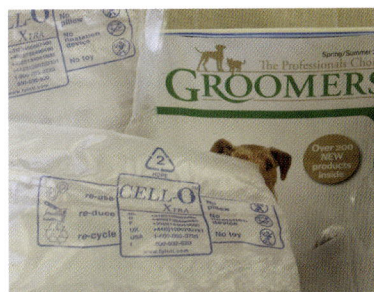

Fig. 7.3.2   *Individually and collectively, we can make a difference to reduce waste. Consider supporting suppliers that are also eco-aware and have made the effort to source recyclable packaging and reduce packing waste.*

◆ Exercise self-control and self-awareness, exerting more control over our urge to buy and use non-essential items because we want to, rather than because we need to.

◆ Reflect on the processes that we go through when making new or replacement purchases, and ask ourselves: Are the purchases as 'green' as they could be? Have we valued durability over disposability? Have we placed enough value on locally produced products?

◆ Resist the 'throw away' culture. Consider extended warranties on equipment so that the next time something breaks, you can get it repaired rather than throw it away. If it cannot be repaired, perhaps the manufacturer can recycle it in part exchange for other recycled goods.

◆ Look for ways that you can recycle and reuse. For example, take equipment apart and salvage any parts that can be used as spares before dumping, e.g. castors, casings, plugs, fuses, etc. Get an electrician to check out and dismantle motors that may well be useful/sellable to replace motors on obsolete older models still in use. Use old newspapers to line cages. Shredded paper can be put into old pillow cases or cushion covers to make warm, cosy 'disposable' dog beds; throw the paper away and re-use the pillow case after washing. Plastic carrier bags can be used as rubbish bin liners. Where an item is heading for the dump, check to see if anyone else is prepared to give it a home and thus keep it out of landfill. The charity freecycle.org matches people who want to get rid of something with people who can use them: http://uk.freecycle.org.

◆ Alert staff and visitors to recycling facilities within your area with a poster in the communal areas. Your post code can be entered into a waste bank locator such as that provided online by recycle-more. co.uk: www.recycle-more.co.uk/banklocator/banklocator.aspx.

◆ With some local authorities either threatening to charge, or already charging, to take waste away, conducting a waste audit at home and at work will give you an indication of the waste produced and the proportion of it that is recycled, together with the cost it represents. A decision to make improvements can then be made.

◆ Demand environmentally friendly service from suppliers. Packaging should be minimized and its recycling insisted upon. Where this is not possible, try not to buy small amounts that are individually packaged (e.g. buy large containers of shampoo rather than several small bottles).

For more information on recycling visit: www.recyclenow.com/what can i do today/start recycling at 2.html

Reducing your impact on forests by cutting your paper footprint

Paper is something that we take for granted. We know it is widely recycled and therefore we use it without much thought because we know we can just pop it in the recycle bin and feel good about our efforts. What we do not very often think about is how we can cut down the amount we are using in the first place. Again, with a bit of thought, our paper waste can be substantially cut down to reduce the amount of forest felling.

Immediately, here are a few ways that you can cut down on paper wastage (and ink!):

◆ Put a sign on the letterbox saying 'No Junk Mail' or sign up to the Mail Preference Service at ww.mpsonline.org.uk.
◆ Send unwanted catalogues back to the sender.
◆ Stop subscribing to publications that you never read.
◆ Share magazines and newspapers and then pass them on to others to read.
◆ Request that all utility bills are electronically managed.
◆ Use electronic messaging systems, and customer email addresses to send business correspondence.
◆ Use supplier websites rather than requesting catalogues.

Table 19   Disposal of grooming room waste.

Product	Disposal method
Dog hair	According to local authority requirements or composted.
Left-over general purpose shampoo	According to the manufacturer's instructions and local authority requirements. Otherwise, dilute well and pour down the drain. Ensure that products used require a minimum volume of water to be neutralized.
Prescription shampoos	According to the manufacturer's instructions and medicine regulations. Ideally, return unused and part-used bottles to the prescribing vet.
Shampoo containers	Investigate the possibility of refills. Buy in bulk to reduce the amount of plastic generated. Where bottles are to be disposed of, rinse well and recycle when possible.
Disinfectant bottles	According to the manufacturer's instructions or rinse well and put in household waste. Consider purchasing refills.
Bleach bottles	Rinse well and put in household waste. Consider purchasing refills.
Left-over floor cleaner and disinfectants	Dilute well and empty into main drain.
Empty aerosol cans	Household waste. Ensure they are CFC-free and seek out environmentally friendly alternatives.
Empty tins	Recycle where possible. Recycling widely available.
Faeces	Clinical waste (yellow bag) for incineration or according to local authority requirements.
Used cotton wool	Clinical waste (yellow bag) for incineration.
Soiled paper bedding	Clinical waste (yellow bag) for incineration.
Paper customer records	Shred and recycle or shred and compost.
Computer software	Recycling widely available.
Computer hardware	Recycling widely available
Broken electrical equipment	Recycling widely available.
Clippers and blades	Recycle (electrical recycling).
Blade wash	Pour into cat litter and put into household waste.
Clipper oil	Pour into cat litter and put into household waste.
Vacuum cleaner bags and waste	Household waste.
Disposable PPE	According to local authority requirements.
Paper and cardboard packaging	Reuse where possible. Compost. Recycling widely available.
Plastic packaging	Recycling widely available. Otherwise put in household waste.

- Do not print out documents from the computer if it is not necessary; if it is necessary, restrict the number of copies to the amount you need and consider printing two pages to a side.
- Where possible, use both sides of the paper when printing and put clear instructions on communal printers and photocopiers explaining how to use the printer settings.

Paper that you buy and use for your business, including toilet paper, kitchen rolls and printer paper, should all be from a recycled source. It is often cheaper to buy and less ink is used to colour the paper.

In some areas the collection of paper, packaging and cardboard is organized by the local authority, but in areas where this is not the case, where possible, try to recycle at a plant within walking distance or at a venue you will be using for another activity such as shopping. Most large supermarkets now have recycling facilities.

Bins should be available for the collection of paper waste and where possible it should be reused before recycling. Old newspapers can be used to line kennels and cages, and all other waste paper can be shredded for stuffing into old pillow cases and cushion covers to make dog beds.

Investigate composting plants in your area. After use, unsoiled paper bedding, along with shredded till receipts, bank statements, paperwork with personal details and envelopes, can be recycled or composted. Landscape gardeners can often make use of your shredding to make compost if you cannot use it yourself. Horse owners that use shredded paper as bedding for their horses are another potential outlet.

Putting control measures in place may well be tiresome to begin with, and notices and reminders will probably be needed as everyone becomes used to the idea, but over time the value and importance of recycling, waste and energy control will become second nature to all of us.

Develop a waste management policy

Table 19 details some of the many different types of waste item produced in the grooming room. Over time, it would be worth developing a policy for each item in order to reduce your waste production footprint. Clearly you have to comply with waste disposal rules and regulations, but you may also discover ways of reducing, reusing and recycling your waste so that your footprint shrinks rather than grows.

Transport policy

Most of you will be working alone or in very small salons, and may feel that this section does not apply to you. That is an understandable reaction because we are, after all, trying to earn a living grooming dogs and may not be interested in transport policies and costs. The intention of this section, therefore, is to be thought-provoking, so that as your business grows and you replace existing vehicles, you may be curious enough to do a little research of your own and in doing so help the environment and your pocket by reducing your carbon emissions. Something else to think about is the fact that, unless you do something about it, the bigger your business grows, the bigger your business carbon footprint will be.

Each salon is responsible for a significant carbon footprint arising through the use of motorized vehicles by both staff and customers. This environmental impact can also be audited and monitored with a view to reducing it. There are a number of possible areas that should be considered when developing a transport policy. Many groomers offer a collection and delivery service for their clients. This makes good business sense, bringing in income for grooming a dog that you may not otherwise have had because the client could not get to you. And then there may also be income from the transportation charges.

Well, you may want to think again! The amount of carbon dioxide produced per kilometre travelled is used to band all cars for car tax purposes. If you are heavily taxed on your company vehicle, then your fuel bill, your emissions and consequently your carbon footprint is higher than necessary. You can maybe add to this the time you spend stuck in heavy traffic, burning fuel but going nowhere (and wasting grooming time), not to mention the costs of maintaining the vehicle (MOT, servicing and repairs, etc). It is a costly exercise both monetarily and environmentally. So perhaps it does not make such good business sense after all!

A number of UK veterinary practices are now taking an enlightened view on promoting environmentally friendly transport options. The 387 Veterinary Centre in Great Wyrley, Staffordshire, for example, proudly makes a donation to the sustainable transport charity SUSTRANS for every client arriving at the practice on foot or by bike. Could you provide details on bus links and other public transport facilities for your clients? Could you promote car share schemes or other environmentally friendly transport ideas to your staff and clients? Could you provide safe parking for staff bicycles?

The European Commission proposed that all new cars should have cut their emissions to below 130g/km by 2012, and that by 2020 this will be reduced further to 95g/km. When you come to replace your vehicle you could consider buying something more environmentally friendly. Currently there are a good number of models producing less than 120g/km and these are listed on the Vehicle Certification Agency's website, together with details of their fuel consumption and exhaust emission figures. It's quite possible your insurance will be less expensive too!

www.vcacarfueldata.org.uk/information/how-to-use-the-data-tables.asp#petrol.

Travel policy questions

1. Does your salon have a transport policy?
2. Does your business actively promote more environmentally friendly modes of transport?
3. New customer packs should include details of how the salon can be reached by public transport, with links to websites listing current bus and rail times where appropriate.
4. Local car sharing schemes should be promoted. This may apply particularly to employees but may be of interest to clients who live close to one another. Your local car sharing site can be found on www.carshare.com.
5. Salons can promote eco-friendly

travel by supporting the work of the sustainable transport charity SUSTRANS and encouraging clients to travel by foot or by public transport.

6. In addition to details on how to get to the salon by road, salon websites should provide details of:
   ◆ bus routes and links to current bus timetables;
   ◆ train routes and links to current train routes;
   ◆ local animal taxi services;
   ◆ cycle routes for staff and volunteers; and
   ◆ local car share schemes.

   A link to the Transport Direct website will allow clients, particularly those who do not have a car, to plan their journey using public transport: http://transportdirect.info/web2/home.aspx?repeatingloop+Y.

7. Details of, and training in, eco-friendly driving could be made available to salon employees who transport dogs (and, indeed, all staff who drive).

8. A driver's driving style can influence a vehicle's fuel efficiency. Drivers should consider the following facts and advice from the Environmental Transport Association (ETA):
   ◆ Driving at speeds less than 15mph causes the most pollution.
   ◆ Pollution decreases as your speed increases, up to 60mph.
   ◆ Travelling at speeds of more than 60mph increases pollution.
   ◆ Switch off your engine if you are likely to be stationary for two minutes or more.
   ◆ Harsh acceleration and braking can increase fuel consumption by up to 30 per cent.
   ◆ Air conditioning use should be limited because it uses more fuel.
   ◆ Stressed driving is more erratic and therefore less economical.
   ◆ Roof racks and open windows reduce wind resistance and burn more fuel.

9. Careful route planning can reduce carbon emissions. ETA's Green Route Finder helps drivers plan their route efficiently and calculates the carbon emissions for the journey. As this service evolves, it is hoped that it will become possible to compare the environmental impact of alternative routes. http//www.eta.co.uk/map

There are many challenges ahead of us if we are to make the sort of headway needed to reduce carbon emissions and combat climate change. The animal care industry and the wider pet-owning community needs to play its part too, and as a respected and caring profession we should try to influence the activities of our partners, suppliers and clients.

Useful websites

campaigns.direct.gov.uk/actonco2/home/on-the-move/top-10-fuel-efficient-cars.html
A government website that, in conjunction with WHAT CAR, provides details on the most fuel-efficient cars in each class.
www.carbontrust.co.uk/default.ct
The Carbon Trust's mission is to accelerate the move to a low-carbon economy by working with organizations to reduce carbon emissions and develop commercial low-carbon technologies.
www.carshare.com/
Allows local car share schemes to be found.
www.communities.gov.uk/planningandbuilding/theenvironment/energyperformance/homes/energyperformancecertificates/
A government website providing details on the Energy Performance Certificates (EPC) that form part of the Home Information Pack for homes built, sold or rented from October 2008.
www.energysavingtrust.org.uk/
A non-profit organization that provides free, independent advice on how people can make energy savings in the home.
www.eta.co.uk/
The website of the Environmental Transport Association aims to raise awareness of the environmental impact of excessive car use.
http://uk.freecycle.org/
The charity freecycle.org matches people who have things they want to get rid of with people who can use them.
www.generationgreen.co.uk/StaffRoom/Secondary/
British Gas's educational initiative (aimed at children) helps promote understanding about climate change and energy efficiency.
www.ipcc.ch/
The International Panel on Climate Change's website provides up-to-date information on the science of climate change.
www.metoffice.gov.uk/research/hadleycentre/index.html
The UK Meteorological Office's website provides detailed and reliable information on the subject and science of climate change.
www.recyclingexpert.co.uk/LocalFacilities.html
Provides information on recycling facilities available in your local area.
www.recycle-more.co.uk/
A comprehensive website allowing local recycling facilities to be identified and providing useful information on what materials can be recycled. A table detailing the different types of plastics and how to identify those that can be recycled is available as a download from: www.recycle-more.co.uk/nav/page689.aspx
www.recyclenow.com/
A very user-friendly website that explains and promotes recycling.
www.reuk.co.uk/index.htm
This online shop supplies an extensive range of energy-saving products for the home and office.
www.sustrans.org.uk/
Sustrans is the coordinator of the National Cycle Network and promotes transport options that benefit people's health and the environment. Sustrans produces a useful low-carbon travel information sheet.
www.vcacarfueldata.org.uk/
The Vehicle Certification Agency (VCA) provides information on new car fuel consumption and exhaust emission figures.

8 First Aid and Emergency Care

All groomers should undertake regular First Aid training and be able to deal confidently with the more common problems they may encounter in the grooming room, regardless of whether the casualty is human or animal. Most groomers work alone and First Aid in any emergency will be their responsibility. This chapter starts by providing a definition of First Aid and outlines its aims, as well as the sort of training that a groomer can look for and undertake.

An accident by definition is an unforeseen event that occurs unintentionally or by chance, so advance planning and good preparation recommend them-selves. You should therefore always ensure that you are prepared for the unexpected and have an emergency action plan with priorities of treatment. A check-list of measures you should consider putting into practice is provided to help you start your preparation.

The list of potential accidents and emergencies is endless and would require an entire book of its own. The next section looks at common illnesses and injuries in human casualties, as groomers can easily find themselves faced with a sick or injured client or member of staff. Building on this, the final sections deal specifically with the common emergencies you can expect to see in dogs, the techniques you should practise, and the equipment and supplies you should buy and keep in your First Aid box.

8.1 FIRST AID – A DEFINITION

First Aid is the care provided to a sick or injured casualty by the first person to reach them. It is therefore the initial care received by the casualty and is usually provided by a non-expert person. The aims of First Aid can be summarized by the three P's:

◆ **P**reserve life.
◆ **P**revent deterioration.
◆ **P**romote recovery.

Whilst the overriding aim of First Aid is to preserve life until medical help arrives, the casualty's condition should not be allowed to worsen as this may endanger life. There are many simple acts that can be performed to help achieve these core objectives. In some cases First Aid can actually initiate the recovery process or even resolve a problem by undertaking a simple but effective treatment (as in the application of a plaster to a small wound).

Training

Within the workplace employers have a legal duty of care towards their employees. In the UK this is covered by the Health and Safety at Work (First Aid) Regulations 1981. Employers are required under this legislation to provide adequate and appropriate equipment, facilities and personnel to ensure their employees receive immediate attention if they are injured or taken ill at work. These Regulations apply to all workplaces, including those with fewer than five employees and to the self-employed.

A booklet entitled 'Approved Code of Practice and Guidance', providing full details of this legislation and the responsibilities it entails, is available from the Health and Safety Executive (HSE) website: www.hse.gov.uk/firstaid/index.htm.

As part of this legislation there is also a requirement to report injuries, diseases and dangerous occurrences. This is covered under the Reporting of Injuries, Diseases and Dangerous Occurrences Regulations (RIDDOR) 1995. Details of this piece of legislation can also be found on the HSE website: www.hse.gov.uk/riddor/index.htm. More information on the HSE and RIDDOR can be found in Chapter 7.

If you find yourself working in another country, you should familiarize yourself with local legislation.

Regardless of the legal position, all responsible citizens have a moral responsibility to undertake First Aid training so that they are suitably equipped to help others in the event of an accident, injury or illness. Situations can arise anywhere and anytime, whether at home or at work, or, indeed, on a journey. The nature of such incidents is that they are unpredictable.

First Aid training provides you with the skills and knowledge to help yourself and others. It needs to be updated every three years and is provided by a number of different organizations in the UK, including St John Ambulance and the British Red Cross. The HSE approves courses for the workplace; these are usually described as 'First Aid at Work' courses and typically last three days. A list of providers of such courses is available from the HSE website.

Whilst such training has traditionally been for the human casualty, there is no reason why it cannot also be for the animal casualty. As a groomer you would therefore do well to undertake training in both human and animal First Aid. Your local veterinary surgery may offer, or be able to point you in the direction of, such courses. Scenario-based training sessions, making full use of role-play situations, can be particularly rewarding and will afford you plenty of opportunities to review your decisions and actions. After any real life situation it is always worth reviewing with your vet what you have done in order to identify those things you did well and any areas you can improve on.

Prevention, preparation and planning

In preparing for the unexpected you need to recognize two things:

◆ Firstly, you are preparing for something that you hope will never happen and doing everything possible to ensure that it does not happen.

◆ Secondly, if it does happen, you are likely to need to make decisions fast and they need to be good decisions: a life may depend on it.

Table 20 provides a summary of the measures you should implement.

Advice on risk assessments and risk management is available from the HSE website and can be accessed via: www. hse.gov.uk/risk/index.htm.

The emergency action plan and treatment priorities

Familiarize yourself with the following emergency action plan(s). There will be no time to look at it when an emergency presents and it is therefore essential that you know what to do. The first example is for the human casualty. Many of the principles described also apply to the animal casualty and these are highlighted and discussed subsequently.

There are several useful mnemonics that can be used to help you remember the priorities of treatment and the emergency action plan: commonly used ones are DR ABC and AB BB.

DR ABC

D = Danger
R = Response
A = Airway
B = Breathing
C = Circulation

DR ABC emphasizes the need to look for danger first, thereby ensuring that you do not become the next casualty. You need to identify dangers and make the area safe. This approach is used in the description of the emergency action plan for a human casualty described below.

AB BB

A = Airway
B = Breathing
B = Bleeding (or burns)
B = Bones

This mnemonic emphasizes the difference between the primary survey and the secondary survey. The first priority is always the casualty's Airway and Breathing (AB). Once you have satisfied

Table 20   Planning and preparation – important things for inclusion in your plan.

Emergency contact numbers	The emergency contact numbers you may need in the event of an emergency should be written on a laminated notice stuck on the wall beside the phone and programmed into all phones. They should include: ◆ 999 for Ambulance, Fire Brigade and Police ◆ Your local doctor ◆ Your local veterinary service ◆ Local animal ambulance services ◆ Local taxi services The sign should clearly indicate your location (address and postcode) so that anyone phoning for help can provide this information precisely.
Admission procedure and health check	All dogs that come in for grooming should only be admitted following an admission procedure and health check. This may be your only opportunity to ask the owners if the dog has any health problems, such as diabetes, epilepsy, heart problems, clotting disorders and phobias or behavioural problems. Remember forewarned is forearmed! The contact details of the dog's veterinary surgeon should be recorded as part of this admission check.
First Aid training	Update your first aid training (human and animal) every three years and practise whenever possible.
First Aid equipment	This should be checked regularly and restocked after each and every use. A weekly or monthly check of the first aid kit should be programmed in the diary. A clear sign in the grooming room should indicate where the first aid kit is located. It should never be locked away in a cupboard or office.
Risk assessment	A risk assessment should be undertaken for your place of work and appropriate steps identified to eliminate or minimize each and every risk, including the risks involved in first aid procedures.
Evacuation procedure	In the event of a fire, or similar emergency, you must have an approved fire exit (or exits) and a designated fire assembly point. If it is safe to do so, your procedure will allow you to evacuate the dogs to a place of safety.
Veterinary care	You should establish a good working relationship with your veterinary surgeon and learn the quickest route to the surgery in the event of an emergency.

yourself that the casualty is breathing, you can undertake a secondary survey that seeks to identify other problems. These checks focus on identifying Bleeding (and also Burns) before checking for broken Bones. This can also be summarized as (BB).

The use of DR ABC will become clearer after reading the description of an emergency action plan for a human casualty given below. After reading this, you should be able to write down your main priorities in order of importance.

8.2 THE HUMAN CASUALTY

The emergency action plan prioritizes the airway and breathing first. All animal life (that includes us!) needs a constant supply of oxygen; if this is cut off, it will result in irreversible damage to the brain cells within three to four minutes. The unconscious casualty does not have control of their airway and it is essential that you protect their airway immediately.

Your First Aid training will teach you how to deal with common human emergencies. These include choking, bleeding, shock, eye injuries, poisoning, burns, broken bones, spinal injuries, heart attack, stroke, diabetes, fitting and asthma. There is not enough room here to deal in detail with these from the human perspective as we now need to focus on the animal casualty. We must also mention the effects of shock and the importance of monitoring both human and animal casualties for this worrying sign. We then discuss

---

APPLYING THE DR ABC EMERGENCY ACTION PLAN TO A HUMAN CASUALTY

Doctor (DR) ABC: Danger, Response, Airway, Breathing, Circulation

Your first priority is to yourself, as you are no good to anybody if you also get hurt. You should therefore start by looking for **Danger** and making the area safe. If, for example, you suspect there has been an electrocution, turn off the power at the mains. Do not take any unnecessary risks.

It is important to call out to the casualty to get a **Response**, so you can make your presence known and establish contact. You need to establish if the casualty is conscious and breathing. This can be done both verbally and then by touch. If they respond, they are, by definition, conscious and breathing. If you don't get a verbal response on approaching a casualty, you should kneel beside them and squeeze their shoulder whilst still talking to them. If they still fail to respond, you are dealing with an unconscious casualty. Shout for help at this point.

The **Airway** of the unconscious human casualty should be made safe by tilting the head back and lifting the chin. This movement will open up the back of the throat and displace the tongue, which is likely to have fallen backwards and obstructed the airway. This done, you should listen carefully for **Breathing**, with your cheek against their mouth and your eyes looking along the line of the chest. By doing this you can hear, feel and see air movement if the casualty is breathing.

If the casualty is not breathing, ring 999 and request an ambulance. You should provide your exact location and specify that you have an **unconscious casualty that is not breathing.** Given that this is likely to be a cardiac arrest (heart attack) patient, you should ask for a **defibrillator.** Once you have requested an ambulance, start cardio-pulmonary resuscitation (CPR). Your training in human first aid will include CPR training.

The current recommendation for CPR is to give **30 chest compressions followed by 2 breaths**. Continue with this 30:2 ratio, changing over with another person if possible (one person cannot sustain CPR for long by themselves) until the ambulance arrives or the casualty starts breathing normally. Compressions are given at 100 per min or to the same rhythm as the Bee Gees' hit record 'Staying Alive'.

The same ratio is used for adults and children. The only difference is that new research has shown that infants can benefit from the administration of five initial rescue breaths as their lungs are proportionally smaller and contain less oxygen than adult lungs. The aim of chest compressions is to compress the chest by about one-third of its depth. In children under a year old this is achieved using two fingers; in those over a year old use one or two hands.

Secondary surveys and the breathing human casualty

If, following your primary survey, you have established that the casualty is not responding to your voice but is breathing, you should conduct a secondary survey to try to identify the cause. This is, of course, easier if the casualty is conscious and can provide you with that information.

If the casualty is unconscious, look for signs of bleeding, injuries and any other clues that could suggest what has happened. Your secondary survey should include the head and neck, shoulders and chest, abdomen and pelvis as well as the legs and arms. Look for any signs of bruising, swelling or deformity.

A thorough systematic survey should reduce the chances of you missing something. As part of your survey you should check the wrist and neck for medic alert bracelets (carried by people with hidden medical conditions such as diabetes and allergies, as well as those taking medication), and the pockets for other helpful clues.

Remember the **D** for **Danger**, however! If you suspect bleeding, you should wear gloves, and take care to avoid any sharp objects, such as needles, in a casualty's pockets.

Where **Circulatory** problems such as bleeding are identified, the cause should be determined and dealt with where possible.

If the casualty is still unconscious, they should be placed in the recovery position to maintain their airway and a 999 call made (if not already done so by someone who responded to your call for help). The recovery position or **safe airway position** keeps the airway open and allows any vomit to drain from the mouth. You will learn and practise this technique during your First Aid training.

wounds, especially dog bites, as these are, quite probably, the most common injury the groomer is likely to sustain during their working life.

Shock

What is shock?

Shock is a condition that can affect both humans and dogs. It is a term that is often misunderstood and often overlooked outside medical circles, probably because the word is so often used to describe a sudden fright that disturbs us and numbs our emotions.

In medical terms shock has nothing to do with a fright; it refers to a state of collapse (or near-collapse) as a response to infection, circulatory failure or a sudden lowering of the blood pressure caused by severe bleeding. In each of these cases the oxygen supply to the vital organs is compromised. The body responds by shutting down the arteries to the less vital parts of the body such as the skin and the intestines.

Dealing with shock in the human casualty:

- ***Do telephone for an ambulance.***
- ***Do speak reassuringly, even if the casualty appears to have lost consciousness.***
- ***Do not move the casualty unless absolutely necessary. It may make the situation worse. Any movement increases the heart rate.***
- ***Do use something to raise the legs so that gravity can assist the flow of blood back to the heart and on to the brain.***
- ***Do loosen tight clothing.***
- ***Do cover the casualty with a thin coat or blanket.***
- ***Do check the pulse and breathing at regular intervals.***
- ***Do not try to give the casualty anything to drink or eat.***
- ***Do not use artificial heat. Even a hot water bottle will attract blood towards the skin, diverting it away from the major organs and causing the situation to worsen.***

Shock in the medical sense is dangerous, and can be fatal. In all cases of an accident or injury, even if the outcome appears to be trivial, the casualty must be monitored for shock; if symptoms occur, medical help must be sought immediately. Signs include:

- pale and cold or clammy skin resulting from the blood vessels shutting down;
- rapid pulse because the heart is trying to maintain circulation;
- weak pulse because the heart cannot beat strongly;
- breathlessness because the casualty has insufficient oxygen;
- thirst because the fluid content in the blood is reduced;
- weakness and possibly fainting because the casualty has reduced blood supply to the brain and muscles; and
- loss of consciousness because of the reduced blood supply to the brain and major organs.

Wounds and dog bites

Groomers are at risk of sustaining a variety of wounds, bites and scratches. These injuries carry with them the risk of bleeding and infection and must be managed appropriately. They are often painful and even the smallest cut can be a nuisance because it can often alter the way you handle your tools so, all in all, in the first instance, these injuries are always best prevented.

Following an injury it may be a good idea to review how the injury happened and how it can be avoided next time. We all make mistakes, but if we learn from them we can ensure that the same mistake is never made twice. You are advised to read very carefully

---

CAUTION: DOG HAIR CONTAMINATION

It is worth pointing out that even clean dog hair is a contaminant; any injury, however small, that breaks the skin, should be kept covered until it has healed. A small cut contaminated with fine hair clipping can easily become a much greater problem should it develop into an infection.

---

the 'safe use of scissors' (Chapter 15) and 'de-matting tools' (Chapter 10) sections so that you understand the risks involved in using these incredibly sharp tools.

Scissor cuts (*see* Fig. 8.2.1) are usually fine lacerations that have cut cleanly through the skin. They are similar in many ways to surgical wounds. This is particularly true of new scissors that are razor sharp and cut easily through the skin, causing minimal trauma to the surrounding tissues. Typically fingers are affected, and the high nerve fibre density in the skin overlying the fingers and especially the finger tips means that these cuts can be particu-

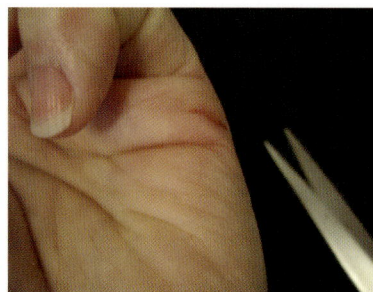

Fig. 8.2.1   Scissor injuries are very common. To cut hair, scissors must be very sharp and unfortunately, if you do get your hands or fingers in the way, the blades will have no difficulty cutting through your skin.

Note: the main causes of scissor cuts are:

- ***Scissors that are too long for you become unbalanced in your hand, so you have less control of them (see Section 15.1).***
- ***The dog moves just as you finish closing the blades and the tips cut you instead.***

---

larly painful and they bleed profusely. **Injuries from de-matting tools** (*see* Fig. 8.2.2) are often more serious as the multiple blades on these tools are exposed and very sharp. They are often also serrated and can result in several deep uneven wounds. These tools are used on dirty unwashed coats and are heavily contaminated so the risk of infection is significant.

In either case the wound should be assessed to ascertain how deep it

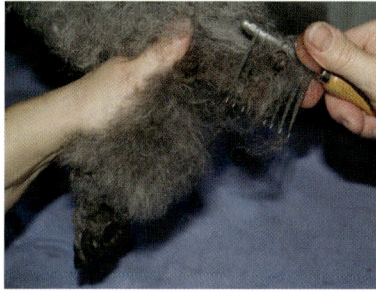

Fig. 8.2.2   The cutting blades on de-matting tools like the one illustrated are very sharp and can cause nasty injuries to both dog and groomer if they are not used correctly and stored in a safe place.

> *Note: the main causes of de-matter cuts are:*
>
> ◆ *Incorrect use.*
> ◆ *They are blunt and you are using too much force to get the tool through the coat.*

is, what tissues are involved and whether the wound is contaminated. If the equipment has been or is currently in use, contamination should be assumed. Only surgically sterilized equipment can be guaranteed free of potential pathogens. When assessing the depth of the injury, the involvement of underlying structures should be considered. Injuries involving tendons, ligaments and joints are particularly serious as infections of these structures can be difficult to treat.

Following an injury, direct pressure should be applied over the wound to stop the bleeding. The wound can then be more easily examined and cleaned. It should be liberally flushed under clean cold running water to remove all contamination. A clean dressing should then be applied over the wound and strapped securely in place. Elevating the affected limb can further reduce the bleeding. For small cuts the wound edges can be brought together by pressing on either side of the wound. This can stop even the most persistent of bleeds. Skin sutures or plasters can then be applied across the wound to keep the edges apposed. Having stopped the bleeding, medical advice should be sought, particularly if the wound is contaminated or deep. If in doubt, consult your GP for advice on

whether to start a course of antibiotics as a precaution against infection.

> *Dealing with cuts:*
>
> ◆ *Initially, apply pressure to stop the bleeding so that the injury can be more easily assessed.*
> ◆ *Flush with cold running water across the wound to remove contamination.*
> ◆ *Secure a clean dressing over the wound and elevate (if necessary) to reduce bleeding.*
> ◆ *Go to Accident and Emergency or to your doctor if stitching may be necessary.*
> ◆ *Monitor for shock.*

Claw (nail) **scratch injuries** (*see* Figs 8.2.3 and 8.2.4) can be both deep and painful. They are associated with both blunt and sharp trauma, and there can therefore be considerable bruising around what may also be a deep cut. Again any bleeding should be stopped by applying direct pressure and the wound liberally and repeatedly washed out. The water should be allowed to flow across the wound rather than into it, as you want to remove contamination rather than wash it deeper into the wound. Nails are typically contaminated with a range of bacteria and other potentially pathogenic organisms. Dogs dig and their paws

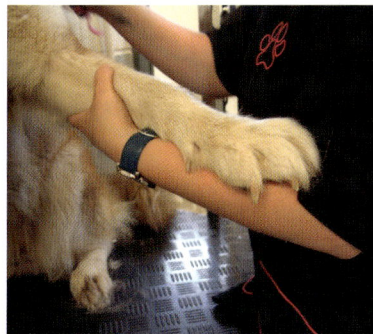

Fig. 8.2.3   Dogs like the Malamute use their nails as crampons to grip the snow and ice. It is natural for this type of dog to grip with its feet, as demonstrated. The nails are very strong, as are the muscles in the foot, and can cause a great deal of damage by breaking the skin and bruising the muscles in the forearm of a groomer.

are in regular contact with the ground; nails should therefore be assumed to be contaminated. The clostridial bacterium responsible for tetanus (*Clostridium tetani*) is prevalent in soil; scratch injuries therefore represent a significant risk for you. All but the most superficial scratches should be taken seriously.

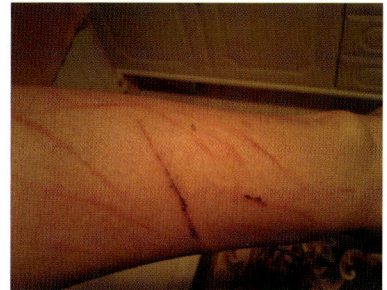

Fig. 8.2.4   The damage done by a dog gripping at an exposed forearm. This injury was caused by the dog's dewclaw.

Cat scratches are potentially more worrying than dog scratches. This is because cat scratches can readily become infected and are associated with a particular bacterial disease called 'Cat Scratch Fever'. This is caused by *Bartonella henselae* and is associated with cat scratches, bites or contact with a cat's saliva. It manifests itself as fever and malaise, and swelling of the draining lymph nodes about two or three weeks after infection. The reader should deduce from this that all casualties should remain alert to, and be carefully monitored for, any such signs in the weeks following a cat scratch or bite.

> *Dealing with nail and claw scratches:*
>
> ◆ *If the wound is deep, apply pressure to stop bleeding.*
> ◆ *Flush for several minutes with running water.*
> ◆ *Assess the damage.*
> ◆ *Dry the skin and apply a clean dressing.*
> ◆ *Cat scratches that have broken the skin need to be taken seriously. Seek medical advice as soon as possible.*
> ◆ *Monitor for shock.*

Bite wounds should always be taken seriously. A dog bite (*see* Fig. 8.2.5) can result in considerable localized trauma to the affected area, as well as mental trauma to the casualty. A bite from a dog generally produces crushing injuries, whereas cat bites are more likely to result in puncture wounds and lacerations to the deeper tissues. The types of injury sustained following a dog bite therefore differ from those sustained following a cat bite and will be described separately.

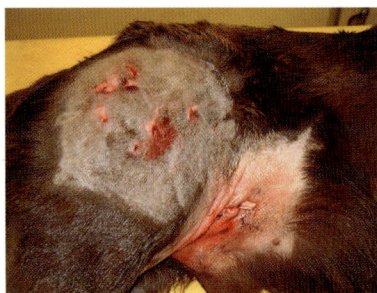

Fig. 8.2.5 This Labrador retriever was attacked by an Akita. There are multiple deep puncture wounds in the upper thigh and considerable trauma to the underlying muscle. The wounds to the thigh were explored and lavaged, and the vet inserted a drain to allow drainage of any inflammatory fluids from the wound. This injury did not happen in a grooming room but it is indicative of the type of injury that could result if dogs that do not know each other are allowed to come into contact.

The jaws of a dog can exert a force of between 250 and 450 pounds per square inch, sometimes more, depending on the breed and head morphology. Dogs with shorter, wider jaws are able to exert the greatest pressure. Such bites crush and tear tissues, causing considerable damage (especially if there has been any shaking). In some cases the overlying skin may be unbroken but the underlying tissues visibly bruised. The traumatized tissues are vulnerable to infection, especially if their blood supply is compromised and the skin has been broken. That said, the incidence of infections following a dog bite is much lower than for cat bites.

Cats tend to inflict damage with their canines, producing puncture wounds. The skin overlying a bite wound tends to be fairly mobile and moves over the underlying tissues; the skin itself there-fore only tears if snagged. The deeper tissues are relatively immobile by comparison and much more prone to lacerations. In addition, a deep puncture wound can result in contamination from a dirty tooth being introduced deep into the tissues. There is no such thing as a clean tooth; you should assume that they carry a mixed population of bacteria that can thrive in a wound if allowed to do so. In particular, cats carry a number of nasty bacteria, such as *Pasteurella multocida*, within their mouths; these can give rise to septicaemia (blood infection), which can potentially be life-threatening.

Never underestimate a puncture wound, even if it appears to have closed over and stopped bleeding. There may be considerable trauma to the underlying tissues and there is a significant risk of infection. The pointed profile of the canine facilitates its entry deep into the tissues, leading to serious complications such as osteomyelitis (bone infection), septic arthritis (joint infections) and septicaemia (blood infection).

Bite wounds should be treated aggressively. The animal should be secured/returned to a kennel, thus making the area safe. The injured limb should then be liberally lavaged with cold running water. The objective here is to remove as much contamination as possible, as quickly as possible. This can be difficult when dealing with a puncture wound. The wound should be allowed to bleed, to help evacuate/clean the affected area. At this point it is probably appropriate to use a disinfectant wash but this should not be a substitute for liberally flushing an area. If you only use a disinfectant you are relying on it killing germs when you should be concentrating on eliminating them (i.e. getting them out). All serious bite wounds should be seen by a medical professional. Antibiotics are likely to be needed and, depending on the extent of any injuries, surgical procedures may be indicated.

Which bite wounds can be left to heal by themselves? This is a difficult question to answer as there are many unpredictable variables and the consequences of complications, such as cat bite fever or joint infections, are very serious indeed. It is always better to err on the side of caution and see a doctor.

Dealing with bite wounds:

◆ *Apply pressure to the wound to stop persistent bleeding as appropriate.*

◆ *Flush with running water across the wound to remove contamination.*

◆ *Assess the injury.*

◆ *If the wound is serious, apply a clean dressing and seek medical advice.*

◆ *For minor wounds, apply a clean dressing and monitor the healing process over the following days.*

◆ *Monitor for shock.*

Whether the casualty is you or another person, the injured party :should always be monitored for shock, even after the smallest of injuries. Everyone responds differently to trauma and it should never be assumed that the casualty will automatically recover without side-effects. A dog bite can be particularly distressing and counselling of the casualty may need to be considered.

8.3 THE ANIMAL CASUALTY

This section deals with the common emergencies that you may encounter in the grooming room, together with some serious ones that, with luck, you will never see, but should be able to recognize and deal with. Table 21 outlines the main emergencies you should prepare for, together with their causes.

In the majority of emergency situations within the grooming room, you will have witnessed the incident and know what has happened. There may, however, be situations where you walk into the kennel area and find a sick or injured dog.

Start with your emergency action plan DR ABC, as this will help you to remember your order of priorities. Check for Danger and make the area safe.

◆ You may need to turn off mains electricity or electrical equipment.

Table 21   Canine emergencies in the grooming room and their likely causes.

Canine Emergency	Cause
Allergic reaction	Chemicals (e.g. shampoo and sprays). Insect bites.
Asphyxiation	Drying cabinets. Hanging from table restraints. Slipping in the bath and drowning. Airway obstruction. Heart failure.
Bite wounds	Dog on dog aggression.
Bleeding *Clotting disorders*	Wounds. Nose bleeds. Vomiting. Coughing .All wounds, including cut nails.
Bruises	Blunt trauma (falls, knocks, etc.) and blasters.
Burns and scalds	Burns from the drier. Contact with other hot surfaces (e.g. clipper blades). Chemical burns. Friction burns (e.g. brushes and rakes). Scalding with hot water.
Electrocution	Water and electricity. Dog biting cables.
Eye injuries	Contamination of the eye during the grooming process. Trauma. Prolapse.
Fitting	Epilepsy. Exposure to toxins (poisoning). Hyperthermia.
Fractures	Trauma to the body (falls, kicks, pathological fractures).
Heart failure	Age-related. Disease-related. Trauma-related. (Bleeding, heat stress, stress).
Heat stress	Bath water too warm. Driers too warm. Drying cabinets. Environment too warm. Sun through windows.
Hyperthermia	Heat stress leading to heat stroke may arise during drying or when left in a car or similar hot environment.
Hypoglycaemia	Diabetes.
Hypothermia	Old or at risk dogs exposed to slow drying conditions after bathing. May be aggravated by shock following an injury or trauma. Exposure to other cold, wet environments and wind chill.
Insect stings	Stings from a bee, wasp or hornet. Other non-insect invertebrates, including some spiders, can produce a nasty bite.
Nail injuries *(if the dog is haemophiliac)*	Nails clipped too short. Nails caught in plug holes and avulsed (pulled off)
Poisoning	Poisons may be ingested, inhaled and absorbed across the skin.
Tail injuries	Tail hitting table legs, etc.
Unconsciousness	Head trauma. Diabetic coma. Electrocution.

- You may need to remove tools or equipment.
- You may need to secure doors to prevent an escape.

Above all, take appropriate measures to ensure you do not get bitten. This may mean wrapping a dog in a towel or calling for someone to help restrain the dog.

If the dog does not **Respond** when approached, called and touched, it is likely to be unconscious. **Shout for help**.

Check the **Airway** by carefully opening the dog's mouth (*see* Fig. 8.3.1). Look for any obvious obstruction, signs of vomiting or fluid at the back of the throat. Where possible, any foreign objects or obstructions should be removed from the mouth and throat

areas. If the dog has strangled himself, remove any collar ties from around the neck.

Having checked and cleared the airway, look, listen and feel for **Breathing.** If the dog is not breathing, get someone to call your veterinary surgery for help and advice. If you are on your own, having a speed dial on your phone is invaluable. Phoning your veterinary surgeon and switching to speaker phone should only take seconds and leaves your hands free to deal with the casualty. If your grooming salon is close to or indeed part of a veterinary centre, help may arrive fast and life-saving measures, including the administration of oxygen, can be instituted. If you are not close to a veterinary surgery, you will have to give the oxygen yourself by providing rescue breaths.

Fig. 8.3.1   Place the handle of a comb across the mouth to prevent it closing whist you examine the throat and airways.

Artificial respiration and cardiac compression

Take steps to protect yourself by cleaning the dog's nose and applying a mask or suitable membrane through which you can administer rescue breaths. Special masks are available for inclusion in human First Aid kits and are to be recommended; if one is not available, a material grooming mask can be adapted (*see* Figs 8.3.2–8.3.4).

Pull the upper lips down to form a seal and place the mask over the top (*see* Figs 8.3.3 and 8.3.4). Air can then be administered via the nostrils. Check to see that the chest is inflating when you blow. You are looking to produce a small amount of chest expansion but must be careful not to over-distend the lungs. Remember that the dog's lungs are a lot smaller than yours; you do not need to deliver large quantities of air, small gentle breaths will suffice.

Do not waste time checking for a pulse. Initiate cardiac compressions if you have identified that the dog is still not breathing. Lay the dog on his right side and place the heel of one hand, with interlocked fingers, over the lower chest wall where the dog's elbow touches the chest (*see* Fig. 8.3.5). An appropriate compression-to-breath ratio would be approximately 10:1

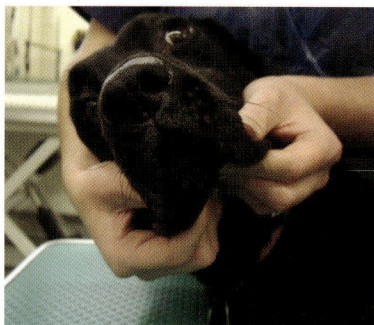

Fig. 8.3.4   *You can now place your mouth over the dog's nose and* puff *gently to mimic the dog panting. The breaths should inflate the lungs but take care not to over-inflate them. Blow several times at one second intervals, then return to chest compressions. If you don't have anything to cover the nose, just blow gently into the dog's nostrils. If you have help, both chest compressions and artificial respiration should be given simultaneously.*

(10 pumps to 1 breath), although the efficacy of this figure has not been evaluated. The chest should be compressed by about a third during each compression. An appropriate compression rate would be 100/min.

If, after some five to ten minutes, the casualty has not started breathing independently, it is likely that they are

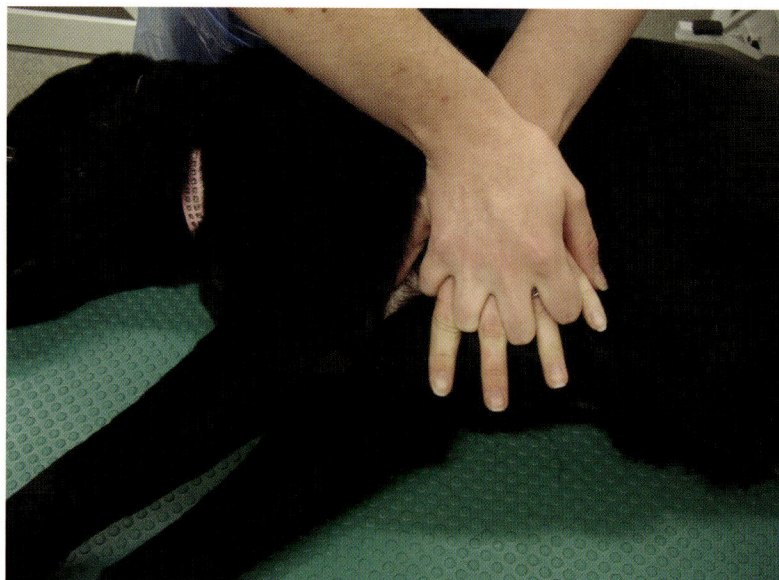

Fig. 8.3.2   *To administer artificial respiration and breathe for the dog, you need first of all to seal the lips around the mouth.*

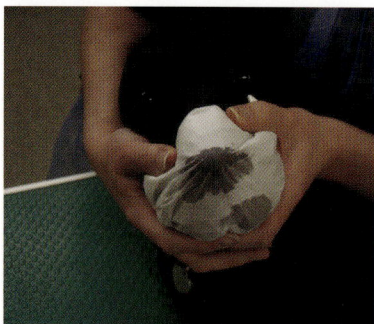

Fig. 8.3.3   *Place something over the dog's nose and mouth (here we have used a paper grooming mask) and lift the head.*

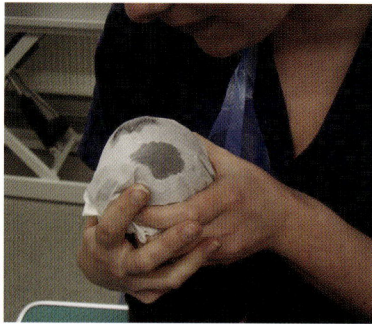

Fig. 8.3.5   *For chest compressions (cardiac massage), lay the dog on his left side and place your hands one on top of the other over the heart, just behind the dog's elbow. Link the fingers of your top hand into your lower hand and push gently into the ribs. If you are on your own, do this three to six times at half-second intervals before you break to give the dog artificial respiration. If you have help, you can maintain the rhythm whilst someone else gives respiration. Lay a towel or blanket over the lower half of the dog to try to minimize heat loss.*

Artificial respiration and attempted resuscitation:

- ◆ **Lay the dog on his right side.**
- ◆ **Place the heel of your hand on the ribs just behind the elbow.**
- ◆ **Apply ten small but firm pushes to the ribcage.**
- ◆ **Stop compressions. Close the dog's mouth with your hand and apply a small breath (a sigh) into the dog's nose.**
- ◆ **Continue the process at a rate of 10:1 for about ten minutes, unless normal breathing resumes.**
- ◆ **Monitor and treat for shock.**
- ◆ **Record all details.**

Note: the normal breathing rate for the dog is between ten and thirty breaths per minute. In the unconscious dog this rate may be less.

dead. If this happens, don't beat yourself up. You have done your best and, very often, without ventilating equipment and veterinary intervention there is little you can do.

Choking should not be confused with breathing difficulties. If a dog has been playing with a toy or is in the process of chewing up his bedding and suddenly starts struggling to breathe, then he may well be choking. If the breathing difficulty has come on gradually, however, it is unlikely you are dealing with a choking.

If the dog is obviously struggling to breathe, and you suspect choking, you should try to relieve the obstruction. Great care is required here as the dog is likely to be very distressed and may bite or struggle. In the first instance a sharp blow with the flat of your hand over the chest (either between the shoulder blades or over the chest wall) may produce an exhalation that can dislodge an obstruction. If this fails, check the mouth to see if there is an obvious obstruction that can be carefully pulled free. You can use the handle of a grooming comb to help prevent being bitten. Place the end of the handle sideways on, as far back as possible between the back teeth and on top of the tongue on one side of the mouth (*see* Fig. 8.3.1). This will prevent the mouth from closing and allow you to look inside and try to remove anything that you can see.

As a last resort an abdominal thrust (the Heimlich manoeuvre) can be used (*see* Fig. 8.3.6). Turn the dog away from

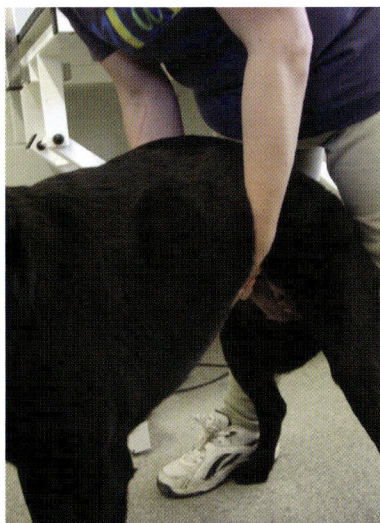

Fig. 8.3.6 If you can't dislodge an obstruction and the dog is choking, the Heimlich manoeuvre can be used as a last resort. Put a towel over the dog's head, covering his face so he cannot see to bite you and to protect yourself if he throws his head around.

you and throw a towel over the top of the dog's head, covering his face, so that he can't see you. This should prevent you from being bitten in the face and will cushion you from bruising if he throws his head around. Stand over the dog with your arms placed around his abdomen. Your clenched fists can then be pulled up under the ribs with a view to producing a forceful exhalation. If it is safe to do so, check the dog's mouth again and attempt to retrieve any obstruction.

If the dog passes out and stops breathing refer to the emergency action plan above.

If a dog is choking, you can try:

- ◆ *A sharp blow with the flat of your hand between the shoulder blades or over the chest wall.*
- ◆ *Carefully remove any visible objects from the mouth and throat.*
- ◆ *The Heimlich manoeuvre: turn the dog away from you. Clench your fists under his ribs and thrust upwards to produce a forced exhalation.*
- ◆ *Carefully remove any visible objects from the mouth and throat.*
- ◆ *Record all details.*

Circulation (bleeding)

Next check the dog's **Circulation** (bleeding). Clearly some forms of bleeding are more serious than others. Profuse or persistent bleeding from any part of the body is referred to as a haemorrhage. In some cases you may be unaware of an injury and it comes as a surprise to see blood on a dog's coat or bedding. You need to identify the source of the bleeding if you are to do anything about it. Don't forget that the blood may have been coughed or vomited up, or may be passed in the dog's urine. Examine the dog thoroughly to determine where the blood is coming from.

An evaluation of the injury that has resulted in the bleeding should give you some idea as to how serious it is. Try to answer the following questions:

- ◆ What caused the injury?
  This may give you an indication of how deep the wound may be.
- ◆ Where is the blood coming from?
  This indicates how much blood is being lost and the extent of the wound.
- ◆ What tissues are involved?
  The wound may be superficial or it may involve muscles and other soft tissue structures.
- ◆ Are any arteries involved?
  Injuries to arteries are very serious and will quickly result in substantial blood loss.
- ◆ Is the dog known or thought to have a clotting disorder?
  Even the smallest wound will need to be seen by a vet in this case.

A half-decent examination should allow you to determine what sort of injury you are dealing with and maybe even what tissues are involved. In this way, if you find that a bleeding dog has a cut pad, for example, you can apply a dressing directly to the pad and then bandage the foot to ensure that pressure is maintained over the wound.

Your first response to a bleeding wound should always be to apply pressure. Initially this can be done digitally (with your finger) or with whatever suitable material you have to hand (e.g. a clean handkerchief or towel). Your objective is to minimize blood loss and ensure that the casualty reaches the vet in the best possible state. **Remember the three P's?** (**P**reserve life; **P**revent deterioration; **P**romote recovery.)

Arterial haemorrhage

If you find yourself faced with a spurting (i.e. pulsating) wound, the blood is coming from a ruptured artery and you may not have much time to save the dog. If direct pressure over the wound fails to stop the bleeding, you should apply pressure above the wound as the blood will be arriving from the heart (*see* Fig. 8.3.7 for arterial pressure points).

Venous haemorrhage

If the blood is oozing more slowly, it is likely to be from the veins, which are generally situated more superficially. Again, apply pressure directly over the

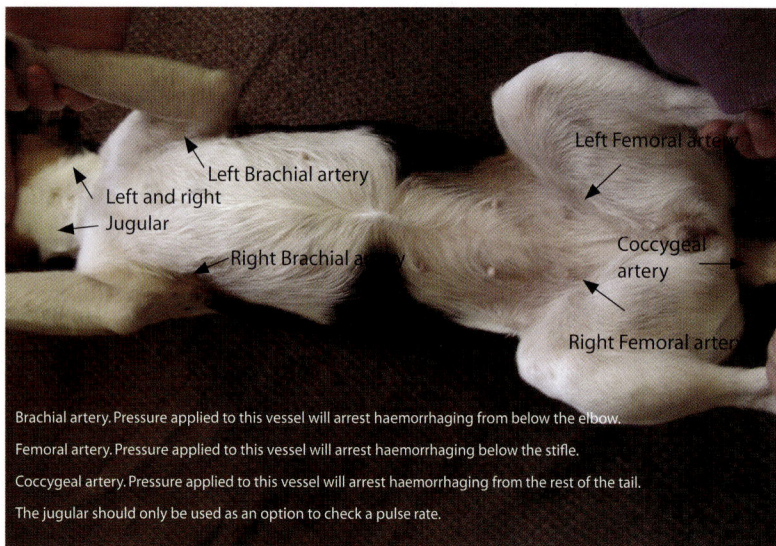

Brachial artery. Pressure applied to this vessel will arrest haemorrhaging from below the elbow.

Femoral artery. Pressure applied to this vessel will arrest haemorrhaging below the stifle.

Coccygeal artery. Pressure applied to this vessel will arrest haemorrhaging from the rest of the tail.

The jugular should only be used as an option to check a pulse rate.

Fig. 8.3.7   The position of the arterial pressure points. Pressure applied to the brachial artery will arrest haemorrhaging from below the elbow. Pressure applied to the femoral artery will arrest haemorrhaging below the stifle. Pressure applied to the coccygeal artery will arrest haemorrhaging from the rest of the tail. The jugular should only be used to check a pulse rate.

wound. If this fails to stop the bleeding, apply more pressure but this time *below* the wound as venous blood is returning from the extremities.

Tourniquets are not recommended as they can cut off the blood supply to an area, causing considerable tissue damage, and can even result in the loss of a limb. In extreme cases, when all other measures have failed, it may become necessary to apply a tourniquet as your last resort. In such cases (and only in extreme situations) it should be tied above the injury and the time of its application recorded. This should give you enough time to get help. If you have to resort to a tourniquet, it should be removed after ten minutes and should never be left in place for more than twenty minutes.

If an innocuous wound such as a small cut or lost nail is bleeding persistently, it is possible that the dog has a blood clotting disorder. Clotting pathways are complex and a clotting disorder can have many possible underlying causes. These can only really be investigated by a veterinary surgeon. That said, if you are dealing with a known haemophiliac, or a breed that is predisposed to this hereditary condition, you should at least suspect this as a cause. This should prompt you to take the persistent bleeding seriously and consult a vet, explaining your concerns. Learning your breed profiles will alert you to the breeds of dog most susceptible to clotting disorders.

Haemophilia is also known as von Willebrand's Disease. It is a sex-linked recessive genetic condition and is therefore mainly seen in male dogs. The gene is carried on the X chromosome, of which males only have one. Females may therefore be carriers of the condition but have to be carrying the gene on both their two X chromosomes to be affected. Almost all breeds of dogs and mongrels have been shown to be affected. Large breeds are more commonly affected and the Doberman Pinscher and German Shepherd Dog are particularly susceptible.

In the event of a dog bleeding:

- ◆ *Apply pressure.*
- ◆ *Identify the location and cause of the bleeding.*
- ◆ *Establish the severity.*
- ◆ *Take appropriate measures to prevent further blood loss.*
- ◆ *Keep the dog calm.*
- ◆ *Monitor the dog for shock and, if necessary, keep them warm and go to the vet.*
- ◆ *Record the details.*

Only use a tourniquet as a last resort and do not leave it in place for longer than ten minutes.

TAKING THE FEMORAL PULSE

The strength of the heart beat is reflected by arterial blood pressure. If the heart beat is weak or you are unable to feel it, you can try feeling for a pulse. In the dog the best place to try is on the inside of the groin. There is less hair there and your finger tips will be against the skin. You should practise this and familiarize yourself with the normal feel of a dog's femoral pulse (see Fig. 8.3.8).

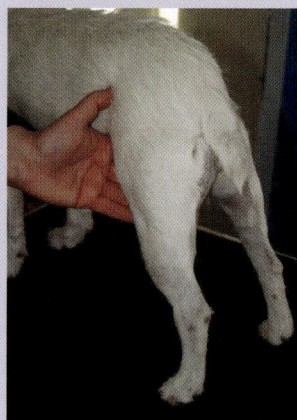

Fig. 8.3.8   Taking a femoral pulse: the first and second fingers are moved across the inner aspect of the thigh until they find a shallow groove in which the pulsing femoral artery can be palpated. Count the number of pulsations over fifteen seconds and multiply by four to give a pulse rate in beats per minute.

The pulse rate of a resting dog is between 70 and 160 beats per minute but can be as high as 180 beats per minute in toy dogs. In the healthy dog the beat is strong and regular. In a shocked dog it may speed up (increased heart rate) and become weak. This is often described as a fast and thready pulse and, if detected, is a cause for concern.

In the human casualty cold clammy skin is a feature of hypovolaemia, but it is not seen in dogs because they do not possess eccrine sweat glands and cannot therefore demonstrate increased sweating.

Other conditions requiring First Aid

Fitting

Seeing a fit, especially for the first time, can be very distressing. The person or animal may start by simply staring into space before convulsing and appearing to lose control of their limbs and, sometimes, their bodily functions. The throat muscles will also often convulse and the casualty may emit a gagging or choking sound. The jaws will either lock rigid or they may convulse, making the teeth chomp rapidly.

If a dog is fitting, do not try to restrain him as you risk being bitten. It is better not to cover the dog with a blanket because the constant scrambling movement of the legs may mean that they become entangled and you will not be able to free them without putting yourself at risk. Move away any items (including loose bedding or blankets if in a kennel – remember the scrambling legs) that could potentially injure the dog, taking care to pad exposed table legs or other hazards with blankets or towels as appropriate. If you have to move the dog, for instance from a bath or grooming table to the floor, lift them from behind with the legs and head facing away from you.

In all instances, dim the lights and turn off any noise to reduce any external stimulation. Allow the casualty to recover in a dark, warm, quiet environment and talk to them quietly, to provide reassurance. When the dog recovers from the fit, he is likely to be tired,

Fig. 8.3.9 Lift the lips of the dog to check the colour of the gums. In a shocked dog the gums become pale and may even discolour to grey.

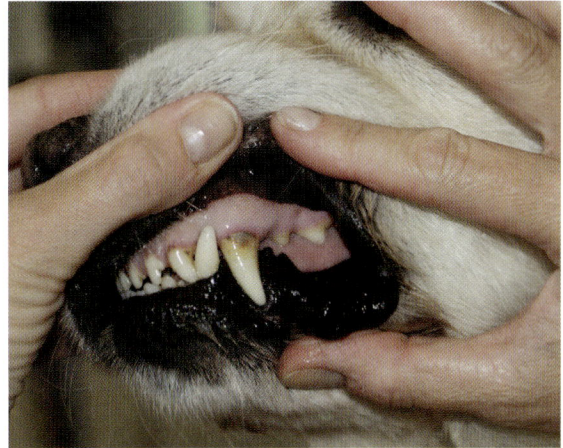

confused and disorientated. He may be distressed if he has urinated and soiled himself, and will have no recollection (or understanding) of what has happened. Now is the time to warm him up if this is needed and to provide further reassurance. It is unwise to continue the grooming process as external stimulation from noise or light may induce another fit. If the fit does not stop, or if further fits follow, you should ring the owner and seek veterinary attention.

Hypoglycaemia

If a known diabetic dog's blood sugar falls very low, he is likely to demonstrate a range of signs, including weakness, restlessness, disorientation and even seizures. In such cases a sugary food item can be applied to the gums in order to boost the blood sugar levels. Suitable products include honey, jam and various preparations of glucose syrup (in the grooming salon, you will probably have sugar in the tea-making area). These can be applied to the inside of the lip and gums, whilst holding the mouth closed. Care should be taken not to get bitten nor to introduce too much into the mouth. Veterinary advice should always be sought, especially if the signs persist.

In casualties with no previous history of diabetes, you as a groomer will certainly have no idea of the cause as hypoglycaemia cannot be confirmed without blood tests. In these cases veterinary advice should always be sought.

Shock

A collapsed or shocked dog can be

alarming to deal with, particularly when it occurs unexpectedly and you are unsure what is happening. You should phone immediately for advice and try to get the casualty to the vet as quickly as possible. Keep the dog warm with a light blanket but do not give him anything to drink.

You may be asked to assess or monitor the dog. A dog in shock experiences *hypovolaemia* (low blood volume). This can arise for various reasons and is characterized by a reduction in blood pressure, colour, temperature changes and consciousness. The body responds to this by increasing both heart rate and respiratory rate. In the human patient and the dog there is also an increase in anxiety (but only the human casualty will demonstrate an increase in sweating).

Lift the dog's lip and evaluate the colour of the gums (*see* Fig. 8.3.9). They should be pink in a healthy dog. In a shocked dog they may be pale or even discoloured (grey or blue, for example). Another test involves applying gentle pressure to a pink area of gum – this empties the capillaries, blanching the gum; upon releasing the pressure, the capillaries should fill rapidly with blood again. In a healthy

---

In the case of the fitting casualty:

◆ *Make the area safe or move the casualty to safety.*

◆ *Do not cover the dog with a blanket.*

◆ *Eliminate or minimize sources of stimulation, such as noise and light.*

◆ *Monitor the casualty but leave him quiet and undisturbed.*

◆ *Allow the casualty to recover and then reassure him and keep him warm.*

◆ *Record all details.*

◆ *Consider asking the owner to return the dog on another day to finish grooming.*

In the case of a collapsed dog: DR ABC.

◆ *If the dog is breathing, keep him warm and phone the vet for help.*

◆ *If the dog is unconscious, phone for help and attempt resuscitation.*

◆ *Record all details.*

---

dog this should usually only take 1–2 seconds. If the *capillary refill time* is slower than this, blood pressure is likely to be low.

Heat stroke

This arises when the body temperature is allowed to increase beyond the body's ability to keep it within normal limits. Dogs left in hot cars or unsupervised under a drier or in drying cabinets can rapidly overheat. They should be removed from the hot environment and cooled down. This can be done using cool (but not cold) water, or by wrapping them in a wet towel. Gently misting or showering the neck area will help cool the blood in the great vessels going to and returning from the head. This is always a temporary first aid measure until you can get to a vet. This condition can be life-threatening and veterinary advice should always be sought.

When phoning the vet for advice, you may be asked to check the dog's rectal temperature. This can provide useful information about the extent of any hyperthermia and allows the dog's condition to be monitored closely. The dog's normal rectal temperature should lie somewhere between 37.9 and 39.2°C. A temperature in excess of 39.5°C (103°F) is therefore high; many dogs suffering from heat stroke will have temperatures in excess of 42°C or even 44°C!

The rectal temperature is taken with a rectal thermometer coated in Vaseline and then gently inserted into the anus. Digital thermometers (*see* Fig. 8.3.10) provide a rapid readout and have the advantage that they do not break and release mercury into the environment. They do, however, contain batteries, which are equally damaging to the environment and should therefore always be recycled.

> **Dealing with heat stroke:**
>
> ♦ **Remove the dog from the heat source.**
> ♦ **Cool the dog with damp towels or cool (but not cold) water on the back of the neck.**
> ♦ **Phone the vet for advice.**
> ♦ **Record all details.**

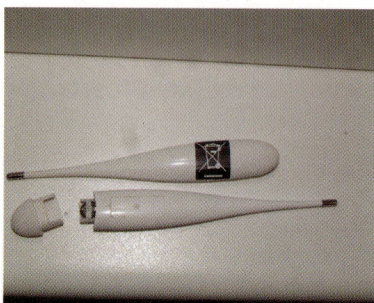

Fig. 8.3.11 *To take the temperature of the dog, first make sure that the dog is secured so that you cannot get bitten. Insert the thermometer up to the bulb and hold it in place for about thirty seconds.*

Poisoning

Dogs should not have access to poisons in the grooming room but accidents do happen. Where a grooming salon is on a business park or industrial estate, there is a possibility that rodenticides may be used to control rats and mice. You should ask about the pest control practices undertaken locally, particularly in areas used by you or your clients as exercise areas, and ensure that dogs have no access to bait. You need to be aware of what pesticide is being used, how long it remains active and how often it is used. Ask for a copy of the COSHH sheet.

Cleaning fluids and disinfectants are also a consideration. They can be licked and ingested, either directly from wet floors, or indirectly either when contaminated paws are licked clean, or

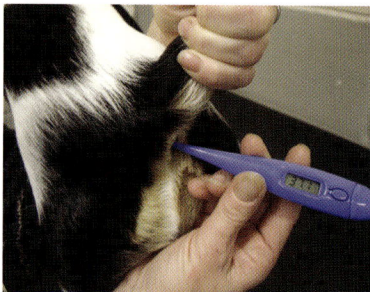

Fig. 8.3.10 *A digital thermometer gives a rapid readout. Digital thermometers cannot break and leak mercury into the environment; they do, however, contain batteries, which should be recycled wherever possible and never disposed of irresponsibly.*

> **TEMPERATURE**
>
> *The dog's temperature should be between 37.9 °C and 39.2 °C. Any reading above 40 °C is cause for alarm and veterinary help should be sought.*
>
> *To take a temperature (see Fig. 8.3.11):*
>
> ♦ *Make sure that the dog is suitably restrained and cannot bite you.*
> ♦ *If you are using a mercury thermometer, shake it to return the mercury to the bulb.*
> ♦ *If you have some, lubricate the bulb of the thermometer with a small amount of KY jelly or Vaseline. If you have neither, a little soap will do.*
> ♦ *Using a rotating action, gently insert the thermometer into the rectum so that the bulb is fully inserted.*
> ♦ *Hold it in place for about thirty seconds or, if you are using a digital thermometer, the time according to the manufacturer's instructions.*
> ♦ *Once removed, a digital thermometer will give you the reading on a display.*
> ♦ *If using a mercury thermometer, rotate it gently until the mercury can be seen against the temperature scale.*
> ♦ *Record the reading.*
> ♦ *Rinse your thermometer in cold water, wipe it, disinfect it and put it away.*

from the coat if a spillage occurs onto the dog's coat.

Where ingestion of a poison has occurred accidentally you should consult your vet immediately and have the product or packaging handy. Once the vet knows what has been ingested, you may be advised to induce vomiting, especially if the poison is rapidly absorbed and best eliminated quickly. Vomiting is not advisable if the material ingested is caustic. If instructed to do so by your vet, you can administer a teaspoon of table salt directly into the

POISONING

In the case of poison being ingested by the dog you should:

◆ *Take the packaging to the phone and call the vet immediately.*
◆ *If you are instructed to make the dog vomit, use a teaspoon of salt.*
◆ *Keep the dog warm and get him to a vet as soon as possible.*

If the poison is on the skin of the dog:

◆ *Remove it as quickly as you can by bathing in clear water for ten minutes.*
◆ *Phone the vet.*
◆ *Keep the dog warm and get him to the vet as soon as possible. Drying is not necessary.*

If a cat has been mistakenly treated with shampoo or insecticidal treatment containing permethrin:

◆ *Clip it off immediately before it has time to be absorbed.*
◆ *Rinse the cat in clear water for approximately ten minutes and seek veterinary advice.*
◆ *If neurological signs develop seek veterinary advice immediately.*

In the event of a fracture:

◆ *Reassure the dog by talking to him.*
◆ *Handle the dog as little as possible and be careful not to get bitten. Muzzle the dog if you are on your own and need to move him.*
◆ *Do not give him anything to drink as he may need surgery.*
◆ *Use a blanket to keep the dog warm (this can also be used as a stretcher to move the dog).*
◆ *Take the dog to the vet.*
◆ *Record all details.*

mon for fine particles of hair and dust to be deposited on the eye and conjunctiva, particularly when you are styling the hairy faces of brachycephalic dogs. Shampoo and bathing products may also enter the eye. These can all be washed from the eye with cold tap water. You should always ensure that the water runs away from the 'good' eye, as you do not want to wash material from one eye into the other.

Where irritant chemicals have entered the eye, copious amounts of

EYE INJURIES

Foreign bodies, chemicals and shampoos:

◆ *Rinse the eye with copious amounts of cold running water.*
◆ *Dry the eye.*
◆ *Monitor the dog until the owner arrives.*
◆ *Advise the owner to monitor the dog and to seek veterinary advice if necessary.*
◆ *Record all details.*

In the event of a prolapsed eye:

◆ *Apply a wet eye pad to keep the eye moist.*
◆ *Secure with a dressing.*
◆ *Seek veterinary help as soon as possible.*
◆ *Record all details.*

mouth to induce vomiting. The use of other products, such as washing soda crystals, is contraindicated as they have been shown to cause damage to the trachea. You should always have the casualty examined by a vet.

Some prescription shampoos may contain harmful ingredients that may be ingested by the dog, either by mouth or via the nose, during bathing. You should therefore always read instructions thoroughly and take extra precautions whilst using these products.

Where a poison has been inadvertently applied to the skin, it should be removed as quickly as possible to limit absorption and/or ingestion.

Fractures

Dogs with fractured limbs are likely to be shocked and in considerable pain. Attempts to stabilize the affected limb(s) can therefore lead to you being bitten and should be avoided. Ring your vet for advice on care and transportation. A stretcher can be improvised using a thick blanket or towel. The dog can be placed on the blanket, which is then folded over the dog and used to support the dog's entire weight when carrying him to the car, and when lifting him in and out. If you have to use a cage, be aware that the dog may be in a lot of pain and getting him in and out of the cage is going to put you at a great risk of being bitten. A voyager cage is better, as the top half can be removed to put the dog in, secured in place during transportation and removed again so the vet has access once you arrive at the surgery.

Eye injuries

In the grooming room it is not uncom-

water should be used to wash them out. Veterinary advice should then always be sought.

Where an injury has been sustained, a soft sterile dressing should be applied over the affected eye. Ideally the eye should also be kept moist. This can be achieved by applying sterile KY jelly or simply moistening the dressing. For severe eye injuries the other eye should also be bandaged to reduce movement in both eyes, thereby reducing further trauma.

In the event of a prolapsed eye (*see* Chapter 2.8 and Fig. 2.8.25), care must be taken not to damage the eye further. Apply a moistened eye pad over the damaged eye and hold it in place with a bandage. Veterinary attention must be sought as soon as possible if the eye is to be saved.

Burns and scalds

These arise when the tissues are subjected to a thermal insult and can look very similar. A burn is generally caused by heat; in the grooming room this may be the result of clipper blades getting too hot or hair-dryers being held too close, and for too long, to the dog's skin. Burns may also be caused by chemicals such as cleaning fluids that have not been left to dry before coming into contact with the dog. Scalds are generally caused by hot liquids such as water but they can also be caused by the production of steam within the dog's coat as it is drying.

The cause of the burn should be identified and dealt with. The temperature of the tissues at the site of a thermal or chemical burn will be raised; it is therefore essential that these tissues be cooled immediately. Cold running water should be used for this. This has the added benefit of removing any chemicals from the area, if you are dealing with a chemical burn. The washing process can be repeated several times.

Burns can be protected from fluid loss and made more comfortable by applying clingfilm to the wound. Alternatively, a new, unused, clear plastic bag may be appropriate. These do not stick to the damaged tissues and are preferable to dry dressings. Do not burst blisters, or apply creams, fats, butter, adhesive tape or dressings to the burn.

All serious burns where there is heat, pain, redness, and perhaps even skin sloughing and ooze, should be seen by a vet.

In the event of a burn or scald:

- **Identify and eliminate the cause.**
- **Flush or wash the affected area in cold running water to lower the skin temperature.**
- **Cover the wound with clean clear plastic and a towel.**
- **Seek veterinary advice.**
- **Take the dog (and, in the case of a chemical burn, any packaging) if necessary to the vet.**
- **Record all details.**

Brush burn

Over-zealous use of some grooming-out tools (such as wire-toothed slicker brushes and moulting rakes) can cause trauma and even lacerations to the skin, particularly over thin-skinned areas such as the hocks. This type of injury is commonly referred to as a 'brush burn'. It may seem an insignificant injury as there is rarely any major bleeding involved but the trauma to the skin will cause irritation and it can become infected.

Brushes and moulting rakes tend to be in use for long periods of time during the grooming out of dense or heavily matted coats; excessive force/pressure can cause very sore areas on the skin, with extensive bruising. The art of using these tools correctly is to apply minimal pressure and not to handle too much of the coat at a time – the good groomer works gradually through the coat until the skin is visible before moving on to another area.

At best, brush burn injuries recover fairly quickly with the help of astringents, such as calamine lotion or distilled hamamelis (witch hazel); at worst, they can cause the dog to lick and nibble at the area, causing yet more trauma and hair loss, not to mention a dislike of being brushed.

In the event of brush burn:

- **Cool the area with either cold water or an astringent, to lower the skin temperature.**
- **In all but the most minor cases, seek veterinary advice.**
- **Record the details.**

Clipper rash/burn

This is a condition caused by clipper blades that are either too hot or damaged, or by clipping too close to the skin.

Clipper rash sometimes occurs on the face and neck of poodle puppies. The young skin is soft and becomes irritated by having the hair removed. This can be prevented by using a slightly longer blade until the puppy has been trimmed several times. It can also occur on dogs that have particularly sensitive skin or a skin disease, and in these cases the same remedy applies – use a longer blade.

As with brush burn, clipper rash/burn can easily be considered insignificant and ignored. In most cases, it will settle down once the skin has cooled. In some instances, however, the skin can be severely traumatized and may become infected. There is then always the risk of the dog developing a skin disease.

In the event of clipper rash/burn:

- **Cool the area with either cold water or an astringent in order to lower the skin temperature.**
- **In all but the most minor cases, seek veterinary advice.**
- **Record the details.**

Wounds

Wounds come in many different forms, shapes and sizes. Sharp grooming tools can very easily cause wounds and injuries if they are used incorrectly or without due care and attention.

A wound can be classified as clean, contaminated or infected (*see* Figs 8.3.12 and 8.3.13). If it is a fresh wound,

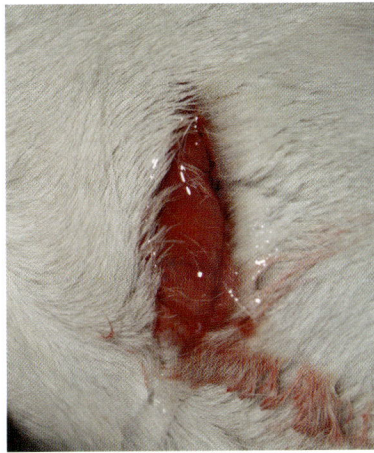

Fig. 8.3.14   Sometimes when you are grooming you will find a wound that has become infected. This dog had an extensively matted coat. After removing as much coat as possible, the dog was bathed in a mild shampoo to soften the scab and scissors were used to nibble at the remaining knot to remove all the debris. The skin was gently washed, really well rinsed and the wound blotted dry with cotton wool. The dog was sent for veterinary treatment.

Fig. 8.3.12   This is classed as a clean wound. It was not done in a grooming room but it is the sort of injury that could occur with a de-matting tool when working on a badly matted coat.

Fig. 8.3.13   A close-up picture shows that the underlying tissue has not been damaged and the wound is fresh, so it has not had time to become infected. The wound was coated with KY jelly to keep it moist whilst the owner travelled to the vet to get treatment.

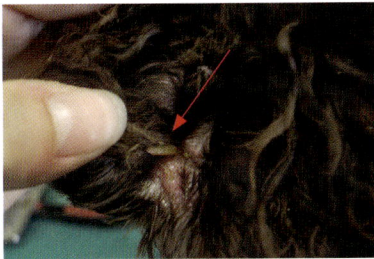

Fig. 8.3.15a-b   This is a wound you are likely to see very often. A grass seed has penetrated the dog's foot and has become infected. The seed was carefully removed with forceps and the wound washed carefully whilst the dog was bathed. A bandage was not applied but the dog was sent to the vet.

In the event of a wound:
Bleeding nails:

◆ **Apply pressure. Apply a coagulant such as 'Quick stop' or a styptic pencil (see Fig. 8.3.16).**

Fig. 8.3.16 If an innocuous cut such as a bleeding toenail bleeds persistently and does not stop with the application of a coagulant, you should consider the possibility that the dog has a clotting disorder.

it should not have had time to become infected. You may, however, find a wound during the grooming process that is infected (*see* Figs 8.3.14 and 8.3.15a-b). A clean wound is one made by a clean object such as a sterilized scissor blade. The dirtier the object, the more contamination is likely to have been introduced into the wound. Contaminated wounds can become infected in a short space of time.

Flush the wound liberally under running water, taking care that the water does not force any contamination deeper into the wound. The wound should then be kept protected until it can be assessed by a vet and receive the treatment it needs. The affected area can be dressed with a sterile dressing, which should be secured in place with adhesive tape or a conforming bandage applied over a layer of padding.

The temptation to introduce creams and disinfectants into a wound should be resisted. Many of these products are damaging to cells and can interfere with wound healing. Products such as TCP should never be used. As a rule, avoid using anything in a wound that you would not be happy to wash your eye in. Water and/or sterile saline are all that you should use to flush a wound. A dilute chlorhexidine or povidone-iodine solution can be used to disinfect the healthy skin surrounding a wound.

Certain wounds are vulnerable to infection and warrant antibiotic treatment in order to reduce the risk. Your vet can advise on specific cases. As a rule you should always consult your vet about wounds, especially if they have been caused by a bite or involve tissue trauma, a penetrating injury or a possible foreign body.

Cuts from scissors or sharp tools:

◆ **Apply pressure to stop bleeding.**
◆ **Rinse for several minutes under running water.**
◆ **Apply a dressing and seek veterinary advice.**

Deep cuts or puncture wounds:

◆ **Apply pressure.**
◆ **If possible rinse for several minutes under running water.**
◆ **Apply a pressure pad, bandage and go to the vet.**
◆ **Record all details.**

Insect stings

These are common at certain times of the year. It helps to know what type of insect has inflicted the sting and you should learn to distinguish bees from wasps (*see* Fig. 8.3.17).

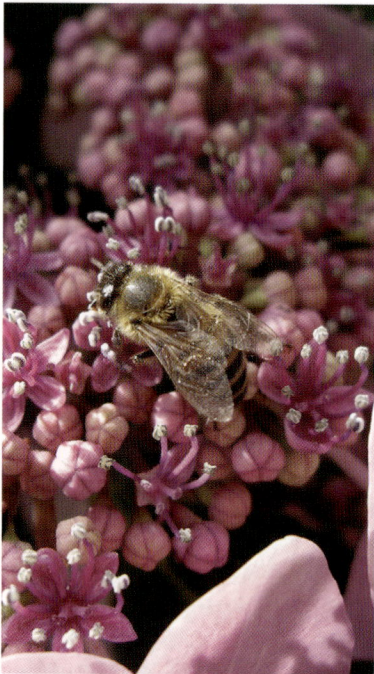

Fig. 8.3.17   Is it a wasp or a bee? It is helpful to know what insect has inflicted the sting. As with humans, some dogs are highly allergic to the venom of some insects, and anaphylactic shock is a possibility. Most owners know if their dog is likely to have a problem but don't take this for granted. If a dog has been stung, monitor him and get him to the vet as soon as possible if he shows even the slightest indication that his breathing is not normal or there is excessive swelling.

Bees leave behind their venom gland (or sac) after stinging. This gland can continue to empty into the tissues and needs to be removed quickly if the amount of venom absorbed is to be kept as low as possible. The gland should never be removed with tweezers as you risk expressing the contents as you do so. Instead, run a hard, straight edge down the affected limb (or area) in a scraping action. A credit card or similar piece of plastic is suitable and will scrape the venom sac away. The affected area can then be cooled down with cold water or an ice pack to help reduce any swelling. The pH of a bee sting is between 5.0 and 5.5. As such, it is acidic and can be neutralized by applying bicarbonate of soda (usually in the form of baking soda or toothpaste). This may provide some relief but may not neutralize the action of some of the proteolytic enzymes found within the venom.

Wasp venom has a neutral pH (6.8 to 6.9) and contains a number of proteolytic enzymes (including phospholipase A and B) that cause mast cells within the skin to release histamine. Other contents of wasp venom, including acetylcholine, stimulate pain receptors within the skin. These proteins are difficult to neutralize. The best response is to counteract the inflammation by applying cold water or ice (e.g. frozen peas, suitably wrapped in a towel) to the affected area. If the affected area becomes particularly swollen, veterinary advice should be sought. If a dog has sustained stings of any description to the mouth, throat or face, such that his airway may become compromised, urgent veterinary attention should be sought. If in doubt, phone for advice.

Some dogs are prone to allergic reactions to insect bites. This should be recorded on the dog's record card on admission. The owner may leave medication with the dog and should tell you how to administer it. In the event of an insect sting, if the dog shows any neurological signs or breathing becomes difficult, seek veterinary attention immediately.

In the event of a bee sting:

◆ **Use a hard piece of flat plastic (such as a credit card), scraping it down the affected area to remove the venom sac.**

◆ **Cool the area down with ice or cold water to reduce swelling.**

◆ **If there are any side-effects, such as breathing difficulties or excessive swelling, veterinary attention should be sought.**

In the event of a wasp sting:

◆ **Cool the area with ice or cold water to reduce swelling.**

◆ **If there are any neurological signs or breathing is affected, seek veterinary attention as soon as possible.**

◆ **Monitor the dog.**

◆ **Record all details.**

Applying a foot bandage

Fig. 8.3.18   It is important to place cotton dressings between the pads to keep them separated so the foot does not sweat.

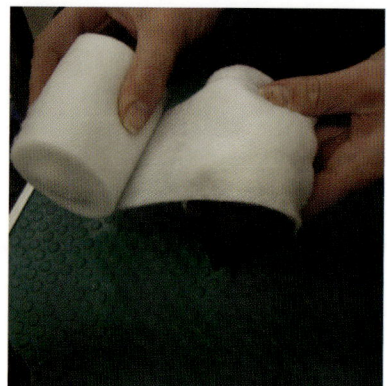

Fig. 8.3.19   We have used Soft Ban, which is easily obtained from your vet. Try not to use cotton wool as it goes hard once it starts to absorb moisture.

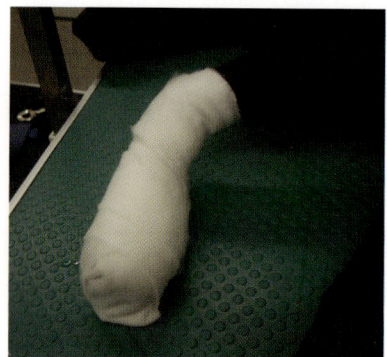

Fig. 8.3.20   Take the Soft Ban® well up the leg to prevent it slipping.

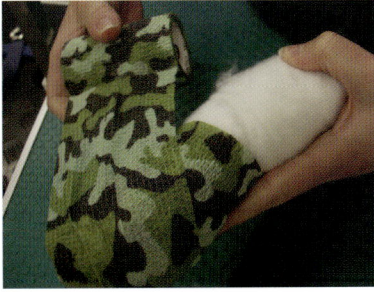

Fig. 8.3.21 If you are using a conforming bandage such as Vetwrap®, make sure that you do not pull the bandage as you apply it. The bandage will be wrinkly when you take it from the package. Those wrinkles should still be there as you place the bandage over the wound. This bandage clings to itself to prevent unravelling. If you use a different type of bandage, use sticky plaster to do this. Never use safety pins – they can get eaten!

Fig. 8.3.22 Conforming bandages stay in place and are light and comfortable. They can be applied easily over most dressings and are waterproof.

8.4 FIRST AID EQUIPMENT

Your grooming room should have one First Aid box for human casualties and a second box for animal casualties. All First Aid boxes should be easily accessible and identified by a white cross on a green background (see Fig. 8.4.1). They should be waterproof and provide the contents with adequate protection from moisture and other forms of contamination. They must be able to close firmly but should never be locked. Notices should identify the location of the boxes.

Contents for a *human First Aid box* are not specified but could include the following:

◆ A leaflet providing guidance on First Aid.
◆ 100 individually wrapped sterile plasters of different sizes.
◆ 6 individually wrapped and sterile

Fig. 8.4.1 A dedicated first aid box should be immediately accessible within the workplace. Its location should be clearly indicated and it should be accessible at all times. You should keep separate first aid boxes for humans and dogs. If you are not using a purposely bought first aid box, you must ensure that whatever you use is green in colour, is totally waterproof and bears a visible white cross on the outer casing. It should close securely but it should never be locked.

medium wound dressings (approx. 10 × 10 or 12 × 12cm).
◆ 2 large sterile wound dressings (18 × 18cm).
◆ 2 sterile eye pads.
◆ 2 triangular bandages, individually wrapped and preferably sterile.
◆ 6 safety pins.
◆ 2 pairs of disposable gloves.
◆ A CPR rescue mask.

The *canine First Aid* kit should also be stored in a clearly identified and accessible location. Ideally it should be clearly distinguishable from the human First Aid kit.

The suggested contents for an animal First Aid kit would include:

◆ 6 individually wrapped (1 × 12cm) sterile wound dressings.
◆ 2 individually wrapped (18 x 18 or 20 x 20cm) sterile wound dressings.
◆ 1 roll of bandage padding.
◆ 2 rolls of conforming bandage or cohesive bandages.
◆ 1 sterile eye pad.
◆ Sticky tape (e.g. Durapore® or Micropore®, 3M).
◆ A silver nitrate stick, 'Quick stop' or a suitable coagulant.
◆ A non-adherent dressing for burns.
◆ 2 pairs of disposable gloves.
◆ A CPR resusci-guard face shield.

Additional materials might include a small pot of table salt and a tube of glucose syrup, jam or honey.

After each use the First Aid box should be restocked (see Fig. 8.4.2). A regular (monthly) check of the First Aid box and First Aid arrangements, etc., should be programmed into the diary.

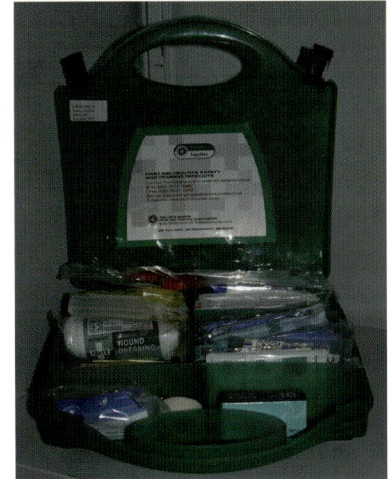

Fig. 8.4.2 After every use the first aid box should be restocked and a regular check should be made in case this has been overlooked.

References and further reading

Nichols, T.C., Raymer, R.A., Franck, H.W.G., Merricks, E.P., Bellinger, D.A., Defriess, N., Margaritas, P., Arruda, V.R., Kay, M.A. and High, K.A. (2010). Prevention of spontaneous bleeding in dogs with haemophilia A and B. *Haemophilia,* 16 (3), 19–23.

Slater, L.N. and Welch, D.F. (2005). Bartonella, including cat-scratch disease. In: Mandell, G.L., Bennett, J.E., Dolin, R. eds. *Principles and Practice of Infectious Diseases.* 6th edn. Philadelphia, Pa: Churchill Livingstone Elsevier, ch. 232.

Smith, P.F., Meadowcroft, A.M. and May, D.B. (2000). Treating mammalian bite wounds. *Journal of Clinical Pharmacy and Therapeutics*, 25, 85–99.

Useful websites

The St John Ambulance website provides details on training courses, general advice and guidance:

www.sja.org.uk/sja/training-courses.aspx

The British Red Cross website provides details on First Aid training courses, together with a collection of useful learning tips and videos:

www.redcross.org.uk/What-we-do/First-aid

9 Handling and Restraining the Dog

Handling dogs *and* restraining *dogs are two different, but closely related, practical subjects. The groomer must become intimately familiar with, and proficient in, both these disciplines.*

Handling refers to the manner in which one lays hands upon, manipulates and utilizes an object or living creature. Dog groomers spend their entire working lives working closely with dogs. As groomers, we are constantly feeling, touching, communicating with, moving, picking up and holding dogs. Usually this is done cooperatively, because the groomer knows how to work with the individual dog. In some cases, if the dog does not cooperate and the groomer's handling abilities are exceeded, restraint becomes necessary. To restrain means to hold back from some action, to deprive or limit liberty or freedom. In the case of groomers, restraining a dog allows a procedure (or a series of procedures) to be conducted safely so that both human and dog avoid injury.

Restraint techniques are the methods by which we maintain control over the dog and stop them from causing harm, either to themselves or to another individual. Techniques range from simple voice commands to enforced restriction, where use is made of collars and leads, muzzles or confinement in a kennel. In extreme cases it may even mean the use of chemical control: where sedation is the safest, kindest (and sometimes only) option.

In the grooming room, these two subjects are intimately bound together because we are a 'hands on' profession and are constantly handling and/or restraining dogs. Grooming practice is both fluid and dynamic. Within a short space of time, we can find ourselves applying a wide range of techniques according to the situation, the dog and the procedure(s) we are undertaking. We need to gauge and interpret each situation and make appropriate choices in terms of the handling and restraint of each individual dog.

These two inter-related subjects can give rise to considerable confusion and misunderstanding. In most cases this confusion stems from a failure to appreciate the different objectives of handling and restraining techniques. This chapter explores this subject in depth and aims to provide the reader with a clear idea of how the wise groomer selects the correct techniques.

9.1 HANDLING

The term *dog handler* is perhaps most often applied to police dog handlers but can mean anyone who works with trained dogs, but *dog handling* describes a more general concept of how a dog is managed, trained and worked with. As such, the concept of handling needs to take into account the objective(s) of the handler. An owner's handling of a dog will therefore differ depending on whether they are playing in the garden or walking along a busy road. In the latter case the handler will be asking the dog to walk on a lead, at heel, in a safe and controlled manner.

A dog groomer's handling will, by contrast, be much more ambitious, for the groomer asks far more of the dog than almost any other handler. It is hardly surprising that dog groomers are often regarded as amongst the very

best dog handlers (McGreevy et al., 2007). Why is this so and what does the novice groomer have to learn in order to develop this level of proficiency?

The simple answer is that you really need to know dogs, know yourself and know your work. This can only come by spending a considerable amount of time working closely with dogs and by developing the vast array of skills that allow you, instinctively, to know how to work with each dog that walks through the door. With time, practice and experience you will learn this fine art. The longer answer is that you need to develop what Aristotle termed phronesis, or 'practical wisdom'. The practically wise groomer will have the wherewithal to do the right thing at the right time, in the right place and in the right way. So what does this mean? It is all about finding the right balance, of doing precisely that which is necessary and sufficient without being excessive

(in any way). A helpful way of thinking about this idea is to reflect on a recent bad (or difficult) experience and play back in your mind the choices (conscious and subconscious) you made when handling the dog:

- Did you rush in or did you hesitate and dither indecisively?
- Were you preoccupied and inattentive or stressed, hyperactive and too attentive?
- Were you too rough/forceful or too gentle (and ineffective)?
- Were you scared/afraid or were you overconfident?
- Were you too loud (noisy) or too quiet?

The practically wise groomer knows how to moderate between these extremes and finds the appropriate balance through applying good and sensitive judgement. In all things we can easily use too much or too little of something (whether that be force, confidence, attention, kindness or the amount of butter on a piece of toast!) … it is for us to learn, however, to get it right.

This should have got you thinking about your approach, and about many of the things you have perhaps always done, instinctively, without thinking. You might think that it is useful, with some dogs, to appear preoccupied (because it makes them less nervous) …this is not the same as being inattentive, though, for you have consciously evaluated the situation and are trying to find the right attitude for the situation. You might think that quiet is good … but is it always? If it is so quiet that you can hear a pin drop some dogs will take fright when a noise is made. Your attitude to handling should always be calm and confident, but you will adapt it, sensitively and subtly, according to the dog and to each unique situation you encounter in practice. A confident, outgoing dog will probably be comfortable being handled by a happy outgoing handler, whereas a dog showing signs of nervousness or anxiety may not appreciate being the centre of your attention and may cope better if you appear preoccupied and uninterested in him. You will need to handle and observe the behaviour of many, many dogs before you find yourself subconsciously (i.e. intuitively) using the right approach and 'getting it right'.

Reflecting on what is going on is therefore crucial to good handling for we need to develop our awareness of:

◆ What is going on for the dog?
◆ What is going on within our own selves and what are we feeling?
◆ What is going on around us?

The first two questions are very much about identifying the emotional state both of the dog and of ourselves. We need to be able to understand how a dog is (probably) feeling in order to behave appropriately towards him. We also need to be monitoring our own emotional state so that we can identify negative states, such as anger, and deal with them before they cause us to act or behave in an unhelpful, or counterproductive, way.

Although dog groomers are not involved in training dogs in the same way as dog handlers, they can benefit enormously from being able to 'read' dogs and situations 'like a book'. This ability allows you to establish a cooperative relationship with most dogs, to train them well and, generally speaking, to work *with them* rather than against them. Learning how to handle each and every dog appropriately minimizes the number of frustrating situations you encounter. This should make 'getting upset' or 'angry' with a dog a rare (or even unknown) occurrence.

It is worth reminding ourselves that when human parents are angry and/or have lost control, they may use corporal punishment on their children. As a result, the corporal punishment of children has become a serious concern and the American Academy of Pediatrics has developed guidelines for disciplining children. It is hardly surprising that similar questions should be asked about how we handle, restrain and indeed discipline animals (Patronek and Lacroix, 2001). The American Humane Association and Delta Society have put together some very helpful guidelines for the training of dogs. These emphasize:

◆ the need to understand the basics of canine behaviour and, whenever possible, to use this to anticipate behaviour;
◆ the need to ensure that dogs are contained and controlled so that they are not a danger to themselves or others;
◆ the need to manage the training environment so that it is not dangerous to dogs or humans; and
◆ the need to recognize the importance of understanding canine behaviour using ethological interpretations rather than anthropomorphic ideas.

In the UK the 'five freedoms' that were developed as guiding principles for good animal welfare on farms are now increasingly applied to companion animals. The reader is encouraged to familiarize themselves with these guidelines.

The Companion Animal Welfare Council (CAWC) argues that these five freedoms are a good starting point but not an end point in defining animal

---

THE 'FIVE FREEDOMS'

The 'five freedoms' were first proposed by the Brambell Committee following a government-commissioned investigation into the welfare of intensively farmed animals in 1965. Following the creation of the Farm Animal Welfare Council (FAWC) in 1979, these guidelines were codified into the list reproduced below:

◆ **Freedom from hunger and thirst.**
    By ready access to fresh water and a diet to maintain full health and vigour.
◆ **Freedom from discomfort.**
    By providing an appropriate environment including shelter and a comfortable resting area.
◆ **Freedom from pain, injury and disease.**
    By prevention or rapid diagnosis and treatment.
◆ **Freedom to express normal behaviour.**
    By providing sufficient space, proper facilities and company of the animal's own kind.
◆ **Freedom from fear and distress.**
    By ensuring conditions and treatment which avoid mental suffering.

---

welfare. The RSPCA has applied these principles and produced a range of publications aimed at improving the welfare of dogs in veterinary practice and when held in kennels.

Although the five freedoms may not have been incorporated into your country's legal system, they remain a good starting point when considering the welfare of animals in your care. You should aim to provide the freedoms as much as possible and you should consider these principles when you are handling and restraining dogs.

Useful websites

The FAWC website provides details on the five freedoms: www.fawc.org.uk/freedoms.htm.

The DEFRA website provides details of the new code of practice for the welfare of dogs and explains how to comply with the provisions of the 2006 Animal Welfare Act: www.defra.gov.uk/publications/2011/03/26/code-of-practice-dogs-pb13333.

Understanding the dog

The dog's sensory world

Cast your mind back over the evolution of the dog, from when they lived as wild creatures in trees to the day the dog moved into our homes. The story started over 400 million years ago but it is only over the last 10,000 years or so that man and dog have become firm friends. It is only perhaps fifty years or so since the dog moved into the house (in some parts of the world the dog is still not welcome indoors). For some breeds, such as the Alaskan Malamute and the Husky, it is only two or three generations (as little as four to six years) since the breed became a 'fashionable' pet. Their 'coming in from the cold' is therefore quite new, in a very literal sense, for they were, until recently, pack members, living outside and working long days in the frozen wastes of Alaska.

The lifestyle(s) of the modern dog reflect the changing roles that have accompanied his integration into human society. The dog has adapted admirably to our new expectations and somehow fits in with urban living. Where human society has changed dramatically in response to technological (and other) advances, the canine brain has remained very much the same. Our canine friends, whilst having to cope with the challenges of modern living, are still likely to view life very simply:

◆ Do I feel safe or threatened?
◆ Am I experiencing pain or pleasure?
◆ Am I hungry? Am I thirsty? And do I need to get it myself?
◆ Am I feeling hot or cold?
◆ Do I want to rest/sleep or do I want to play?

The dog, as both a hunter and a social animal, had to develop a refined ability to read the intentions of, and anticipate the actions and movements of, other animals. Dogs therefore have an incredible ability to watch and read human body language and to use humans to their advantage. The communication that goes on between man and dog is therefore quite different from that which humans have come to rely upon themselves.

Humans and human society have become particularly reliant on language as a means of communication. Language is, however, only one of many communication channels used to exchange information. The various channels available to us are opened (receptive) and closed (non-receptive/blocked) subconsciously; this has implications for how well we receive and understand the information available to us. When communicating with dogs (or indeed humans), it is therefore worth considering which of our communication channels are open and being actively used and which are closed. Are we only picking up certain messages and not others? What non-verbal messages are we ourselves relaying without realizing it?

Human emotion is particularly evidenced through our body language. And dogs can read this, in some cases becoming aware of our emotional state even before we are! This occurs because their communication channels are very much open, where ours may be closed. When we express our emotion in this way, we present the dog with information and the opportunity of responding. The dog's response can be either positive or negative, for, ultimately, from the dog's perspective, the emotion (body language) that you are conveying is, very simply, either friendly or unfriendly or neutral (i.e. somewhere in between).

Formative experiences

In seeking to understand both humans and dogs, we need to pay attention to the experiences that inform and structure the individual's understanding of the world. From the moment of birth, before the eyes and ears are open (see Fig. 9.1.1), the dog's sense of smell, together with his sense of touch, provides information on his world and structures his experiences. It is through these sensory learning experiences that a dog learns how to survive. At that young age life is at its most simple:

◆ A soft, gentle touch and warm surroundings are safe.
◆ Hard and rough touches are not safe.
◆ Appeasing pheromones from the glands around the bitch's mammary glands exert a calming effect on the young suckling puppies.

Once the eyes and the ears are open, life becomes more complicated and the dog learns two more very important survival tricks: to watch and to listen!

◆ Soft eyes are friendly (see Fig. 9.1.2); hard eyes are not (see Fig. 9.1.3).
◆ Soft relaxed bodies are friendly, tense hard ones are not.
◆ Soft noises are friendly, loud noises are not.

Fig. 9.1.1   From the moment of birth, even before the eyes and ears are open, the puppy learns that soft hands and a gentle touch are safe.

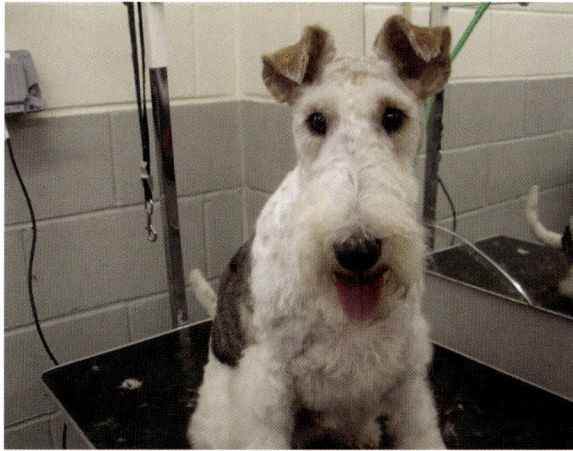

Fig. 9.1.2 Terriers are known for their sharpness of character. This dog's expression is alert but the eyes are soft and not threatening.

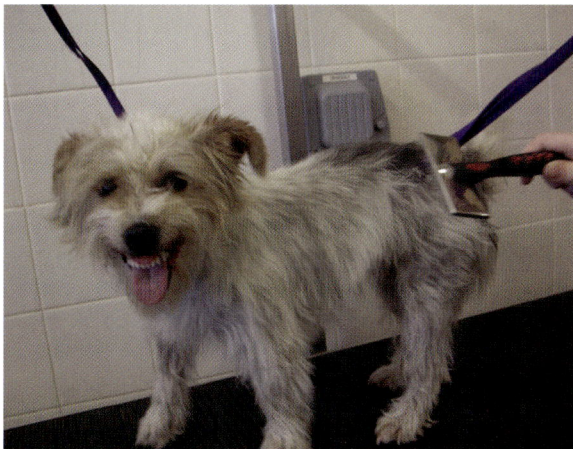

Fig. 9.1.3 The expression in this dog's eyes is hard and businesslike, clearly threatening the groomer.

As the dog grows, these simple principles continue to keep him safe. The best advice I can give you on the subject is to pay attention to these same simple principles. If you want trust and cooperation from the dog, handle him with soft hands, look at him with soft eyes and keep your voice soft!

It takes confidence on both sides when you meet a dog for the first time. If you are confident, and maintain a soft quiet aura, you are more likely to be greeted by one. If you are nervous, you will become hard and aggressive in your mannerisms and stance, and you are more likely to get off to a bad start.

Dogs cannot participate in a rational argument or discussion; this makes it difficult for them to understand the cause(s) or motive(s) that may explain why humans change their moods and their attitudes. But the dog is very much able to establish a connection between fear and aggression. Dogs understand that if they feel afraid or threatened, their body becomes tense and ready to react (it becomes a 'hard' body). They

recognize this state in themselves and they probably recognize it in others. If you are tense, you are telling the dog that you are ready to react and he will interpret this in one of two ways:

◆ You are afraid of him, and if he stands his ground you will leave him alone.
◆ You are a possible threat, so action needs to be taken.

He almost certainly does not see that the cause of your tension has nothing to do with him. He senses that you are tense and becomes tense himself. This is not at all helpful as you now have a tense dog, who may be on the defensive (and therefore a danger to you), as well as being tense yourself.

Communicating with the dog in the grooming room

Body language

You need to keep your body language quiet, positive and confident at all

---

SOME HELPFUL HANDLING RULES FOR THE GROOMER

Rule 1
As a groomer/handler, you are an educator and you must educate the dog to understand that there is a job to be done and that they have no choice in the matter. It is not a battle of wills and there is nothing personal involved. You cannot get the dog to willingly do what you want through domination or rough contact. You cannot buy obedience, so bribery is also out of the question. If you keep feeding treats to get a response, then once you run out of treats, there may be no response!

You achieve rule 1 by following rule 2!

Rule 2
You need to get the dog's attention and teach them to watch you so that you can communicate with them; they will soon understand how they are expected to react. Clear, consistent directions ensure that the dog understands what he needs to do next. Make sure that you always approach a dog from within his area of vision (see Chapter 2.8). He will watch what you are doing with your body and your hands, and process the expression in your eyes and your voice.

Rules 1 and 2 are enforced by following rule 3!

Rule 3
Once you have put your hands on the dog, you must maintain the connection by keeping the contact. If the dog knows where your hands are, and can feel the expression in them, he knows what is happening. Most dogs are comfortable with that; they like to be kept informed! Once the dog loses track of your hand, they can also lose track of how they are supposed to behave, and this is when it can become dangerous and you can be bitten.

times, and be relaxed and soft in everything you do. This will serve two major purposes:

◆ It tells the dog that you are not a threat and that what is about to happen is quite normal. You are not afraid or anxious, so why should he be?

◆ If, by chance, it goes wrong and the dog does react, you will be able to move out of the way with swiftness and agility. If you are rigid with fear, you will not be able to move easily.

Soft eyes

Remember that the dog will notice everything you do, and this includes watching your eyes. Your eyes need to be soft and yielding all the time. If you become angry or irritated, your eyes will become hard and your expression purposeful. To the dog, this signifies a threatening situation and he may feel the need to respond. Eye contact need not, however, be threatening, as is often considered to be the case. It is the expression in the eye that conveys the threat. If you have a dog at home I am sure that you can look them in the eye without causing an argument. This is probably because your eyes will be expressing affection, playfulness and love so they will be soft and yielding. Your dog will not take offence at this. Harden your expression and your pet will react quite differently: he may become unsure of himself, avert his gaze and try to move away from you. A well-adjusted dog is not overly troubled by direct eye contact. In the nervous dog, by contrast, this is not the case, but nor is it helpful to ignore them completely. The deliberate use of discreet sideways glances can calm and reassure an apprehensive dog, in much the same way that blinking can be used to reduce the perceived threat of a stare when working with cats.

Voice

Your voice should be soft and calming, whilst remaining confident and positive. It does not matter what you say or how much you say, because the dog responds to the tone of your voice and the way that you use it rather than to anything that you do say. You can try this out by using the same pitch and tone to relate several different sentences to the dog. He will respond in the same way to each sentence whatever you have said because the language is not important to him. During training, voice commands are given by pitch and tone and supported by body language, so listen to the way the owner speaks and try to replicate it when you later have to give the dog commands (such as stand, sit and stay). Remember that your voice resonates through your body and even a deaf dog can be calmed or agitated by the volume and tone of your voice if you are maintaining contact with him through your hand.

Hands

How we use our hands when working with a dog is extremely important. The dog, like all other living creatures, is sensitive to touch. If a fly were to land on the dog, he would be aware of its presence even through a substantial coat. It should not ever be necessary to exert a hard grip on a dog during handling. Indeed, were you to do so, this could give rise to problems. An example of this would be the use of an over-firm grip on a dog's foot whilst cutting the nails. The dog perceives this as a trap. Remember the dog cannot reason. A trapped foot means that the dog cannot escape, so he feels threatened and vulnerable. The dog will fight not against you but against the situation he finds himself in – trapped by the foot! Relax your hand and moderate the force needed for the task, seeking to use the bare minimum, and you will experience the difference (*see* Fig. 9.1.4).

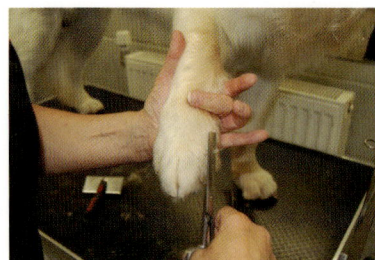

Fig. 9.1.4   Here you can see how lightly the groomer is holding the dog's foot. Her hand is open but supporting the foot with her thumb and her centre finger. The hand is soft and relaxed but still in control.

When you approach a dog, keep your hands low and relaxed by your sides, and when you touch the dog for the first time keep them soft, relaxed and on the dog, preferably around the shoulder area.

Keep your hands soft whilst you groom the dog with just enough pressure to hold your tools safely. By lightly holding and handling the dog, you can guide and direct him into the position(s) that you need him to adopt.

> ### HOW MUCH PRESSURE IS JUST ENOUGH?
>
> *To give you some idea of the pressure that you need to exert when handling the dog, particularly his feet:*
>
> ◆ *Place a sponge in a bowl of water.*
> ◆ *Remove it and turn your hand over and over, without dropping the sponge and without squeezing out any water.*
>
> *This is enough pressure!*

Another point about using your hands is to remind yourself regularly of the way in which the joints of the dog move (*see* Figs 9.1.5 and 9.1.6). Consciously take note of how you are holding limbs and keep checking how you are manipulating joints whilst you are working. Are you working with the dog? Your hands are very strong and pulling knees sideways, twisting hips

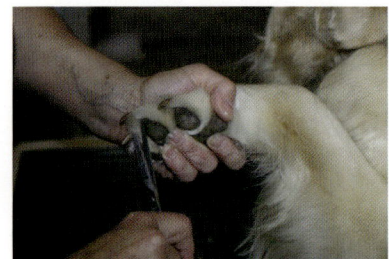

Fig. 9.1.5   Stay conscious of how the various joints move. The groomer here is holding the foot too tightly and is twisting it from the carpal joint in a way that it does not have a great deal of flexion. An arthritic dog or a growing puppy would find this very painful and you could possibly do damage to the joint.

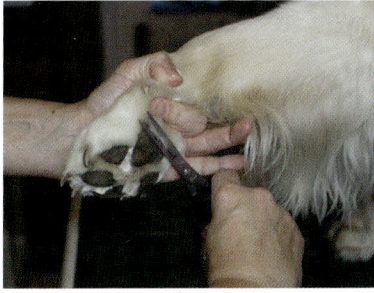

Fig. 9.1.6   The groomer has relaxed her hold and the angle at which she is holding the foot. She may need to bend down to see under the foot now but the dog is more comfortable and less damage can be done.

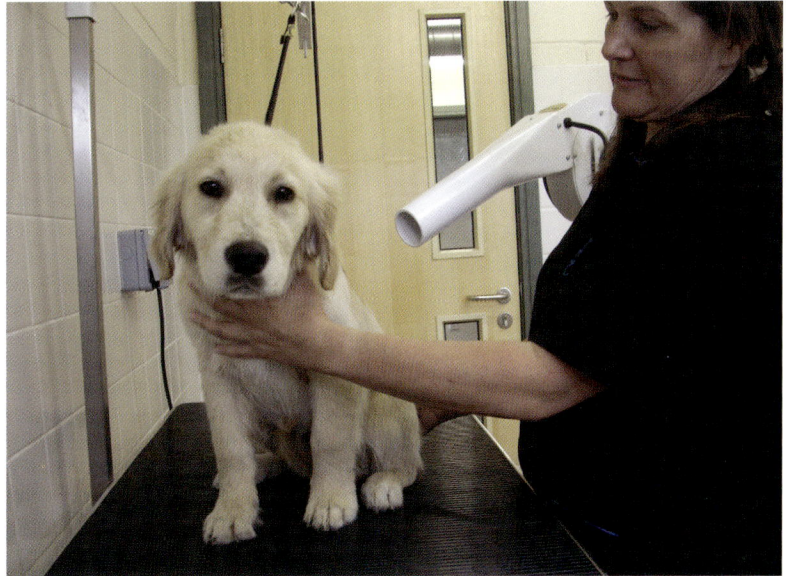

Fig. 9.1.7   Puppies and young dogs need to be given time to get used to new experiences and need plenty of voice encouragement.

at odd angles and turning feet in the wrong direction are all easily done when you are busy concentrating on what you are trying to achieve. Whilst you may not have noticed that you are asking a lot of a joint, the dog will have. So pay attention! You must remain alert at all times. You need to recognize immediately when you are asking too much of a dog as this can cause them discomfort and even pain, leading to the loss of trust and cooperation.

Squeezing the foot whilst trying to gain access between the toes is another practice best avoided. The many joints in the foot make it supple and easily manipulated, but squeezing the toes hurts and causes distress, particularly as the dog ages and stiffens. Keeping your hand relaxed and soft prevents this and the dog stays calm and settled.

I think it is safe to say that, although the principles of handling are the same for all dogs, each dog does have to be handled differently according to his age, health and temperament. Certain breeds also sometimes need modifications to the basic handling principles.

Young dogs

Young dogs (*see* Fig. 9.1.7) need plenty of time to become familiar and comfortable with each new situation. You must allow them the time they need to cope and learn, so that what initially appears threatening becomes less so. Providing they are not overwhelmed, young dogs learn that grooming is not something they need to be fearful or

wary of . . . and they can afford to relax. In this way the young dog will treat any subsequent experience with little apprehension, for he has learnt to cope and is comfortable with the grooming process.

Growing joints can be easily damaged and sometimes they can be painful simply because they are growing. Pups and young dogs need plenty of reassurance, so good use of the voice is necessary and hands should be kept very soft and supple and on the dog at all times.

Old dogs

Older dogs often have diseased joints or muscle injuries, and should therefore always be handled with extra care and consideration. You may also encounter blind dogs, and should treat them with respect and understanding, remembering that they cannot see you to read you. Hearing problems may also be encountered and similarly require you to adapt your approach. Dogs with such disabilities benefit enormously from knowing where you are when you are working with them: maintaining physical contact is especially reassuring, so keeping your hand on them is vitally important. Even a deaf dog can respond to your voice through the vibration in your hand as long as you remember to keep one hand on the dog at all times.

Brachycephalic dogs

These types of dog have restricted vision so again it is important to stay within the dog's area of vision when you are handling them (*see* Chapter 2.8 and Fig. 2.8.4). If the dog cannot see you approaching, you risk startling them and they will be more likely to defend themselves. Once you have approached the dog, place your hands on him near the shoulders so that he can see and feel what you are doing. These dogs have short necks and cannot easily see behind them; they are also more likely to stand their ground and defend themselves. You are therefore advised to keep one hand on the dog all the time you are working with them; failure to do so reduces the quality of communication between you: once you have removed the contact, you are likely to startle the dog and may get bitten (or at the very least upset the dog). This can easily happen if you suddenly put a hand on the centre of their back (or somewhere else out of sight) without warning.

Terriers

Terriers were developed as vermin hunters (*see* Fig. 9.1.8). They are sharp witted and always watchful of what is going on around them, reacting quickly to the slightest movement. These dogs need to kept informed of what you are

Fig. 9.1.8   Terriers are sharp-witted vermin hunters that react instantly. They need to be kept informed of what is happening. If you take your hand off the dog, he will consider the job done. Something has caught the attention of this little dog and the groomer has broken contact with her. Startling the dog by suddenly touching her without forewarning could result in you getting bitten. The dog won't wait to consider whether you are a rat or not!

doing and where you are doing it. If you take your hand off a terrier, he may consider the job 'done'; if you then put your hand back on again, he can react very sharply indeed. He may not mean to bite you but, equally, he may not stop to consider the possibility that your hand is not a rat or a snake. The terrier cannot afford to wait for an explanation: their quick reactions are instinctive!

Problem dogs: when handling has to give way to restraint

This section on handling has emphasized the importance of a sound and well-developed understanding of the canine subject. You need to read and understand dogs, and communicate clearly with them. There are, however, situations when a dog refuses to cooperate and cannot be handled. Sometimes this is because you have not achieved the right level of communication with the dog or competency in this subject area. Sometimes this is down to nerves or inexperience. When the groomer is still developing their communication skills or has suffered a bad experience and lost confidence, this is often reflected in their body language. Time and more favourable experiences will help the groomer to overcome such challenges. In the meantime, the assistance of another, more experienced, groomer should be called upon, allow-ing you to learn, stay safe and develop your confidence. You will improve with time, practice and experience. In other cases the dog would be a challenge to the most experienced and proficient groomer. You need to recognize these dogs and know when it is not safe to attempt to groom them without some form of restraint.

There are several reasons why dogs may not enjoy grooming and may refuse to cooperate. Generally speaking, they result from experiences that have marked (i.e. mentally scarred) the dog. Dogs that have been mishandled or badly handled remember the experience and associations may be formed. People, places, smells and objects can all become associated with a bad memory and trigger an aversive response.

Dogs that are fearful of the grooming salon, of the groomer and of the grooming process may need to be restrained for both their safety and your own. Before discussing restraint, however, it is essential that we say a few words about preventing such fears.

Grooming initiations

When a puppy has his first encounter with brushes and combs, he has absolutely no idea what is going to happen. This 'first time' visit to the grooming salon can be as significant as a child's first day at school. It is an event that has a bearing on how the dog responds to grooming throughout the rest of his life. Whenever possible, encourage new owners or owners of new puppies to bring the puppy to the salon for its first groom rather than to attempt the first groom themselves because this is where most problems start.

It is easy to get the first grooming experience wrong – sometimes very wrong. New (first time), inexperienced, incompetent or anxious dog owners attempting to groom a wriggling puppy without proper knowledge of what they are doing can easily traumatize the puppy. Holding the young dog firmly between hard hands so that they cannot move, pinning them down, working against them and failing to recognize that the reason they are struggling is because they are afraid and feel trapped is almost guaranteed to store problems up for the future.

In some cases the owner or an inexperienced person gives up after several failed attempts and several fights with the dog. It is often then the case that the dog is left for some time before the help of a groomer is sought. The pup will be traumatized and scarred. He will also have learnt how to be evasive and be a highly adept wriggler. This can make it very difficult indeed to get the job done! Puppies learn quickly and do not forget. A puppy that has learnt to be evasive and is afraid of being handled presents the groomer with a challenging problem that may take some time to overcome.

It may be that rough or hard handling has overstretched or strained the developing skeleton, causing pain or damage to growing joints. The puppy will not forget such uncomfortable, painful, stressful and sometimes terrifying experiences. It may take many grooming sessions before the puppy learns to trust the groomer and ceases to anticipate further nasty experiences. For this to happen, the old experiences need to fade away and be replaced by positive ones that restore trust and confidence.

Incorrect handling is the most common cause of dogs becoming defensive about being groomed. Sometimes it takes many years to overcome the problem. In rare cases the dog never forgets the bad experiences and always remains distrustful of the process.

9.2 RESTRAINING THE DOG

For most owners, the word restraint immediately conjures up an image of their pet looking miserable, muzzled and tied up tightly on a grooming table. This is a horrible image – and rightly so for it is wrong in so many ways!

It would be incorrect and irresponsible of me, however, to suggest that you should never, under any circumstances, use a muzzle, or that dogs should never be held in table restraints. Not doing so could put you and the dog at risk of injury.

The dogs that you groom are not ornaments; they move around, fidget, and may be more interested in what is happening to the dog on the next table. And it must never be forgotten that all dogs are capable of defending themselves if they feel pain, or feel threatened. There are no exceptions: even your own trusty dog can bite should the need arise!

Each individual dog decides what he perceives to be a threat, so their viewpoint counts; it is the final arbiter! In the grooming room the 'threat' could be the whole experience (especially if the 'first groom' proved to be traumatic and unbearable). Not all dogs want to have the hair removed from their feet or have their toenails cut. To some dogs having a bath is unacceptable/too much; for others the hair-drying experience is one they would rather forgo.

Whatever the dog perceives as 'a threat' can put you, the dog and others at risk of being harmed; there are therefore times when restraining the dog for everyone's sake is the best option. And there are, of course, times when the dog needs to be restrained so that it is kept safe and out of mischief whilst waiting to go home.

There are many ways in which restraining the dog can be enforced so this section looks at the options and the advantages and disadvantages of each.

First of all, restraining the dog simply means keeping it under control. In the grooming salon dogs need to be under control for several reasons:

- to keep you, your staff and any visitors safe;
- to keep the dog safe whilst in your care;
- to keep other dogs safe; and
- to prevent the dog from escaping.

Keeping dogs under control is normally achieved by the use of a collar and lead when you are moving them from one place to another, by table ties whilst you are working with them, and by confining them to a cage or kennel when you are not working with them. There are times, however, when you need to use additional control measures whilst grooming, either for the safety of the dog or the safety of the groomer. The dog has to be restrained so that you can do what needs to be done, whilst respecting the comfort of the dog.

The least amount of restraint necessary for safety and control should be applied. Measures should never be excessive or disproportionate and you should always be seeking to reduce/minimize them. If the dog feels threatened because he is uncomfortable or feels overpowered, he will resist; it then becomes a test of willpower and a trial of strength. The dog will not give in easily; the more you restrain him, the harder he will resist and the more dangerous and disagreeable the experience becomes. It is so much easier to work *with* the dog and help him learn how to work with you.

As emphasized above, the minimal amount of restraint should always be used. It is therefore appropriate to start by discussing the ways in which the groomer can use their voice and hands before discussing the aids they may need to pull out of a drawer in more extreme situations. Some of the techniques and aids may be more familiar as handling aids than as restraining aids – this reflects the difference in the objectives of the dog and the dog handler, and the handler's ability to work with rather than against the dog.

The voice

Sometimes a dog can be calmed and

CAUTION: MAKE SURE THAT YOUR CHOICE OF CONTROL IS SAFE TO USE

Whatever form of control you choose to use, make sure that all straps and tie-up leads are constructed of a material that can be cut through with a normal pair of trimming scissors and that all fastenings can be released in an instant. This is essential as it allows you to release the dog in the event of an emergency (such as a slip, fall or epileptic fit).

Before fitting a restraint, you should also check all straps, buckles and fastenings for signs of wear and tear. Buckles are particularly difficult to release if they are rusty, and worn stitching can break easily under stress.

comforted by just the voice. It is, after all, the way that owners communicate with their dog and the way that they communicate with each other. It is the tone of the voice that alerts the dog to whether it is being praised or whether it has done wrong.

The tone of the voice can signify alarm, joy, pleasure, disgust and anger. It can also comfort the dog if it is hurt or anxious. Learn to use your voice in a calm, quiet but confident manner. What you say is not as important as how you say it and many dogs respond well to voice tone; this is often enough to settle them for grooming. Dogs have a very short concentration span and the use of the voice can help keep them alert and interested in what you are expecting them to do.

Arms and hands

These too are very handy when restraining the dog (*see* Fig. 9.2.1). Both arms and hands can be used to hold a dog still whilst someone else performs a necessary task. This can be anything from cutting nails to clipping feet or cleaning out ears. Generally this is the restraint method of choice for securing young puppies; it is kind and gentle, as long as the supporting person keeps their hands and arms soft.

Puppies do not appreciate being held in a vice! The disadvantages of this method is that the dog can bite; he may also learn that, with a bit of a struggle and noise, he can be held cosily every time he needs to have his nails clipped, ears cleaned or feet trimmed! Avoid having the owner as the second pair of hands: the owner's anxiety will be transmitted to the dog (and you!) and the method can become dangerous if the dog tries to get away.

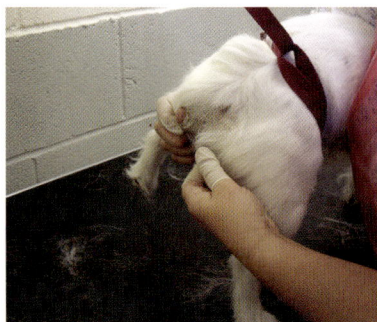

Fig. 9.2.1   Arms and hands are being used here to restrain this little dog whilst his rear end is hand-plucked for the first time. If the groomer is relaxed, the dog will stay confident and is more likely to accept the procedure.

The collar and lead

Most, but not all, dogs are used to a collar and lead of some description (*see* Fig. 9.2.2). Dogs are generally used to wearing their collars all the time and they recognize the addition of the lead as a routine procedure, which usually signifies that they are being taken out of their usual environment. The use of a lead can often be sufficient to settle a dog. They associate it with security because they are used to being kept secure by their owner whilst wearing the lead. They also know that, whilst wearing the lead, they are required to respond according to certain control instructions. For instance, they usually know that they have freedom to the length of the lead and should not fight to pull away. They may also know that being on the lead means that they should not interfere with other dogs or people.

Collars should be fitted so that two fingers can be slipped comfortably between the collar and the dog's neck (*see* Fig. 9.2.3). It is important to remember that brachycephalic dogs have par-

Fig. 9.2.2   Collars and leads are accepted by most but not all dogs. They should be checked for wear and tear before you use them and they should fit so that the collar cannot slip over the dog's head.

ticularly thick necks, which are often larger in circumference than the head! Collars should not therefore be relied upon for securing these dogs as they can slip over the head if the dog pulls away.

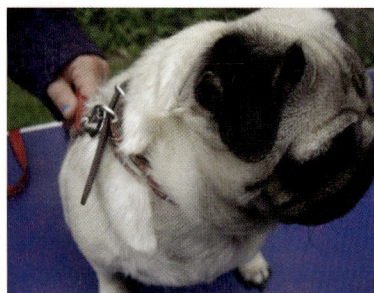

Fig. 9.2.3   With many brachycephalic dogs, the neck is thicker in circumference than the head. This picture illustrates how this collar, which fits the neck of the dog well, will slip over the head if the dog pulls away.

Leads or ties, used correctly, are a good way to keep a dog relatively safe when you are working on them. Care must, however, be taken to ensure that the dog cannot hurt or injure himself whilst tied up, and you should never leave them unattended.

Chains – tethering chains and chain collars

Tethering chains for tying up a dog in the salon are an acceptable and use-

ful means of restraint; the dog cannot chew the chain and a strong dog is less likely to break it. The tethering chain is secured to an immovable surface (such as the wall), but should be attached to the dog by means of a collar that can be easily cut through, if necessary.

The use of a chain as a restraining collar ('choke' or 'check' chain) is not, however, suitable in the salon. Any weight from the dog against the 'choke chain' will cause the restraint to continue tightening around the neck (*see* Figs 9.2.4 and 9.2.5). If the dog were to lose his footing in the bath, or step off the table, the chain would automatically tighten and the dog could hang himself in seconds.

Metal chains rust in water and can warm up quickly with the heat of dryers or cabinets. A hot chain could potentially burn either the dog or the groomer.

A further problem with chain collars

Fig. 9.2.4   A check-chain collar should not be used as a restraint in a grooming room.

is that, if they are not put on correctly, they will lock rather than releasing automatically. This again carries with it the risk of a dog choking because, in an emergency, they cannot be loosened or cut away from the neck.

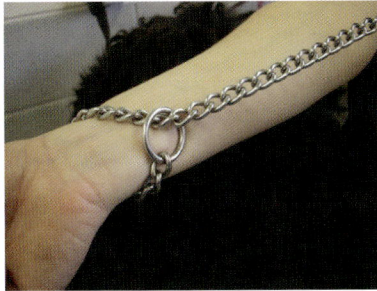

Fig. 9.2.5   The check-chain will tighten relentlessly around the neck as soon as pressure is applied.

Slip leads

Slip leads (*see* Fig. 9.2.6) are made from a length of rope or chain with a ring at one end through which the opposite end can be passed to make a loop. They work in the same way as choke chains and tighten when the dog pulls against them. Unless well trained to walk to heel, dogs pull against whatever is restraining them as they seek to run or walk faster. Pulling in this way against a tightening rope can damage the throat and cause breathing difficulties. A dog should never be left unattended when tied up on a slip lead, and these leads should never be used to restrain a dog on the table or in the bath.

Fig. 9.2.6   This dog is wearing a slip lead and is leaning away from the handler. The lead will tighten further as the dog pulls against it. Slip leads should never be used in a grooming room to restrain a dog if it is in the bath or on the table because there is a risk that the dog could hang himself if he loses his footing, suffers a fit or has a heart attack.

Table and bath restraints

Table ties (*see* Figs 9.2.7 and 9.2.8a) and bath ties are used to prevent the dog jumping, falling or slipping. On the table the dog should be restrained with both a neck restraint and a belly restraint. The neck restraint should be fitted short enough so that the dog can stand with the head in a natural, relaxed position. The belly restraint should be fitted short enough so that the dog can stand comfortably without straining the abdomen. If table ties are being used, two restraints must be fitted. If the belly restraint is not in place dogs can step off the table and hang themselves (*see* Fig. 9.2.8b).

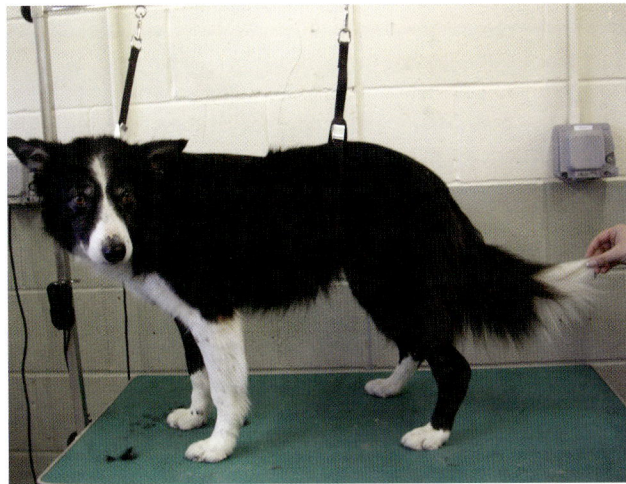

Fig. 9.2.7 Table ties are fitted so that the dog can stand in a natural position. The straps should not be too tight around the neck and abdomen.

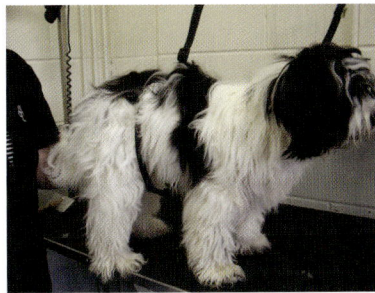

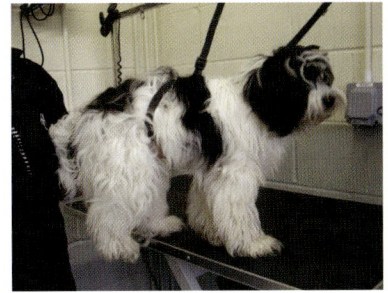

Fig. 9.2.8a and Fig. 9.2.8b   The belly strap on this dog has been fitted too loosely. You can see how the dog could step off the table and lose his footing. It would only take seconds for the dog to hang himself and die.

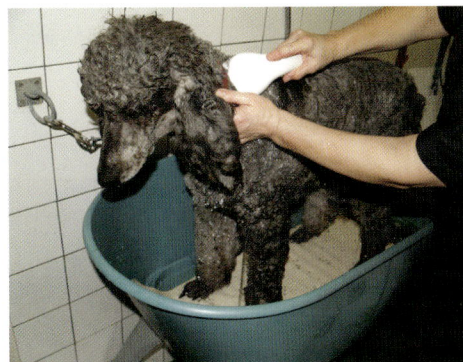

Fig. 9.2.9   This dog is restrained in the bath by a neck strap attached to a tethering ring on the wall.

> ### CAUTION: METAL CHAINS AND CABLES
>
> *Think twice about using any neck or belly restraint that is either made from or contains a metal chain or a metal cable. In the event of an emergency the weight of a possibly unconscious dog will make the chain difficult to release and the dog could strangle itself. Rusting of the metal is also something to be aware of, as it weakens the chain and rust particles can cause damage to the skin.*

Bath ties tend to be restricted to just the neck (*see* Fig. 9.2.9), to prevent accidental drowning if the dog should slip into the water and to prevent him from jumping out of the bath.

The advantages of both table and bath ties are that they can reduce the risk of accidents. The only disadvantage is that some dogs tend to lean on the neck restraint, making them prone to gag and cough (similar to when the dog pulls on the lead).

Slings

An alternative to neck and belly straps are slings (*see* Fig. 9.2.10). These help to support the weight of the animal and are particularly useful for disabled dogs that cannot stand easily, or for lazy dogs that do not want to stand. The main disadvantage of slings is that they restrict access to the body. They can also encourage lazy dogs to 'get lazier' but otherwise they serve a useful purpose.

Fig. 9.2.10   A sling is an alternative option to neck and belly straps and is particularly useful for disabled dogs or those who prefer not to stand!

Muzzles

CAUTION: PROTECT YOUR FACE

Remember that in the grooming room the dog is on a table in a position that places his face very close to your own. Even the best-behaved dogs may bite if they become frightened, hurt or anxious. If you are concerned (or doubtful) about a situation, early application of a muzzle can often save time and injury.

Muzzles need not be unpleasant for the dog to wear. If a muzzle is fitted correctly (*see* Figs 9.2.11 and 9.2.12), it should not be uncomfortable, nor should it restrict the dog so much that he panics through fear of not being able to breathe adequately. All muzzles have a buckle that is secured behind the ears (as you would a collar); some also have a centre strap coming up over the bridge of the nose and over the head to meet the collar strap. There are many designs, varying in size, shape and material, but basically they are either closed-fronted, open-fronted or full face.

Open fronted means that the foreface is covered but the front of the muzzle is open to allow better breathing and sometimes drinking, and also allows vomit to escape (*see* Figs 9.2.11 and 9.2.12). *Closed fronted* means that the entire foreface of the dog is enclosed. The dog can neither drink nor eat. Vomit cannot escape and, sometimes, breathing can be marginally restricted (*see* Figs 9.2.13 and 9.2.14). *Full-face* muzzles cover the entire face of the dog so that the dog has either limited or no vision. They cannot drink and vomit cannot escape (*see* Fig. 9.2.15).

New designs are constantly becoming available so the following discussion focuses on the most common designs. When purchasing muzzles, consider the materials used to manufacture the muzzle and the design.

Careful choice and correct fitting of muzzles are vitally important for the

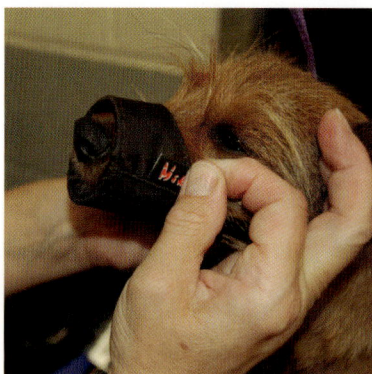

Fig. 9.2.11   The open-fronted muzzle does not restrict airflow so the dog can breathe comfortably. It should be fitted so that the mouth can open enough for the dog to pant. You should just be able to slide your finger into the side of the muzzle.

safety and comfort of both the dog and the groomer, whilst also making it possible for you to get the job done.

Fig. 9.2.12   This muzzle is too big. The dog would be able to get his mouth open wide enough to bite the groomer.

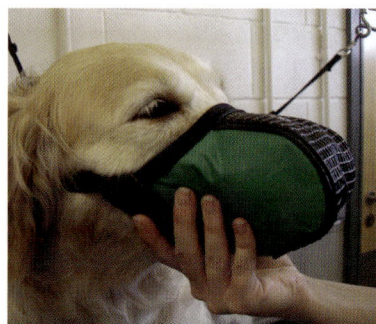

Fig. 9.2.13   This closed-front muzzle is made from a soft, breathable fabric. It will stop you getting bitten but restricts access to the foreface.

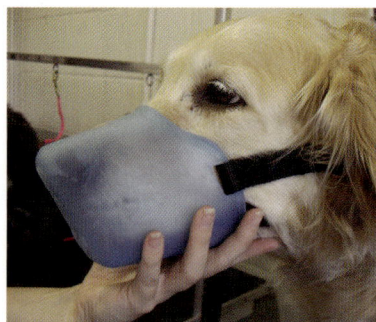

Fig. 9.2.14   A moulded plastic full-face muzzle. It is safe and comfortable for the dog to wear and offers the groomer protection from being bitten. A slight disadvantage with these muzzles is that they can cause nasty bruising if the dog throws himself around and hits you with the corner of the muzzle. They have also been known to break unexpectedly at the point where the neck strap is attached, if the dog stresses the attachment by rubbing or clawing at the muzzle.

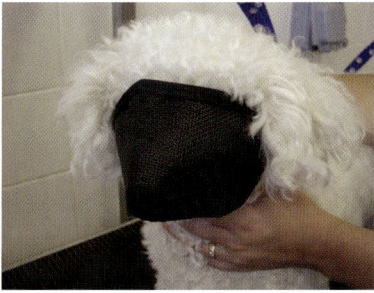

Fig. 9.2.15   A full face muzzle that can be used on either a cat, a brachycephalic dog such as a Shih Tzu or on breeds that have overly large eyes such as the Bichon Frise. The muzzle covers the eyes so they are protected from damage caused by either the edges of the muzzle or debris from the grooming process.

Fabric muzzles are soft and washable; fitted correctly, they are comfortable for the dog and safe for the groomer. The neck strap is nylon and does not stretch or break. The muzzle is easily washed and does not rot with constant wet use. You should, however, periodically check the stitching for deterioration. Material muzzles can be either open- or closed-fronted. From a grooming perspective the disadvantage of material muzzles is that the hair on the foreface cannot be pulled through for cutting; in extreme cases you may therefore have to leave this bit untrimmed.

Plastic muzzles are of either an open lattice design (*see* Fig. 9.2.16), made up of plastic strips moulded together, or a closed-fronted, solid design with air ventilation holes. The former, known as a Baskerville® muzzle, is generally comfortable for the dog and allows the dog to drink with it on. It also has the advantage that the dog can vomit through it, and the groomer can pull hair through the lattice design to trim the foreface. The solid version, by contrast, does not have any of these advantages but is comfortable for the dog, if fitted correctly. Fitting of these muzzles should ensure that they do not touch or cause trauma to the eyes, or pressure on the nose. Another advantage of both types is that they do not rot if they get wet so washing them clean is not a problem. These muzzles leave little possibility of the groomer being bitten, providing they are not loose. Their main disadvantage is that the plastic has been moulded with hard-

ened edges so that the muzzle holds its shape. This can cause bruising to the groomer if caught when dogs throw their heads around.

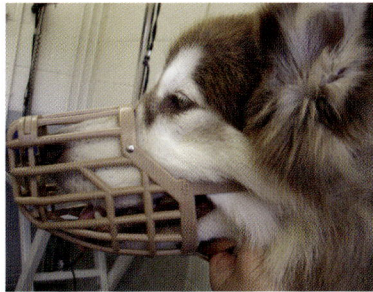

Fig. 9.2.16   Open-lattice muzzles are comfortable and have the advantage that dogs can drink whilst wearing them. If the dog had facial furnishings, you would be able to reach them without removing the muzzle by using a comb to pull the hair through the lattice.

Leather muzzles are of either an open lattice design consisting of leather straps, or closed-fronted with ventilation gaps. In my opinion, a leather muzzle is not the best option for the grooming room. The former type does have the advantage of allowing you to pull hair on the foreface through the straps for trimming, but this is outweighed by the disadvantages of the manufacturing material. Leather needs a lot of attention to keep it in good order. It needs to be oiled periodically to keep it soft and comfortable. It reacts badly to the chemicals in shampoo (and vomit) and even the best leather will harden and rot if it gets wet and is not dried out properly. Washing these muzzles is consequently also a problem. If leather becomes too dry, it disintegrates, leaving the possibility of the muzzle falling apart during use. The other disadvantage is that the leather neck strap, if fitted, can stretch and you may find that the dog has managed to remove the restraint.

Wire cage muzzles are also generally not a good investment for the groomer. Whilst they provide good ventilation and are good for pulling facial hair through for trimming, the metal rusts after a while and the joints, in particular, become weakened. They are also usually fitted with a leather neck strap that will stretch and deteriorate. These muzzles should be checked after every use to make sure that the wire design

has not broken at any of the joins. Such breaks can leave a pointed piece of wire free to cut or dig into the dog's face. The groomer should also check that the muzzle has not changed shape as this could cause damage to the face and eyes.

Full face latex mesh muzzles are very good for use on brachycephalic, or short-nosed, dogs as they are not close-fitting around the foreface and allow the dog room to pant. They also fit well above the eyes so rubbing or trauma to the eyes is rarely a problem. They are usually constructed of a soft latex (or nylon) mesh and are fitted with nylon neck straps. These muzzles also protect the dog's eyes from hair clippings and dust particles. The disadvantage is that the dog cannot vomit or drink, and you cannot monitor the dog satisfactorily because you cannot see his eyes. It is difficult to pick up on any signs of stress other than heavy panting, which may be normal for the dog. This means that you may have to remove the muzzle periodically to check the dog, and getting it back on again can be problematic. That said, it is better to be safe than sorry and, used with care, these muzzles are generally very useful.

Emergency muzzles

In the absence of a muzzle, it is possible to make an emergency muzzle from a length of non-stretchy bandage, or perhaps a nylon lead. Such emergency muzzles can readily be put together in a hurry, especially if there is a risk of the dog trying to bite you. The handler ties the two ends in a half-hitch, making a loop that can be used to competently 'noose' the muzzle of an unpredictable or uncooperative dog from behind. There are two ways in which the emergency muzzle is commonly used: traditionally, veterinary surgeons and nurses position the half hitch knot in the loop on the top of the nose. This is then tightened to close the front of the mouth and the tape ends passed under the mandible before the tape is finally tied behind the head. In the grooming environment, the half hitch is placed under the muzzle and tightened, between the lower mandibles; this closes the back of the mouth. The head is then brought down towards the chest before the long ends of the tape are tied at the back of the dog's head. Fitted in this way, the restraint provides sufficient control and access for the groomer to clear the hair from the lips and the foreface, without being bitten. Care and practice are required to use the technique correctly.

It is, however, a short-term solution, and should not be left in place for longer than a few minutes. Firstly, the knot can work loose and you could be bitten; secondly, and most importantly, dogs do not appreciate having their mouths tied shut. It is uncomfortable and can restrict breathing, and this type of restraint should be avoided where possible. Always keep a pair of scissors handy to cut the tapes in the event of the dog becoming stressed or panicking.

You should practise and perfect this technique (soft toy dogs are useful here) so that, if you have to resort to this form of restraint, you know exactly what you are doing.

Elizabethan collars

The Elizabethan collar (see Fig. 9.2.17) is a funnel-shaped tube that surrounds the dog's head, just like the pleated ruffs worn by the gentry in Elizabethan England. It is secured by the dog's collar and prevents the dog swinging his head around to bite you. They are generally made of plastic so they are easily washed and dried. You will need several sizes, but note that as the size

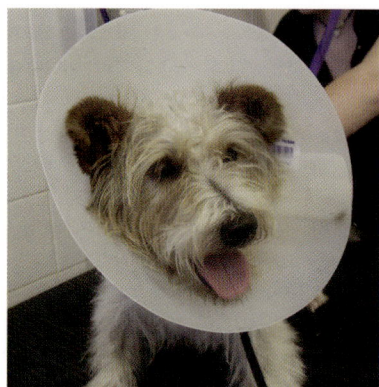

Fig. 9.2.17   An Elizabethan collar offers the groomer some protection but only as long as you are working behind the protection of the collar. It will not protect you if the dog is facing you. Make sure that the depth of the collar is greater than the combined length of the dog's head and muzzle.

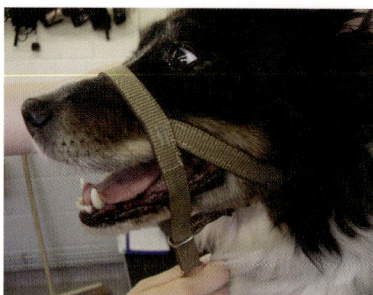

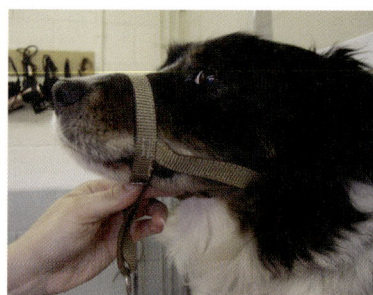

Fig. 9.2.18a-b   The Halti® is useful for restraining dogs that are not aggressive but may give you a nip. It can be tightened as required and is useful if you have facial furnishings to deal with.

gets bigger, so does the depth of the collar. This can mean that larger sizes make grooming difficult.

It is a good alternative to the muzzle and is excellent for use on brachycephalic dogs. It will, however, only protect you if your hands stay outside the circumference of the collar. If they intrude inside it, you can be bitten.

Halti®

A Halti® (see Figs 9.2.18a-b) is quite useful for dogs that are not aggressive but may nip. The Halti® fastens behind the ears and the nose strap can be tightened under the lower jaw when required. It is handy to use on dogs that have facial furnishings because, by holding the nose strap tight, the hair on the nose can be groomed and trimmed. The disadvantage of the Halti® is that the nose strap needs to be held to be secured; should the dog struggle, causing you to release your grip, the dog is no longer muzzled and you can be bitten.

Caging and kennelling

There are endless varieties of cages and kennelling available to suit the requirements and pockets of just about everyone. A good choice of cage will prove an excellent way of restraining animals in your care and keeping them safe.

Cages

Metal cage banks (see Fig. 9.2.19) can be expensive but are usually excellent quality, hard-wearing and easy to clean. The doors are usually large and allow easy access. They are, however, cold, and they echo. *Plastic or fibreglass cages* can be expensive but they do not echo

Fig. 9.2.19   A bank of cages is a space-saving option to keep dogs safe whilst they are waiting.

and are warmer than the metal variety. Cleaning them is also easy. You should check that door fastenings are secure and easy to operate in an emergency.

Wire crates (see Fig. 9.2.20) are suitable for use when the groomer needs a spare cage or when space is limited. They vary in price and design, and do not offer any protection from the environment or from airborne dis-

Fig. 9.2.20   Collapsible wire crates and cages are ideal if you are limited for space because they can be easily stored when not in use. Make sure that the design you choose has a large door so it is easy to get dogs in and out.

ease transmission. The doors are often small and can make access difficult, whilst fastenings can sometimes be difficult to operate. They are, however, useful and allow the groomer to see the dog at all times if monitoring is required.

Material collapsible cages should not be used for dogs that do not willingly come out of the cage. The doors are small and, should the dog retreat to the back of the cage, it would mean that you have to put yourself at risk by leaning into the cage to get hold of the dog to remove him. They are also unsuitable for dogs that need to be monitored as viewing through the mesh ventilation 'windows' is limited, for obvious reasons. They are clearly unsuitable for dogs that are destructive.

Plastic cages are useful for stacking; they are also warm and exclude drafts. They are constructed in two halves that come apart easily for cleaning and storage. Their disadvantages include their very small doors, and door fastenings that are not always easy to secure; they are not suitable for dogs that need monitoring. The inside of the cage sometimes has one half overlapping the other, leaving an edge that can be chewed through by a destructive dog.

Kennelling

Correctly built kennelling (*see* Fig. 9.2.21) does not come cheap. If your grooming practice is part of another business (such as boarding or breeding kennels), you may be fortunate enough to have good kennels/runs at your disposal. The flooring should be concrete and easily hosed down and the dog should have somewhere it can get under cover from the sun or wet weather. Doors and gates should be metal and escape-proof. The advantages are that the dog has plenty of freedom and is kept safe whilst waiting to be attended to. The disadvantages are that kennels take a lot of cleaning and, if correctly cleaned between dogs, they can take some time to dry out again. They are also expensive and take up a lot of space.

Wooden kennelling is neither cheap nor easy to maintain; it is difficult to clean and can harbour both infections and parasites. It is also chewable. Careful consideration should be given before choosing this option; although it is less costly than metal kennelling, this may prove to be a false economy.

Straddling

Straddling is the term used when the dog is standing on the floor and the groomer places a leg either side of the dog, at the point of the waist, to hold the body still. The dog is facing forward and the groomer steps around the dog from behind. This is an excellent way for the groomer working alone to restrain a large dog whilst performing a task such as cutting nails. It can also be achieved with one person straddling the dog whilst another performs the task. The advantages are that a good level of restraint can be achieved to keep the dog still and the position can be released immediately after the job is completed. The disadvantage is that, on its own, it does not stop the dog from biting. The dog's face may be very close to your own, so care must be taken and a muzzle applied if you are in any doubt about the dog's reactions.

Sedation

Chemical restraint (sedation) is generally used as a last resort for dogs that have a history of being severely traumatized by grooming, somewhere along the line. Often the dog's past remains unknown; this is particularly true of dogs that have been rehomed and may have had several owners. Many dogs have not been well socialized as puppies and have been allowed to develop a range of dysfunctional habits that reflect their dysfunctional lives and the fact that they have not learnt to function comfortably in everyday life.

The groomer is likely to see many heavily coated dogs that are 'unmanageable', and where sedation is needed. These individuals have perhaps been passed through many homes, or have been left until their coats are in a terrible state before someone has attempted to groom them. 'Rescued dogs' also sometimes require sedation for grooming if they have been ill treated and abused. In this case it is not so much the grooming that the dog is afraid of, but more the handling. Quite often, sedation is only required once. Once the coat has been removed, regular daily attention encourages the dog to accept being handled and groomed. Sedation may also be indicated in situations where a heavily coated dog has been badly injured in an accident and grooming becomes necessary before the dog has completely recovered.

Modern sedatives in veterinary practice today can minimize side-effects by combining drugs from different

Fig. 9.2.21 If your grooming practice is part of another business, such as kennels or doggy day care, you may be fortunate enough to have the use of purpose-built kennelling.

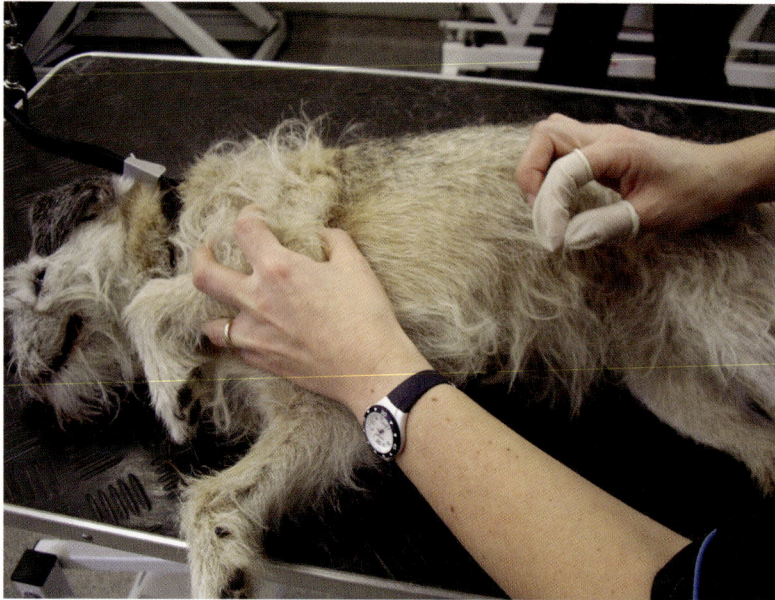

Fig. 9.2.22   This dog is not sedated; she is unfazed by the work of the groomer. In circumstances where grooming is necessary but the dog is of unstable temperament and cannot be handled safely, chemical restraints allow you to groom a dog whilst it is recumbent.

classes. Small doses can be given and the dog can be 'woken up' with a reversing agent as soon as the job is complete. Sedation is not, on its own, a guarantee that you will not be bitten, as many dogs have been known to bite when coming round, catching the vet or nurse off guard. A plastic cage muzzle can be fitted in such situations; this will prevent you being bitten but the dog can still vomit and you can still monitor them.

The advantage of sedation is that the dog can be groomed safely without further stress and trauma. The disadvantages are that the dog has to be groomed lying down (*see* Fig. 9.2.22) and bathing is not possible.

Modifying your restraining methods

When and why you restrain a dog depends on the situation you are dealing with. If, for instance, you are taking the dog from the kennel area to the grooming room, it makes sense to put the dog on a collar and lead. If the dog is too big to carry but is able to walk, then a collar and lead will guide them safely to where you want them to be. If you are carrying the dog it still makes sense to put a collar and lead on the dog, so that they understand you are in control, but it is not absolutely necessary.

Each situation needs to be assessed in order to identify and evaluate the risks involved. There are times when you may need to modify the way in which you use your restraints. Examples include:

◆ Bitches in whelp must not be made to stand for long periods of time. Neck straps need to be loose to allow her to sit, whilst belly straps should not be used. In such cases a table positioned against a wall is a good idea because the dog cannot fall off the back and you will be watching the front so the dog will be safe. You could also consider using a sling (*see* Fig. 9.2.5).

◆ Dogs with bladder problems should not have a belly strap because this puts pressure on the bladder. A belly sling is a better option.

◆ Old or disabled dogs may not be able to stand for long periods of time, so belly straps must be removed regularly to allow the dog to sit and rest.

◆ Some dogs become stressed if they are made to wear a muzzle. If you really need to protect yourself, you could perhaps try putting a towel over the dog's head so he cannot see you. Another option would be to use a neck tie as usual, but with a second restraining strap running from the collar to the side arm of the holding frame; this ensures the dog cannot swing round and bite you.

◆ In hot weather material muzzles need to be removed regularly to allow the dog to pant and drink. It is not, however, always easy to get the muzzle back on again. In such cases, you should consider fitting a Halti® underneath the muzzle so that when you are ready, you can close the dog's mouth again and re-fit the muzzle safely.

This list could go on because each and every dog has different requirements. The most important thing to remember is that everyone must be kept safe, restraint should not exceed that which is necessary and sufficient for any given situation, and the dog's physical and mental well-being must be respected.

Safe lifting

Manually lifting the dog is going to mean handling and restraining it, but before you endeavour to lift it, you must do a temperament assessment to establish whether or not the dog will need muzzling or any extra restraints. Remember that you will be working close to the dog and your face will be vulnerable to injury.

Fig. 9.2.23

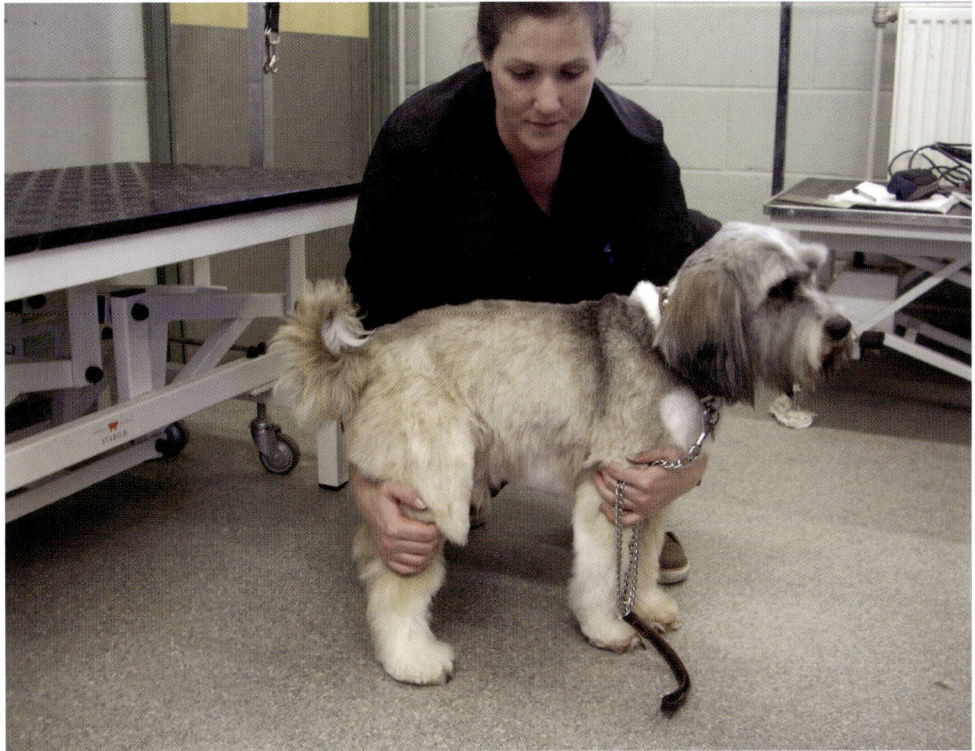

Lifting is a means of supporting or transporting a load upwards from or to ground level from another supporting platform and in our case it usually means moving the dog by bodily force. About a third of accidents in the workplace are caused by lifting and your employer is legally responsible for preventing lifting accidents, but you have a duty to yourself to undertake your own risk assessment to prevent personal injuries. Employers must take all appropriate measures to avoid the need for manual lifting. Where it is unavoidable it is necessary for them to minimize the risk of injury, particularly to the employee's back. With planning, training and controls in place, safe systems of working can be applied and injuries can be reduced. This involves a risk assessment, where hazards are questioned and identified and will include looking at:

The task

This concerns where the object has to be moved from and to. In our case this is usually from the floor to the grooming table or bath and back down to the floor again and we need to consider whether we as individuals can perform the task without undue twisting, stooping or straining that may cause us injury.

The load

The load to be lifted in most cases will be the dog, but on occasions, will be the grooming table. We need to consider if the load is stable and likely to shift (a dog wouldn't be stable because it is a moving object), and whether it difficult to grasp (that would depend on the size of the dog).

The working environment

In our case this is the grooming or bathing room where slippery floors and space constraints are often a problem.

The individual's capability

Is the individual correctly trained in lifting techniques, wearing suitable clothing and footwear, physically able to reach the height required and physically strong enough to lift the load?

In the grooming room, it is sometimes very difficult to have definitive answer to these questions because for instance, a Bassett Hound is short on its legs so it is not very tall so one could presume that it would therefore be classed as a small dog. However, it is in fact a breed that is very heavy and difficult to lift because of its length and may need two persons to lift it. By contrast, a Lurcher that may be very tall and leggy could be much lighter in weight and often easier to lift by one person. In both cases the risks are increased when the dog moves in your arms. Both breeds will become unstable and the force of movement will make them both much heavier in your arms.

In the grooming room it is usual to adopt one of two lifting methods for manually lifting the dog. A one-man lift is where the groomer lifts the dog without assistance (Figs 9.2.23 and 9.2.24); a two man lift is where another person is required (Fig. 9.2.25).

Lifting techniques

To lift the dog from ground level:

◆ Put your table up to a height where you can place the dog without bending to release the lift.
◆ Place your feet apart with your leading leg slightly forward to give you a balanced stable base.
◆ Adopt a good posture by bending the knees, and keeping your hands at waist level. Keep your back straight, chin in, shoulders level and lean slightly over the dog.
◆ If working alone, place one arm around the back end of the dog and one around the chest keeping the dog's centre of gravity and the

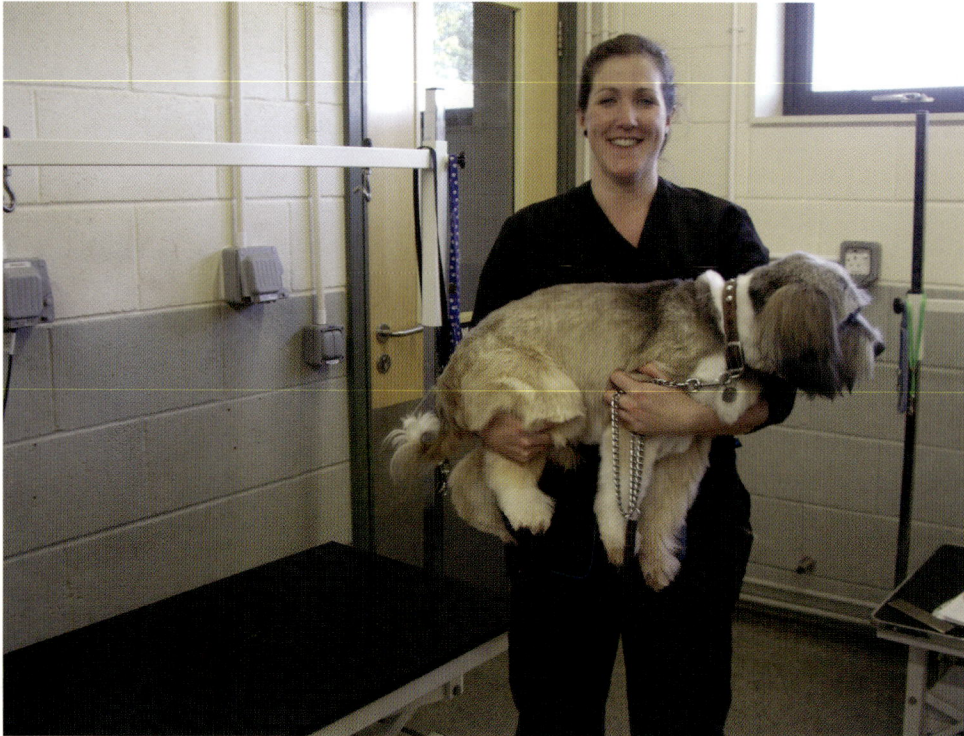

Fig. 9.2.24

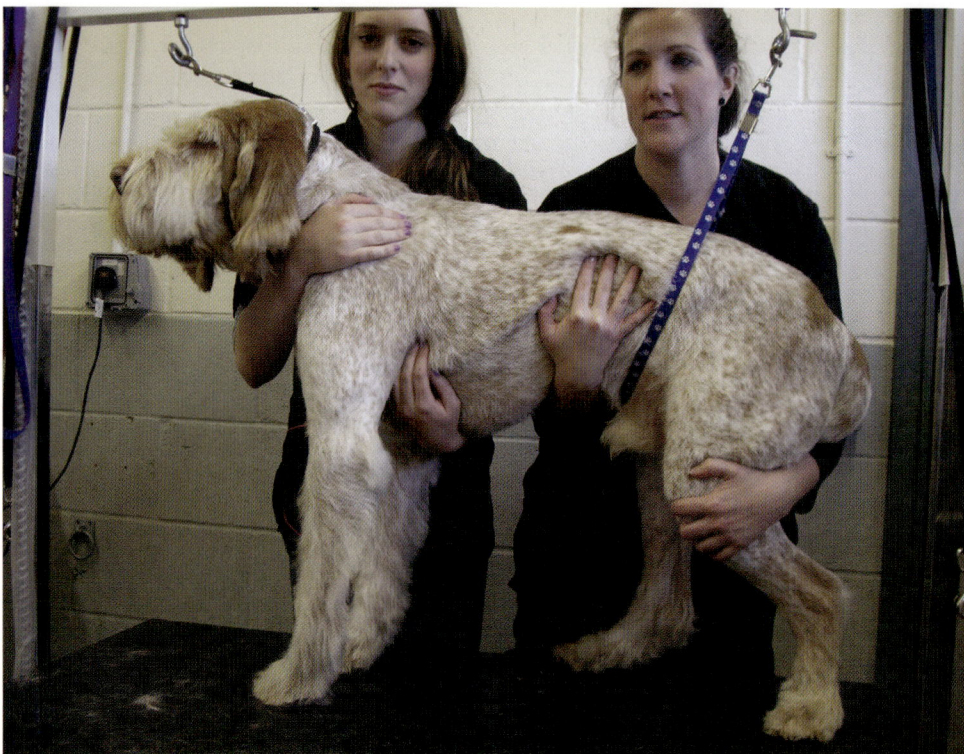

Fig. 9.2.25

heaviest part of his body (the rib-cage) against your body.

◆ If using a two-man lift, stand side by side. One person will have an arm around the front of the chest and one arm under the dog supporting the ribcage. The other person will have one arm under the abdomen and the other around the back of the dog. Keep the dog close to your bodies.

◆ Keeping the dog close to you and your arms within the boundaries formed by your feet, lift the dog (count yourselves in so you lift together if there is two of you) and stand upright.

◆ Carry the dog as smoothly as possible and without twisting your body if you turn sideways. If working as a pair, shuffle your feet as you turn.

◆ Lower the dog's feet onto the table

and stand upright as soon as the dog has found his balance.

To lift from a height to ground level:

◆ Adopt a good posture with your feet slightly apart to provide a balanced, stable base.

◆ With your arms securely around the dog's chest and rear end (supporting the body if there are two of you), move backwards if necessary before turning sideways.

◆ Walk smoothly, keeping the dog close and bend the knees before gently lowering the dog, holding it secure until its feet are firmly on the ground and it has its balance.

There is no such thing as completely safe manual handling and lifting, but you can help to protect yourself by considering your own stature and physical abilities before you decide whether or not you can lift alone or you require assistance. It is worth pointing out here that according to the law as at October 2012, there is not a legal maximum lifting weight. Whilst the Manual Handling Operations Regulations (1992) (UK) provides recommended guidelines to the maximum weight an individual can lift, they are only guidelines and you must not feel that you are obliged to lift a weight that is too heavy for you.

References and further reading

Ballard, B. and Rockett, J. (2009). *Restraint and handling for veterinary techni-cians and assistants.* Clifton Park, New York: Delmar Cengage Learning.

Chadder P, Duncan, M. and Heighway, P. *Health and Safety at Work Essentials.* 7th edition. 2012 . Lawpack Publishing Ltd.

Hubrecht, R. (1995). The welfare of dogs in human care. In: J. Serpell (ed.), *The domestic dog, its evolution, behaviour and interactions with people.* Cambridge: Cambridge University Press, pp. 179–98.

McGreevy, P., Hawke, C., Celi, P. and Downing, J. (2007). Learning and teaching animal handling at the University of Sydney's Faculty of Veterinary Science. *Journal of Veterinary Medical Education*, 34 (5),

Patronek, G.J. and Lacroix, C.A. (2001). Developing an ethic for the handling, restraint and discipline of companion animals in veterinary practice. *Journal of the American Veterinary Medical Association*, 218 (4), 514–17.

Rooney, N.J., Gaines, S.A. and Bradshaw, J.W.S. (2007). Behavioural and glucocorticoid responses of dogs (Canis familiaris) to kennelling: Investigation of mitigation of stress by prior habituation. *Physiology and Behaviour*, 5, 847–54.

Rooney, N.J., Gaines, S. and Hiby, E. (2009). A practitioner's guide to working dog welfare. *Journal of Veterinary Behaviour: Clinical Applications and Research*, 4 (3), 127–34.

Sheldon, C.C., Sonsthagen, T. and Topel, J.A. (2006). *Animal restraint for veterinary professionals.* Mosby, Elsevier.

Useful websites

www.kenneldesign.com/products/blueprints/legislation.php
Provides information on kennel design legislation and useful links depending on the country you are working in.

www.defra.gov.uk/publications/2011/03/25/dogs-and-cats-welfare-pb10308/
Provides information on the transportation of pets and how to ensure that an offence is not committed under the 2006 Animal Welfare Act.

10 Equipment and Tools

Setting up your work space and purchasing your tools is exciting – but it can, at the same time, be very daunting. Your challenge is not only to buy equipment that fits within the area you have available; it also has to suit your budget and your needs. Additionally, in the case of bathing facilities, it also has to fit and correspond with the plumbing available within the building and meet environmental rules and regulations.

For the new groomer, selecting equipment can be a minefield. Open a catalogue or visit a grooming supplies website and you will find an incredible collection of tools to choose from. Open another catalogue, visit another website and you may find another, equally impressive but different selection. There are hundreds of possibilities and choices, so where do you start?

The best way to start is by asking yourself some questions and answering them!

Note: Clippers and blades are covered in Chapter 14; scissors are covered in Chapter 15.

What am I buying it for?

Establish why you are buying any equipment in the first place. The pet owner whose work and needs are limited to their own dog(s) may only need to invest in the tools that will allow them to maintain their own animal's coat. A few pieces of equipment may suffice and it need not cost you the earth. By contrast, the person wanting to make a living from grooming must deal with a wide range of dogs, of varying breed sizes and coat types, and will need to invest in a correspondingly greater variety of equipment and paraphernalia.

How much grooming will I be doing?

Do you just want to groom your own dog(s) every six or seven weeks, or do you want to work commercially, grooming a variety of dogs every day? If you intend grooming large numbers of dogs you will need to invest in a more comprehensive range of good-quality tools and equipment to withstand heavy use.

How do I know which are the best tools and equipment to buy?

Grooming is very physical work and you may find some techniques difficult if you have limited mobility in your wrists, elbows or shoulders. With this in mind, I have covered the various options of tool design available to help you work more comfortably, safely and efficiently.

Consider the following points:

- It has to suit *you* personally and feel comfortable for you to use and operate. If you have small hands, bulky clippers and large heavy scissors will make life very difficult for you. Similarly, if you have restricted wrist, elbow or shoulder movement, you should choose equipment that makes allowances for your lack of mobility.
- The most expensive or the most popular item is not necessarily the best buy for you personally.
- Each tool or piece of equipment will have umpteen different designs and variations that all do the same job. Buy the design most suited to you. You certainly do not need all of them!
- Do not buy tools or equipment just because someone has told you they are 'the best'. Try each one out for yourself and make up your own mind. If you intend buying on-line, try before you buy: either go to a dog show where the equipment will be on display, or ask for 'sale on approval' so that you can handle the tools before you commit yourself.

How much will I have to spend?

Whether you are grooming your own dog(s) or starting a business, you need to work to a realistic budget. Decide on the budget you have to play with and what your spending priorities are. Try to ensure that your money is well spent and that your purchases dovetail with your immediate requirements. Any tools and equipment that you buy will need to pay for themselves sooner rather than later, and if you plan to work commercially this has to be accounted for in your outgoings. To begin with, your grooming business may be slow to take off because it takes time to build up your confidence, develop your skills and establish a client base.

The cost of tools can vary considerably between suppliers and manufacturers; in many cases you can make savings by changing your supplier or selecting a different design. The importance of buying tools that are well suited to you cannot be overstated. Beware of items that look good or have an attractive price tag: it does not matter what it costs – if you don't get on with it, it is money wasted!

Do I have to buy it all at once or can I just buy the essentials?

This depends on why you are buying the equipment. If it is for the purpose of grooming your own animals, you may find that you can put the purchase of certain tools on hold. For instance, if you plan to regularly clip your dog and you are buying your tools in the summer, you can get away with buying just the clipper blades that you require for a summer trim, leaving the acquisition of winter-length blades until you need them. If you are beginning a commercial venture, you need to equip yourself for the variety of work that you will be dealing with on a daily basis; the essentials are therefore a must, and anything extra is a matter of matching up your needs and your budget. You may, for example, wish to purchase equipment that you do not anticipate using straight away, especially if you are offered a very good deal on a large order.

Buy wisely and treat your tools and equipment as an investment.

The following pages look at the different types of equipment currently available, starting with the essential equipment of tables, baths and driers. The next sections look at the different grooming tools available to help you choose the designs best suited to you and your needs.

When you have drawn up your 'shopping list', shop around and find yourself a supplier who is both helpful and reliable and provides excellent after-sales support. If you plan to work commercially, you cannot afford to be without your equipment for too long should it need to be replaced, repaired or sharpened.

Left-handed groomers

There are few tools available specifically for left-handed persons, although they are starting to make an appearance. Several designs can be suitably adapted from right to left-handed use and these are pointed out as we go through the list.

ESSENTIAL EQUIPMENT

There are a few pieces of equipment that are essential either if you are going to groom your pet in a manner that is comfortable for you both, or if you are going to work commercially to earn a living. You need easy access to the dog whilst you are working on them, somewhere to bath them and some way of drying them. The first part of this chapter will deal with these important (and most expensive) pieces of equipment.

10.1 TABLES (OR 'SOMETHING TO PUT THE DOG ON'!)

In all cases – for your own safety, the safety of the dog and to ensure your subject is adequately controlled and restrained – it is advisable to groom the dog on a table or a workbench.

Your choice of table is vitally important because it is one of the costlier and bulkier items that you are likely to purchase. Essentially you want a

table that makes your work easier, safer and enjoyable. Should you choose the wrong table, or an unsuitable one, you may end up regretting it, especially if it results in you injuring yourself or having to sell it on. Should the latter be necessary, you may even lose money and have to pay for it to be moved.

There are many different types of table to choose from. Table specifications can vary considerably in terms of their height range, tabletop size, construction and mobility. Tables can also vary considerably in price but there will usually be one to suit your budget, even if this means hunting around or sourcing one second-hand. If you are only planning to groom your own dogs, you will probably only want to invest in a portable table that can be stored when not in use. If, however, you plan to work commercially, you really should invest in a lifting table to protect your back from injury when working with heavy dogs.

Workbenches

If you are only grooming your own dogs, it is possible that you can manage using a worktop or workbench already in place in a garage or utility room. The height of the work surface should be the same as you would have in your kitchen so that you are not bending or overstretching whilst working. This may cause problems if your dog is either very short on his legs or very tall, but it may save you an expense if you find that it 'does the job'. The important point to remember is that the top should have a non-slip surface. Smooth or shiny surfaces can be made safe by standing the dog on a rubber bathmat, with suckers attaching it to the worktop to prevent it slipping.

Even whilst grooming your own dog, you must have some way of securing his lead either to a wall fastening or to a portable grooming arm so that he cannot fall off and hurt himself. Restraining your dog in this way is necessary and very important because he knows you very well, and is more likely to lead you a merry dance if he decides he does not want to be groomed today, or tries to jump off or escape.

Consider the width of the workbench too. If it is too narrow, you may not be able to stand the dog where you want him to be, and if it is too wide, he can flatten himself against the wall so that you cannot reach him comfortably.

For the commercial groomer, a fixed-height, fixed-width workbench does not allow you the flexibility that a lifting table provides. It may also present you with height and weight restrictions as you may not be able to lift up heavy dogs, and it may make it difficult for you to see the underside of short-legged dogs or over long-legged dogs. Furthermore, such tables may well compromise your health. Having said that, there are many groomers working on workbenches and managing very well so it does depend on the type of work you plan to do.

Portable tables

Portable tables (*see* Figs 10.1.1 and 10.1.2) are ideal not only for the pet groomer and the mobile groomer, but also as an extra table in the salon. They fold flat for storage or transportation and are fitted with carrying handles. They are available in a choice of tabletop sizes, from small to salon size, and a range of heights, unless of course you opt for adjustable height. The rubber tabletops are often available in a choice of colours. All portable tables can be fit-

ted with a detachable restraining arm which makes for easy storage. Salon-size tables can be fitted with a detachable 'H' frame. The main disadvantage of the portable table is that you are restricted to the size of dog that you can groom:

◆ Small tabletops restrict you to toy-sized dogs and small terriers.
◆ Medium-sized tabletops will allow you to trim a dog up to Cocker Spaniel size.
◆ Salon-size tabletops are suitable for larger dogs but require you to lift the dog onto the table, unless you have a ramp or steps that the dog is able and willing to walk up.
◆ Portable tables are lightweight so that you can carry them. Consequently, they can sometimes be a little unstable. Any instability will be particularly apparent when working with the largest dogs your table can accommodate, or if it is positioned on an uneven floor.

Fig. 10.1.1   A folding portable table suitable for a mobile groomer or the pet owner.

Fig. 10.1.2   A small folding table suitable for pet owners with a small dog.

A NOTE ABOUT WORKING ALONE

One point to consider here is that, if you are working alone, you will also be restricted to the size of dog that you can safely manage on your own – a portable table may therefore be sufficient for you.

Trolley tables

These tables (*see* Fig. 10.1.3) have all

the benefits of the portable table but they are fitted with wheels and a pulling handle instead of a carrying handle, so that they become trolleys. This can be very useful for mobile groomers who have to transport grooming equipment from their car boot into a customer's home, and also for taking to dog shows. They are not available in as many sizes or colours. Their main disadvantage is that you are again restricted to the size of dog that you can groom for the same reasons that apply to the portable table.

Fig. 10.1.3   This folding table has all-terrain wheels that transform it into a trolley, making it a good option for mobile groomers.

Lifting tables

For the salon-based commercial groomer a lifting table is recommended but not essential. These tables drop down to as little as 8 inches (20cm) from the floor, allowing larger dogs, in particular, to step on to the table. The table can then be raised, either electronically or hydraulically, to a suitable working height. This not only makes your life easier, it also significantly reduces the chances of you suffering a back injury, as well as reducing the risks to the dog.

Lifting tables are available as either hydraulic (*see* Fig. 10.1.4), or electronically operated (*see* Figs 10.1.5 and 10.1.6) units. They are all suitable for fitting with either control arms or 'H' frames. Table sizes vary a little, and prices can vary considerably. A lifting table is a wise investment, however, and you are therefore advised to find one that you can afford. These tables are much more sturdy than portable tables and most will safely take a weight of 300lb or 150kg, making them suitable for most breeds.

Push-button controls allow the table height to be adjusted instantly, either via a hand-operated control unit or at the press of a pedal. Such controls allow the dog to be raised or lowered

Fig. 10.1.4 For a commercial salon a lifting table is an excellent investment. The hydraulic table is reasonably priced and useful if electrical power points are limited.

Fig. 10.1.5 The electric lifting table is more expensive but benefits from a smoother lifting action.

Fig. 10.1.6 A folding electric table may be the purchase of choice for the mobile groomer. It has the advantages of being portable and operating smoothly, but care must be taken to check cables and connections every time the table is moved as they can be easily damaged by constant re-locating.

according to the groomer's requirements during the grooming process. The other advantage of a lifting table is that in a multi-groomer environment, where tables are shared, the table can be altered instantly to suit the height of one groomer and then changed equally quickly when someone else takes over at the workstation. This is not a convenience afforded by a portable table.

In terms of performance, the main difference between hydraulic and electric tables is the smoothness of action. An electric table glides gently up and down whereas a hydraulic table tends to have a less smooth action due to the foot-pumping mechanism. Most dogs will happily get used to either. The only obvious disadvantage to the electric table is its reliance on electricity. Power cuts prevent the use of the lifting mechanism, and broken or damaged cables prevent the use of the table. In the event of this happening, for safety reasons the table should not be used

until it has been checked and repaired. If you are employing staff, electric tables also need to be PAT (Portable Appliance Tested) by a qualified electrician annually.

'H' frames/bars, restraining arms and restraining straps and slings

'H' frames or bars (see Fig. 10.1.7) and restraining arms (see Fig. 10.1.8) are adjustable metal tubes that can be altered in height to suit the dog so that both the neck strap and the belly strap are relaxed but not loose when the dog is in a standing position. The 'H' frame is supported by side pillars with a cross-bar that forms the 'H', whereas the restraining arm is supported by a single pillar either fitted to the side of the table or to the centre back. Both designs have either hooks or rings for attaching restraining ties or straps. Most dogs will bear down on the straps so, whichever you choose, you must make sure that your restraining arm or frame is sturdy and that the screws that alter the height are tight otherwise the aerial bars can collapse on the dog. You can have either a fixed holding frame that is welded or bolted to the table, or a removable frame that is fitted to the

Fig. 10.1.7 An 'H' frame is so called because of its shape. It can be either bolted to the table or fitted with clamps as shown.

Fig. 10.1.8 A single arm restraint offers better access to the front or rear end of the dog as you need to move it less often when styling.

Fig. 10.1.9 Tie-up nooses are a safety feature that reduce the risk of accidents to both groomer and dog. Make sure the design that you choose can easily be cut through should there be an emergency.

CAUTION

In case of an emergency, all neck and belly straps should be easy to cut through with a normal pair of grooming scissors, thus allowing the immediate release of the dog. Nylon webbing or straps of similar construction are therefore recommended.

Chains are sometimes used on heavier breeds. They have several disadvantages:

- *They cannot be cut through in the event of an emergency.*
- *It may be impossible to release them whilst they are carrying the weight of a large collapsed dog.*
- *A neck chain can damage the airways and cause suffocation.*
- *The metal gets very hot when exposed to heat and may burn either you or the dog.*

table with clamps. Restraining straps (see Fig. 10.1.9) can be constructed either of nylon webbing, chain or cord, and are fitted in pairs: one at the dog's neck to support the front end of the dog, and the other around the belly to support the back end. Slings offer more support than straps because they hold the whole body. This makes them a good option for elderly or disabled dogs that cannot stand for long periods of time. The disadvantage is that the body of the dog is covered so grooming is more difficult.

Left-handed?

The tables themselves are suited to either left- or right-handed use but the electricity supply to electric tables is not. If the table has an electric socket fitted to it, try to find one fitted onto the left hand side of the table or ask your wholesaler if the socket can be moved. This avoids clipper and hair-dryer cables crossing your body when in use. If this is not possible, you should ensure that wall sockets are fitted on the left-hand side of the table.

10.2 BATHS

The bath is probably the piece of equipment that causes most problems, partly because they require a lot of space and partly because they are usually at a fixed height. The height of the bath can be of considerable concern as, if the bath is at the wrong height for the dog you are bathing, it can make for backbreaking work!

As with everything else, you need to choose a bath that suits your requirements. Bathing your own dog at home is usually possible using the family bath or, alternatively, for small dogs, the kitchen sink (see Fig. 10.2.1) or a baby bath. For the commercial groomer, however, these are not viable options and you need to think about what is best for you.

Fig. 10.2.1   The pet dog can be bathed in the household bath or a utility room sink.

Start with the plumbing!

You have many options to consider when buying a bath but you need to start with the plumbing because this is undoubtedly more expensive to install than the bath itself and will be difficult to alter once the work has been completed.

Where will your water supply be coming from?

Are you on a mains water supply or well water? Is the water in your area hard or soft? Limescale from hard water may have an effect on your plumbing system and shower equipment; you may therefore want to consider investing in a water softener.

If it is possible, you can make life easier for yourself by installing the water inlet (and consequently your hose) on your preferred working side. Right-handed people, for example, will find it easier to work with the hose in their right hand, so it is better to have the water inlet installed on their right-hand side. This may not, of course, always be achievable but it certainly helps to make the bathing process more user friendly.

How are you going to heat the water?

The priority is to ensure that you can maintain the water temperature during the bathing process. It is important to choose either a system that can be controlled by a thermostat, allowing you to warm a tank of water to a specified temperature, or a system that you can set to warm the water as it passes through the heater (see Fig. 10.2.2). In practice (as explained in Chapter 7.3.1), water temperature can be set as low as 30°C.

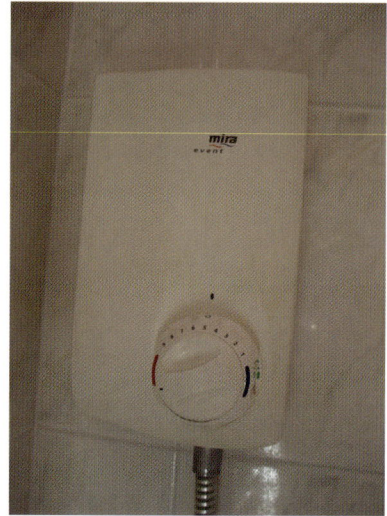

Fig. 10.2.2   Standard wall-mounted water heaters can be set to the required temperature.

CAUTION: TAP CONNECTORS

Tap connectors are not suitable because not only can they become disconnected during use, but the movement and bending of the rubber hoses can stop the flow of water from one tap. If the cold water hose is occluded, you could easily scald yourself and the dog.

Pet owners without access to a fixed temperature shower hose would be wiser to use jugs of water, prepared in advance and sitting ready for use in a few buckets at the right temperature.

Where is the waste going to drain to?

Ideally, the waste needs to drain directly into main drains that will take it away from your property. If you are bathing lots of dogs, draining into a septic tank will fill the tank quickly, requiring it to be emptied frequently. Draining into mini sewerage plants may mean that the chemicals in the shampoos you are using could damage the plant. Similarly, chemicals allowed to drain into rivers can damage the environment and could mean you are breaching environmental laws.

See Chapter 7 for more information on environmental issues.

How easy is it to unblock the drainage pipes?

It doesn't matter how careful you are with pre-bath grooming, a certain amount of hair always comes away from the dog during the bathing process. An accumulation of sludge and oils from the shampoo will also build up within the drainage pipes. All of this will be washed down into the drains, and you need to stop it as close to the bath as possible.

You can help reduce the risk of blocked drains by:

◆ using a wider pipe than is usual for domestic waste (if you are installing your plumbing from scratch);
◆ fitting a 'bottle trap' under the bath that you can unscrew to clean and empty easily (*see* Fig. 10.2.3);
◆ using a hair trap (*see* Fig. 10.2.4) over the plug hole (highly recommended); and
◆ running clean hot water through the bath outlet for several minutes at the end of the day to remove any oils and shampoo scum from the pipes.

Fig. 10.2.3   Fitting a bottle trap under the bath gives easy access to clear pipes of hair and shampoo residues.

Fig. 10.2.4   A hair trap is also a good investment.

Plumbing sorted? Options for a bath!

If you are making use of an area that already has plumbing, look for a bath that fits into the area you have available. If, however, you are starting from scratch, you have more options. In a commercial salon you may even find it easier to have the bath built.

See Chapter 12 for bathing the dog.

Domestic baths

These are widely used by groomers, and you need not necessarily buy a new one as your local recycling depot may well be able to source one for you. The domestic bath can be a bit cumbersome and take up a lot of room but you may be lucky enough to pick up a ¾-sized bath, which would be an excellent find.

The positive aspects of a domestic bath are that they can be very cheap and big enough for even the largest of dogs. They are also robust and unlikely to break or get damaged. On a less positive note, recycled baths may be old, so check the size of the pipework to make sure it is compatible with modern plumbing. They should preferably be made of steel or fibreglass rather than polythene, which scratches easily and is difficult to clean. Steel baths are very slippery so mats will be needed to prevent the dog from slipping.

The bath needs to be fitted at a suitable height, which means having it fitted into some form of framework. This may be costly. Even when fitted within a framework, the depth of the bath can make your job difficult as you will be leaning forward over or into the bath; care must therefore be taken to avoid backstrain and injury (*see* Fig. 10.2.5).

Shower trays

Shower trays can be an excellent alter-

Fig. 10.2.5 Domestic baths can be bought cheaply from recycling centres. This picture demonstrates the strain on the back of the groomer when the bath is too low. If possible, have your bath raised.

native to a traditional bath (*see* Fig. 10.2.6). They are available in a variety of sizes and widths, so you should be able to find one that fits your designated space. They are affordable and easy to plumb in, but will need some form of framework to lift them to an acceptable height. A frame can easily be built out of breeze-blocks and tiled over. Selecting the right height can be difficult because dogs come in so many different sizes. If space is available, an easy solution to this is to build a two-tier bath, with a small tray fitted at worktop height for small dogs and a larger tray lower down for larger dogs.

Shower trays have a number of advantages:

- They are easy to clean.
- They usually have an embossed base to prevent slipping.
- It is easy to get the dog into it because they are shallow, thus eliminating the need to lift the dog over the side.
- They do not require you to reach down into the tray, thereby reducing a potential cause of backstrain.

Shower trays do present some disadvantages, though:

- The shallow rim means that water can easily splash over the side and get you and the floor (and your feet) wet.
- If you are using a wide tray, the dog is likely to hug the wall furthest away from you, meaning that not only are you definitely going to

get wet, you are also working in an awkward position.

A cheaper and very effective alternative to fitting shower trays is to build the same framework and a rim out of blocks and tile the whole thing. This is a very popular option where an area is difficult to fit with standard baths or trays. If you do choose to do this, remember to have the builder drop one end of his design slightly towards the plug so that the water drains easily.

Moulded polypropylene booster baths and wash tubs

These are purpose-built, lightweight, portable and affordable, and can be free-standing or fitted into holding frames (*see* Figs 10.2.7a-b). They are built from strong moulded polypropylene with rubber inserts on the floor. Access is easy, either through an open end or a sliding side door, and ramps are included so lifting the dog is not necessary. The static height version sits on removable pedestal legs which can be dismantled for moving. This might well be a good option for pet owners who may want to take the bath apart for storage between bathing sessions or for mobile groomers.

An electric version of the polypropylene bath is also available. This bath sits on an adjustable chassis that lifts and lowers the bath to adjust the height.

There are many positive points to the polypropylene bath and they certainly outweigh the negative points. One point to consider is that the design of these baths does mean that, although they are very strong and sturdy, they can be a little on the narrow side for either large overweight dogs or larger dogs that are reluctant to be bathed, so be prepared to get wet!

Fig. 10.2.6 These three shower trays are at a student training college. They are raised on breeze blocks covered in tiles and are designed to make them easy for students of different heights to work at.

Figs 10.2.7a-b Booster baths are robust and affordable. They are also easily moved and transported if you need to relocate. Fitted with a ramp, they can accommodate quite large breeds, as demonstrated by this Standard Poodle.

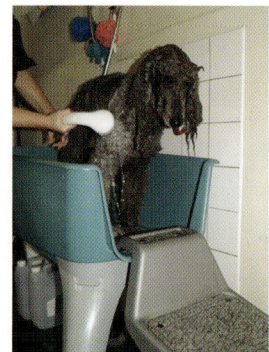

Stainless steel bathing stations

Manufactured from high-grade stainless steel, these baths are designed for heavy duty use in a commercial salon (see Fig. 10.2.8). They are large, roomy and have a sliding access door. Some of these baths have shower (remember to check that the plumbing fits!) and blasting attachments within the bath, plastic mesh on the floor to aid drainage and high backs to protect walls from water and spray. The static bath sits on fixed-height stainless steel legs so, if you are small in stature, make sure that you can comfortably reach over the front of the bath without straining.

An electric version sits on a lifting chassis allowing the bath to be lowered so that the dog can walk straight into it. It can then be raised to the correct height for the groomer to work without the risk of backstrain (see Fig. 10.2.9).

Fig. 10.2.8 A stainless steel bath will give years of service and can be purchased with an attached shower unit. This bath has a sliding panel to allow easy access and accommodates a ramp for larger breeds.

Fig. 10.2.9 A stainless steel bath with an electric lifting function.

Hydro baths

Hydro baths® are an excellent design, particularly in an age where we all have a responsibility to be increasingly environmentally friendly and reduce our carbon footprints. These baths have two integral tanks, one containing diluted shampoo and the other containing cold water from an inlet hose. The idea is that the water is heated as it leaves the water tank and after drenching the coat it is filtered back into the tank. After applying the diluted shampoo, the recycled water is then reused to rinse the dog. The water is then emptied out and changed before you bath the next dog. Both tanks are fitted with high-pressure hoses for maximum penetration of the coat, so you can reduce the amount of water and shampoo you apply. Recycling reduces the amount of water you use and it is heated as you need it; the shampoo is pre-prepared to a weak dilution, allowing you to economize on shampoo and reduce the amount of chemical waste produced by your salon. The baths are also lightweight and portable.

There are a few points to consider. You must exercise good hygiene and make sure you change the water and disinfect the bath between dogs to reduce the risk of cross-infection. It is recommended that you use company-specific chemicals and shampoos in the unit. These are all environmentally friendly but you may want to check the reliability of the supply. If you are discharging the water into anything other than mains drains you must check that the shampoo chemicals will not harm your waste unit. If you live in a hard water area, limescale could pose a problem with the hydro bath's recycling unit, so check descaling requirements with your supplier.

> **CAUTION: ELECTRICITY AND WATER**
>
> *Electricity and water do not mix, so it is imperative that the plugs and cables on the lifting baths are kept in good condition and regularly checked by a qualified electrician. You must make sure that the plug is kept dry at all times, particularly if your bath is mobile and has not completely dried out when you move it. The spray caused by using a blaster whilst the dog is in the bath is another potential hazard with electric baths. Power cuts may also be a problem. If you are buying your electric bathing unit from another country, check that the power supply and fittings comply with your own power supply.*

Purpose-built baths

Building a bath to suit your needs is also an option. If the bath is to be placed in an area that will not accommodate a commercially manufactured bath, it is possible to design your own, with the help of a builder (see Fig. 10.2.10). Plumbing permitting, any shaped bath can be built from breeze blocks and covered with either fibreglass or tiles. This allows you to fit a bath into any available space.

Fig. 10.2.10 A purpose-built bath can be made to fit your premises. This bath is made of breeze blocks covered in fibreglass. The builder has fitted it with tie-up rings and has included a ramp in the design for large dogs.

10.3 DRYERS AND DRYING EQUIPMENT

High-absorbency cloths

These work by soaking up several times their actual weight in water, in much the same way as chamois leather. Used properly, they can reduce drying time considerably, benefitting both the dog (as their skin is exposed to heat for less time) and your pocket because the dryer is not running for long periods of time (*see* Fig. 10.3.1).

Fig. 10.3.1 Super-absorbent towels like the Aquasorb remove many times their own weight of water to reduce drying time.

Towels

Towels are often overlooked as drying equipment but they are just as important as the electrical stuff. Invest in towels that are not too large or too thick, because they take too much laundering and take too long to dry once washed. Very soft towels should be avoided as they do not absorb well. Lastly, make sure that new towels are laundered before you use them for the first time, so that they do not bleed colour onto the dog.

Blasters and hair-dryers

Blasters and hair-dryers are grouped together here because they operate in a similar way and have the same considerations. Blasters and dryers are used to remove water and moisture from the coat after bathing by the velocity (force) and/or temperature (heat) of the air flow. They do serve different purposes and can be purchased as individual pieces of equipment or as combined machines.

Blasters

The purpose of a blaster (*see* Fig. 10.3.2)

is really to save time in the busy salon. Blasters have a high-velocity (very powerful) air flow that literally blasts the water and dead undercoat out of the coat. Once a dog has had a bath, a blaster is used to render the coat 'drip free' before being dried by heat. There are a variety of blasters available, ranging from moderate velocity to extremely powerful. Because they are used close to the bathing area on very wet dogs, they have a long 'snake-like' hose attachment with a directional nozzle to aim the air flow.

Some blasters have a heating element to warm the air flow; if not, you need to purchase a hair-dryer as well. The power of the air flow can make the blaster noisy and the use of ear protectors may be necessary, although technology is improving in this area. Have a good look round to see what is available and switch them on before you buy.

Fig. 10.3.2 Blasters with exceptionally high velocity airflow simulate the dog shaking to remove water from the coat by centrifugal force.

Hair-dryers

Hair-dryers differ from blasters in that they are not as powerful and they all contain heating elements. Some form of hair-dryer is essential and a busy grooming salon will quite possibly have several, all of which have their uses. Hair-dryers are available as hand-dryers, stand-dryers and cabinet-dryers. Your choice must take into account both the design of the dryer and your budget.

Hand-dryers are the basic type that you would buy for use on your own hair (*see* Fig. 10.3.3). They are cheap, versatile, usually fairly powerful, transportable and easily stored. For pet groomers and mobile groomers they are ideal, and they can be attached to the grooming table with a stand that acts as a second pair of hands. The small motor also means that they are fairly cheap to run. Hand-dryers usually have a selection of speeds and heat settings and they tend to be made from lightweight fabrics that are durable and do not fracture easily if the dryer is dropped. They are very useful for nervous dogs and noise-sensitive dogs because the switches are on the handle and you can distance the dryer or switch it down a speed instantly, if necessary, just by moving your fingers, without taking your eyes off the dog.

Fig. 10.3.3
Hand-held dryers are cheap and versatile.

The disadvantages of a hand-dryer are that, without a stand or second pair of hands, it is difficult to brush the dog with one hand, hold the dryer with the other and manage to lift legs to get to awkward areas, so a dryer-holder is a good investment (*see* Fig. 10.3.4). They also have a relatively short guarantee because using them for prolonged periods of time without resting tends to burn out the motor. For these reasons alone you may choose to use a more powerful commercial dryer in the workplace, although most groomers still have a hand-dryer amongst their equipment.

There are many designs of *stand-dryer* (*see* Fig. 10.3.5) to choose from. The advantages of stand-dryers are that they leave both hands free for handling and brushing the dog, and they are designed to withstand heavy use, so they can work for many hours

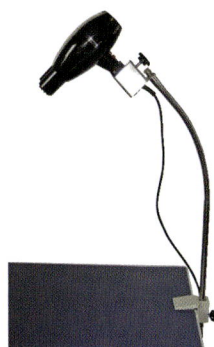

Fig. 10.3.4
Dryer holders allow you to use both hands whilst you are working – one to hold the dog, the other to hold the brush.

without damaging the motors. Stand-dryers have a much more gentle air flow than blasters but are more powerful than hand-dryers; they come into their own when drying wool or heavily coated dogs. When choosing your stand-dryer an important factor is stability. They generally fit on spring-loaded adjustable stands that have five legs and castors for easy manoeuvrability. Most dryers have either a single- or a double-speed air flow and a range of temperature settings. The dryers have an extending arm that brings the air flow closer to the dog without restricting your working space, and quite often they have nozzle attachments. The only disadvantage may be the circumference of the base. It needs to be large enough to stabilize the dryer but in a small salon this will take up limited floor space. Nevertheless, their versatility and value really do make up for this inconvenience.

Fig. 10.3.5
Commercial groomers also need to purchase a stand dryer. Designed to be workhorses, stand dryers are powerful and robust, and leave your hands free to work on the dog.

Combination dryers (*see* Fig. 10.3.6) are dryers and blasters combined. Very useful in the smaller salon, these machines have a variable air flow that is used first at its highest setting as a blaster. Once the coat is drip-free, the air flow is reduced and the air flow warms up so that it can be used as a hair-dryer. They sit on stands similar to the stand-dryer and they often have a flexible hose that is attached for the blasting process. They are very useful for new groomers starting out, especially where funds or space are limited.

Cabinet dryers are a useful investment as your business grows. Drying cabinets are designed to securely house one or two dogs (within partitions), whilst warm air circulating with-

Fig. 10.3.6
Combination dryers offer the groomer a blaster and a dryer all in one. They are powerful and versatile, have a high velocity airflow and are ideal for small salons where space is limited.

in the unit dries them (*see* Fig. 10.3.7). Drying cabinets are now widely used in salons; since their debut, they have undergone many improvements and design changes so that, providing they are used with care, they are safe. They generally have two or more motors

Fig. 10.3.7
Drying cabinets are popular with commercial groomers. They can be time-saving and are safe if used correctly but they should never be left unattended whilst a dog is being dried.

10.4 NON-ELECTRICAL TOOLS FOR GROOMING OUT OR REMOVING THE COAT

delivering the power to the fans that generate the air flow. They are temperature-controlled. Some (not all) cabinets are time-controlled and some (not all) have emergency stop switches. The doors may be sliding or hinged, and are made of Perspex (or transparent plastic), allowing you to see in and the dog to see out.

Drying cabinets are popular with groomers because in effect they provide you with an extra pair of hands. Cats in particular love them, probably because they like the gentle heat flow and of course they are safely confined; few dogs object to them. The disadvantages are that they take up quite a lot of room and, if you want to produce a good styling finish, all dogs apart from smooth coats need to be finished with a stand-dryer to stretch and straighten the coat. Additionally, the dog (or dogs) within the cabinet should be carefully monitored at all times, so someone has to keep an eye on them. They are expensive to buy and expensive to

run, so you should consider whether your business can justify the cost of purchasing, running and maintaining a cabinet dryer.

Undercoat rakes and shedding tools

The purpose of *shedding tools* is to remove loose hair either from the coat or from the root without cutting the coat. They should remove the complete hair. If they cut the hair instead of removing it, a portion of dead hair will be left behind. This can compromise the health of the skin and the quality of the coat.

There are basically two types of shedding tool: rakes and blades. Both types are available with either straight handles that give rise directly to the teeth, or ergonomic handles where the operational part of the tool crosses the handle to form a 'T' shape. Removing an undercoat can be hard work and can put strain on the wrists and elbows of the groomer so, if you anticipate problems, it may be better for you to opt for the ergonomic handles.

Rakes (*see* Figs 10.4.1 and 10.4.2) resemble combs, and the rake is used in the same way as a comb but the design of the teeth makes it more effective and easier to use on dense undercoats. The teeth can be short in length and large in diameter, or they can be long, with alternating shorter teeth. The teeth are always made of metal, whereas the handles may be plastic or wood. Rakes can also be purchased with rotating teeth which spin as they move through the coat. This gives less pull on the coat, so it is perhaps easier on the dog but it can be harder for the groomer as it is marginally less effective and takes longer.

Fig. 10.4.1 Undercoat rakes remove all loose hair and dead coat from double-coated breeds such as Border Collies.

Fig. 10.4.2   An undercoat rake with an ergonomic handle and longer teeth. This tool doubles up as a moulting comb.

Shedding blades (*see* Fig. 10.4.3) are a series of cutting blades often referred to as Furminator®s, *Shed stoppers* (*see* Fig. 10.4.4) or Coat King®s (*see* Fig. 10.4.5). It is perhaps questionable if they are correctly categorized as undercoat removers because they can cut the coat. These tools have ergonomic handles which come in several designs. The Coat King® is perhaps the more popular and is available with different blade sets, ranging from six to twenty teeth. The teeth are long and curve into themselves (like a series of hooks); they work by cutting through the undercoat with the blades, whilst the curved design of the teeth hooks the hair and pulls it away from the coat. The Furminator® has a flat blade (resembling the base plate of a clipper blade) that has a series of very short teeth; it works by catching the hair between the blades and dragging it away from the coat.

These types of tool are suitable for both left- and right-handed use.

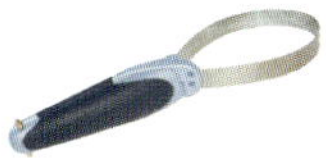

Fig. 10.4.3 Shedding blades are used in a dragging motion to remove hair from smooth coats.

Fig. 10.4.4   Shed stoppers and similar tools should be used with care and skill otherwise they can cut the coat rather than remove it from the hair shaft. A close look at this tool reveals the sharp cutting edge between the teeth.

Fig. 10.4.5   Coat Kings® are popular with professional groomers but their handles and operating motion are not suited to everyone. The ergonomic design is ideal for groomers with limited mobility in the wrist and elbow and can help to reduce joint strain.

CAUTION: THESE TOOLS CAN CAUSE HARM

Shedding tools need to be used with care. The raking action required to remove the coat can very easily cause skin trauma if not applied with patience and care. The skin is naturally more sensitive than usual as a result of the shedding/moulting process so monitor it carefully. Do not use excessive pressure with your tools until you are well practised and have developed a smooth atraumatic technique.

To remove an undercoat properly you must avoid cutting it. If you do cut the hair, you will leave some behind and thus fail to remove the undercoat completely. The residual hair can mat, clog up the coat and may compromise the health of the skin. Failure to remove the undercoat properly can also result in the hair growing back unevenly – possibly denser than when you started. If the coat has been cut instead of removed, you may also find that, in some breeds, you will lose the richness of colour as you would if you were clipping the coat.

If you are using a tool with blades, you must keep your wrist straight (as if it cannot bend) and drag the tool through the coat. Do not use a flicking action, as you would if you were combing, because this can damage the coat.

CLEANING AND MAINTENANCE OF SHEDDING TOOLS

After use, check the blades for damage. Carefully wash the tools in warm soapy water and leave to dry. Once dried, place the tools in either an ultraviolet light sterilizer or a liquid sterilizer. If using the latter, you should ensure that the tools are dried carefully before storing or using them again on another animal.

Rubber mittens (mitts) and pads

These are based on an adaptation of the rubber curry comb used to remove hair and massage horses. They include rubber grooming gloves and rubber sponges brushes (*see* Figs 10.4.6 and 10.4.7) and are used to remove loose or moulting hairs from smooth or short-coated dogs. Normal brushing is not sufficient to take out these hairs as they tend to slip between the teeth or bristles of the brush. Anyone who has ever owned, or knows, a Labrador or a Jack Russell Terrier will relate to the amount of hair that needs vacuuming up on a daily basis: some of these dogs appear to be in perpetual moult, and brushing just does not allow the hair to be removed and the problem managed.

Fig. 10.4.6
Rubber grooming
mitts are not only
satisfying to use,
they are excellent
for removing hair from smooth-coated breeds.

Fig. 10.4.7
A variation of the
rubber mitt is the
rubber sponge
pad. The pad is
gripped in the
hand rather than the hand being used flat.

The superior performance of rubber tools can be explained by the fact that the rubber warms up slightly during use, providing additional traction that gives just enough grip to pull the loose hair from the coat.

Rubber mitts fit onto your hand like a large glove and they generally have two different surfaces. One side has longer, softer nipples for use on the slightly longer coats of breeds like the Labrador or dogs with little muscle cover. The other side has dumpy, firmer nipples for use on shorter-coated, more muscular dogs like the Staffordshire Bull Terrier.

Rubber sponge brushes often have nipples on one side and a dense rubber pad on the other. The textured side removes the hair and the pad is used to remove any dander that has come to the surface.

Rubber mitts and pads are used in a circular motion. Working forward towards the head and against the coat growth has the greatest effect on coat removal. Some dogs may object to this, however, especially if they have very sensitive skin. If this is the case, start behind the head and work your circles with the lie of the coat. Either way, the action benefits the dog in three ways:

◆ you are lifting the coat to get at the under hairs.
◆ you are removing dead skin cells (dander).
◆ you are massaging the dog, encouraging blood flow to the skin and facilitating the removal of toxins.

The technique is easy to learn but new groomers need to take it steady as their shoulder muscles are unlikely to be prepared for what is satisfying but very hard work! Groomers with small hands may find the mitts too big to be comfortable and may prefer to use a pad instead.

Rubber brushes are not quite as good at the job as you cannot use them in a circular motion. They work by brushing the hair against the coat growth. They have a handle attached to a pad of nipples and are perhaps a better option for those groomers with restricted shoulder or elbow movement.

> ### CLEANING AND MAINTENANCE OF RUBBER MITTS AND PADS
>
> *After every use, remove hair that has collected between the nipples, and then wash the mitts and pads in warm soapy water to remove grease. Rinse well and then leave to dry. Once dry, they should be placed in an ultraviolet light sterilizing cabinet to ensure they are safe to use on another dog. Liquid sterilizers may cause the rubber to perish.*

Both pads and brushes can be used effectively in either hand. The mitt, however, may need to be used on both hands by both left- and right-handed operators because the nipples on each side perform differently. Using a mitt can be hard work and the advantage of learning to use both hands means that your shoulders share the workload!

10.5 BRUSHES

> *The next stage after removing the loose hair is to break up the coat further so that the hairs start to separate. We do this using one of a variety of brushes to suit the coat we are working with. On some breeds, such as a Poodle with a short coat, only one type of brush – the slicker – is needed, but on others, like a Cocker Spaniel, you may need to use a slicker to break up the long feathering on the legs and a softer bristle brush on the shorter body coat to bring up a shine. The length of the coat you are working with also has a bearing on the length of the pins your brush needs to be able to work its way through the length and density of the coat.*

Slicker brushes

These brushes (*see* Figs 10.5.1 and 10.5.2) are designed to open up the coat by separating the individual hairs, whilst at the same time stretching the hairs to remove kinks and curls. They are sometimes called carding brushes.

Fig. 10.5.1   A basic
slicker brush, with a
user friendly handle
and medium length
metal pins that are suited to most coated breeds.

Fig. 10.5.2   This
slicker has longer
pins to help the
groomer penetrate
longer coats.

The slicker is the most commonly used brush and is generally used on all coat types except perhaps the long silken show coats of breeds such as Yorkshire Terriers or Afghan Hounds. That said, even these coats can be groomed with a soft slicker brush, providing it is used carefully.

Traditionally, these brushes have a rectangular head fitted with a rubber cushion pad that holds fine metal wire-like pins, all bending towards the handle. The handle is made of either wood or plastic, and there are various different designs, all of which feel quite different in the hand. Slicker brushes are available in a variety of sizes and pin length to cater for the size of dog and coat density. The length and thickness of the pins determines the 'drag' on the brush, which can range from soft or gentle to quite firm. The firmer brushes may appear harsh or unkind to the new groomer but they are often needed on very thick coats, such as that on a full-coated Chow Chow or a densely coated Standard Poodle. They do, however, need to be used properly so they don't cause abrasions on the skin (brush burns). It should also be pointed out that the bigger and stronger the brush, the more drag there will be on the wrist and elbow of the operator.

The slicker has recently been redesigned to have a reversible, flexible head with straight pins on one side and bent pins on the other. This design may be more suited to groomers with restricted wrist or elbow movement. There is also an excellent version with extra-long pins allowing better penetration of longer coats.

Fig. 10.5.3   A curved head slicker produces less drag on the coat and less strain on the wrist of the operator.

When buying a slicker there are a few things you need to consider:

◆ The size of brush you need and whether you need it to be gentle or firm.

CAUTION: BE CAREFUL HOW YOU USE YOUR SLICKER

In order to avoid damaging the dog's skin, the slicker must be used with the pad FLAT on the coat to use all the pins together. The pins are bent towards the handle and if you tip the brush so that you are only using the pins on the outside edge, they will bend in the opposite direction and dig into the skin. Before you use a slicker for the first time, try the technique – and the wrong technique – on the palm of your hand.

Fig. 10.5.4   This damaged slicker brush should not be used. The pins are not all bent and facing in the same direction. The pins on this brush can badly scratch the dog's skin, leaving it vulnerable to infection and disease.

Check the pins before each use. If they are damaged, the brush should not be used (see Fig. 10.5.4). Brushing too firmly, or for too long, over the same area can cause brush burns, particularly on areas that are not protected by body fat like the hock and lower legs for instance. You should always monitor the dog and its skin for signs of trauma whilst you are brushing and stop if the skin becomes reddened or sore.

◆ What shaped handle feels most comfortable for you to use.
◆ Whether you are physically comfortable using a fixed head slicker or whether a flexible head would be more suitable for you.

To use the slicker brush correctly, you separate the coat in layers and work either up or down the body, brushing from the root of the hair to the tip. When one layer is completed, you separate an adjoining layer and repeat the brushing process. This method allows the operator to separate the dog's hair without too much drag on the coat. Excessive drag can cause trauma to the skin of the dog or strain to the groomer's joints.

When brushing the coat downwards, it is best to hold the brush like a lollipop in your hand with the pins facing the dog. When brushing the coat against the coat growth, it is better to hold the brush upside down, with the handle between your fingers and the pad in the palm of your hand with the pins still facing the dog. This reduces joint strain for the operator and doesn't restrict the groomers' view of the skin (see Fig. 10.5.3). Slicker brushes are suitable for left- or right-handed use.

Pin brushes

These are sometimes called porcupine brushes because they resemble a porcupine with its spikes sticking rigidly upright on its back (*see* Figs 10.5.5a-b). They are generally used on delicate coats or coats that are not having the undercoat removed. They look very much like a standard human hair brush and are manufactured from either plastic or wood. The rigid pins are set into a rubber cushion pad and are usually spaced quite far apart. The idea is that they separate the coat without removing any hair, although on a moulting coat there will be some hair collection. These brushes are not ideal for dogs with matted or knotted coats as they are not able to break through the density of the wadding to remove the problem. They do, however, work well on mat-free, heavy, double-coated breeds, like the Pomeranian and the Samoyed, if used regularly. You often see show dog handlers at the ring side using these brushes on double-coated breeds to lift the coat from the body and give it volume, without removing even the loosest of hair.

The easiest way to use a pin brush is to turn the dog so that it is facing away from you. Start behind the back

Fig.10.5.5a-b Pin brushes or porcupine brushes with handles (left) are better for using on coats that are brushed towards the dog's head (Pekingese), whereas the palm brush (right) is more suited to coats brushed towards the tail (Briard). The palm brush produces less drag as it works through the dense coat to lay it flat.

of the head and work from one shoulder across the back to the opposite shoulder, brushing the coat in layers forward towards the head. Work down the body layer after layer until you reach the tail and the knickers. The tail can also be brushed in layers upwards towards the tail root. The knickers are similarly brushed in layers, one side at a time, by using a wrist flicking motion (flicking the wrist towards you as if you were whipping cream), known as whipping up the coat. Once the dog has had a good shake, the coat will settle back into place.

This is a lovely way to make a double coat look full and well groomed with a minimum of effort from the groomer. It is only suitable, though, for well-groomed double coats. There are no adaptations to the design of the pin brush to cater for mobility problems but the method of using the brush requires very little in the way of excessive joint movement for the operator. It is suitable for right- or left-handed use.

Bobble brushes

Bobble brushes (*see* Fig. 10.5.6) are a modified pin brush. They are generally of the same design and made from the same materials. The difference is that each pin is topped with a 'bobble' of plastic. The idea is that the pins are less damaging to very fine soft coats and that the skin on breeds with little or no undercoat is protected. The Yorkshire Terrier is a good example of a breed that has a coat that often benefits from the use of a bobble brush. The coat is very fine and often the sparsely protected skin is visible.

The bobbles can occasionally get caught up in long hair so for this reason the bobble brush should only be used in a downward motion, working with the hair growth rather than against it. This type of brush is not ideal for use on double coats or wool coats as the bob-

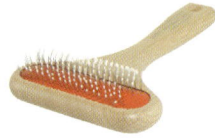

Fig. 10.5.6 A flat wooden-handled bobble brush, showing the flexible pad holding the pins. The pin heads are coated with a 'bobble' of resin to protect the skin on fine-coated breeds such as the Yorkshire Terrier.

bles do tend to 'snag' and get caught up in the coat, but you can give it a try, as long as you go carefully. Bobble brushes are suitable for right- or left-handed use.

Bristle and part-bristle brushes

Pure bristle brushes (*see* Fig. 10.5.7) are very expensive and difficult to find, but this is one area where you may not be able to find a cheaper alternative. It is a type of brush that would probably not be used in a commercial capacity as they tend to be bought for a specific dog – usually a show dog. The brushes are generally of two designs; one is a handled brush with or without a rubber cushion pad fitted into the head to hold the bristles, and the other is a round brush that is held in the palm of the hand and is called a palm brush. They are available in different sizes to suit your breed and your hand size. The bristles are derived from the hair of the boar or wild pig, and as they work through the coat they condition the hair with natural oils. Because of this, they are most suited to silk-coated breeds that are groomed so that their hair falls sleek and smooth.

Part-bristle brushes are a cheaper option and will be more useful to you, particularly if you plan to work commercially. They are available in the same designs as the pure bristle but are a combination of bristle and nylon, or bristle and pin (see Fig. 10.5.8). The nylon bristles or metal pins help to

remove mats and wadding in the coat, breaking it up into single strands of hair, which are then conditioned by the boar bristles.

Fig.10.5.7 A pure bristle brush.

Fig. 10.5.8 A bristle and pin brush.

These brushes are generally used in the same way as pin brushes, by turning the dog away from you and brushing the coat forward in layers. After completing the groom through, the coat is then brushed following the coat growth to produce a sleek finish. The nylon in these brushes can occasionally cause static in the coat but generally the oil from the natural bristle is enough to counteract this. They are suitable for left- and right-handed use.

Nylon brushes

Nylon brushes are available in the same designs and sizes as the aforementioned brushes. They can be effective and have the advantage of being considerably cheaper than the bristle

> ### CAUTION: STATIC
>
> *The static build-up caused by nylon brushes not only makes the coat difficult to manage, it can also cause a cracking or snapping noise and has been known to produce mild electric shocks. These mild shocks are random and unlikely to do any damage to the dog but they could alarm him, so be careful not to be bitten.*
>
> *The problem can be avoided by ensuring that the nylon bristles are damp; whilst you are working, periodically wet the brush with water and tap it on a towel to get rid of any drips.*

or part-bristle brushes. The major disadvantage with pure nylon brushes is that they can produce a lot of static in the coat, which may make the grooming of silk coats very difficult, particularly if you are working under a hairdryer where the static generated by the drying process further compounds the problem.

Nylon brushes are used in the same way as pin, bobble, bristle or part-bristle brushes, and are suitable for left- and right-handed use.

Combination brushes

Combination brushes (*see* Fig. 10.5.9) are two brushes sitting back to back on one handle. They have nylon bristles on one side and metal pins on the other, both set into rubber cushion pads. These brushes are very popular with pet owners as it means they do not have to buy more than one brush. Each brush works as effectively as its singular counterpart and, like the others, the combination brush comes in different sizes to suit the size of your dog and your hand size. These brushes are often used by commercial groomers but they have a slight disadvantage in that they are bulky and, when you are concentrating on the brushing movement with the bristle side, the pins are facing in the opposite direction and can get tangled in the coat.

Fig. 10.5.9 Combination brushes effectively offer two brushes on one handle. These are perhaps favoured more by pet owners and show dog owners.

The combination brush is used in the same manner as its singular counterparts, and is suitable for left- and right-handed use.

Terrier pads

Terrier pads (*see* Fig. 10.5.10) are included here because they are used for brushing the dog, although we do not refer to them as 'brushes'. The terrier pad is a rubber pad containing metal pins that sits in the palm of your hand. It is used to flatten the coats on wire-coated breeds by brushing following the coat growth. They can only be used in one direction and work in the same way as the slicker brush, by separating the individual hairs so that they lie evenly. There is no reason not to use a terrier pad in a commercial environment, although the slicker is more adaptable as it can be used either with or against the coat growth. For the pet owner with a terrier it is a very rewarding tool to use as the design requires you to stroke the dog, which is always enjoyable and makes for good bonding time.

Fig. 10.5.10 A terrier palm pad works like a slicker but allows the groomer to contour the dog's body whilst using the brush.

> ### CLEANING AND MAINTENANCE OF BRUSHES
>
> *Brushes and terrier pads should be cleaned free of hair after every use and checked for loose or damaged pins. They should be washed in warm soapy water to remove grease and well rinsed before being left to dry. Once dry, place them in an ultraviolet light sterilizer. Using a liquid sterilizer may rot or rust the pins or bristles.*

> ### CAUTION
>
> *Washing alone is not sufficient to stop the spread of disease. Bacterial and fungal organisms are not killed by soap and water and can develop at the base of pin and bristle shafts and within damaged areas of the rubber pads so sterilization is absolutely necessary.*

To use the terrier pad, secure the strap around your hand and 'stroke' the dog in a smooth motion following the direction of the coat growth. It is suitable for left- and right-handed use.

10.6 DE-MATTING TOOLS

> *Some groomers use these tools before they brush the dog, whilst others prefer to brush first, but either way these are the tools that split up, separate and remove knots and tangles from the coat. These tools are arguably the most dangerous tools that groomers use. The nature of the tool means that it is designed to get rid of difficult and sometimes very dense wadding; this is achieved by cutting through and slicing the hair so that it can be removed. All of these tools therefore possess very sharp blades and need to be handled with care and used with caution.*

There are several designs of de-matter and three different techniques for using them, depending on your chosen tool.

Basically the designs have either short blades, long blades or singular blades. Each of these is available with a straight handle or an ergonomic handle, so again you need to consider your physical ability when making your choice. 'In the trade' each different design has its own name, as explained below; they all come under the heading of de–matting tools, however, because that is what they do.

Mat breakers

This is the name used for tools with short teeth that are used on medium-length coats (*see* Fig. 10.6.1). They have a series of sharp, hooked blades that slice through the mat or knot and remove it by hooking it out of the coat. Mat breakers are designed with either a plastic, wooden or rubberized handle and, just like the Coat King®, come in a variety of blade sizes; they are not, however, available as an ergonomic design. The handles are straight, with a thumb rest or resting place indented into the handle. The handles vary in diameter so again make sure the model you select is comfortable in your hand.

To use a mat breaker, hold it firmly in your hand with your thumb on the guard or in the thumb rest groove.

Fig. 10.6.1   A short-toothed mat breaker suitable for medium-length coats.

Fig. 10.6.2   The mat master has longer curved blades for working longer coats. The ergonomic handle gives a dragging action rather than a combing action, and the serrated blades saw rather than slide through the coat.

Once you have located the knot, hold the hair above the knot out of the way with your other arm or hand. The blades of the mat breaker are inserted behind the knot. A sawing motion can be achieved by rolling your wrist such that the tool cuts through the matted hair. The tool can be taken out and repositioned if necessary, whilst at the same time gently pulling the knot towards you. The blades will cut the knot and split it into manageable pieces, a process that can be further aided by manually teasing out the knot. Final removal of the knot is achieved by repeating the process or by means of a slicker brush.

The blades of the mat breaker, although curled into themselves, have blunt ends and are therefore unlikely to cut the dog. They do, however, pose a danger to you. Injuries may be sustained when failure to use the thumb rest results in the tool rotating in towards the hand as the tool leaves the coat.

LEFT-HANDED?

This tool is manufactured with the cutting edge of the blades facing in one direction only and it is usually marketed in the position used by right-handed operators. The blade unit can be removed by a simple screw, usually found in the centre front of the tool. The blade unit can then be turned around to face the other way, thereby making it suitable for left-handed use. If the tool has a thumb guard, simply swivel it over to the other side of the tool, then replace and tighten the screw.

Mat Masters

An adaptation of the mat breaker, Mat Masters (see Fig. 10.6.2) have the same shaped blades fitted into an ergonomic handle. The Mat Master is suitable for groomers with restricted mobility. The handle is quite chunky, making it easy to hold.

To use the Mat Master, first locate the knot and expose it by holding the rest of the hair away with your supporting arm or hand. Insert the blades of the Mat Master into the back of the knot and drag it towards you gently. This tool works with a raking action rather than a rolling action. The Mat Master will not rotate in your hand because of the handle design. It can, however, cut into your supporting hand if you are pulling hard and you allow the tool to come away from the coat with force. It is suitable for both left- and right-handed use.

De-matting comb

This is the name we use for the long-toothed tools, which are used to de-mat long coats (see Fig. 10.6.3). The de-matting comb has a series of long serrated blades mounted on a straight handle. The tool is fitted with a thumb guard, whilst the blades are blunt ended but not curved. They are designed to saw through the matted fur and separate the wadding into manageable pieces for brushing. The handles come in designs varying from slim to chunky, and can be wooden, plastic or rubberized, so try holding them before you buy so that you find one that is comfortable for you to use.

Fig. 10.6.3   The de-matting comb has long serrated blades for working long coats. They are used with a sawing motion to reduce the drag when removing large knots and wadding.

To use, hold the de-matting comb firmly in your hand with your thumb on the guard. Once you have located the knot, use your supporting hand to hold back the hair to keep the knot exposed, and insert the de-matting comb behind

the knot. Use a sawing action to slice through the knot and at the same time pull the tool gently towards you. The tool will come out of the coat. Look at the knot and decide whether you need to repeat the process or whether the knot has been broken up enough to be brushed out.

This tool is marketed ready for use by right-handed operators, but it is manufactured so that it can be reversed. Release the screw at the end of the blades (it doesn't have to be removed) and rotate the blades and the thumb guard until they are facing the other way. Tighten the screw securely. It is now ready for use.

Single-blade mat splitters

These are excellent little tools for getting into tricky areas like behind the ears or between the toes (see Fig. 10.6.4). They consist of a very sharp honed steel blade that is fitted into a protective cover. There are two designs for this tool; one has a handle with the blade set at right angles (like a scythe), and the other is set onto a flat holding case. Both designs make use of a tapered guide to protect the dog; this extends beyond the blade so that the tool can slide into the coat safely.

Fig. 10.6.4   The single-blade mat splitter picks its way through knots.

When using the handled tool, hold it firmly in your hand. Insert the blade, tapered end first, into the coat behind the knot. Hold the hair behind the knot against the skin with your fingers; this helps to neutralize any pull on the individual hairs that make up the knot and thus prevents tugs being transmitted to the skin, which is then at risk of becoming sore. The blade should then be pulled firmly but not roughly towards you. To use the design with the holding case, a similar technique is used but with the tool held between the thumb and the first finger. The process can be repeated several times until the knot or mat is sufficiently broken up to respond to brushing.

This tool is suitable for both left- and right-handed use.

CAUTION: EXTREME CARE IS REQUIRED WHEN USING THESE TOOLS

De-matting tools are invaluable and essential to the work of the groomer but they are very dangerous and can cause deep, nasty cuts if they are not used correctly. Make sure you use the thumb rests and guards if the tool is fitted with them.

It is essential that the blades are kept sharp so that you are not tempted to use them with extra force. They should not be used if the blades are rusty.

When not in use, store them in a safe place where they cannot do any harm and NEVER leave them on the grooming table.

CLEANING AND MAINTENANCE OF DE-MATTING TOOLS

After use, check the blades for damage. Wash in warm soapy liquid and rinse well. Dry your de-matter by tapping it on a rolled-up towel and leave it somewhere safe to dry. Once dry, it can be placed in an ultraviolet light sterilizer. If you are using a liquid sterilizer, dry your de-matter well before storing or using on another dog.

Do not store it unprotected in a grooming trolley, grooming case or grooming box, where it could cause harm when you put your hand in to retrieve tools: sooner or later you will forget to look and cut yourself.

10.7 COMBS

Once the undercoat and any mats have been removed, the next stage is to comb the coat to break it up and separate it further. Combs are used a lot from this stage forward so it is essential that you buy robust and effective combs that are comfortable to use and do not make your hands sore. Some combs have very pointed teeth and can damage the dog's skin if they are used too harshly, so beware of this when you are using them.

Combs basically have two purposes: to divide the individual hairs, leaving them free of knots and tangles; and to arrange the hair and comb it 'into place'. It sounds simple enough but the choice of combs available is phenomenal. All combs are suitable for either left- or right-handed use.

Combs are available in four grades of tooth spacing, extra fine, fine, medium and wide, and in different tooth lengths. They can also be purchased as combinations where two different tooth spacings are available, either back-to-back or side-by-side, on the one shaft or spine. Some have two different, alternating, tooth lengths, and some have rotating teeth. They can be made of metal, plastic or wood, and have either a rake handle, a straight handle or no handle at all. They come in different shaft (or spine) lengths. They can be treated with an anti-static coating. Lastly, they come in all sorts of different colours – the choice is yours!

Tooth spacing – what's the difference?

The wider the spacing between the teeth, the more hairs go through each gap. After brushing a coat through to remove knots and debris, you should use a wide-toothed comb to break down the coat further, followed by a medium-grade comb to break it down further still. This ensures that the coat is completely groomed out before being bathed; this can be achieved with either two combs with differently spaced teeth (*see* Figs 10.7.1a-b) or a single comb that has different spacings at either end (*see* Fig. 10.7.2).

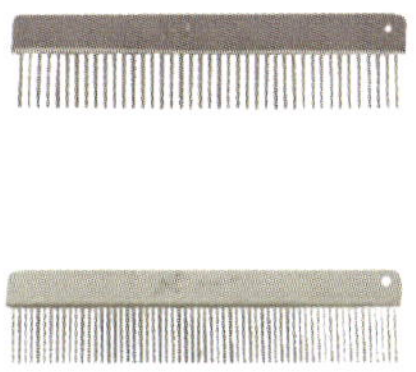

Fig. 10.7.1a-b You need a coarse comb and a medium comb.

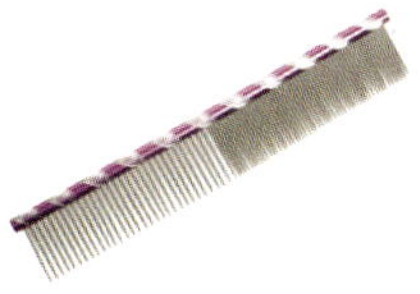

Fig. 10.7.2 An alternative to using two combs is to use a combination comb that has two different width combs side by side on one spine. These are sometimes called 'greyhound' combs.

CAUTION: FINE COMBS

Be careful when using a fine comb on a dirty coat. The individual hairs will be thicker than they are when clean and the comb may pull the coat out, possibly causing trauma to the skin in the process.

Once the dog has been bathed and dried, the coat is prepared for styling by combing with a medium comb followed by a fine comb. At this stage the coat is totally separated into individual hairs and there should be no sign of clusters of hairs or tangling. Fine combs are often referred to as finishing combs. They are generally not used on dirty coats because hairs coated with grease and dust are too thick to pass comfortably through the tooth gaps. Once the coat is clean, however, a fine comb will slide through easily, disentangling any missed hairs.

Extra fine combs are often referred to as flea combs because they are used to remove fleas and flea eggs from the coat. These combs are not suitable for general grooming as they are too fine and can pull the hair out, leaving the skin sore.

Tooth lengths

The length of tooth needed depends on the length of coat being groomed. Medium-length coats on terriers or spaniels require a tooth length of about 2–2.5cm, whereas the longer coat of the Old English Sheepdog or Briard may need a comb with teeth 3.5cm in length. The longer the tooth, the more 'drag' there is on the comb as it works its way through the coat. This may put more strain on the wrists of the groomer and create more pull on the skin of the dog.

Handles

As with other tools, the choice of handles or no handles depends on the mobility of your wrists and whether you suffer from restricted use of your hands. *Straight-handled combs* (see Figs 10.7.3a-b) can have either a metal, rubber, plastic or wooden handle that provides you with varying degrees of comfort in a closed hand position. The chunkier the handle, the more comfortable you may find the comb to use. Metal handles are narrower and, by nature, are harder in composition so they can not only be uncomfortable in the hand but can also be tiring to use over a long period because of the tighter grip needed. They require a flicking rolling wrist action so are not always suited to persons with restricted wrist movement.

Fig. 10.7.3a-b You may prefer to use a handled comb. There are various different-shaped handles to choose from so try them out to see which design is most comfortable in your hand.

Rake-handled combs (see Fig. 10.7.4) have the teeth set across the handle, making an ergonomic 'T' shape. They usually have wooden or plastic chunky handles for comfort and are very helpful to those with restricted wrist or elbow action. They are easily used in a downward raking action but are difficult to use if you want, or need, to lift the hair against the coat growth, as is sometimes required when styling. If you need to use this design of comb you should practise 'lifting' the coat against the growth so that you can find a technique that suits you and your mobility.

Fig. 10.7.4 An ergo-dynamic handle makes this comb useful for those with restricted wrist movement. The comb also doubles up as a rake.

Combs without handles (compare Figs 10.7.1a-b and 10.7.2) have the teeth inserted into a metal shank that is held in the hand. The size of the shank can vary from very small and flat to large and round with a circumference up to 2–3cms; you need to hold them in your hand to see which is most suited to you. Sometimes a small shank can give the groomer wrist ache or cramp in the palm of the hand, especially if the comb is in use for a long period of time. These combs are very popular with groomers as they are light in the hand, easy to use and are available as combinations of two different tooth spacings. This last advantage provides the groomer with a dual-purpose comb. The handle-less comb can also be purchased in different shank length for use on small, medium or large dogs and of course different coat lengths. The point you need to consider here is that the longer the comb, the more drag it will produce through the coat, which may be difficult if you have wrist or joint problems.

Single, combination or double?

Combination combs are available either with handles or without handles (see Fig. 10.7.2), but they are not currently available as rakes. Your choice of comb largely depends on whether you are buying it for use only on your own dog (and how much hair it has) or whether you are planning on doing a wide range of dogs. For your own dog, you may get away with a double comb that has a coarse comb and a medium-width comb back to back on one spine (see Fig. 10.7.5). Alternatively, you may prefer to purchase a combination comb that has two different tooth spacings at either end of the spine.

If you are planning to work commercially, you will need all three tooth spacings, either as individual combs or as combinations to suit you.

Fig. 10.7.5 A double comb with a different comb on either side of the spine. These combs are often favoured by pet groomers who do not require a large selection of tools.

Alternating tooth length combs (moulting combs)

These combs are manufactured with two different tooth lengths, with the idea that the shorter teeth comb through the undercoat whilst the longer teeth comb through the topcoat (see Fig. 10.7.6). They are available in fine, medium or coarse spacing and always have a handle, which is made from either wood or plastic and is usually quite chunky in the hand. The nature of the combing action on both topcoat and undercoat together does mean that these combs can have quite a drag on the coat, particularly if they are being used to remove undercoat. Prolonged use of such combs can therefore prove very tiring for the groomer and care must be taken not to strain the wrist and hand.

Fig. 10.7.6 A comb with teeth of alternating lengths helps to groom away any remaining hairs from a moulting coat after brushing has been completed. Note: this comb has teeth that are two different lengths but it does not serve the same purpose as using a coarse comb followed by a medium-toothed comb when grooming out the coat.

Rotating toothed combs

These are excellent combs to help take the strain out of grooming out undercoats and matting. The rotating teeth are set into either a handled or a straight shaft and roll their way through the coat as you are combing. They are gentle on the dog and gentle on your wrist, but are really only suitable for grooming out. Because of the rolling action, they are not suited to whipping up a coat to make it light and fluffy for styling, so you still need a fixed tooth comb for this purpose.

Composition

The teeth and the shanks of nearly all combs are made of either steel or a metal alloy. The differences have quite a bearing on the suitability, weight and strength of the comb.

Which comb you choose should depend firstly on how comfortable it is for you to use and, secondly, on your reasons for buying the comb (i.e. what you intend using it for). Prices can vary considerably. Always make sure that the comb you choose is well made and does not have any rough or sharp edges.

Anti-static combs are coated with Teflon to eliminate static build-up in the coat and may be a good option to consider.

Using combs

All combs are used by inserting the teeth at the base of the hair and pulling the comb gently towards you. For general grooming out the comb is used in a downward motion following the natural growth direction of the coat. On long-coated breeds, it is easiest to start at the feet and work upwards. Use one hand to lift the coat upwards and comb the underlying hair downwards. Keep lifting and combing, and by working up the legs towards the body, and working the body coat in the same way towards the head, you will get a good view of the skin and the hair roots and be able to see any tangles or knots at the base of the coat.

> **CAUTION**
>
> *If you are teaching yourself, make sure that you comb the coat from the root or base as the majority of knots begin further along the hair shaft and you need to get behind the knot to remove it. With long or dense coats, it is very easy to miss the first couple of centimetres of coat growth when combing and overlook the tangles by only combing the ends of the hair.*

Back combing

Sometimes, when a coat is being prepared for styling and scissoring, the coat has to be encouraged to stand away from the body so that an even cut can be executed. This is done mainly, but not exclusively, on wool coats. We call this lifting or 'whipping up' the coat because it is done by using the wrist in a whipping action (as if you were whipping cream in a bowl).

Start by inserting the comb about 1cm from the lowest point of the leg. Pull the comb towards you in a downward motion until the comb is about halfway along the length of the hair, then turn the comb by flicking your wrist so that the points of the teeth are facing you. Then, keeping the wrist still, move your hand and the comb in an upwards motion; this will stretch the hair against the growth direction and leave it fluffy. Reinsert the comb about 1cm higher up the leg from our starting point, repeat the action and keep going. Eventually, with practice, you will be able to do this with a rhythmical whipping action of the wrist.

Alternating tooth length combs are not suitable for use as styling combs as they do not lift the coat evenly, and rotating toothed combs do not stretch the coat sufficiently. These combs should therefore only be used for grooming out.

> **CLEANING AND MAINTENANCE OF COMBS**
>
> *Check the teeth for damage. Wash combs in warm soapy water after use and sterilize by ultraviolet light. Alternatively, if using liquid sterilizing solutions, rinse and dry well before storing or using on another dog.*

10.8 TROLLEYS AND GROOMING BOXES

> *Where you keep your tools is going to depend on whether you are a pet groomer or a commercial groomer, and whether you are working at home, in a salon or in a mobile unit. The most important factor is that your tools need to be kept safe, whilst remaining accessible.*

For the pet groomer, grooming bags are available (see Fig. 10.8.1) or you may prefer to have a simple tack tray, plastic tool tray or plastic box. Whatever you choose, it is wise to have a lid on it: this helps to keep dirt, water and humidity out. You should also be able to wash it out easily.

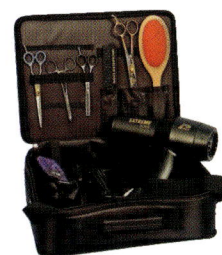

Fig. 10.8.1 For the occasional groomer, or the groomer who occasionally needs to groom away from the salon, a canvas tool case holds everything that you need and is easily washed out.

Mobile groomers, or those wanting to use their equipment at shows, should opt for a metal carrying case, which offers the best protection for travelling. There are many to choose from; all are lightweight and have either carry straps or handles. Make sure that it has adequate holding points or compartments to prevent your equipment from moving and that it has somewhere to hold any liquids such as blade or clipper oil that you may need to take with you (see Fig. 10.8.2).

Fig. 10.8.2 An excellent travel bag for mobile groomers: it is robust, lightweight and roomy.

For the commercial salon there are several designs of trolley to choose from. Make sure that you are comfortable with the layout and the depth of the drawers. The design should allow

Fig. 10.8.3 In a commercial salon a trolley on wheels is invaluable for moving between tables. It keeps your tables free of equipment and keeps your tools safe.

the trolley to be easily cleaned out and any hair accumulating around the wheels and casters should be easily removed (*see* Fig. 10.8.3).

It is worth spending a little bit of time choosing your tool boxes or trolleys because it can be frustrating if your tools are not readily available when you are busy.

NOTE: TRANSPORTING SCISSORS AND BLADES

Scissors and blades do not travel well. If you intend using your equipment away from home, it is wise to invest in a proper scissor case or wallet, and a blade box for your blades.

10.9 STERILIZING EQUIPMENT

If you are working commercially, you must sterilize your equipment between dogs. Which method you use is not as important as making sure that you make the time to do it. Sterilizing your equipment is essential to prevent the risk of diseases spreading in your grooming room and amongst the dogs visiting your salon. So consider your options carefully as some methods take longer than others. There are two ways to do this, either by ultraviolet (UV) light or using a sterilizing solution.

Ultraviolet light (UV) sterilizing cabinets (*see* Fig. 10.9.1)

These cabinets are by far the easiest way to do this job and they have the advantage that they kill most, if not all, micro-organisms. The unit does not heat up so it cannot burn any of your equipment, and you do not have to wait for the cabinet to reach a certain

temperature before it sterilizes, so it is quick to set up. User manuals on each product advise you on the recommended time for sterilizing equipment but it is generally around 30 minutes. The equipment is ready for use as soon as it comes out of the sterilizer.

Fig. 10.9.1 An ultraviolet (UV) sterilizing cabinet.

Other advantages of sterilizing cabinets are that they do not leave any residue on the equipment, and they need very little maintenance except the odd vacuum cleaning to remove any loose hairs that may have collected. The ultraviolet bulbs are easy to replace and last a very long time. As the unit does not heat up, electricity consumption is minimal, and there is no risk of corrosion or damp damage to grooming equipment as no liquids are involved.

The disadvantages are that they are not cheap to buy, so the pet owner may not find them cost-effective, and they will not work if there is a power failure.

NOTE: STERILIZE ALL SURFACES

To be effective the light has to reach all surfaces. This means that equipment such as scissors need to be open when placed in the cabinet and turned over so that the light can reach the other side. Brushes, combs and de-matters also need to be turned over.

Ultraviolet light scanners (*see* Fig. 10.9.2) are an adaptation of the UV sterilizing cabinet. This battery-operated scanner claims to kill 99.99 per cent of bacteria and viruses, including salmonella, MRSA, H5N1 (bird flu) and E coli. This little machine operates on a

Fig. 10.9.2 The NANO UV light scanner claims to kill 99.99 per cent of bacteria and viruses within ten seconds, making it a useful appliance for scanning grooming tunics and shoes as well as tables and equipment.

ten-second timer and works by killing germs as it scans an area.

The UV scanner can be very useful for the grooming salon and also for the pet owner. It is very reasonably priced and does all that the sterilizing cabinet can do. It is worth remembering, though, that the machine is only as good as the person operating it, so any area not scanned will not be treated. As with any piece of equipment, the manufacturer's instructions should be studied and carefully followed. Particular attention should be paid to any scientific control studies demonstrating the efficacy of such equipment and their limitations.

Sterilizing solutions

These are disinfectants (*see* Chapter 7) that are useful for combs, scissors, blades and forceps if used in a container. They are effective and, once made up to the correct dilution, can be made readily available in the busy grooming room. The concentration and prescribed contact time should be noted on any container.

They are reasonably cheap to purchase and some contain rust inhibitors that help to protect your equipment. The disadvantages are that these solutions cannot be used on electrical equipment, clothes or shoes, and brushes may not fare very well as bristles and rubber both deteriorate when wet. Care must also be taken to dry combs and blades well before using them on a dog with sensitive skin that may react to the disinfectant. Sterilizing solutions are useful for the mobile groomer and they do work in power cuts!

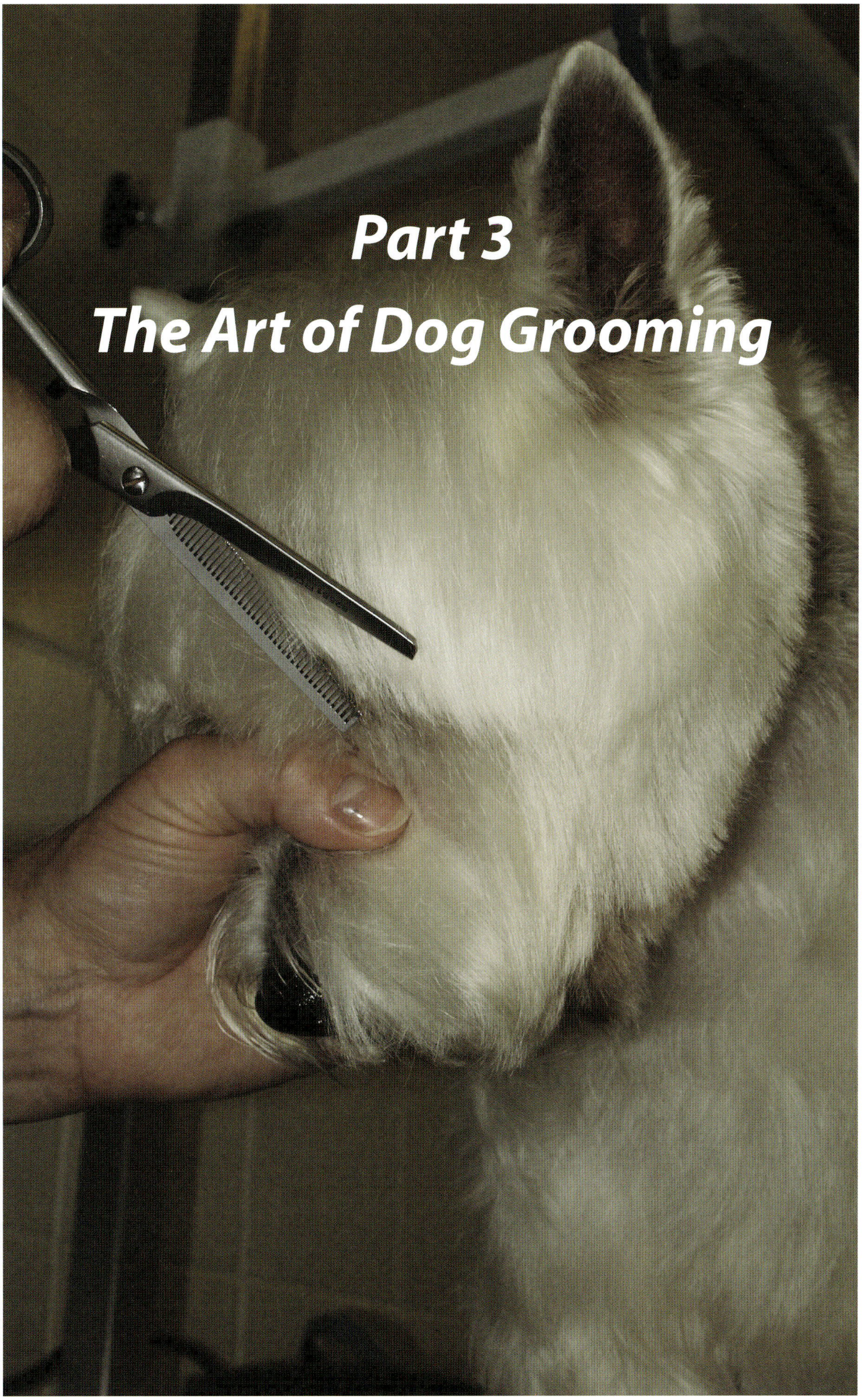

Part 3
The Art of Dog Grooming

Groomers are artists! A professional groomer is skilled and practised in the art of sculpting and uses imagination and sensitivity to create a work of beauty from a raw material, namely the coat of the dog. Artistry can be defined as a fusion of technical skills: essentially this is where all your many technical skills come together in practice to create a quality piece of work. Proficiency in each of the skills must be developed first, however. This section is all about practice and is very much the fun bit!

In this section you will learn how to take care of the dog's coat and how to use your tools to create or sculpture your own unique piece of 'art'. I say unique because you will never create two pieces the same. Every dog you present will be different, and every time you present that same dog the results will be different (even smooth coats will look different, as you will see later on!). It is for this reason that I have refused to include an 'it must look like this' breed styling section in this book. The piece of art that you will create will depend on too many factors to put dogs into such precise categories.

I am not suggesting that you do not need to know how a breed should be presented. Learning about the variety of breeds will help you to recognize what a pedigree dog is expected to look like and, once you have mastered the use of your tools, you will be able to present each breed according to the specified criteria/requirements. As a commercial groomer, you are, however, more likely to style dogs according to the owner's requirements and lifestyle, and their choice may be nothing like the recognized breed presentation. The owners are paying the bills so, as long as you meet their requirements, you will have the freedom to use your imagination and creativity to place your own personal stamp on the grooming and styling of your subjects. This is why grooming is such fun. You can create whatever you want as long as you have the coat to work with and the owner's permission to do so.

The health and temperament of the dog do have a bearing on your options but, basically, common sense should prevail and you should opt for a creation that is sympathetic to these issues, whilst taking into account the lifestyle and the general grooming requirements of the individual dog.

The only rule that you must abide by is that the health and welfare of the dog must take priority at all times.

This section follows through the grooming process from stage to stage, although there are no hard and fast rules that dictate when you should perform these tasks. This is because they are tasks that should be and can be done regularly either during grooming or in between grooms. It therefore makes sense to give each stage its own chapter. This should help the reader locate the relevant information for each stage. At the end of this section I have included a chapter on preventative care. This is about cutting nails, cleaning teeth, cleaning ears and looking after anal sacs.

Once upon a time dogs looked after their own grooming requirements because they could. Their coats were short and dense and seasonal changes determined when the shedding of the coat was necessary. To remove his shedding or moulting coat the dog would rub himself along bushes and tree trunks or roll on his back on the grass; many dogs display similar behaviour today, except that in most cases the bushes and trees have been replaced by furniture and the grass by carpets and rugs. So, to an extent dogs have lost their grooming tools and the alternatives are not nearly as efficient. Instead of removing the coat, the substitutes produce static that encourages the hairs of the coat to cling together and form wadding or knots.

Most dogs have also lost the seasonal changes as well. Nice warm houses, double glazing and central heating mean that the dog no longer needs to keep himself warm: we do it for him. In Chapter 2 we learnt that the dog can shed or throw his coat as soon as his body temperature begins to rise. This means that every evening when the central heating comes on, there is a good chance that the dog will shed some of his coat and in the morning, when the heating goes off again, he will stop shedding. You don't even need the central heating to do this: closing the doors and windows to take the chill off the house and to stop draughts has the same effect. The fact is today's dog can experience several different environmental (*or seasonal*) changes (*temperatures*) within any 24-hour period of modern living and he just can't keep up with his grooming requirements. Owners of indoor-living Labradors and Jack Russell Terriers will be more than familiar with the amount of shed hair that needs to be vacuumed on a daily basis – sometimes more than once a day. The same dogs would not shed nearly as much, or as often, if living outside in an unheated kennel with a blanket to snuggle into when cold, but that they can wriggle out of when feeling warm again.

And then there is the bath! When dogs groomed themselves, they did not need to have a bath. As the coat shed, dirt and debris came out with it. Rivers and streams would have been useful to cool off in the heat of the summer but soap? I don't think so! Besides which, Stone Age man probably had more important things to worry about than a smelly dog outside the cave, and it is likely that the smell of the dog would help to deter predators. Now the dog lives inside the 'cave' and, rather than fending off predators, he is one of the family and included in social occasions with the neighbours so his personal hygiene is important, not so much to him but to you. It would not do to be the gossip of the neighbourhood just because the dog did not smell too healthy. In fairness though, the modern cave is fitted with expensive furnishings and carpet cleaning is costly, so it is perhaps prudent and cheaper to bath the dog regularly. And here is another thought: who is it next to you on the bed when you wake up in the morning?

And what about fashion? To stay in vogue, we have provided him with longer, thicker, fluffier or silkier 'clothes' that may look superb but, boy, are they high maintenance! In most cases a dip in the river, a game in the mud or rolling in the nearest cow-filled field fills most owners with absolute horror and probably results in perhaps the second or third bath in a week, not to mention trying to preserve the fashionable haircut!

Generally, humans are proud of their dogs and like to share their homes and their lives with them. To suit the modern environment, the dog has been developed to fit with modern trends, fashions and lifestyles and that means that, as we are responsible for modernizing him, we are also responsible for helping out with the grooming. Indeed, any fashion-conscious dog demands it!

Aesthetically, having your dog groomed may be viewed by some as a status symbol. It may also be seen as an extravagance. It is arguably both. More importantly, it is essential to the health and well-being of the dog. We made him like he is, so we have to look after him. Grooming takes time and it has to be done regularly.

Grooming your own dog is a valu-able and rewarding experience that, as well as helping to build the relationship between you, is both therapeutic and relaxing for dog and groomer alike. And, when the job is done, the soft eyes and wagging tail of the well-groomed dog are worth a thousand thank-yous.

This section covers the various stages of grooming and caring for the coat. Starting with assessing the work to be done, we will look at removing dead hair, mats and knots, removing shedding coats, bathing and drying, and finally how to use your tools to trim and style the coat.

I can explain to you, I can show you – but ... I cannot practise for you!

Learning can be hard at times but it is always satisfying to see the end results as you become more proficient. Do not get too stressed as you engage with the learning process ... this feeling of anxiety soon passes as your confidence grows. If you make a mistake, learn by it and do not do it again.

Keep yourself relaxed, practise some breathing exercises, hum a tune or sing to the radio whilst you work and remember: this is the fun bit!

11 Grooming Out the Coat

We groom dogs because we like them to look nice but there are other reasons that are often overlooked. Hair is a dead material but it is produced by living cells. It grows from the skin because it is produced by hair follicles that are part of the skin. Hair, as we learnt in Chapter 2, is grown by mammals for a range of reasons, including camouflage, insulation, protection and social communication. All hairs have fine nerve fibres at the base of the follicle that respond to stimulation; they can also be raised and moved by a set of muscle fibres (the erector pili muscle). Hairs that are knotted and tangled are not able to function normally. In such cases the dog is less able to function effectively and may be placed at a social disadvantage in the world he inhabits. The health of the dog's largest organ, the skin, may also be compromised – if the skin is suffering, so is the dog!

A well groomed coat is aesthetically pleasing to look at, but, more importantly, the process of grooming has significant health benefits for the dog. It

- *stimulates blood flow to remove toxins from the body;*
- *separates the hairs so they can be raised when needed, as well as allowing them to supply sensory information to the nervous system;*
- *removes dead coat to optimize body temperature control;*
- *removes dead coat to make way for new coat growth;*
- *removes knots and tangles to help prevent skin trauma and disease;*
- *separates individual hairs so that the coat (and the dog) can move freely; and*
- *helps with parasite control.*

Dogs are mammals and, as such, all have hair, even those that appear hairless. All dogs therefore benefit from being regularly groomed. Depending on the type of coat the dog carries, grooming routines can last from minutes to hours and may be needed on a daily or weekly basis. The health and condition of the skin should be checked before grooming begins and it should be in the same condition (or better) when you have finished grooming!

This chapter explains how to groom out the various coat types, either as part of day-to-day coat maintenance or to prepare the coat for bathing and styling. The reader is first provided with a reminder of the different 'coat types' as this has a direct bearing on grooming out. The process of grooming out the coat is then discussed in detail.

Important note

You are advised to familiarize yourself with the sections in Chapter 2 relating to the skin and its appendages (2.10) and also hair and 'coat types' (2.11). These will provide you with an understanding of the structure and behaviour of the coat. You may also want to have a quick look at Chapter 18, which focuses on the care of ears, teeth, eyes, skin folds, nails and anal sacs. These procedures can be undertaken at any time and should be carried out whenever they are required.

In this chapter we focus on grooming out the coat and so I have not included or discussed preventative care. Do bear in mind, however, that these two chapters can and do complement each other.

With the exception of a few breeds, it is usual for dogs to have two hair structures that make up the coat. The coarser hairs are called the 'topcoat' because they make up the outer covering and provide weather resistance. The hairs of the topcoat are often referred to as 'guard' hairs. The finer downy hairs are called 'undercoat' because they lie underneath and provide insulation. Undercoat hairs differ from guard hairs because they are hollow; they do not have a medulla, so air is trapped inside the hair, greatly increasing its insulation value. Largely through man's interference, there are some breeds with coat formations that do not necessarily behave as originally intended. Two examples of this are the Afghan Hound, whose coarse topcoat does not lie on the top, and the Poodle, whose undercoat does not always moult out.

For grooming purposes, we categorize all dogs under one of five different 'coat type' headings according to the structure, behaviour and grooming requirements of the coat. Groomers have named these categories 'Wire', 'Silk', 'Smooth', 'Double' and 'Wool' (with 'Corded' coats being a subcategory of the 'Wool' coat). Each coat type category includes a great variety of dogs and breeds.

The Airedale Terrier, for example, possesses a 'wire coat' because it is harsh to the touch and has a specific coat growing cycle. The very much smaller Norfolk Terrier is also in the 'wire coat' group, as is the Irish Wolfhound. These dogs have different backgrounds and hold different places in our society; they are of different sizes and shapes – but their coats are of similar texture and behave similarly, and they are therefore groomed in the same manner with the same tools.

Newcomers to grooming are often confused by the many variations within the 'coat type' categories. The differences are strongly influenced by the amount of undercoat. It is easiest

Fig. 11.0.2 The opposite extreme of the smooth coat is the Labrador Retriever. Note the longer length and the density of the hair on the neck and thighs.

to demonstrate this with the smooth coats. The Dobermann has a very short and very fine topcoat without an undercoat, and the skin is clearly visible through the topcoat, whereas the Whippet (*see* Fig. 11.0.1) has an equally fine topcoat but also possesses a very fine, sparse undercoat on the body, though very little undercoat on the lower limbs and undercarriage. The Labrador Retriever, by contrast, also has a smooth coat but the topcoat hairs are much longer and the undercoat is dense and abundant (*see* Fig. 11.0.2). The coats on these breeds range from very fine to very dense, but they are all groomed and maintained in the same way.

Before you begin grooming check the entire coat – including between the toes, between the pads, under the groin and sanitary areas, as well as any long furnishings – so that you can have

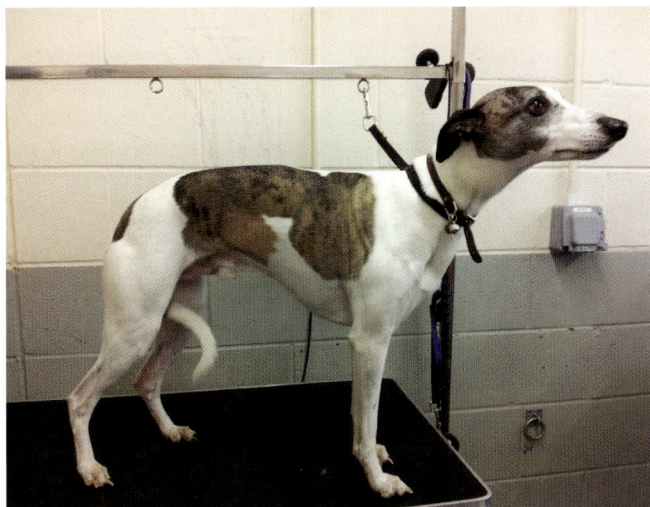

Fig. 11.0.1. The Whippet has a very fine, short, smooth coat. The coat is so fine that there are areas on the lower hind limbs, the feet and under the chest where you can often see the skin.

NOTE: GROOM FROM THE SKIN OUTWARDS

Grooming from the skin outwards towards the ends of the hairs not only allows you to monitor the skin whilst you are working, it also ensures that you have done the job properly and the coat has been separated right down to the base of the hairs.

all the tools that you need available and handy.

11.1 REMOVING THE UNDERCOAT

At some point the anagen (growing or developmental) phase of the hair growth cycle ends and gives way to the catagen phase. During this next phase each hair detaches itself from the underlying matrix from which it developed and will be held in the fol-

licle only by friction. Such hairs are thus no longer anchored, and fall out easily. This applies to both guard hairs and undercoat hairs and it is true of all dogs. In fact it happens to all mammals. In some cases the hairs simply fall out or shed without help; this we refer to as moulting. Where the hair fails to shed, it remains *in situ* until it is actively removed or pulled out. Those coats that behave in this manner are referred to as non-moulting.

Whatever stage the coat has reached within the growth cycle, it is the undercoat that dictates the amount of grooming a coat needs and how it is groomed. Until you have gained some experience, and have learnt to recognize the challenges that undercoats present, knowing what tools to use and where to start can appear baffling.

The undercoat is the most complex and problematic of the two hair structures because:

◆ undercoat hairs are more numerous than topcoat hairs;
◆ the amount of undercoat hair depends on the environment that the dog (or type of dog) originally inhabited (domestication and geographic mobility are still relatively new to the dog and evolutionary changes take time);
◆ undercoat hairs are deciduous so they die or shed when they are surplus to requirements or need to be replaced;
◆ their number fluctuates according to the season;
◆ the sex of the dog can also have a bearing on the undercoat density;
◆ neutering can affect the behaviour of the undercoat; and

249

◆ previous grooming and styling can also affect the undercoat.

All of these factors can influence the undercoat. Varying densities of soft, often dirty, coat may be seen. If this does not shed from the hair follicles and fall free from the coat, it typically can become horrendously knotted. The resulting mats and wadding will need to be groomed out.

For each new dog the learner should consider:

◆ The breed profile. What 'type' of coat does the breed have and how should it behave? What are the daylight hours and temperatures of the geographical region in which the breed developed, and how will these have affected undercoat behaviour?
◆ The effect that different grooming and styling methods have on undercoat behaviour compared to topcoat behaviour. (This is covered more fully in Chapters 14, 16 and 17.)

There are several ways to remove the undercoat, depending on the length and condition of the hair. Chapter 10 discusses the tools and equipment used for each stage of the grooming process and should have helped you to select the tool designs that will suit you best for each task.

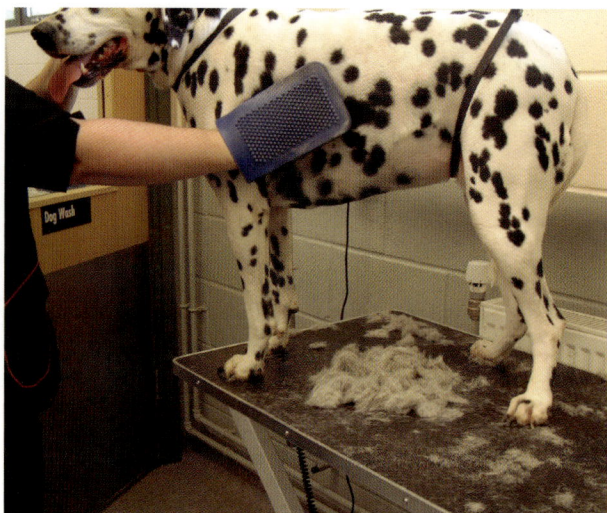

Fig. 11.1.1 On fine coats use a rubber mitt or glove and start working in a circular motion towards the head. You need to keep going until there are no more hairs coming out of the coat.

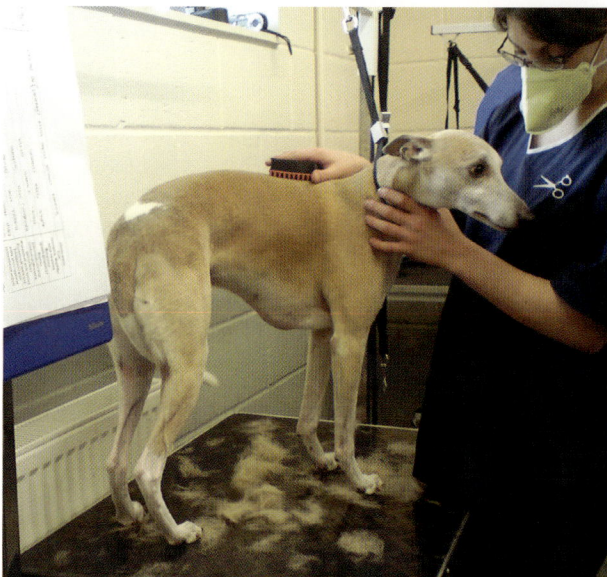

Fig. 11.1.2 A rubber pad does the same job as a mitt or glove. Use the nippled side first and then stroke the hair in the direction of growth with the sponge side.

CAUTION

It is during the grooming-out process that most accidents occur, both at home and in the grooming room. This is because sharp tools are being used. Make sure that you use them correctly and handle them with respect, to reduce the risk of injury to both dog and groomer.

Skin trauma is also common through excessively harsh grooming methods and over-zealous use of grooming tools. It is likely that many skin diseases and infections could be minimized or prevented by groomers using their tools correctly and with consideration.

Massage

Suitable tools: rubber glove, mitt or pad

These tools all do the same job. They are used on smooth coats because they are gentle on the skin and effectively massage the dog to remove the hair. The tools are used in a circular motion and the friction caused by the rubber on the coat warms the rubber, making it adhere to the fine hairs.

This method of grooming allows a considerable amount of dirt and dander to be removed at the same time as the hair. You are therefore strongly advised to wear a face mask.

Technique

The glove, mitt or pad is used in a circular motion, starting on the dog's thigh and working forwards towards the head so that the coat is separated and removed at skin level (*see* Figs 11.1.1 and 11.1.2). The rubber tool can be used in an up and down motion on the legs, pinna and tails if you find that easier. It is safe to use these tools on the face but a little caution is needed to prevent hairs and dander from entering the eyes.

Raking

Suitable tools: rakes, Furminators®, combs

The rake does as its name suggests and rakes the coat away from the skin. These tools can be very harsh if used with too much vigour as the tapering teeth are hard and can be sharp.

Technique

On a short coat, lift the coat up the 'wrong' way with your supporting hand. You may or may not be able to see the skin easily at this point. Insert the tool gently into the coat and, without using too much pressure, drag the tool gently along the coat in the direction of coat growth (*see* Fig. 11.1.3). Make your strokes short so you are not pulling the coat too hard. You should frequently check the skin below your working area, especially if the teeth on the rake are longer than the depth of coat (*see* Fig. 11.1.4). If the skin is becoming sore, move to another area to rest the skin before going back to it, and practise using less pressure on your rake.

On a very dense, longer coat, you need to change the angle at which you insert the rake when you begin until the coat starts to break up and separate. Lift the coat with your supporting hand and insert the rake sideways on into the coat (*see* Fig. 11.1.5) and pull it out towards you. This enables you to use the rake to pick your way down through the depth of coat until you can safely reach and see the skin.

On very dense but shorter coats it may be easier to use a coarse comb to rake out and break up the undercoat.

De-matting and removing knots

Suitable tools: fingers, de-matters, mat splitters, mat breakers, thinning scissors, clippers and blades

Mats, tangles, knots and wadding are all terms that are used to describe a formation where some hairs have become intertwined and tightly locked to their neighbours. The severity of this problem can vary considerably, ranging from a tangle of a few hairs to a large knot involving large areas of coat. Although it may well appear that it is the topcoat that is responsible, it is more often than not the undercoat that is the culprit!

Mats, *tangles* and *knots* tend to be a confused mass or cluster of hairs hanging either within or from the coat. They can often be isolated for special attention and they are usually removed by splitting up the mass with de-matting tools and breaking it down by brushing until it eventually disperses.

Wadding tends to be used to describe undercoat hair that has come away from the skin and formed a thick felt layer within the remaining coat. It is generally harder to remove because it covers large areas and can sometimes be very dense. Where the hair has come away from the skin, tools can be inserted behind the wad and gently dragged through the coat. If, however, the wad has not entirely left the skin, its removal is far more challenging: the hair will be tight and in some cases the skin may be raised in some areas by the tightening hairs. The skin is likely to be traumatized and care must be taken not to make the situation worse.

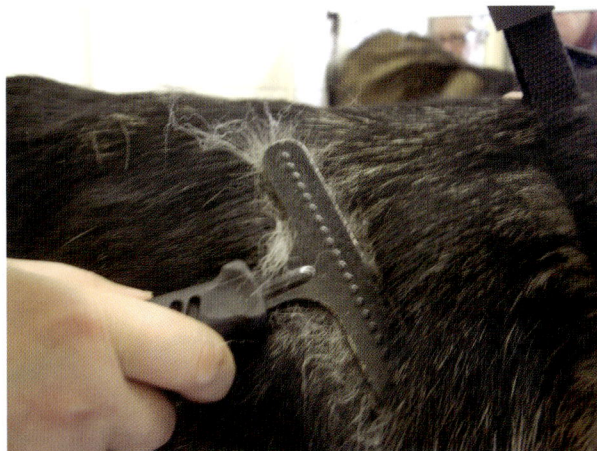

Fig. 11.1.3 Insert rakes gently into the coat, and without applying too much pressure drag the rake a short distance in the direction of coat growth.

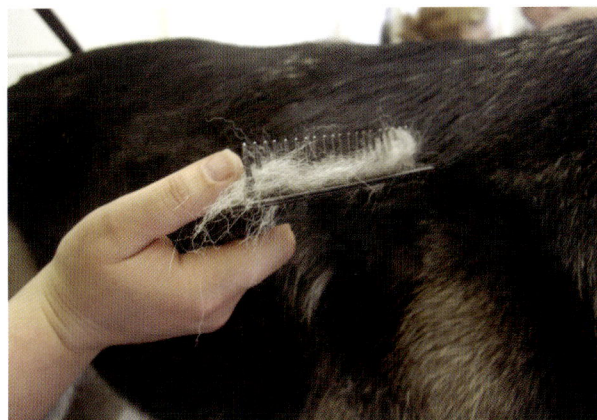

Fig. 11.1.4 The teeth on raking tools are long and may be longer than the depth of coat, so check the skin under your working area frequently.

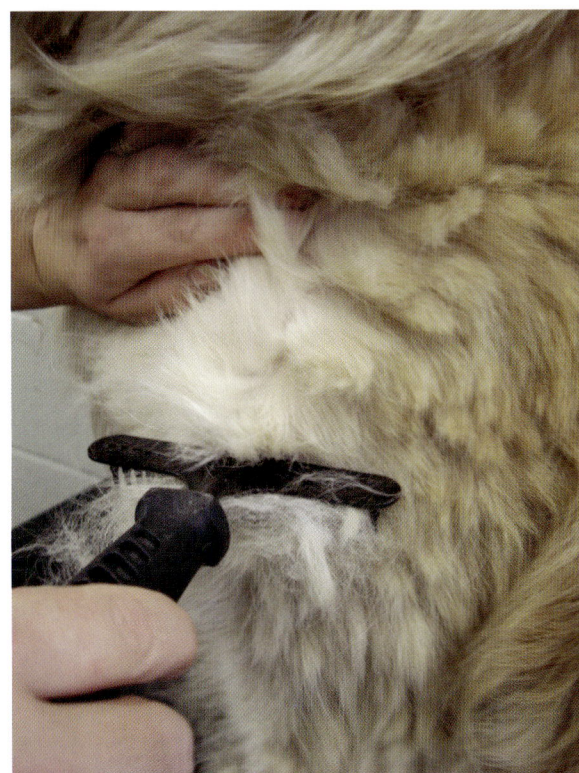

Fig. 11.1.5 On very dense coats, insert the rake sideways on and use it to pick your way gradually into the coat so that you can work your way safely down to the skin.

Fig. 11.1.6 There is a selection of tools available to de-mat the coat.

NOTE: AN IMPORTANT POINT TO REMEMBER ABOUT DE-MATTING

Whatever method and tool you choose to use, with the exception of clippers that remove the coat entirely, you should always aim to split the mass along the length of the hair, not across the hair. This encourages the mat to move towards the ends of the hair so that it can come out of the coat. Cutting across the coat leaves shorter hairs that once damp or dirty will entwine themselves around any longer hairs to form further knotting.

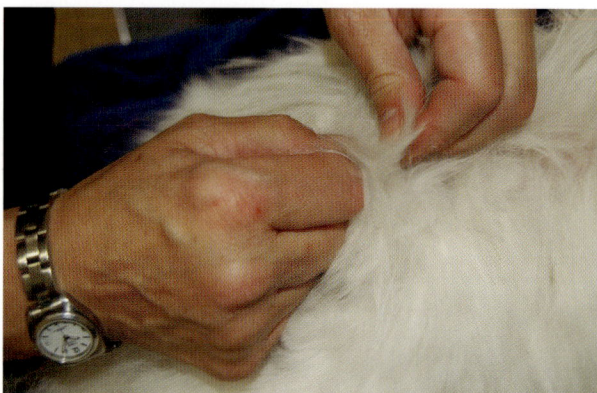

Fig. 11.1.7 Your fingers are the best tool to start with, particularly if the mat is small or close to the skin.

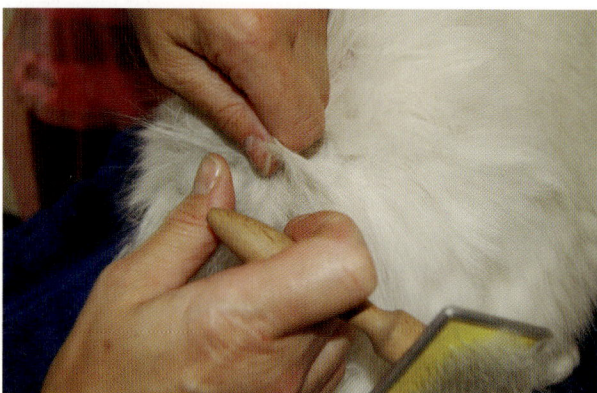

Fig. 11.1.8 Once the mat starts to come apart, use a slicker brush to break it up further and disperse it.

You have a selection of tools to work with here (*see* Fig. 11.1.6). De-matting tools are very sharp, so make sure you hold them firmly and correctly as you will experience some resistance from the coat as you try to remove the tangled masses.

Technique

The first method to try is teasing it apart with your fingers. Sometimes, if the mat is not too large, or if it is close to the surface, it is possible to break it up with just your fingers (*see* Fig. 11.1.7).

As the mass starts to break down, use a slicker brush to break it up further and disperse it (*see* Fig. 11.1.8).

If possible, try to isolate the mass from the surrounding coat so that you can concentrate on a specific area (*see* Figs 11.1.9a-b). If the mat is small, and you have a good view of the mass, insert a de-matter behind the mat and, using the tool according to the required blade action (either slicing or sawing), work the tool towards the end of the coat. The mat should come away reasonably easily (*see* Fig. 11.1.10).

If the mats are compacted and cover

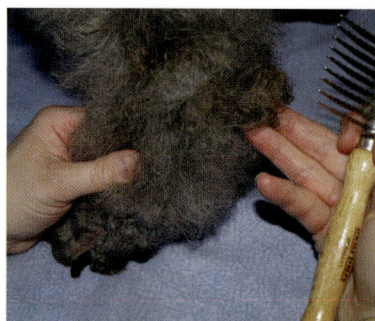

ABOVE AND BELOW: Fig. 11.1.9a-b If possible, try to isolate the mass from the surrounding coat so that you can concentrate the tool you are using on a specific section of coat.

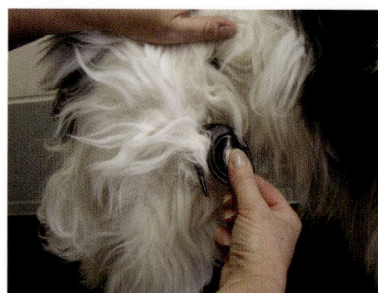

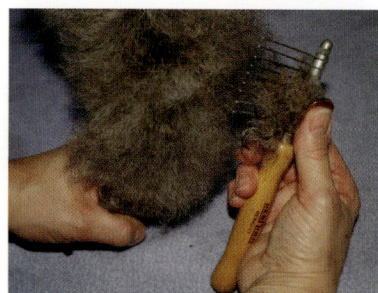

Fig. 11.1.10 If you use the correct action for the tool that you have selected (this de-matter has serrated blades so requires a sawing action), the mat should come away quite easily.

large areas of coat, you need to select one area at a time and, by inserting the de-matting tool, start to pick your way through to the skin. In these cases a *short-toothed mat-breaker* (*see* Fig. 11.1.11) may be preferable because the blades are easier to insert into the coat and the action allows you more control over where the blades are cutting. This reduces any tendency you may have to pull too strongly or forcefully.

Another method involves the use of *thinning scissors*. These are particularly useful when you are working in an area where it is easy to cut the skin, or if you are working on a dog that will not stand still. In Fig. 11.1.12 the dog has a very tight knot that is pulling the skin away from the body. A single cut from the thinning scissors can be used at the base of the knot, close to the skin, to reduce the density of the hair. The knot was then brushed with a slicker to break it up, and finished with a de-matter. The other ear was more difficult and the thinning scissors were used several times

Fig. 1.1.11   If the mat covers a large area, it may be better to use a short-toothed mat breaker. The curved blades are easier to insert into the mass and work with a slicing action.

along the length of the knot (*see* Figs 11.1.13a-b). The knot was then teased apart with fingers and then brushed with a slicker (*see* Fig. 11.1.14). At this point it became possible to insert a de-matter behind the knot to break it down further.

There are times, particularly if you are working with badly matted wool coats, when de-matting tools simply cannot get into the coat. In such cases you may need to use *clippers* and remove either part of the coat or, indeed, all of it (*see* Fig. 11.1.15).

On a healthy dog, it would be a rare thing to have to clip off the entire coat. On older dogs, however, where muscle formation is poor, it may be an option worth considering. This is mainly because grooming out is often so time-consuming; the dog must brace himself against the pull of the brush or comb and this can easily exhaust an old dog. Another option, of course, would

*Fig. 11.1.12
Thinning scissors are particularly useful for removing mats in difficult areas or when your subject won't stay patiently still.*

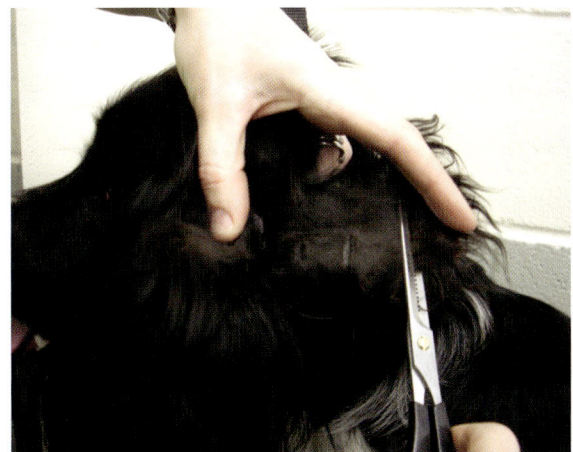

Fig. 11.1.13a-b   Here, the thinning scissors are used several times along the length of the mat, working outwards towards the end of the ear.

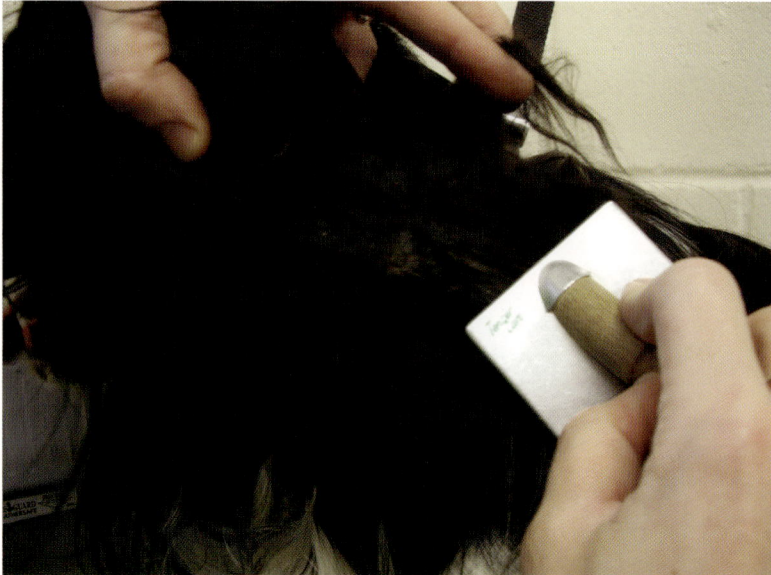

Fig. 11.1.14   The mat is then teased with the fingers and worked with a slicker brush to break it up.

Fig. 11.1.15   In some cases you may have to clip the coat off.

CAUTION: *DO NOT* IMMEDIATELY REACH FOR YOUR SHORTEST CLIPPER BLADE

The following two points should be considered first:

The time of year: if the coat is very dense, and you clip the coat down to the skin in the middle of winter, the dog may become ill. In the height of the summer the dog needs some coat to provide protection from sunburn. Try to leave as much covering as possible.

The skin under a heavy coating of mats and wadding will be very tender and sensitive: a short clipper blade may therefore more readily cause clipper burn and rashes.

In essence, you need to try to leave a good covering of hair unless it is absolutely necessary to expose the skin.

---

be to groom the dog over several sessions.

Clipping off a badly matted coat is not always easy and it is not a job that can be done in a hurry. Sometimes it is not easy to see any areas of skin, so you may have no idea of what you are going to find.

There are two ways to remove a coat in this condition.

Method 1

Start by selecting a medium-length skip-toothed blade (*see* Chapter 14). Make or find a gap in the coat to insert your clipper and start clipping *slowly* (*see* Fig. 11.1.16). If you try to clip in a

---

If you have never used clippers before, read through Chapter 14 on clipping first, otherwise you may damage the dog, yourself or the clippers!

---

hurry, forcing the blade through, it will snag and pull on the skin. The blade may struggle to slide through the coat, placing unnecessary strain both on the skin and on the clipper motor.

If the blade is struggling, try using a slightly shorter length. You may have to change blade length a couple of times before you find a length that will cut the coat, but do remember to try to leave a covering of hair. In many cases the coat will come off in large pieces (*see* Fig. 11.1.17).

Method 2

Sometimes, even a clipper with a fine blade will struggle to get into the coat and clip it off. It is most likely to be a wool coat that presents you with this problem because the coat is long, dense and very sticky (*see* Fig. 11.1.18). The hairs will still be firmly attached to the dog (as they do not moult) and there will be a fair amount of dirt and debris contributing to the mess. To make things even more difficult, a heavy coat may present to you damp because once it gets wet, it is often unable to dry out properly and becomes more easily knotted.

Have a good feel of the dog to establish the depth of coat. Use an old pair of

Fig. 11.1.16   *Find a gap in the mats to insert the clipper blade, and start clipping very slowly because you don't know what may be underneath the matted fur.*

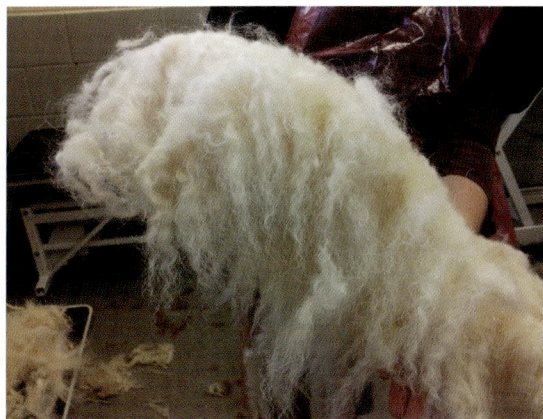

Fig. 11.1.17   *In many cases the coat will come away in large pieces.*

Fig. 11.1.19 *Use an old pair of scissors to cut down some of the coat length. Don't attempt to rush or to cut it down too far, because you don't know what is underneath.*

Fig. 11.1.18   *Sometimes even a clipper will struggle to get into a coat. This young dog had a coat where the knots were approximately 12cm deep. Brushed out, the coat is likely to be three or four times that length.*

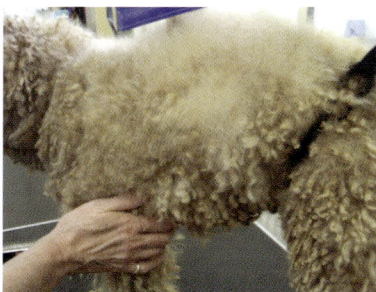

Fig. 11.1.20   *Once you have removed some of the length, brush the coat with a slicker…*

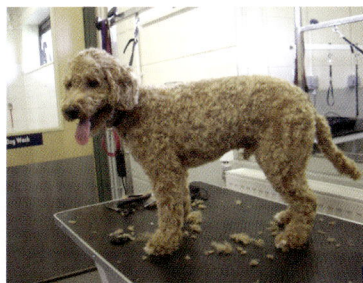

Fig. 11.1.21   *…and then trim the long fuzzy ends off.*

scissors to cut down some of the coat length (*see* Fig. 11.1.19). Brush the coat with a long-toothed slicker. This will start to break up some of the hair and long fuzzy strands will start to stretch out from the coat (*see* Fig. 11.1.20). Cut the long fuzzy strands down and brush again.

Continue doing this until the coat has either broken up enough to get a clipper blade into it or until you have trimmed it down short enough to brush the remaining mats out (*see* Fig. 11.1.21). If you opt to brush, do so with care because the skin may be sore or very sensitive, and it will be within reach of your brush strokes. This is particularly important if the dog arrived with a wet (and dirty) coat.

Brushing

Suitable tools: slicker brush, pin brush, bobble brush, bristle brush

Brushing is a vital part of grooming out a coat and should be done several times during the session. The purpose of the brush is to separate the hairs so that they can be combed. For the dirty coat, the slicker and the pin brush are the most effective because the long teeth or pins penetrate deep into the hair. Care must be taken, particularly when using a slicker brush, to moderate the vigour of your brush strokes as it is easy for the fine teeth to scratch the skin.

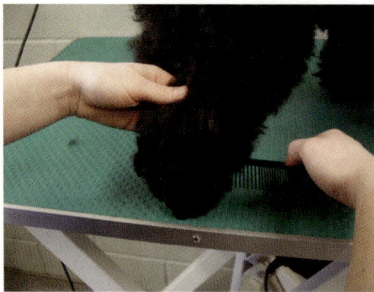
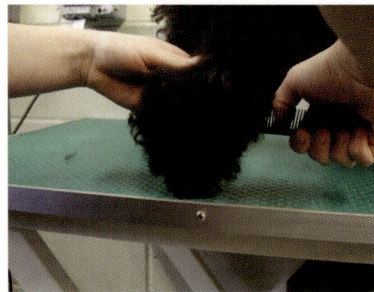

Fig.11.1.22a-c   To backcomb the coat, insert your comb with the teeth facing towards the table. Slowly turn the teeth of the comb towards you, and then continue turning the comb upwards until it leaves the coat.

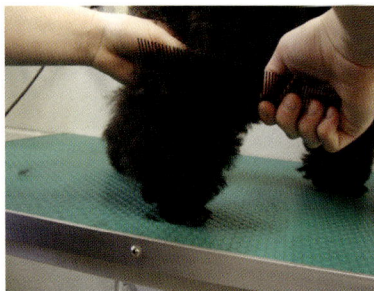

Fig. 11.1.2.23   Reinsert the comb slightly above the hair just combed and repeat the backcombing action. As you speed up, your wrist will be working as if you are whipping cream.

Technique

The brush you use depends on the coat type and the amount of undercoat to be removed. The coat should be brushed in layers starting from low down on the legs and working upwards towards the body. On the body, start with the dog facing away from you and brush the coat in layers towards the back of the head. This will provide easy access to the undercoat and allows you to see the skin between the layers. Once you have brushed the entire coat, the hair can be brushed back o lie in its resting position, close to the body.

Combing

Suitable tools: coarse comb, medium comb, combination comb, moulting comb

The comb is the groomer's best friend. It is the most versatile tool and it is used throughout every stage of the entire grooming and styling process. It is often the first and the last tool that you use. On some short but dense undercoats it can be used instead of a rake, but in most instances you use the comb after removing all knots, dead coat and wadding and after having brushed the coat through. The use of a coarse comb followed by a medium comb will find and remove any stray tangles that have been overlooked.

Technique

It may be possible for you to use a moulting comb (which has two different length teeth placed alternately along its spine), providing the comb will work through the coat without causing a dragging effect that is uncomfortable for the dog or for yourself. If this proves to be the case, the alternative is to use a coarse comb followed by a finer toothed comb. The comb can be used to remove the undercoat from short coats that are so dense that a rake will not suffice.

Being methodical in the way you comb the dog gives you the opportunity to check the skin one last time. This is particularly important if the coat was in poor condition when you started and the skin has had to endure some stress.

Start on a back leg and lift up the hair with your supporting hand away from the table top so that you have a good view of the foot. Use your comb to gently comb the hair back down again in layers, remembering to comb the inside of the leg as well as the outside. Work your way up the leg towards the body. With the dog sideways on to you, use your supporting arm to lift up the hair from the undercarriage towards the dog's back and comb the hair down again in thin layers.

Do the same to the front leg and then repeat the process on the other side.

There are two ways to use your comb, either in a downward motion that serves the purpose of grooming out knots and tangles, or to back-comb the coat so it is lifted away from the body (*see* Figs 11.1.22a-c and 11.1.23).

Carding

The expression 'carding' often causes some confusion in discussions, depending on the opinion of the groomer, their interpretation of 'carding' and the era of training. In my training days it simply meant grooming the coat out. The tool of choice was a slicker brush, which was an adaptation of the wooden carding tool used to card out and separate the wool of the sheep ready for spinning. Much to the confusion of many, it is now used within the grooming world to mean something completely different.

Carding now refers to a method of styling the coat by removing the undercoat with the aid of a stripping knife, a fine-toothed blade or a tool such as a Furminator®. The idea is that the undercoat is either thinned out or removed, and it is in effect an alternative (but not necessarily quicker) method of grooming out a dead undercoat by hand plucking (*see* Chapter 16).

It may be suggested by some that it would be more appropriate to include carding in the styling section but I have chosen to include it in this chapter because, however you choose to interpret its meaning, carding is still a method of grooming out the hair by separating and removing the undercoat, rather than styling a coat by altering the topcoat.

In principle, carding does have some merits:

◆ it is easier on the hands and fingers than hand plucking;
◆ you do not need to know how to hand pluck in order to do the job;
◆ the end result can be achieved over several grooms rather than all in one go; and
◆ it can help to restore a clipped silk coat to a silky texture.

As long as the job is done well, the coat should remain easy to manage and aesthetically pleasing to look at. If it has not been undertaken correctly, however, the effect is quite the opposite.

The main reason for this is that the tools used to drag the dead undercoat out from the topcoat are sharp and will cut the coat if used incorrectly. If you are going to cut the coat, you may as well save yourself a lot of effort and use clippers!

If you do choose to remove the undercoat by this method, before you start take a close look at the tool you will be using. Both the stripping knife and the Furminator® resemble a comb blade from a very fine clipper blade. They are formed of short metal teeth and the junction between the teeth is sharp, and it is this sharp metal at the junctions that will cut any hairs crossing its path. If the tool is in an upright position, the hairs will be dragged between the teeth and they will either be cut clean across their shafts at some point or, worse still, there will be many lacerations along the length of the shaft, causing weakening of the hair structure and multiple split ends.

If you have used either tool in this way, the finished effect today may be acceptable but in a few weeks' time, as the coat grows, you will be able to see how the hairs and the coat have been damaged. The damage often presents itself as dullness in the coat, where the split hairs continue to grow until they reach the stage where they are naturally discarded. During this time the damaged hairs have a rough/harsh feel to them because natural oils cannot coat the hair properly. Consequently, the coat may lose its glossiness, and waterproofing may be affected. In addition, unless the coat has reached the catagen stage of development, where it is ready to be discarded, undercoat hair will not have been removed from the follicle. It will, instead, have been cut across the shaft, leaving it very dense at the point where it emerges from the skin. The shortened hairs may not be able to move sufficiently to control the temperature of the skin, which may cause bad odours or, worse still, skin trauma through overheating.

The coat needs to enter and complete a new growing cycle before the damage can be fully rectified.

Consider these points:

◆ On double coats, the coat should be in catagen – it has moulted so the undercoat hair comes out with a bit of tension. If it is not in catagen, the coat will not come out easily and the tools will almost certainly cut the coat close to the skin rather than removing it.
◆ On smooth coats, these tools will most definitely cut the topcoat hairs as they work their way through to the undercoat.
◆ On wool coats, they do not work because the coat is too dense.
◆ On wire coats you risk cutting the coarse thick topcoat hairs.
◆ On silk coats, the hairs are fine and will slide easily between the teeth, so the method works if you use the tools properly.

My advice is that you only card a double coat that has moulted or the silk coat of spaniels and setters if it is absolutely necessary! I would also recommend that you use a blunt stripping knife, which is less likely to cut the coat. By necessary, I mean as an alternative method to stripping out errant undercoat hair. I have described the method for carding below.

Technique

The technique is simpler to explain than it is to execute and it needs lots of practice!

◆ First, assess the skin thoroughly because of the design of the tools. They can scrape or scratch the skin and any existing problem will be aggravated.
◆ Use a blunt, well worn tool.
◆ Place a coarse (wide) toothed stripping knife *flat* on the coat so that it rests against the hair (*see* Fig. 11.1.24).
◆ Keeping the tool flat, use short dragging strokes to pull the tool along the coat in the direction of coat growth. Check that you have removed the full length of the hairs. If you twist the tool slightly (*see* Fig. 11.1.25), the teeth will enter the coat and will cut.
◆ Continue over the area to be cleared (*see* Figs 11.1.26a-b).

Fig. 11.1.24 Place a coarse stripping blade flat on the coat so that it is resting against the hair. Keeping it flat, and pushing it down onto the coat, drag the tool along the length of the hair to pull the undercoat out from the coat.

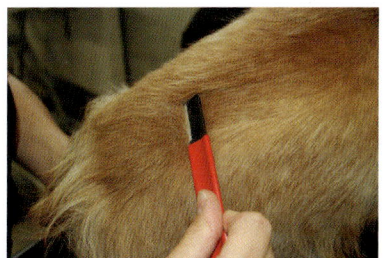

Fig. 11.1.25 If the tool is kept flat it should not do any damage, but if you twist the tool so that the teeth are facing down into the coat, the hairs will slide to the junction between the teeth and will be cut. This photo shows the teeth of the tool facing into the coat and you can see the short cut hairs.

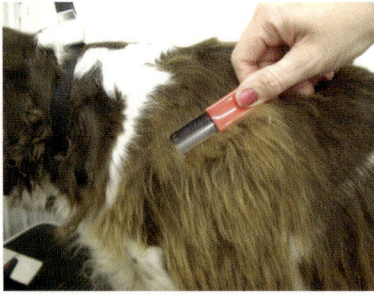

Fig. 11.1.26a-b   The errant undercoat on an English Springer Spaniel (left). Continued carding of the coat has restored it to its natural colour and texture (right).

◆ Depending on the stage of coat growth, you may have to repeat the process in a few weeks.

11.2 GROOMING THE SMOOTH COAT

The Coat

This is the most deceptive of coats. It is often believed that the smooth coat requires little or no grooming and looks after itself. To an extent, the coat does look after itself and the dog that is wearing it achieves this by moulting profusely; this is particularly true of dogs that live in the house. Anyone who has owned (or knows someone that owns) a Labrador Retriever or a Smooth Jack Russell Terrier will be able to relate to the amount of hair that these dogs can shed on a daily basis.

It is untrue, however, that the coat does not need grooming. It may well be the easiest to groom but it is often the most time consuming. On a good note, it does not mat or knot up, partly because it is not long enough but also because it is abundantly supplied with oily waterproofing that tends to keep the hairs apart.

The topcoat hairs are short, vibrant in colour and very glossy. They are quite coarse when handled as individual hairs and the growing tip can easily penetrate your skin. Handle multiple hairs by stroking along the coat as it lies flat and the overall feel is of sleekness and softness. Any undercoat hairs are very fine and dull in colour, and they can range from a sparse covering to very thick covering indeed. The smooth coat offers various degrees of waterproofing depending on the breed of dog.

The skin

The skin on the smooth-coated dog is surprisingly vulnerable and easily damaged if it is groomed without consideration. The smooth coat can moult almost to order so there is always some action taking place either at skin level or just below the surface level. This can make the skin sensitive and susceptible to damage, particularly if the protective topcoat barrier is breached. Use the minimum of force when grooming a smooth coat. There are many rubber grooming tools available that do an excellent job without the risks involved with using metal brushes and combs. It is also a good idea to use the mildest of shampoos for bathing.

It is common for owners and groomers to use undercoat rakes and Furminators® to remove the ever-moulting coat but considerable care must be taken here. These metal tools are unforgiving. They have hard ends to the teeth and the teeth are long enough to penetrate deeper than the depth of the coat, risking chafing and scratching to the skin. This damage can result in bacterial infections, particularly as the

tools can become contaminated during use and the contaminant is then in a good position to challenge the defences of the damaged skin. Bruising is also a consideration and carries a high risk. The same risks apply to the use of a slicker brush.

If you do choose to use an undercoat rake or a slicker brush, use it with as little force as possible to minimize the impact on the skin. Use a gentle raking action on the muscled areas of the dog only; this can be achieved by inserting the tool or the slicker brush gently into the coat and dragging it without pressure through the hair. If you choose to use a Furminator® the same considerations need to apply, with further thought being given to the action of the tool. The tool is made up of very fine teeth (similar to the comb plate of a clipper blade) that can cut through the coat rather than pull it away from the dog. This may not damage the skin but it can have the same effect as cutting or clipping the coat.

To groom a fine or very short smooth coat (*see* Fig. 11.0.1), you need:

◆ a rubber mitt/glove or pad; and
◆ a bristle brush or velvet grooming glove.

If the coat is slightly longer and denser (*see* Fig. 11.0.2), you may also need:

◆ a rake;
◆ a medium and a fine comb; and
◆ a slicker brush.

You need to keep grooming until all of the loose hairs are removed; this may take some time but it is important that you do not cut corners and give up too soon (*see* Fig. 11.2.1). This is particularly

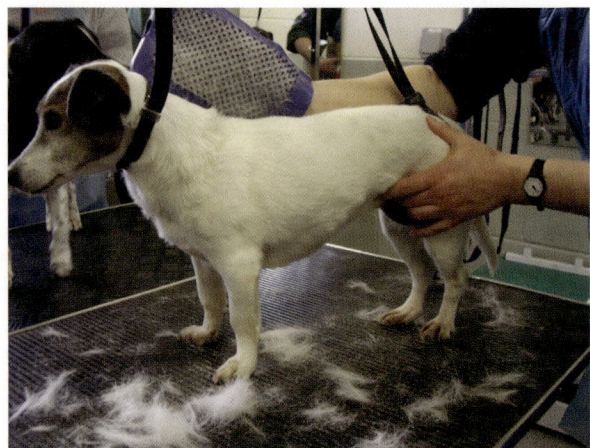

Fig. 11.2.1   On a smooth coat, you need to keep grooming until all the loose hairs have been removed.

Fig. 11.2.2   It is particularly important to groom the smooth coat properly if the dog is going to be bathed. This dog has shaken several times and you can see some of the expelled hair on the tiles.

Fig. 11.2.3   This hair came from the dog in the previous photograph and demonstrates the likely impact loose hair can have on your plumbing and drainage systems.

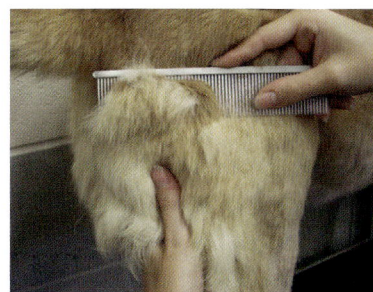

Fig.11.2.4   On denser coats like that of the Labrador, you need to use a rake or a medium comb to break up the wadding caused by loose hair.

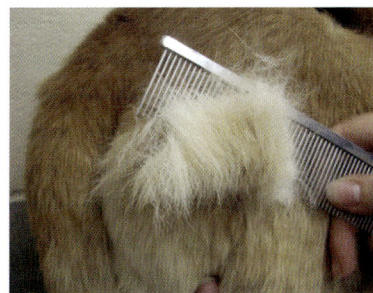

Fig. 11.2.5   The hair will be thickest on the back of the thigh, the tail and the neck, and there will be considerable drag on the comb so take care not to damage the dog's skin or hurt yourself.

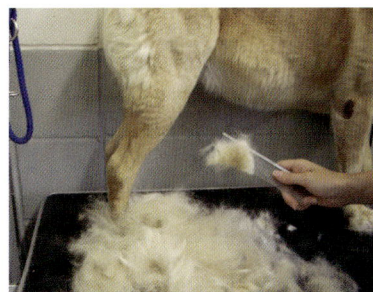

Fig. 11.2.6   A considerable amount of hair may be removed.

significant if you are going to bath the dog. Any loose hairs will come away in the bath (*see* Fig. 11.2.2) and many will be washed away with the bath water. This can lead to blocked pipes and drains (*see* Fig. 11.2.3) that are costly to fix or, worse still, may result in flooding in your salon.

Once all the loose hairs are removed, use the slicker brush to lay the coat down again; the dog is then ready for the bath or for 'polishing' with a bristle brush. To 'polish' the dog, use your bristle brush all over the body in the direction in which the coat is lying. This will remove all traces of dander and dust and will bring a natural lustre to the coat. An alternative to the bristle brush is a piece of velvet or, if you are lucky enough to find one, a velvet grooming glove.

Using a rubber mitt, glove or pad in a circular movement, start on the thighs of the dog and work towards the head. There will be a slight drag on the rubber and some dogs take a few minutes to get used to this so be gentle. Work your way over the top of the head. When you do the face, take care not to get any dirt, dust or loose hairs in the dog's eyes. You may want to keep a bit of clean damp cotton wool handy, just in case you need to wipe the eyes. The legs are the bit the dog least enjoys so it is best to leave them until last. The grooming tool can be used in an up-and-down motion on both the inside and the outside of the legs. The tail can be groomed in the same way.

If the coat is slightly longer and denser, you may need to start with a rake or a medium comb (*see* Fig. 11.2.4). The hair is thickest on the backs of the thighs (*see* Fig. 11.2.5), on the tail and on the undercarriage. There will be considerable drag on your comb or rake so take care not to make the skin sore or to hurt yourself by taking too much hair into the grooming tool. It is better to take less hair and do less harm. A considerable amount of hair is likely to be removed from the dog (*see* Fig. 11.2.6) but, once the raking and combing is finished, a slicker instead of a bristle brush should be used to bring out any small loose hairs that remain. If you prefer, you can at this stage use a rubber mitt in a circular motion to remove these random hairs but it is very hard work because of the coat length.

You should now use your slicker brush to brush the entire coat, taking particular care to reach the legs and undercarriage. Once brushing is complete and there are no more hairs coming out of the coat, the dog can be bathed or polished.

General maintenance

If the dog is healthy, the coat should adjust itself according to the environment that the dog inhabits. This may mean that it needs daily grooming, or a complete groom once or twice a week. The coat is constantly shedding to cope with environmental pressures, and in doing so cleans the skin of dead squames and dirt. If this is regularly removed by grooming out the loose hairs, the dog should maintain a clean, odour-free coat and bathing will only be needed occasionally. If this material is left in the coat, together with the loose hairs, the coat will start to smell and the dog will need to be bathed more frequently. If a smooth coat shows signs of heavy dander loss, or smells despite grooming, a veterinary check-up is advised.

Fig. 11.3.1   *The Irish Setter has long straight silky furnishings on the legs and undercarriage.*

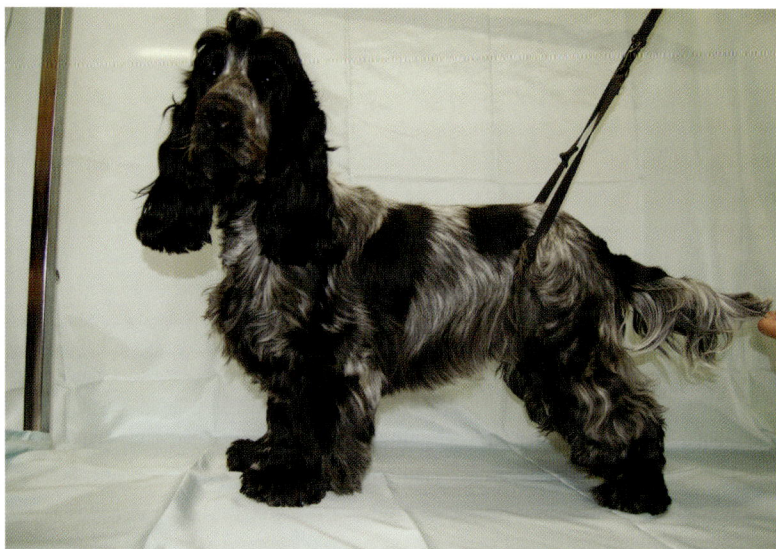

SUMMARY

To groom a smooth coat:

- ◆ *Use a rubber mitt or pad, possibly an undercoat rake, a slicker brush, a bristle brush, a hound glove or similar.*
- ◆ *Assess the coat for moulting.*
- ◆ *Start at the rear end of the dog and, if required, use a moulting rake to break up and remove undercoat.*
- ◆ *Use your rubber mitt or pad in a circular motion, working up towards the head, to remove loose hairs.*
- ◆ *Keep going until you have removed all the loose hairs.*
- ◆ *Use a bristle brush with the direction of coat growth to lay the coat down again.*
- ◆ *Bath, or polish with the bristle brush and then the hound glove.*

Fig. 11.3.2   *The silky-coated English Cocker Spaniel has a shorter wavy coat.*

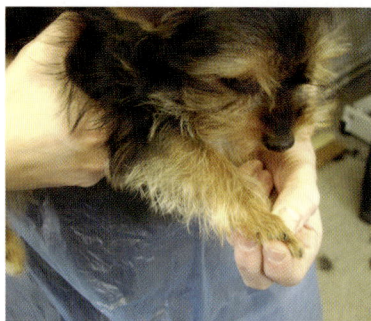

11.3 GROOMING THE SILK COAT

The coat

The silk coat should feel sleek and silky to handle. The coat appearance, though, ranges from the very long straight coats of the Afghan Hound and the Irish Setter (*see* Fig. 11.3.1) to the short wavy body coat and long flowing furnishings of the English Cocker Spaniel (*see* Fig. 11.3.2). Although it is not always apparent, the silk-coated

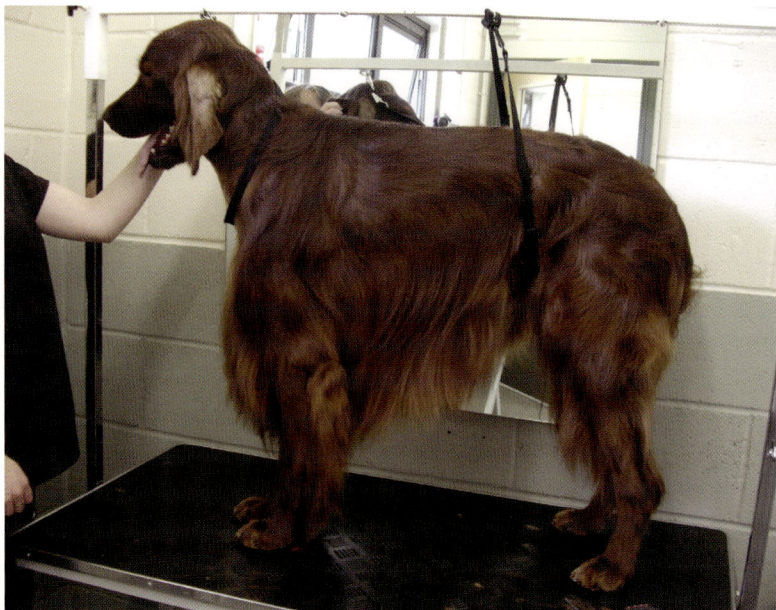

Fig. 11.3.3a-b   *On a Yorkshire Terrier puppy (left), you can see the undercoat close to the skin between the silky leg hairs that are just beginning to gain some length. On the adult Yorkshire Terrier (right), undercoat is most visible on the ears.*

dog does have an undercoat. It is very fine and sparse but if you look carefully, you will be able to see it close to the skin. In the Yorkshire Terrier it is obvious in puppies (*see* Fig. 11.3.3a) and on the tips of the ears (*see* Fig. 11.3.3b) and often on the feet of older dogs. On the Australian Silky it is obvious on the muzzle and on the lower portion of the legs, below the hock on the hind and the carpal joint on the front. Generally, the silky hairs are reasonably tough, again like our own hair, with the exception of the Afghan Hound and the Saluki, whose coats are reversed. The topcoat is short and very glossy and can be seen on the face and saddle of the Afghan Hound (*see* Fig. 2.11.10) and close to the skin over the rest of the body, and on the face and body of the Saluki Hound. In both breeds, but more apparently so on the Afghan Hound, the longer length hair is in fact undercoat hair. It is dull, slightly woolly to the touch and extremely fragile, much as a shorter undercoat would be.

Silk coats do not moult in any significant quantity. Generally the hairs grow to a length and then break. If the coat is left long and cared for, it will remain silky but, with the exception of the Afghan Hound, once the coat is clipped down, the undercoat will do its job and often begins to grow longer and denser, giving the silk coat a woolly, dull appearance.

The skin

The skin on silk-coated breeds is generally quite resilient and robust in terms of how it protects the dog. This is in part because the hair covering is generally not particularly dense and itself offers little protection. The skin on some silk-coated breeds, though, is fine in texture and can tear and damage easily if subjected to harsh grooming; this is especially the case on the ears and the hocks, and groomers should modify their technique accordingly.

Some wire-toothed brushes are harsh and unforgiving when coming into contact with the skin. The lack of any significant undercoat makes it more likely that these brushes will do damage by scratching or scuffing the skin. Bruising is also a possibility. If you have to use a wire brush, make sure that it is well worn, so the pad holding the pins is more flexible; alternatively, use a soft touch brush or a pin brush. Use all brushes with minimum pressure.

In some breeds the coat is parted down the centre spine (*see* Fig. 11.3.4), leaving the skin exposed to sunlight; during the summer months this area is vulnerable to sunburn. When this is evident, take particular care not to break the skin or cause further trauma by using your tools with too much vigour.

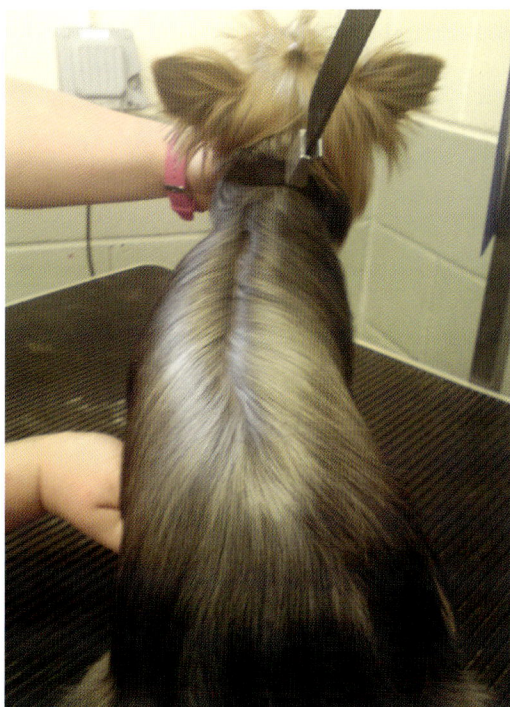

Fig. 11.3.4   In some silk-coated breeds the coat is parted down the centre back. This can leave the skin exposed to sunlight during the summer months and may cause sunburn.

The technique used when working with de-matting tools can be particularly damaging to the skin on some silk-coated breeds if they are used incorrectly. If the tool is designed to saw (up-and-down action) through the coat then it will exert too much strain on the skin if it is dragged or pulled through the coat, causing bruising and tearing. Check the cutting action of the blade that you are using.

To groom out the silk coat you will need:

◆ a pin brush (preferably);
◆ a soft-touch slicker (alternative);
◆ a de-matting tool (possibly); and both
◆ a wide comb and a medium comb.

The pin brush is preferable to a slicker, but a bristle brush, despite its gentle action, is more likely to cause static, resulting in the coat becoming unmanageable and even knotting up in some cases.

Check the coat for mats and tangles. If possible, use your fingers to tease mats apart and then use your brush to work them out; if they are stubborn, you may need to use a de-matter. Work gently from the skin towards the end of the coat length and then brush the knot away.

Start on a hind leg and use your supporting hand to lift the coat upwards towards the body, so you can see the skin underneath the length. Use your brush to go through the coat in layers, working up towards the top of the leg. Continue over the other legs and then brush the body coat with the way it falls, usually straight towards the ground. Use your wide comb to work through the coat in the same manner and then follow it with your medium comb. (A fine comb is likely to be too severe on these coats and may pull the coat out rather than groom it through.) The coat is now ready for bathing or rough clipping (*see* Chapter 14).

Coat maintenance

This depends on the breed and lifestyle of the dog. A dog in full coat needs regular daily brushing and will need to be bathed at least once every two weeks. If the coat is styled, as is often the case with pet dogs, the coat needs to be groomed at least once a week and will need to be restyled approximately every ten to twelve weeks, with bathing as required.

SUMMARY

To groom a silk coat:

◆ *You need a pin brush or a soft-touch slicker, possibly a de-matting tool, a wide comb and a medium comb.*

◆ *Assess the coat for mats and tangles, and remove them.*

◆ *Using the pin brush or slicker, start low down on a back leg and brush the coat in layers up towards the body. Continue over the entire body.*

◆ *Using the wide comb, go back to where you began and comb in layers.*

◆ *Repeat the process with the medium comb.*

◆ *The dog is ready for bathing.*

11.4 GROOMING THE DOUBLE COAT

The coat

The double coat can range in length from short (Malamute) to quite long (Old English Sheepdog) (see Figs 11.4.1a-b), and in density from quite thick and open, meaning that you can still see the skin on parting the coat (as in the Border Collie), to profusely dense,

Fig. 11.4.2   *The double coat moults once or twice a year, losing almost the entire undercoat.*

where you cannot see the skin if you part the coat (as in the Chow Chow).

Groomed regularly, this coat can be a pleasure (and the easiest) to look after, but the double coat moults, losing almost the entire undercoat once or twice a year (*see* Fig. 11.4.2). In between times, there is very little noticeable change in the coat status and owners often forget to groom the dog. For this reason the double coat can often prove very hard work when it arrives for grooming.

Once the undercoat comes away, it will remain caught up in the topcoat if it is not groomed out. The lifeless undercoat is dry and, without oils to separate the hairs, they tangle easily. Dirt and debris collecting in the coat adds to the problem, often by forming a nucleus for the hairs to bind to – and

very soon you will have a major job on your hands!

On the bright side, because it has become detached from the dog, with patience the majority of the coat should groom out reasonably well but it requires much effort. The major problem that you face is knotting and tangling, particularly in areas where the hair is extra long, such as on tails, knickers (see Figs 11.4.3a-b), leg furnishings and undercarriages. It helps to remember that the matted hair in these areas is also detached from the dog so, by working from the skin outwards, mats can be broken up and will often work loose and come away.

Grooming out these coats requires a lot of effort from the groomer but also from the dog. This is a point often overlooked by both groomers and owners.

Figs 11.4.1a-b   *The double coat can vary from short (left) to very long (right).*

Fig. 11.4.3a-b   The main areas of tangling on a double coat are where the hair is extra long, such as on tails, knickers and undercarriages.

Every time the groomer exerts effort into a brush or comb stroke, the dog has to brace himself against the pull. This requires a considerable amount of muscle movement and consequently energy. Some dogs become very tired, even quite exhausted, after a long, hard grooming session!

The skin

This coat type is the most problematic for the health of the dog's skin and groomers need to be particularly vigilant because the double coat moults excessively, leaving the hair follicles tender and the skin sensitive until the new undercoat begins to grow. If the dead hair is not removed, it forms a barrier within the coat that prevents effective thermoregulation. The temperature of the dog may rise to dangerous levels if the dog cannot cool himself. The skin is also at risk of overheating.

When double-coated dogs arrive for grooming, check the status of the coat and, if the undercoat has formed such a barrier, make sure that the dog is not contained in a holding area where he may succumb to heat stroke. Provide plenty of ventilation and drinking water, and do not leave the dog unattended. This applies particularly to farm collies that live outside and are only generally groomed once a year; in summer, when temperatures are higher, these working dogs will not be acclimatized to indoor environments.

If water seeps through the barrier of discarded hair, it cannot escape nor can it evaporate effectively and skin scalding is a possibility. The warm moist environment also makes the skin vulnera-

ble to bacterial infection. Urine seeping through the barrier of discarded hair is also unable to evaporate away from the skin, which can cause urine scald (*see* Fig. 11.4.4) and again bacterial infections. Wear disposable gloves when grooming out these areas because you may be at risk from infection from the stale urine and any bacterial infection on the skin.

Take care when you begin grooming, particularly if you cannot see the skin. Work slowly through the coat and be particularly cautious if the coat is wet. In wet areas, brace the skin with your supporting hand so the pulling action of your tools is reduced and skin

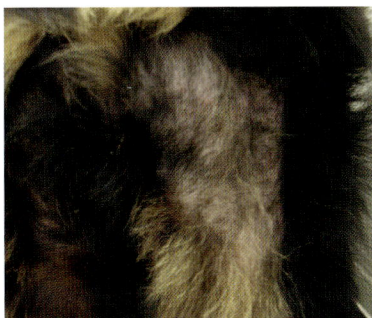

Fig. 11.4.4   Urine seeping into a matted undercoat leaves the skin wet for long periods of time. This can cause urine scald and bacterial infections, and may damage the skin, preventing new coat growth.

trauma is kept to a minimum. Be extra careful if you are using any equipment that can scratch or damage the skin surface.

It is not unusual for the entire undercoat to moult out to the extent where

bald patches or areas of very sparse hair cover appear. This leaves the skin vulnerable to environmental influences and possibly disease. Take care when using any tools that can scratch or damage the skin. Bruising is also a cause for concern here because the skin in certain areas is tender and exposed, so work carefully over the dog. The dog may also be very aware of your

---

CAUTION: GROOMING HEAVY DOUBLE COATS

These coats, particularly very heavy double coats, can be daunting for a newcomer to tackle, and if you do not work systematically you may fail to completely groom out the coat. This in itself can cause problems for the dog and his skin; it will also be extremely difficult to bath the dog properly and get the skin and coat clean. A further problem will be that of getting the dog dry again. Make sure you work to a routine, and complete each stage of the grooming-out process properly. Perform a 'check' at the end of each stage before you move on to the next tool and process.

---

tools because of the increased sensitivity of the exposed skin.

To groom the double coat you need:

◆ a de-matting tool;
◆ an undercoat rake;

◆ a slicker brush;
◆ possibly a bristle brush;
◆ possibly a pin brush;
◆ possibly a moulting comb; and
◆ a wide comb and a medium comb.

Before you begin, assess the coat thoroughly for mats and wadding. Check to see if the undercoat has come away, leaving a gap between the skin and the dead coat. Start by removing any mats and knots with your de–matter (*see* Fig. 11.4.5). These are most likely to be found in the longer hair of the tail and knickers.

Once these are removed, use your

Fig. 11.4.5   On longer double coats start by using a de-matting tool to remove mats and tangles. The undercoat is not attached to the skin so it should come away without too much force.

undercoat rake. Start on the back legs at about the level of the stifle, where the coat starts to thicken and lengthen. The rake can be used on the shorter facial and lower leg hair but you must be careful not to exert any pressure into the tool because you risk bruising the dog. When you are learning, it is perhaps better to use a coarse comb and then a slicker brush in these areas until you have become more proficient.

Insert the rake as close to the skin as possible, taking care not to bruise the skin with the hard tips of the teeth. Brace the dog with your supporting hand and, using short combing strokes, work the undercoat rake from the skin towards the ends of the hair. Work small pieces of coat at a time to reduce strain on your wrists and trauma to the dog. Work in layers up towards the back and then continue over the entire dog, including the areas where you have used your de-matter.

Once the rake has removed all the visible undercoat, the coat can be brushed. Use a slicker if the dog is still moulting, otherwise a bristle or pin brush can be used. Start at the same place on the back leg (the skin will have rested by this time) and again work in small manageable layers, making sure that you continue until you can see the skin between each layer. Work up the leg and then over the entire body.

Once you have brushed the dog all over, using the same method and starting in the same place, the coat can be groomed through with either a moulting comb (if the coat has lost its density) or otherwise a wide comb (*see* Fig. 11.4.6) and possibly a medium comb, depending on the density of the remaining coat and how dirty it is.

The coat is now ready for bathing.

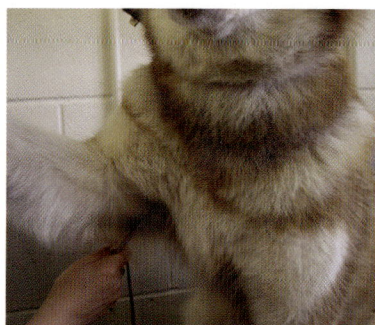

Fig. 11.4.6   When all the undercoat has been removed from the double coat, after brushing you should be able to work a moulting comb or a coarse comb easily through the coat.

Coat maintenance

The coat should be brushed through at least once a week. When the coat shows signs of moulting, it needs the attention of an undercoat rake before being brushed and combed, and needs daily attention until shedding has finished. If a double coat is groomed regularly, it may only need bathing after the coat has shed unless the owner prefers otherwise. (Try this: before you groom out a double coat, smell the dog from very close. The coat may well smell musty and even dirty.)

If the dog is healthy, once the coat

has been totally cleared of dead hair and the debris that will come away with it, the dog will have a perfumed coat that is specific to that dog. If you have done your job properly, the smell will be fresh and pleasant and it is often not necessary to bath the dog.

SUMMARY

To groom a double coat:

◆ *You need a de-matting tool, an undercoat rake, a slicker brush, a wide comb and possibly a medium comb.*
◆ *Start by assessing the coat for mats, tangles and dead undercoat wadding, and remove them with the de-matter.*
◆ *Starting on a hind leg at about the level of the hock, use your undercoat rake to rake through the coat in layers. Work on small areas at a time until you can see the skin, and progress methodically all over the body.*
◆ *Go back to your starting place on the back leg and repeat the process with your brush.*
◆ *Repeat the process with a comb. No more hair should come out.*
◆ *The dog is now ready for bathing if required.*

11.5 GROOMING THE WOOL COAT

The coat

The wool coat is perhaps the most time-consuming to look after because it requires constant attention. The coat is very soft to the touch and lacks any significant lustre or glossiness. This is because the coat is made up predominantly of undercoat hairs with – if you look closely – sparsely distributed but very wiry topcoat hairs included in the mix (*see* Fig. 11.5.1). Because the coat is made up in this way, it does not repel dirt and debris as effectively as the other coat types (with perhaps the exception of the Afghan Hound). Even with regular grooming, the coat very

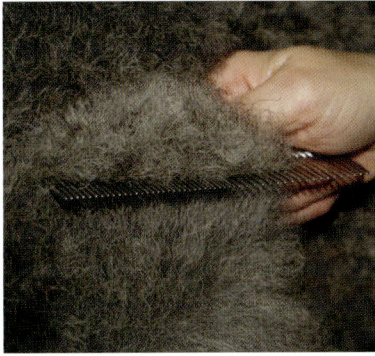

Fig. 11.5.1   *If you look closely into the wool coat of this Poodle, you can see the sparsely distributed wiry topcoat hairs within the woolly (undercoat) hairs.*

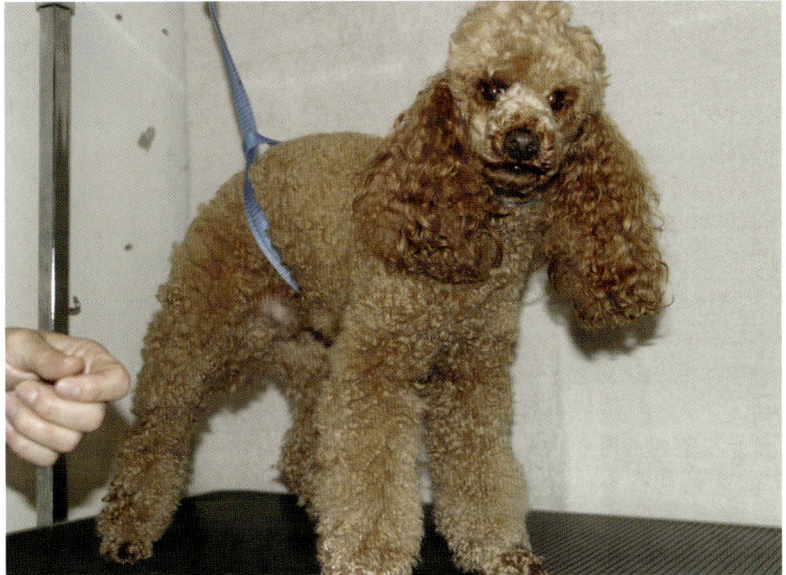

Fig. 11.5.2   *Most wool coats grow in curls or spirals. This contributes to the problems of knotting and tangling.*

quickly becomes sticky and dirty, and soon develops mats and knots. Most wool hairs grow in a curl (*see* Fig. 11.5.2) or spiral rather than straight, thus adding to the problem because each hair is then naturally inclined to interfere with its neighbours, so knots are easily encouraged. The coat is incredibly waterproof but sebaceous oils have a tendency to make the coat adhesive to dirt and grime rather than assisting with repelling debris as other coat types do. This is perhaps because the topcoat hairs, which would be the glossy guard hairs, are few and far between.

The skin

The condition of the skin on wool coated breeds depends largely on the condition of the coat. A well-groomed wool coat is open, with all the hairs standing independently from their neighbour, allowing the skin plenty of freedom and good ventilation. A knotted coat is, however, a different matter. If the coat is knotted, the knots will not budge of their own accord, so they put constant tension on the skin. This can cause bruising and soreness. Try to arrange that the dog is groomed by the owner several times a week and that they visit the groomer regularly (typically every four to eight weeks).

Knots and mats also prevent movement of the skin, causing a degree of trauma. As the dog moves, the skin is pulled or restricted, resulting in bruis-

ing and soreness. This again can be prevented or minimized if the dog benefits from a regular grooming programme.

Condensed wadding prevents heat loss (*see* Fig. 11.5.3). This is something that is often overlooked as a potential cause of heatstroke. The *erector pili* muscles attached to each follicle within the skin raise the hairs from their resting position to either trap or release heat. The hairs cannot move and let heat come away from the body if they are prevented from doing so by a barrier of wadding within the coat. This can result in skin damage through over-

heating, and can predispose to heat stress and even heatstroke.

Condensed wadding may retain water or urine, causing scalding and bacterial infections. Take particular care if you are grooming out a dirty, wet coat. Any scratches or chafing to the skin will increase the risk of infection.

Grooming out knots and wadding causes trauma. Grooming, especially when trying to remove hairs that are fixed firmly in their follicles, needs to be done with a great deal of care and consideration.

From a grooming perspective the

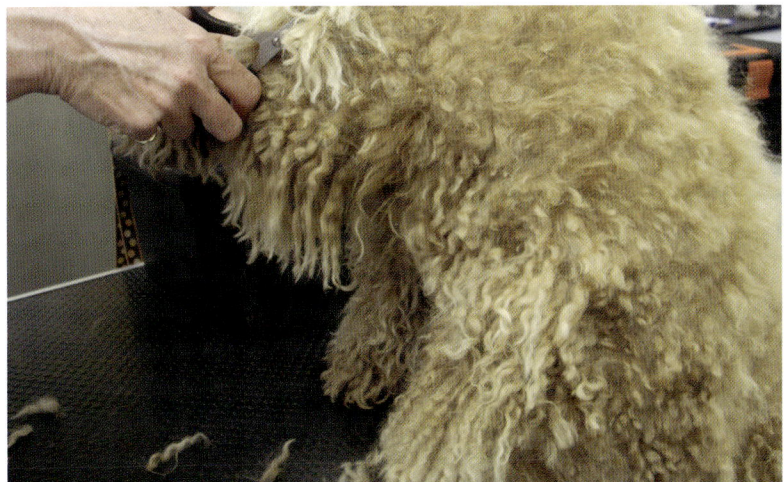

Fig. 11.5.3   *The wool coat does not moult so the knots can begin forming close to the skin and will stay there gaining density. This results in condensed wadding that prevents heat loss. Wadding is considered by many as coat neglect, but is overlooked as a cause of heat stroke which is life-threatening and much more serious.*

coat is generally stretched and groom-ed against the direction of hair growth and it is encouraged to stay that way. Try to use the minimum of force when brushing against the natural direc-tion of the coat because this in itself is traumatic to the hair follicles that are designed to lay a coat close to the skin.

To groom the wool coat you need:

◆ a de-matting tool of your choice;
◆ a slicker brush;
◆ a wide comb; and
◆ a medium comb.

Start by assessing the coat for knots, mats, wadding and dampness. A wool coat grows profusely between the footpads, so check this area well for knots, debris and sore skin.

Begin grooming on a hind leg of the dog and use your slicker to brush the coat in an upwards direction. At this stage you may not be able to see the skin so proceed with caution and remain vigilant. After brushing the entire body, use your de-matting tool on any areas where the brush has not removed the wadding or knots. Then go back to your starting point and brush the coat again.

Using a wide comb and a back-comb-ing action (*see* Fig. 11.5.4), start low on the hind leg, combing the hair gently in thin layers up the leg towards the body. You should by now have a good view of the skin between each layer. The coat should be lifted well away from the body. If the coat permits, repeat the process with a medium comb. (Be aware that the individual hairs on a very dirty coat will be coated in debris, which may make the use of a medium comb difficult.) Long ear furnishings should be combed with a coarse comb down the length of the pinna.

The coat is now ready for bathing.

Coat maintenance

Owners of wool-coated breeds should be prepared to groom their dogs sev-eral times a week and it may be ben-eficial for you to demonstrate the basic grooming techniques. To help ears remain healthy, it is important that dropped pinna, such as those of the Poodle, can move to allow ventilation. Precautions should therefore be taken

SUMMARY

To groom a wool coat:

◆ *You need a de-matting tool, a slicker brush, a wide comb and a medium comb.*

◆ *Assess the coat for knots, mats and wadding, and check between the pads of the feet.*

◆ *Starting on a hind leg, use your slicker brush to brush the entire dog against the direction of coat growth to break up the coat.*

◆ *Use your de-matting tool to remove any knots the brush has left behind, then brush the coat again.*

◆ *Go back to your starting point and use the wide comb in layers to back-comb the entire coat to leave it lifted from the body.*

◆ *Repeat the process with a medium comb.*

◆ *Comb the hair on the ears from the base down the length of the pinna on both sides, double-checking behind the ear for knots.*

◆ *The coat is now ready for bathing.*

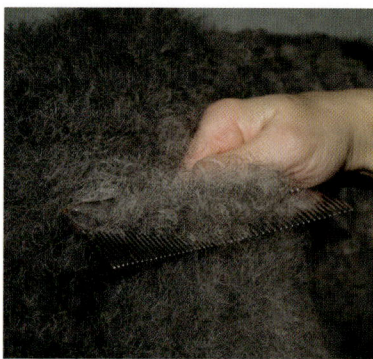

Fig. 11.5.4   After wads and mats have been removed, brush the coat and then use a coarse comb to backcomb the coat, starting from the bottom of the leg and working upwards. You then work in the same manner up towards the head. When the comb goes through the coat, the dog is ready for the bath.

to prevent the hair knotting badly in this area. A rolled collar will help if the coat is very long, or you could consider trimming the hair short around the entrance to the ear canal.

The hair between the footpads grows quickly and is exposed to all sorts of terrain, so the feet should be checked every time the dog is groomed.

11.6 GROOMING THE WIRE COAT

The coat

This is the type of coat that you are most likely to find on Terriers and Terrier crosses. The topcoat is coarse and harsh to the touch, covering what can sometimes be a substantially dense

downy undercoat (*see* Fig. 11.6.1). It is often referred to as a 'broken coat' because it appears to break away from the skin when it has completed its growing cycle, but the wire topcoat does in fact come away from the root as it dies, much in the same way as any other coat that moults or sheds. It usually tends to remain *in situ*, however, rather than noticeably falling out.

New coat growth is glossy and rarely causes problems with knotting or mat-ting, but as the coat grows in length, it loses its glossy (oily) coating and starts to dry out. It is then that the wire coat can become problematic, particularly in areas where the coat grows to a con-siderable length, such as on the legs and foreface.

The selection of tools needed to groom a wire coat depends on the stage of coat growth, but note that it is usual for the undercoat to moult at a different time from the topcoat. It also depends on the breed, as some grow a coat that is the same length all over,

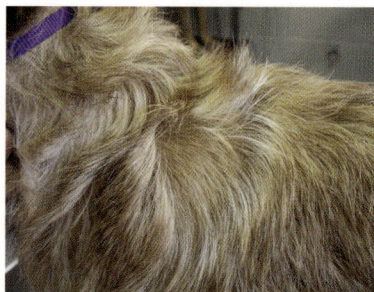

Fig. 11.6.1   The coarse harsh topcoat and downy undercoat of the wire-coated Border Terrier.

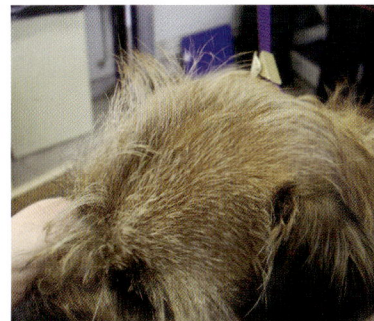

Fig. 11.6.3 *When the topcoat of the wire coat dies and is ready to be removed, a new glossy coat is already on its way through. The long wispy hairs in this picture are the dried-out, faded hairs of the old topcoat. The newly growing topcoat is visible, as is the undercoat.*

Fig. 11.6.2 *Some wire coats are styled to leave longer hair on heads, undercarriages and legs. These areas are where regular grooming is most important.*

whilst others have longer leg and facial hair.

For our purposes, it is convenient to separate the two types, referring to them as *natural* and *styled*. A *natural* wire coat is the sort of coat that is found on the Border Terrier, the Wire-coated Jack Russell Terrier and any other breed or crossbreed that grows a coat all over at the same length. These coats reach the same stage of growth at the same time over the entire dog so the whole coat is ready to come away at the same time. Because these coats all grow at the same speed and to the same length, the individual hairs lose their glossy coating at the same time and the coat begins to look dull and tired. If the coat is not removed from the dog at this stage, it will start to knot.

A *styled* wire coat is the sort found on dogs that have longer leg and facial furnishing, like the Airedale Terrier or the West Highland (*see* Fig. 11.6.2), and any others that have been styled so that the coat is of two different lengths (e.g. a Cairn Terrier trimmed into a West Highland style). These coats are cut down in length rather than removed, so not only is it more difficult to gauge the stage of the growing cycle without the protective topcoat, but the growing cycle is often altered to cope with environmental pressures. A further prob-

lem is that of the different coat lengths. The longer leg and facial furnishing is not removed from the dog but is left to 'add style and shape', leaving *in situ* dried-out dead hair that makes ideal matting and knotting material.

The skin

The skin on a wire-coated dog is tough and robust and, with the exception of some wire-coated breeds that are predisposed to skin disease, these dogs generally present for grooming with good healthy skin. The nature of the coat cycle and the way in which groomers deal with the coat will, however, have an impact on the skin's health, condition and maintenance.

In wire-coated breeds the skin may become vulnerable when the topcoat dies and is ready to be removed; however, where these dogs differ from other moulting breeds is that the new coat begins to grow before the old coat is cast (*see* Fig. 11.6.3). They do not lose their undercoat at the same time as they lose their topcoat, which means that the skin is never left unprotected. But skin damage can still occur if grooming tools are used too vigorously; the sharp teeth on wire brushes and the unforgiving tips of the teeth on metal combs are particularly to blame.

However, in wire-coated dogs it is equally likely that any damage to the skin will be caused by the way that the coat is maintained. It is suggested by many people that trimming the wire coat by clipping makes the coat easier to look after but this is not always the case. Removing the coat by pulling it out when it is ready reduces the length and the volume of hair because it is being physically removed from the follicle, as would happen during a moult, thus making way for a new glossy coat to grow (*see* Fig. 11.6.3). In contrast, clipping the coat reduces the length of the hair but it does not make the coat any less dense. In fact it is often the case that the coat becomes denser because the undercoat thickens to compensate for the loss of topcoat protection. It is also often the case that the coat becomes compacted because both topcoat and undercoat are now the same length. This in turn can make it difficult for the dog to adjust his skin and body temperature. It is quite possible that overheating of the skin may occur, which may contribute to some skin problems. To reduce this risk and to help prevent the onset of skin and coat problems, the trimmed wire coat needs to be maintained by regular grooming to separate the coat and prevent wadding and mats from occurring.

To groom the *natural* wire coat you need:

- a slicker brush;
- possibly an undercoat rake;
- possibly a moulting comb;
- a medium comb; and
- possibly a fine comb to remove moulting undercoat.

Check the coat through by giving a few topcoat hairs a slight tug. If they come away without lifting the skin, the coat is ready to be removed. Likewise, check the undercoat hair by giving a slight tug. If the hairs come away in your fingers, then the undercoat is moulting.

Start by using the slicker brush gently against the lie of the coat to lift the hair away from the skin. This gives you a good view of the skin and brings any abnormalities to your attention. If the undercoat is coming away, use your undercoat rake to lay the coat down again by starting just above the tail and working in layers up towards the head. Work up the legs from bottom to top.

Comb through the coat in the direction of growth with either the moulting comb or the wide comb, followed by the medium comb and finally, if necessary, the fine comb.

This coat is now ready to be bathed if desired, or stripped/plucked (*see* Chapter 17) if the coat is ready to be removed. The coat needs to be removed whenever a few topcoat hairs come away with a minimal tug.

To groom the *styled* wire coat you need:

- a slicker brush;
- possibly a de-matter;
- possibly a moulting rake;
- possibly a moulting comb; and
- a wide and a medium comb.

Check the coat through on the legs and facial furnishings for signs of mats or wadding. Check a clipped body coat by tugging gently at a few hairs to see if the undercoat is moulting.

Start by giving the dog a good brush with your slicker, taking the coat against the direction of growth to lift it from the skin. Next use your de-matting tool to remove or break up any knots or mats. Use your slicker on these

SUMMARY

To groom a natural wire coat:

- *You need a slicker brush, possibly a moulting rake, a wide toothed comb and a medium comb.*
- *Assess the coat for evidence of moulting.*
- *Brush the coat thoroughly to break up the longer hairs.*
- *Use your moulting rake to remove any moulting hairs from the body.*
- *Comb the coat through with the wide toothed comb and repeat the process with the medium toothed comb.*
- *The coat is ready for bathing or plucking.*

To groom a styled wire coat:

- *You need a de-matting tool, a slicker brush, possibly a moulting rake, a wide comb and a medium comb.*
- *Assess the coat for evidence of moulting and for knotting of the longer furnishings.*
- *Start on a hind leg and use your slicker brush to break up the coat.*
- *Use your moulting rake to remove any moulting hairs on the body.*
- *Use your de-matting tool to remove any knots in the furnishings that the brush has left behind.*
- *Brush the coat again.*
- *Go back to your starting point and use the coarse comb in layers to back-comb the entire coat to leave it lifted from the body.*
- *Repeat with a medium comb if appropriate.*
- *The coat is ready for bathing.*

areas again to remove loose hair and debris from the knots. Now use your moulting rake on the body if it is required to remove undercoat, and then the slicker again on the body, taking the coat in the direction of growth. Finally comb with the moulting comb or the wide comb, followed by the medium comb, until no further coat comes away.

This coat is now ready for bathing or styling.

General maintenance

The clipped wire coat can become very dense and will compact on the skin. The coat requires grooming with a slicker and combs at least twice a week to break up the compaction, thus aiding thermoregulation. Unlike the smooth coat, squames and debris cannot work their way easily through the wire coat so they will be caught up in the hair, resulting in a coat that becomes sticky with oils, encouraging knots and bad odours. The coat needs clipping down every ten to twelve weeks to keep it

manageable, but bathing may need to be done in between trims.

11.7 PUPPY COATS

Puppies go through many developmental changes within the first year of their lives, including the change from a puppy coat to an adult coat. In both males and females, the coat changes somewhere between the ages of nine and twelve months. Before the puppy reaches this age, the coat is in its first growing cycle and, regardless of the coat type, it is most likely that the coat will have an extra thick undercoat (*see* Fig. 11.7.1). The puppy coat also appears to have extra waterproofing properties; this is, of course, to keep the puppy warm during his development. Whether it actually is more waterproof, or whether it appears so simply because the coat has a different texture from that of the adult is difficult to determine for sure. You will discover, however, from experience that it is more difficult to soak a puppy coat than it is an adult coat!

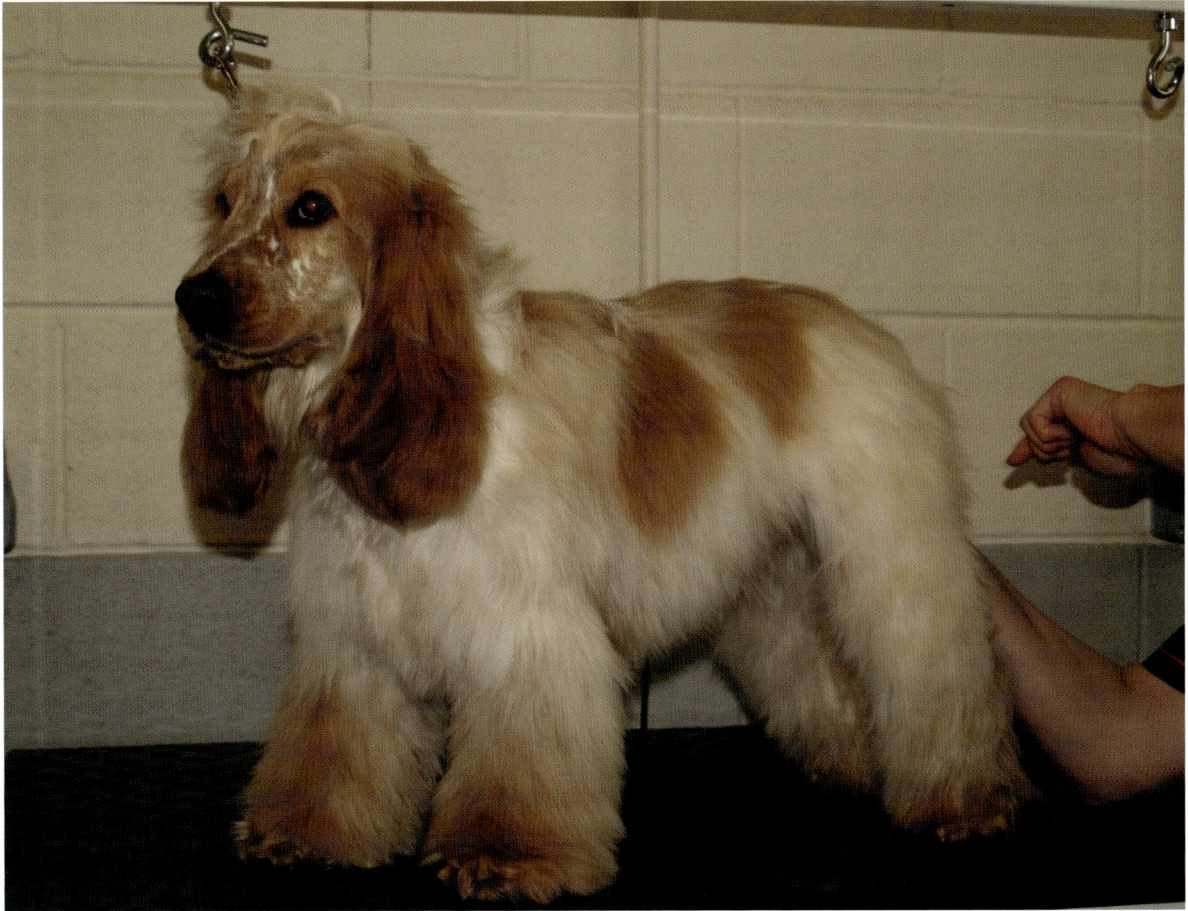

Fig. 11.7.1   A Cocker Spaniel puppy demonstrating the extra amount of undercoat that puppies carry. The Cocker Spaniel is a silk coat, but here it is fluffy. The undercoat will not come out on its own and, although the puppy is not destined for the show ring, the coat needs to be stripped out to reveal and encourage the silky coat underneath.

A puppy coat is very easy to look after as even a long coat will not knot up easily and there is no moulting undercoat to worry about. You can use this to your advantage! The puppy needs to get used to being groomed and it will be much easier to convince him that grooming is a good experience if you do not have to work for hours removing knots and tangles on his first time.

Arrange for the puppy to be groomed daily by the owner and every couple of weeks by a groomer for just a few minutes so that the sessions are short and frequent and become an 'everyday, nothing-to-worry-about routine'. It is a good idea to get the puppy used to having baths and accustomed to a hair-dryer. Modern shampoos are formulated to be kind to the skin so bathing will not do any harm and it is best to make the experience a familiar one whilst the puppy is a manageable size (*see* Fig. 11.7.2).

In contrast, as the puppy coat reaches the end of its first growing cycle and begins to change to an adult coat, it becomes much more difficult to look after, and this unfortunately remains the case *until the coat change has been completed*.

When the coat starts to change, moulting breeds lose some of the undercoat hairs. Other coats that do not moult change colour, becoming lighter and faded, and they also change in texture, becoming dry and lifeless. The skin at this point may well be slightly traumatized because, as with many other new developments the dog experiences as he grows up, the coat change is a 'first time' event and the skin has to adapt, so take extra care when grooming out.

Changing *smooth coats* are the easiest to recognize because the coat moults for the first time and loose hairs will appear around the house. Some undercoat comes away first, soon followed by a portion of topcoat hair. The coat replenishes itself almost immediately and retains its glossy character.

Silk coats lose their lustre and the coat becomes dry and brittle, and breaks easily. Knotting will begin if the coat is not groomed, and as the knots are groomed out, the hairs break easily somewhere along their length. The problem this poses is that the hairs are then all of different lengths and it is thus more likely that the coat will continue to knot up as the different length hairs move against each other.

When *double coats* experience their first major moult, it is likely to be a huge moult – remember that there is more undercoat to come away than normal. This can sometimes be unexpected because it is not always governed by a seasonal change. It may also be a hormonal change. If a bitch puppy has her first season in a wintry November,

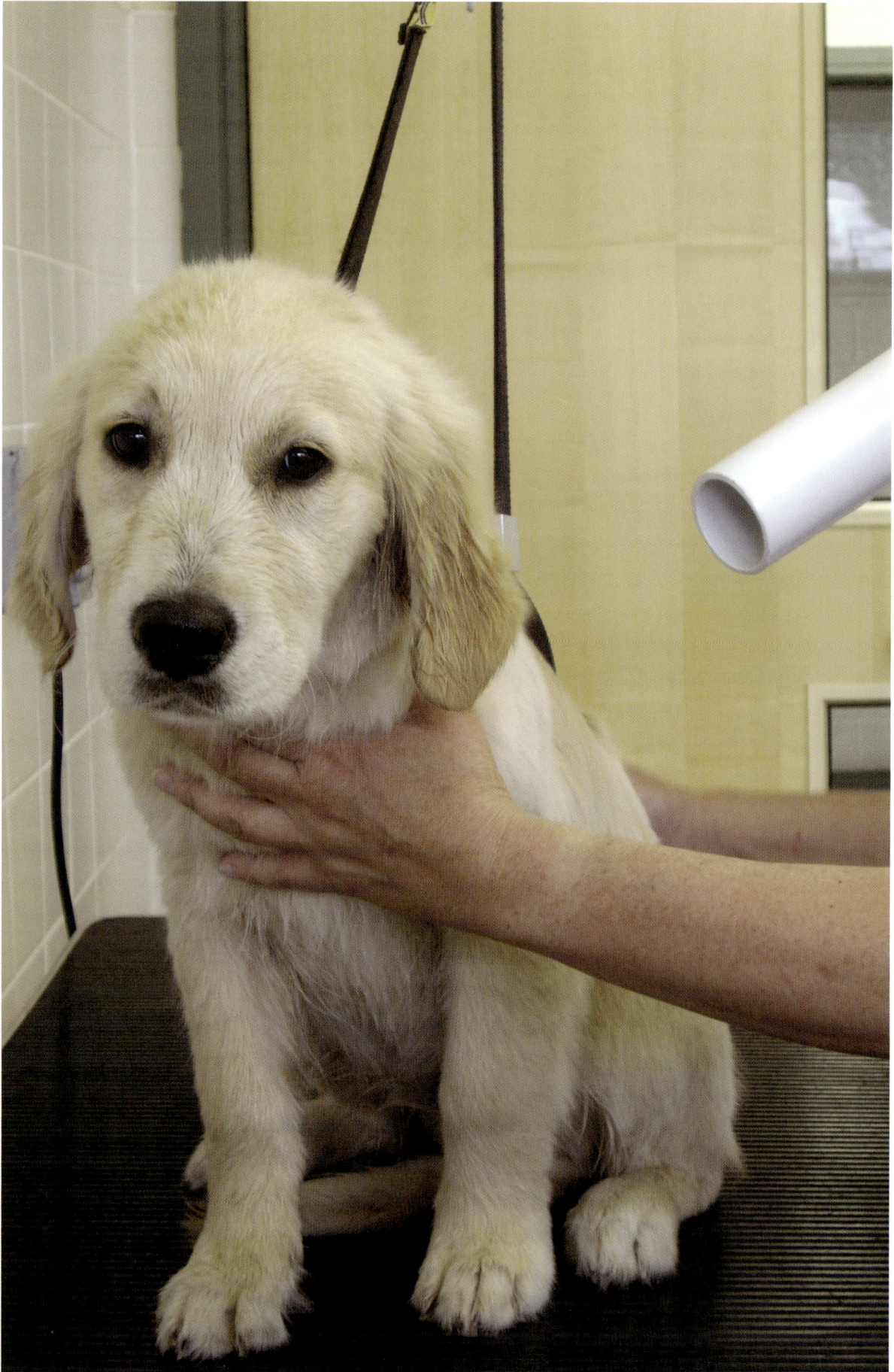

Fig. 11.7.2   It is a good idea to get puppies used to the bath and the hair-dryer whilst they are a manageable size and the job doesn't take too long. The puppy then learns to enjoy the experience.

she may have her first moult to coincide with the time she would be having puppies if she were mated – about nine to ten weeks later, around the end of January. It is not unusual for bitches particularly to lose nearly all of their undercoat, leaving a very sparse covering. This is normal for a first moult, but it is just as normal for the moult occasionally to be very insignificant. You do not need to worry too much, but should be more concerned if things appear abnormal at a second moult. Heavily coated male dogs may not be overly affected by seasonal changes if the climate is mild, so again the moult can occur when the dog reaches maturity rather than according to the weather. The undercoat needs to be removed as soon as it starts to come away.

Wool coats are the most problematic. The puppy wool coat is incredibly soft, light and buoyant. Before the coat change it is quite glossy, and even when dirty it rarely knots significantly, although it may take on an odour. This coat does not moult but it does die, and it loses all of its glossiness, becoming sticky, dull and lifeless. Then it knots up, mats up, forms wadding, smells and ... it will do all of this within a few hours of grooming – every day, for weeks!

This happens because the coat is predominantly undercoat and, as with the other coat types, there is a lot of undercoat wanting to come out but

unable to do so. It has to be groomed out and this can only be done once the hairs have become fragile enough to come away from the hair follicle. An added problem is that, whilst the old hairs are dying, new hairs are already growing from the same follicles; if left ungroomed, the two coats (old and new) merge and can become troublesome, resulting in the obliteration of the daily grooming effort! Perseverance is the answer if you want to keep the coat long, otherwise this is one occasion where most owners often ask for the coat to be removed. On the bright side, it will grow again – very quickly.

Wire topcoats die, fade and start to curl and separate. This normally starts to happen at around five months of age but it does depend very much on the breed. The dying hairs need to be removed or they may obstruct the new coat trying to grow through the same follicles. On wire-coated breeds that grow furnishings, the longer hair may not reach its full length until the puppy is around a year old and, as the coat reaches this stage it may start to knot up in places, although it is more likely that slight wadding will occur because of the presence of dead undercoat.

Puppies differ greatly in their development according to their breed but, generally speaking, all puppies begin adolescence once their adult teeth are

in place, so coat changing can begin any time after about five or six months of age.

It is commonly thought that clipping a puppy coat off too soon may damage the coat, although this is not possible because the coat grows from the inside out, so the growing roots cannot be reached to be damaged, and that clipping the coat changes the structure of the coat. There are two main reasons for this:

◆ Clipping silk and wool coats encourages the coat to grow thicker simply because the hairs will be stronger and will not break or be damaged as easily as hairs that have been left to grow and become brittle or weaken with age.
◆ Clipping wire coats makes the coat thicker and possibly paler in colour. The coat might also appear softer and may even continue to grow with a curl to the hairs. If the coat is left to moult out and regrow, it can more often than not be returned to its correct texture, although this could take quite a few months.

With this in mind, it is always best to confirm with the owner whether the dog is destined to be a pet or a show dog, and whether the puppy is going to be styled traditionally (hand plucking) or pet trimmed.

12 Bathing

The idea of bathing a dog conjures up images of copious amounts of soap suds and water everywhere, and most people can recount an occasion where they have got as wet as the dog. Few people take the exercise seriously and few understand the importance of doing the job properly. In fact, bathing the dog is perhaps the most important part of the grooming process because it is the part where a significant number of skin irritations and problems begin. Remember: skin irritation – leads to scratching and biting – leads to knot formation – leads to skin trauma – leads to sores and abrasions.

As discussed in the previous chapter, accidents and rough handling or incorrect use of tools can result in skin trauma and even cuts and abrasions; these are visible, however, and you can see the damage as it happens. The damage that occurs when a dog is incorrectly bathed is, by contrast, much more subtle, and largely invisible in the early stages. In most cases there is very little, if any, evidence of the damage for several days. For this reason, damage inflicted through incompetence in the grooming salon, or through lack of experience by the owner, is often overlooked as a possible cause of skin irritations.

This chapter discusses shampoos and bathing. An historical account of shampooing is presented first, paying particular attention to our growing understanding of how shampoos interact with and affect the skin and hair coat. This is followed by a discussion of the different purposes and appropriate uses of shampoos, their composition (content) and a consideration of how they may best be used. This section therefore ends with a close look at bathing the dog.

12.1 SHAMPOO

There are lots of myths and old wives' tales about bathing dogs, perhaps the most common being that it should not be done unless absolutely necessary because it is 'unnatural' or because it damages the skin by removing essential oils. But what is 'natural' and to what extent is it damaging?

Before the 1970s human hair was washed once a week or less, and then just with soap. Shampooing one's hair every day was arguably therefore 'unnatural' for humans. Today, there are few people in the west who would view washing one's hair every day or every other day as unnatural – clearly views and perspectives on what is 'natural' change. Today's pet dog lives within the home and there is a clear need for the dog to be kept clean, healthy and free from external parasites. Shampoos can be used to achieve all of these objectives.

Shampoo – a short history

The word 'shampoo' derives from the Hindi word 'champo', from 'chāmpnā' meaning to 'knead', and originally it referred to a head massage that was often performed using some form of hair oil. Indian head massage, and consequently the words 'chāmpo' and 'shampoo', were introduced to the UK when a Bengali entrepreneur called Sake Dean Mahomet introduced the practice to a London bathhouse in the early 1800s (Fisher, 1997). In the 1860s the meaning of the word changed as soap was increasingly applied to hair.

Soap was shaved and boiled and then mixed with herbs to produce the early shampoos and confer shine and fragrance to the hair. Soap is an ancient product with early records of its use dating back to Ancient Egypt and beyond; it is derived from animal or vegetable oils or fats combined with alkaline solutions. The oil used to produce the soap accounts for many of its characteristics. Savon de Marseille (Marseille soap), for example, is made entirely from olive oil and is renowned for its mildness. Originally soap and shampoo were very similar, both containing the same naturally derived surfactants (a substance that can reduce the surface tension of a liquid, thereby allowing it to penetrate solids).

Modern shampoos tend to contain synthetic surfactants or detergent-based liquids that are designed to cleanse the skin and coat and, in the case of medicated shampoos, act as a vehicle (or carrier) for the active ingredients (Curtis, 1998). Modern shampoos have evolved considerably as our understanding of the skin and hair coat has developed and as developments have been made within the chemicals industry.

You may be surprised to learn that the shampoo a dog requires is a lot different from the shampoo you require. The pH balance (acidity/alkaline ratio) of the dog's skin is not the same as yours so, whilst it may not hurt to use your shampoo a couple of times on your dog, after repeated use you may well start to notice ill-effects on the dog's health and skin condition, particularly if the dog requires frequent bathing.

The pH balance of the dog's skin ranges between 5.5 and 7.2, whereas human skin pH typically ranges between 4.5 and 6.0 (Meyer and Neurand, 1991; Matousek et al., 2003a). Canine skin is therefore more alkaline (higher pH) than human skin. Some researchers have found even higher pH readings on canine skin: Ruedisueli et al. (1998) reported an average pH over the flank area of 7.48, whilst Matousek et al. (2003b) found pH ranging between 6.4 and 9.1 on the skin along the mid-back (the thoracolumbar or spinal area). Skin pH probably varies with location on the body as well as with a range of other factors, including breed, coat colour and sex.

In humans, skin pH is generally higher in skin folds and areas where two areas of skin are in close contact. It is thought that this higher pH can predispose to skin infections such as bacterial pyoderma, candidiasis and nappy rash. Similarly, in dogs the high pH has been proposed as an explanation for the dog's greater susceptibility to skin infections compared to humans and cats.

Shampoos, soaps, detergents and other cleaning agents have the potential to cause considerable irritation and damage to the skin, as well as to other sensitive parts of the body. Baby shampoo is specifically formulated to be less irritating to the eyes than regular shampoo. Baby shampoo is also designed to be mild so that it does not dry out the delicate skin of babies. Baby skin is both thinner and has a higher water content than adult human skin. It is essential that the skin stays hydrated if it is to stay healthy. Canine skin is similarly thinner than adult human skin and is vulnerable to drying. Shampoos that are highly acidic also have an effect on the protective qualities of the dog's coat as valuable oils may be removed and the skin may begin to dry out.

In summary, then, it is clear that shampoos were developed in order to perform a cleansing action. Unfortunately, their use has not been without problems and in further developing and refining shampoos so that their performance is enhanced and their negative effects minimized, we have had to develop our understanding of how skin structure and physiology are affected by the various ingredients found within shampoos.

You should now be aware that shampoos have the potential to cause damage to the skin and hair coat if poorly formulated and used incorrectly. Your role as a groomer is to ensure that the shampoos you use are appropriate to the individual dog, that you remain alert to any potential problems and that you consider the effects of using the shampoo, or a combination of shampoos, on your own skin.

Shampoos and their uses

Legal Status

Shampoos for dogs can easily be purchased over the counter in most pet shops or sourced from grooming suppliers. Certain shampoos are also available on prescription from the dog's veterinary surgeon. It is important for the groomer to have an understanding of the differences in intended use for these shampoos, as this determines their legal status.

The former are non-medicinal shampoos for general grooming use and contain a range of ingredients that are intended for use on all dogs with a healthy skin and coat. Such products are usually classed as cosmetics (although the precise legal classification should be checked in the country in which you are working). As such, they are products that are applied to the body in order to cleanse, beautify or alter its appearance.

The latter are shampoos that contain a medication (the active ingredient) that is intended to treat a specific medical condition. As such they are veterinary medicinal products, as defined by the Veterinary Medicines Directorate (VMD). This means that they contain ingredients that have properties for treating or preventing disease in animals, or they are administered to animals with a view either to restoring, correcting or modifying physiological functions by exerting a pharmacological, immunological or metabolic action, or to making a medical diagnosis.

Broadly speaking, this means that a shampoo classed as a veterinary medicinal product has been tested and approved for the treatment or prevention of disease, or has been shown to exert an effect on the immune system or body metabolism and thereby resolve a skin problem. As such, veterinary medicinal shampoos are to be distinguished from shampoos that may support skin health. These will not have been subjected to the same degree of testing and cannot claim to treat a skin condition. This is a significant distinction because there are many shampoos that make loose claims to help resolve skin problems (*see* Fig. 12.1.1). In conclusion, it is important to appreciate that veterinary shampoos are medicinal and should be treated with the same respect as all prescription drugs or medicines.

Fig. 12.1.1 The label on the front of this bottle is typical of a cosmetic shampoo, i.e. one that is not an approved veterinary medicinal product. The wording suggests there may be some benefit if used on dogs with skin conditions, but without specifying what sort of condition. Shampoos formulated with emollients and humectants may help to hydrate the skin and reduce irritation associated with the skin drying out. As such, this usually alleviates the clinical signs associated with a skin condition, rather than treating the condition. The claims are non-specific and it is important to appreciate that a diagnosis from a veterinary surgeon should be sought and such shampoos are not a substitute for veterinary treatment where a specific disease process has been identified.

Fig. 12.1.2 The label on the back of this shampoo bottle clearly indicates that this product is a UK Approved Veterinary Medicinal Product (red arrow) and has been designated as an 'Authorized Veterinary Medicine on the General Sales List (AVM/GSL) (black arrow).

In the UK these shampoos are clearly labelled as 'UK Authorized Veterinary Medicinal Products' and feature a number of letters in a small box, specifying the legal category that the shampoo has been accorded (see Fig. 12.1.2). Human prescription medicines are labelled with the letters POM (Prescription Only Medicine). Veterinary prescription medicines display the letters 'POM-V' or 'POM-VPS'. These shampoos are only available on prescription and are intended for use on a specific dog under a veterinary surgeon's care. The way in which the product is to be used by the owner (and in some cases, the groomer) will be prescribed by the vet.

In some cases a shampoo may be classed as a veterinary medicinal product but be available over the counter from a vet, pharmacist or suitably qualified person. Such products are given the designation 'NFA-VPS', which stands for 'Non Food-producing Animal – Veterinarian, Pharmacist, Suitably Qualified Person'. In other cases, anybody is able to sell the product, and such products are given the designation AVM-GSL, which stands for Authorized Veterinary Medicine – General Sales List'. You should look on the back of the bottle to find the legal category of any shampoo containing a veterinary medicinal product.

Further information on the legal categorys of shampoos in the UK is available from the National Office of Animal Health (NOAH): www.noah-compendium.co.uk/Compendium/Overview/-42802.html

Intended uses

As groomers, we are spoilt for choice when it comes to buying shampoo as there is an amazing selection of excellent products to choose from, all of which have been formulated with the health of the dog's skin and coat in mind. In order to make the selection simpler for you, shampoos for general use can be divided into five categories: cleansing, conditioning, insecticidal, medicated and prescription.

Cleansing shampoos are widely available from pet product retail sources. They are generally suited to all breeds but they may be subdivided into subcategories that describe the action of the chemical constituents:

- *Mild*. Contains a weaker chemical solution that is indicated for use on puppies and dogs with sensitive skin or poor coat condition.
- *De-greasing*. Contains a stronger detergent to act against excessive amounts of grease (oil) and dirt in the coat.
- *Skin moisturizing*. Has added moisturizers to help prevent the skin becoming dry from frequent shampooing and the repeated use of hair-dryers.
- *Colour enhancing*. These are general cleansing shampoos with the addition of colour enhancement chemicals to either stain the coat, whiten the coat or reflect the light.

Conditioning shampoos are also widely available from pet product retail sources. They have added conditioners to noticeably soften the coat and help with the maintenance and grooming of long coats or coats that do not moult heavily (wool coats particularly). The conditioning agents in these shampoos are able to smooth the cuticle scales on the hair, thereby ensuring that the hair does not tangle and helping to eliminate static electricity when the hair is dried.

Insecticidal shampoos are widely available as an alternative treatment for fleas and ticks in pet product retail sources. They contain a powerful chemical that assists with the control of fleas and ticks. These, by definition, are veterinary medicinal products and many are categorized as AVM-GSL products. One of the main criticisms of such treatments is that they offer little residual protection against fleas once they have been washed off.

CAUTION: HEALTH RISKS

If using an insecticidal shampoo, you are advised to check what risks any active ingredients pose to your health. Certain active ingredients such as organophosphates and amitraz are toxic and can have significant side-effects.

Think carefully before agreeing to use a product containing such toxic ingredients, even if you are provided with the necessary protective clothing. Repeated exposure may be damaging to your health.

Medicated shampoos are available from veterinary surgeries, pharmacies and pet product retailers. They contain alternatives to conventional medicines and can be effective in the control/management of some skin conditions. Where the active ingredient is a veterinary medicinal product, these shampoos are generally classed as NFA-VPS unless they are prescription medicines (*see* below). Where the active ingredient is exerting a purely physical effect (i.e. the effect is not achieved by exerting a pharmacological, immunological or metabolic action), the active ingredient is not viewed as a veterinary medicinal product. Many shampoos marketed for the treatment of seborrhoea are therefore widely available and are good examples of the sorts of medicated shampoo you may see advertised. They are usually quite expensive and should only be used for specific indications (i.e. specific skin problems), as recommended by the manufacturer and the dog's veterinary surgeon.

Prescription shampoos are only available on prescription from a veterinarian. These shampoos are veterinary medicinal products that are typically administered as part of a treatment programme for a skin problem. Some ingredients, for example, will be anti-

---

NOTE: INSECTICIDAL SHAMPOOS ARE NOT RELIABLE

These shampoos can be excellent as an aid to the prevention of fleas and ticks but you should monitor the situation for signs of infestation or skin intolerance. They should not be considered a reliable substitute for the proper management of fleas and ticks, and they may not have any effect on other skin parasites such as mange mites and lice.

NOTE: ALWAYS SEEK ADVICE BEFORE TREATING A SKIN CONDITION

For any dog with a skin condition, however mild, veterinary advice should be sought by the owner of the dog before a choice is made between a prescription shampoo and an alternative over-the-counter treatment. The choice/decision should be that of the owner in consultation with their veterinary surgeon. It should not be yours.

bacterial, others anti-fungal. They are classed as either POM-V or POM-VPS medicines.

Malaseb® is an example of a POM-V shampoo that you may come across. It is only available on prescription from a veterinary surgeon. It contains two active substances: Chlorhexidine digluconate and Miconazole nitrate. It is specifically licensed for the treatment and control of seborrhoeic dermatitis associated with *Malassezia pachydermatis* and *Staphylococcus intermedius* in dogs.

In conclusion, there are many different sorts of shampoo available for you to use. You are most likely to find yourself using cleansing or conditioning shampoos, but you may come across the other types. With the exception of prescription shampoos, you will need to try shampoos from several different manufacturers before you decide on the products that suit you and your business best.

Before you make your choice, consider the number of dogs that you are likely to be bathing and the amount of exposure that your skin will have to the shampoo. It probably makes good sense to buy all your shampoos from the same manufacturer, since they are likely to have used the same basic formula for all of their products and you can then minimize the number of chemicals that you handle and are exposed to. With this in mind, and also for the sake of the environment, it makes sense to buy products that contain as few chemicals as possible.

Shampoo ingredients explained

To persuade us to buy a particular shampoo, it must look good, smell good, be thick and creamy and produce a good lather. And, lest we forget, the purpose of a shampoo is to clean the hair, but not to clean it so well that the hair is stripped of its natural oils. Manufacturers therefore need to formulate a product that achieves all these things. To this end, manufacturers combine many different ingredients, most of which seem to have ridiculously long, confusing names. The following section provides a little insight into what some of these ingredients actually do.

*Detergents***:** A detergent is a surfactant or mixture of surfactants with cleaning properties when in solution. They are the active cleansing ingredients used to clean the skin and the hair. They are sometimes referred to as sulphates. Detergents work best in water that is low in calcium and magnesium, as these minerals bind to the detergent and produce an insoluble scum. Commonly used detergents include ammonium lauryl sulphate, ammonium lauryl ether sulphate, ammonium laureth sulphate and cocamidopropyl betaine (very mild). By adding a milder detergent, such as cocamidopropyl betaine, to the formula, the amount of harsher detergents is proportionately reduced.

Tetrasodium EDTA (EDTA = **e**thylene**di**amine**t**etra**a**cetic acid) is a chelating agent, used to mop up and decrease the reactivity of metal ions that may be present in a product. It is therefore able to mop up the calcium and magnesium ions in the water so that they rinse away without forming a scum.

Humectants are ingredients added to the shampoo to add moisture to the hair. Unlike emollients (*see* below), they rehydrate the skin without using oils. They act by drawing in moisture from the air and from the animal's own (deeper) tissues. Humectants may be neutralized by the active detergent. Carboxylic acid, propylene glycol and glycerine are common humectants.

Emollients are substances that add oil to the skin and help to make the hair softer. They also help to sooth itchy, dry or irritated skin. The application of baby oil to a baby's skin immediately after a bath, in order to trap in moisture, is an example of the use of an emollient. Common emollients include coconut, safflower, olive and almond oils.

Emulsifiers are used to help two or more non-mixable substances bond together, such as an oil-based ingredient with a humectant. Common emulsifiers include cetyl alcohol, stearyl alcohol, laureth 5, lechathin and stearic acid.

Medications are added to shampoos, which then serve as a vehicle (or carrier) for a topical treatment (one that is applied to the skin surface) for certain skin conditions.

Insecticides are sometimes added to shampoos. A common example is Pyrethrin, a contact poison that penetrates the nervous system of insects and causes their death, but has a high safety rating amongst humans and other animals.

Citronella is often added to shampoos that contain only natural ingredients. It is an example of an insect repellent.

Cocamide DEA, MEA or *TEA* are foaming agents that help produce lather. They also act as a viscosity booster and help the ingredients to bond together and produce a thicker liquid.

Vitamins and *pro-vitamins* give relatively little benefit to the hair or the skin as they are washed away with the water when rinsing. They do, however, look good on the bottle!

Fruit acids and alpha-hydroxyl acids have little or no benefit to hair or skin care but may add to the scent. They also increase advertising blurb/verbiage.

Botanical extracts add to the scent but have little or no other value to skin or hair care.

Silicone oils such as dimethicone and cyclomethicone coat the hair and aid softness and manageability. They also reflect light and thereby promote shine, creating a sheen or gloss.

Guar hydroxypropyltrimonium chloride promotes smoothness and volume.

Designer water has no benefit to the skin and hair as it is washed away with ordinary shower water!

Antioxidants have no benefit to skin or hair care although they do increase advertising verbiage.

Perfume is added to disguise the smell of the detergent and to make the product more appealing to the consumer.

Pearlescent brighteners and *colour enhancers* are added to some shampoos to reflect the light away from the hair shafts, giving the illusion of added colour.

Having just read the above list, you may well ask yourself what continuous exposure to these various chemicals can do to your health. This is a sensible question to be asking, as your own skin will often be exposed to the chemicals for as long, if not longer, than the dog's skin. You may also wish to consider the extent to which these ingredients have been (and continue to be) tested on animals. These two questions are very different. At the end of the day we need to know that the products we use are safe for ourselves, our staff and the animals we are working with, but we do also want to be sure that they do not continue to be tested unnecessarily on animals.

The following websites provide further information on some of these issues:

www.legislation.gov.uk/uksi/2008/1284/contents/made
Provides details on the Cosmetic Products (Safety) regulations 2008.

www.safebeautyassociation.com/
The Safe Beauty Association provides information on safety issues within the beauty industry. Many of these are relevant to dog grooming.

www.ewg.org/skindeep/
The Environmental Working Group's 'Skin Deep' website provides a comprehensive online resource and database on cosmetics and their ingredients.

www.buav.org/
The British Union for the Abolition of Vivisection continues to campaign against the use of animals in the testing of cosmetic products.

Use and storage of shampoo

Before a shampoo is marketed for use, it must have undergone rigorous testing to ensure that the chemical contents are stable and do not work against each other. The way that the chemicals relate to one another is key to the safety of the product. In most cases individual chemicals do not mix well, and they are not particularly friendly to us either. They bond together and become 'friendly' only when they are mixed with other 'peace-keeping' substances. The 'friendship' is referred to as being 'chemically balanced 'or 'chemically stable'.

Once the user alters the chemical balance (i.e. adds water to dilute it), the product will have a short lifespan before the ingredients start to break down and the diluted product becomes chemically unstable. The chemicals revert to type and may become dangerous. Other factors such as direct sunlight may also cause a product to become chemically unstable. Light can break down the chemical stability, as can heat. Chemicals react differently at different temperatures, and can either break down and separate or react against each other. Extreme cold can have the same effect.

Because we trust manufacturers to keep us safe, we often become complacent when using everyday products like shampoo and we forget that we are handling a cocktail of chemicals that can be dangerous if they are not treated correctly. So:

◆ Always read through the instructions *every time* you open a new bottle (*see* Fig. 12.1.3). This is particularly important when using prescription shampoos. Ingredients change, and so do health and safety warnings.

◆ All operational precautions and Standard Operating Procedures (SOPs) should be followed (e.g. the use of PPE).

◆ All dilution rates should be followed and respected.

◆ Unused shampoo should be discarded at the end of the day because the chemical stability will have broken down by the following morning.

◆ Never put unused diluted shampoo back in the bottle with concentrate. The added water affects the chemical balance of the shampoo concentrate and could do harm.

◆ Dispose of the shampoo according to either the manufacturer's instructions or the recommendations of your local council/government.

◆ All shampoo bottles should be stored away from heat and direct sunlight (some products specify a temperature range for storage).

◆ Shampoo bottles should be kept off the floor and safely out of reach of dogs.

◆ Shampoo bottles should have their caps firmly secured at all times to prevent spillage.

◆ The use of a particular shampoo should be stopped if an animal repeatedly experiences irritation or develops new skin lesions following the use of that particular product.

◆ All POM-V and POM-VPS shampoos should either be given back to the owner or stored in a secure cupboard.

Fig. 12.1.3
Read shampoo labels carefully every time you open a new bottle because ingredients and health warnings can change without notice. PPE may include gloves, arm protectors, a plastic apron and possibly a face mask.

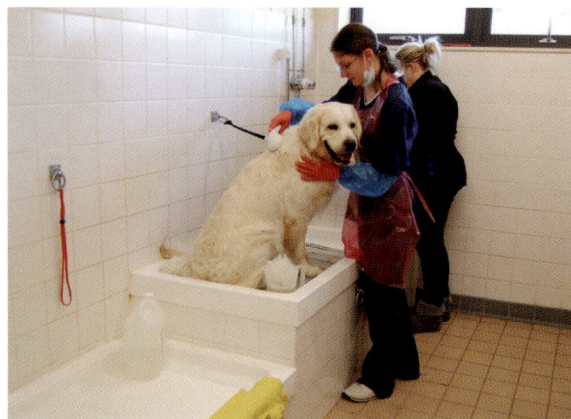

Diluting shampoo

Shampoo is diluted to ensure the safe use of the product. Ignoring dilution rates means that you are compromising the health of both yourself and the dog(s) you work with through over-exposure to the chemicals within the product. This is both unnecessary and potentially unsafe as you will both be at risk of chemical damage or possibly chemical poisoning. It is also wasteful, makes little economic sense and is potentially damaging to the environment.

Water quality

The type of water in your area will have an effect on the amount of lather that your chosen shampoo will generate. Hard water produces fewer suds than soft water, and it is a common mistake to use shampoo at a lower concentration rate in hard water areas to try to produce a better lather. This can overdose the dog and yourself with the active ingredients and can lead to skin damage. Shampoo does not work better if it produces more lather as the detergent that does the cleaning will still do its job.

Example:

A dilution rate of 12:1 means that you should use 12 measures (units) of water to 1 measure (unit) of concentrated shampoo. The ratio is always written with the water ration first.

SAFE USE OF PRESCRIPTION SHAMPOOS

Although widely used, these shampoos must be used with care and the utmost consideration as they can cause harm if used incorrectly. Prescription shampoo bottles are marked with VPOM (Veterinary Prescription Only Medicine), POM-V or POM-VPS, if the shampoo is for use on animals only, and can only be obtained from the prescribing vet. In some (exceptional) cases the shampoo may be a human prescription product marked POM (Prescription Only Medicine). In such cases you should double-check that it has indeed been prescribed by a vet for the dog in front of you. Under no circumstances should you use a human POM product supplied by the owner without veterinary authorization.

In both cases the prescription shampoo will be for a specific 'named' dog as part of a skin treatment programme. The bottle should be marked with a detailed label that provides the name of the dog, the address of the owner, the conditions of use (frequency and duration, and any specific instructions or other requirements), the date it was prescribed, and the name and address of the prescribing practice. The bottle will also display the name of the manufacturer, a batch number and a use-by date, and operator and recipient health and safety warnings.

You should request and retain a data sheet for these shampoos (for risk assessment). If you are keeping the shampoo on your premises, it should be kept safely in a cupboard. You should not retain any shampoo that is no longer required and any surplus should be returned to the owner when the treatment is finished.

These shampoos may contain chemicals and medicines that may be harmful to you, so you must observe all safety warnings and use PPE where indicated/advised (see Fig. 12.1.3). Never use the shampoo when it is out of date.

Any adverse affects should be recorded in the accident book and medical help should be sought as soon as possible.

These shampoos should be treated with the same respect afforded to all prescription drugs and should never be used on any other dog except the dog for which they are prescribed. You should never take the initiative and use one on any other dog just because you think that you recognize the skin complaint. This constitutes a diagnosis and the prescribing of medication. This is an illegal practice and you could be prosecuted. If you are not a registered veterinarian, you cannot diagnose a medical condition or prescribe medication.

12.2 COAT CONDITIONERS

Coat conditioners can be either a stand-alone product, or they can be integrated with a shampoo to form a two-in-one 'conditioning shampoo'. Groomers and hairdressers use conditioners as an aid to protecting the hair from environmental damage and to render the hair easier to brush and comb. Hairs have rough edges, which not only attract dirt and debris (*see* Fig. 12.2.1), but also make it easier for individual hairs to dry

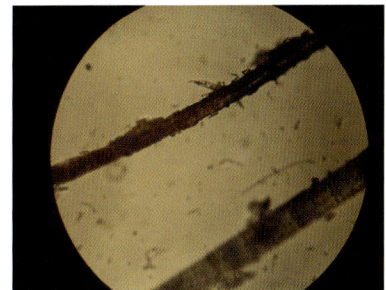

Fig. 12.2.1 A silky hair from an English Springer Spaniel before the dog was bathed. You can see the rough edges to the hair shaft and the dirt and debris clinging to it.

Fig. 12.2.2 After bathing and conditioning, hair from the same dog is smooth, sleek and clean.

out, snag and break. Conditioning the hair applies a coating that smooths the edges so it is more difficult for dirt and debris to attach itself; it also helps to prevent damage (*see* Fig. 12.2.2).

The contents of conditioners fall into five categories:

◆ Moisturizers: these contain humectants to hold moisture.
◆ Reconstructors: these are rich in proteins that penetrate the hair shaft to strengthen the hair.
◆ Acidifiers and detanglers: most detanglers are acidifiers. Acid added to a conditioner alters the pH of the product to close the cuticle layer of the hair. This allows the hairs to separate more easily and adds shine and buoyancy.
◆ Thermal protectors: these are polymers that redistribute heat to protect the hair from heat damage.
◆ Glossers: these are very light oils (*dimethicone* or *cyclomethicone*) that attach to the individual hairs to give a smooth coating to each hair that reflects the light.

Some conditioners are category specific, whereas others perform several functions. We use them to soften the coat, to aid grooming and to help with the maintenance of coats that knot easily. They are particularly beneficial on wool coats that have a continuous growth pattern and grow to a great length but do not moult excessively. These coats are prone to tangles and knots. Silk coats also benefit from conditioning. The individual hairs are delicate and easily damaged. Extreme moulting is rare in silk coats and continuous grooming is required. Conditioning adds protection to the fragile hairs and helps to reduce knots and tangles.

Conditioners are less important on smooth and double coats as they moult regularly so knots and tangles come away more easily. Conditioning a wire coat will make it unnecessarily soft and the coat will attract dirt and debris more easily.

Conditioners add weight to a coat. This may not always be what you want so, whereas a conditioning shampoo (a shampoo with conditioning properties) is applied to the whole coat, a separate conditioner can be applied

only to certain troublesome areas of the coat (e.g. ear feathers and furnishings, which hang from the body and are especially prone to knotting); these will benefit from the extra weight added by conditioning agents left in the coat.

12.3 BATHING

There are a few very important points to think about before you embark on bathing the dog. Firstly, if the dog is not bathed properly, you are most certainly compromising the health of the dog's skin. Take pride in every part of the process and make sure it is done well!

Remember that the dog's skin is at a lower pH than yours. This means that human shampoo is far too strong (alkaline) to be used on the dog so buy him his own!

You may like a hot shower but it is not good for your dog. The water should only be tepid/lukewarm – about 30–35ºC. This is slightly lower than the dog's own body temperature and is perfectly adequate. If it is too warm the dog will start to overheat very quickly. Hot water also loosens hair (as does a warm weather spell), inducing an impromptu moult, and the coat can start to shed and mat whilst it is being bathed. Hot water also softens the skin and renders it vulnerable to further insult.

The fewer chemicals you use the better. If you have to use two different shampoos on a dog, rinse the first off completely before using the second. Likewise, conditioners contain chemicals that are different from the chemicals in shampoo. You should therefore rinse the shampoo completely from the coat before applying conditioner to prevent any interaction. Chemicals within the shampoo can damage both the dog's skin and yours if they are not used correctly. You must read the instructions on shampoo bottles and follow them.

The only way you are going to get the dog's skin clean is if the shampoo can reach it. All dead hair, knots and tangles should be removed before putting the dog in the bath. If tangles, dead hair and knots are present they may prevent the water from properly drenching the coat; this means the

shampoo cannot work through the coat properly and it will concentrate only on the areas it can reach.

Shampoo can accumulate within knots and seep onto the skin below. As the heat from the dog and/or the hair-dryer dries the coat, the shampoo residue will dry onto the skin. Thorough rinsing may remove the shampoo from the coat, but it may not remove the shampoo from the knots. This puts the skin at risk of a chemical reaction to the concentrated chemicals in the shampoo residue, and the dog will begin to scratch, lick, nibble and even self-mutilate.

Tangles and knots get tighter once they are wet, and pull on the skin as they start to dry. As the knots get tighter, they pull the skin in several directions at the same time, resulting in trauma, irritation and, in some cases, lesions to the skin.

If the skin is not properly cleaned and rinsed it will become itchy and irritate the dog, who will scratch, making himself sore and damaging his skin. Soap attracts dirt so the coat will get dirty more quickly than usual, which will also cause itching.

After bathing, the coat should be drip free before the dog leaves the bath and goes under the dryer. If there is too much water left in the coat it will heat up under the dryer and result in a build-up of steam within the coat that can scald the skin.

Shampoo is for use on the outside of the dog, not the inside, so care must be taken not to get shampoo in the eyes, ears, mouth or genitals. If you do have a mishap, clear water should be applied liberally for three to four minutes to dilute the chemicals as much as possible. If shampoo gets into the eyes, flush them immediately with clear lukewarm water.

Washing the head and ears last may help reduce the shaking reflex in some dogs.

Getting started

Start by preparing the coat correctly (*see* Chapter 11). The condition of the coat after grooming out will give you a good idea which shampoo to use and whether the coat would benefit from a conditioner. Now get everything you need ready:

- Prepared shampoo in a dispenser or jug.
- Conditioner.
- Waterproof apron and rubber gloves.
- Bath ties.
- Non-slip mat.
- Jug and buckets of clean water if you are not using a shower hose.
- Sponge or body scrubber to work the shampoo.
- Towels.

Prepare your drying area ready to receive the wet dog, so that you do not need to leave him unattended in the bath, even if he is tied up, in case he slips and hurts himself. It is also unwise to handle hair-dryer plugs with wet hands so have them plugged in ready.

Hair grows very close and profusely around the entrance to the ear canal and this area is often very dirty, sometimes requiring more than one wash. To prevent water entering the ear, you can, if you wish, insert cotton wool into the entrance of the ear canal (*see* Fig. 12.3.1). Otherwise use your hand to shield it (*see* Fig. 12.3.2).

Secure the dog in the bath, on a non-slip mat and with a neck strap (*see* Fig. 12.3.3). Test the water temperature on

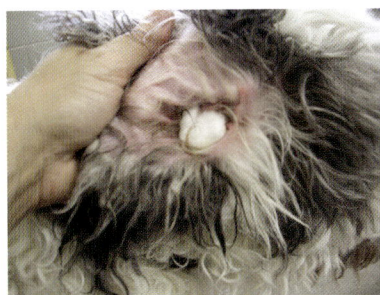

Fig. 12.3.1   Cotton wool placed in the ears can prevent water entering the ear canal during bathing.

the inside of your wrist. It should ideally be tepid or lukewarm, which will feel a little on the cold side to you. Some dogs who do not like baths settle better in colder rather than warmer water. You may not like working in it, but it will not harm the dog as long as the water is not freezing cold. Dogs often happily jump into very cold rivers or the sea at all times of year and neither is heated! What dogs do not like though, is rain!

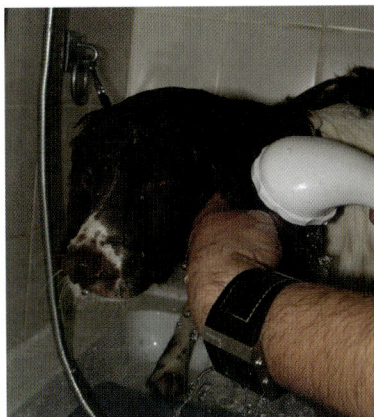

Fig. 12.3.2
Alternatively, you can use the back of your hand to cover the entrance, or place your thumb in the entrance.

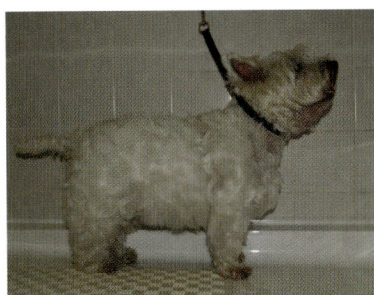

Fig. 12.3.3   Use a non-slip mat to prevent slipping and a neck restraint to stop the dog jumping out.

In my experience, trying to get most dogs out to do their business when it is raining is very difficult. Along with other animals, dogs are very sensitive to anything landing on their body (even a virtually weightless fly landing on their back) and many dogs do not like the feel of rain, or water pitter-pattering on their backs like rain. When you start to wet the dog's coat, keep the

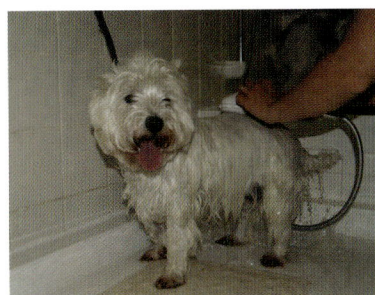

Fig. 12.3.4   Start wetting the dog from the rear end, making sure you get the water under the coat. Keep the hose on the skin to get maximum penetration from the water flow.

shower hose on the dog so that you maintain full water pressure and flow control, thereby ensuring water gets into the coat (*see* Fig. 12.3.4). By keeping the shower head against the dog, you also avoid simulating rain and this is usually much better tolerated by the average dog.

> ## NOTE: FIRST BATHS
>
> *When you introduce a young dog to his first bath, do not rush him. Make sure that the experience is a pleasurable one, because you may be bathing him for many years to come. Make sure that the non-slip mats do their job and are firmly fixed so that they do not slip if he struggles to get out. It also helps to ensure that your bath ties keep the dog in place. Stay calm and quiet but positive and confident in your actions and talk reassuringly to the dog as if being bathed is quite normal.*

The dog's coat is designed to be waterproof and lies flat as it gets wet, thus allowing the water to cascade off the dog and keep him dry. To get him wet, you have to run the water against the lie of the coat so that it runs under the coat and wets the dog from the skin outwards. Start drenching the coat from the back end, working forwards towards the back of the neck, lifting the coat with your fingers and the water pressure as you work. Leave the head and ears until the body has been shampooed. Once the head and ears are wet, the dog will shake more readily and you will get wet. The dog also loses a lot of his body heat through the ears, therefore leaving them until the last minute helps to maintain body temperature.

Keep checking that the coat stays wet. Greasy or very waterproof coats (particularly woolly coats) expel the water very quickly (*see* Fig. 12.3.5) so it can sometimes help to pour just a little shampoo onto the coat whilst wetting it. This breaks down the waterproofing and allows the coat to hold the water. The dog should be completely drenched before you begin shampooing, and you should be able to see

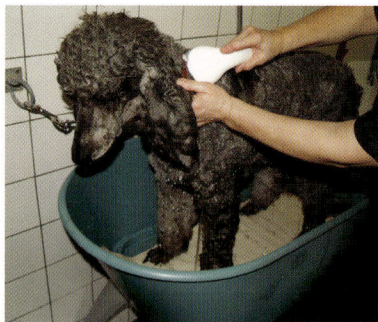

Fig. 12.3.5   Some coats, particularly wool coats, are very waterproof and repel water. A little shampoo will help to break down the waterproofing so that you can drench the coat.

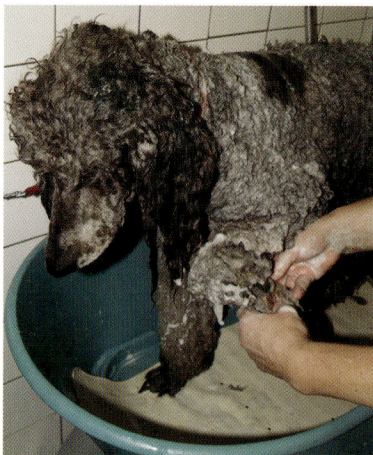

Fig. 12.3.6   The skin of an English Springer Spaniel showing through his drenched coat. This dog has much less undercoat and a silk coat that is not waterproof so it is easier to get it wet.

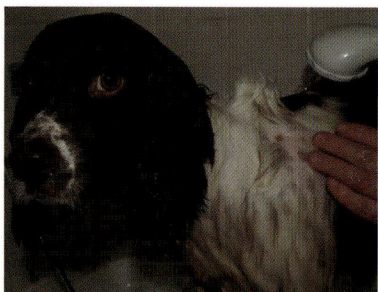

Fig. 12.3.7   Start shampooing at the shoulder and use your fingers or a body rubber on short-haired dogs in a circular motion. On longer coats just use your fingers so that you can penetrate the hair length and reach the skin. A body scrubber on a long coat only encourages tangling and knots.

the skin through the wet coat (*see* Fig. 12.3.6).

A good place to start applying the shampoo is on top of the shoulders, as any excess seeping away whilst you wash drains through the dog's

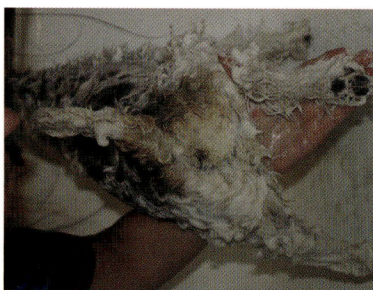

Fig. 12.3.8   Wash carefully between the toes and the foot pads.

Fig. 12.3.9   Washing the back end and the feet.

CAUTION: A NOTE ABOUT BODY SCRUBBERS

Body scrubbers are excellent on smooth-coated dogs because there is very little hair to penetrate before you get to the skin. On longer coats, however, they can induce tangling and sometimes they do not reach the skin surface, so check as you work that you are washing the skin as well as the coat. You may have to revert to using your fingers.

body coat and into the leg hair, so you can catch it further down rather than it running straight off the dog and wasted. Using your fingers, a sponge or a body scrubber (*see* Fig. 12.3.7), work the shampoo well into the coat, moving down the body towards the tail. You can work the shampoo in circles on shorter-coated breeds but work up and down or backwards and forwards on longer coats as circles encourage

knots to form in long hair. Take care to wash between the pads of the feet (*see* Figs 12.3.8 and 12.3.9), between the toes and the rectal area. If the anal sacs need emptying, this is the time to do it (*see* Chapter 18).

This done, you can now wet and shampoo the head, face and ears, making sure that the coat is again thoroughly drenched (*see* Figs 12.3.10 and 12.3.11). A small sponge or your fingertips can be helpful here to get the shampoo into the facial hair (*see* Figs 12.3.12 to 11.2.14) but avoiding the eyes, nose and mouth. The ears are better washed with your fingers, particularly if they have furnishings. Make sure you wash the hair at the entrance to the ear canal well as this is where dirt and grime typically accumulate (*see* Fig. 12.3.15).

Rinse the dog well, starting with the

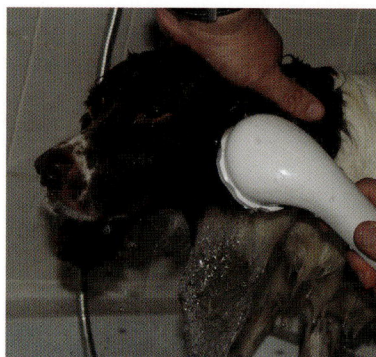

Fig. 12.3.10   Start wetting the head on the sides of the face, keeping the hose close so that you have control of the water direction.

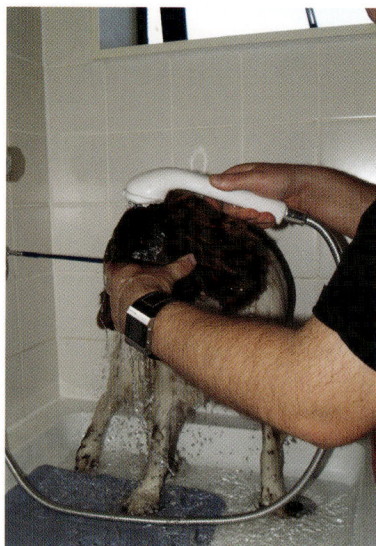

Fig. 12.3.11   Tip the head downwards and use your hand to shield the eyes and the nostrils.

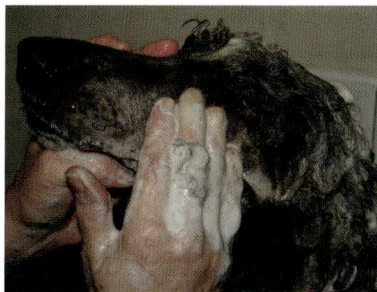

Fig. 12.3.12   Use your fingers to wash the face to give you more control of the soap suds.

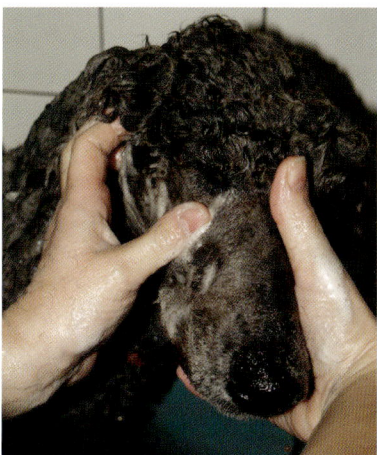

Fig. 12.3.13   Make sure you wash well into the corners of the eyes to remove any discharge.

Fig. 12.3.14   Beards and facial furnishings may need extra washing, Take care not to get shampoo into the dog's mouth by holding it firmly closed.

face. Keep the shower hose on the face to direct the water flow and use your hand to shield the eyes and nose. Rinse the head next. The water will run off the head easily, and you can shield the eyes with your hand. Dropped ears protect themselves at this point, whilst for pricked ears you can insert your thumb into the entrance of the ear canal to prevent water entering.

Pay special attention to rinsing ear furnishings and the areas around the ear canal entrance. Next work your way

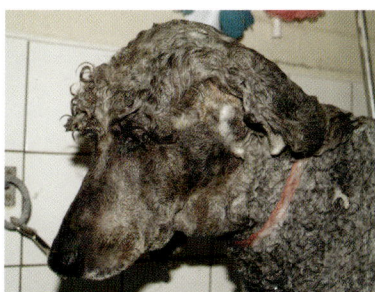

Fig. 12.3.15   The area at the entrance to the ear canal may need a second shampoo to remove grease and ear cleaning preparations. The hair on the pinna may also need a second wash.

down the neck (*see* Fig. 12.3.16), along the back towards the tail and down the legs (*see* Figs 12.3.17 and 12.3.18). The shampoo by this point will have accumulated underneath the dog's body and between the legs. Rinse under the neck, the undercarriage, the groin area, around the genitals and under the tail, and when you think these areas are soap free, check and rinse them again.

If the dog was very dirty, you can repeat the process; otherwise, keep rinsing until the water runs clear and the coat squeaks whilst resisting the movement of your hand as you slide it down the dog's back.

If a conditioner is to be applied, either all over the dog or in specific areas, the dog must be thoroughly rinsed again afterwards (do not forget to check and double-check the underside of the dog). After conditioning, the water should still run clear but you may not get the squeaking effect: this is down

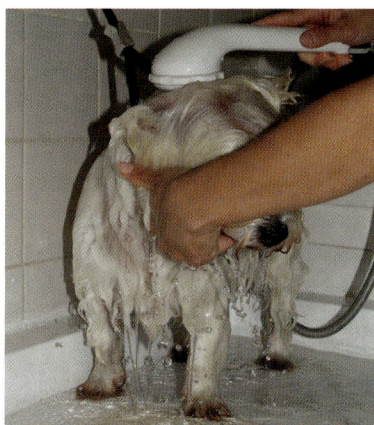

Fig. 12.3.16   Start by rinsing the face thoroughly so that you minimize the risk of shampoo going into the eyes or being ingested. Then rinse the head and start to work your way down the neck towards the tail.

Fig. 12.3.17   Keeping the hose on the dog, rinse the back for several minutes to allow the water to disperse the shampoo detergents.

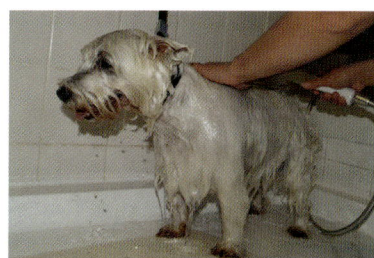

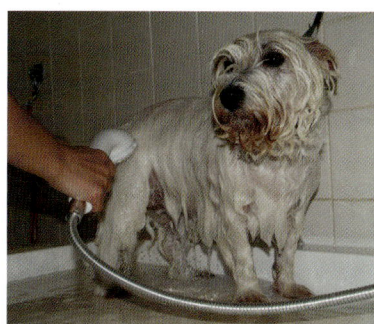

Fig. 12.3.18   Finally rinse the legs and the undercarriage, including between the back legs until the water runs clear.

to the oils in the conditioner.

Bathing over, the coat must now be squeezed with your hands to start to remove the water and then blotted with either a high-absorbency towel (*see* Fig. 12.3.19) or a terry towel. It is important here to blot the coat rather than rub it in circles, as this removes the water but does not encourage knotting of the coat. How long you continue this depends on whether you are going to continue with towels or use a blaster to help disperse the water. Either way, the dog should not be dripping when he comes out of the bath.

Fig. 12.3.19   Use a high-absorbancy cloth to remove as much water as possible so that the dog is 'drip dry' before you use a blaster or apply heat.

BATHING BRACHYCEPHALIC BREEDS

The position of the eyes on these breeds means that they are constantly moving their heads to be able to see you. As they do not have any length of foreface, bathing the face can be difficult. Figs 12.4.1–12.4.9 show you how to do this safely and confidently.

Fig. 12.4.1   The position of the eyes on a brachycephalic dog mean that it has to constantly move its head to keep you within its field of vision. Turn the dog away from you so that it is not looking up at you because it can see you within its peripheral field of vision.

Fig. 12.4.2   Shield the eyes and the nose whilst you are wetting the top of the head.

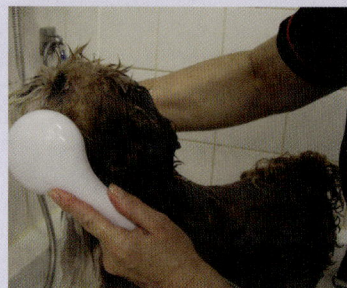

Fig. 12.4.3   Keep the hose on the cheek as you wet the sides of the head.

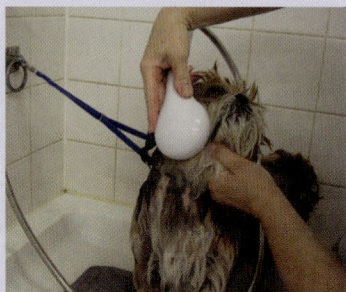

Fig. 12.4.4   Hold the hair under the chin to stop the dog looking downwards so the water can't seep into the eyes.

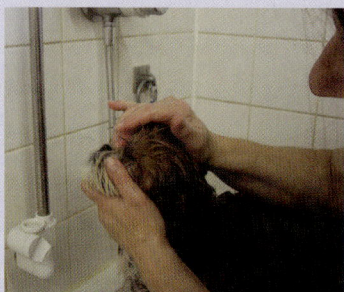

Fig. 12.4.5   Use a small amount of shampoo taken from the back of the neck and use your fingers to wash the bridge of the nose, with the dog still facing away from you.

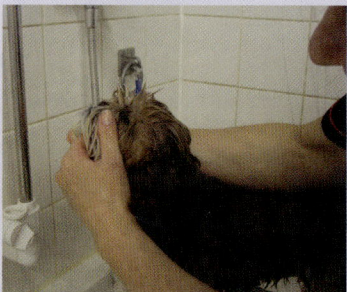

Fig. 12.4.6   If you wash both sides of the face at the same time, the dog will be less inclined to turn to face you or to look up.

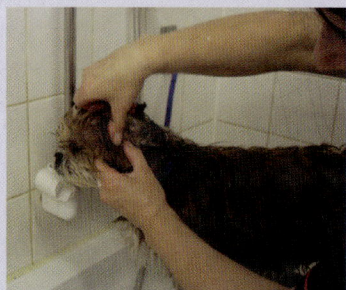

Fig. 12.4.7
Most of the brachycephalic dogs you will encounter have small heads so it is easy to work both hands at the same time to both wash and keep the head in a level or downward position without unduly restraining the dog.

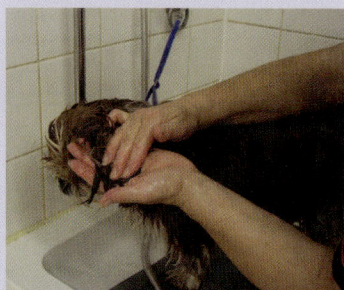

Fig. 12.4.8   The same applies when you are washing the ears.

Fig. 12.4.9   Bathing over, the face is rinsed in the same way as it was drenched, making sure that the hose is kept close to the skin at all times and that you use your hands to shield the eyes and the nose.

CAUTION: LIMIT THE RISK OF SPREADING DISEASE

Clean and disinfect the bath before the next dog, and do not re-use the towels until they have been washed.

If water has got into the ear canals, dry them out with dry cotton wool, and do not forget to tell the owner if the dog has ingested shampoo or if shampoo got into the dog's eyes.

BATHING PROCEDURE CHECK-LIST

◆ *Prepare the dog by grooming out all excess undercoat, debris and knots and insert cotton wool into the ears (if this is your preference).*

◆ *Prepare the bathing area with towels and shampoo ready for use.*

◆ *Secure the dog in the bath with ties and have a non-slip mat or towel for him to stand on.*

◆ *Check the water temperature on the inside of your wrist. It should be tepid or lukewarm.*

◆ *Soak the dog thoroughly, starting at the rear end and moving towards the head, with the water running under the hairs onto the skin. Leave the head until last to prevent the dog from shaking excessively.*

◆ *Apply the shampoo and wash in a circular motion for smooth coats and an up and down motion for long coats.*

◆ *Now wash the head, face and ears, taking care to avoid getting shampoo in the ears, eyes or mouth.*

◆ *Rinse thoroughly from the head towards the tail until the coat is 'squeaky' clean and the water runs clear.*

◆ *Apply another shampoo if necessary, or a conditioner, and rinse again.*

◆ *Check that there are no soap suds left in the coat, particularly on the dog's undercarriage, under the throat and between the back legs.*

◆ *Squeeze the water from the coat with your hands and towel dry with a super absorbent cloth.*

◆ *Use towels or a blaster to make sure that the dog is 'drip dry' before leaving the bath.*

◆ *Dry according to the required finish.*

Note: soaking the coat should be done from the rear end moving forwards towards the head, whereas rinsing is done from the head first, down towards the tail.

References

Curtis, C. (1998). Use and abuse of topical dermatological therapy in dogs and cats. Part 1. Shampoo therapy. *In Practice*, 20, 244–251.

Fisher, M.H. (1997). *The travels of Dean Mahomet: An eighteenth-century journey through India*. Berkeley: University of California Press.

Matousek, J.L., Campbell, K.L., Kakoma, I., Solter, P.F. and Schaefer, D.J. (2003a). Evaluation of the effect of pH on in vitro growth of Malassezia pachydermatitis. *J. Canadian Veterinary Research*, 67, (1), 56–59.

Matousek, J.L., Campbell, K.L., Kakoma, I. and Schaefer, D.J. (2003b). The effects of four acidifying sprays, vinegar and water on canine cutaneous pH levels. *J. Am. Anim. Hosp. Assoc.* 39, (1), 29–33.

Meyer W. and Neurand K. (1991). Comparison of skin pH in domesticated and laboratory mammals. *Arch. Dermatol. Res.*, 283, 16–18.

Ruedisueli, F.L., Eastwood, N.J., Gunn, N.K., Watson, T.D.G. (1998). The measurement of skin pH in normal dogs of different breeds. In: K.W. Kwochka, T. Willemse and C. von Tscharner (eds). *Advances in Veterinary Dermatology*. Vol 3. Oxford: Butterworth-Heinemann, pp. 521–522.

13   Drying the Dog

After bathing the dog, the coat needs to dry. This is very important and serves to take moisture away from the skin, thereby preventing chafing and protecting the dog from either:

◆ hypothermia, should the wetting of the coat reduce the dog's ability to stay warm. A wet coat is less able to trap air and protect the dog from draughts and a drop in the environmental temperature. In extreme cases moisture in the coat may freeze and turn to ice crystals.

◆ overheating (or even scalding), should the temperature increase as the moisture heats up.

Having bathed the dog, we must take responsibility for making sure that he is able to get his coat dried. There are several ways that this can be done, which both meet the needs of the dog and, if required, help to prepare the coat for styling and shaping.

It may be argued that, as long as the coat is dry, it is sufficient to meet the needs of the dog. If the dog has been bathed because he was dirty but not in need of a trim, then the argument has some merit, although the counter-argument is that, for the sake of the dog, a long coat still needs to be groomed whilst it is drying. Either way, it can only be of benefit to the dog if the coat is dried in a manner that leaves the coat in a knot-free, manageable condition.

If the dog is to be trimmed and styled, the quality of the finished article will definitely depend on how well you have dried the coat and the method used. Any existing knots or tangles will tighten as the hair dries, so it is in the interest of the dog and its skin to remove these before bathing, or during drying if they are discovered at this late stage.

Even the best styling skills will be compromised if the coat has not been prepared correctly. Styling and shaping will be difficult and will challenge even the best stylist. Your work will be seen by many and may attract disapproval and criticism.

This chapter looks at the different drying methods, and the effects they have on preparation for styling and shaping. Chapter 10 covered drying equipment: this chapter deals with how and when we use that equipment.

Drying is the process of removing moisture from the coat. For the purposes of grooming and styling, the coat is dried in order to both prevent a long coat from curling and knotting as it dries, and to prepare the coat for its final presentation (either styled or unstyled). Drying anything, including the dog's coat, can only be achieved by:

◆ *Evaporation:* a natural process where water changes from the liquid state into a vapour or gas and disperses into the atmosphere. This occurs quickly as soon as the water temperature is raised above freezing point. Below freezing point it becomes ice; it will still evaporate but much more slowly. The body temperature of the dog causes water to evaporate and disperse.

◆ *Centrifuge:* a process where the water is repelled by force. This is naturally achieved when dogs shake themselves vigorously.

◆ *Draught:* where the movement of air forces moisture to be removed.

This occurs naturally when the wind blows or moves the dog's coat.

Before we go any further, attention needs to be paid to the effect that drying the coat has on the skin of the dog. The skin, as we know, is designed for protection and aids thermoregulation. It is tough and robust but can be easily damaged when it is exposed to harsh treatment and conditions.

The dog naturally repels water from the skin by body heat and from the coat by centrifugal shaking. This requires energy to create the body heat and substantial shaking from the dog to create centrifugal force. Shaking excessively or unnecessarily can pose the risk of injury to pendulous ears and may put extra strain on the joints

of some dogs. It may be argued that shaking is the natural way for dogs to dry themselves; this is true of the dog that has taken a dip in the sea or a river (*see* Fig. 13.0.1). It is not quite correct, however, of a dog that has just come out of the bath.

Fig. 13.0.1   *After a winter swim in the sea, Tulip was unaffected by the cold and came out of the water to give her ball back before going back in again.*

The difference is that the sea does not contain shampoo, so the dog swimming in the sea is not exposed to chemicals (however mild) that may remove or reduce the ability of the natural oils in his skin and coat to repel water. The natural oiliness of the dog's skin and hair coat help to protect the dog from becoming sodden or drenched (see Fig. 13.0.2) and naturally repel water. By contrast, the detergents in shampoo drastically reduce this repellency. The dog coming out of the sea is therefore far less waterlogged than the dog coming out of the bath, and requires a lot less shaking to dry the coat.

Fig. 13.0.2 Even before she had a shake, her coat was wet but not saturated. The grease in the coat repelled most of the water, showing that her natural waterproofing is unaffected.

A coat that has lost its waterproofing, albeit temporarily, needs a lot more shaking and the dog must expend a lot more energy to dry it. So, when we remove the waterproofing by bathing the dog, it is only fair that we give the dog a hand to get dry again.

Aiding the drying process must be done with consideration because applying excessive heat or prolonging exposure to artificially generated heat can:

◆ dry and damage the skin;
◆ risk burning or scalding the skin; and
◆ interfere with thermoregulation and the skin's natural ability to cool the dog.

Before applying any heat source, natural or artificial, it is vitally important that you remove as much water as possible after bathing the dog. This can be achieved firstly by using your hands to squeeze excess water from the coat, and then by using high-absorbency cloths or towels to 'blot' the coat until it is drip dry. At this point there should no longer be any drips falling from the end of the hairs.

Removing excess water serves three purposes: it reduces the risk of the dog overheating when the water heats up; it reduces the risk of steam building up between the layers of the coat as it dries, thereby reducing the risk of scalding the skin; and it reduces the time that the skin is exposed to artificial heat, therefore reducing the risk of drying out the skin and causing permanent damage. The time spent drying with any sort of hair-dryer needs to be minimized and temperature settings kept as low as possible.

In essence, the more water you remove from a bathed dog before you begin drying the coat, the better and safer it is for the dog. And, on a practical note, it is also cheaper on electricity for you!

13.1 DRYING SYSTEMS

A 'drying system' is the arrangement and coordination of one or more pieces of drying equipment to provide you with different methods to achieve your desired end result. A variety of drying equipment is available to you, giving you the flexibility to choose from several systems to get the coat dry, starting with high-absorbency cloths, and finishing, perhaps, by drying the coat, either naturally or with generated heat of some kind. You may require the versatility of more than one drying system and a range of drying techniques if you are working commercially in order to meet the needs of different breeds. The choices you make depend on your budget, the space that you have available and the number of dogs you expect to be grooming. The final presentation of the dog depends on how you have prepared the dog and, critically, how you have dried the clean, washed coat.

The drying options available to you are:

◆ towels and high-absorbency cloths
◆ blasters
◆ hand dryers
◆ stand dryers
◆ drying cabinets
◆ fresh air!

Your decision about how to dry each dog will depend on many factors:

The skin condition of the dog

If the skin is in poor condition, it may be advisable to avoid using a blaster to remove excess water. The use of artificial heat to dry the coat may also be contraindicated. Check with the dog's vet!

The anatomy of the dog

Dogs with shortened nasal passages (brachycephalics) should not be put in drying cabinets. A portable dryer (hand or free standing) should be used instead. If the dog has poor muscle condition, using a blaster may be unwise as it could cause bruising. The dog may also chill easily, so a drying cabinet may be a good option.

The health of the dog

Dogs with known heart conditions or breathing problems should not be put in a drying cabinet. Use a portable dryer instead or consider natural drying in extreme cases. Likewise, dogs that suffer from fits and convulsions should not be placed in a drying cabinet. Use a portable dryer instead or, in extreme cases, consider natural drying.

Old or infirm dogs should be dried as quickly as possible as they can chill easily. Consider using a drying cabinet if the dog is otherwise healthy but ensure the dog is supervised and monitored at all times.

The temperament of the dog

If the dog is sensitive to noise, a blaster would be unsuitable, as would a noisy portable dryer. Consider using a drying cabinet. If the dog is very nervous and panics easily, a drying cabinet would not be a wise option, whereas a portable dryer can be switched on and off, or moved away from the dog where necessary.

A dog that shows signs of aggression should not be put into a drying cabinet in case you cannot get him out again.

The type and quality of the coat

A coat that needs to be dried straight

for styling will go curly very quickly in a drying cabinet and the quality of your work may be compromised. Very long coats may become knotted by the velocity of a blaster, and long coats may form into 'whip' knots when exposed to the circular airflow of a drying cabinet.

Very dense coats benefit from the use of a blaster whereas finer coats may be easily damaged.

Short coats will not lie sleek on the body if they have been blow dried against the natural direction of the coat growth by drying cabinets or portable driers.

The dog may have a coat that requires two different methods of drying if it is to be styled. For example, the English Cocker Spaniel has a short smooth body coat but longer leg, ear and body furnishings that need to be stretched and dried straight for more even trimming.

13.2 DRYING METHODS

There are several methods or procedures that can be used to dry the dog:

- towel drying
- blasting
- cabinet drying
- natural drying
- stretch drying
- fluff drying.

Each one serves a different purpose and each gives a different finished or final effect. The method you choose depends on how you intend to complete the grooming session, and whether you will be styling or trimming the coat after the bath (and therefore need to prepare it correctly), or whether the dog is just being bathed to clean his coat and preparation for styling is not necessary.

In either case, you need to make sure that the dog is drip dry before he leaves the bath.

13.2.1 Towel drying

Towel drying is something that must be done in the first instance before the dog leaves the bath. The reasons for this are twofold. First, if the dog leaves the bath dripping water everywhere, the floor will become wet and slippery, which is dangerous for all concerned.

DRYING BY ARTIFICIALLY GENERATED HEAT

When you are drying the dog with any form of artificially generated heat, the coat at the point of airflow contact should be moving at all times. You can achieve this by using your fingers to move the coat or by working with your brush to cross the airflow as it focuses on the coat (see Fig. 13.2.1). There are a few reasons for this:

- *If you cannot feel the heat arriving on the dog, you are failing to monitor the heat at skin level and the dog risks getting burnt. By holding the brush in your hand and using it to cross the airflow, you can feel and monitor the heat of the drier.*
- *Steam can build up in the coat if the hair is not moved during the drying process (see Fig. 13.2.2). This can result in scalding of the skin. The brush or your hand should therefore be moving the hair at the point of airflow contact.*
- *Brushing with the help of an airflow separating the coat gives you a very clear view of the skin so you can monitor for burns or scalds. You may also find any abnormalities of the skin that your health check may have missed. You should be watching and monitoring the skin and coat whilst you are working so you should not miss anything!*
- *Make sure that you are brushing (and watching) where the airflow makes contact. If you are brushing elsewhere, the skin is likely to get burnt (see Fig. 13.2.3).*
- *It is a waste of effort, energy and time if you are brushing a wet coat in order to dry it straight whilst the coat is being dried curly by the hair-dryer in an area that you are not brushing. A drier with a large output nozzle spreads warm air over a large area. This may result in areas being inadvertently exposed to heat and the hair drying without being brushed.*
- *Once the coat has dried curly, you cannot straighten it without wetting it again so your coat presentation may not be good enough to style correctly.*
- *The warmer and stronger the airflow, the quicker you have to work. The coat will dry much more quickly than the skin once heat is applied and you must keep the coat moving to prevent a build-up of steam and obtain your desired drying finish.*

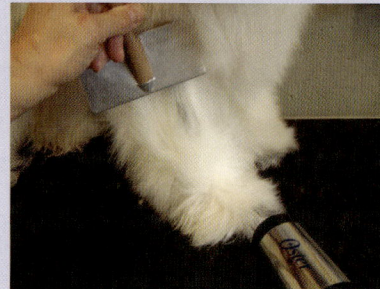

Fig. 13.2.1   Move the coat by working your brush across the airflow as it focuses on the coat.

Fig. 13.2.2   Here you can see that the brush is holding the hair down to dry it straight rather than moving it. This will very quickly cause a build-up of steam within the density of the coat, which could scald the skin.

Fig. 13.2.3   Make sure that you are brushing at the point of heat contact. If you are brushing somewhere else, the skin is unmonitored and could be burning.

Secondly, in order to protect the skin, as much water as possible needs to be removed before exposing the skin to artificial heat.

There are a few things to consider when you are drying a dog with towels:

◆ If the skin is very sore or the hair coat is very thin (alopecia), do not rub with your towel. Instead, blot the coat and keep blotting until the coat is as dry as possible.
◆ If the dog has a long coat, use an up-and-down motion with your towels rather than a circular motion, as the latter will knot the coat.
◆ A short-coated dog can be dried with either a circular motion or an up-and-down motion, in both cases lifting the coat towards the head to dry the skin.

You need a high-absorbency cloth (this type of cloth is used damp, and can absorb many times its own weight in water; it will need wringing out frequently) and at least one dry towel.

With all dogs that have some length of coat, you should restrict yourself to blotting the coat with your towel or working in an up-and-down motion. Rubbing the coat in circles will promote knots and tangles. Smooth-coated dogs won't have this problem, so circles are fine!

Start by drying the head and face first, particularly with longer-coated breeds so that water does not drip into

the eyes. This is particularly important if you have used a conditioner because these products often leave a residue after rinsing to protect the hair and aid grooming. A similar situation may arise following the use of a VPOM shampoo, which is designed to leave a chemical/medicinal residue in the coat (*see* Figs

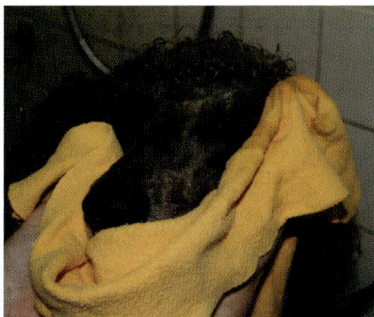

Fig. 13.2.4   Towel dry the face and the head first, particularly with coated breeds, so that water doesn't drip into the eyes. This is very important either if a conditioner has been used because it often leaves an oily residue behind after rinsing, or if VPOMs have been used that are designed to leave a chemical medicine in the coat.

Fig. 13.2.5   Once the face and around the ears are drip dry, the dog will not feel the urge to shake quite as violently or as often.

13.2.4 and 13.2.5).

Dogs shake to remove the water from their head and ear regions, so once the face and ears are dry, they are less inclined to shake violently or as often. This helps you keep control over where all the water goes, rather than

leaving it up to the dog!

From the head, work your way down the back and the body using your cloth in a backwards-and-forwards motion (head to tail and back again). Gravity pulls water down towards the feet so the back tends to dry quite quickly. This does mean, though, that drying the legs and feet is more time-consuming whether the dog has a long or short coat.

Blot the legs repeatedly, wringing out your cloth frequently, particularly if you are drying long coats (*see* Fig. 13.2.6). The longer back legs can be blotted or rubbed up and down, but remember to resist the temptation to make circles over the rump and the tops of the legs (*see* Fig. 13.2.7). When there are no longer any drips coming from the coat, use your towel to repeat the process (*see* Fig. 13.2.8). The dog is now ready for blasting or drying.

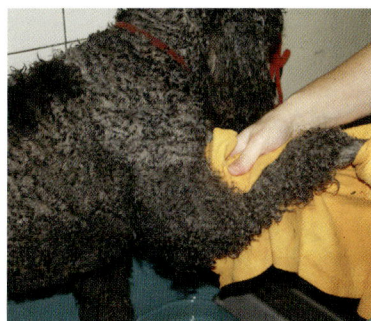

Fig. 13.2.6   On coated dogs blot the coat or squeeze it in a high-absorbency cloth to extract the water. Rubbing encourages knotting.

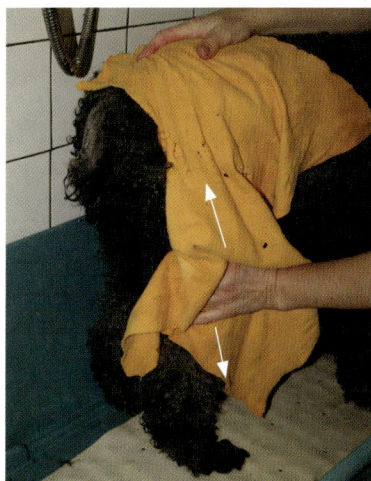

Fig. 13.2.7   You can either blot the hair on the long hind legs or you can rub up and down but try not to make circles with your cloth.

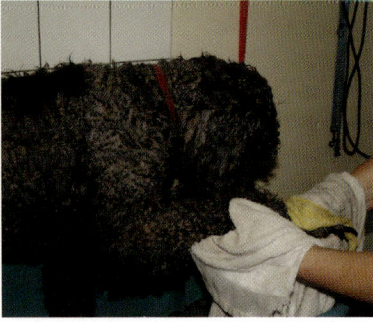

Fig. 13.2.8   You can see here that there is no water dripping from the coat. A terry towel is being used to sop up any final droplets. This coat is now ready for blasting or drying with a hair-dryer.

There are some instances where it is not possible to use any form of heat. This includes dogs with skin conditions that will be aggravated if heat is applied (*see* Fig. 13.2.9). Sometimes dogs that are very sensitive to noise may need to be towel dried from start to finish if the dryer cannot be tolerated. It is acceptable to leave the dog to dry, providing the environment is warm and free of draughts, but in winter it may be necessary to use towels to dry the dog. You are likely to need several towels but good use of a high-absorbency cloth will help to reduce the amount that you use.

Towel drying should be interrupted periodically to brush the coat so that any developing knots are removed.

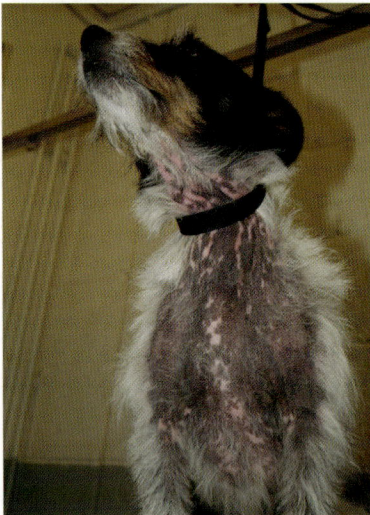

Fig. 13.2.9   This Jack Russell Terrier has hair loss and lichenification of the skin over the neck and chest. The skin is inflamed and will benefit from being dried without any form of artificial heat. This dog was dried with towels only.

Confine the dog to a bed covered in towelling. Evaporation from the warming skin will help to finish the drying process. Change the towel frequently so that the dog is not lying on a wet patch and encourage the dog to turn over and lie on the opposite side when the bedding is changed. If it is not possible to get the dog completely dry with towels, pay particular attention to the drying of the ears, and the lumbar back region, as these are the areas where the dog will feel the cold first. Keep the dog in a warm room until drying is complete. If the dog is long coated, it may be wise to brush or ruffle the coat periodically to lift it from the skin, thus allowing the skin to dry as quickly as possible.

Towel drying is the preferred way to dry damaged skin, and it minimizes skin damage from over-exposure to a heat source. The disadvantages are that it is time-consuming and generates a lot of laundry, and a naturally dried coat is not necessarily prepared correctly for styling.

13.2.2 Blasting

Blasters are a very useful addition to the grooming environment. Used correctly, they simulate the centrifugal action of the dog shaking. With the nozzle held adjacent to the coat, with the airflow aimed across the coat in two opposing directions (up and down, or side-to-side), they repel large quantities of water and any loose hairs. In addition, the high-velocity airflow helps to remove the water by draught, saving the commercial groomer valuable time, a lot of effort and less towel laundering. Long coats can be brushed whilst you are using the blaster to help prevent knots forming. Blasters can be very noisy, so they are not suited to all dogs, and some models are so powerful they are not suitable for use on puppies, old or disabled dogs, or those with poor muscle tone.

Some blasters have a heating element that produces warm air to help the drying process but others blow cool air only. The latter do little to dry the coat, unless used for a prolonged period, but they do disperse the majority of water from the coat. Another drying method is needed to complete the job.

You need:

- a blaster;
- a brush to suit the coat type;
- ear protectors for the groomer;
- a face-mask for the groomer; and
- possibly cotton wool for the dog's ears.

Switch the blaster on and let the dog get used to the noise before you apply it to the coat. Start near the rear end of the dog with the nozzle at a distance from the coat (*see* Fig. 13.2.10). A spare pair of hands may be useful if it is the first time the dog has experienced a blaster.

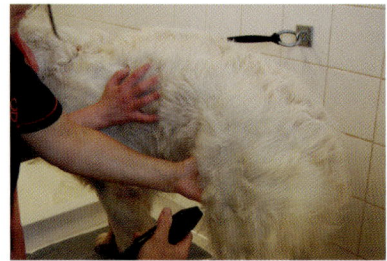

Fig. 13.2.10   Start the blaster and give the dog a few minutes to get used to the noise. Then start using the blaster near the rear end. If the dog is not used to a blaster, a second pair of hands on the dog can be useful to reassure him.

When the dog is settled, turn the nozzle sideways on so that it is parallel to the coat and wave it slowly from side-to-side, either very close to the coat if the dog is short haired, or from a distance that allows the coat to blow straight if the hair is long (*see* Fig. 13.2.11). If you move the nozzle too fast, it encourages long coat hairs to turn around on themselves and knot-

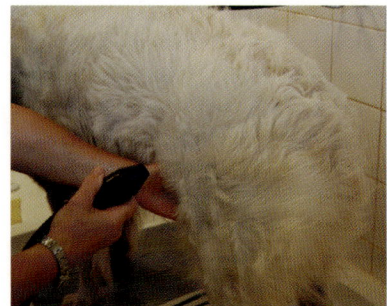

Fig. 13.2.11   Keeping the nozzle parallel to the coat, move it slowly from side to side, leaving enough room between the dog and the nozzle for the coat to blow out straight.

ting will start. If there is a lot of water being displaced, you can hold a towel behind the area that you are working on to collect the moisture before it is expelled into the environment of your bathing room.

Work slowly and methodically over the dog, working towards the front, with the coat always being blown in the direction of hair growth (*see* Fig. 13.2.12). If you blow the coat in the wrong direction with the force of a powerful blaster, you risk traumatizing and bruising the skin. Take care not to use the blaster on sensitive areas such as the undercarriage, the throat, around the genitals and the face, and stop if the dog shows any signs of stress or discomfort.

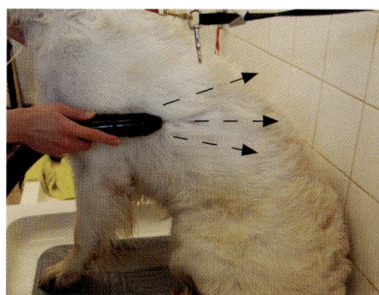

Fig. 13.2.12   Work slowly and methodically over the coat, working towards the front of the dog.

The advantages of blasting are that it saves on towels and drying time. The disadvantages are that it can cause bruising and skin trauma if used incorrectly (see Figs 13.2.13a–13.2.13b) and can cause damage to the bathing room environment (*see* Fig. 13.2.14).

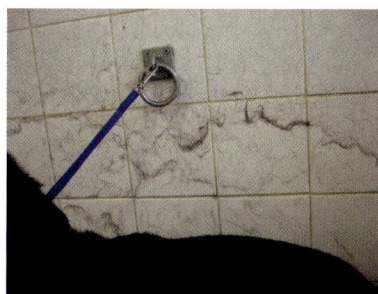

Fig. 13.2.14   Some of the wet loose hair blown out of the coat in a few seconds by a high-velocity blaster. Water will have blown from the coat at the same time. This picture demonstrates the damage that a blaster can do to your environment, and highlights the need to wear a face mask.

A WORD OF CAUTION ABOUT BLASTERS

Blasters are an extremely useful addition to the commercial grooming salon as long as they are used correctly. Before you use your blaster, however, you should think about what you are trying to achieve and the dog that you intend to use it on.

Blasters remove the water from the coat in the same manner as the dog shaking himself. When the dog shakes, the hairs are moved across the body in two opposing directions, so that water droplets can travel the length of the hair shafts and be thrown off at the ends. The strong air current from the blaster causes a draught and does the same as the breeze or wind by separating the coat to remove the moisture.

You need to simulate this action with the blaster by moving the coat from side to side with the help of the air flow. Aiming the blaster directly at the dog concentrates the air flow into a small area, and the skin, rather than the coat, takes the impact. Water particles are not forced along the hair length to disperse because the air flow covers less area on the coat length.

It is worth remembering that the dog's skin is covered by hair for a reason. As a living organ, it was not designed to be, nor should it ever be, directly exposed to an extremely high-velocity air flow aimed directly at one small point on its surface. Using a powerful blaster incorrectly may not only dry out and bruise the skin, it can also, in some cases, cause muscle damage to the dog, so exercise caution and remember the risks when you are using one. Used correctly, they are safe and extremely useful.

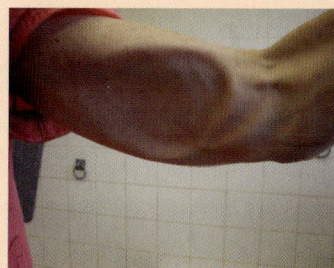

Fig. 13.2.13a-b   These two pictures demonstrate the force of the high-velocity blaster. The photo on the left shows the indentation caused in well-developed muscle by the blaster pummelling the skin at close range. The photo on the right shows the arm of a mature person and the effect of the same blaster on the same setting from a distance of about half a metre. The muscle structure is weaker and this lady actually suffered nasty bruising from the demonstration.

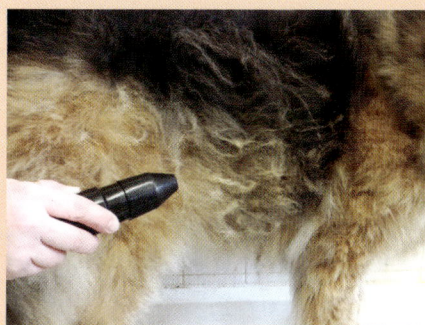

Fig. 13.2.15   Aiming the blaster directly at the dog has the same effect on his muscle and skin

Note: whip knots
Aiming the strong air current from the blaster across the coat can cause 'whip knots' to form, where a long coat tangles as it blows. These are not nearly as damaging to the dog (or his skin) as the injuries that can be caused by the blaster being aimed directly at the skin. On long coats, using the blaster further away from the dog helps to reduce 'whip knots' by giving room for the hair to straighten out as it blows. This also allows the water particles to be blown right to the end of the hairs, from where they can disperse.

13.2.3 Cabinet drying

Cabinet dryers are very popular with commercial groomers. They are costly to buy and not particularly cheap to run, but in a busy establishment they can save time. (They can also waste time: if you require a straight coat for styling and the dog is not removed before the coat dries curly, the coat will have to be damped down again and redried.)

Drying in a cabinet is a good option for:

◆ smooth-coated dogs that do not require a special coat finish;

CAUTION: FATALITIES DO OCCUR IN DRYING CAGES

Brachycephalic dogs like the Pug (see Fig. 13.2.16), the Cavalier King Charles Spaniel, the Shih Tzu, the Lhasa Apso, the Pekingese and the Bulldog should NEVER be put in a drying cabinet. These dogs have restricted breathing and the environment within a drying cage is extremely dangerous to their health and welfare.

Fig.13.2.16   Brachycephalic dogs should not be put into a drying cabinet because they have restricted breathing.

Dogs with known or suspected heart conditions or epilepsy should also not be dried in a drying cabinet because the environment is unsuitable. The groomer may not always be aware of these conditions, but careful questioning of the owner on admission, combined with breed knowledge, should alert you to those individuals and breeds vulnerable to heart disease. As a precautionary measure, these dogs should not be placed in a cabinet.

◆ dogs that are only being bathed and not styled;
◆ dogs that are noise-sensitive or nervous of the hair-dryer; and
◆ starting the drying process before using another drying method.

Once bathing is complete, dry the dog until he is drip free and place him in the dryer. You need to watch the dog throughout the drying process and remove him immediately if he becomes stressed, starts panting, or shows any signs of becoming unwell. In addition, you should regularly remove him to check that there is no steam within the coat, as this can burn the skin, and to brush the coat through so you can keep a check on progress. If you want the coat to dry straight, remove the dog before his coat is fully dry.

The main advantage to cabinet drying is that it allows the groomer to do something else whilst the dog is drying. Be very wary of this apparent benefit, though, as it can lead to inattention and even fatalities. The disadvantages

Fig. 13.2.17   This dog has just been removed from a cabinet after ten minutes. The coat has dried and gone curly.

Fig. 13.2.18   Even after attempting to straighten the coat, the wrinkles are still evident and have spoilt the finish on the style.

of drying cabinets are that they are expensive pieces of equipment to buy and costly to run, they are not suitable for all dogs, they must be monitored by someone all the time, and, unless care is taken, the coat finish may be substandard if the coat has been left to over-dry (see Figs 13.2.17 and 13.2.18).

CAUTION

NEVER put a dog wearing a muzzle in a drying cabinet. Muzzles restrict breathing and can increase the risk of suffocation. If the dog cannot pant sufficiently, he can easily overheat or suffer heatstroke. If he starts to suffer the effects of either of these problems, you will be faced with the dangerous situation of a distressed, panicking and potentially aggressive dog fighting for survival. His distress can render him difficult to remove from an enclosed area, and you cannot rely on the dog being able to get himself out of the cabinet. Additionally, you may not be able to safely remove the muzzle.

13.2.4 Natural drying

Natural drying is, as the name implies, the process of drying the dog naturally, without the aid of generated heat and without interfering with the coat by brushing whilst it is drying. It is a procedure used mainly on short-coated breeds (see Fig. 13.2.19) that can be left in a warm place to dry their coats with the aid of their own body heat or sunshine. Some coated breeds are also encouraged to dry naturally so that their coats dry with natural curls and waves in. The soft silky coat of the Irish Water Spaniel, for example, dries in natural curls (see Fig. 13.2.20).

You need:

◆ a high-absorbency cloth;
◆ a towel;
◆ a blaster if desired;
◆ a dry day if drying outside; and
◆ a brush or comb to suit the coat type.

The coat should be towel dried until

Fig. 13.2.19 *Some dogs, like the smooth-coated Labrador, can be left on a nice day to dry naturally in the sunshine.*

Fig. 13.2.20 *The Irish Water Spaniel (pictured) and the Kerry Blue Terrier both have a silky coat that is left to dry naturally after bathing so that the coat curls whilst drying. They are then combed out with a wide-toothed comb and trimmed to show off the curly coat. (Photo: Michael Trafford)*

there is as little moisture in the coat as possible, and blasting can be done, providing it does not affect the coat presentation.

Once you have reached this stage, brush or comb the coat through gently so that you separate the hair out or lay it down, depending on the coat length. Take care when doing this because the skin is vulnerable and tools used with too much vigour can be damaging.

The dog can be left to run around

in the sunshine, or put in a warm area where his body temperature will dry him from the skin surface outwards. If it is a windy day, you would be wise to periodically check a long coat for tangling.

If the dog is to be confined whilst drying, make sure that the area provided is large enough for him to move around in, as he needs to generate heat in order to keep warm.

There are several advantages to natural drying. The coat dries from the skin outwards, so moisture can escape rather than increase in temperature. It is therefore less likely that the dog's skin will be harmed. The coat dries to exhibit its natural structure. Smooth coats lie sleekly on the body, whilst long coats display curls and waves. It is useful for drying nervous dogs, especially any that are particularly noise-sensitive, and it is very economical!

The disadvantages are that it can take a long time for the coat to dry if the dog is heavy-coated, and long coats may start to curl and may even form knots, particularly if the dog rolls around on the grass in an effort to speed up the process.

If you are allowing your pet to dry naturally within the home, do not forget to keep him away from carpets, beds and chairs. Even a drip-free dog can be very wet!

> **CAUTION**
>
> *If you decide to dry a dog in the sunshine, he must be able to move out of the sun if he wants to. Either leave him loose to move around or, if you are restraining him, make sure that shade is available within reach. Water must also be within reach at all times and the dog should be checked regularly.*

13.2.5 Smooth drying

This method is used to dry the coat flat against the body to enhance body shape whilst leaving it lying glossy and 'smooth'. It is achieved by first lifting the coat to dry the dog's skin and then laying the coat down as the coat hair dries so that it conforms to the dog's body shape. Short-coated dogs like Labradors are dried with this method to leave the coat sleek and 'velvet' to the touch. It can also be applied to breeds where the hair has a little more length to it, such as German Shepherds. There are many silk- and double-coated breeds that are presented with their body coats smooth-dried close to the body to enhance the long flowing furnishings on legs and undercarriages. Irish Setters, English Cocker Spaniels (*see* Fig. 13.2.21), Golden Retrievers and Border Collies are some of the breeds presented in this way. The Border Collie has a much longer and denser coat but it is also smooth-dried so the body coat lies flat.

To smooth-dry your dog you need:

◆ a high absorbency cloth;
◆ a towel;
◆ a blaster if desired; and
◆ a hair-dryer.

Begin by squeezing water from the coat and using a towel until the coat is drip free. A blaster can be used if appropriate. The dog can be placed in a drying cabinet for a short time if desired, but if you choose to use a cabinet to start the process, use it for only a few minutes because the coat will not lie smooth if it has dried in the wrong direction. A hand dryer or a stand dryer can be used with the aid of your fingers to ruffle or move the coat so the skin can dry. Finish by smoothing the coat

Fig. 13.2.22 *After being smooth dried so that the coat lies flat, this Border Collie cross was brushed with a bristle brush to bring up the shine on the coat.*

as it is drying towards the tail with your hand or a brush.

When you think the dog is dry, leave him to cool for five or ten minutes and then run your fingers through the coat in the wrong direction to check for damp. Keep checking the dog for signs of chilling, particularly during the colder months.

Once dry, brush with a bristle brush to achieve a smooth glossy finish (*see* Fig. 13.2.22). Sacking can be applied to help to keep the hair straight on dogs whose coat has a tendency to curl again as soon as moisture reappears within the coat.

The advantages of smooth drying are that short-coated breeds develop a beautiful natural lustre to the coat and their coat sits close to the body, the dog's body shape and muscle structure are more defined, and it enhances the furnishings of some breeds. The disadvantage is that it can take a lot longer

SACKING

Sacking is the term used when a breathable mesh coat (see Fig. 13.2.23) is put on a dog during or immediately after the drying process to help to keep the coat free of waves and curls. The mesh coat is often applied to show dogs that have coat textures which deviate from the desired breed requirements.

Fig. 13.2.23 *This Golden Retriever is wearing a mesh coat to keep the coat smooth for showing. The coat has been smooth dried but moisture in the environment will make it wavy. The mesh coat prevents this happening. This practice is called 'sacking'.*

than one might think to thoroughly dry a short, thick coat like that of the Labrador. This is because moisture can continue to build within the coat for some considerable time as oily sebum is absorbed into the skin and excess water is pushed upwards from the surface layers of the skin.

Stretch drying

Stretch drying is a method used to straighten curls and waves from the coat, leaving it as straight as possible

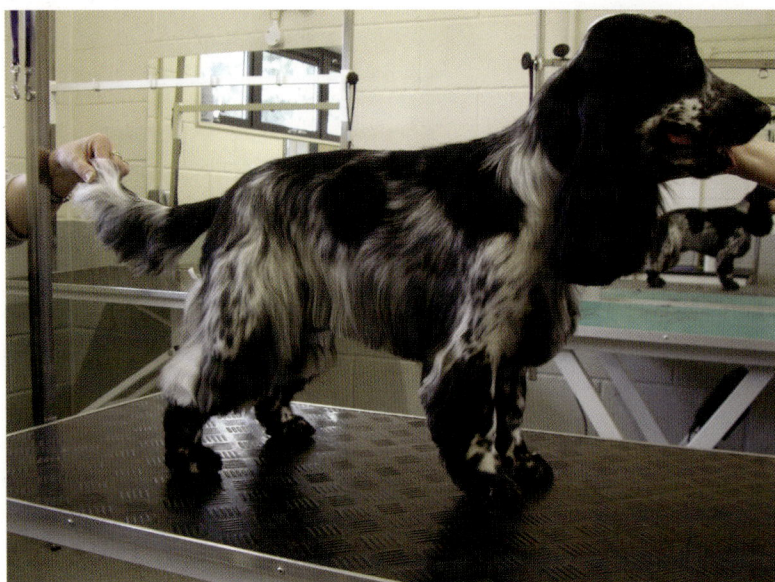

Fig. 13.2.21 *The body coat of this English Cocker Spaniel has been smooth dried so that it lies close to the body.*

once dried. It can create the illusion that the coat is longer than when you started. Whilst this method can be used in any circumstances where the coat needs to have the curl or wave removed, it is most often used on the feathers and furnishings of gundogs such as Spaniels (*see* Fig. 13.2.24), Setters and Retrievers. In these dogs, the longer hair on the legs, ears, undercarriage and tail (*see* Fig. 13.2.25) can be styled evenly. It is also indicated for wool coats like that of the Poodle and Bichon Frisé, where the coat needs to be curl free for styling.

When hair is wet it reverts to its natural structure, so any curls or waves become apparent; if the coat is left to dry naturally, these curls and waves will tighten up and become more exaggerated. Stretch drying is achieved by continuously brushing the hair in the direction in which it grows until it is dry (see Fig. 13.2.26). The hair then remains straight until it becomes damp, when the curls and waves will start to reappear.

This method of drying is used over the entire body, or on parts of the body, on any breed where a curl or wave in the coat prevents the groomer from styling the coat evenly. In the case of very long silk coats like that of the Yorkshire Terrier, some Afghan Hounds, the Shih Tzu and the Lhasa Apso, the hair is stretched and then parted down the middle as soon as it is dry.

Ideally a dog's coat needs to be styled as soon as the coat is dry, as any 'resting' time will ruin your drying efforts.

Curls or waves in the coat give the impression of a shorter coat as the length of the individual hairs is taken up by the diameter of the curl. Straightening the coat therefore lengthens the individual hairs, giving a more accurate indication of the actual length of the coat. Trimming a coat that is curly will result in uneven cut lines.

You need:

♦ a high-absorbency cloth;
♦ towels;
♦ a brush to suit the coat type; and
♦ a hair-dryer.

To achieve this method, the coat has to be brushed continuously throughout the drying time. The coat is brushed in the direction of the coat growth and the groomer should continue brushing until the coat is absolutely dry.

Begin by towel drying the coat until it is drip dry. A blaster is not recom-

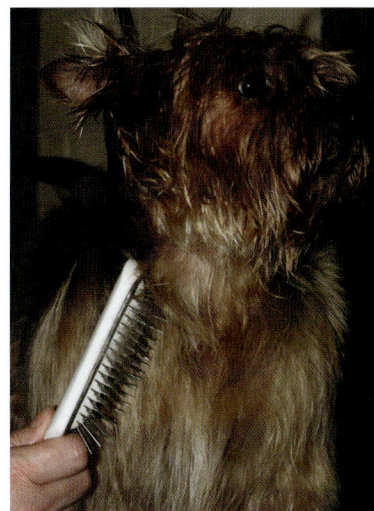

Fig. 13.2.26 *The coat should be brushed continuously in the direction in which it grows. A pin brush is being used on this Yorkshire Terrier to put a slight tension on the hair as it is stretched.*

the dryer temperature and brush the coat continuously as it is drying with the direction of growth. These coats are fragile and generally do not carry a short undercoat that will offer the skin protection from the heat. You need to work fairly fast, taking your brush the full length of the hair.

If you are stretching a wool coat, you should again lower the dryer temperature. To stretch-dry a wool coat you need to reverse your brush strokes and work against the direction of hair growth (the opposite way) so you are exposing the skin. For this you need to work even more quickly (crossing the airflow at about one brush stroke per second).

There are several advantages to stretch-drying the coat: the individual hairs are stretched to their maximum length; it allows the silk coat to lie sleek; it takes the curl out of wool coats (albeit temporarily); and it is easier to judge length when styling and easier to cut 'true' trimming lines rather than cut lines that are uneven because the coat curls or waves. The disadvantage is that the groomer must work quickly so the coat is stretched before it dries.

The coat will remain straight until moisture causes the hair to return to its natural texture, so you need to get the coat trimmed as soon as possible after drying.

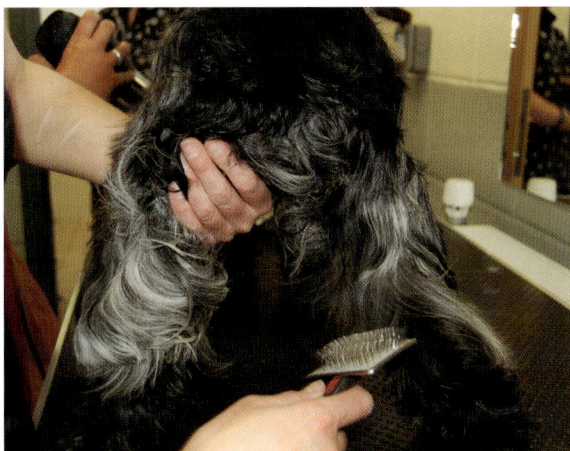

Fig. 13.2.24 *The trousers on this Cocker Spaniel are stretched dried to remove the wave in the coat so that the hair can be cut straight and even.*

Fig. 13.2.25 *The tail on this Golden Retriever has been stretched to maximum length for restyling.*

mended on long silk coats because they are fragile and can be damaged but it is fine to use on wool coats. A drying cabinet is not recommended if you want to stretch-dry a coat because even minimal use will start curling a wool coat and cause shrinking or knotting in a silk coat. Using a hand or stand dryer, start by ruffling the coat with your fingers so that it is lifted off the body. This helps the skin to start to dry.

If you are stretching a silk coat, lower

Fluff drying

Fluff drying is an effect rather than a method. It is, in fact, a stretch-dried coat that has been brushed in reverse! By brushing against the natural direction of growth whilst stretching it, the coat is encouraged to separate and stand up straight rather than lie on the body. This leaves the coat light and plump, giving the impression of added density and volume. The coat looks quite solid and it is firm and springy to the touch if patted very lightly.

To achieve a good 'fluff dry' effect, the entire coat must be continuously brushed in the wrong direction whilst it is being stretch-dried to ensure that the hair dries from the root and all curls are removed from the root outwards. Reducing the curl reduces the weight and the hairs will no longer hang down because they are straight and buoyant, and instead rise upright and support themselves by standing up against each other. This gives the coat an impression of greater volume.

This technique is generally the pre-ferred and recognized method for drying the wool coats of Poodles, the Bichon Frisé and Bedlington Terriers. It can also be used on double coats, the appearance of which benefits from the volume that fluff-drying achieves.

It is a difficult drying skill to master, partly because it requires a lot of effort from the groomer and partly because you have to work quickly so that you can get the coat straight before it dries. You also have to maintain the reverse brushing action in difficult places, such as the insides of the legs. Brushing against the natural direction of the coat can be hard work because there is more drag on your brush than there would be if you were brushing the coat the other way. Wool coats also dry very quickly so speed is of the essence.

You can achieve a good 'fluff-dry' finish with either a stand dryer or a hand-held dryer. A drying cage dries the coat too quickly and it will not have the straight, buoyant, voluminous texture that you require. It requires a fair bit of practice before you get it right, but it is well worth the effort.

You need:

- a hair-dryer;
- a slicker brush or a pin brush;
- a medium comb to finish with; and
- a spray bottle of water to dampen coat that has dried curly.

Until you have mastered the fluff-drying technique, you may find that wool coats in particular dry more quickly than you can work; they may therefore dry curly. It is a good idea to keep a spray bottle of water handy to dampen the coat slightly. Be careful not to apply too much water, though, because the dog will be warm and the moisture can quickly turn to steam in the coat.

Hold your brush lightly in your hand and use a light flicking action with your wrist as you brush, rather than a hard, forceful action, using your whole arm (imagine that you are whipping cream or beating eggs with a back-hand motion). Watch where you are drying. A dryer with a large outlet nozzle will spread the heat over a large area. Maintain a brushing rhythm of about

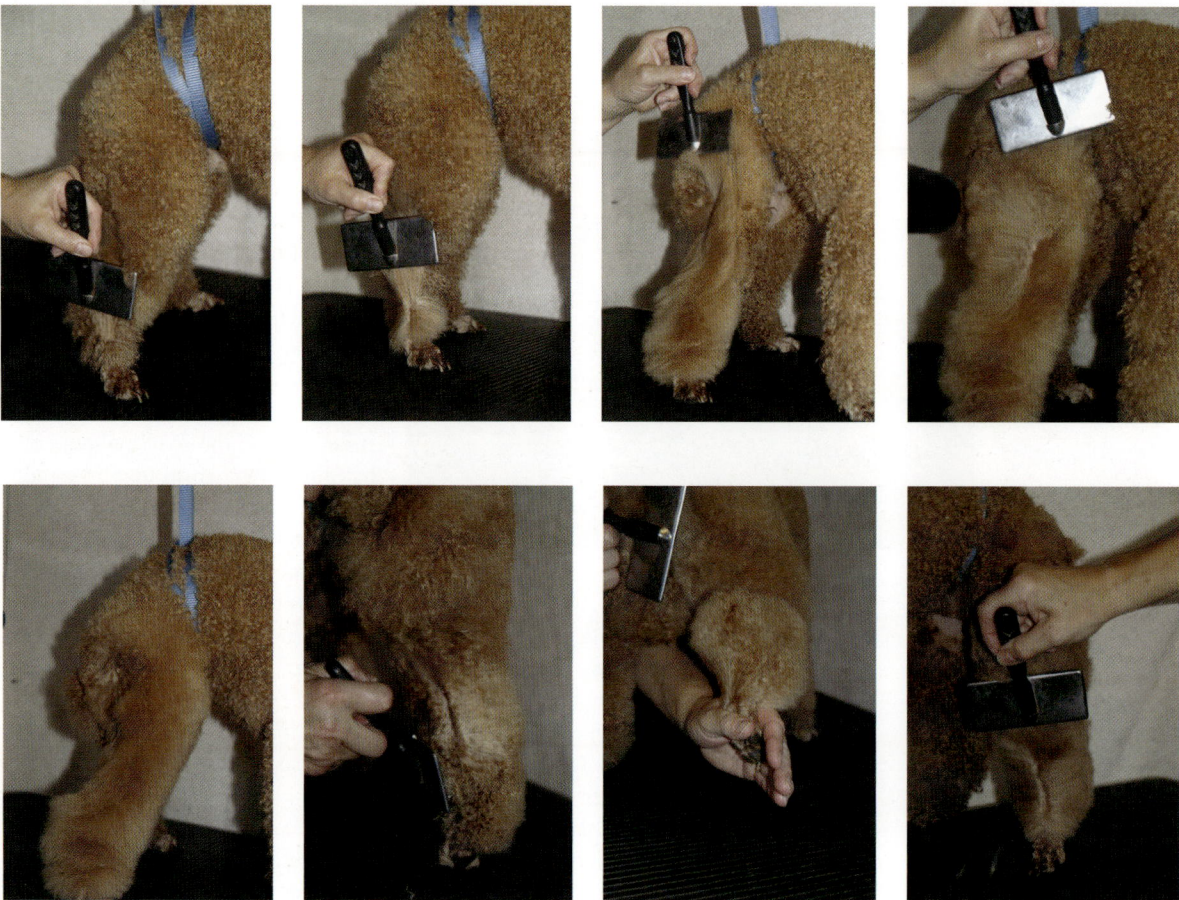

Figs. 13.2.27a-s The technique of fluff-drying

one stroke per second and cross the airflow with your brush at every stroke so that you can monitor the heat from the dryer on the back of your hand and straighten the coat at the point of heat contact before it curls.

If the heat reaches areas that you are not watching and monitoring, it may result in the coat drying curly; more seriously, it may cause the skin to overheat or burn.

It is best to start at the bottom of

the leg and work upwards. If you start at the top, the fluffed-up hair will fall over the wet hair and get damp again. Steam can get trapped in the underlying damp hair and may scald the skin. Starting at the bottom and working

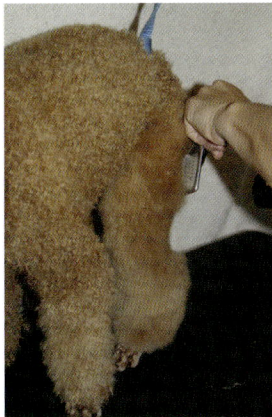

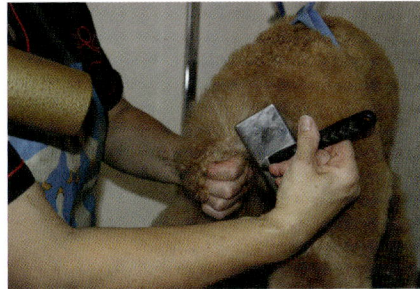

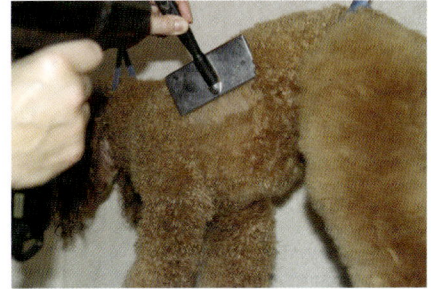

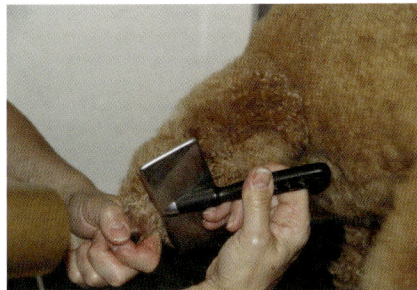

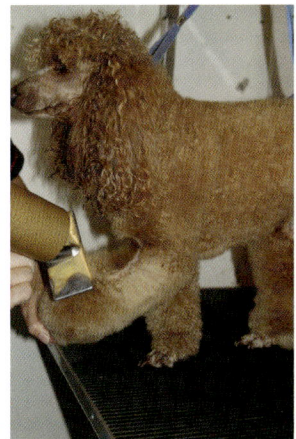

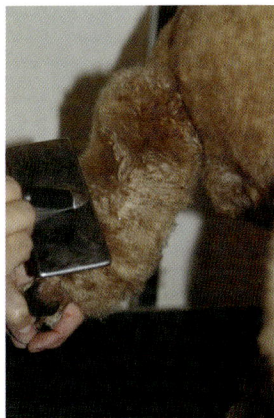

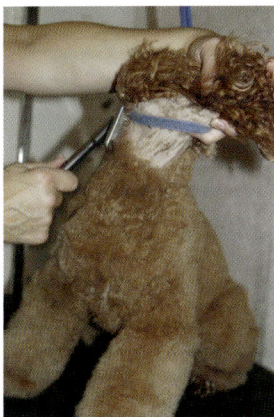

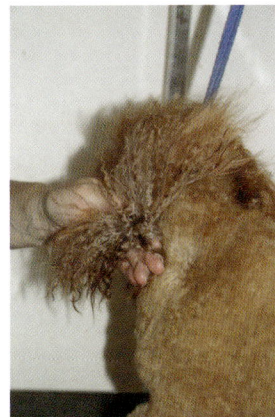

upwards gives you a better view of the skin so you can monitor it more easily whilst working. It also encourages an upwards brushing motion.

Be methodical in your work. Start by drying a small area, and do not move on to the adjoining area until the coat is completely dry, straight and buoyant. Short hair will dry more quickly than long hair so dry these bits first. Remember to dry the insides of the legs and the bits that you cannot easily see or reach. The hair still needs to be brushed upwards in these areas. Ear furnishings should also be brushed upwards on both sides of the pinna. The hair underneath the ear, if left curly, will knot very quickly, and the ear furnishings must be continuously brushed straight so ringlets cannot form. Lastly, tails should be brushed towards the dock.

Once dried straight and fluffy, the coat should be back-combed from the bottom upwards, to bring up the pile.

The advantage of fluff drying is that the coat will be light and buoyant in texture, dense in volume and straight in structure, so it is ideal for 'sculpting' by trimming and styling as long as you have dried it properly. The disadvantage is that if you do not dry it properly, the coat can become troublesome. Whilst it is the preferred way of drying

the wool coat, these coats dry curly very quickly.

It takes practice to perfect the technique of brushing more quickly than the coat is drying to prevent any kinks or waves appearing. Curls and kinks spoil the end result and the coat will have an uneven trim that not only looks unsightly, but may also cause the coat to knot up more easily. This happens because the shorter hairs curl up again very quickly and wrap themselves around any longer, straightened hairs causing tangles and, very soon, mats.

The sculptured styling on the fluff-dried coat of the Poodle or Bichon Frisé can only be successfully achieved if the coat has been dried absolutely straight without curls or kinks in the coat. This includes areas that you cannot always see, such as underneath the dog and on the insides of the legs.

NOTE: DRYING CABINETS AND FLUFFY COATS

It can be counterproductive to start drying a coat in a cabinet dryer if you intend to maximize the effect and the quality of a fluffy coat for styling. You may think you are saving time by using a cabinet to start the coat drying but it may mean you have to spend more time working the coat with a brush and hair-dryer to get the coat straight enough for a good fluff-dry finish for styling. You may even have to resort to dampening the coat if it does not straighten sufficiently with brushing. You are better to skip the drying cabinet stage and get going with a brush and hair-dryer as soon as the coat is drip free.

NOTE: DRYING THE COAT AGAINST *THE DIRECTION OF COAT GROWTH*

To enable water to run off the topcoat and keep the dog dry, the hair follicles direct or grow the hairs towards the tail and towards the ground. Brushing the coat in the opposite direction can be traumatic to the skin, so you should use as soft a brush as possible and brush with as little vigour as possible, watching the skin the whole time you are working. With the coat being brushed 'the wrong way', the skin is also left vulnerable to the heat from the dryer. Burning of the skin and overheating can easily occur.

Try this on your own hair: pull a few hairs in the direction that it grows and then pull the same hairs in the extreme opposite direction – it hurts! This is what is happening when you brush a coat in reverse.

Conclusion

The procedure you use to dry the coat affects the end result of your work, so you need to select the best option for your required finished product.

The most important points to remember when drying the dog are:

◆ Drying the coat can only be achieved by removing the water either by evaporation (including draught) or centrifuge.
◆ Evaporation can cause steam to form within the coat layers, causing scalding and overheating.
◆ Centrifugal forces produced by shaking or with the aid of high-velocity driers and blasters can cause bruising and injury.
◆ Moving the hair against the direction of the natural growth can cause skin trauma.
◆ A dryer with a large outlet nozzle spreads heat over a larger area. This can cause skin burns on areas that you are not working on.

To minimize these risks:

◆ After bathing, the coat should be blotted dry with towels or high-absorbency cloths until it is drip dry.
◆ Blasters should be aimed across the coat not at the skin, and hair-dryers should be on a low heat and used for as short a time as possible.
◆ The coat should be moving all the time that artificial heat is being applied so steam cannot build up within the coat and scald the skin.
◆ Brush the coat where the air from the hair-dryer contacts the hairs (remember the skin is underneath and will be heating up at this contact point). Brushing elsewhere leaves the skin vulnerable to being burnt.
◆ Monitor all areas that are being affected by the dryer air flow.
◆ Make sure that the coat is moving if you are using a drying cabinet.

In the majority of instances you will be drying the dog according to the trimming style for the breed but there are always exceptions. Some dogs have poor quality coats or they may be cross-bred dogs that look like one parent but have the coat texture of the other. In these instances the coat needs to be dried according to the coat structure and texture rather than the coat style.

14 Clippers, Blades and Clipping

In my experience as a teacher, I have found that clipping is the part of the course students most look forward to and cannot wait to get started on. It is also the bit that terrifies them the most! It is exciting because this little machine can clip off the right bits very quickly to make an amazing transformation – but it can also clip off the wrong bits very quickly, and that is scary!

The first attempt at clipping often finds students forgetting to breathe and holding themselves absolutely rigid with fear and concentration. In fact, clipping is generally fun and produces fast results – but even the rapid removal of a coat by electric power will not be achieved quickly enough to prevent you passing out through lack of oxygen. So, before you start, promise yourself that you will remember to breathe – not least because there may not be anyone else around to finish the dog! Remember, too, that the dog responds to your body language and if you are terrified, how do you think the dog is going to feel?

There are two points to remember that may make clipping less scary:

- *Clipping a coat off in the wrong place has never to my knowledge killed a dog – so it is not life-threatening.*
- *One thing you can be absolutely sure of is that the coat will grow again, so that is not life-threatening either.*

Very few of the dogs that present for grooming need clipping but those that do will require you to use your clippers safely and skilfully.

14.1 CLIPPERS

A history of clipping

The verb 'shear' derives from the Old English word 'sheren' and the Nordic word '*skera*', meaning to cut, and was commonly used to describe the removal of wool from sheep. The word 'clip' did not come into use until the fourteenth century, when it was used in a maritime sense (a 'clipper' being a fast sailing boat that cuts or slices its way through the water) rather than in the context of describing cutting or shearing; it is therefore uncertain as to when people began to use 'clipping' to describe the cutting of hair.

The removal of wool from sheep first began in about 3,500BC, when man first learnt how to spin wool. It was done by hand, using a heavy tool resembling a pair of scissors. Sometime around the early seventeenth century, during the reign of Louis XV of France, the trimming of dogs gained popularity and the first grooming salons began to appear in the streets of Paris. The tool used to remove the hair was still hand-operated, and continued to be so until 1865, when an Irishman, Frederick York Wolseley, a wool grower living in Australia, developed the first practical mechanical shear. His invention was patented in 1868 but it was a further five years before the first machine was manufactured. Sadly, it was not very successful. In 1884 Wolseley joined forces with Robert Pickup, and together they produced and patented the first cog-gear universal joint to drive a motor. The prototype for the clippers we use on animals today had made its debut. Wolseley died in 1899 but by then his machine was becoming widely used in the wool industry and by the turn of the century, 'shears' had been modified for use on dogs.

Thanks firstly to the invention of elec-tricity and then to the desire to remove hair from sheep, horses and dogs at a faster speed with less effort, Wolseley's invention has developed into a precision piece of machinery that does the job faster and more efficiently, whilst making light work of it. As the popularity of clipping dogs to remove or style their coats has grown, so has the selection of clippers, trimmers and cutting blades of different lengths. The choice is now vast and there is something for everyone.

Generally speaking, the machines used to remove the bulk (or all) of an animal's coat are referred to as *shears* or *clippers*. By contrast, the much less powerful machine that is used to tidy up small areas of coat, such as on the face and the feet, is referred to as a *trimmer*. Both machines actually do the same job, and both operate by cutting the hair between two blades, although the clipper is more robust than the trimmer as it is expected to cover larger areas. The two blades are pressed together with a spring and are known as a blade set. The bottom plate is actually a comb because it does not cut, but rather combs through the hair to a length that will remain in situ. The sharpened top plate slides across it from side to side and is the cutting blade.

Buying clippers

There are two reasons for buying an animal clipper or trimmer: either you want to trim your pet(s) or you want to work as a groomer. In either case the machine you choose will probably be determined by your finances or style preference but there are a few points that you may like to consider before making your selection.

The machine must be comfortable to hold in your hand, and it should not be too heavy or too bulky for your hand size, but must be capable of doing the work you want them to do. It should not vibrate excessively when in use because this is not only uncomfortable, it may also cause muscle stress to your hands and arms. Nor should it be excessively noisy or high pitched when running. You may have to listen to it for long periods of time when you are learning or working on a large dog and prolonged use could affect your hearing. Excessive or unpleasant noises may also be stressful to and upset certain dogs. You should make sure that the blades can either be sharpened or replaced easily. If you are working commercially, and require more than one clipper, make sure that they have the same blade attachment so the blades are interchangeable.

Clippers can be used in either the left or the right hand.

Fig. 14.1.2a-b   Commercial clippers are powerful and engineered for optimum performance. They are robust and can work their way through any coat type.

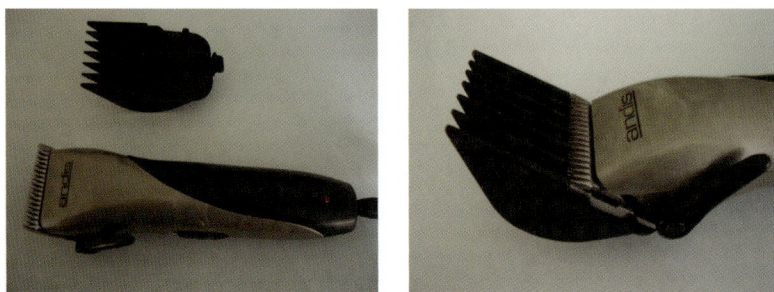

Fig. 14.1.3a-b   The domestic clipper usually has a set of plastic blade extensions to provide a longer length clip. The extensions are easily fitted to the blade.

Pet clipper or heavy duty?

There are several differences between these two types. The pet clipper (*see* Fig. 14.1.1) will be less expensive and the price is a good indication that the machine is not designed to do a lot of work. The pet clipper will happily trim one or two dogs every couple of months, but the motor is not robust enough to work its way through a variety of different coat types on a daily basis. This amount of work requires a heavy duty commercial machine (*see* Figs 14.1.2a-b). Pet clippers tend not to have a choice of running speeds. This is adequate for the pet trim but would not be sufficient for commercial trimming.

The pet clipper is usually fitted with an adjustable tapering blade which allows the operator to change the length of the blade without changing the blade itself. The choice of blade

Fig. 14.1.1   A domestic (pet) clipper with a single adjustable blade. The clipper blade is adjusted by moving the arm on the side of the clipper housing up or down.

lengths is limited. Attachment combs (plastic or metal extensions that fit onto the blade) are usually provided and are necessary when clipping longer length coats (*see* Figs 14.1.3a-b). In contrast, heavy duty clippers use a selection of different length detachable blades. Attachment combs are optional.

Fixed blade or detachable blade?

This depends on the reason for buying your clipper. If you only require the clipper for occasional use, such as on your own dog every few months, you will probably only need a fixed tapering blade and you will be able to manage with blade attachments (sometimes called extensions or combs). The advantage of the fixed blade for the pet groomer is, of course, the lower cost, as you do not need to buy a selection of blades. There are a couple of disadvantages, however. The tapering handle that is used to change the blade length can often work loose, allowing the blade to change length during use. You may find yourself with a sudden bald patch! Using an attachment comb is not always easy, and they do not work well if the fixed blade is blunt or the wrong length, or if the coat is too dense, too curly or poorly prepared.

In a busy grooming salon you certainly need robust clippers with detachable blades. This is necessary to give the variety of clipping lengths. It is a lot quicker to change the blade than to fuss about with a lever arm to regulate blade length and secure attachments (and you should remember that fixed blades can be unpredictable). The disadvantage here is, of course, the cost of purchasing individual blades. If you plan to work commercially, you will need a wide selection of blades and a minimum of two sets so that you always have a sharpened set available. It is also important to consider that you also need a spare pair of clippers, so remember to make sure that your blades are compatible with both clippers.

Cable or cordless?

This may well depend on whether or not you need your clipper to be mobile. If you are buying your clipper for use at dog shows, or if you intend to work away from a salon base, you may need a clipper that can be battery charged so you are not dependent on an electricity supply (*see* Fig. 14.1.4).

The *cordless clipper* is battery operated and can be useful if you do not have a socket near your grooming

Fig. 14.1.4
Rechargeable clippers are popular with commercial groomers. They are versatile and very useful for clipping dogs that do not stand still because there are no cables to worry about. They are also useful if you do not have many power sockets in your grooming room.

table, or if you are a mobile groomer. Their manoeuvrability makes them very versatile for trimming a reluctant model that will not stand still despite being restrained, especially as you do not have a trailing cable to worry about. Another advantage with a cordless clipper is that, to an extent, it is unaffected by power cuts and electrical storms.

The disadvantages are that you must always have a charged battery available, particularly if you are away from the salon, and the battery does add extra weight to the clippers, making them a little on the heavy side for some groomers.

The *cabled clipper* is generally the preferred option for professional groomers because it does not have the problem of the battery running down. It does, however, have two significant disadvantages: they do not work in a power cut, so if you live in an area with an unreliable electricity supply or where there are significant numbers of electrical storms, this may be problematic. The cables can fracture mid-wire or detach from the clipper, and will need to be repaired. Correct storage and maintenance should prevent this but accidents do happen and the cable can be damaged.

Single speed or multi-speed?

For the pet owner, or trainee groomer, a single speed is probably adequate. The motor drives the blades slowly, so you are less likely to be afraid of the clipper running away with you and clipping off more than you intended. It also has the advantage that, because of the slower motor drive, the blades do not heat up as quickly. This can be beneficial because when you are learning clipping skills, you probably won't be working at any great speed so the

clipper will be running for a long period of time. The major disadvantages of a single-speed clipper are that the low-powered motor can sometimes struggle through heavily matted coats and, because the blades are running more slowly, they can produce clipper lines. (There are also other reasons for clipper lines, which I will discuss later in this chapter.)

As your skills improve, and your business grows, you may want to upgrade to a multi-speed clipper. This gives you the benefits of faster clipping and a stronger motor that is more suited to heavier or matted coats, and also gives a much better finish on the clipped coat.

Clippers are expensive items to purchase and buying without handling is a big mistake. Once you have decided on your requirements, you should either travel to a supplier if possible or visit a dog show where clippers are on display. You can then ask for advice on which machines are suited to pet use and which are heavy duty, thereby tailoring your purchase to your needs.

Clipper check-list. Always check:

♦ the weight;
♦ the size;
♦ the position of the on/off switch – it should be easily operated but not in the way;
♦ the shape of the clipper and the covering;
♦ the vibration and the noise (by switching it on);
♦ how easy it is to obtain spare parts and repairs;
♦ how easy it is to maintain; and
♦ the warranty and after-sales care available.

Remember that all groomers have their favourite, but it is suited to them and is their personal choice – it may not be the right choice for you!

Handling your clipper

All clippers are suitable for both left- and right-handed use. To get the best results when you are clipping, your clipper should be an extension of your hand. When you use your hand to stroke or caress the dog, your hand is soft and your wrist movement is smooth and supple. The palm of your

hand lies flat on the dog as you slide it over the coat to stroke him. When you are clipping, your hand should be just as soft when you hold the clipper and your wrist movement should be just as smooth and supple. The blade of the

> **NOTE: GAUGING THE STRENGTH OF YOUR GRIP**
>
> *Put some water in a bowl or sink and drop a sponge in it. When the sponge is full of water, pick it up in your hand and hold it without squeezing any water out of it. Now turn your hand over and back again several times without letting go of the sponge and without squeezing any water out of it. When you have done that, using just your wrist wave your hand up and down then side to side, still holding the sponge and still not squeezing any water out of it.*
>
> *That is the amount of pressure you need to have in your hand whilst holding your clipper and that is the amount of flexibility you need in your wrist.*

clipper becomes the palm of your hand and should be flat on the dog as you slide it over or through the coat.

The clipper must be held firmly and securely in the hand but not so tightly that it restricts your wrist movement (*see* Fig. 14.1.5). You should be able to roll your wrist in a circle whilst holding the clipper, and you may find it easier to hold the clipper with your fingers rather than in the palm of your hand (*see* Fig. 14.1.6).

If you hold your clipper tightly, your hand will be hard and your clipping movement will be heavy. Remember that the hair on the dog is attached at one end to nerve fibres and that the coat is very responsive to signals sent out by the nerves. If the clipper is pushed heavily down onto the coat and puts pressure on the skin, the nerves will respond and the dog will react to move away from the pressure. You then have a dog that will not stand still or may become troublesome to clip so keep everything light and soft and – do not forget to breathe!

LEFT: *Fig. 14.1.5   This groomer is holding the clipper with a 'hard' tight grip. This will restrict her wrist movement and her work will be affected.*

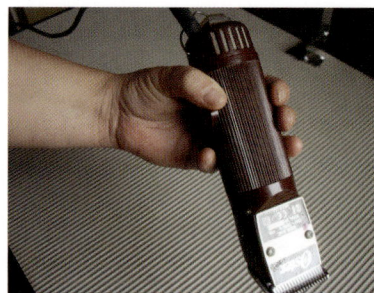

RIGHT: *Fig. 14.1.6   Relaxing her hand and changing her grip on the clipper, the groomer will still have good control of the machine but her hand will be soft and her wrist flexible.*

CARE AND MAINTENANCE OF CLIPPERS

When you buy your clipper, it will be supplied with guidelines for maintenance and it is absolutely vital for your safety and the safety of others that you follow the manufacturer's instructions. It may be recommended that you do some limited maintenance yourself but the clipper will need to be returned to an agent for servicing. Never try to open a sealed unit. If it doesn't open, you are not supposed to access it!

   Day to day maintenance and care:

- **Be careful never to drop your clipper as this could cause a fracture in the casing; not only could this be dangerous, it will also let the damp in.**
- **Cables, plugs and switches should be checked before and after every use.**
- **When storing your clipper, never wrap the power cable tightly around the machine as this can fracture the wires inside the cable (see Fig. 14.1.7).**
- **After each use, hair should be removed from the blade station with a small brush (see Fig. 14.1.8) and the air vents should be brushed clean (see Fig. 14.1.9). The clipper can then be placed in an ultraviolet light unit for sterilizing.**
- **Never store your clipper anywhere where it can get damp.**

If it is recommended that you lubricate your clipper:

- **make sure that the clipper is unplugged;**
- **lubricate the clipper motor only if it develops a 'squeal'; and**
- **add a few drops of manufacturer's oil to the recommended points and only use the recommended oil.**

If it is recommended that you grease your clipper:

- **you will need to access the gear housing (for clippers with name plates, such as the Oster, the gear housing is found under the name plate; remove the cover and the gear linkage, see Fig. 14.1.10);**
- **insert a small amount of manufacturer's grease into the hole on the top of the gear post and reassemble.**

The tone of the clipper will tell you when this needs doing.

If it is recommended that you change carbon brushes:

- **There will be instructions for access to the carbon brushes, and you should be able to remove them for inspection.**
- **Compare the length of the square section with the length of the round section. When the square section has been reduced to the length of the round section, the brushes need replacing.**
- **Always replace both carbon brushes at the same time.**
- **When reinstalling the brushes, make sure that the sharp corners of the brushes are aligned correctly in the spring assembly, so that they will fit comfortably back into the clipper housing.**

Servicing (and PAT testing) should be done once a year by a recommended agent unless the clipper is not functioning properly. This is particularly important if you are employing staff.

Fig. 14.1.7   To prevent damage to the cable and the cable connections, remember not to wrap cables tightly around your clipper when you store it.

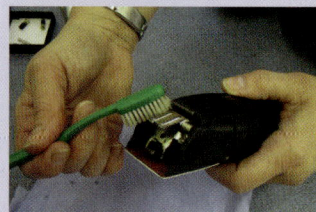

Fig. 14.1.8   Brush the clipper with a small brush to remove all traces of hair before placing the clipper in a UV sterilizer.

Fig. 14.1.9   Remove the filter cover to clean away hair and grease.

Fig. 14.1.10   If the manufacturer recommends greasing the clipper's gear housing, you can access it under the name plate.

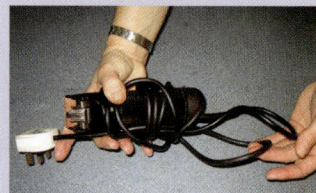

14.2 BLADES AND THEIR USES

The type of clipper you purchase will determine the sort of blades you need to buy. Most clippers have interchangeable blades that are compatible with other brands, but one or two manufacturers use specific blades for their machines. This section focuses on the flat blades that are interchangeable between most of the popular clipping machines.

Blades are referred to as 'sets' because there are two of them, a static base plate and a movable top plate that slides from side to side over the bottom plate. Both plates have 'teeth' cut out of them, which are sharpened to enable the blade to cut; they are also fitted with a tension spring to hold the blades together and a socket that attaches the blade to the clipper.

The teeth of the bottom plate are graded at different lengths and widths, so that the length of the remaining coat can be regulated as the clipper passes over and removes some hair. The back edge of the base blade is referred to as the heel and the front edge is the toe. The blade also has a left and a right edge. The top plate has short teeth and regulates the quantity of hair that is cut. Apart from very fine surgical blades, most blades have the same length teeth on the cutting blade (*see* Fig. 14.2.1).

Fig. 14.2.1   *Apart from very fine surgical blades, most blades have the same-sized cutting blade. It is the comb blade that determines the length of cut.*

Skip-toothed blades

Blades are defined as either skip-toothed or finishing blades ('F' or 'FC' blade depending on the manufacturer). These definitions are determined by the formation of the teeth on the base plate. On a skip-toothed blade every second tooth on the comb blade is shorter in length, giving the impression that it has teeth missing (*see* Fig. 14.2.2). There are two reasons why you may select a skip-toothed blade: they are very effective at feeding dense or matted hair through the gaps in the teeth, producing much less strain on the clipper motor, and the variable tooth length effectively cuts the hair at two different lengths, layering the coat and reducing the density effect. This makes them very useful if you want to reduce the bulk of a heavy coat or want it to lie flat on the body, particularly if you are clipping spaniels. Medium and long length body blades give you the option of a skip-toothed version.

Fig. 14.2.2   *Here you can see the difference between an 'F' (finishing) blade and a 'skip-toothed' blade. On the blade on the right, every alternate tooth is shorter, giving the impression that it is missing a tooth. This is the 'skip-toothed' blade. As it cuts through the hair, it layers the coat by cutting it at different lengths. Layering prevents the coat from becoming denser because the longer hairs lie flat on top of the shorter hairs. If the hairs are all cut at the same length, they pile up on top of each other, making the coat deeper (or thicker) in depth.*

One disadvantage of using a skip-toothed blade is that it may leave clipper lines ('tramlines') if too short a blade length is used on a dog with a dense undercoat. This is because the teeth will cut layers into both the topcoat and the undercoat. Another disadvantage is that skin folds can get caught between the teeth, causing injury. To prevent this happening, the skin should be kept taut by stretching it slightly with your supporting hand whilst you are clipping. Throughout this process you should never force the blade through the coat.

Finishing ('F' or 'FC') blades

Finishing ('F' or 'FC') blades have all the teeth on the bottom plate the same length (*see* the no. 5 blade on the right in Fig. 14.2.1) , and the 'F' or 'FC' is the alternative option for medium and long length blades (the body blades). These blades also have three advantages: the even teeth on the comb plate of these blades prevent layering and produce a much finer finish; they are less likely to leave clipper marks; and they are less likely to catch skin folds.

The disadvantage with these blades is that the hair is all cut at the same length; it will not have been layered and consequently thinned out. This is quite acceptable on a Poodle coat because the Poodle does not have a dense undercoat and the dog will still be able to regulate his body temperature. But on dogs such as a heavily undercoated West Highland Terrier the density of the coat could quite possibly contribute to overheating and consequent skin problems. These blades do not always produce the best result on silk-coated breeds (such as the English Cocker or Springer Spaniel) either, as the coat may not lie flat and retain its silky effect.

Toe blades

Toe blades are blades that have a number of teeth in the centre of the blade only. As their name suggests, they are used for trimming in between the toes of breeds such as Poodles and Bedlington Terriers. Their size means that they can be easily manoeuvred around toenails and between the pads of the foot and, although many professional groomers manage quite well without them, they are very useful for the nervous or anxious groomer who is worried about such a delicate job.

Blade attachments

These are manufactured from chrome, stainless steel or plastic, and they attach to the base plate of a fine clipper blade (*see* Figs 14.2.3a-b). The idea of the attachment is to allow the groomer to leave a length of coat on the dog which is longer than can be accomplished with a standard blade. This would normally be achieved by styling the dog with scissors but this is a time-consuming job for a very busy salon.

To get the best results from using an attachment, the groomer must make

Fig. 14.2.3a-b Attachment blades for commercial clippers are generally made of chrome to make them more robust. They are designed to leave a longer length coat than can be achieved with standard blades. Fig. 14.2.3b shows how they are easily attached to the blade.

sure that the coat has been correctly prepared and is clean, totally dry, mat free and, if possible, stretched so that it is free of wrinkles or curls. Because the attachment is fitted to a very fine blade, it means that if the clipper snags or gets caught in the coat, the hair could well be cut at the length of the cutting blade rather than the length of the attachment, and this may be very, very short! The same problem can occur if the coat is not consistent in density. Thinner patches quite often mean shorter hair!

Attachments take some getting used to and they do serve a purpose but, as your trimming skills improve and you become more adept with the use of your scissors, you may well prefer to style the coat by hand. I think it would be fair to say that, although many groomers find blade attachments invaluable, overall you can achieve a far superior finish with scissors or thinning scissors.

Metal or ceramic?

Blades are available in metal alloy or ceramic. Metal blades tend to get very hot from the constant movement of the metal cutting blade, especially when they have been in use for a prolonged period of time. By contrast, a ceramic cutting blade helps the comb blade stay cool for longer. The reduced temperature tends to keep the ceramic blade sharp for longer than its metal counterpart. One unfortunate disadvantage of the ceramic blade is that it is more likely to break if you drop it.

With all blades you must constantly monitor the temperature of the base plate and spray it with a cooling lubricant when necessary. Keeping the blades well oiled is also a necessity if you want them to perform properly and you want them to last. A good indication of whether the blade needs oiling during use is the tone of the clipper. Dry blades put extra strain on the clipper motor and it will begin to labour and sound noisy.

Definitions of blade cutting lengths

Surgical-length clipping is done using very short blades cutting against the coat direction to remove as much hair as possible from the skin. It is generally only used in veterinary surgeries but may be used in some breeds for the show ring, for example to remove errant hairs from normally hairless breeds.

Very fine clipping is used on some show dogs such as Poodles and Bedlington Terriers, where the faces and feet are clipped very short. The dogs

Assembling a blade

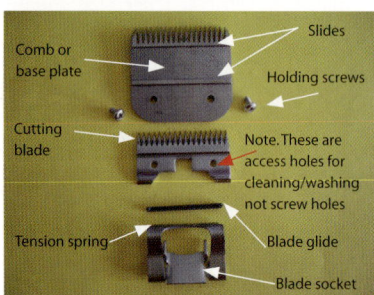

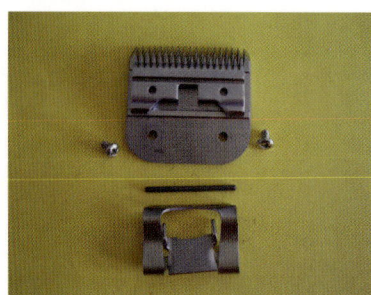

Fig.14.2.4 The clipper blade consists of a comb or base plate with two raised slides, a cutting blade, a blade glide to ease the lateral movement of the cutting blade, a blade socket to attach the blade to the clipper, a tension spring and holding screws to hold the blade secure.

Fig. 14.2.5a-b To reassemble your blade, lay the cutting blade on top of the comb plate so that the teeth of both blades are aligned and the back of the cutting blade sits on the slide.

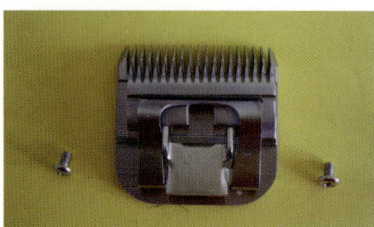

Fig. 14.2.6a-b Replace the blade guide on the front of the tension spring and rest it in the groove on top of the cutting blade. The screw holes underneath the tension spring should line up with the screw holes in the comb plate. Hold together and fasten the holding screws from the underside.

are regularly clipped with this length blade so the skin is used to being exposed with little or no hair covering.

Fine clipping involves cutting against the direction in which the coat lies and is usually executed with a very short blade. Fine clipping is usually restricted to the face, feet and tails of breeds such as the Poodle and Bedlington Terrier. It is also used on sanitary areas and when clipping for surgery.

Medium-length clipping is achieved by using a medium-length blade following the coat growth direction and is usually confined to the body. There is an exception to this general rule. When trimming the top of the head of an English Cocker Spaniel, it is acceptable to use a medium-length blade in the reverse direction to achieve a smoother cut.

Long-length clipping is when you use the longest of blades or a blade comb attachment following the direction of the lie of the coat to leave a substantial length of hair still in place on a clipped coat.

Table 22 is a guide to the uses of each blade length. As you progress, and become more adventurous, you can experiment using different blade lengths on different coat types from those suggested so that your work becomes more personalized.

Attaching and detaching snap-on blades

To attach the blade:

◆ the blade stay on the clipper should be in the open position;

◆ slide the stay into the blade socket;

◆ switch the motor on to centre the cutting blade;

◆ when it is securely in place, snap the blade down onto the clipper.

To detach the blade:

◆ switch the motor off;

◆ turn the clipper so that you are looking at the blade;

◆ push the blade spring on the clipper towards the blade with your thumb on the hand holding the clipper;

◆ remove the blade.

If the blade stay snaps closed, insert a screwdriver *under the side* of the stay to lift it open again.

Attaching and detaching clipper blades

LEFT: Fig. 14.2.7   To attach the clipper blade, make sure that the blade stay is in the open position.

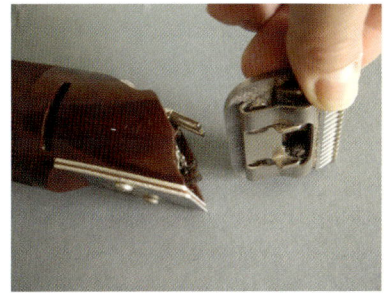

RIGHT: Fig. 14.2.8   Switch the motor on and slide the stay in the blade socket.

Fig. 14.2.9a-b   Once the blade stay is fully inside the socket, push the blade down so that it sits down flat onto the clipper.

Fig. 14.2.10   To detach the blade use your thumb to push the spring forward towards the blade. The spring will release the blade stay and the blade can be removed.

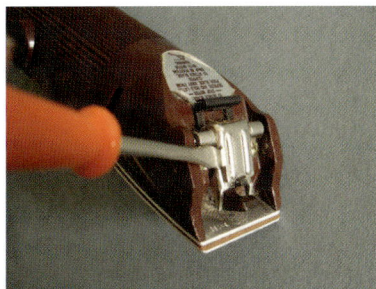

Fig. 14.2.11   If the blade stay snaps closed, use a screw driver under the side of the stay to lift it open again.

CARE AND MAINTENANCE OF CLIPPER BLADES

See 'Checking that your blades are balanced' and 'Parts of the blade'.

New blades: check that new blades are correctly balanced before you begin clipping. To do this, run your finger up the front edge over the teeth from the base plate to the top plate. If there is an apparent 'ledge', or any rough edges, the blades need to be loosened and the top plate moved so that the two blades together form a smooth front edge. You also need to wash the blade in blade wash to remove any preservatives that have been applied to prevent rusting, and you should run the blade without using it for about fifteen minutes so that it can 'bed' in comfortably.

All blades: after every use, slide the top plate halfway across the bottom plate and brush away the loose hairs (see Fig. 14.2.17). Then slide the top plate the other way and brush the other side. It is advisable to sterilize the blade in either an ultraviolet light unit or in a sterilizing solution. The blade can then be either oiled and stored ready for re-use or stored in a lubricating blade wash.

Checking that your blades are balanced

Fig. 14.2.12   Your clipper blades will not cut properly if they are not correctly balanced. This means that the cutting blade must line up as closely as possible with the teeth on the comb plate. When you use blades for the first time, even if they are new or have just been re-sharpened, you should check the balance. To alter the position of the cutting blade, loosen the screws slightly and wriggle the cutting blade into a new position. Hold it firmly between your finger and thumb whilst you tighten the screws again.

Fig. 14.2.13   This cutting blade is sitting slightly proud of the comb plate.

Fig. 14.2.14   This cutting blade is sitting behind the comb plate.

Fig. 14.2.15   The cutting blade has moved off the slides on the comb plate and is sitting lopsided. The blade glide is also not sitting in the groove of the cutting blade so it cannot move the cutting blade properly.

Fig. 14.2.16   The same blade after being adjusted.

Fig. 14.2.17   After every use, slide the top blade halfway across the comb blade and brush it to remove the hair, then slide the blade the other way and do the same. The blade can now be sterilized by UV light or put into blade wash.

Before using the blade, any sterilizing solution or blade wash should be wiped off the blade and a small amount of oil should be applied to the runners between the two plates.

During use, the temperature of the bottom plate should be monitored and a cooling lubricant applied as necessary. If the blade is in use for a prolonged period, you may need to apply more oil to the runners. This keeps the blades running smoothly and should dislodge any hairs that collect between the plates.

Blades are ready to be sharpened when they snag or catch in the coat or start to cut unevenly. Sometimes, depending on how they have been used, blades wear more on one side than the other. This is generally the fault of the groomer (not using them flat on the coat) rather than a manufacturing fault.

If your blade stops cutting, remove it from the clipper and clean it. Blades are small and cut hairs from a heavy, damp or dirty coat can clog them up. If they still won't work, they probably need sharpening. When your blades get older and need to be replaced, mark the old ones with nail varnish and save them for removing coats in poor condition, rather than using your good blades.

Blade attachments should be washed and sterilized after use but, because they are manufactured from plastic or stainless steel or are chrome-coated, it is not necessary to store them in blade wash or oil. They should be stored in a safe place where they cannot be damaged or broken. When in use, oil is applied to the movable cutting blade in the usual manner but not to the attachment as it does not have any moving parts.

Table 22   Blade chart (Andis, Oster, Laube, Aesculap Fav 5 and Wahl).

Surgical	Very fine	Fine	Medium	Long

Blade number	Uses
50#	An ultra-fine surgical blade used by veterinary surgeons and nurses (to prepare a surgical site) but also suitable for use with a blade attachment.
40#	A very fine blade used for clipping prior to surgery, as well as on the face and feet of some show dogs, or it can be used with a blade attachment.
30#	Slightly longer but fine enough for use as a surgical blade or it can be used for fine clipping the face, feet and tail on show Poodles and Bedlington Terriers. Can also be used with a blade attachment, although a number 40 or 50 would be preferable.
15#	Still a fine blade but slightly longer. Suitable for pet Poodles that have been used to having their face, feet and tail clipped short for some time.
10#	A medium-fine length that is used on the face, feet and tail of Poodle puppies or other breeds whose skin needs to be conditioned to fine clipping. Also suitable for clipping shapes into Poodle body cuts, Terrier and Spaniel heads and ears, armpits and groin areas.
9#	Slightly longer but still a short blade used for clipping the body on heavily coated breeds, particularly Spaniels.
8.5#	A short- to medium-length body blade used as a body blade on Spaniels, Terriers and some clip-offs.
7#	A slightly longer medium-length skip-toothed blade that is suitable for summer body cuts on most breeds. An excellent blade for removing badly matted or knotted coats.
6F#	Slightly longer than the 7#, this is a finishing blade, used mainly by specialist groomers to enhance coat texture.
5#	The longest of the medium-length skip-toothed body blades. A 5# is suitable for all breeds wanting a little more coat left on, or those with very fine coats. Ideal for use on the body of Yorkshire Terriers.
4	A long body blade used on all breeds. A popular length with owners who require their pets to have winter trims and also very useful for dogs with sensitive skins or those that do not normally get trimmed down.
3	A very long body blade used on all breeds when a little more length is required.
7F, 5F, 4F, 3F	These are finishing blades that have a cutting length corresponding to their counterparts but leave a finer, smoother cut.
5/8#, 7/8#	These are toe blades. The cutting edges of the plates are reduced in size to make them less bulky for trimming feet and delicate areas.
Attachments	Plastic extensions attached to very fine blades and used to create a very long natural effect.

14.3 CLIPPING

Very few dogs need clipping, but the ones that do will require you to be able to use your clippers safely and skilfully. Clippers do the same job as scissors but more quickly, and in the majority of cases they produce a smoother, more precise finish to the coat. Generally they are safer too, particularly if you are styling a dog that does not stand patiently or in instances where the coat has to be taken to skin level. Your clippers will soon become your best friend.

How to use your clipper

The clipper blade is designed to remove all the hair at the same length. The only way that this can be done is by maintaining the same pressure on the blade throughout the clipping process and by ensuring that the surface being cut is flat and even. This is achieved by using the weight of the clipper to provide the pressure and by using your supporting hand to stretch and move the skin to keep it flat.

Using a set of clippers is a bit like using an upright vacuum cleaner to clean a rug! When you use a vacuum cleaner, you switch it on and guide it gently in the direction that you want to go. The power and drive of the motor take the vacuum cleaner across the rug, maintaining the contact to collect dust

Think about what you are doing. Blades should always be kept sharp and clean. Do not use blades with broken teeth or rusty blades because they are dangerous and could cut or graze the skin. Blades are sharp but they rarely cut the skin if they are used properly. The most common type of accident happens when you are using a skip-toothed blade because skin folds can be caught between the gaps in the blade teeth. If the skin is kept taut and pulled so that it is flat at all times, this should not happen. Extra care is, however, needed when clipping under the front legs and on the sides of the groin area.

Clipper burn/rash: clipper burn is sometimes more correctly referred to as clipper rash and it is actually caused by the blade, not the clipper. It is in fact a rash caused by clipping too close to the skin with a short blade. The drastic removal of the hair and associated trauma causes the skin to react and become inflamed. The condition usually presents itself as localized reddening or colouring of the skin, possibly with an increased skin temperature, whilst the dog is still in the salon. The problem can get progressively worse over the next 24 hours, during which time the dog may scratch and mutilate the area.

You can help the dog in the first instance by dousing the area with distilled witch hazel (Hamamelis) to cool the skin and relieve the irritation, leaving the solution to dry on the skin. Be wary of using cream preparations as they can heat up on the skin and further aggravate the problem. Record the details and inform the owner so that the dog can be monitored at home.

Ways to reduce the risk of clipper burn/rash:

- *If the skin does not look healthy, do not use a short blade (see **Fig. 14.2.18**).*
- *Use a fine (10# or 15#) blade rather than a very fine blade on the face, feet, tail and groin areas of pink-skinned Poodles and similar breeds.*
- *Never clip the genital areas too short because the skin is very sensitive in these areas.*
- *Start young Poodles, Bedlingtons and puppies of other breeds that have clippers used on their heads and faces with a 10# blade on the clipped areas as early as possible. The breeder will usually have given the pups their first clip at about six weeks old.*
- *If you have to clip the coat off a breed that does not normally have their coat removed, do not cut it down to the skin unless it is absolutely necessary.*
- *Do not use a short blade on a wet-coated dog (in fact you should never clip a wet dog!). The skin will be more sensitive so, apart from the risk of electrocution, you are compromising the health of the dog.*

Once the dog has been clipped several times, the skin very often becomes more tolerant and a shorter blade can then be used.

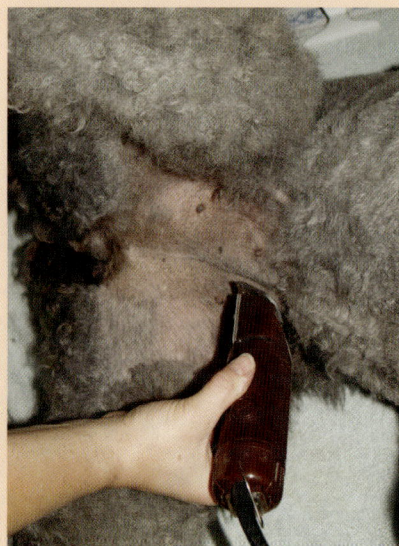

Fig. 14.2.18   *This dog is already showing signs of skin trauma so her groin area is being cleared with a 10# which will leave a covering of hair but still keep her clean.*

and dirt as it travels. But if you push it, it will ruffle up the rug, causing pleats or folds to form, and then stop moving. If you lift the back edge of the vacuum off the floor, the front edge digs into the rug and the machine not only stops moving, it may also get rug fibres tangled around the beater. Likewise, if you lift the front of the vacuum off the floor, it will not remove the dirt from the rug.

Using a clipper is very similar, if you imagine the clipper as the motorized vacuum, the blade as the vacuum beater and the dog's coat as the rug. Push the clipper and the skin wrinkles up. Lift the back edge (heel) of the blade off the coat and the front edge of the blade digs into the skin; it stops moving and keeps cutting any hairs touch-

ing the blade. Lift the front edge (toe) of the blade off the coat and the teeth do not cut any of the coat.

Direction of cut

There are two ways to clip the coat, and the direction you choose to cut depends on the clip, the skin and the breed.

- *Following the direction of the lie of the coat (see* Fig. 14.3.1). *This smooths the coat down onto the body and cuts the hair at the length you have selected by your blade number. It is usual to cut the coat in this direction on the body of the dog but is also an option for clip-

ping any sensitive areas or for dogs with damaged skin when a fine blade is being used. Pink-skinned dogs also may need clipping with the coat direction to prevent sunburn and rashes.

- *Against the direction of the lie of the coat (see* Fig. 14.3.2). *This positions your blade underneath the lie of the coat and lifts the hairs as the clipper travels through the coat. This cuts the hair shorter than the length suggested by the blade number. It is usual to cut in this direction on the faces and feet of Poodles and Bedlington Terriers. Puppies having their first clip can also have their faces clipped this way, though a longer blade (10#)

may be preferable until their skin toughens up. Clipped spaniels look particularly smart with the top of their heads and their faces trimmed with a 7F# used in reverse (against the coat direction).

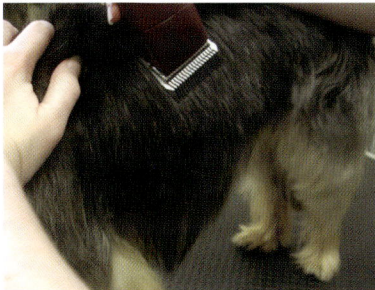

Fig. 14.3.1 Clipping with the direction of coat growth.

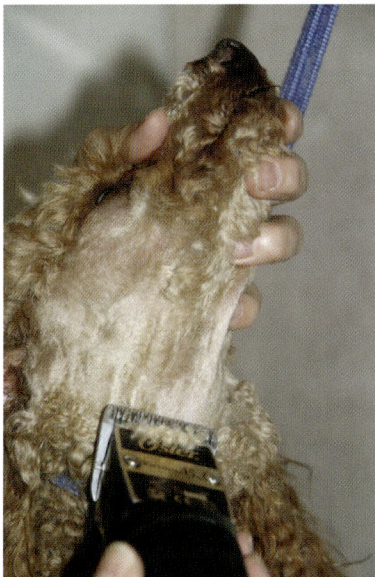

Fig. 14.3.2 Clipping against the direction of coat growth. The cut will be much shorter.

If you cut *across* the direction of coat growth, you will make short cut lines with the two outside teeth of the clipper blade, which can be removed to an extent but not entirely, so it is best to avoid this.

Clipping the coat

Practice over, have a proper go! Here are a few pointers to get you started with clipping skills:

◆ When you first begin clipping, start on the dog's body (*see* Fig. 14.3.3). Use a long-length blade that leaves a

good coat covering. This is less likely to frighten you, and, especially if you are nervous and hard with your hands, starting with the body ensures that you do not alarm the dog, as might happen if you chose to start with their rather more sensitive feet.

◆ Start with the dog facing away from you and work your first clip down the spine towards the tail. The spine is straight so you should be able to follow it, and make your first clipper line straight.

◆ Keep the skin taut. Take a handful of skin (not too firmly) at the base of the neck and put the toe of the clipper into the coat slightly further down the spine at about the area of

the withers, where the skin is now taut. If necessary, you may need to grip the skin in this way over the entire body to keep it flat.

◆ Insert the toe of your blade into the coat first and then flatten the blade so that the heel and the toe are resting on the dog to get an even cut (*see* Fig. 14.3.4).

◆ Do not push the clipper through the coat; instead let the motor do the work, let the weight of the clipper keep it on the skin and draw the clipper towards you. Use your other hand to keep the skin taut and flat (remember the rug!) by easing the skin away from the clipper (*see* Fig. 14.3.5) so that the clipper can glide through the coat without causing ruffles and pleats in the skin. The dog has very pliable skin that slides easily over and around the torso, so by using your hand to do the moving, it should not be difficult to keep it stretched and smooth.

◆ Clip with short strokes, about 10cms at a time.

◆ At the end of each stroke, do not stop abruptly but scoop the blade in a sweeping motion off the coat. This is less likely to leave a severe cut line.

◆ For the second stroke, overlap the end of your last stroke by starting before the finishing point to make sure that you blend the clip line and do not miss any hair.

◆ Once you start to work away from the spine, overlap the last cut line by about a third of your blade width; again this helps to blend the cutting line.

◆ Try not to cut *across* the coat because the cut will be uneven.

◆ To start with, along the spine, your clipper is working towards the tail, but as you work down the body and legs, it will be working towards the table (*see* Fig. 14.3.6).

◆ When you reach areas where the coat is left on, such as on leg and undercarriage furnishings, use your supporting hand to move the hair away so that you do not accidentally clip into it (*see* Figs 14.3.7a-b to 14.3.8a-b). Watch the coat and clip in the direction that it grows. As you come off the spine onto the sides of the body, the coat starts to change direction.

◆ Look out for whorls in the coat, the chest area, the throat and under the tail, where the coat grows in the opposite direction to the main coat (*see* Fig. 14.3.9). Shorten your blade strokes around these areas to a centimetre or so for each stroke until you become familiar with the coat pattern. Apart from whorls on the body, which are random, all dogs have the changes of coat direction in the same place.

◆ If you do cut the coat too short in these areas, do not panic! It is difficult to hide the mistake but the hair will grow again; you may have spoiled your work, but you will not have damaged the dog. Own up if it is not your dog and learn by your mistake so that you do not do it again.

Fig. 14.3.6   As you work down the body and legs, you will be clipping towards the table rather than in the direction that you started on the back.

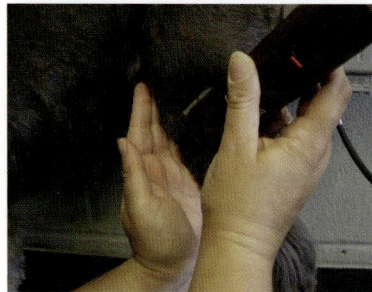

Fig. 14.3.3   Start on the body with a long length blade that will leave a good covering.

Fig. 14.3.7a-b   When you get to the part where you need to leave leg furnishings, use your supporting hand to move the hair out of the way so that you don't clip it off by mistake.

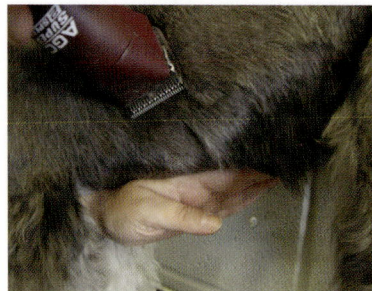

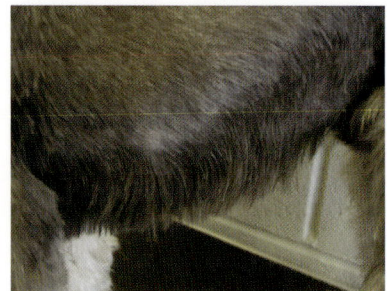

Fig. 14.3.4   Insert the toe of the blade into the cut and then flatten the blade, keeping the heel and the toe on the dog so that the blade can cut evenly.

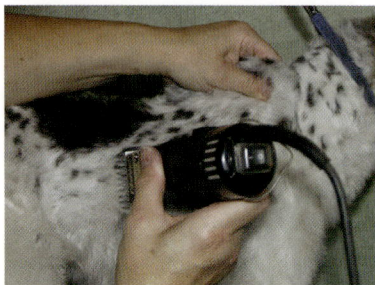

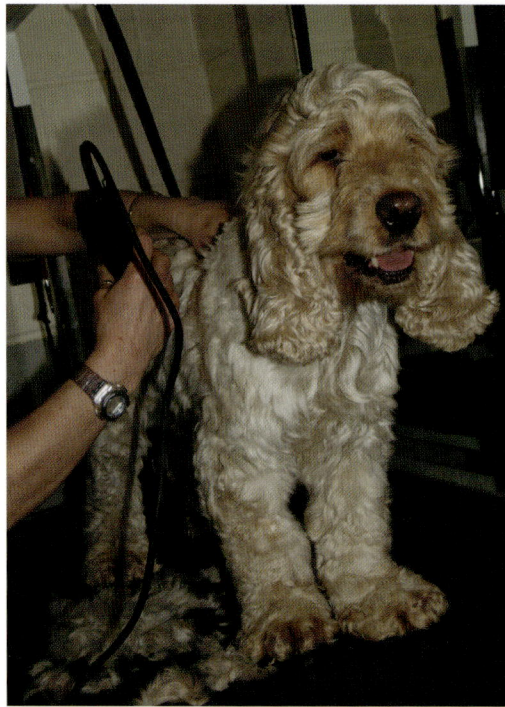

Fig. 14.3.8a-b   The same technique can be applied when you are leaving furnishings on the undercarriage.

Fig. 14.3.5   Keep the skin taut by taking up the loose skin and holding it whilst the blade works in the opposite direction.

Fig. 14.3.9   This poodle has been clipped short to show the different directions of coat growth on the chest area. Unless you plan to cut very short, you need to change your direction of clipping frequently around this area.

You are now on your way, and it gets easier with practice. Fine clipping of the face and feet is quite tricky when you first start, so there are illustrations to help you with this in Figs 14.3.22 to 14.3.36.

Once you have mastered the method of using clippers you can experiment with different blade lengths and eventually work your way to fine clipping against the direction of hair growth.

Selecting blade length

Novice groomers are always apprehensive about the amount of coat to cut off when clipping or scissoring. The following points may be helpful.

◆ The hair on clipped areas can help you to decide how much hair you are going to remove. The hair tends to grow at the same speed all over the body, so if you are clipping 1 cm in length of re-growth hair in a clipped area, where the coat is taken down to the skin, such as a Poodle's face or the groin area, this means that there will be 1 cm of hair to be trimmed from everywhere else either by clippers or scissors.

◆ When clipping, always opt for a longer blade as a starting point because you can go over your work again with a shorter blade if necessary but you cannot put the hair back on again if you have cut it too short.

◆ Always treat puppy skin or the skin of dogs that are not generally clipped with extra care and avoid clipping too short. Until you are more experienced, I would recommend that you do not use anything shorter than a 10#, particularly on faces and sanitary areas.

◆ Make notes on your customer card so that you know exactly what you have done, and list the blades you used for each trim, so you can repeat or modify future trims.

Asking the owner is not always helpful as they often hold up their fingers and reply that they want 'about this much left on' or 'about this much taken off' or, worse still, 'oh, do what you think, I'll leave it up to you'. That may be adequate when you have been doing the job a while but until you get to that

stage here are a few points for you to think about that will help you decide.

The age and health of the dog

◆ Is he a young or an old dog, and how much does he move around?
◆ Does he suffer from immobility problems that restrict him from moving around?
◆ Does he have age-related problems that may affect heat retention or temperature control?
◆ Does he suffer from a medical condition that may affect coat re-growth?

An active dog, whatever his age, is more likely to have good muscle tone and is more likely to keep warm. If the dog is old or inactive, you may be better to select a long blade (4# or 3#) so that the dog does not get cold, particularly in the winter months. Some medical conditions affect the coat re-growth but not necessarily the skin; you should still err on the side of caution and opt for a longer blade.

Skin condition

◆ What colour is the skin?
◆ Is it a good texture?
◆ Is it in an acceptable condition?
◆ Are the areas you want to clip sensitive?
◆ Is the breed known to be predisposed to certain skin problems?

Paler skin and/or fine-textured coats can be affected by the sun (sunburn) so they need to have a fairly good covering of hair for protection. Sensitive skin (especially the groin area) is more prone to trauma, and irritation can be caused by short clipping. Some breeds are more susceptible to skin trauma than others. If the dog in front of you is high risk, it would be wise not to clip short even if the skin appears perfectly normal. Select a medium or long blade (5#, 4#) so that you do not irritate the skin.

The breed of dog

◆ Is it a breed that is usually clipped?

Breeds that are generally clipped with short blades, such as the Poodle, Bed-

lington Terrier and Cesky Terrier, are clipped from a very early age and the skin becomes more tolerant of short clipping. Breeds that are not generally clipped have more sensitive skin.

Select the longest of the fine blades (10#) or a short medium blade (7#) for any short clipping and a 5# (or longer) as a body blade. It is unwise to use short or fine blades on any breed for their first trim. If the skin is irritated, the dog will scratch or rub himself along surfaces such as carpets to relieve itching and may make himself sore.

Coat type and density

◆ What type of coat are you dealing with?
◆ Does the dog have an undercoat?

Fine silk coats are better with a 4# or longer for the body blade because the skin needs the length for protection. A thicker coat can take a shorter blade. If you are in any doubt, start with a long body blade and, if you are not happy with the effect, drop to a shorter blade length. If the dog has a very dense undercoat, try not to use a skip-toothed blade for any rough clipping (see below) as it will cut into the undercoat and make tramlines.

Environment

◆ Where does the dog live – inside or outside?
◆ Does he live in the town or the country?

If the dog is living outside or in the country, you may need to select a long blade (4#) to keep him warm, particularly in the winter, although during the summer months you can use a shorter blade, depending on the age and mobility of the dog.

Dogs living in town areas normally live in the house and there is a tendency for them to be trimmed more often, so let the coat density decide whether a long blade is required or whether it would look neater with a slightly shorter blade length.

Maintenance

◆ Do the owners groom the dog?
◆ Is the dog good to groom?

◆ Will he be brought to the salon regularly for grooming?

If the answer to any of these is 'No', you would be better selecting a medium-length blade (5# or 4#) or a shorter blade (7# or 8.5#), especially if the dog is not good to groom.

Owners' wishes

◆ Are the owners being realistic with their requests?
◆ Can they physically cope with grooming their pet?
◆ Are they prepared to put the time, effort and expense into keeping a longer coat?

If the answer to any of these questions is 'No', it is best to opt for a medium-length blade (7# or 5#). This gives the dog a nice covering but will be easy to maintain.

CLIPPING OFF A COAT FOR THE PURPOSE OF 'COOLING' THE DOG

Points to consider before you make your choice of clipper blade length.

A short clipped coat will not necessarily keep the dog cooler because the shorter the hair, the more difficult it is for heat to be released from the coat. A slight length of coat allows the hairs to move with any air movement (breeze) and the movement of the dog, whereas a coat clipped tightly to the skin will not move freely and may concentrate heat on the skin.

If you live in an unpredictable climate, another point to consider is that if the dog does need to warm himself up for any reason, i.e. in a spell of colder weather, a coat clipped very short will not be able to trap and warm air between the skin and coat.

Lastly, if the dog becomes very wet from rain or from swimming, a short clipped coat may not move enough when shaking to remove the water and allow the dog to dry before it loses body temperature.

Clipping before or after the bath?

There are advantages and disadvantages to both.

Clipping before the bath is called 'rough clipping' because, as the name suggests, it roughly removes some of the coat to make bathing easier (*see* Fig. 14.3.10). The coat may be marked out into a 'rough' style with shape lines (*see* Fig. 14.3.11), but the overall effect is not meant to be good enough for an end result. Rather, it seeks to reduce the amount of time spent on the dog and the resources used. It can also be effective in removing badly knotted coats to reduce stress and discomfort to the dog.

The advantages of removing some of the coat before bathing are that:

◆ Pre-bath grooming time is reduced;
◆ there is less coat to bath so it is easier to clean the skin and coat;
◆ less shampoo (and conditioner) will be needed; and
◆ drying time will be reduced.

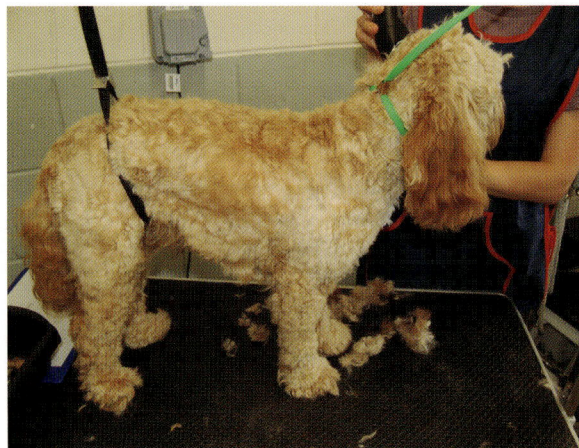

Fig. 14.3.10 This Cockapoo is being rough clipped all over before having a bath. The blade being used is a 4F#; after the bath the dog will be reclipped with a slightly shorter 5F#.

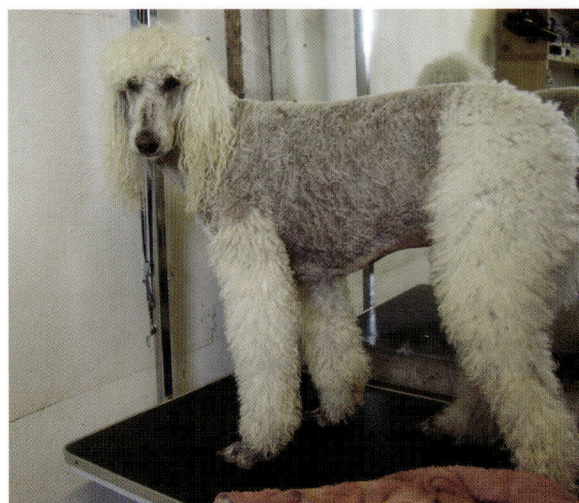

Fig. 14.3.11 This Poodle has been 'rough clipped' into a shape before being bathed to save drying time.

The disadvantages are that:

◆ it may blunt the clipper blade and strain the clipper motor if the coat is very dirty, wet or badly knotted;
◆ clipping a dirty coat is more likely to cause aggravation to sensitive skin;
◆ the unclipped coat and the coat around the clipping lines still need to be groomed before the bath, and this may take longer than you expect;
◆ drying is not always quicker. Some long coats dry better and more quickly if the coat can move under the airflow of the dryer. This also applies to the clipping of double coats, which always dry better if there is some length to help the coat move;
◆ if the coat has been cut short, you may not be able to dry it to the best effect, particularly if you want the coat straight. The shorter it is cut, the more difficult it is to get it straight; and

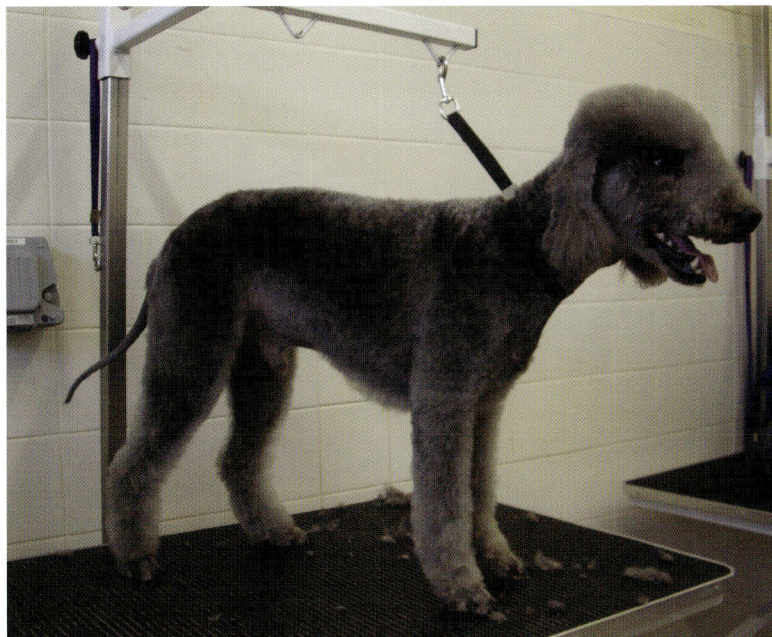

Fig. 14.3.12   *The body of the Bedlington Terrier is often styled by scissoring. To save time, the body of this dog was clipped after the bath with a 4F# once the coat had been stretched and fluff-dried. It is an acceptable alternative to scissoring.*

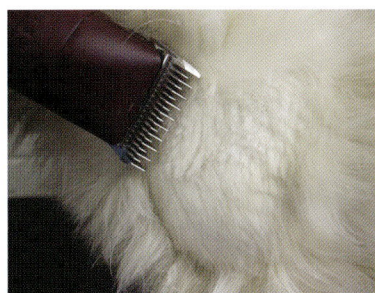

Fig. 14.3.13   *Not only has the skip-toothed blade cut into the undercoat of this dog to leave 'tramlines' in one direction, the blade has crossed the coat causing an uneven cut across the direction of coat growth. When clipping before the bath, these lines will still be apparent after drying.*

CAUTION

A dirty, matted coat is more likely to pull on the dog's skin as it is being removed; you therefore risk potential skin aggravation. If your decision is to go ahead and clip, you must do so with the same care and consideration for the skin as you would use if you were grooming out the knots.

- you will need to spend time re-clipping once the dog is ready for styling. A coat that is clipped before the bath nearly always requires an after-bath clip! An important point to make here is that, if you are going to clip before bathing, you should use a blade length longer than you intended to use because the coat will need clipping again after drying. It will have curls and it probably will not have clipped off evenly, and, of course, to get a good finish on your dog, you need some coat to style.

Clipping after the bath also offers several advantages:

- there is less stress to the dog's skin, minimizing skin aggravation;
- there is less stress on the clipper motor;
- it does not blunt the clipper blade;
- you have a good indication of the length your blade will leave the coat; and
- you reduce clipping time because you only clip the coat once (*see* Fig. 14.3.12)

The disadvantages are:

- bathing and drying may take longer to complete;
- if the coat is not totally dry, the clip-

pers will collect damp hair and the blade will stop cutting;
- a damp coat will blunt the blade more quickly; and
- a damp coat will cause the blades to rust.

Blocking is a term used for skimming over parts of the coat to save scissoring time on terriers and some wool-coated breeds. When clipping the body, with the blade resting on the dog, instead of taking the blade off the coat when you reach legs or furnishings, release the pressure on the blade so that it lifts almost entirely off the coat and you run the blade down the remaining length of hair (see Fig. 14.3.14) to remove just the ends of the hair. You can use long fixed blades or attachments, but gain some experience before you attempt this. A steady hand is essential, and the dog needs to stand very still. If you put any pressure on the coat, the blade will cut the hair to the length of the comb blade. The idea is to cut just the ends of the hairs.

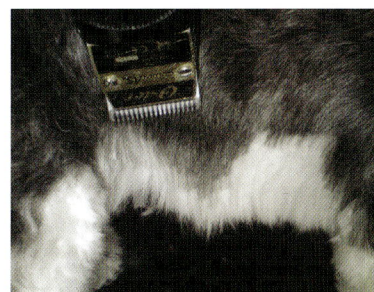

Fig. 14.3.14   *Blocking is a term used for clipping to remove some of the hair on the legs and furnishings to save time. Once the clipper leaves the body, you release the pressure on the clipper but continue clipping down the remaining hair, taking just the ends of the hair between the clipper blades.*

Clipping tails

If you are clipping the body coat off a dog, it makes sense also to remove the coat from the upper few centimetres of the tail to improve hygiene in the sanitary area (*see* Fig. 14.3.15). It is important to remember that, unless the dog is a breed that is usually clipped, the skin will be sensitive the first time this is done, so do not be too heavy-handed with your clippers on the underside. The coat should be clipped in the direction of growth unless the dog is of a breed that is usually clipped otherwise (these include Poodles and Bedlington Terriers).

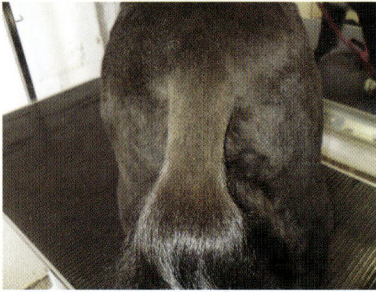

Fig. 14.3.15   If you are removing the body coat of a dog, it makes sense to remove the top of the tail to improve hygiene of the sanitary areas. On breeds that are not normally trimmed, the clipping should be done following the coat direction.

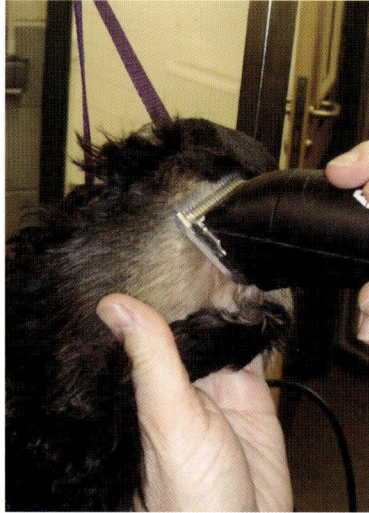

Clipping ears

Some breeds benefit from having the hair removed from the inside of the pinna. Spaniels and Poodles are particularly prone to ear infections, and removing the hair from the inside of the pinna may help to reduce this.

Fig. 14.3.16   When clipping the inside of the pinna , always work with a fine blade from the centre outwards so you do not cut the edges of the ear or the skin flaps.

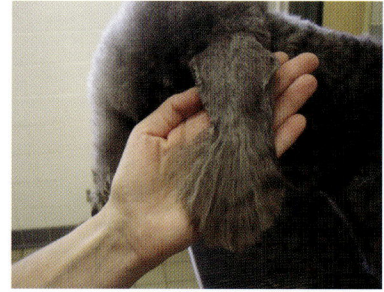

It is important to remember to clip from the centre of the ear towards the outside edge (*see* Fig. 14.3.16) when you are clipping the inside of the ear so that you do not cut the skin folds. It is also best to use a fine blade or a finishing blade and always clip in the direction of hair growth. If you use a skip-

Fig. 14.3.17   Rest the pinna on your hand when clipping it so that you have it supported if the dog wants to move it.

toothed blade the fine edges of the ear can get caught between the teeth.

When you are clipping the pinna, you must hold it with your supporting hand so that you have it secure if the dog moves. This is very important on fine-skinned dogs like the Bedlington Terrier, because not only does the pinna move easily, but the fine skin cuts easily as well (*see* Fig. 14.3.17).

The following illustrated step-by-step guides to 'Clipping the body', 'Clipping feet' and 'Clipping a Poodle face' show you how to handle your clipper and how to hold the dog whilst you are working.

Clipping the Body

These photographs show the stages to follow when clipping the body. This dog will be left with furnishings, but in a total clip-off you can clip down the legs and remove the undercarriage.

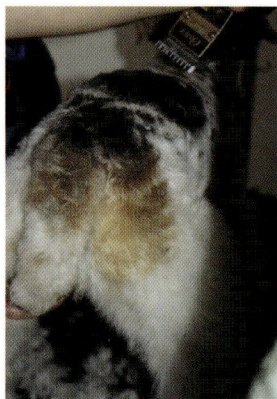

Fig. 14.3.18a-c   Select a body (medium to long) blade and start on the centre back at about the area of the withers. Work down the centre of the back. Go over your work again and then start to work off the spine.

Fig. 14.3.19a-b   Work off the spine following the way the coat grows. Be sure to overlap your cutting lines.

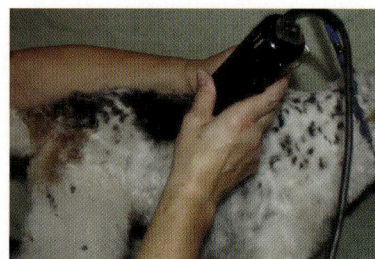

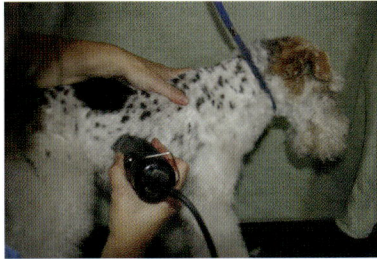

Fig. 14.3.20a-b   Clip one side, leaving any leg or undercarriage furnishings, and then turn the dog to do the other side.

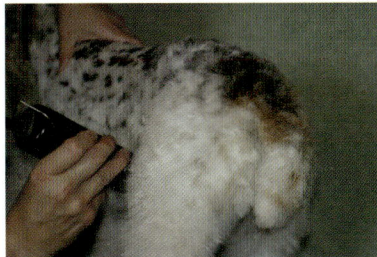

Fig. 14.3.21a-b   Clip towards the table when you are clipping near the loose skin of the groin so you don't catch it in the clipper blades, and stretch the head forward when you are clipping the neck. This lets you see which way the hair is growing.

Clipping Feet

At some time or other you will have to clip feet. Poodles have webbed feet (arrow) so it is easy to spread and separate the toes. This is done by putting your centre finger under the foot in between the pads and using your thumb to push down gently on the top of the foot. Keep a soft hand at all times.

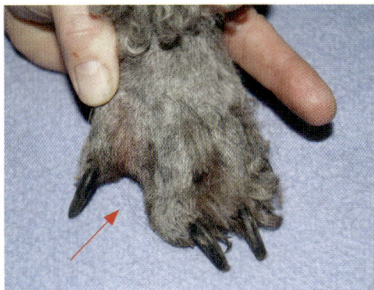

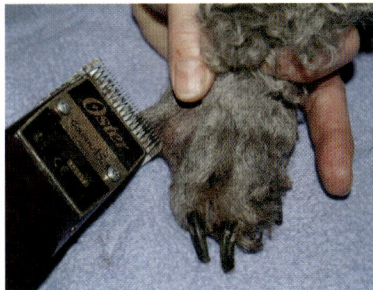

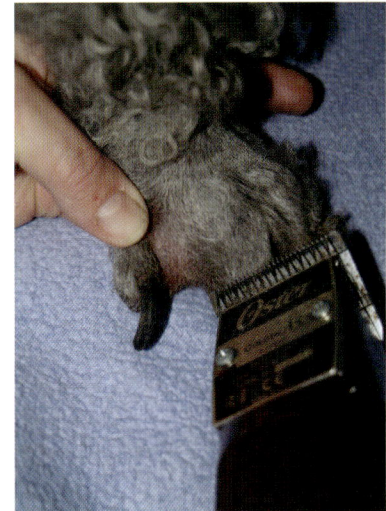

Fig. 14.3.22a-b   Use a fine blade or a toe blade. It is not easy to cut the dog with these blades if you use them to just touch the coat rather than push the blade into the skin. Try to use the left and right edges rather than the whole blade. Clip against the direction of hair growth.

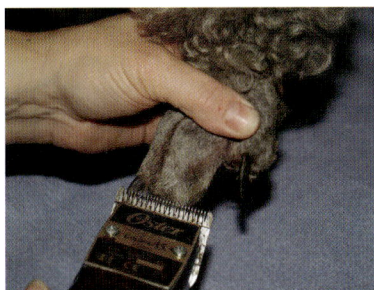

Fig. 14.3.23   The right edge of the blade trims the right side of the toe, the left edge of the blade the left side (shown).

Fig. 14.3.24a-b   To make the foot as tidy as possible, use the blade edges or the centre of the blade to pick up the hairs around the nail bed.

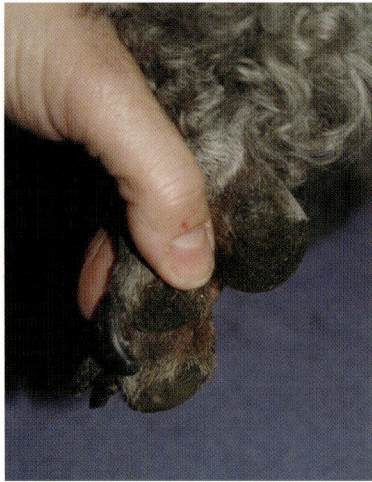

Fig. 14.3.25a-c   To open the foot so that you can trim the underside, hold it with your index finger on the top of the foot between the two centre toes, and wrap your thumb gently around one outside toe and your second finger around the other outside toe. Push the two centre toes down and gently pull the two outside toes upwards. The foot will open.

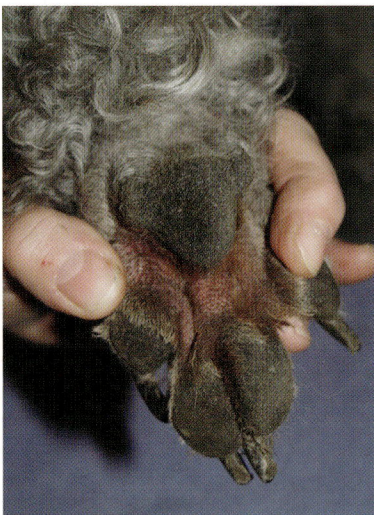

Fig. 14.3.26a-b   Keep a soft hold and remember only to bend the joints in the direction that they naturally bend, and do not force the bend. Keep hind legs well under the body when clipping back feet.

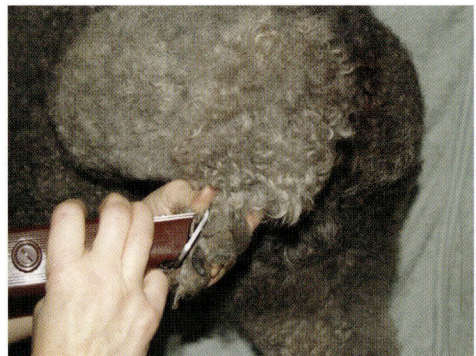

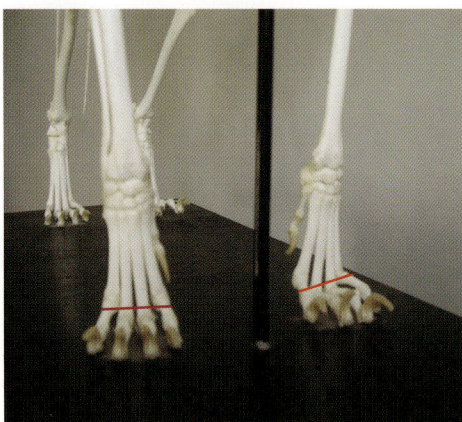
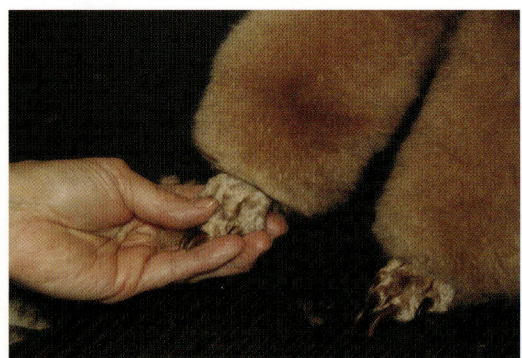

Fig. 14.3.27a-b   The whole of the foot on the Poodle is clipped to the junction of the carpal/tarsal and metacarpal/metatarsal bones. When the leg hair is trimmed, it will show a nice neat foot.

Clipping a Poodle face

Clipping a Poodle face for the first time is daunting, but there are in fact little discreet markers to help you. Use a fine blade and clip against the direction of hair growth.

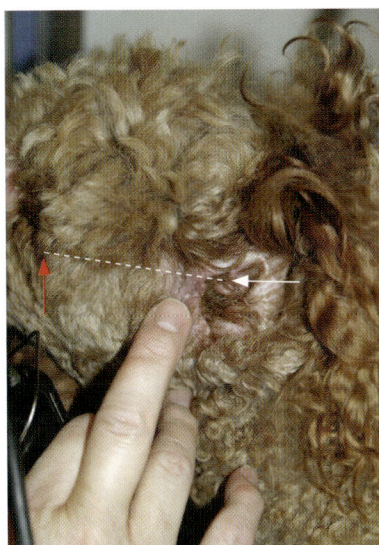

LEFT: Fig. 14.3.28   The first 'marker' (white arrow) is a tiny skin crease at the top of the inside ear. This is your starting point and you are heading in a horizontal line to the outside corner of the eye and your second 'marker' (red arrow).

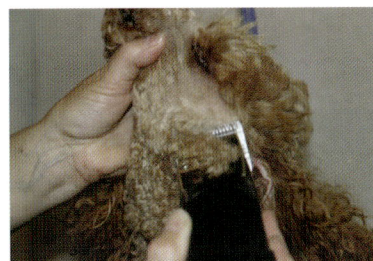

RIGHT: Fig. 14.3.29a-b   Clipping against the hair the whole time, remove the hair from in front of the ear and the cheek.

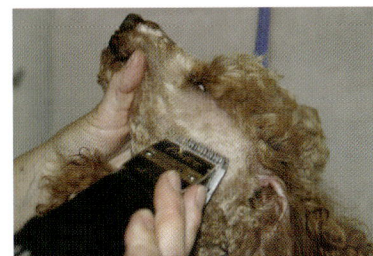

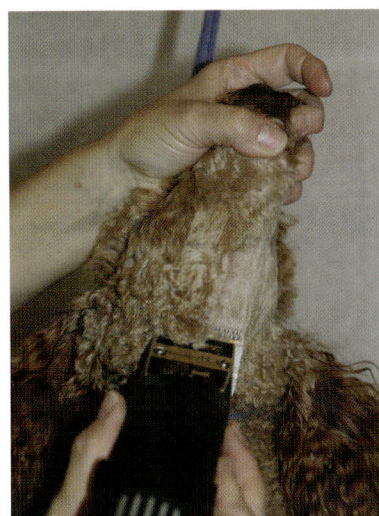

RIGHT: Fig. 14.3.31   Using the same markers, clip the hair from the ear to the corner of the eye on the other side of the face.

LEFT: Fig. 14.3.30   Tilt the head towards the ceiling and clip around the throat at about the level where the collar sits (another marker).

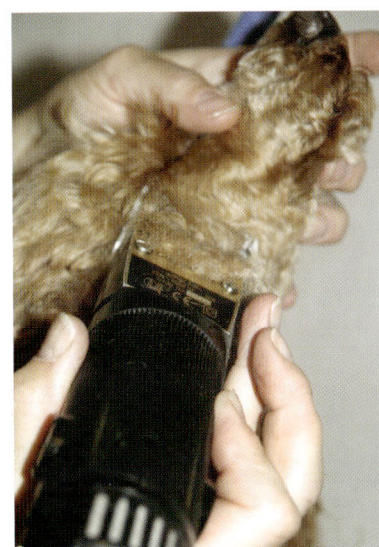

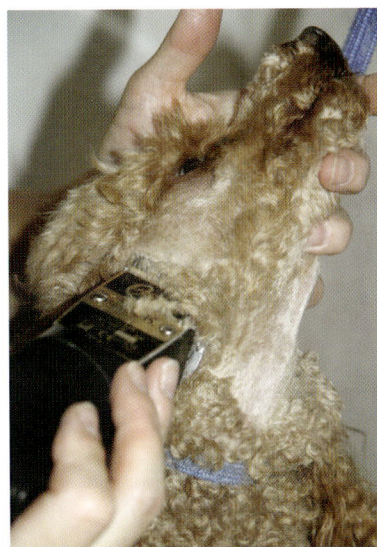

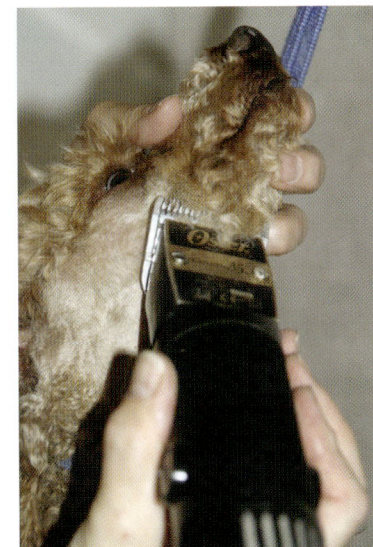

Fig. 14.3.32a-c   Continue clipping against the hair to remove all the hair on the cheek.

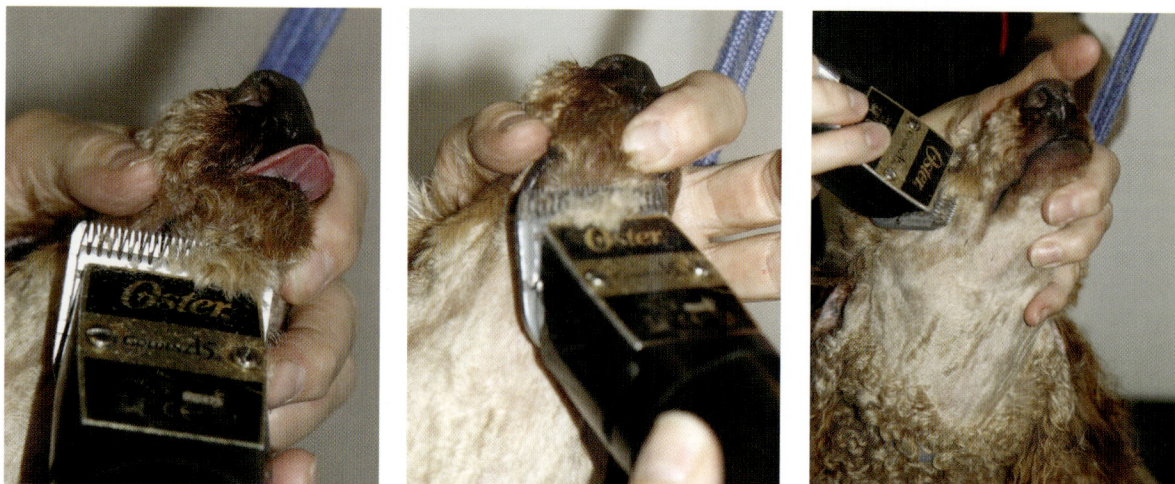

Fig. 14.3.33a-c   When you start to clip the nose, most dogs start to lick in response to the air disturbance caused by the clipper blade movement tickling their nose. Use your finger to keep the mouth closed. Clip the lower jaw and start to work your way onto the top of the nose.

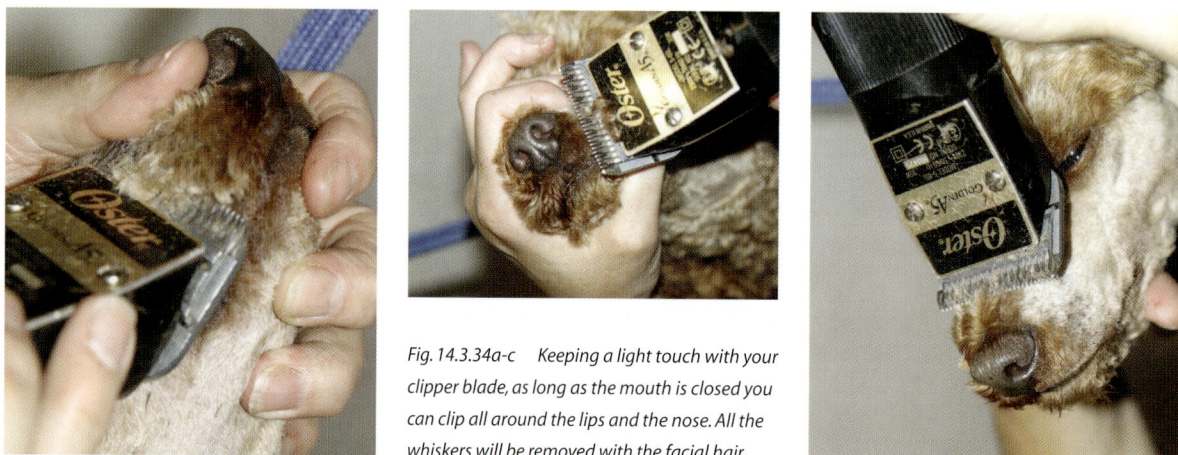

Fig. 14.3.34a-c   Keeping a light touch with your clipper blade, as long as the mouth is closed you can clip all around the lips and the nose. All the whiskers will be removed with the facial hair.

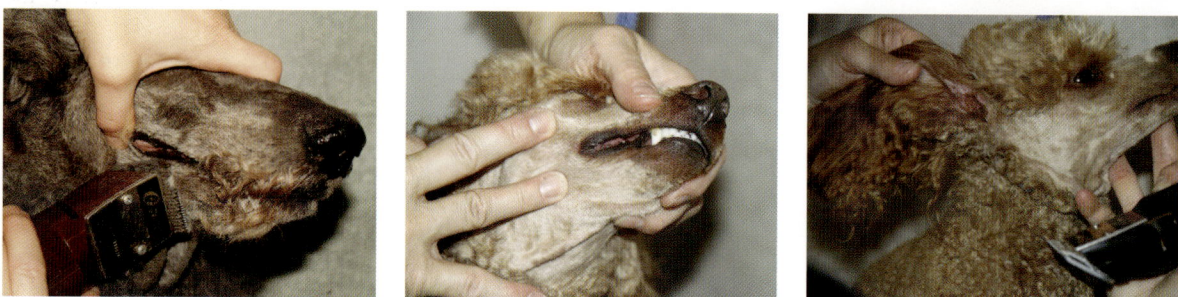

Fig. 14.3.35   To clear the hair away from the lips of this Standard Poodle, the groomer is using her thumb in the corner of the lip to stretch the skin so the lip folds can be clipped free of hair.

Fig. 14.3.36a-b   Once you have finished, check your work for any missed bits and for any signs of clipper rash or irritation.

Clipping is fun. Once you have learnt to use your clipper with confidence, you not only reduce the workload on your hands from using manual tools, you can also save yourself valuable time. Start on the dog's body, using longer-length 'F' blades (4F or 5F) because they are more forgiving. As you improve, go over your work with the next blade to further shorten the coat. When you feel more confident, try out the effects of skip-toothed blades. The first time you use a fine blade on a Poodle face or feet, opt for a 10# and, when you are comfortable and confident, providing the dog's skin is not showing signs of trauma, go over your work with a 15#. Every coat is different and a blade that works well on one coat may not work so well on another. Only time and experience will help you to make the right choice but, if you make a mistake, do not panic. The coat will grow back!

15   Scissors and Scissoring

Learning how to use your scissors is where you can really start to enjoy yourself. Once you have mastered the skill of cutting, you will be able to create whatever style you want, as long as you have the coat to do it with. Using a pair of scissors is really not very difficult and I am sure you will have used them many times to cut many things; it will not therefore take you long to understand the principles of cutting. What does take time is developing a steady hand, and good eye and hand coordination.

This is where practice comes in. The more practice you get, the sooner you gain confidence in your ability. You need something to cut (it does not need to be a dog to begin with) so that you can master scissor control, but you also need to learn to really look at and beyond the outline of the object you are cutting, so that you can improve your eye/hand coordination.

In my experience, the mistake students most often make is buying the wrong scissors. If the tool is not suited to your hand, it is uncomfortable to use, and even with practice it will take a long time to build confidence in yourself and dexterity with your scissoring hand. With this in mind, this section starts by looking at some of the scissors available.

15.1 SCISSORS

There are hundreds of scissors (sometimes also called shears) to select from, hundreds of suppliers to buy from and you can choose whether to spend your pocket money or re-mortgage the house!

Scissors are actually quite simple (*see*

Fig.15.1.1). The job of scissors is to cut hair. Despite the vast range available, they are all based on one design – and a very good design it is too. They have two handles, each with a hole in them. In one hole you insert a finger and in the other your thumb. They are operated by the movement of the thumb and directed by the angle of the hand and wrist.

The handles extend and flatten out to become two blades that are joined somewhere along their length with a screw; this allows them to work in a cross-cutting action to cut something – in our case: hair! It could not be simpler.

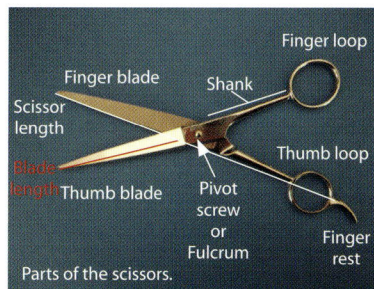

Fig. 15.1.1   Parts of the scissors.

The complication comes in the number of variations to this basic design. Scissors do perform differently, and some have certain modifications that make them more suited to some tasks (and operator) than others but, whilst you may need several pairs of scissors, you do not necessarily need as many variations as you do in brushes and combs. You certainly do not need to buy every pair in the catalogue, and you do not need to stretch beyond your budget unless you want to. Your first pair should

not be too expensive as, without doubt, you will not use them or handle them with precision, but eventually you will want to invest in the best you can afford; if you look after them, they will serve you well. Scissors are like old slippers: once they become comfortable, they are hard to replace and even another pair of the same make and design will not feel the same.

When selecting your scissors you need to consider what you want to use them for, what size and wieght you need, and how much you are prepared to pay. There are a few basic facts that apply to all scissors.

◆ Firstly, they must be sharp! The most expensive pair of scissors is not going to help you if they are blunt. Not only will they not cut properly, they put extra strain on hand tendons and joints, causing fatigue and possibly injury. Surprisingly, it is also easier to cut the dog with blunt scissors as you exert more pressure on the cutting action in an effort to make the scissors work, and you may not be able to feel the extra density as fine skin slips between the blades (particularly if you are cutting through dense or matted hair!).

◆ They must fit your hand (*see* 'Fitting your scissors'). When you are holding the scissors in your hand with your thumb in the thumb loop and either your second or third finger in the finger loop, the palm and the back of your hand should be as flat as possible with your fingers still sitting in their natural side-by-side arrangement.

Fitting your scissors

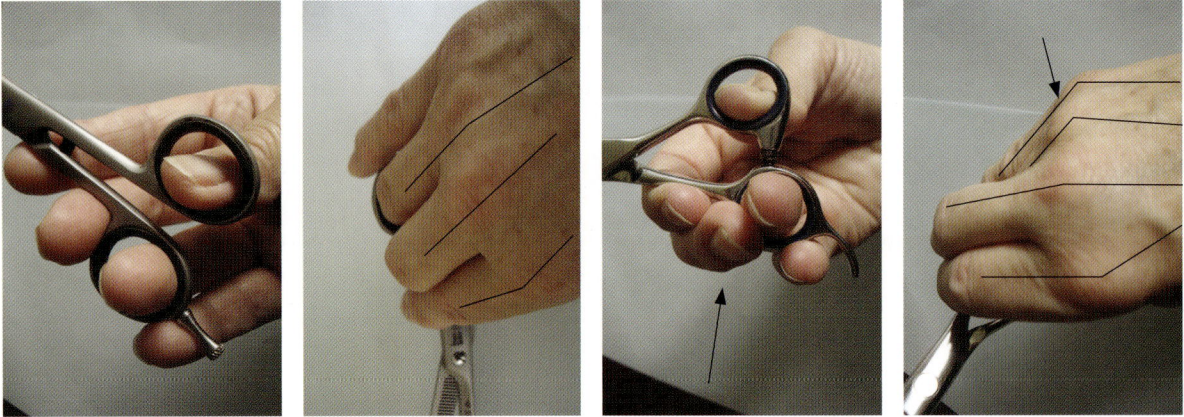

Fig. 15.1.2a-b   For a correct fit and to help prevent injuries such as Carpal Tunnel Syndrome (CTS) and Repetitive Strain Injury (RSI), your fingers should stay in their normal side by side formation when you are holding and working with your scissors.

Fig. 15.1.3a-b   These scissors with asymmetric handles don't fit this groomer's hand. The index finger is being pulled into its neighbour and the third (ring) finger and the little finger are being pulled across the hand. This would cause injury in a very short period of time at the point of the arrow.

CAUTION

If your metacarpal bones and your fingers are being pulled across one another, it puts a strain on the joints, tendons and muscles in your hand. In many cases, after a few years the damage will be irreversible and you are at risk of developing carpal tunnel syndrome (CTS) or repetitive strain injury (RSI). When buying scissors, the length and width of your hand and your wrist mobility are always more important than the brand name or popular design.

Scissor balance

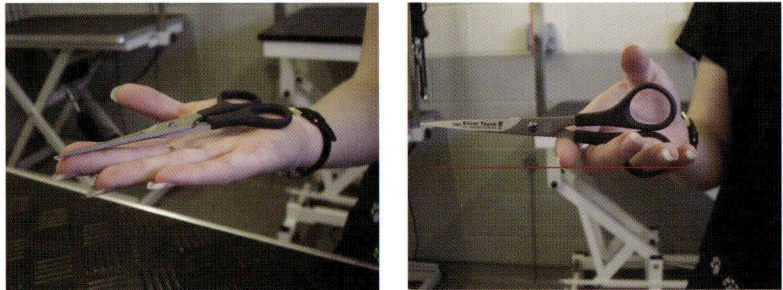

Fig. 15.1.4a-b   This groomer has a small hand. These 6.5-inch scissors are the same length as her hand, with the pivot about half-way along the length of the scissors. When the groomer removes her thumb from the thumb ring, the fingers are in their natural position and the scissors stay horizontal (balanced) in her hand. This is a good pair of scissors for this groomer.

- They must be balanced in your hand (*see* 'Scissor balance'). Scissors with long blades tend to have short shanks. This means that the weight of the scissors is not in your hand. To test the balance, hold your scissors and line them up parallel to a flat surface. The scissor should not pull your index finger out of alignment if your thumb is removed from the thumb loop and the scissor should remain parallel to the surface. The more the scissor drops, the less balance you will have.
- They are operated by the movement of the thumb only and they are directed by the angle of the hand and wrist.

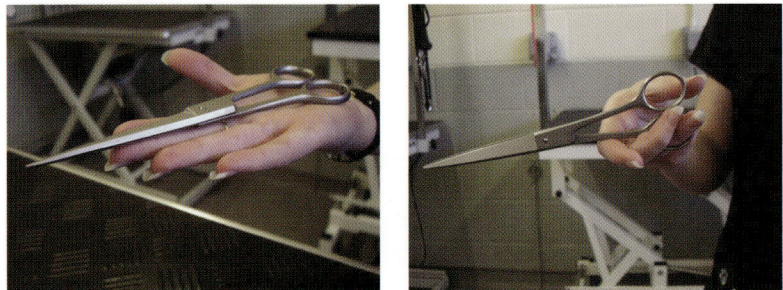

Fig. 15.1.5a-b   These scissors are 8 inches in length, lightweight, with the pivot approximately halfway along the length and with symmetrical finger loops. When the thumb is removed from the thumb ring, the scissors will pull the index finger towards the table and the holding finger upwards, straining the tendons of the hand. They are too long for this groomer and they are unbalanced in this hand.

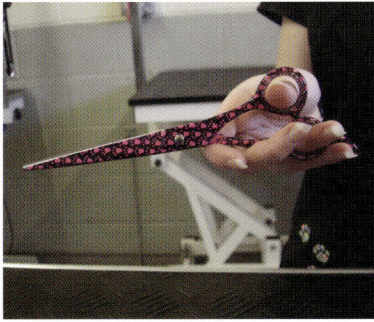

Fig. 15.1.6a–b   These are 7-inch scissors and the pivot screw is about central to the length of the scissors. The scissors have asymmetric finger loops, meaning the thumb loop is further forward than the finger loop. Remove the thumb and the weight of the blades will unbalance the scissors in this hand enough to drop the index finger and raise the holding finger.

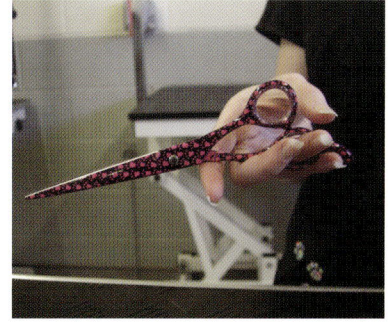

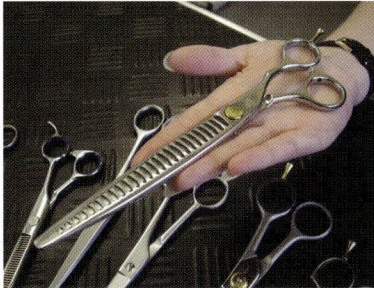

Fig. 15.1.7a–b   These are very lightweight blending scissors, despite their very long length. They are not a good investment for this groomer because even with her thumb still in the thumb loop, the length of the blade is pulling the hand out of shape. The health of your hands is important. The most popular or the most expensive type is not necessarily going to be right for you, so buy for fit rather than for fashion.

- Scissors are generally manufactured in stainless steel (steel combined with chromium) or other alloys to reduce the risk of rusting. Carbon-steel scissors are prone to rust if they are not kept well oiled. The blades are often ice-tempered for optimum strength and durability, and to keep them sharp for longer. Some scissors have an anodized, oxide or Teflon film coating applied to the non-cutting parts for protection.
- Most, but not all, scissors have one blade with a polished edge and the other micro-serrated (*see* Fig. 15.1.8). This means that one blade has minute notches along the length to catch and hold the individual hairs for cutting.
- Scissors are manufactured in different lengths (*see* Fig. 15.1.1), measured from the outside edge of

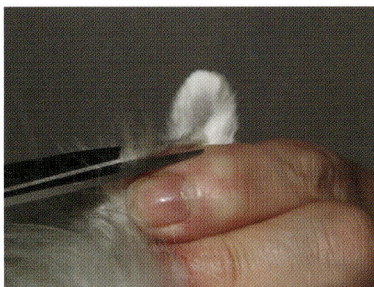

Fig. 15.1.8   Illustrated here are the micro-serrations on the edge of the scissor blade holding the hairs for cutting.

the finger handle to the tip of the blade. Scissor blade length is different from scissor length. To produce a longer blade and a wider reach between the blades, scissors often have a shorter handle-to-blade length ratio. These scissors are useful for breeds like the Standard Poodle, where you have large areas to cover.
- The size of the scissors determines their weight: the wider and longer the blade length, the heavier the scissors. Wider blades, sometimes referred to as 'Filipino' scissors, are often preferred for styling heavy dense coats like that of the Labradoodle, whereas finer coats (such as the furnishings on Setters) benefit from lightweight scissors. The weight can be reduced by having plastic handles or holes in the blades.
- Finger and thumb loops can be reduced in size by the addition of finger guards (rubber rings that are fitted to the loops). These reduce the risk of blistering to the skin on your fingers, but if the loops fit too snugly around the finger, they can restrict the movement of the scissors in your hand.
- Some scissors are designed with convex blades that bulge outwards to give them a crisp, effortless cut, which also extends the life of the blade edge.

- The tension on these scissors must be adjusted before use as it varies between coat types and depth. The tension screw is located in the centre of the blades and it allows you to tighten or loosen the tension as required to maintain performance. The point where the tension screw is situated is sometimes referred to as the pivot or fulcrum.
- Scissors are precision made so that the blades meet and cut evenly. Once dropped, scissors can be permanently damaged, so for your first pair of scissors, you are advised not to spend too much money. Practise your trimming skills before upgrading to better quality scissors.
- Sharpening is more likely to damage poorer quality scissors but even good quality scissors can be ruined by an untrained technician with the wrong equipment. Have your scissors sharpened by a reputable company.

Types of scissors

Straight scissors (*see* Fig. 15.1.9) are the ones that you will use more often than not. They range in size from 4.5 inches (11.5cm) to about 9 inches (22.5cm), and they range in weight from lightweight to heavy duty. They also have a variety of handle sizes and shapes to suit everyone's personal preference. Although they are referred to

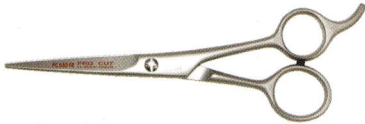

Fig. 15.1.9   *Straight scissors can be purchased either with or without the finger rest. They vary considerably in size and weight.*

as straight scissors, a skilled groomer often uses these scissors to cut circles and pompoms as well as steadily cutting straight lines on long legs.

The point allows you to be very precise with your cutting line and lets you cut very close to the skin. A general rule is that the tighter or smaller the area you are trimming, the smaller the scissors you need. For example, between the foot pads try 4.5 inch scissors and 7 inch scissors for the body. Using small scissors on a large area means you will be applying many more scissor cuts to the coat and it is more difficult to get an even trim, particularly when you are learning.

To cut between footpads, around the genitals and close to the ears, you can purchase short scissors with an enlarged, rounded, blunt end, called 'bullnose' scissors (see Fig. 15.1.10). The rounded end lessens the risk of puncturing the skin. Nevertheless, when using bullnose scissors, do not become complacent and think that you cannot

Fig. 15.1.10   *Bullnose scissors have a rounded end to prevent the scissors puncturing the skin when trimming the difficult area between toes and pads.*

cut the dog. Care must still be taken. The tips of the scissors may not puncture the skin but the blades are still very sharp and can still cut, causing injury.

Curved scissors (*see* Fig. 15.1.11) are designed to help you cut circles and around corners, making it easier to style pompoms, tubular-shaped legs and round heads, like those of the West Highland Terrier and Bichon Frisé. They are available in the same sizes as straight scissors, and the smaller size can also be purchased with a bullnose adaption. They do take a bit of getting used to but they can help with wrist mobility problems. The main point to remember with these scissors is that they do not cut straight lines so, whilst you are happily snipping away, beware: should you inadvertently try to cut a straight line, the points will dig into the coat and you will make a hole in your handiwork.

Fig. 15.1.11   *Curved scissors are designed to make the trimming of circles (Poodle topknots) and rounded head shapes (Bichon Frisé) easier for the groomer.*

Bent shank scissors (*see* Fig. 15.1.12) are very helpful for those groomers who have wrist mobility problems or have difficulty learning how to keep their hand and fingers away from the coat when scissoring. The handles on these scissors are offset and have a bend in them to allow you a better eye line; this is particularly valuable when you are scissoring along the length of the dog's back (top line). It may take a while to get used to using bent shank scissors because you hold your hand further away from the coat and cut at a different depth than you would if you were using straight scissors. It also takes a little while to coordinate your eye line with your hand position. Once very popular, these scissors can be difficult

Fig. 15.1.12   *Bent shank scissors are useful for groomers with restricted wrist movement because they help to distance their hand from their work.*

to get hold of now as they have fallen out of popularity and are being overlooked in favour of straight scissors with ergonomic scissor handles. They are still available, however, although you may be limited to only a few sizes.

There are two further tools that come under the heading of scissors purely because they are of a similar design and have the same action. Their principal function is different, however. *Thinning scissors* (*see* Fig. 15.1.13) are, as their name suggests, designed to thin the coat. The basic design is the same as the traditional scissors but the blades are divided up into teeth. As you open the scissors, the blades open to face each other with symmetrical teeth spaced at intervals along the blade, each of which has a small 'V' or notch cut into it. When the thinning scissors are placed into the coat, close to the skin, and closed, the hairs that fall between the gaps in the teeth escape the cut whereas the hairs caught within the notch are cut, thus thinning the density of the coat by that amount of hair.

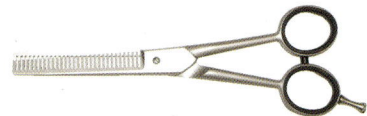

Fig. 15.1.13   *Thinning scissors with two toothed blades thin the coat by reducing the density of the hairs with each cut, but without automatically reducing the length.*

Thinning scissors are not generally used twice in the same spot as repeated use in one area eventually results in all the hairs being cut. The action is usually performed only once or twice in one spot with the next cut in an adjoining area until all the required coat has been removed. By using this method, and working methodically over the area you wish to thin out, you can achieve an even finish. Care must be taken not to overuse thinning scissors as they do not remove the hair totally: they merely cut it off, close to the base of the hair shaft, thereby simulating a false moult. The hair will continue to grow and sometimes the coat can even be encouraged to grow more thickly. These scissors are widely used to thin out heavy coats, particularly on the leg furnishings of Cocker Spaniels, but they can also be used to thin the body of heavily coated breeds such as the Bouvier des Flandres.

Blending scissors (*see* Fig. 15.1.14) have one straight cutting blade and one fine-toothed thinning blade. They can produce a lovely finish, particularly on dogs that have been partially clipped, where the clipper line needs to be softened and blended into the furnishings. They are also very useful on breeds such as Old English Sheepdogs in full coat, where there is a desire to remove a couple of inches of hair but not to use clippers. These scissors work by selecting a few hairs between the teeth and cutting them off with the straight blade. The best way to use them is to insert them into the coat close to the skin and make three or four single cuts at different intervals as you bring the scissor towards you and towards the end of the length of coat. This will layer the hairs and blend your cutting line. If you make the three or four cuts without moving the scissors, you will remove a large portion of hair and probably create a hole in the coat cut. It does take practice but the result is worth it. It needs to be remembered that, if used excessively right at the base of the coat, you may have the same problems with regrowth as you would with thinning scissors.

Fig. 15.1.14   *These blending scissors have a straight blade and a toothed blade to help the groomer blend the cutting lines in the coat by thinning and tapering the edges of the scissor cut.*

Both thinning scissors and blending scissors are often referred to as fine or coarse, depending on the number and size of the teeth. The number of teeth also has a bearing on the length of the blades. For example, a pair of 46-toothed single-edged thinning scissors 6.5 inches in length will produce a fine finish, whereas a pair of 28-toothed scissors of the same length will produce a coarser cut because the teeth are wider and so are the gaps between them. You need to experiment to determine which ones are most suitable for you.

Scissors are now available in hundreds of variations of handle designs, metals and alloys (and even colours) to make them comfortable for you to use. Some scissors come with finger rests to help you balance them, and some can be fitted with finger guards to reduce blistering and prevent them sliding in your fingers. There are even scissors with larger finger holes for men.

Design and technology is moving on all the time. At the time of writing (2013), modifications have been made to the design of the thumb handle on scissors, allowing the thumb ring to rotate, thus reducing the amount of movement needed by the thumb to operate the scissors. This design may well be very useful in extending the working life of groomers with carpal tunnel syndrome or repetitive strain injuries, and in helping to prevent these problems for new groomers.

The best advice I can give you is not to pay too much for your first pair of scissors as they will no doubt have a hard time. When you are ready to buy a better pair, try out several handle designs to find a pair that is right for you and your budget. Remember that you will not be cutting many absolutely straight lines because, apart from the spinal column, the dog does not have any, and even the spinal column is not very straight! You need to learn how to cut curves, around bends, underneath and over the top of the dog whilst he remains standing. You cannot turn the dog upside down to reach those difficult bits! To do this, you need to develop dexterity and smooth operational skills to obtain the maximum benefit and the best possible finish. The simple exercises described and illustrated later in this chapter (*see* section 15.3) will help you acquire flexibility in your body and convince your hands that they can use scissors upside down and the wrong way round!

CLEANING AND MAINTENANCE

Your scissors need sharpening as soon as they show signs of not cutting, or of snagging or catching in the coat. It is not unusual for scissors to become blunt at the tips but not further along the blade. This is because we use the tips of the scissors more often than the whole blade. Make sure that when you send your scissors for sharpening, they are attended to by a reputable, qualified technician.

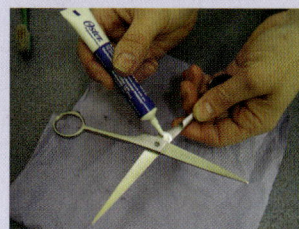

Fig. 15.1.15   *Oil the scissors at the pivot to maintain a smooth cutting action.*

Scissors should be sterilized after every dog, either by ultraviolet light or by immersion in a liquid sterilizing solution. Dry them well before storing or re-using. Oiling your scissors is essential if you want to maintain maximum performance. Wipe a little oil along each blade, making sure that you wipe from the screw (or pivot) towards the tip, so that you do not cut yourself, and put extra oil around the screw. Do not forget to wipe it off again before use. Scissors are precision balanced, so you should store them in individual pouches; if you are storing them for a prolonged period of time, it is best to oil them and store them in waxed paper inside the pouch.

CAUTION: BULLNOSE SCISSORS

Do not become complacent when using bullnose scissors. Their design means that they may not be able to puncture the skin but the blades can still do damage. All scissors are – and should be – sharp, so handle them with respect and never leave them with the blades open or in an area where they can cause harm when they are not in use.

15.2 HOLDING AND OPERATING SCISSORS

Scissors are held with the thumb resting within one handle and the second or third finger resting in the other (*see* Fig. 15.2.1). If a finger rest is being used, it will rest on the next finger along. The anatomy of your hand will decide whether the scissors are more comfortable for you to use between the thumb and your second finger or your thumb and your third finger. Remember that to reduce the risk of RSI and CTS your metacarpal bones should be as flat as possible and should not be pulled out of their natural alignment. Look at what is happening to your fingers and then decide.

Do *not* use your index finger as not only will you exert too much pressure, but the scissors will not balance well

Fig. 15.2.2   *This groomer is demonstrating the loss of scissors control by using her index finger in the finger loop instead of using it to help with balance. The extra strength in the index finger means that the cut lines are hard and noticeable.*

Fig. 15.2.1   *The scissors are held with the thumb in one loop and either your second or third finger in the finger loop. The index finger is free to slide along the shank to balance the blade in your hand.*

in your hand (*see* Fig. 15.2.2). Scissors are not operated by a pincer action, so keep your hand and fingers still and operate the scissor by using the thumb only. This keeps the pressure on the scissors to a minimum and your hand is relaxed, allowing your hand muscles to stay supple and soft. Hard muscles reduce the feeling in the hand and may result in muscle strain.

Your thumb and finger should be inserted into the rings to the first joint. This is the position that you need to maintain whilst you are working. Using the last third of your finger puts the lightest amount of pressure with the most amount of control into the cut. If the scissors slip down your finger, your hand will become hard and you will not be able to use the scissors effectively.

If you find it difficult to maintain this

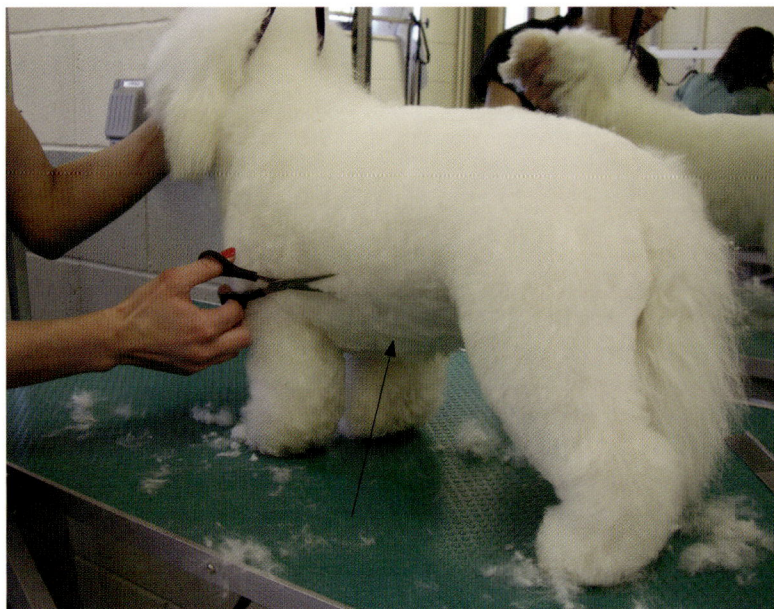

position, rubber scissor guards can be fitted into the control rings to make them smaller and help to hold them in place.

Cutting

A beautifully styled coat is achieved by the smoothness of your cutting lines. As you practise, try to keep your hand steady and relaxed so the hair you are cutting has a moulded or sculptured appearance without dips and dents in it. Any deviation in coat lengths, such as where styled legs meet the body or where legs and undercarriages are graced with furnishings, should be blended in a smooth invisible transition. This is done by using either straight scissors, blending scissors or thinning scissors, and in some cases a combination of them all. With all scissors, both sides of the blade are used.

A *forehand cut* (*see* forehand cutting) is when the *front* of the scissor blades is parallel to the coat. (The front is the side facing away from your palm when you are holding the scissors.) The scissors can be used in any direction but always cut with the front of the blades.

A *backhand cut* (*see* backhand cutting) is when the *back* of the scissor blades is parallel to the coat. (This is the side closest to your hand when you are holding the scissors.) The scissors can be used in any direction but they always cut with the back of the blades. Your thumb blade will bring the hair to meet the other blade and the two blades will cut the hairs from both sides as they meet.

Turning your scissors sideways to the coat will result in a hard, straight cut line rather than a smooth cut line (*see* Figs 15.2.3a-b).

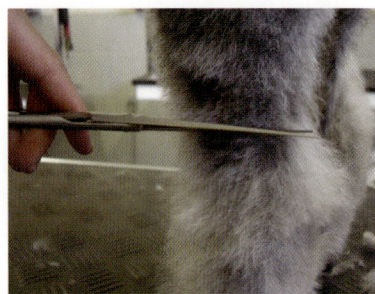

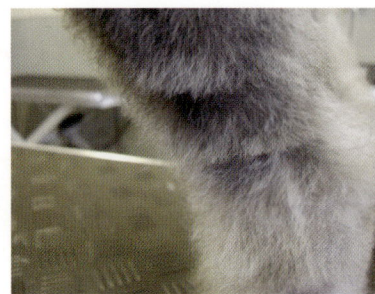

Fig. 15.2.3a-b   *If you turn your scissors sideways on to the dog, you will cut unsightly hard lines.*

Forehand cutting

Any scissors can be used. The cutting is done by the front of the scissor blades with the blades parallel to the coat. The scissors can be on any angle but the cut is always done with the front of the blade. Take note of the angle of the scissors and the position of the hand.

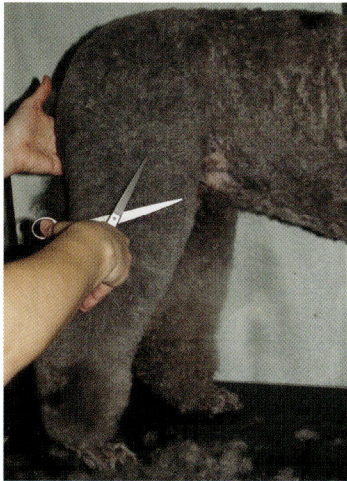

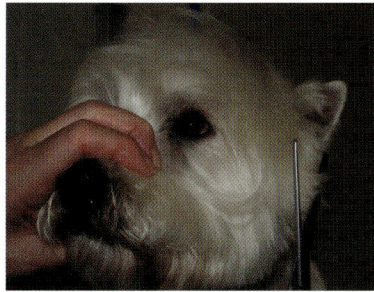

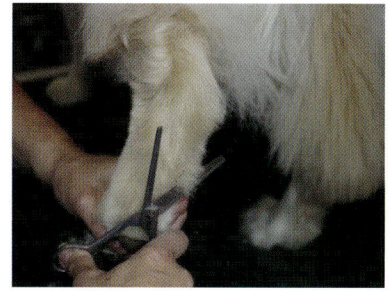

ABOVE: Figs 15.2.5a-b   A forehand cut being used by a right-handed groomer using blending scissors to shape the left side of the head of a West Highland Terrier and the hocks of a Golden Retriever.

LEFT: Fig. 15.2.4   The front of the scissors is the side facing away from your hand as you hold the scissors, whether you are left- or right-handed.

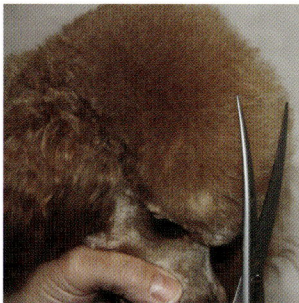

Fig. 15.2.6   A forehand cut with curved scissors on a Poodle topknot.

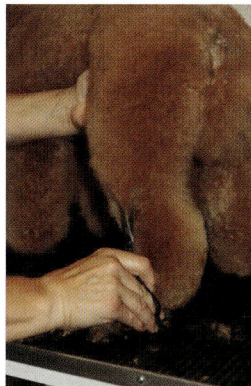

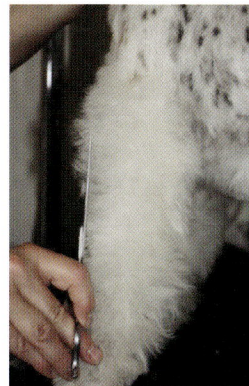

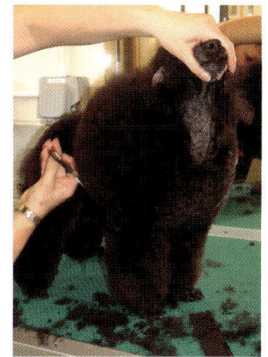

Figs 15.2.7a-c   The first two pictures illustrate the groomer working on the side of a left hind leg and the back of a right hind leg. In the third picture you can see how the scissors are at 90 degrees to the hand to shape the underside of the Poodle's body coat.

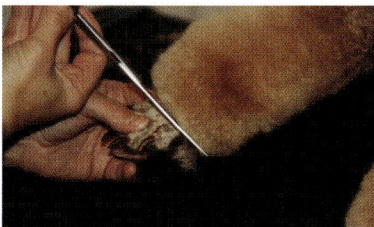

Fig. 15.2.8   To shape the bottom of the leg, the scissors are again at a 90 degree angle to the hand.

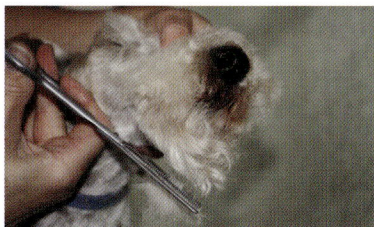

Fig. 15.2.9a-b   Forehand cutting is used here to style and shape with blending scissors the beard of a Fox Terrier and the tail of a Golden Retriever.

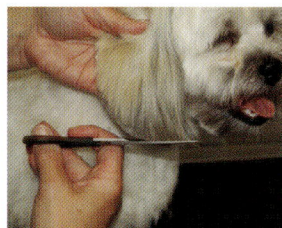

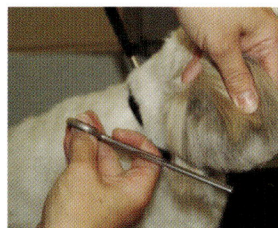

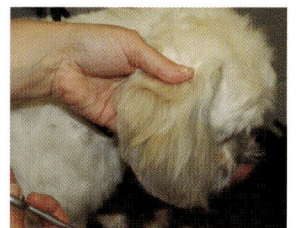

Figs 15.2.10a-d   The ears of this pet Lhasa Apso have been cut and shaped first of all with straight scissors and then the edges have been retouched with thinning scissors to give a softer look.

Backhand cutting

Backhand cutting is when you are cutting with the backs of your scissor blades parallel to the coat. Any scissors can be used, and they can be used at any angle but they will always be cutting with the backs of the blades.

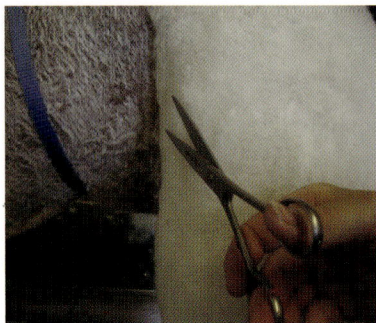

Fig. 15.2.11 The back of the blades is the side closest to your hand.

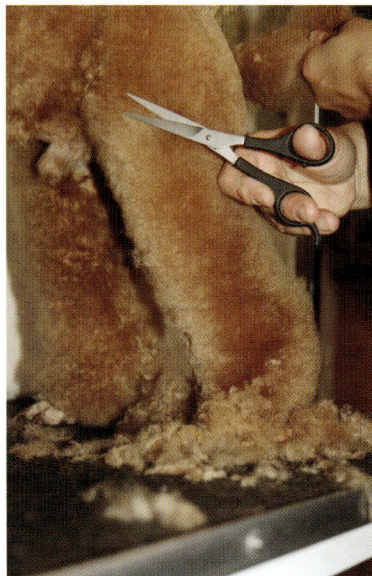

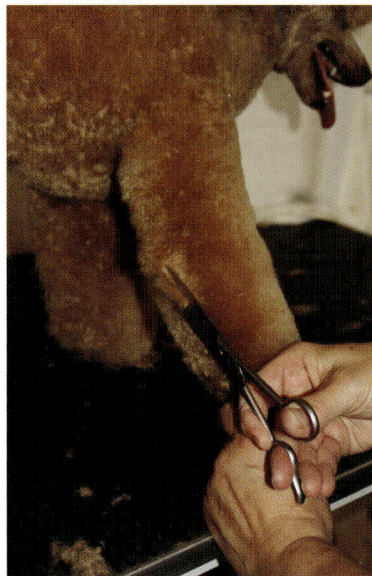

Figs 15.2.12a-b These pictures illustrate how the groomer has changed to a backhand cut as she works around the legs. This is not only a more comfortable position to work in, it gives an uninterrupted view of the cutting area.

Fig. 15.2.13 A backhanded cut to shape the undercarriage of a Wire Fox Terrier. Note that the scissors are being worked towards the elbow, rather than towards the groin.

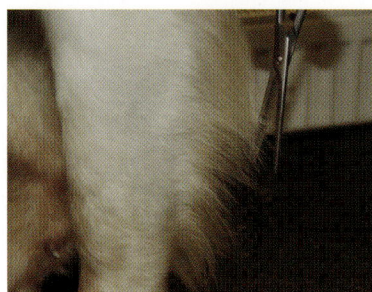

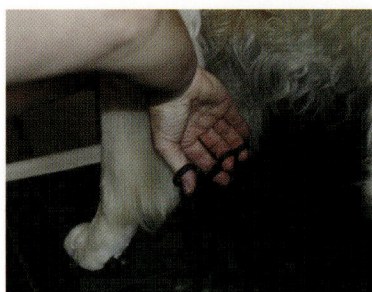

Fig. 15.2.14a-b The hair on the legs of the Retriever hangs towards the ground so the hair is cut with a backhand cut with the scissors pointing in the direction that the hair lies.

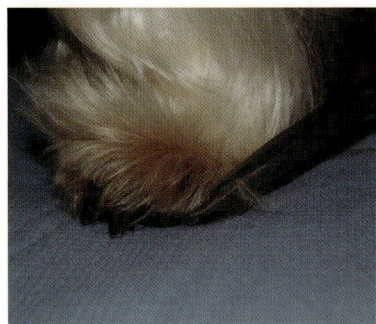

LEFT: Fig. 15.2.16 A backhanded cut being used to trim around the feet.

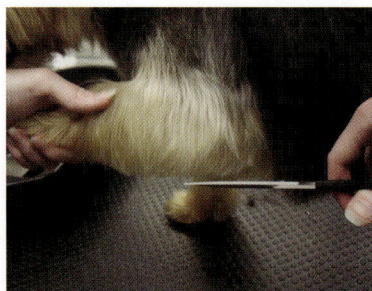

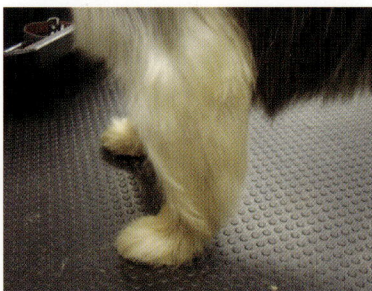

ABOVE: Fig. 15.2.15a-b An alternative way to trim leg feathers. The leg is held up and shaken so the hair falls naturally. A backhanded cut is used with the points of the scissors facing the foot. This is the equivalent of the foot being on the table and the scissors pointing towards the table. When the foot is let down, the feathers will fall gracefully.

Left-handed groomers use the same two cuts, but where the right-handed groomer uses a forehand cut, the left-handed groomer uses a backhand cut, and where the right-handed groomer uses a backhand cut, the left-handed groomer uses a forehand cut.

Direction of cutting

Generally speaking, whichever cut you are using, if you are styling a coat that has been dried straight and fluff-dried to give it volume, as in the case of Poodles, Bedlington Terriers, Bichon Frisé and other woolly coats, position the tips of your scissors on or above the horizontal. This is so that the bottom blade lifts the coat as it cuts, rather than flattening it. This helps to keep the coat buoyant.

When trimming leg feathering on breeds such as Spaniels and Setters, where the hair grows downwards, cut with your scissors pointing downwards to keep the coat falling gracefully in its natural direction. When cutting leg feathers, try to open your scissors wide enough to span the width of the feather so that you make a single cut in any given place, rather than several cuts. Every time you place your scissors, even the lightest touch will move the hair so your second cut may not be cutting the hair that you want it to. If you have to make a second cut, comb the hair first.

When cutting the undercarriage, try to work your scissors towards the elbow rather than towards the groin. Not only will you get a better view of where you are working, but you are less likely to nip the hanging skin in the groin area.

When shaping long ears, work downwards away from the ear, as this means you are less likely to nick the base of the ear. If you are trimming close to the pinna, as in West Highland Terriers and

NOTE: CURVED BLADES

Remember that the curvature of the blade means they cut curves, not straight lines! Remember to change to flat blades if you want a nice flat finish (a mistake often made when you first start using them).

CAUTION: TO MINIMIZE THE RISK OF CUTTING THE DOG

- *Never cut where you cannot see.*
- *Never leave your scissors on the table within reach of the dog. He might stand on them.*
- *Never leave your scissors open anywhere! They are very sharp and can cut easily, even without pressure on the blades. Store them closed and somewhere safe.*
- *When trimming feet, always hold the leg or put pressure on top of the withers to keep the foot on the floor.*
- *Always make sure that your scissors are sharp to avoid putting too much hand pressure into blunt blades.*
- *Never pull the hair away from the skin to cut it because you will also be pulling the skin from the body and you may cut it by mistake.*
- *Try to cut away from the groin and armpits rather than towards them, where the skin is loose and hanging.*
- *When cutting around eyes, always have the tips of your scissors well past the edges of the eye and never cut towards the eye.*
- *Try always to cut away from the base of the ear, working towards the end of the pinna.*
- *Never point your scissor tips into the ear canal. (They should not be in there anyway because you should not cut the hair in the canal – it should be pulled out.)*
- *Do not bounce with your scissors because you have less control of the pressure there will be when your scissors meet the coat. Apart from cutting dents in the coat you can cut the skin.*
- *Keeping your hands soft means you are more likely to be able to feel what is between the scissor blades. Skin between the blades feels different from hair.*
- *Try not to use large, heavy scissors unless it is necessary. A smaller, finer pair cuts less hair, so you will be using less pressure, thus protecting your hands; you are also less likely to cut skin.*
- *Sculpt the coat by sliding and gliding your scissors over small areas at a time, taking off a small amount of hair from the coat surface and gradually working deeper where you need to.*

breeds with clipped-off ears, hold the edge of the ear between your finger and thumb so you can feel where it is when you cut. Always cut away from the base of the ear for safety and so that you can see where you are cutting.

15.3 EXERCISES

Most people are familiar with the saying 'A bad workman always blames his tools'. The scissors may do the cutting but you are the operator and you do the styling. A good, well-balanced pair of scissors undoubtedly helps, but you need practice to improve your standard of work and you should do exercises to improve your suppleness!

Scissors may be operated by the hand, but the scissoring motion comes from the knee and it works up your body through the hips, waist and shoulders and finally down to the wrists and hands. Your body should sway from side to side and up and down, rather than relying on your arm and hand to do all the work. Your body needs to be 'soft', relaxed and supple in order to move freely so that your scissors and your hand glide smoothly over the coat. If you are stiff in your lower torso, the stiffness extends through your body and your scissoring will be uneven.

So, exercises! No half-marathons, just a few simple exercises to help you get grooming fit. Do them gently, and do not force anything that does not want to move. The important point is to find out where your stiffness is and to start to gently work it loose. If you have difficulties doing any of these exercises,

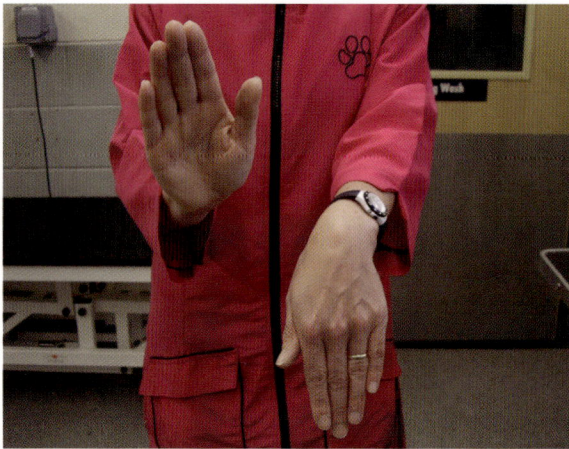

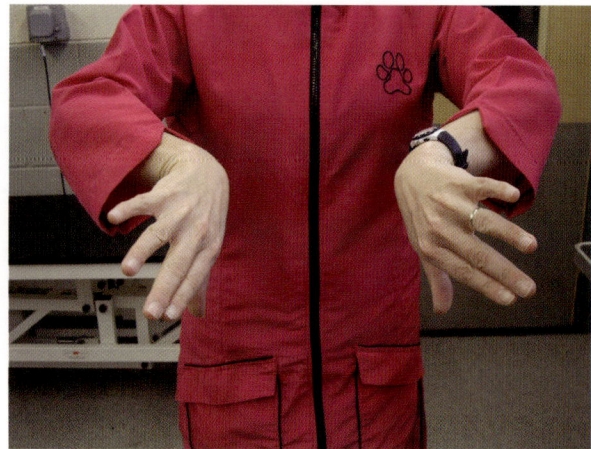

Fig. 15.3.1a-b   Do some simple exercises to loosen up your wrists so they become flexible. It doesn't matter what you do, the important thing is to get them moving up and down, in circles, and from left to right in a fluent movement.

speak to your doctor, who may be able to suggest alternatives that suit you better.

Loosen up your wrists

Stiff wrists will give you hard hands and restrict your hand movement. It does not matter how you choose to do this but the important thing is to get both wrists moving up and down and in circles, rotating both to the left and to the right (see Fig. 15.3.1a-b). You can do this exercise at any time – when watching television or chatting on the phone. The more you do this, the softer the movements become.

Loosen up your elbows

This exercise is similar to the wrist exercise: move your lower arms up and down, as if you are directing traffic, and in circles.

Loosen up the shoulders

Pretend that you are swimming. Front crawl and back stroke both loosen up the shoulders and the neck. Breast stroke loosens the muscles in your chest and upper back. These exercises not only help with suppleness, they also strengthen your upper back, which helps you maintain balance when you are bending at odd angles.

Bend the waist

This will help to stretch your muscles

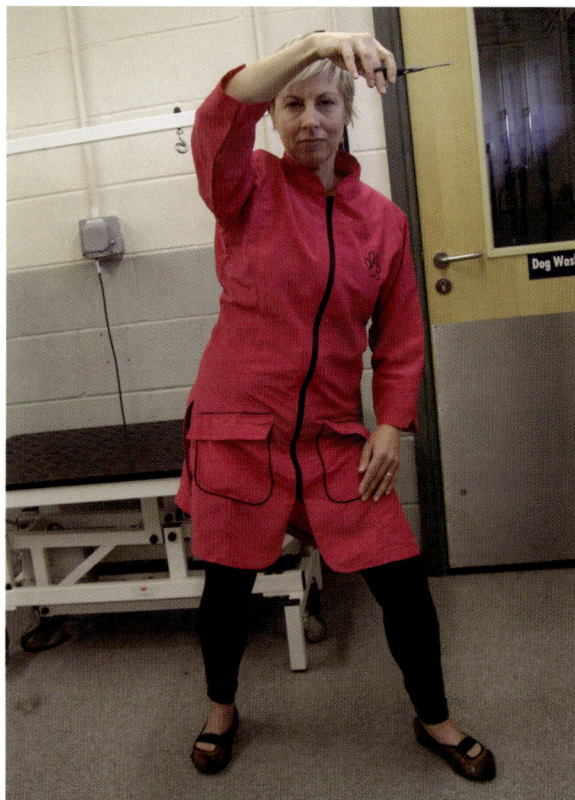

Fig.15.3.2   Get your knees and your waist moving. It is easier to work around the dog than to work the dog around you, so you need to be flexible and as supple as possible. Your body movements come from the knee, the hip and the waist, so any movement to loosen them up and strengthen them will help you.

and start to strengthen them. With your feet slightly apart and planted firmly on the ground, bend to the left and to the right. If you are able, rotate your torso in a sort of circle, but if your balance is poor or your back weak, use one hand on a chair back or tabletop to support you and do not push yourself beyond your capabilities.

Trim the door frame (*see* Fig. 15.3.2)

This may sound odd but this little

exercise will demonstrate to you the amount of movement that your body will be doing and the odd angles at which you are working your scissors. You need to be able to cut where you want at whatever angle you are working at (*see* Fig. 15.3.3). As you practise this exercise, keep your centre finger on the door frame to help you with coordination, to learn to keep your scissors parallel with your subject, to balance your scissors and to steady your hand by stopping you bouncing the scissor

Fig. 15.3.3 Look at how the groomer is balancing her scissors backwards from her hand to trim the hock of the dog. Using scissors in this way is not difficult but it will be unfamiliar to you and you must practise to make your scissoring movement fluent and precise.

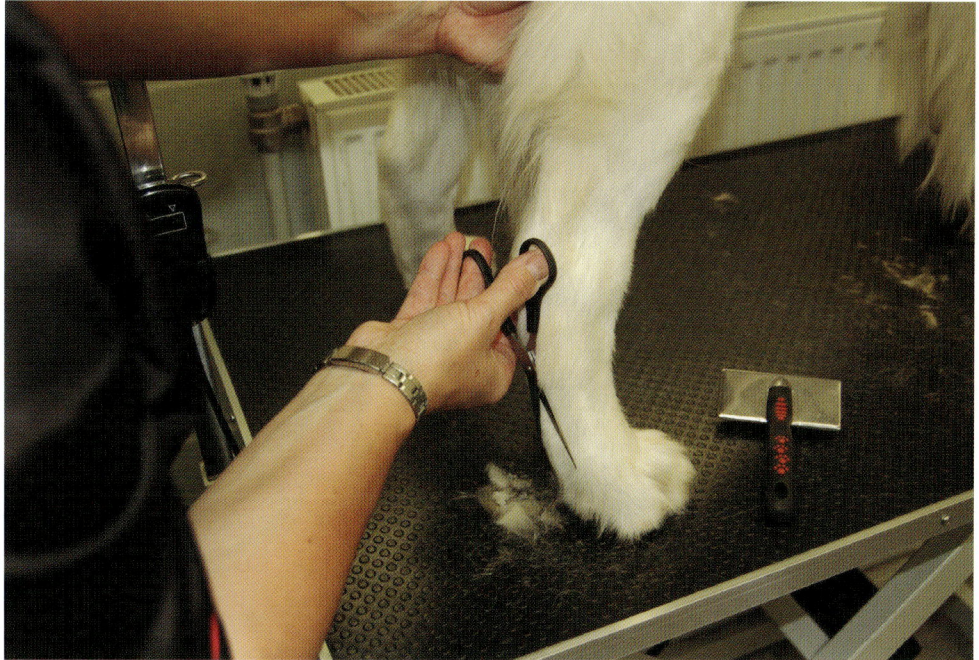

blades as you cut (this prevents dips and dents in your work).

With the door open, stand with your feet slightly apart, facing the door frame. Holding a pair of scissors in your hand, put your hand close enough to the door frame so that the finger in the finger loop is very lightly touching the frame, with the scissors (*see* Fig. 15.3.4) parallel to the frame, facing towards the ceiling. Using your thumb to work your scissors, 'scissor' up one side of the frame (simulating the dog's hind leg) to about shoulder height and then turn your scissors so that they are parallel to the floor and trim a straight line across

the top of the frame to the other side (simulating the dog's back). Following the bottom of a window frame with a forehand cut will simulate trimming the undercarriage (*see* Fig. 15.3.5).

Close the door. Now work back the other way. Turn your hand over so that your finger is touching the door and the scissors are pointing towards the ceiling. Scissor across the door to the frame and then turn your hand so the scissors are pointing towards the floor. With your finger still on the frame, work down the frame to about knee height.

When you have 'trimmed' the door frame, do the same with tables and cupboards – in fact anything that gives you a template to follow. It all helps.

Pompoms

This is by far the best exercise you can do; it is excellent for improving eye/

hand coordination, scissor skills and your balance.

Make a big pompom (*see* Figs 15.3.6a to 15.3.12b). With an old pair of scissors in one hand (do not use your trimming scissors because you will make them blunt), hold the pompom in the other hand over a waste bin. Without moving the pompom at all, follow its shape and trim it into a perfect circle. Take your time and work around the whole of the pompom, using both sides of your scissors and bending your body so you can see where you are cutting. Keep going until the pompom is very small – and then make lots more. You need the practice and the more you can get, the better.

Figs 15.3.4 To begin with, you may think that this is a silly exercise but it does help you coordinate your eye and hand so that you can learn to be precise with your scissor cuts. Start with the door and then use lots of other shapes as templates to work around, keeping your centre finger on the article so that you cut smoothly and do not bounce with your scissors.

Fig. 15.3.5 Keeping your scissors parallel to the floor, practise trimming straight lines but with a forehand cut. Make your cutting action fluent, keep your scissors level and remember not to bounce the scissoring movement.

Making a pompom

Cutting pompoms will help you to get scissor control, scissor balance and supple wrists. You need some cardboard, some wool, something to mark the cardboard and some scissors.

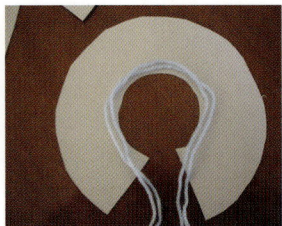

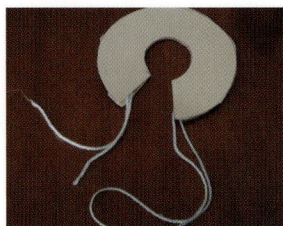

Figs 15.3.6a-b   Cut two circles out of the cardboard with an opening gap and a small centre circle. Cut a length of wool, double it and lay it on top of one of the circles leaving the two strands hanging out. You need these to tie the pompom together.

Figs 15.3.7a-b   Place your second circle on the top to make a sandwich and start to wind your wool through the centre and around the pieces of card.

Figs 15.3.8a-b   Keep going until the wool is quite thick. Cut the wool free and tie the two strands.

Figs 15.3.9a-b   Make sure you have tied and knotted the strands as tightly as you can. Slide the scissors between the two pieces of card to cut them apart.

Figs 15.3.10a-b   As you cut, the wool will start to form the pompom. Slide the card away and you have your pompom.

Figs 15.3.11a-b   Hold the pompom by the ties. Do not move the pompom at all. Work around it to practise and get the feel of your forehand cut ...

Figs 15.3.12a-b   ...and your backhand cut.

16 Hand Stripping and Plucking

At some time during your career you may be asked to hand strip or pluck a coat. This is a process that removes a percentage of the dog's topcoat or guard hairs (which will be rapidly replaced by new growth), whilst leaving the undercoat hairs untouched. The art of hand plucking and stripping is effective and can produce a lovely finish on a coat if the groomer has taken the time to master the techniques, but it is time-consuming in the early stages of your learning.

It should not be confused with 'carding' (see Chapter 11), which is a useful method of removing the dog's undercoat. Plucking, by contrast, is a method of stripping out or shortening the dog's topcoat. It existed long before the invention of clippers and the skill is still very much sought after today, by both pet owners and exhibitors of show dogs alike.

16.1 HAND STRIPPING AND PLUCKING

This is a controversial subject! Hand stripping and plucking are considered cruel, stressful and unnecessary by many people who either have been misinformed, do not understand the benefits of hand stripping or have experienced poor work by a groomer. A knowledgeable groomer who understands the concepts of stripping and hand plucking will be able to put those fears to rest. If the job is done properly and at the correct time, it is far from cruel and stressful (*see* Fig. 16.1.1). The groomer is simply removing an amount of hair that the dog would otherwise remove themselves, if they still lived in an environment where they were able to do so, by rolling on grass or gravel and using hedges, rocks and other pack members to pull out the dead coat.

The first point to make about this styling method is that the coat will only come away from the skin if it has reached the end of the catagen stage. The hair at this stage is held in the follicle by friction alone and comes out very easily. It will have separated itself into strands, a condition we refer to as 'blown' (*see* Fig. 16.1.2). If you pull gently at one of the strands (*see* Fig. 16.1.3), it comes away easily from the skin as a strand. If you have to put any pressure into your fingers to pull the hair, or the skin lifts at the time of pulling, the coat is not in catagen and it must be left or trimmed by an alternative method.

The second point is that, if done correctly, it is by far the best way to maintain a healthy skin and coat, and

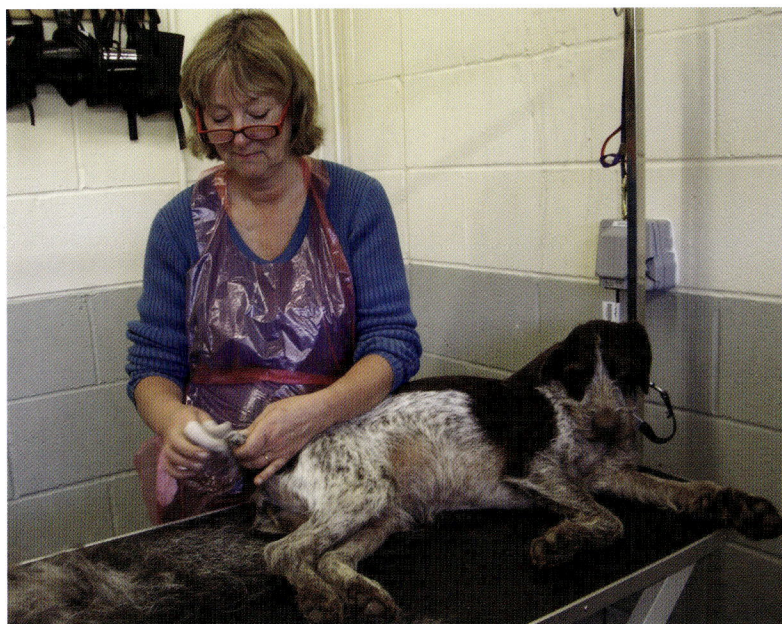

Fig. 16.1.2 When the coat is ready for plucking, it will be a the end of the 'catagen' stage and will separate into strands.

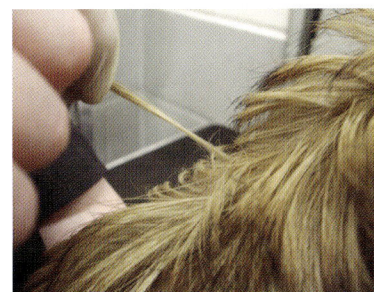

Fig. 16.1.1 If the job is done properly and at the right time, plucking is far from cruel and stressful!

Fig. 16.1.3 If you pull gently on one of the strands, it should come away easily in your hand.

it benefits the skin, the coat and therefore the dog in several ways:

◆ It thins out (*see* Fig. 16.1.4) the coat to a volume suited to the time of year and the dog's living environment. This ensures that skin temperatures are maintained at a suitable level and overheating of the skin is avoided. In contrast, clipping merely shortens the coat and does not reduce the density at skin level. The shortened coat does not respond in the same way to temperature changes and very often the undercoat may not moult, causing the coat to become denser.

Fig. 16.1.4 The dog's coat adjusts itself to the seasons. Plucking removes the discarded coat and thins it out.

◆ Thinning the coat also helps to reduce the risk of skin problems caused by moisture and humidity within the coat. The hairs within a very dense coat are less likely to separate and move, so allowing air to dry the moisture from the skin. The moisture and the skin temperature produce a warm damp environment, ideal for bacteria to grow.

◆ It retains the texture of the coat. The dog has a coarse waterproof layer of topcoat that is designed to repel water. The denser undercoat is designed for warmth rather than waterproofing. Clipping shortens the topcoat to the same length as the undercoat; therefore the coat is no longer waterproof and the sparser, coarse topcoat becomes lost amongst the soft downy undercoat (*see* Figs 16.1.5–16.1.7).

◆ Dirt and debris are removed with the topcoat so bathing is rarely necessary. Dirt and debris are collected by the coarse topcoat. During catagen, the old coat is removed, taking

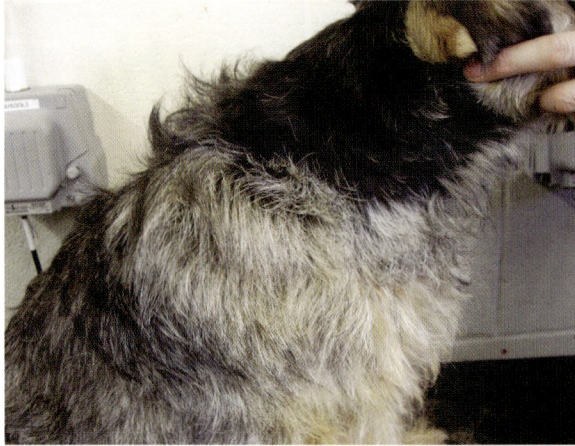

Fig. 16.1.5 At this stage the coat on this dog has only been plucked and you can see that only the soft undercoat remains.

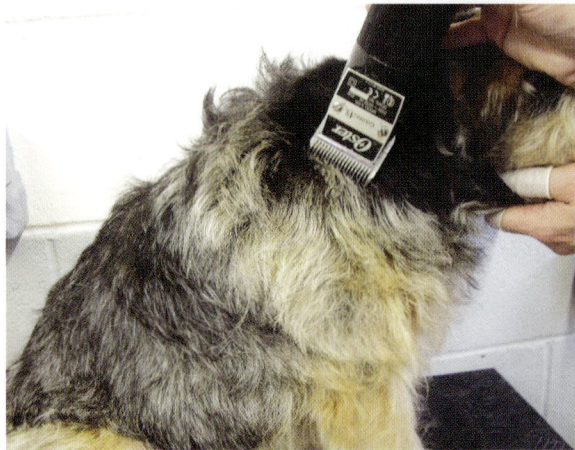

Fig. 16.1.6 Clippers are applied to a small area of the coat to reduce the length to that of the undercoat.

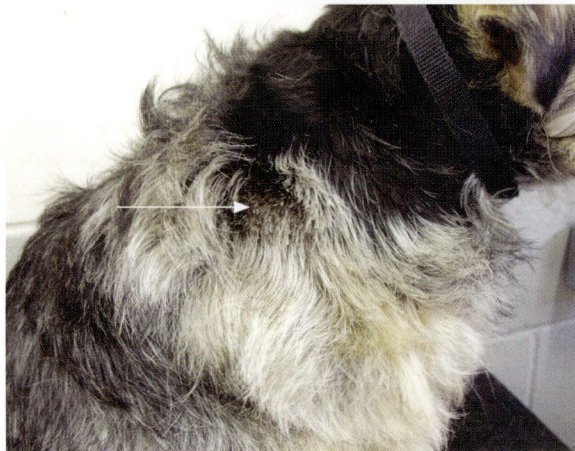

Fig. 16.1.7 Look closely at the clipped area and you can see that the topcoat hairs are still in place, only shorter, and you can also see that there are many more undercoat hairs than there are topcoat hairs. If the coat is clipped all over, the coat will lose colouring simply because the bulk of the hair will be undercoat coloured, and it will lose texture because it will be soft undercoat textured.

with it the grime. At the same time a clean glossy new coat is developing. Once the dead coat has been removed, the dog will be clean and bathing is unnecessary, thus preserving the natural oils coating the new topcoat hairs and eliminating the exposure of the skin to bathing chemicals and heat from dryers.

◆ It maintains the colour of the coat. There are more undercoat hairs than guard hairs, so the richness in the colour of the topcoat is lost if the coat is clipped. Loss of colour is mainly aesthetic but it does demonstrate the suppression of growing guard hairs or topcoat and consequently the loss of waterproofing.

◆ It restores a damaged coat to its natural condition so that it serves the dog as it was designed to do (*see* the Lakeland Terrier sequence in Figs 16.1.8 to 16.1.11).

Hand stripping a Lakeland Terrier's previously clipped coat

This six-year-old Lakeland Terrier's coat was hand plucked when the dog was young but, after neutering at the age of two, hormonal changes interrupted the coat development cycle and the coat became soft, dense and woolly.

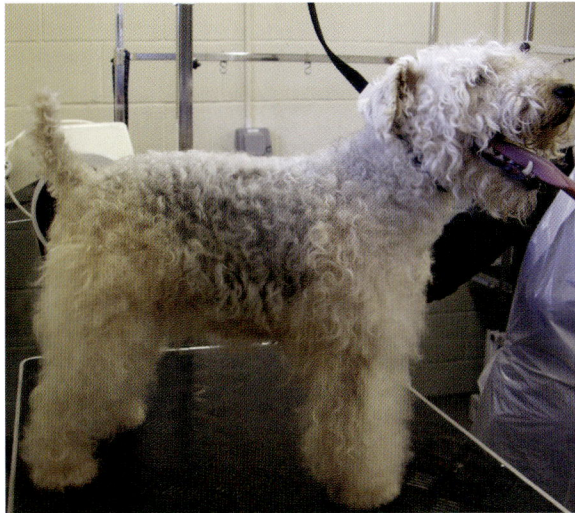

Fig. 16.1.8   The dog was clipped for about three years but the owner would now like his coat restored. Since the last clipping, the undercoat has been regularly groomed through on a weekly basis with a very fine comb to reduce the density.

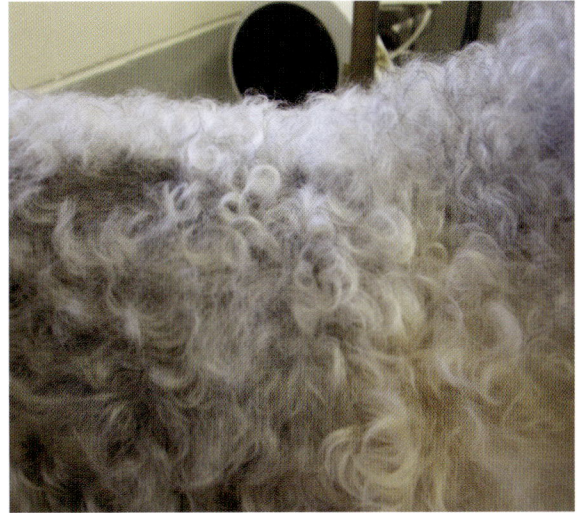

Fig. 16.1.9   The coat has been left for approximately a year without being trimmed to make sure that the old undercoat had definitely reached the end of the catagen phase and the new topcoat was just starting to grow. This is important to gain control of the future development of the coat. The topcoat must be encouraged to grow and needs a head start before it is swamped again under new undercoat. Removing all of the existing undercoat will allow this to happen.

Fig. 16.1.10   The dog is going to have a full strip on his back and his head will be clipped with a 8.5# Oster clipper blade. You can see that the dead undercoat and topcoat hair is coming away relatively easily to reveal the new coat. The emerging topcoat is sparse but is a good colour and texture. The new undercoat is at this stage still shorter than the topcoat.

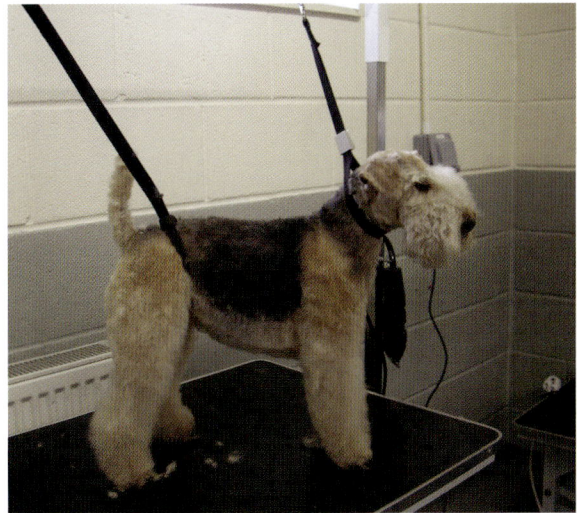

Fig. 16.1.11   The coat now looks and feels encouraging. The dog was bathed and the coat fluff-dried on this occasion only to make sure that all the dead undercoat was lifted from the skin and removed. The coat will need to be managed carefully and the dog will be brought back to the salon on a monthly basis to remove errant undercoat. In approximately four months the topcoat should be the longer of the two coats and it will be maintained by rolling.

Fig. 16.1.12   For the show ring, the coat of the wire-coated West Highland Terrier is plucked to maintain its coarse texture.

Hand plucking also has aesthetic value:

◆ It is the desired presentation for wire-coated breeds entering the show ring, where the texture of the coat must be demonstrated (*see* Fig. 16.1.12).

◆ It retains the sleek effect by thinning out the coat on silk-coated breeds such as the Cocker Spaniel (*see* Fig. 16.1.13 and the picture sequence 'Hand plucking or stripping a silk coat', Figs 16.1.16 to 16.1.20).

◆ It enhances the dog's assets by tactfully removing certain areas of hair, such as a 'saddle' down the centre of the back of the Afghan Hound (*see* Fig. 16.1.14) to reveal the short glossy hairs over the shapely spinal area, the ear fringes on a setter to show a neat head shape, or the neck to give an elegant head carriage.

◆ It can help to restore a coat that is not responding to a normal growing cycle. This may be through illness, hormonal changes and clipping, amongst other reasons (*see* Figs 16.1.15a-b).

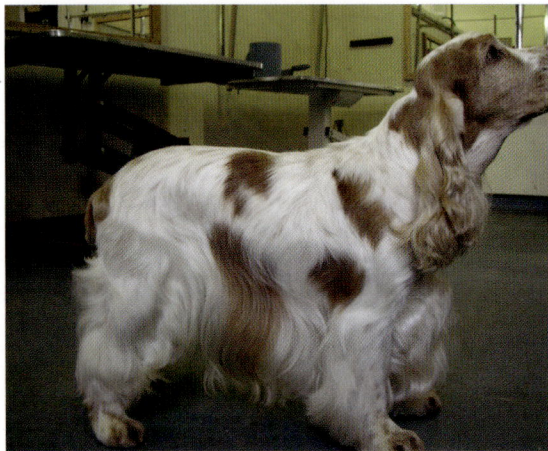

Fig. 16.1.13   The English Cocker Spaniel is silk-coated. The coat is plucked for the show ring to remove all errant undercoat so that the coat retains colour and silkiness.

Fig. 16.1.15a-b   The coat on this Saluki is not following a normal growth cycle and has stayed in Anagen until the growing undercoat has far exceeded the length of her topcoat. The reason for this is unknown. Maddie had her undercoat removed by plucking to begin restoring her coat to its naturally fine, silky texture. If the coat continues to grow in this way, a veterinary check-up would be recommended.

Fig. 16.1.14   The saddle on this beautiful Afghan Hound has been stripped to reveal the short glossy hairs along the spine.

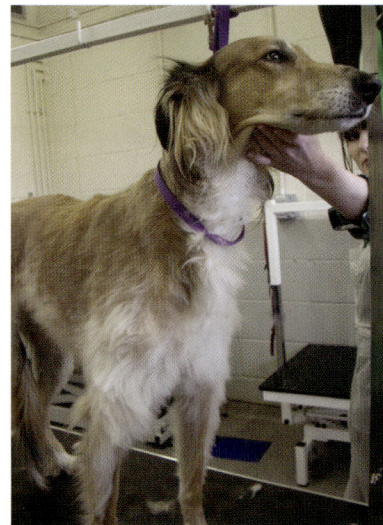

Hand plucking or stripping a silk coat

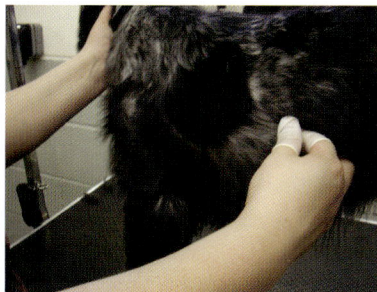

Fig. 16.1.16   Long undercoat hairs will often spoil the effect of the glossy silk coat

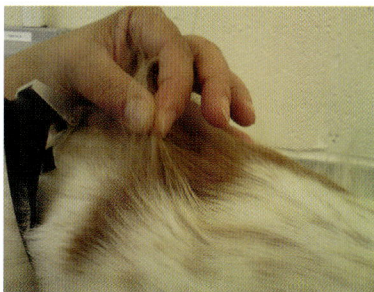

Fig. 16.1.17   The hair will come away easily by hand plucking or by carefully using a stripping tool

Fig. 16.1.18   Here you can see how undercoat hairs often grow extra long on coloured spots or 'ermine marks' but can easily be plucked out.

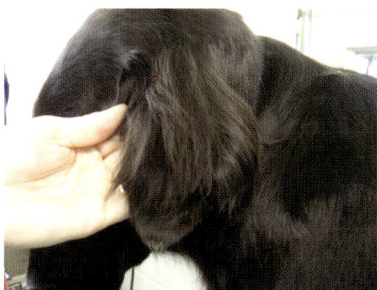

Fig. 16.1.19   The dead coat on the ears of a Flatcoated Retriever will be plucked to restore a smooth finish to the pinna.

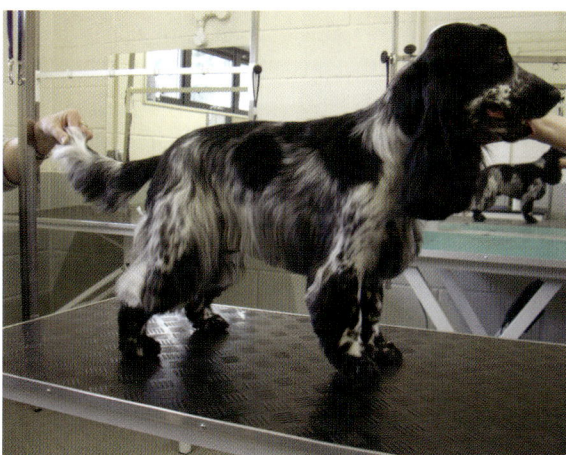

Fig. 16.1.20   This shows the finish that can be achieved by plucking a silk-coated English Cocker Spaniel that has just had his first trim.

So there is merit to stripping and plucking a coat, but there are a few points to consider before you start. Skin quality is essential. If the dog's skin shows signs of trauma or instability, the coat should not be stripped until the dog has seen a vet and the process has been sanctioned. (In some cases a vet will suggest plucking a very dense coat, even on a dog with a skin condition, as the thinning process may be beneficial to the management of the condition but never take this for granted. Seek advice first.)

Stripping and plucking should not be attempted on a coat that is not ready to be removed. The individual hairs should come away without the skin pulling away from the body. Even coats that are regularly stripped or plucked need to reach this stage before you can remove them without causing trauma to the skin. When deciding whether a coat is suitable for stripping or plucking for the first time, try pulling a few hairs with your finger tips. If gentle plucking does not extract the hair easily, either leave the coat for a few months and try again, or consider using an alternative method of grooming.

Stripping and plucking can be time-consuming (it may take a couple of hours or more) and the health of the dog needs to be taken into account before submitting him to a lengthy grooming process.

16.1.1 Hand stripping tools

The nature of this method of trimming means that you do not use electrical equipment to style the dog. It is all done by hand, either with or without grooming aids to help you. The tools are basic and inexpensive, but the small amount you do spend is, arguably, the best investment that you can make (*see* Fig. 16.1.21).

Most of the work is done by your fingers. These are free and readily

Fig. 16.1.21   A variety of modestly priced aids are available to help you and they will be a worthwhile investment.

available, though you do not have a choice of size and the state of your own skin has a bearing on your work. Very fine plucking around ears, tops of heads and sanitary areas can be difficult for groomers with large hands or restricted joint mobility. Wire coats are very coarse and can cause blisters until the skin on your hands has hardened.

Finger protectors

These are either rubber thimbles or latex 'cots' or 'condoms' that fit onto the ends of your finger and thumb to give you extra grip. The thimbles can be purchased with breathing holes on one side of them and dimples, or nipples, on the other side to grab and hold the hairs as you pull. The 'condoms' (or 'cots') are smooth but grab onto the hair as they warm up. Some groomers use rubber gloves, but your hands will get warm whilst plucking and rubber gloves tend to overheat the hands and become slippery on the inside, which can cause blisters.

Stripping knives

Look closely at a stripping knife and you will see that it is indeed a blade with a row of teeth, the bases of which, if not used correctly, are sharp enough to cut the coat. They are designed as an aid to stripping, or removing, the coat. The trick is to keep your wrist rigid whilst executing a pulling action to remove the whole hair from the follicle, rather than a flicking action that cuts the hair off somewhere along the hair shaft.

Stripping knives are available for both left- and right-handed groomers. Left-handed groomers should check when buying knives that the bevelled side of the blade is facing them when holding the tool in their left hand.

The choice is wide, but basically stripping knives are available in extra fine, fine, medium and coarse blades, although unless you specialize in stripping and it forms the bulk of your work, it is unlikely that you will need them all. When you start out, or if you are trimming your own dogs, a medium and a coarse will probably be sufficient. The important point is to find a handle that is comfortable in your hand. Plastic handles can make the palm of your hand sweat, making the knife difficult to use; some of the wooden handles may be too bulky for the small hand, and the slim handles may be too small for the larger hand. You need to hold the handle in your hand before making a decision, but make sure you are holding the tool correctly. The handle should be held in the palm of the hand with the index finger bent and resting on one side of the blade and the thumb resting either in the thumb groove, on the cutting blade, or against the side of the cutting blade.

Stripping Stones

Synthetic pumice stones are available usually in black for darker coats and white for paler coats. The stone can either be dragged following the coat growth direction to remove short fine hairs or rubbed through the coat against the growth direction to leave a residue in the coat, giving more traction to the hairs and making for easier pulling.

Chalk and fuller's earth

Chalk is widely used to give traction to the coat. You simply dip your fingertips into the chalk to coat them and away you go. Chalk cannot be used if you are using finger condoms or thimbles. Being white, it does, of course, have an obvious downside, so for darker coats fuller's earth is sometimes preferred. The disadvantage with using either of these is the amount of product that is left in the coat and on the skin. You must make sure that the entire product has been removed from the skin, particularly if the dog is a pet and you may not see him again for some time.

The principal advantage of chalk on show dogs (West Highland Terriers particularly) is that it does enhance the coat colour and texture. It is also in the interest of the show dog owner to check that the skin is not compromised and the chalk is removed after showing.

Lava blocks

As the name suggests, these are pieces of lava with a coarse-grained surface that can also aid traction. Hold the block in your hand and grab the coat between your thumb and the block. Pull gently in the direction of coat growth and the hair should come away easily. Lava blocks can leave a residue in the coat and this may need to be removed by bathing when you have finished.

16.2 PLUCKING OR STRIPPING: WHAT IS THE DIFFERENCE?

Whilst the terms plucking and stripping are often used interchangeably, a distinction can be made inasmuch as stripping is achieved with the aid of a tool known as a stripping knife (*see* Fig. 16.2.1), whereas plucking is achieved by extracting the hair with the fingers (*see* Fig. 16.2.2). You need to assess the condition of the coat and your own physical ability before you decide which

COAT PREPARATION

The coat is more easily plucked or stripped if it has not been washed. A clean coat is soft and glossy and traction to hold the hairs is therefore more difficult to obtain. If the dog has an excessively greasy coat, it is better to wash the coat about three or four days before you intend plucking or stripping it so that it can regain its texture. It may also be advisable to speak to the dog's vet. An overly greasy coat is not normal and, whilst there may be little evidence of skin sores or trauma, the grease may indicate an underlying problem.

In most cases it is not necessary to bath the dog after it has had the coat plucked or stripped because the dirt is removed with the hair. The decision to bath is up to the individual.

method to use. If it is done with care, stripping with tools can be as effective as hand plucking, but if it is done badly the coat will look awful and will be very problematic to maintain.

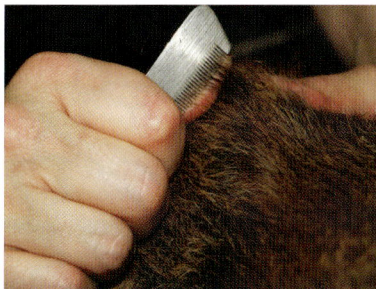

Fig. 16.2.1   Stripping is done with the aid of a tool called a stripping knife.

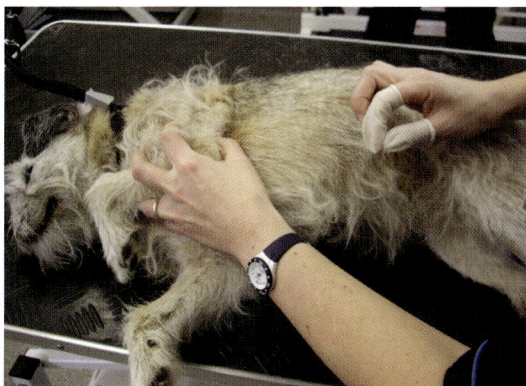

You must choose and perfect the technique that suits you best, and make your own decisions as to the tools and aids that you use to help you.

Plucking

Plucking is generally considered to be the best method as the desired coat can be removed from the roots with little damage to the individual hairs if you are only using your fingers. If the coat is ready to be removed there should not be any discomfort to the dog but the groomer may experience sore fingers or finger muscle strain if the job is a lengthy one.

Your first attempt at plucking is likely to take you many hours, and your hands and forearms will no doubt ache for several days but do not let this discourage you. You may want to spread the job over a couple of sessions. If you do, do not leave it too long between sessions as the coat is continuously growing and even a week may make a difference when it comes to plucking the dog for his next trim – some hairs will be ready to be removed and some will not! Split your sessions over a couple of days at the most.

Building up muscle strength in your hands and forearms takes time, but with practice you will speed up and gain confidence. It is well worth the effort. Not only is stripping and plucking beneficial to the dog, it has a commercial advantage: it does not use electricity and no tools other than perhaps a stripping knife so there are very few maintenance overheads. A skilled groomer can hand strip a dog in almost as little time as it takes to groom by clipping, and can charge a lot more money for the service. I have trained many groomers who have had little desire to learn scissor and clipping

Fig. 16.2.2   Plucking is done with your fingers. This groomer is using finger condoms as an aid.

skills and have built their entire businesses on plucking and stripping only.

It is not essential but it is easier to start to learn plucking on a smaller breed. A Border Terrier (*see* the picture sequence 'Hand plucking the Border Terrier', Figs 16.2.4 to 16.2.25) is a good candidate as this breed usually has a slightly longer topcoat; when it is ready for removing, the coat will blow and start to curl and separate into strands. Since almost the entire topcoat is removed with only a minimum of styling to be done on the face, styling mistakes are not easily made. The topcoat comes out cleanly and the difference in effect between plucked and unplucked is satisfying to see and encouraging to reflect on. Another small breed to start with would be a Wire Haired Dachshund (see Figs 16.2.26 to 16.2.37).

To check if the coat is ready, there is no need to brush or comb the coat unless you want to. Turn the dog so that he is facing away from you, and take one of the strands between your thumb and index finger. Pull gently towards you in the direction of coat growth and the strand should come away easily with very little movement of the skin.

Note that the whole of the hair length will have been removed; in many cases the withered 'bulb' at the base is just visible. If you hold the hair too far down the shaft, you risk pulling out the undercoat as well as the dead topcoat (see Fig. 16.2.3). Not only does this hurt the dog, but the skin will become sore and the dog may end up with bald patches.

Although your main tool is your fingers, you can get more grip on the coat with the help of chalk or fuller's earth.

Fig. 16.2.3   The hair on the left has been held too far down the shaft and undercoat has been removed along with the topcoat. This will hurt the dog and make his skin sore.

Hand plucking the Border Terrier

Fig. 16.2.4   It is easier to start your hand strip from the head and work towards the tail because the coat grows in that direction.

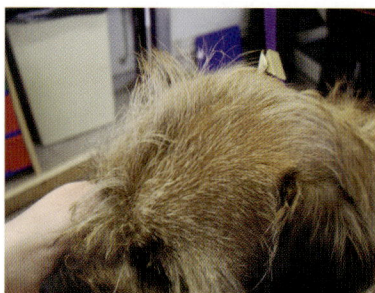

Fig. 16.2.5   Start with the top of the head, just behind the eyebrows.

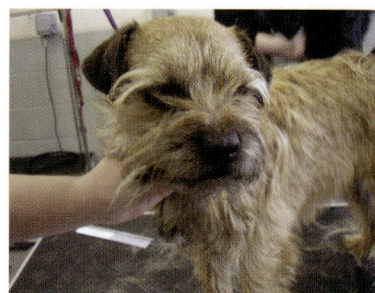

Fig. 16.2.6   Working towards the neck, clear both the inside and the outside of the pinna, both sides of the face and under the jaw.

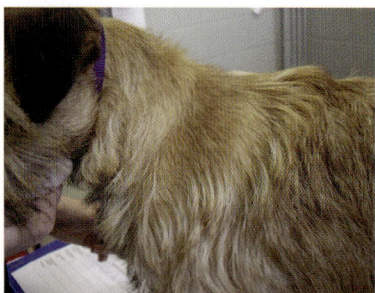

Fig. 16.2.7   Work down the body pulling the hairs towards the tail.

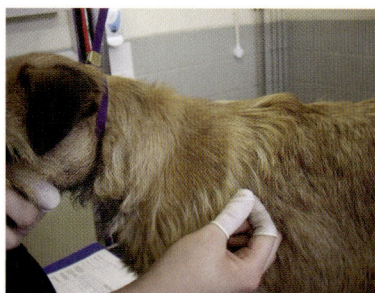

Fig. 16.2.8   Work in narrow strips crossing the spine from one side to the other.

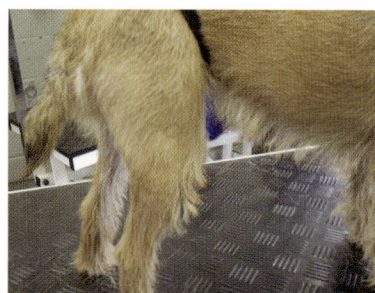

Fig. 16.2.9   Clear all the dead coat from one strip before making another. Work off the spine over the side of the body.

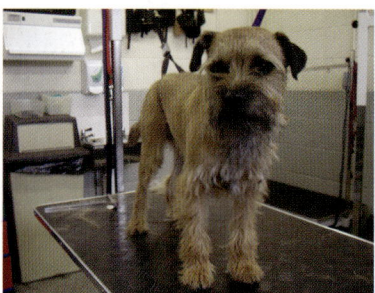

Fig. 16.2.10   Continue down the body, and work down the hind legs. It is best to leave the legs until the body has been completed because it is during the plucking of the leg fur that the dog is most likely to become anxious about the procedure.

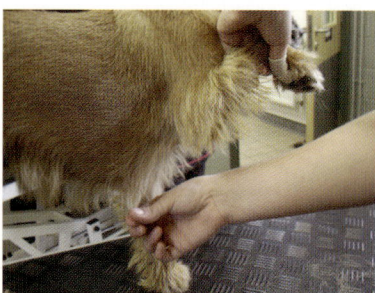

Fig. 16.2.11   Remove the hair from the undercarriage and the 'underarm' area.

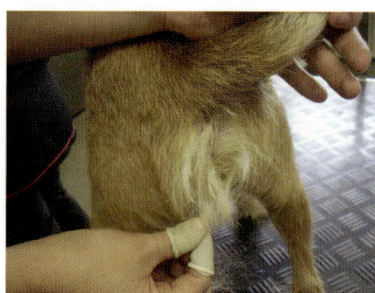

Fig. 16.2.12   Then clear the tail and around the bottom.

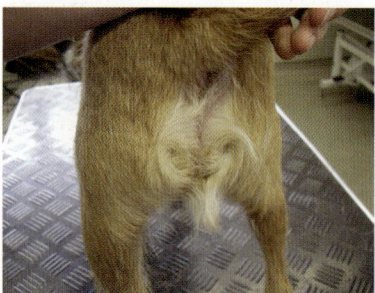

Fig. 16.2.13   All the dead hair will come away, leaving the sanitary area clean and hygienic.

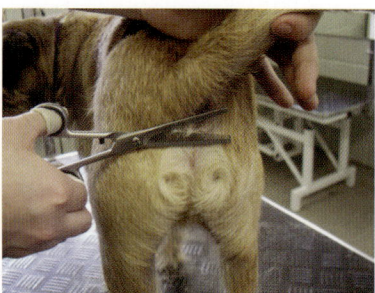

Fig. 16.2.14   Thinning scissors may be used to tidy or shorten the hairs close to the rectum.

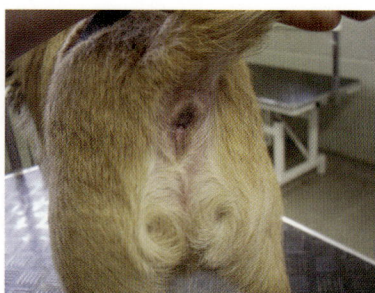

Fig. 16.2.15   A neat, clean rear end.

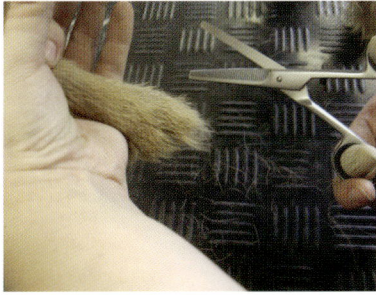

Fig. 16.2.16   Once the hair has been stripped from the legs and feet, thinning scissors can be used to tidy and shape the foot, taking care not to make your cutting lines too severe.

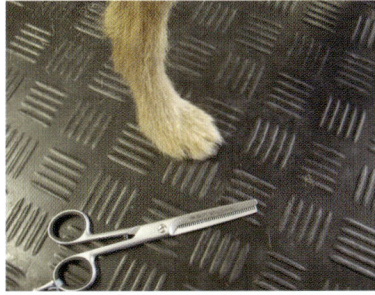

Fig. 16.2.17   The idea is that you cannot see the trimming that has been done. Tidy any hair underneath the feet with straight scissors

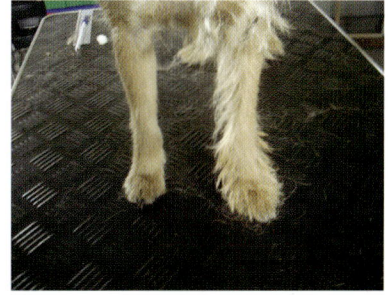

Fig. 16.2.18   When stripping or plucking the Border Terrier, expect all of the hair to come away from the legs leaving then neat and without the hint of feathering.

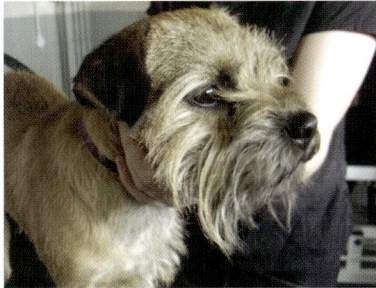

Fig. 16.2.19   Now finish the head to finish styling the face.

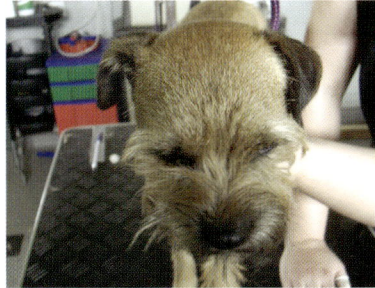

Fig. 16.2.20   The face of the Border Terrier should resemble the face of an otter and it will naturally shape itself. Over the eyebrows, remove only the hairs that will come out without using too much tension.

Fig. 16.2.21   Use a comb to straighten the facial hair so you can see the longest hairs.

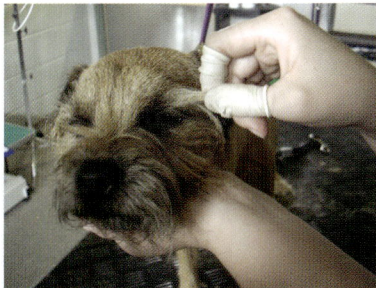

Fig. 16.2.22   Pull out only the longest hairs on the eyebrows until there is no more hair coming away in your fingers.

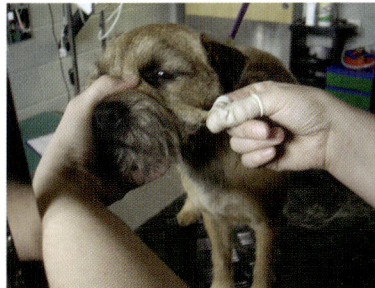

Fig. 16.2.23   When styling the beard , start by removing only the long hairs that come away with the minimum of pulling

Fig.16.2.24   If necessary, tactile trimming can be done with blending scissors but don't over trim.

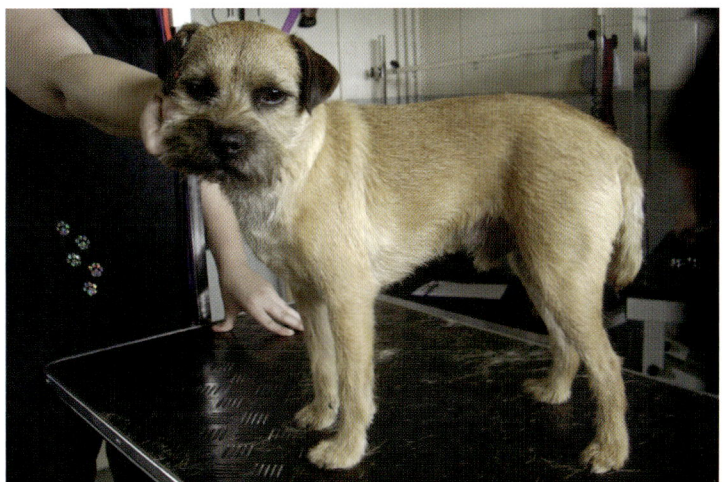

Fig. 16.2.25   Nails done, ears cleaned, eyes wiped and ready to go home.

Hand Plucking a Miniature Wire Haired Dachshund.

Fig. 16.2.26   The coat has blown and is ready for stripping.

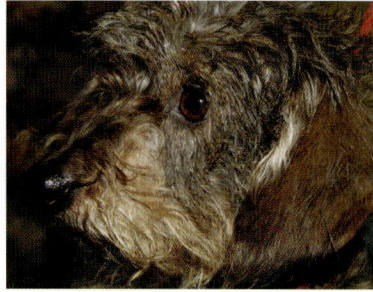

Fig. 16.2.27   Start with the head, just behind the eyebrows.

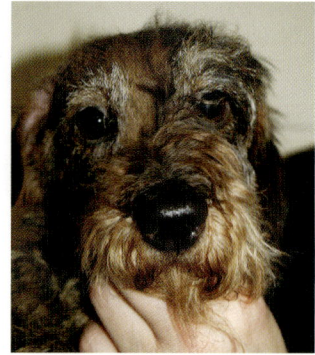

Fig. 16.2.28   Here you can see that half of the head has been stripped.

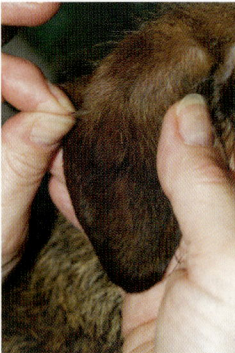

Fig. 16.2.29 Support the ear whilst you gently pull out the dead guard hairs to leave it smooth.

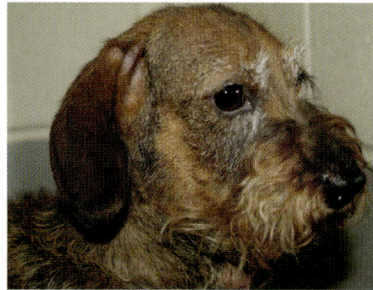

Fig. 16.2.30   After clearing the head and ear, start working down the sides of the face.

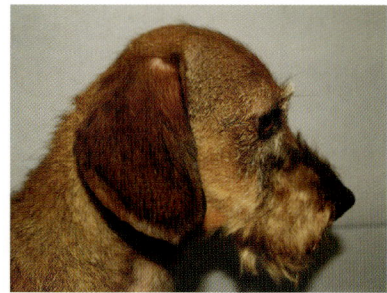

Fig. 16.2.31   The finished head.

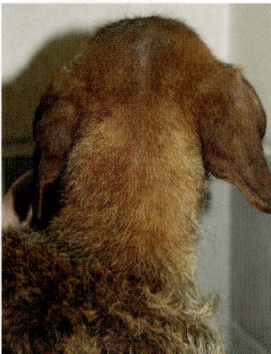

Fig. 16.2.32   Continue working down the neck onto the back, working in strips across the coat from side to side so you don't leave a hair behind.

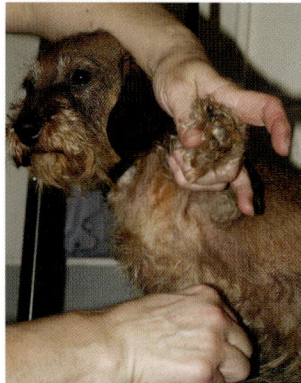

Fig. 16.2.33   Lift the leg to clear under the arm and the chest.

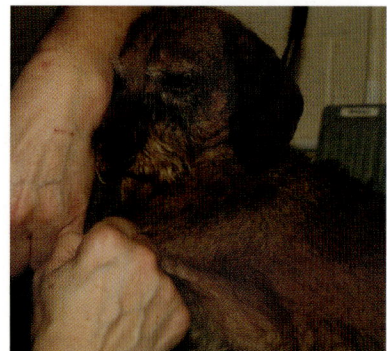

Fig. 16.2.34   Clearing behind the arm.

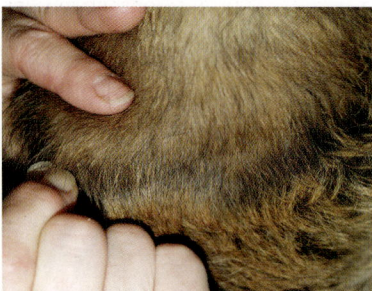

Fig. 16.2.35   Continue stripping the whole coat. Any dead hair will come away easily. Any hair that does not come away easily should be left behind, e.g. on the lower leg.

Fig. 16.2.36   Use thinning scissors to touch up in front of the eyes, under the pads and round the feet.

Fig. 16.2.37   One down, one to go! Here we have the before and after.

CAUTION

Bear in mind that you are using chalk or fuller's earth because the coat has been washed and it is too soft for you to get a grip, not because the coat is not ready and you need to grip harder to pull it out. This is when problems occur and hand plucking becomes cruel.

Also remember that if you put chalk into the coat, you must get it out by bathing. Chalk soaks up moisture from the skin and dries hard like clay, causing all sorts of problems.

Stripping

You may want to consider stripping as an option if you have restricted movement or pain in your fingers. Stripping with a knife will be easier for you, and may be quicker. It may also be an option if the hair length is very short and difficult to get hold of, particularly on the top of the head and on the pinna. If it is done properly, you need not cause damage to the coat.

The disadvantage of stripping with a knife is that if the knife is used incorrectly, the blade can cut the coat (*see* Fig. 16.2.38) – in which case, you may as well have saved yourself the effort and used clippers because the effect will be the same. The coat has not been removed from the follicle and the density of the coat has not been reduced.

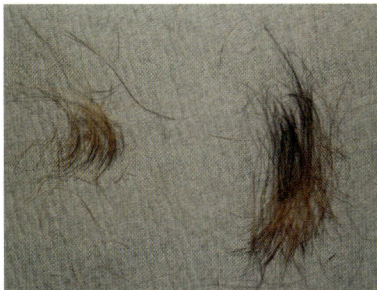

Fig. 16.2.38 *The disadvantage of using a stripping knife is that if you use it wrongly it will cut the coat. The hair on the left has been removed with a flicking action of a stripping knife. The hair on the right is from the same dog and has been removed by plucking. You can clearly see the difference between the two lengths. The shorter hair has been cut mid-shaft and the remainder of the hair has been left within the coat.*

USING A STRIPPING KNIFE CORRECTLY

Use a well-worn knife so the cutting edge is less sharp and less likely to cut the hair. Once you have the hair between the blade and your thumb, draw the knife towards you without turning your wrist or flicking your hand; this will withdraw the full length of the hair (see Fig. 16.2.39). If the knife is used purely to aid traction with the coat, using a straight wrist action when pulling prevents the teeth of the knife turning and cutting into the coat. If you twist or flick your wrist as you pull, this results in the hairs catching between the teeth of the tool and being cut (see Fig. 16.2.38).

Fig. 16.2.39 *When using a stripping knife, grab the hairs between the knife and your thumb and pull straight towards you with a straight wrist. If you flick the wrist or twist as you pull, you will cut the coat.*

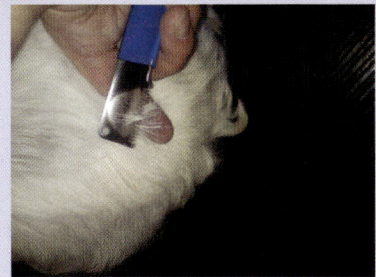

Fig. 16.2.40 *This is the result of twisting the wrist when pulling the hair.*

Practise on a small area that is not easily visible until you have mastered the technique. Check your work to make sure that you have removed the entire length of the hair (the 'bulb' at the base should be visible), and that you have not cut the hair along the shaft.

In some areas, for example under the eyes, and for layering a coat a stripping knife is used with a flicking wrist action. This allows the blade to cut and shape the coat by altering the length gradually so that the coat holds the style you wish to achieve.

Stripping knives are available in many designs and are graded from fine to coarse so, if you intend to strip rather than pluck, you will need to experiment with the different types and their effects. When you are using a stripping knife, it is unlikely that you will need to use chalk, fuller's earth or finger cots because the soft pad of your thumb grips the knife blade sufficiently.

16.3 MAINTENANCE OPTIONS

There are two options for stripping and plucking the coat. You can either perform a full strip, which involves straight removal of the entire dead top coat, or you can 'roll' the coat. The former, as the name suggests, extracts all of the coat that is ready for removal, leaving just the undercoat and any new top-coat hairs. The latter involves a monthly treatment, removing just a portion of the hair. The decision depends on whether the dog is being groomed for the show ring or for the pet home.

Full strip

Face the dog away from you, and check the coat for readiness by gently pulling or stripping a few strands. Check that you have taken the complete hair, including the root or bulb. If the coat is ready, start on the top of the head, leaving the eyebrows. Take a few hairs at a time and work a small area at a time, making sure to remove all the long hairs before moving to an adjoining area. Work across the top of the skull in rows from ear to ear. When the top of the head is completed, remove the hair from the sides of the face, leaving the desired facial furnishing, such as a beard. Work down from beneath the jaw to about the point of the breast bone. Remove any undesired hair from the pinna. To do this, hold the pinna in one hand and gently pluck or strip with the other. Do not do either without holding the pinna because you can bruise the skin. Then work down the back of the neck in rows towards the shoulders.

Continue working across the dog in rows from left to right (or right to left if you are left-handed). This results in neat work and you should be able to follow your previous line easily. Continue along the body to the tail. Where you go from here depends on the breed of dog you are styling. The important point to remember is that you must remain methodical. If you start to randomly pull out bits of coat without following your previous lines, you will soon lose your way and leave hair behind. This not only looks unsightly, but the coat will not grow back evenly and the next visit to the groomer will prove to be a nightmare as some coat will be ready to come away (the bits that you left behind) and the rest will not (because it has not been left long enough).

Rolling

Rolling a coat is something that is done purely for the purpose of dog showing and it is unlikely that you will ever be asked to do this because show dogs are very valuable and most handlers prepare their own dogs.

It involves a constant stripping of dead hairs to keep the coat in year-round show condition and is achieved by a continuous three-monthly grooming cycle that requires a portion of the coat to be removed each month. It takes a complete four-month cycle before the coat is settled into a routine and the task becomes straightforward. The easiest way to remove a random number or proportion of the coat is to take a portion of skin and hold it in your fingers to make a 'tent'. The hairs then stand away from the skin and you can remove as many as you wish.

At the beginning the dog has a full, untouched coat. Let's say that the top-coat is 5cm in length and we want to reduce it to 2–3cm.

Month 1: make your tent and start by taking the longest hairs to remove about a third of the topcoat hairs with-

> **CONFUSED?**
>
> *It may take a while to understand the concept of rolling a coat. It is much easier in practice! (See 'Rolling the coat'.)*

in your hand. Continue over the area you wish to strip. You will be left with the undercoat and the rest of the original coat in place.

Month 2: use the same technique and remove about half of the remaining longest hairs. You will be left with the undercoat and two different lengths of topcoat. Some hairs will be the regrowth of the hair removed in month 1 (which will be about 1cm in length), the rest are from the original topcoat, still at 5cm.

Month 3: remove the last of the longest hairs. The undercoat is still intact and you will still have two different lengths of topcoat. The replaced hair from month 1 will be approximately

2cm in length, and the replaced hair from month 2 will be about 1cm long, approximately the same length as the undercoat.

Month 4: the undercoat is still intact unless it is in catagen. The replaced hair from month 1 is now 3cm long, the replaced hair from month 2 is 2cm long and the replaced hair from month 3 is about 1cm long. The long hairs from month 1 are now ready to come out again. If you continue the process, the styled coat will be maintained at 2–3cms in length.

The undercoat will partially moult out and replace itself according to the seasons, but the topcoat will be made up of two different lengths. This allows it to sit flat on the body and leaves the dog with a topcoat.

Depending on the breed and the desired coat length, this method can be spread over a three-, four- or five-month cycle. Over five months the same effect is achieved but less hair is removed at each month's grooming, leaving the hair to grow slightly longer before it is removed.

16.4 CONCLUSION: STYLING GUIDES

Within this chapter, I have included step-by-step styling guides for several dogs. Their coats are all different, as is the style of the trim, so you can see the different shapes that can be achieved simply by using your fingers. Whatever the breed or type, the

> **CAUTION**
>
> *Monitor the skin throughout the stripping and plucking routine. Remember that the coat should only be removed by this method if it is ready to be removed. This means that each hair has completed its life cycle and is only being held within the follicle by friction. Dead hairs can be plucked without pulling the skin away from the body. If the skin is being pulled, the styling session should be abandoned and the coat re-checked for suitability after a couple of weeks.*
>
> *If there are signs of inflam-mation, stop immediately and rest the skin. When performing this styling technique for the first time on any dog, it is advisable to ask the owner to check the skin for the following few days as there can sometimes be a delayed response to the pulling. Distilled witch hazel (Hamamelis water) has a general sales licence, is safe for use on animals, is available over the counter at most chemists and is a good astringent to help with mild irritation of the skin after plucking. It should not, however, be used if the skin has broken into open sores.*

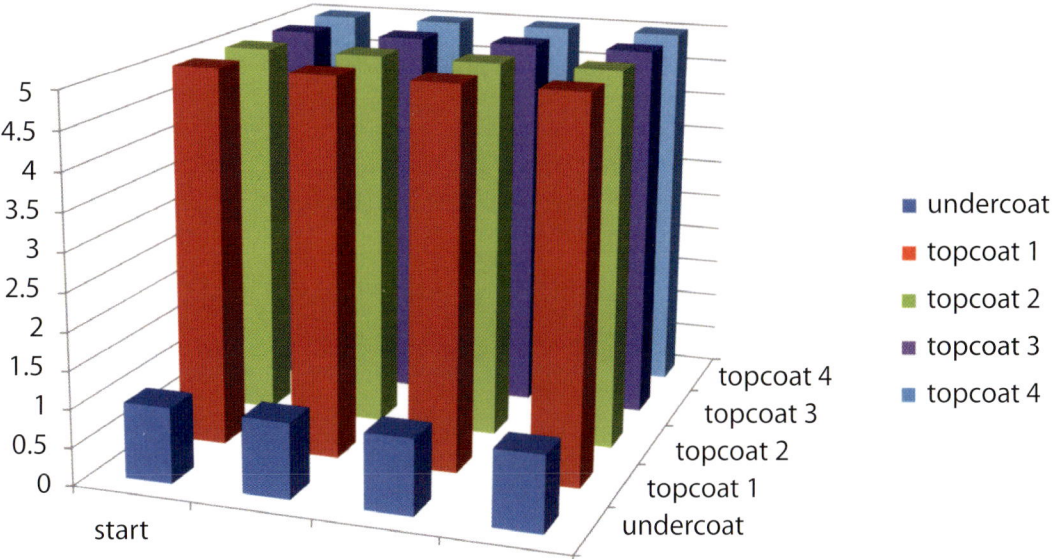

Fig. 16.4.1

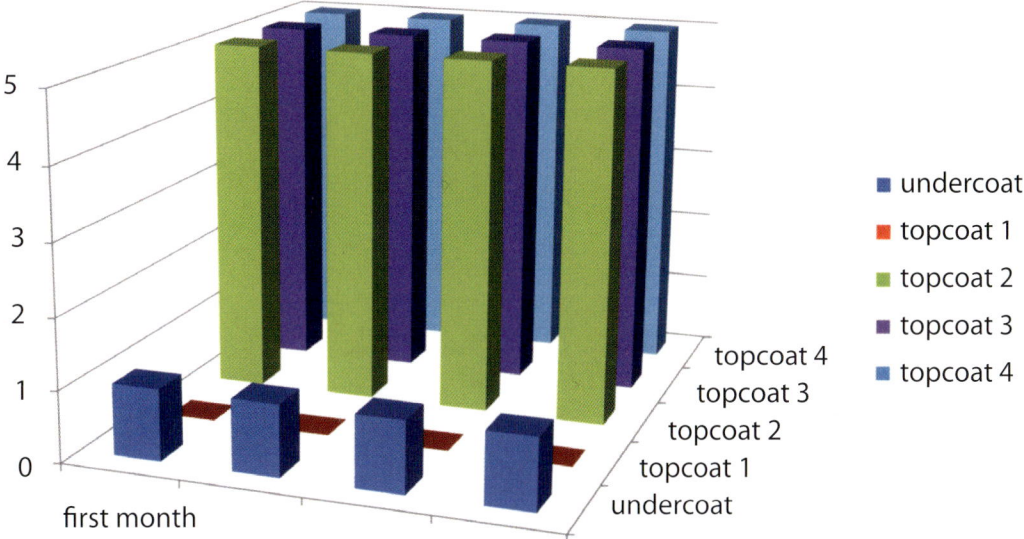

Fig. 16.4.2

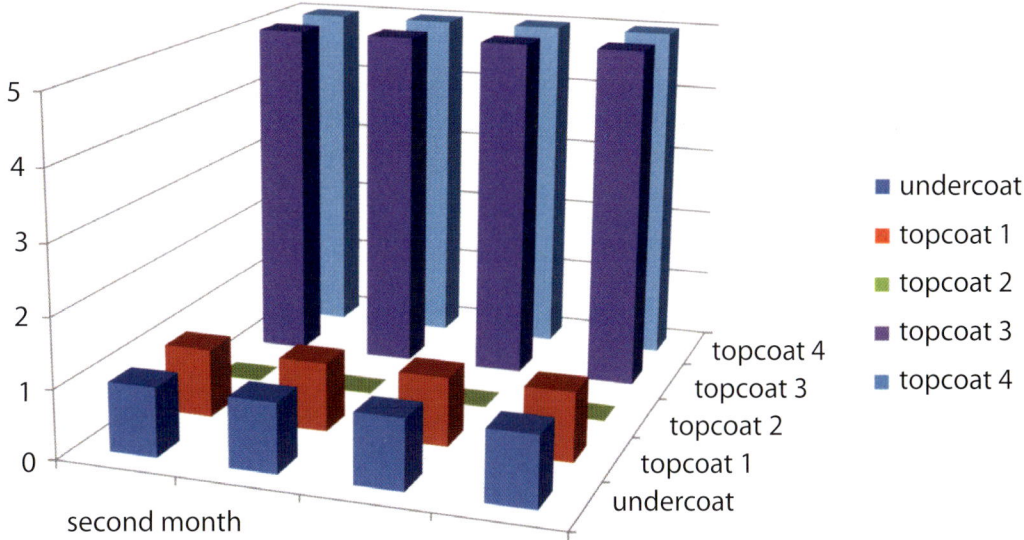

Fig. 16.4.3

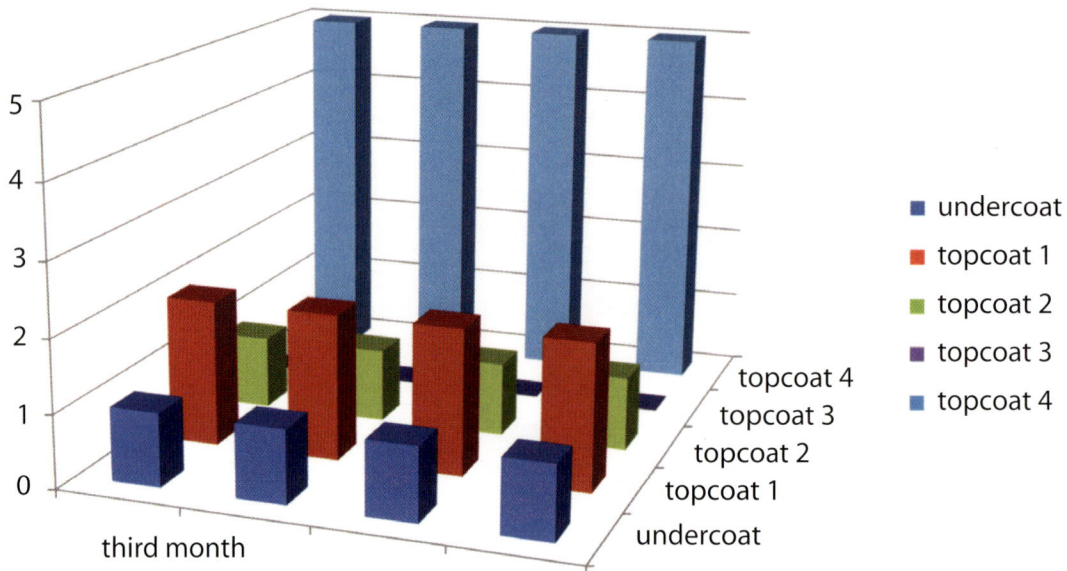

Fig. 16.4.4

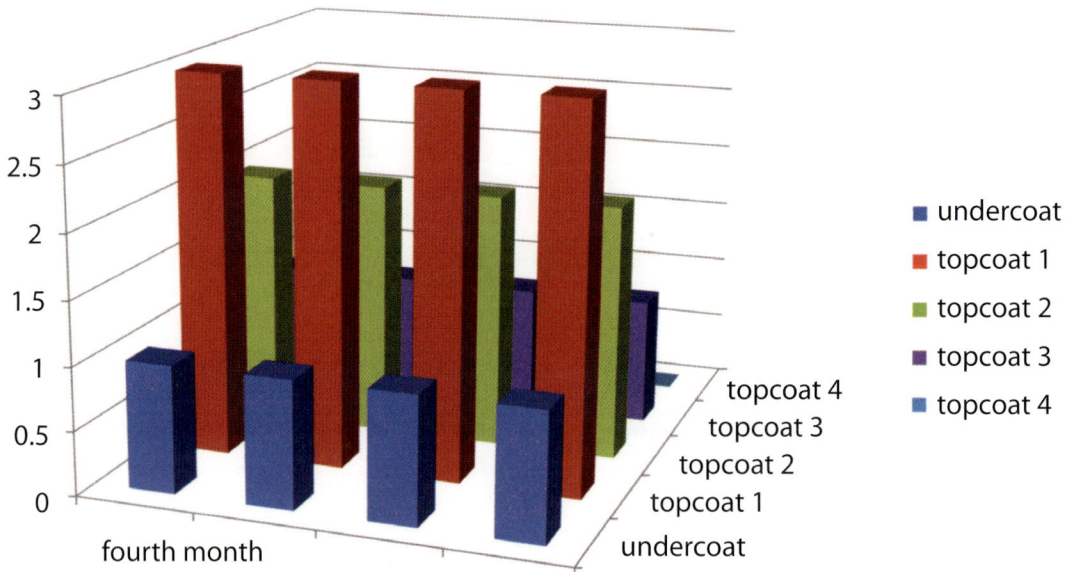

Fig. 16.4.5

principles of stripping and plucking remain the same.

The finishing touches are completed according to either the breed specifications or the owner's requirements, and usually involve either touching up the feet and facial furnishings with thinning scissors, or trimming the legs with straight scissors.

Please remember that this book is not a book about styling: it is about teaching you how to use your skills and equipment to achieve any style!

Maintaining the coat

Once removed, the coat re-grows at approximately 1cm per month. We are aiming to reduce the coat from approximately 5cm to 3cm and then to maintain it at 3cm.

To make the graphs easier to understand, the topcoat hairs are in four different colours. Each colour represents a monthly portion of coat. Topcoat 1 will be the first portion to be removed and so on.

At the beginning the dog has an undercoat (blue) and a full topcoat (the other four colours) that is roughly all the same length (5cm) and at maximum density. The coat will be standing off the body instead of lying down.

When the coat is ready, remove approximately a quarter of the topcoat in the areas you want to shape. Do not touch the undercoat. You should be leaving approximately three-quarters of the topcoat *in situ*.

In the second month remove approximately a third of the original topcoat. The first pulling (topcoat 1) has been replaced with new growth and the undercoat is still *in situ*. The topcoat is three-quarters of its original density and will be starting to lie closer to the body.

In the third month remove half of the remaining original topcoat. Topcoat 1 has grown to two-thirds of its eventual length, and the second month's pulling (topcoat 2) has been replaced by new growth. The density of the topcoat is three-quarters of the original depth and the undercoat is still in place.

In the fourth month remove the last of the original topcoat. Topcoat 1 is now on its way to its final length of approximately 3cm. Topcoat 2 has two months' growth and topcoat 1 has been growing for one month. The coat remains at three-quarters of its original density and now lies flat in place with the texture preserved. Next month the cycle will restart with topcoat 1 being removed. It should be easy to now keep the coat at this 3cm length.

Fig. 16.4.6   *The Scottish Terrier with a rolled coat ready for showing. (Photo: Michael Trafford)*

17　Styling

> *Styling is the act of transforming something into a 'design' or a particular 'appearance'. The art of styling is when the stylist uses the mastery and fluency of skills to create an individualistic expression, or image, from their working media: in the groomer's case, the dog and his hair coat.*
>
> *Styling is neither difficult nor is it a mystery. The trick is to 'see' each dog as an individual so that you can select and adapt the style best suited to his morphology. You also need to appreciate how each dog's coat grows and behaves so that you can choose the most suitable styling method for your creation.*
>
> *The only difficult bit involves investing the time and effort required to learn breed profiles; this ensures you know what the dog should look like. These profiles can then be adapted to the individual dog, according to their individual anatomy and your evaluation of what style would work best for the framework of the dog. This creates your 'mental' template and makes it easier for you to use the coat that is in front of you to enhance the dog's best features and your work.*
>
> *The only mystery is how one groomer can make a dog look 'right' and another can make the same dog look 'wrong'. It takes many months, maybe even a couple of years, of practice for some groomers to develop good hand and eye synchronization and to achieve mastery and fluency in the use of their tools.*
>
> *It is not essential to have an enormous amount of coat to work with, and nor is it essential that you use a book of diagrams to show you how to style the dog; every dog is different so you need to be flexible in your styling. The shaping for one spaniel may not be suitable for another, even if they are both destined for the show ring!*
>
> *Styling and shaping the coat is essentially achieved by:*
>
> - *clippers and blades to cut the coat, either following the coat direction or working against it;*
> - *scissors (of some description) to cut the coat with either a backhand cut or a forehand cut; and*
> - *fingers or stripping tools to pluck the hair from the follicle.*
>
> *Helpfully, there are only a few coat types to deal with and all coats lend themselves naturally to just a handful of hair styles.*
>
> *This chapter is not intended to cover all breed styling. If you have learnt your breed profiles, you should be familiar with breed styling. My intention is to simplify the styles available to you, to explain what to do and when you can do it. You can create any style you want if you use your tools properly and really 'look' at the dog.*

The type of styling a commercial groomer produces depends on the requirements of the clientele. A town or city practice may be supported by dogs that are exercised in parks and live within the home so they are often groomed and bathed regularly and styled for an 'image'; full clip-offs may be few and far between. A country practice, by contrast, may be patronized by dogs used for country sports, farm work and guarding; clipping off entire coats once or twice a year may therefore be more routine, with fewer clients requesting a traditional hairstyle for their pet.

The quality of the styling a commercial groomer produces depends on their motives for becoming a groomer and whether the aim is for perfection and job satisfaction, or simply to trim as many dogs as possible within as short a time as possible. Your motives inevitably have an enormous impact on how much effort, practice and research you put into your work.

Styling is created from a number of shapes: a body shape, a head shape, a foot shape and a tail shape, for all of which there are just a couple of options to choose from. By mixing them up a bit to suit the dog and his coat, it is possible to find or create something for everyone, even the scruffiest of mongrels and cross-breeds. What is more, despite extensive research I have not been able to find a law anywhere saying that all dogs have to be styled to represent their breed image.

This is good news for owners, because they can happily have their dogs styled to suit them and their lifestyle. It is good news too for the dog because this means that his coat can be managed in accordance with his health, lifestyle and temperament. It is also good news for groomers because it means we can promote health and minimize distress for the dog by encouraging suitable coat management.

It also has financial benefits to the groomer because a well-groomed and/or styled coat needs to be kept in shape, meaning more trips to the groomers. The other piece of good news is that the job need never become boring because every owner has different requirements, so every job comes with its own challenges.

You may be asked to maintain a coat for the show ring. This, whilst it may be a bit more challenging, is by no means beyond your aspirations and capabilities. It is essential, however, that you know the breed standards and requirements. Once these are learnt, a quick glance at a picture of a current show dog will remind you of what you are aiming for, but do check with the

Fig. 17.0.2   This Wire-haired Fox Terrier is heading for the show ring so the coat has been plucked and there is more hair length to the legs. The facial furnishings are sharper and more tailored.

owner when the dog is being shown so that you can plan a timeline, since any drastic reshaping or styling needs to be done in time for the coat to grow again (*see* Chapter 16, 'Rolling the coat').

The style of the show dog is not always that different from the pet dog styled to the breed image. The styling method for show dogs is, however, different. For example, with Wire Fox Terriers a pet can be clipped (*see* Fig. 17.0.1)

across their body, whereas a show dog needs to be hand plucked (*see* Fig. 17.0.2). For some breeds the styling between show dogs and pet dogs differs vastly. A pet Lhasa Apso may be clipped and scissored into a short manageable haircut, whereas the show dog has his coat left long and untouched, with only the hair under the feet lightly trimmed.

There is also a tendency to leave a longer coat on many show breeds. For breeds that are scissored, you need a steady and practised hand, and you must familiarize yourself with the styling methods of other breeds, many of which require a more subtle approach to their coat presentation. Equally important, you must remain up-to-date with the presentation of the breeds you are maintaining, for styles differ from year to year and between countries.

17.1 BALANCING A STYLE

'Balancing a style' is a term used by groomers and show dog handlers; it refers to the way in which the dog is

put together and whether the coat styling enhances or detracts from the dog's natural shape. For example, a dog that has been trimmed tight or very short on their body but with the head left under-trimmed gives the overall impression that the dog has an overly large head. Another example is a dog that is very true to type and shape being made to look longer or shorter in the body, or longer or shorter in the leg because the groomer has either left too much hair or too little hair in the wrong places (see 'Balancing the dog').

By arguing or implying that this does not matter if the dog is a pet, you are suggesting that the owner does not recognize the quality of their dog against the breed requirements but you may well be fooling yourself. For the same reason that you use a hairdresser who styles your hair to enhance your image, the dog owner will be drawn to a groomer who enhances and does justice to their dog's image.

Fig. 17.0.1   The style of the pet dog is not always that different from the show dog. It is the styling method that is significant. This pet Wire-haired Fox Terrier has been clipped.

'Balancing' the Dog

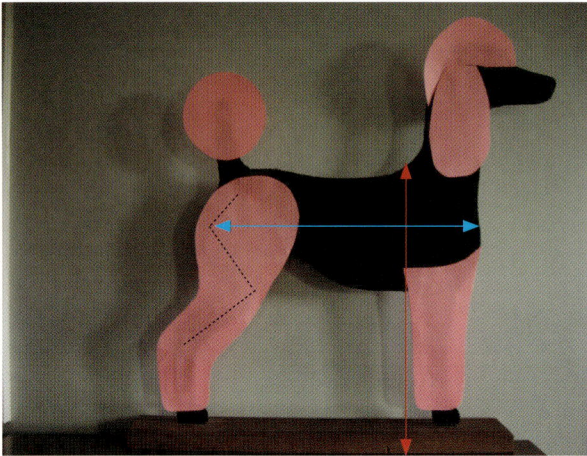

Fig. 17.1.1   The shape of a dog can be altered either dramatically or subtly by an inexperienced groomer who is unfamiliar with the shape of a particular breed. Here I have used a model of a Miniature Poodle in a lamb trim to demonstrate this to you. The Miniature Poodle should give the impression of being 'square'. This means that the height at the withers (red arrow) is the same as the body length of the dog (blue arrow). The neck should be long and elegant and the hind leg should be well angulated (black dashed line). The black areas are the clipped parts of the body and the coloured areas are the scissored areas.

Fig. 17.1.2a-b   Fig. 17.1.2a shows the finished style. Fig. 17.1.2b shows how the style fits on to the frame of the dog and where the hair has been cut away or left on to enhance the shape. Note that the hair on the hip has been cut close to the dog (black arrow) and the hair on the backs of the legs is roughly equal to the length of the hair on the front of the legs. The dotted line shows the visual length between the legs.

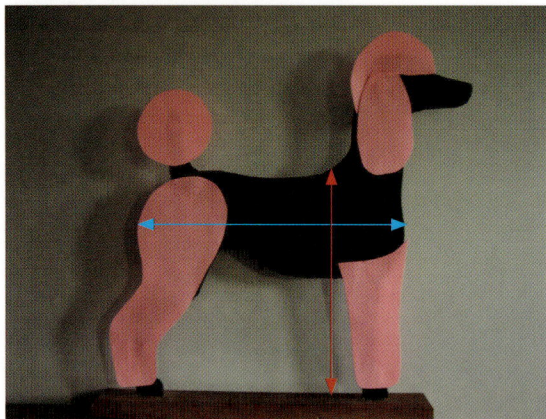

Fig. 17.1.3a-b   This is, of course, the same model so the morphology has not changed but visually the dog in Fig. 17.1.3a looks longer in the body than the dog in Fig. 17.1.2a. Fig. 17.1.2b shows how the hair has been left on the back of the hip (black arrow) to lengthen the body, and also there is more hair on the back of the hock and on the front of the foreleg, thus throwing both legs further apart (dotted line) than in Fig. 17.1.2a.

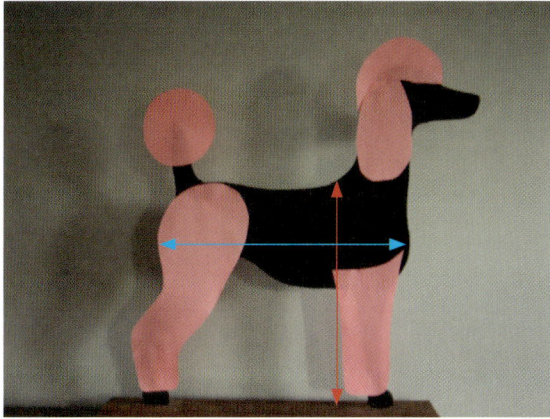

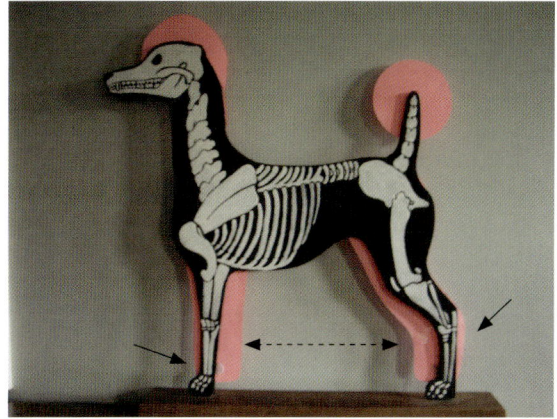

Fig. 17.1.4a-b   Fig. 17.1.4a shows the dog looking taller than it does in Fig. 17.1.2a. Fig. 17.1.4b shows how the hair has been cut too close on the back of the hock and the front of the foreleg (black arrows) and that there is too much hair left on the front of the hind leg and the back of the front leg, thus shortening the gap between them and making the dog look taller.

Fig. 17.1.5a-b   Fig. 17.1.5a shows how the angulation in the hind leg has been lost and the dog looks too heavy on its back end. Fig. 17.1.5b shows where the morphology of the dog has not been followed and too much hair has been left on (black arrows).

Fig. 17.1.6a-b   Fig. 17.1.6a is unbalanced because the pompom on the tail is too small. This makes the dog look 'weak' on its rear end. Fig. 17.1.6b is unbalanced because the topknot on top of the head is too small. This makes the head look too small for the body.

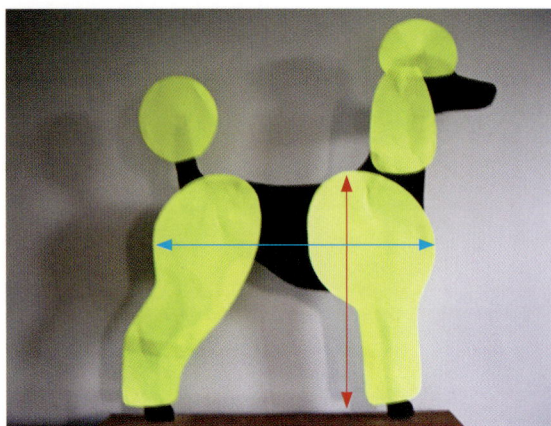

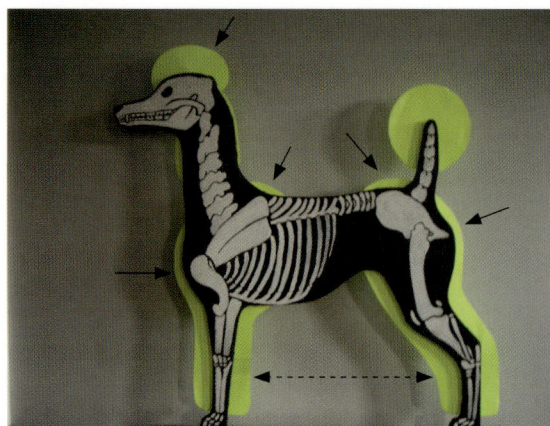

Fig. 17.1.7a-b   Fig. 17.1.7a shows the same model in a different style, called a Royal Dutch Haircut. It is slightly more extravagant than the basic lamb trim but not as flamboyant as a show trim. This style lost popularity for many years but it is slowly making a comeback, particularly on Standard Poodles. The black areas are clipped very short and the scissored coloured areas are trimmed to a length that 'balances' the morphology of the dog. The arrows on Fig. 17.1.7b show how the height of the dog has been increased by leaving hair on the topknot, the withers and the croup; to balance the dog, the same amount of hair has been left on the hip and the chest. The legs have an equal amount on the backs and the fronts.

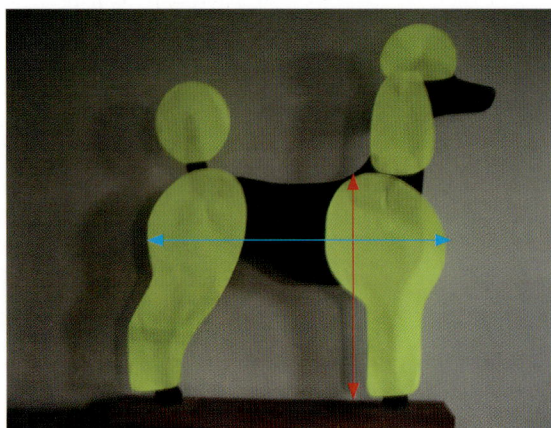

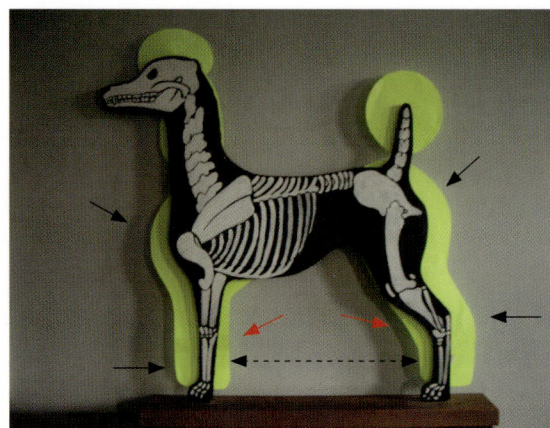

Fig. 17.1.8a-b   Fig. 17.1.8a shows the dog longer in the body and shorter in height. The black arrows in Fig. 17.1.8b show where the hair has been left too long and the red arrows show where it has been cut too short, thus visually extending the gap between the legs.

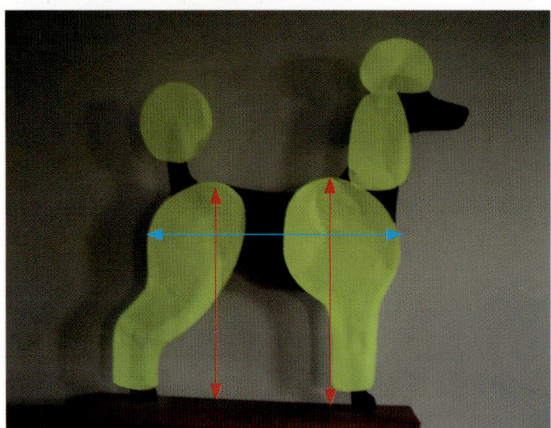

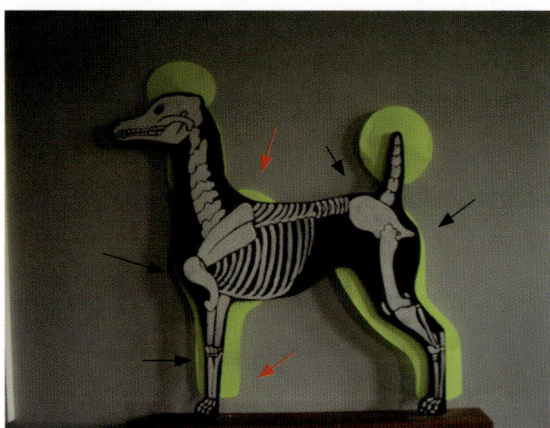

Fig. 17.1.9a-b   In Fig. 17.1.9a the dog is too tall on the front end, and the black arrows on Fig. 17.1.9b show how the hair has been removed from the chest, the front of the foreleg and the hip to shorten the length of the dog and from the croup, which lowers the back end. Leaving the hair on the withers and the backs of the front legs (red arrows) has given height to the front end.

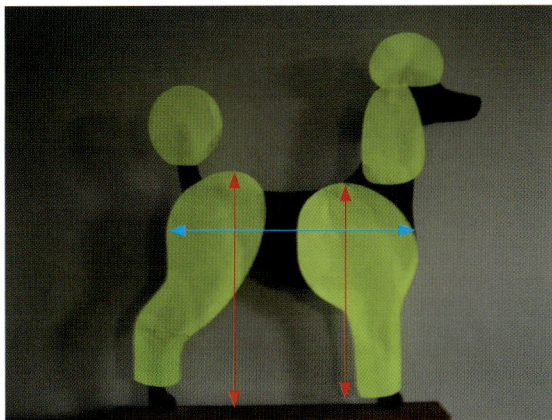

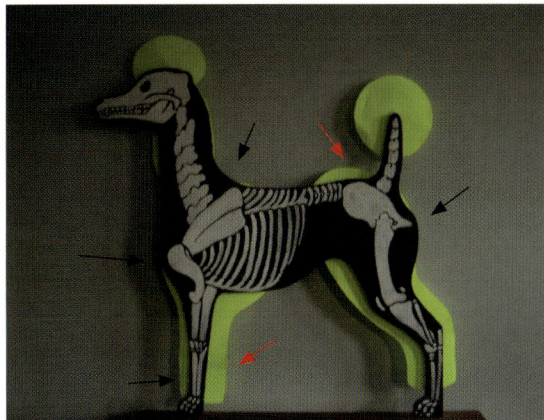

Fig. 17.1.10a-b   Fig. 17.1.10a shows the dog looking too tall, particularly at the back end. This lowers the front end, making the chest look heavy and the neck look abnormally long. The black arrows in Fig. 17.1.10b show how the hair has been removed from the front of the chest and from the withers. The red arrow shows where the hair has been left high on the croup and on the back of the front legs, further shortening the dog's length.

NOTE: LEARN TO 'LOOK' AND 'SEE' THE DOG

Start with pedigree dogs because they have a set of 'standards' that breeders are trying to meet.

You can train your eye to 'balance' the dog by arming yourself with a copy of a breed standard and getting yourself to some dog shows where you can see scores of dogs of your chosen breed. Make good use of such opportunities to observe these dogs closely. When they are side by side in the ring, you will see the differences. They may all be the same breed but the dogs will be very different.

Take note of how they all relate to the breed standard. Which dogs are longer in the body, which are longer in the leg? Start to think about what you could do to change what you are seeing. If the legs are long, would longer belly furnishings make the legs look shorter? If the dog has a long body could more hair be taken off the chest or the knickers? Take note of how the different coat colourings affect the overall image and how some colours (particularly patches – black patches, for example, look smaller than white patches) can give a false image by distorting what you are seeing. Learn to see through this.

Once you have learnt to 'see' a pedigree dog, you should be able to visualize where the shape you are styling needs to be altered to 'balance' or enhance the physique or shape of the dog. When you have achieved this skill, styling all dogs, including cross-breeds, becomes much easier.

17.2 SELECTING A STYLE

You need to select your style before the dog is bathed and dried so that the coat can be prepared appropriately. The preparation may include the use of a conditioner, and you may need to make decisions as to whether the coat is smoothed, fluffed or stretched whilst drying (see Chapters 12 and 13).

Selecting a style is really quite easy. There are only a handful to select from, but several factors can influence your decisions about the length of hair for the chosen style and the styling methods required.

◆ The quality and condition of the skin. If the skin is diseased or in poor condition, you may be restricted to clipping the coat off, thereby removing as much hair as possible so that the skin can be treated. You may not be able to pluck the hair or use fine clipper blades, and you would not want to leave a hair length that will easily knot up as this can lead to further skin trauma.

◆ The coat condition. This to a large extent depends on how much grooming is done between salon visits but it also depends on the health, diet and lifestyle of the dog. In addition, it depends on whether the coat has been damaged by chewing and scratching (self-mutilation) or parasite infestation.

◆ The coat available. This depends on whether the coat has moulted, whether the dog comes in regularly for styling, whether the owner has had a go at cutting the hair between visits to the salon and whether the coat was previously clipped right off. Whatever the reason, you may only have enough hair length to outline a new hairstyle or tidy an existing one.

◆ The coat quality. In a healthy dog the coat should be strong and glossy (unless it is a wool coat, which should have lustre). If the coat is well groomed and maintained between salon visits, the structure and density of the coat should remain consistent and undamaged from the removal of knots and mats. If the coat density is not consistent, it may ruin the shape of your style.

◆ The coat texture. The texture of the coat establishes the styling processes available to you. Wire and silk coats can be plucked, clipped or scissored, whereas wool coats and double coats can only be clipped or scissored. An owner with a pedigree dog may not be able to have the dog styled in the recommended procedure for the breed if the dog's coat is not true to the breed requirements. A Cairn Terrier, for example, should have a wire coat and it is suggested that the breed should be hand plucked, but if the coat is not of the correct texture, it needs to be clipped or scissored.

◆ The coat behaviour. This is particularly important if you intend to clip down a double coat. These coats moult, and if the coat is clipped at the time the dog has just come back into coat, the undercoat hair may take many months (sometimes as long as a year) before it is renewed and starts to regrow. Whilst the undercoat remains short, a very sparse topcoat may grow after the clipping, giving the impression of poor coat quality and alopecia. The coat will be restored once the undercoat regrows. Another point you need to consider is the growth rate of non-moulting coats. A rough estimate is approximately 1cm per month for wool, wire and silk coats during the months of longer daylight hours, and slightly less during the months of shorter daylight hours.

◆ The owner's requirements. The owner is paying you to work for them so their requests need to be met, but whether or not this is possible depends on all of the above. If the dog is in poor health, is not groomed or if exercise time is spent hunting, swimming and foraging, a beautiful, extravagant 'hairdo' may well not be the best option! You therefore need to discuss and agree on an alternative. A compromise is essential to keeping everyone, including the dog, happy.

A NOTE ABOUT FIRST GROOMS

When a customer makes a booking for a young puppy to have his first groom, unless you are told otherwise you should always assume that the dog is to be eventually styled to its traditional breed image. Owners may later decide to show their dogs, and you may need to encourage the development of a show quality coat so do not be too eager to cut it off before the puppy matures.

When deciding upon your styling approach for any given dog, you should first consider the condition of the skin after the dog has been prepared. This is particularly important if you intend to use fine clipper blades or chemical coat preparations that are designed to aid scissoring or clipping. Bear in mind the following points.

For a pedigree dog:

◆ Do you know what the breed should look like? This is essential if you are to know what you are aiming for in terms of 'style'.

◆ Do you know the breed standards so that you can evaluate and try to 'balance' the dog? Cast a critical eye over the dog to pick out his good points, as well as his bad points. This allows you to find a balance between what you have and what you should have.

◆ Does the dog in front of you have a 'good' coat for styling or is it of poor quality and therefore likely to be difficult to style?

◆ Which tools and styling systems are likely to produce the best effect on the coat that you have been given to work with?

For a cross-breed:

◆ Does the dog look like either of his parents?

◆ What shape are the feet, the head and the tail?

◆ Does he have short legs or long legs?

◆ What coat do you have available? Some, but not all, cross-breeds favour the coat type and hair growth pattern of one of the parents.

◆ Does the dog have coat features that grow naturally, such as eyebrows, beards and leg furnishings? (If they do, select a style that allows you to leave them on unless you are told to take them off. They can be trimmed shorter but leave them on – in the absence of a pedigree, they can often contribute significantly to the dog's identity.)

◆ What texture is the coat? If it is woolly coated, it can be clipped or scissored, and if it is wire coated it can be clipped or hand plucked.

The choice here often comes down to the owner's preference and budget.

There are not that many styles to choose from, and all cross-breeds fall into one of the categories available to pedigree dogs because essentially all styles are variations on a theme. The eyebrows may be from one hairstyle and the legs from another, but your choices are limited.

The more critical you are of the dog's anatomical deviations (i.e. departures from what is standard for the breed), the easier it becomes for you to recognize where you need to make adjustments and which of the styles would be most suited to each individual dog.

STYLING OR SCULPTING: WHAT IS THE DIFFERENCE?

Styling makes sympathetic use of the dog's natural coat style to enhance his body shape and features. A good example of this is the English Springer Spaniel. If the dog is clipped to remove all of the coat and its furnishings, the dog is strong, muscular and workmanlike. Leave the natural furnishings on the dog and they provide elegance and beauty.

Sculpting is when you use the coat as a modelling media to fashion or make a shape that does not necessarily follow the dog's natural body shape. A good example of this would be the Poodle. Left in its natural state, a Poodle coat falls into hanging curls or cords about the entire body. Fluff dry and stretch the coat and you can sculpt or mould it into any shape you want – not necessarily even dog shaped, as creative styling demonstrates!

Another example is the 'Lion Trim' – a shape that can be either modelled with clippers to remove the hair on the hind legs, as on a Portuguese Water Dog or a Lowchen, or shaped with scissors into the long buoyant coat of the show Poodle.

17.3 COAT CHARACTERISTICS AND PATTERNS

Dogs can be divided into sections for styling, focusing on the shapes of the body, feet, head, face, ears and tail. As most dogs have all or at least most of these parts, they all require a style from each category. It is the morphology of the dog and the coat type that determines which of the styles the dog ends up with. The dog's coat naturally grows in one of four patterns, and all dogs fall into one of these categories:

The smooth coat: this, of course, does not require styling since it is in itself a 'style'. This being the case, it also lends itself to being the result of styling, as it would be in a complete clip-off where the entire coat is removed to a fraction of its natural length. Thus totally clipping off a coat is an acceptable way to style the dog.

The short and curly: the short and curly coat found on breeds such as the Curly Coated Retriever is generally coarse in texture and often lends itself to restyling. By clipping off or hand plucking the coat you can temporarily create a smoother style.

The furnished coat: the furnished short coat is where the body coat is short or medium in length, whilst the legs, undercarriage, chest, ears and tails are furnished with longer hairs. This is the sort of coat found on Spaniels, Setters and many double-coated breeds. Dogs with this coat pattern can be styled to emphasize these furnishings, whilst shortening the body coat to enhance and neaten the physical appearance of the dog.

The long coat: this category covers a huge range of breeds, from the dense silky coat of the Kerry Blue Terrier to the corded coat of the Hungarian Puli, the fine silky coat of the Yorkshire Terrier and the long corkscrew curls of the Poodles and Bichon Frisé. The coat reaches lengths that, if desired, can be trimmed and shaped into whatever style the owner requires/requests.

It is the last two coat formations that have led to the styling and presentation practices that we see on dogs today.

17.4 HAIRSTYLES

You have two choices on how to present your work. You can leave the coat as natural as possible and limit any styling to light tidying of the feet, eyes and sanitary areas. For this effect the coat is groomed out, bathed and dried; minimal trimming is then undertaken to tactfully remove any hair that spoils a shape or may cause health problems. The *natural effect* is a style in itself but you may be surprised to see how a little tactful trimming of leg feathers or around the feet adds that finishing touch.

The alternative is to transform the dog by reshaping or restyling the coat. For coats that require more styling or a complete transformation, there are surprisingly few styling options to choose from; each of these is, however, quite distinctive.

Both choices are immensely satisfying and both have their place within the grooming industry.

Spaniel style

This style is fashioned to create an image of softness in the expression of the dog, combined with sleekness and elegance. We call it the Spaniel cut because it is what Spaniels look like even before they are styled.

This style exploits the *furnished coat* characteristics where the body coat is short or medium in length, with longer furnishings present on the ears, the chest, the backs of the front legs, the front of the upper hind leg, the back of the thigh, the undercarriage and the tail. The position of the furnishings is the same for all dogs with this coat formation, irrespective of breed, although the length and density of the furnishings varies greatly.

The body coat is sometimes made shorter by clipping or plucking, and the furnishings are styled to enhance the dog's shape or to suit his lifestyle. The head and face are cleaned of stray hairs, and the tail is either trimmed to the same length as the body coat if it is docked, or left with a natural flag or pennant shape if it is undocked. There are many other breeds that sport this coat formation, including the silk-coated Setters and the double-coated Retrievers and Border Collies. These breeds often require minimal styling but they can be clipped and styled into a shorter-length spaniel cut should you be asked to do so (*see* Fig. 17.4.1).

You can create this style on dogs that do not have this coat formation simply by creating your own cutting lengths and lines. It does not, however, work well with a wool coat because the growing style of the coat and the texture do not lend themselves to long, sleek (or even straight) furnishings. The style can be created by clipping (*see* Fig. 17.4.2), plucking (*see* Fig. 17.4.3) or rolling (*see* Fig. 17.4.4) depending on the coat type, the effect that you want to achieve and the owner's preference(s).

Fig. 17.4.1   The Border Collie has a 'furnished' coat formation, meaning that the coat has long furnishings on the legs, undercarriage, chest, tail and knickers. If you are asked to clip the coat off, the coat lends itself to a 'spaniel cut'.

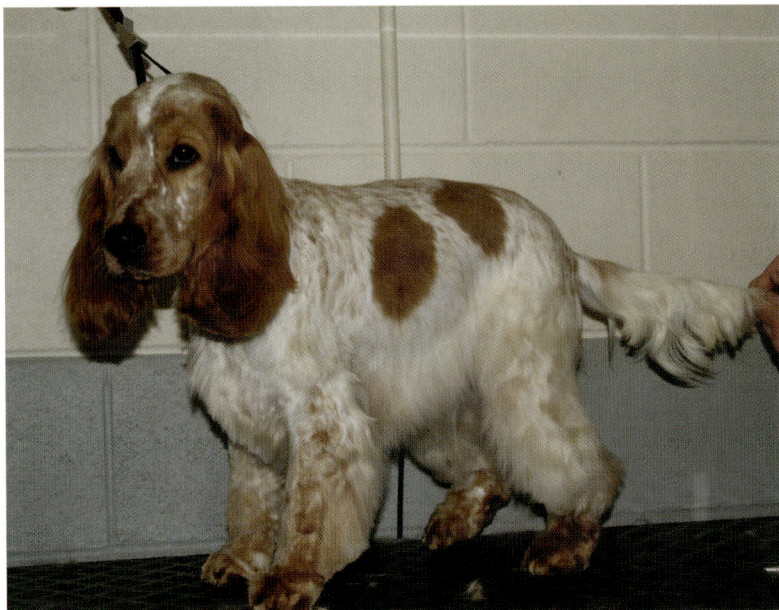

Fig. 17.4.2   This puppy is not destined for the show ring and has had its first clip. He is exercised in the countryside so his leg furnishings have been cut well up from ground level to help with maintenance. His long tail has been styled into a flag.

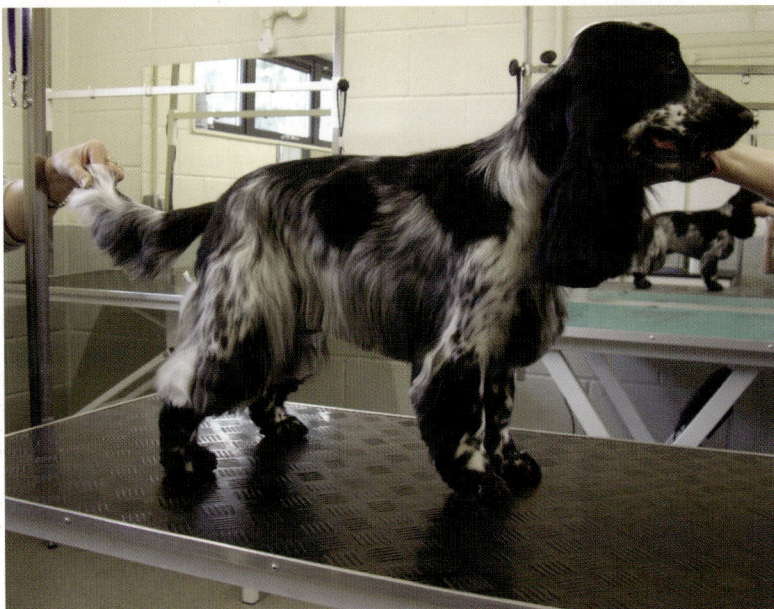

Fig. 17.4.3   This spaniel has been plucked. The dog is not shown but the owner likes to keep the coat as is recommended for the breed. The owner has requested that the furnishings are trimmed well off the ground to help with maintenance. The undocked tail has been styled in a flag.

Fig. 17.4.4   The coat of this young spaniel has been 'rolled' for the show ring. The coat is plucked monthly to maintain the length. The dog gains elegance as the furnishings grow and the added length helps to straighten the curl.

STYLING THE SPANIEL

Clip or pluck the hair to leave a clean head

Use thinning scissors to nip the hair, leaving an indentation in the coat that will emphasise the occiput

The top ⅓ of the ear is clipped with a fine blade in reverse

The foreface should be cleared by clipping or plucking

Pluck or strip the back far enough down the body to enhance the shape of the ribcage

Docked tails should be neat

Ear furnishings should be long and full

Clip the hair with the hair growth from the chin to the breast bone

Clear the rectum

Chest furnishings are thinned to allow them to hang. Clear the armpits

Furnishings are styled to suit the dog and its' lifestyle. Transition lines between the body coat and the furnishings should be subtle and well blended

Stray hair on the foreleg is plucked to the length of the natural coat length

The hair is shortened enough from the hock down to give a solid 'chunky leg

Trim between pads and 'round' feet leaving plenty of hair on top of the foot

Fig. 17.4.5   (Photo: Michael Trafford)

1. Head. *Clear the head, cheeks and foreface of any excess hair. Use thinning scissors to make an exaggerated occiput.*

2. Throat. *Clip the hair in the direction of the coat growth from the chin to the breast bone.*

3. Ears. *If the dog is a pet, clip the hair from the inside of the pinna. Clip the top third of the pinna (until you have cleared the fold) on both sides of the pinna. On Cocker Spaniels the ear furnishings can be trimmed neatly. On Springer Spaniels they are left natural.*

4. Back. *Clip or pluck the back. Take the sides low enough to enhance the shape of the ribcage. Blend the transition line into the skirt of the undercarriage.*

5. Rear end. *Clear the hair under the tail until the two rosettes are visible (over the points of the hip). Clear all hair around the rectum and shorten the hair around the sanitary areas. The tail should be neat and tidy if docked or flagged if undocked. Trim the knickers into an inverted 'V' to end at the hock.*

6. Chest. *Thin the furnishings if necessary so that they drop from the breast bone. They should blend into the undercarriage. Clear under the armpits.*

7. Feet. *Clear between the pads. Shape a 'round' foot, leaving enough hair on top of the toes to form a soft pad.*

8. Forelegs. *Clear any excess hair on the front of the leg to the length of the naturally shorter coat. Use thinning scissors to blend the sides into the furnishings.*

9. Hind leg. *Shorten the hair from the hock to the foot enough to give a stocky or 'chunky' appearance to complement angulation and to balance the style.*

It is completed with scissors and thinning or blending scissors.

Long-legged terrier style

This is, to an extent, a fashioned style that exploits the coat characteristics of a medium or long coat. It requires a certain amount of length on the coat so that it can be shaped onto any long-legged dog, including those with wool coats, silk coats and wire coats.

This style probably got its name because it best describes the shape or style created on long-legged dogs such as the Airedale, Lakeland, Irish and Welsh Terriers and the Wire Fox Terrier. Traditionally the style is recognized for its clean-cut lines and an image of defined sharpness, as you would expect to see on any long-legged terrier; it is, however, a style that can be adapted to any long-legged dog (*see* Fig. 17.4.6). Two significant aspects of this style are that the body coat is styled shorter than the length of the hair on the legs

and any furnishings on the undercarriage are shaped at an angle to accentuate the deep chest and the shape of the tucked-up undercarriage.

The legs are styled to show a sturdy cylindrical foreleg and to exaggerate and enhance the well-defined muscular shape of the hind leg. On a terrier the trim includes styling a clean head and ears, with a breed-specific beard and eyebrows. On non-terriers, however, the head shape may be adapted to suit the dog.

Fig. 17.4.6 The long-legged terrier cut is associated with the crisp clean cut lines of the wire-coated terriers but here you can see how it has been adopted for the silk-coated Kerry Blue Terrier. The style is the same but the coat is curly rather than harsh. (Photo: Michael Trafford)

Fig. 17.4.7 A variation of the long-legged terrier cut has been adopted by all three sizes of Schnauzer. The style is the same but the furnishings on this Miniature Schnauzer have been left very long, giving a soft impression to the style. The body coat is coarse, and styling methods are the same as for the terrier. (Photo: Michael Trafford)

An example of a variation to the long-legged terrier cut is the Schnauzer, a breed that resembles a terrier in appearance but does not in fact belong to the Terrier Group (*see* Fig. 17.4.7). The Schnauzer comes in three sizes: the Miniature (36cm), the Standard (USA) Schnauzer (48cm) and the Giant (65–70cm). They all adopt this hairstyle, with the only notable difference between them being that the Miniature has a tendency to grow longer hair on the furnishings. The physique and the morphology of the breed make it easy to adapt this style, and on the 'salt and pepper' coloured dogs the difference in the coat colouring can actually help you place your styling lines. The beard furnishings are left longer than on a traditional long-legged terrier and the eyebrows are shaped differently.

Another breed that adopts this style is the Kerry Blue Terrier (*see* Fig. 17.4.6). Unlike the sharp tailoring of wire-coated breeds such as the Airedale, the Kerry has a soft, silkier coat that is dried naturally to form tight curls before styling, resulting in a much softer style.

STYLING THE LONG-LEGGED TERRIER

Fig. 17.4.8

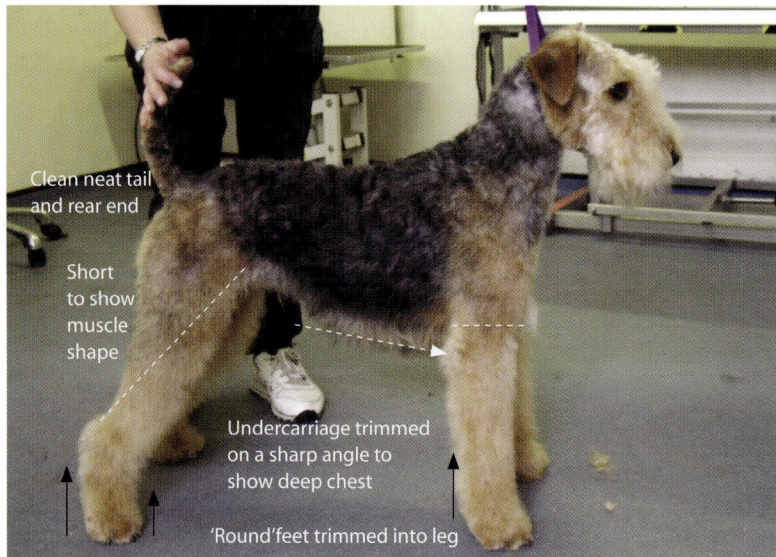

Clean neat tail and rear end

Short to show muscle shape

Undercarriage trimmed on a sharp angle to show deep chest

'Round' feet trimmed into leg

1. *All long-legged terriers have the same hairstyle, apart from their faces (see eyebrows and beards).*
2. Head. *The top of the head and the ears are clipped or plucked smooth. Check your breed profile for cheek, eyebrow and beard shaping.*
3. Throat. *Clip or pluck the hair short from the throat to the breast bone.*
4. Chest. *The chest furnishings are short and neat and should meet with the undercarriage. Clear the hair under the armpit.*
5. Back. *The back is clipped with a medium length blade or plucked. Take your lines right around the ribcage leaving a thin strip of furnishing on the undercarriage. The shoulders can be trimmed slightly shorter to give the impression of 'narrowness'.*
6. Forelegs. *The forelegs are trimmed straight and finish at the groove above the elbow. Scissor upwards and then comb downwards.*
7. Hind legs. *Blend the tops of the hind leg into the body but take plenty of hair from the thigh to show the muscle shape. Trim the furnishings on the front of the leg downwards, and trim the hocks upwards.*
8. Feet. *Remove the hair between the pads and trim 'round' feet, shaping them into the legs.*
9. Tail. *The tail is trimmed short and neat to the length of the body coat.*
10. Rear end. *Clear the hair well away from the rectum and neaten it around the sanitary areas. The groin area can be clipped.*

Styling the Poodle in a blended lamb trim

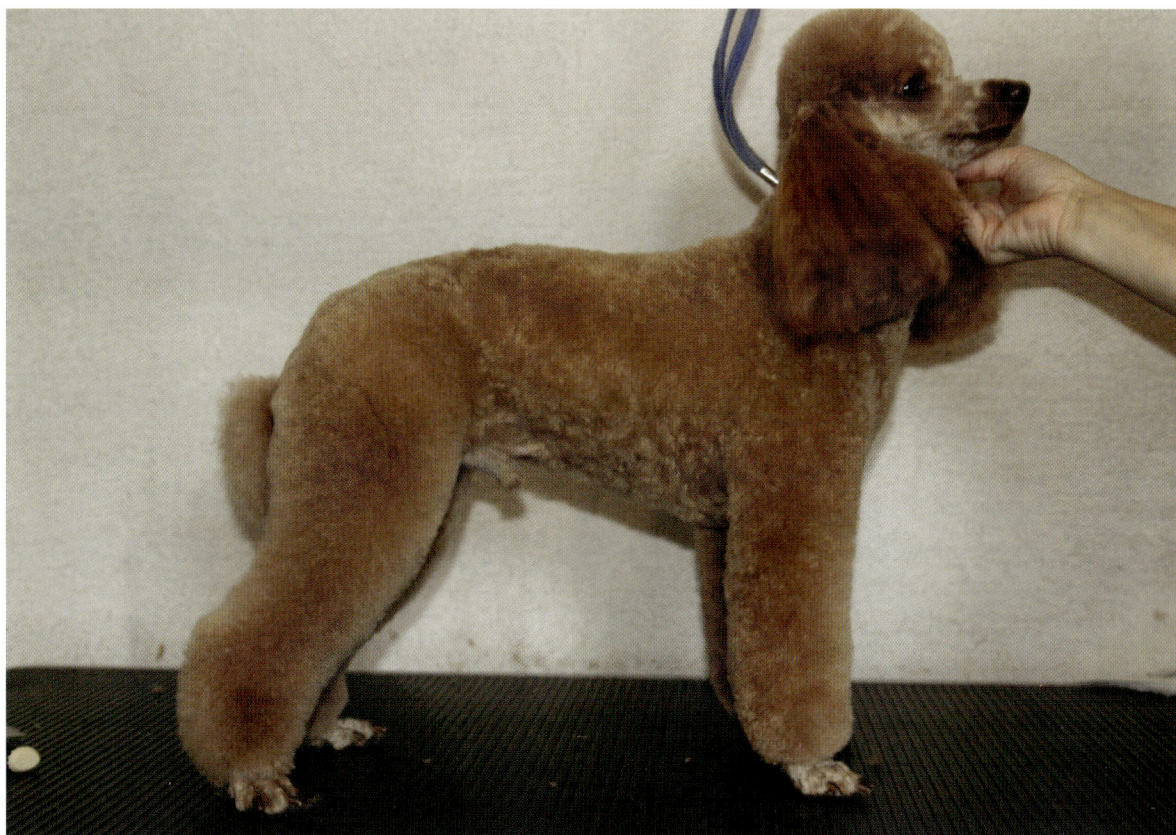

Fig. 17.4.9   This Poodle's trim is another variation of the long-legged terrier cut. In the UK the Poodle in a lamb trim is styled with the feet clipped, a pompom on the tail and the ear furnishings left in situ. In Europe this style often has the feet left untrimmed and rounded into the leg, the tail is trimmed without a pompom, ear furnishings are removed and the face is styled with a full beard.

The length of the hair left on the dog to create this style depends on the owner's requirements. On this dog, the back is clipped and the legs are blended into the body at the hip and shoulder. The front legs are cylindrical in shape and the back legs have the same circumference as the front legs up to the stifle. The leg hair then tapers in length towards the hip. The top knot is scissored to blend into the nape of the neck and the tail is docked so it has a pompom. The face, feet, groin and base of the tail have been clipped with a fine blade.

Before you begin, the coat needs a good bath and to be stretch-dried to its maximum length.

You will learn most from these photographs if you concentrate on the angle of the groomer's scissors and the cut she is using. The groomer styling this dog is right-handed. If you are left-handed, take a close look at the cut the groomer is using and use the opposite cut. The first few photographs should draw your attention to this.

The skills used to achieve the style on this dog are the same as those used for styling any wool coat. To achieve the effect of fullness, you need always to be cutting against the lie of the hair, and, apart from around the bottom of the legs, you will always be cutting with your scissors facing up the coat.

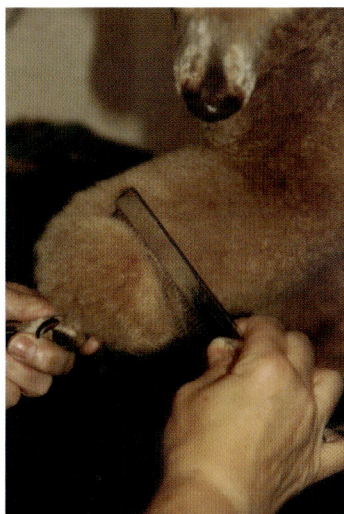

Fig. 17.4.10   Comb the hair down over the foot.

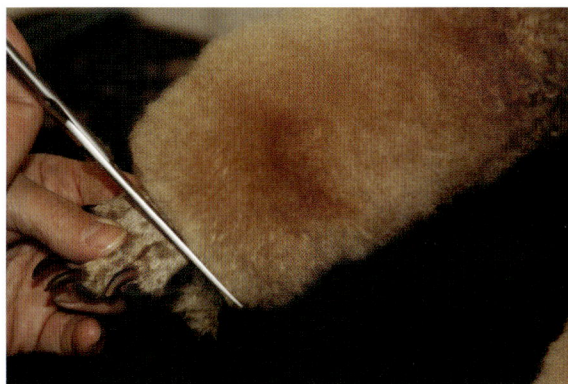

Fig. 17.4.1   Whether you are right- or left-handed, you will be using both backhand (shown) and forehand cuts to shape the hair in a neat line around the bottom of the leg.

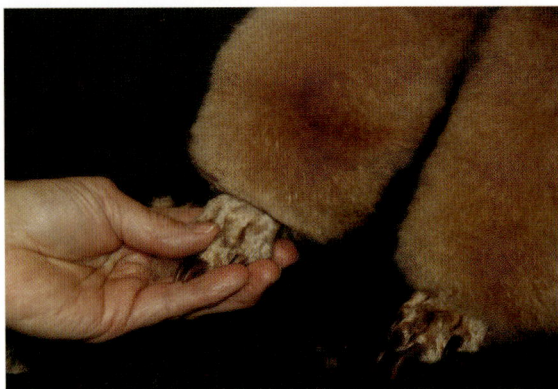

Fig. 17.4.12 *The hair is neat around the foot. Comb the hair and shake the leg to restore the hair to its fluffed-up position.*

Fig. 17.4.13 *Hold the foot to lift the leg. From the bottom of the leg, with your scissor tips facing up the leg, start to trim off some of the hair in a straight line. The groomer in this picture is right-handed so a forehand cut is being used on the inside of the leg. If you are a left-handed groomer, you will be using a backhand cut. At this point you are removing a first layer of hair and you will need to scissor the leg again after combing.*

Fig. 17.4.14 *To get to the inside of the other leg, the right-handed groomer now needs to use a backhand cut, whereas the left-handed groomer would be using a forehand cut.*

Fig. 17.4.15 *Keeping your scissoring smooth, work your way up the leg.*

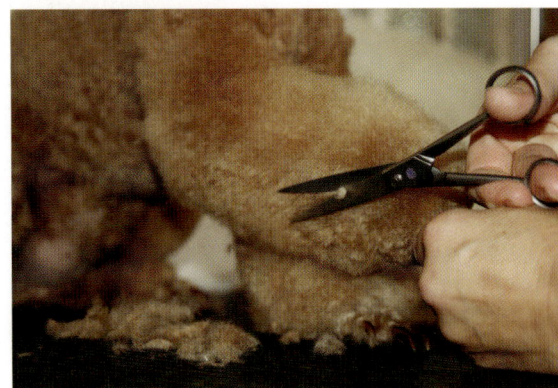

Fig. 17.4.16 *Continue to work around the outside of the leg. The right-handed groomer is using a backhand cut on this leg. A left-handed groomer would be using a forehand cut.*

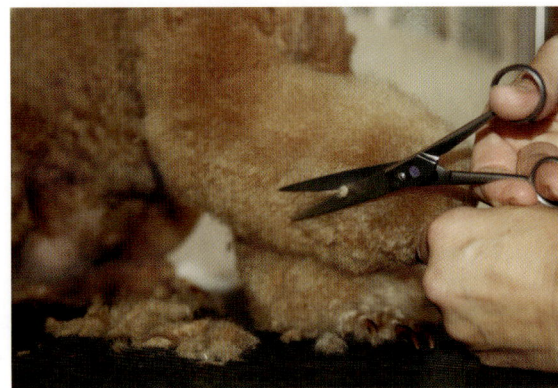

Fig. 17.4.17 *To work around the outside of the opposite leg, the right-handed groomer is now using a forehand cut, whereas the left-handed groomer will be using a backhand cut.*

Fig. 17.4.18   The front of the leg can be trimmed by standing the dog sideways on to you, and with the leg taken slightly to the side. This gives you a good view of your cutting line, and lifting the leg allows you room to manoeuvre your scissors. By the time you reach this point, if you keep moving your line of vision slowly around the leg, you should be able to see the difference in length between the cut hair and the uncut hair. Note the forehand cut on this leg …

Fig. 17.4.19   … and the backhand cut on the other leg.

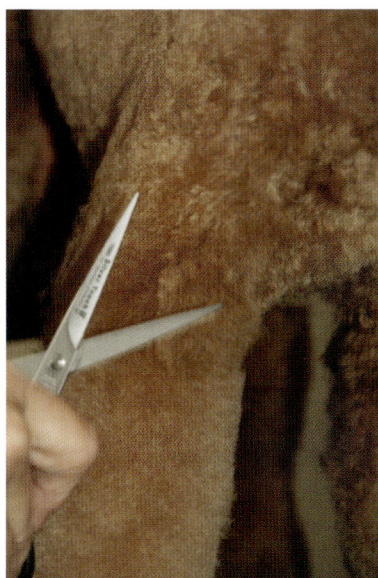

Fig. 17.4.20   With the foot back on the floor, blend the top of the leg into the body

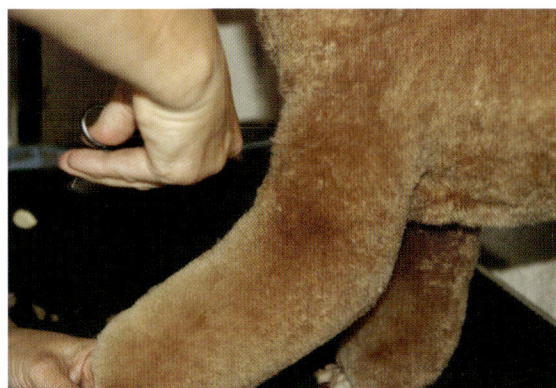

Fig. 17.4.21   Comb the leg, give it a shake to free up the hair and then tidy up any long ends that spring out of place.

Fig. 17.4.23   To style the back leg, you start in the same way by combing the coat down towards the foot and trimming the hair level around the bottom of the leg. Then start to work your way up the leg.

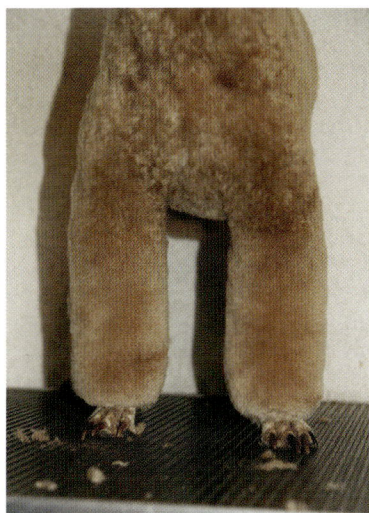

Fig. 17.4.22   Both legs finished. They are similar width without any long ends remaining and they are blended into the body coat.

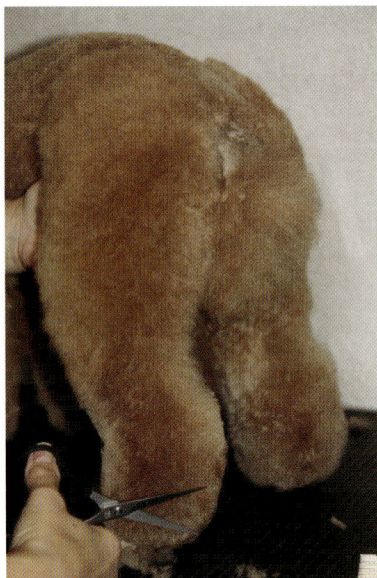

Fig. 17.4.24 You are aiming at styling the leg to the same circumference as the front legs up to the level of the stifle, where the thigh muscles make the leg thicker so the hair length needs to be reduced. As soon as you have room to manoeuvre your scissors, the foot can be placed back on the table.

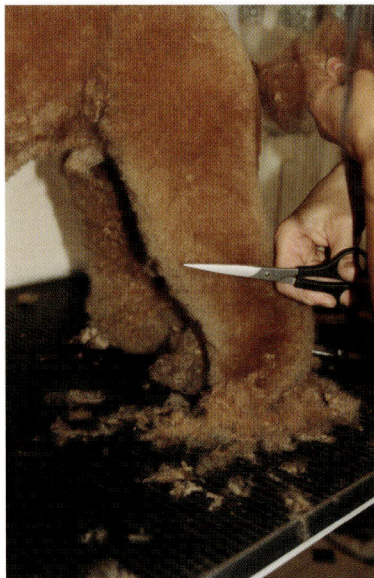

Fig. 17.4.25 At this point, this groomer has crossed her hands. She is using her right hand for a backhand cut to work up the front of the leg; to be able to hold the tail out of the way, she has to cross her hands and will be looking over her left arm to see her work.

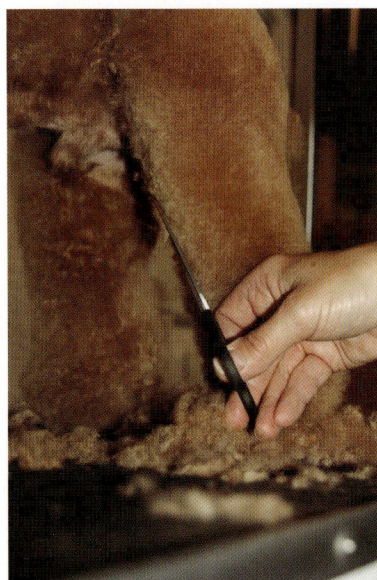

Fig. 17.4.26 This right-handed groomer will continue to use the backhand cut to trim this part of the leg into the groin area. Note how well the scissors are balanced in her hand, with just the very end of the thumb being used to operate the cutting action. This allows her to keep her hand as far away as possible from the coat.

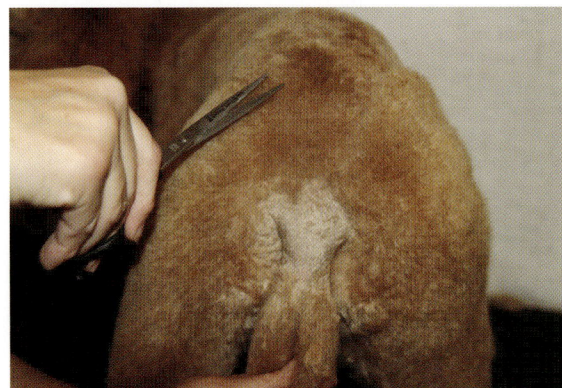

Fig. 17.4.27 Blending the leg into the hip.

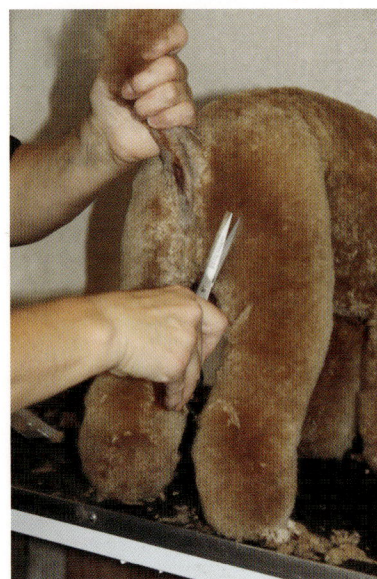

Fig. 17.4.28 Styling the second back leg is easier because you can turn the dog to face away from you and then you have the shape of the first leg to copy.

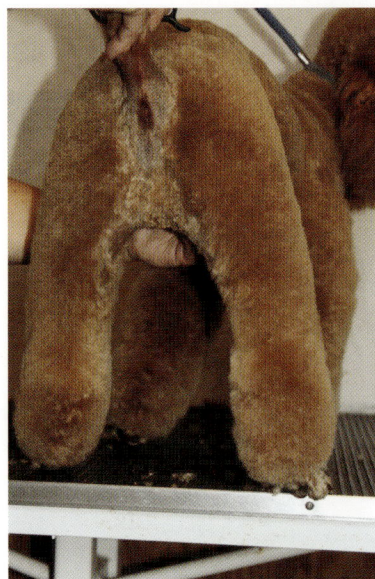

Fig. 17.4.29 Both back legs are finished. Note that by tapering the tops of the legs as you work towards blending into the hip, the leg maintains the same circumference for its full length.

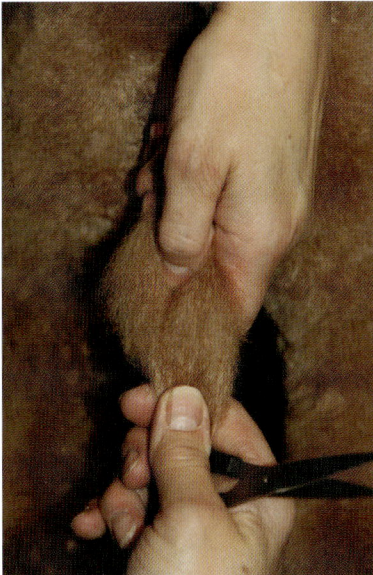

Fig. 17.4.30 To trim the tail, comb all the hair towards the tip to gauge the length of hair.

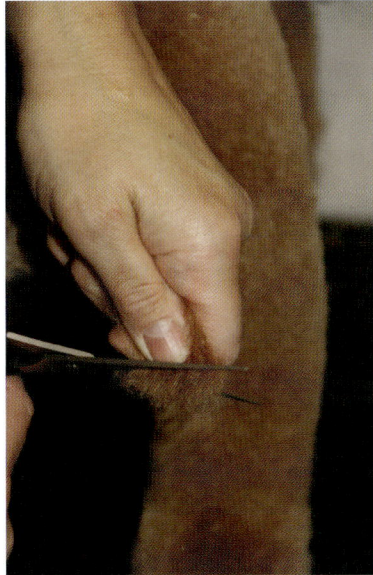

Fig. 17.4.31 Holding the hair between your finger and thumb, slide your grip a few centimetres along the hair and cut away any excess.

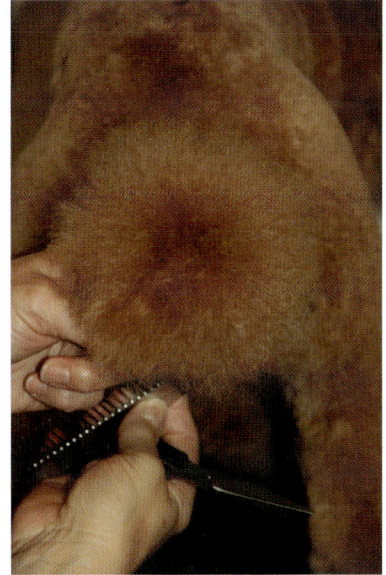

Fig. 17.4.32 Release the hair and comb it.

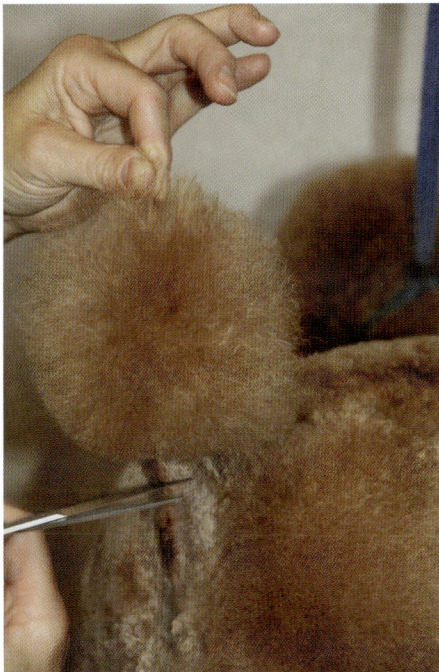

Fig. 17.4.33 Hold the tip of the tail by a few hairs and starting from the bottom, style it into a pompom.

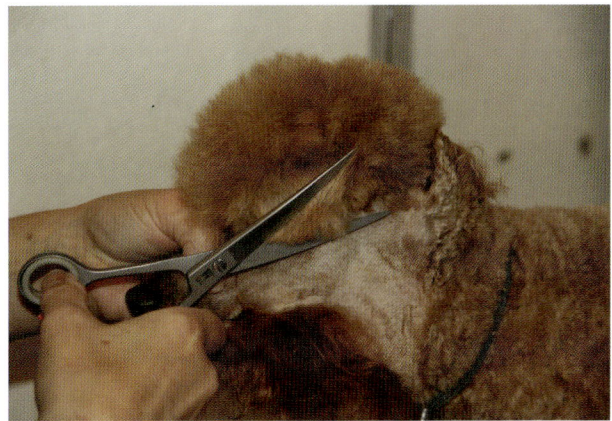

Fig. 17.4.34 To shape the topknot, first comb the hair well. Take one ear around the back of the head and hold it with your supporting hand to keep it out of the way. With your scissors parallel to the cheek, cut away the excess hair and round the hair upwards towards the top of the head.

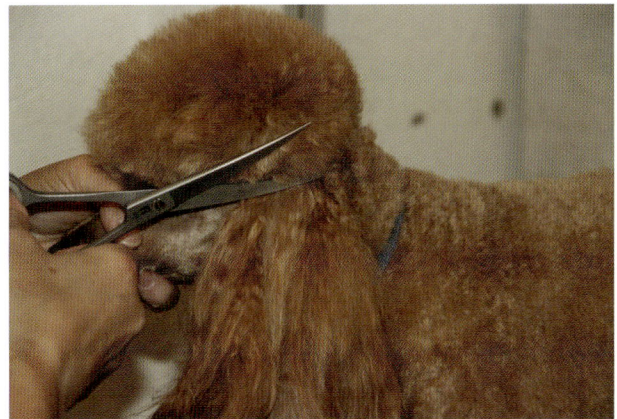

Fig. 17.4.35 Drop the ear back into place to trim across the top towards the back of the head.

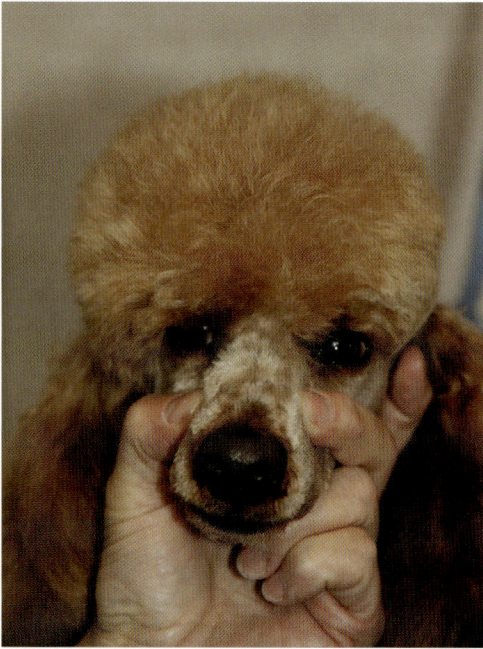

Fig. 17.4.36   One side finished, now to do the other side!

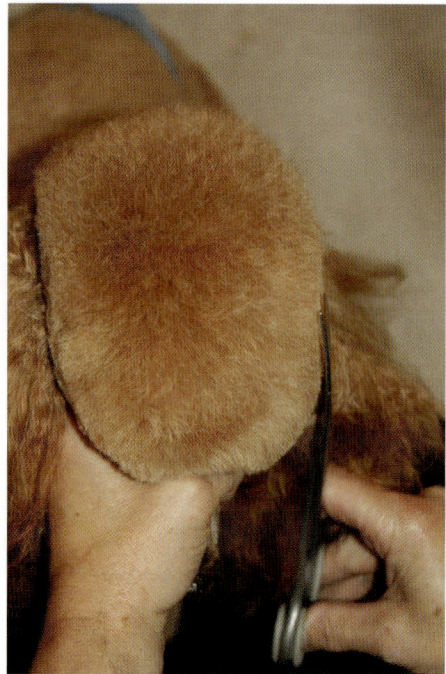

Fig. 17.4.37   Looking down onto the top of the head, you are aiming at shaping a circle.

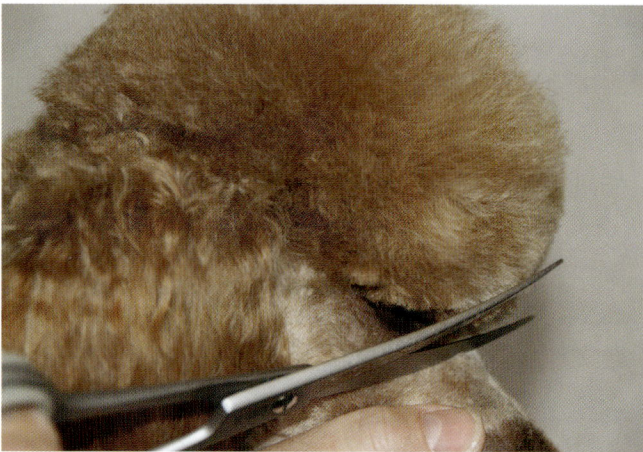

Fig. 17.4.38   Here curved scissors are being used to shape the front of the topknot up towards the top of the head.

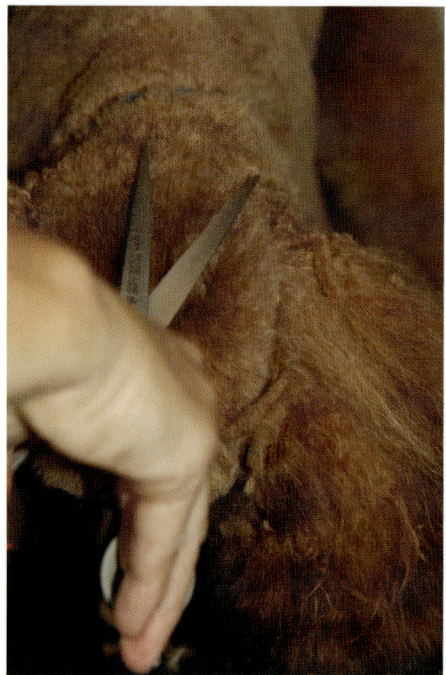

Fig. 17.4.39   Work over the top of the head keeping the shape rounded from all aspects.

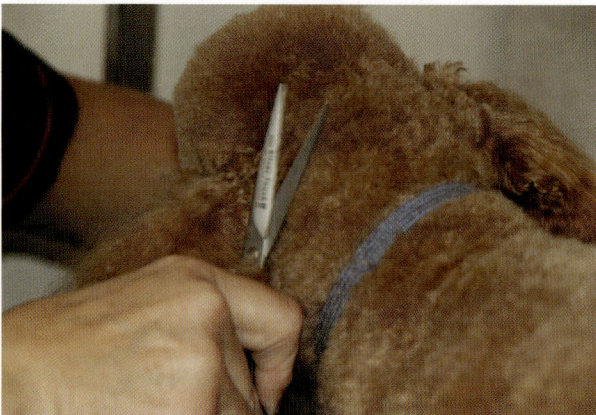

Fig. 17.4.40   Blend the back of the topknot into the neck.

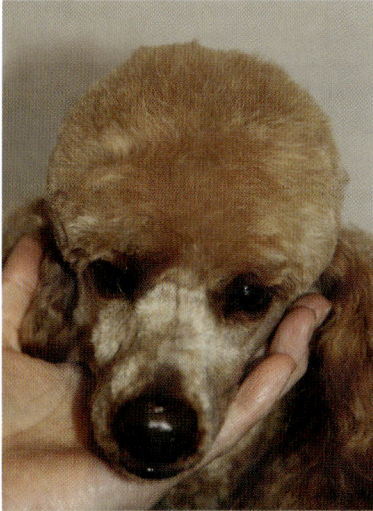

Fig. 17.4.42   To finish the style, the ends of the ears have been lightly trimmed to tidy then up.

You may be surprised to learn that a Poodle in lamb trim (*see* 'Styling the Poodle in a blended lamb trim') is another variation of the long-legged terrier cut. The front legs are cylindrical in shape and the hind legs are shaped to show off angulations and physique. In the United Kingdom it is fashionable to clip the face and the feet of the Poodle and to leave tail furnishings, ear furnishings and a topknot. In Europe the Poodle is often styled with the feet unclipped, the tail hair and ear furnishings removed, a beard or moustache left on the face and a topknot on the head. Apart from the topknot, this makes the style very similar to the long-legged terrier trim.

The style can be created by clipping, plucking or rolling, depending on the coat type and the owner's preference. It is completed with scissors and thinning or blending scissors.

Short-legged terrier style

This is another fashioned style that uses a long coat to enhance and exaggerate the depth of the undercarriage and the strong, sturdy, shortened legs of the short-legged terrier (*see* Fig. 17.4.43). The furnishings on the undercarriage are left long and are styled parallel to the ground, or on a very slight rising angle from the elbow towards the groin. This style can look very different on different dogs because the body furnishings can either reach ground level or they can be styled to show a little length of leg.

The Scottish Terrier (*see* 'Styling the Short-legged Terrier – 1') has particularly short legs and profuse furnishings, and is styled with very long, heavy furnishing on the undercarriage that sweeps the ground. By contrast, the Sealyham Terrier (*see* 'Styling the Short-legged Terrier – 2') is a little longer in the leg, as is the West Highland; a slight length of leg is therefore evident in the styling.

*Fig. 17.4.43
The short-legged terrier style enhances the sturdiness of short-legged breeds by exaggerating the depth of the undercarriage and the strong short legs.*

STYLING THE SHORT-LEGGED TERRIER – 1

The underside of the tail is trimmed short with a length of hair left on the body side.

The body is stripped or clipped to a medium length and blended at the transition lines with the neck and head

Hair on the thighs is trimmed into the body coat

The back is blended into the furnishings which are always trimmed parallel to the ground. The length will depend on the breed, the leg length and the amount of hair available.

The coat is cleaned of hair to the breast bone. The front of the shoulder can be taken shorter than the body coat.

Feet are trimmed under the pads and rounded into the legs

Fig. 17.4.44   All short-legged terriers are trimmed similarly but the heads are different and some have less furnishing. The Scottish Terrier has profuse furnishings and very short legs. (Photo: Michael Trafford)

1. Head. *The head is styled according to the breed.*
2. Back. *The back is clipped to a medium length following the hair growth direction, plucked or rolled. The back is trimmed to an area about halfway down the ribcage. Transition lines with the head and throat should be blended.*
3. Throat. *The throat is clipped short in the direction of hair growth. If desired, the front of the shoulder can be taken shorter than the body coat.*
4. Forelegs. *The forelegs may or may not have profuse furnishings.*
5. Feet. *The hair is cleared between the pads and the feet are styled into neat circles to round off the leg. Cut nails if required.*
6. Hind leg. *The hind leg is blended into the body at the hip.*
7. Tail. *The underside of the tail is trimmed short and close, with a length of hair left on the body side. The tail should taper from base to tip.*
8. Rear end. *The rectum should be cleared and the sanitary areas neatly trimmed for hygiene.*

The coat is styled to leave a significant amount of furnishings on the sides, legs and the undercarriage of the body, with just the centre back and the top half of the ribs (or thereabouts, depending on the dog) being styled to a shorter length. Tail furnishings are generally styled to the length of the body coat so they are tidy, but not tailored like that of the long-legged terrier. Head shape on this cut varies according to the breed. The groomer may thus discover a wide range of shapes, from the round pompom head of the West Highland Terrier to the defined beard and eyebrows of the Scottish Terrier.

Variations of this style are often applied to breeds such as the Lhasa Apso or Shih Tzu when owners request a short pet trim (see Fig. 17.4.46). The head shape of these breeds suits the spherical pompom shape of the West Highland head, whilst the dense hair on their short muscular legs is easily styled into shape. The main variations to the style are that the undercarriage is styled shorter and the tail furnishings are left *in situ*.

This style can be used on any short-legged dogs, including those with wool coats, wire coats and silk coats. The style can be created by clipping, plucking or

rolling, depending on the coat type and the owner's requirements, and is completed with scissors and thinning or blending scissors.

It could be argued that the styling of the American Cocker Spaniel is another adaptation of the short-legged terrier style (see Fig. 17.4.47). The silky coat texture gives the style a different visual effect from that of a coarse-coated terrier, but take a closer look and you can see the shape of the style. The chest, abdomen and legs of the American Cocker grow more furnishings than other spaniels. The long silky hair is clipped or stripped from the back and

STYLING THE SHORT-LEGGED TERRIER – 2

The bone coat is taken down to a medium length and blended into the furnishings of the undercarriage

The tail is trimmed close on the underside and the body side is left with a pad of hair

Hips and thighs blended into the body coat

The throat is cleared of excess hair to the breast bone

The undercarriage furnishings should be straight but can be styled on a very slight angle to show a length of leg

The feet are trimmed round and neat

Fig. 17.4.45   All short-legged terriers are trimmed similarly, with variations in the length of the furnishings and in head shapes. If the dog has shorter furnishings, like this Sealyham, the leg is shaped into the style.

1. Head. *The head is shaped according to the breed or the morphology of the dog.*
2. Back. *The back is either clipped with a medium-length blade in the direction of coat growth, plucked or rolled. The back is trimmed to complement the shape of the dog and blended into the furnishings of the undercarriage.*
3. Throat. *The throat is cleared of excess hair to the breast bone and blended into the chest furnishings.*
4. Forelegs. *The forelegs are trimmed to a neat and tidy length that balances with the hind legs.*
5. Feet. *The hair is cleared from between the pads and the feet are rounded into the leg.*
6. Hind leg. *The hind legs are blended at the hip and thigh into the body coat. The legs are not styled to show angulation.*
7. Tail. *The tail is trimmed short and close on the underside and left with a pad of hair on the body side.*
8. Rear end. *The rectum is cleared of hair and the sanitary areas are trimmed neatly.*

the top half of the ribs, leaving the underside of the dog heavily coated. The feet are rounded up into the legs as they would be on a Scottish Terrier or a West Highland Terrier, the undercarriage is styled parallel to the ground and the tail, if docked, is trimmed to the length of the body coat. The main difference is that the ears are styled as in other spaniels and a 'quiff' or 'rosette' is styled onto the top of the head to enhance a clearly defined 'stop'.

Some general comments

In summary, most styling is based on these three basic haircuts, with variations and adjustments to suit the dog or the breed that you are styling. What makes the shape of each breed look so different is the styling of the head, ears, feet and tail of the dog and the length of the hair left on the hairstyle.

There is an argument that not all breeds fall into these categories, because each and every breed has its own specific style. My counter-argument is that they do, since all styles exploit the character of the dog's natural coat and body shape (created by the dog's musculoskeletal apparatus).

All breeds, and in fact all dogs, can and do therefore fall into one of these three categories.

The character of the coat is simply adapted by styling it to suit breed preference and the morphology of the dog, or the coat is sculptured into a shape that suits the desires of the owner. Examples of this practice are where we change the natural character of the coat to suit our own preferences. By selectively breeding dogs with the alopecia gene, for example, we are able to produce dogs with very little hair. Another example is provided by the selective breeding of the Bichon Frisé

Fig. 17.4.46   This ten-month-old Bichon Frisé X Shih Tzu has been styled into a variation of the short-legged terrier cut, as are lots of pet dogs of similar stature, including the Lhasa Apso and the Shih Tzu. The puppy is going through a coat change. The coat is soft and knots up easily, so to help with grooming until the coat matures, the excess hair on the undercarriage has been removed and the head has been styled into a short pompom or round shape.

Fig. 17.4.47   It could be argued that the American Cocker Spaniel is styled in a variation of the short-legged terrier cut. Notice how the body furnishings resemble those of the Scottish Terrier. When the tail is undocked, it is trimmed like that of the Sealyham. The main difference is that the ears are styled like those of other spaniels. (Photo: Michael Trafford)

to change the character of the coat from being fine, silky and falling in soft corkscrew curls to a woolly coat, so that we can fluff dry it straight and style or sculpt the coat as we wish.

The breeds most commonly associated with sculpting are the Bichon Frisé and the Poodle. The reason for this is that their coats are naturally long and shapeless, but once cleaned and stretch-dried straight to remove the curls the coat becomes very dense and buoyant and can be fashionably sculpted and shaped. The styling of these two breeds in particular is interpreted by the individual talent and creativity of the groomer.

And it is all about fashion and preferences. Although the Bichon Frisé (*see* Fig 17.4.48 and 17.4.49) is now often styled and shaped for the show ring (see 'Styling the Bichon Frisé'), it

is not in fact a requirement as the dog can be shown in a natural untrimmed coat. In the United Kingdom it is recommended that the Poodle is shown in a

traditional 'lion' haircut but this again is not essential and Poodles can be (and are) shown in other styles, if the owner so wishes.

Fig. 17.4.48   The Bichon Frisé has a coat that is stretched and fluff-dried for styling. Whilst it could be argued that the style is unique and cannot be categorized into any one of the recognized coat styles, take a second look. The style is based on the body and leg styling of the long-legged terrier with a round or pompom head shape! (Photo: Michael Trafford)

Styling the Bichon Frisé

The Bichon Frisé has a soft woolly coat that doesn't moult and usually falls in long gentle curls; we can dry the coat straight and fluff it up so that we can style it. There is no hard and fast rule as to how the Bichon should be styled, and the pet style can be very different from the showing style. Show dogs tend to have a lot more coat, which is styled to give the impression of a solid, chunky little dog without any hard lines in the trim.

Fig 17.4.49 On this show dog you can see the gentle curves that are styled into the long coat to give that chunky impression. The shape is a variation on the long-legged terrier style with the body shape being hand scissored because the wool coat cannot be stripped, and the feet blended into the leg hair. The style exaggerates the angulation of the hind leg and shows a well-developed chest. Note the angle of the undercarriage, styled to give the impression of a deep ribcage. The spherical head shape is adapted to blend with a gentle curve into the body coat on the withers, giving the impression of a solid chunky neck. Whereas the impression of the long-legged terrier is for sharpness and elegance, adapting it to leave extra length gives the dog the appearance of stockiness and substance. (Photo: Michael Trafford)

Fig. 17.4.50 Styled with the same technique as used on the Poodle coat, from the back view you can see how the legs have been shaped to blend into the body coat at the hip. The hair is again left long to give the impression of chunkiness.

Fig 17.4.51 From the front you can see the cylindrical legs, again chunky, full and blended into the shoulder. The ears are shaped into the spherical style of the head, and the hair has been trimmed back a little to clear the eyes.

The length of hair left on this dog would be problematic for most pet owners, so generally you will be asked to cut the hair shorter. From clipped bodies to clipped faces to clipped feet, all are possible because, like the Poodle's, this coat can be styled into whichever shape the owner requires. (Photo: Michael Trafford)

It is possible to leave a long coat looking untrimmed but considerably shorter than its natural length by carefully layering the coat. The style retains the long and natural effect but the hair length is actually very much shorter (*see* Section 17.5).

Heads and faces

Heads and faces can be styled on any dog that has a hair growth pattern that produces either total or partial covering of the head and face. There are several options for you to choose from here.

The spherical (*round*) *head* (*see* 'Styling a spherical head shape') is the style given to dogs that have their facial hair left *in situ* and styled into a round pompom shape. It is generally the recognized style for the Bichon Frisé (*see* Fig. 17.4.52) and the West Highland Terrier (*see* Fig. 17.4.53), but it can also be used on some Poodles, pet-trimmed Yorkshire Terriers, Shih Tzus (*see* Fig. 17.4.54), Lhasa Apsos, Dandie Dinmont Terriers (*see* Fig. 17.4.55) and also on the fashionable Cocker Spaniel cross Poodle – the Cockapoo. This style works best on dogs where the length of the skull and the length of the nose are about equal, or on brachycephalics where the excessively short nose and long skull produce a natural spherical shape. Long-nosed dogs are more challenging to shape correctly.

The *egg-shaped head* (*see* 'Styling a Bedlington Terrier head shape') is given exclusively to the Bedlington Terrier. The hair is prepared like that of the Poodle, stretched and fluff-dried, and the sides of the face and the lower mandible only are shaved, leaving the hair on the maxilla. The head is then scissored into an 'oval' or 'egg shape'.

Fig. 17.4.52 *The spherical head shape of the Bichon Frisé. (Photo: Michael Trafford)*

Fig. 17.4.54 *The spherical head shape of brachycephalic breeds like the Shih Tzu shape easily into the round style.*

Fig. 17.4.53 *The spherical head shape of the West Highland Terrier. When you are shaping this style on a West Highland in the grooming room, the coat will be soft from bathing and it may not hold this round pompom or 'apple' shape. A tiny bit of chalk brushed into the coat and then brushed out again helps the coat stand firm.*

Fig. 17.1.55 *The round head style of the Dandie Dinmont Terrier.*

Styling the West Highland Terrier (spherical) head

This head shape is the same shape as the pompoms you have been practising with. From whatever angle you look at this head, you should be able to visualize a sphere. The length of the nose has an influence on the length of the hair that you need to leave on the dog to maintain the round shape, but take care not to compromise shape for untidiness. If the hair is too long, it will be too heavy to hold the shape and will hang down from the cheeks, giving the head a long, narrow appearance. This head shape can be used on any dog that has a spherical head shape and enough coat to style, including Yorkshire Terriers, Shih Tzus and Lhasa Apsos in pet trim.

Fig. 17.4.56 *Start by clipping or stripping the hair from the top of the pinna to approximately a third of its length. Keep the index finger on your supporting hand level with the clipper blade so the pinna is sandwiched between the two whilst you are doing this to prevent the ear bending away from the blade as you try to clip.*

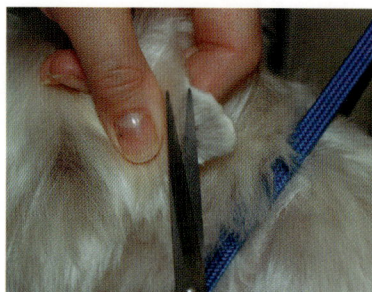

Fig. 17.4.57 *Comb the hair up the length of the pinna and, using either straight or blending scissors, carefully cut the hair from the back of the pinna so that it makes a clean transition edge with your clipping.*

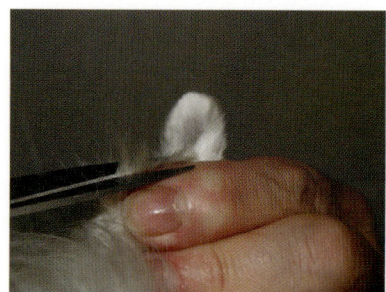

Fig. 17.4.58 *Comb the hair up around the ear and trim it all to the level of your clipper line.*

Fig.17.4.60   Starting on either side of the head, comb the hair down and, using either straight or blending scissors, and with the clipper line as your starting point, visualize an arc to end at the tip of the nose and cut your shape.

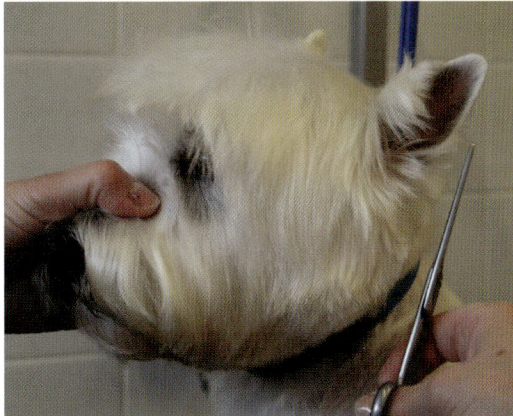

Fig.17.4.61   Here you can see the trimmed left-hand side of the head and the untrimmed right-hand side.

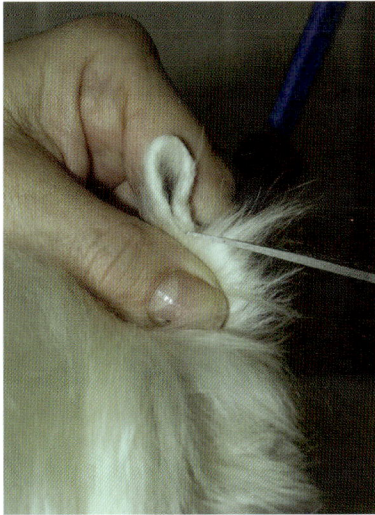

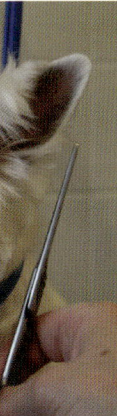

Fig .17.4.59   Comb the hair upwards from the cheek and trim any long ends level with your clipper line. The clipper line indicates the outer edge of your sphere, and the length of the hair between the skin on the head and the clipper line indicates how much hair you need to leave on to make the round head shape.

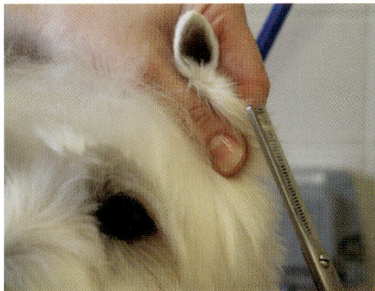

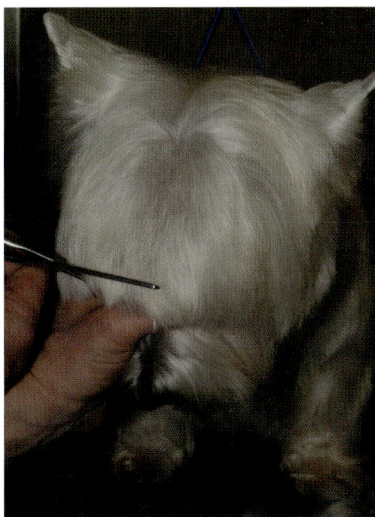

Fig.17.4.62   Complete the other side of the head first by combing and then by cutting an arc from the tip of the nose to the clip line on the pinna.

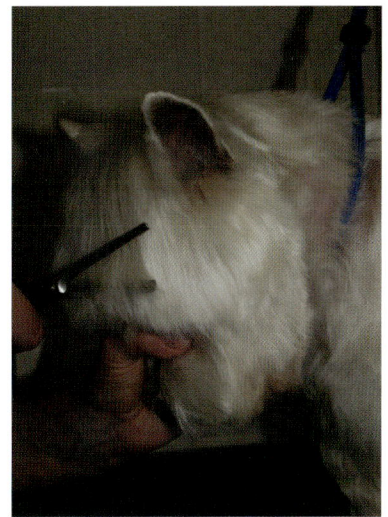

LEFT: Fig.17.4.63   When you are working towards the ear, use thinning or blending scissors for safety and hold the pinna firmly to prevent the ear from flinching.

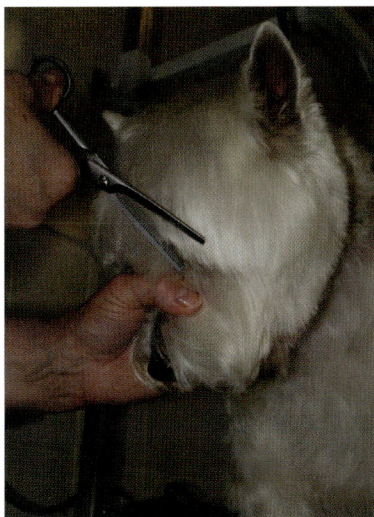

Fig.17.4.64   Comb the hair from the cranium forward. Rest the side of your thumb against the stop to give you a guide and cut a straight line long enough to just span the bridge of the nose. From this marker line, you will be able to shape the front sides of the head into the cheeks when the dog puts his head up.

Fig.17.4.65   Comb the hair forward again and, from your front marker, shape the fringe into the cheeks.

Fig.17.4.66   Use blending scissors or thinning scissors to taper the front edge of the head.

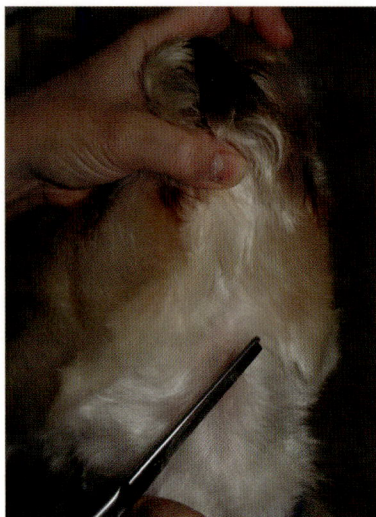

Fig. 17.4.67   Remove the hair between the mandibles to give a neat throat.

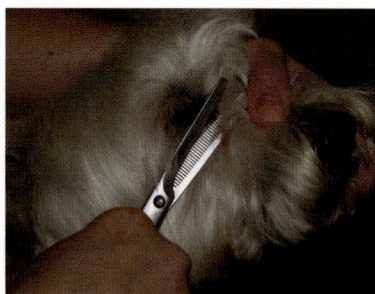

Fig. 17.4.68   Use thinning or blending scissors to clear the hair from in front of the eyes. Note how the centre of the scissor blade is doing the cutting, with the blade tip placed well past the eye for safety.

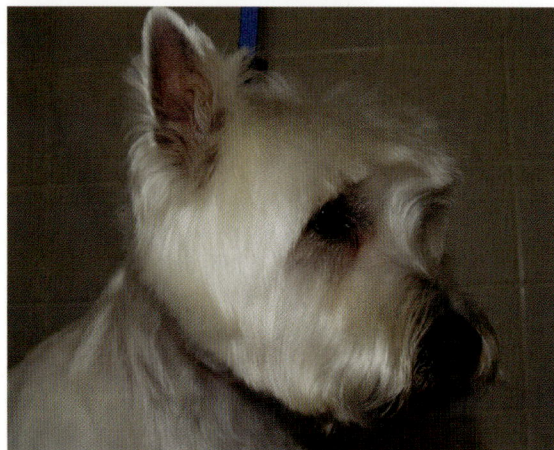

Fig. 17.4.69   Tidy the hair in a straight line across the nape of the neck and comb the whole head forward to show up any missed hairs. It is silky coated and slightly long in the nose for a perfect sphere, but the head on this dog is neat and as round as possible.

Styling the egg-shaped head – the Bedlington Terrier

This head shape is exclusive to the Bedlington Terrier. The coat is prepared by drying it straight and fluff-drying. The Bedlington has a soft 'linty' wool coat that wrinkles and curls as soon as it attracts any damp, so you will need to keep using your comb to straighten out the coat. Some groomers find it easier to shape the head after grooming it through and allowing the dog to shake so the coat is in a natural position. Others prefer to comb the hair from side to side to style it. Try both ways to find which suits you best.

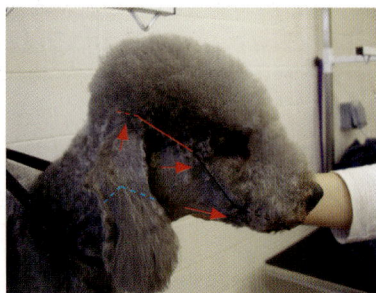

Fig. 17.4.70   Start by combing the hair thoroughly. Using a fine clipping blade in reverse, clip a line from the junction with the ear to the outside corner of the eye (red line). Clip the cheek to a line from the outside corner of the eye to the junction of the lips (black line). Clip the hair away from the lower mandible (black dotted line). Clear the sides of the cheeks. Using the same blade in reverse, clip the pinna to the root of the ear (red dotted line), leaving an inverted 'V' (blue dotted line) at the bottom.

RIGHT: Fig. 17.4.72   When you look down on the head you should be able to visualize your 'egg' shape with the nose being the pointed end of the egg.

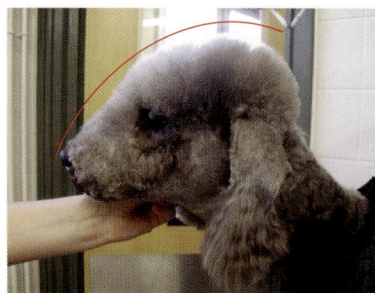

Fig. 17.4.71   From the side aspect, you are aiming at styling an arc from the tip of the nose over the top of the head to the occiput. The back of the head is rounded into the neck by continuing the arc.

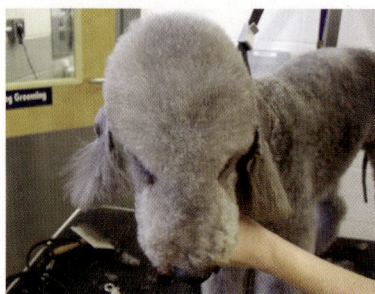

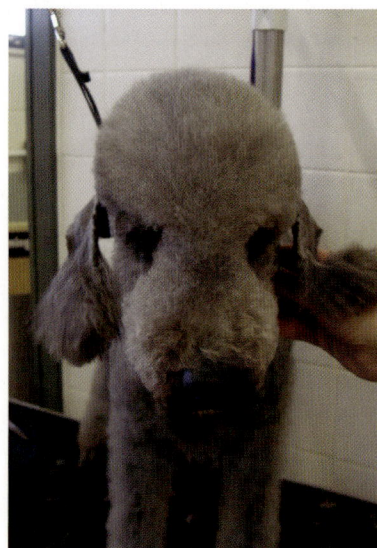

Fig. 17.4.73   The head shape should not have any hard edges or give any impression of sharpness to the shape. It has rounded edges, just like the egg it represents. Here you can see the hair has been cleared around the eyes and curved gently around the upper foreface. The ears have been finished by styling the lower edge into a 'V' shape.

The *topknot* is the name given to the fluffy dome styled onto the top of the Poodle's head. The topknot can be shaped either into a 'cap', where the dome is separated from the back of the neck with a cutting line, or into a 'helmet', where the back of the dome is shaped into the hair on the back of the neck.

A variation of the topknot is styled onto the Dandie Dinmont Terrier. In this breed the topknot is not fashioned in the same sculpted manner as it is in the Poodle; this is because the coat is soft and silky. It is left longer than the Poodle topknot and is styled tactfully to reduce the length of the hair as required. This is achieved by gently pulling out stray or extra long hairs so that the topknot blends into the hair on the foreface and falls gracefully onto the neck and over the top of the ears.

A topknot is also the name that groomers use to describe the tying-up of the hair on the top of the head with bands or ribbons. Traditionally this was a method used by hunters working with Poodles, when a length of coloured rag was tied into the dog's head hair for identification. Nowadays, however, it is used for keeping long hair away from the eyes of the dog and can often be seen on Poodles, Bearded Collies, Maltese Terriers and Yorkshire Terriers in the show ring.

The *clean face* (*see* Chapter 14: 'Clipping a Poodle face'), as its name suggests, removes all the hair on the foreface of the dog to leave a smooth finish, usually by clipping, although wire coats and silk coats can be plucked. It does not mean removing the hair from the top of the head.

The *clean head* is where the skull of the dog is either clipped or plucked to remove all the hair, including eyebrows. The head of the English Cocker Spaniel is a good example of this practice.

The *Rosette* (*see* Figs 17.4.74a-b) is the shape styled onto the front of the cranium of the American Cocker Spaniel. Exclusive to this breed, the rosette is shaped in a semi-circle, reaching back from the outside corner of one eye to the outside corner of the other. The edges of the circle are tapered to blend into the short-clipped head.

Fig. 17.4.74a-b   The rosette styled onto the cranium of the American Cocker Spaniel. Fig. 17.4.74a shows the rosette spanning from the outside of one eye to the outside of the other. Fig. 17.4.74b shows the back edge blended into the clipped skull.

Eyebrows

These fall into three basic categories:

◆ **Long split,** where the eyebrows extend down the length of the nose but are trimmed to separate between the eyes. The part of the eyebrow that crosses the outside corner of the eye can be trimmed shorter so that the dog can see. These eyebrows are seen on the Scottish Terrier (*see* Fig. 17.4.75) and Schnauzers.
◆ **Short split,** where the eyebrows are trimmed short. The eyebrows are separated by removing the hair between them. Some breeds have short hairs on the bridge of the nose that are left in situ to form only a slight definition between the eyebrows. Short split eyebrows are seen on Airedale Terriers, Wire Fox Terriers (*see* Fig. 17.4.76) and most other long-legged terriers.
◆ **Centre fall,** where the eyebrow extends well down the foreface towards the nostrils and is not separated between the eyes. The side of the eyebrow, the bit crossing the eye, can be trimmed shorter so the dog can see more clearly. These eyebrows are seen on Lakeland Terriers (*see* Fig. 17.4.77), Soft-Coated Wheaten Terriers and Kerry Blue Terriers.

Fig. 17.4.75   The long split eyebrows of the Scottish Terrier. Note how the hair is very long at the inside corners of the eye but the eyebrows are styled shorter just across the eye, to clear the area of vision. The style is also used on the three sizes of Schnauzer.

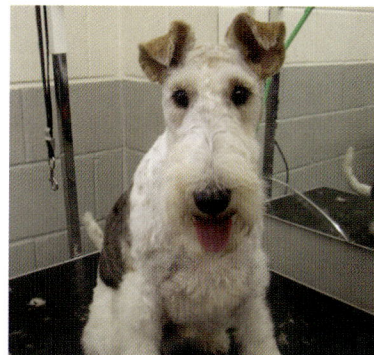

Fig. 17.4.76   Short split eyebrows on a Wire Fox Terrier. The hair between the eyes is shortened to show two definite eyebrows, and the eyebrows themselves are styled short, following the natural curve of the brow with either blending scissors or by plucking. This style of eyebrow can be used on any dog that has facial furnishings but always check if you are styling terriers to their breed requirements as eyebrow shape differs between breeds.

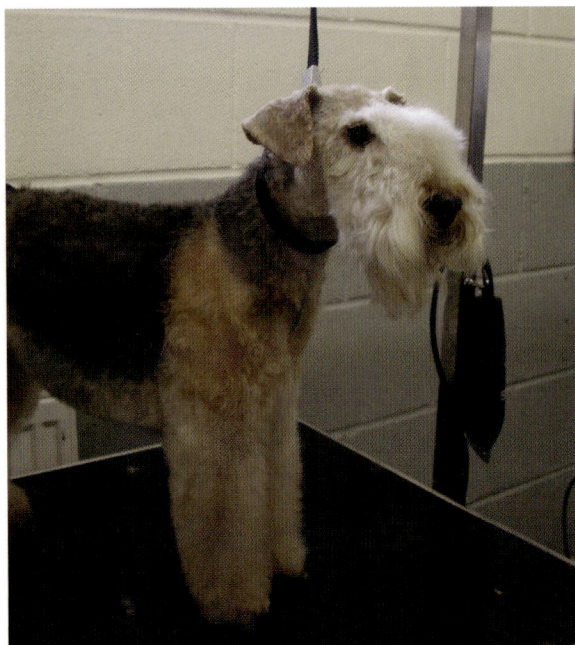

Fig. 17.4.77 *Centre fall eyebrows do literally as their name suggests; the hair is left to grow over both eyes and span the stop. Just enough hair on the sides of the brow is removed so that the dog can see.*

◆ *Round:* this is a shape that is styled onto a breed rather than growing into a natural shape. It was once very common on Poodles but in the UK the style has almost died out, although it remains very popular on the continent. The sides of the face are clipped, leaving the fore-face covered in hair to give shape to a full beard (*see* Fig. 17.4.80). The hair is then styled into a circle around the mouth (*see* Fig. 17.4.81). The shape can be transformed into a 'moustache' by simply removing the hair from the lower jaw (*see* Fig. 17.4.82).

Fig. 17.4.80 *The round beard is styled on Poodles by clipping the cheeks and the bridge of the nose, but leaving the hair where a natural beard would grow.*

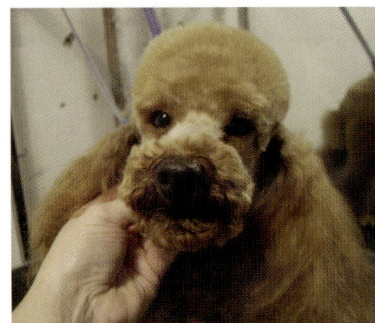

Beards

Beards can be tailored, full or round.

◆ *Tailored:* this is where the hair has been removed completely from the cheeks and is left to start taper-ing in length as it comes down the sides of the foreface. The hair cover-ing the back half of the lips is quite short, with the hair on the front half of the lips being left longer to reach its longest point right at the very front of the mouth (*see* Fig. 17.4.78). From the side aspect, the beard is styled into a triangle, tapering from the side of the lips to the front of the mouth. From the front aspect, the beard squares off the foreface, giving a rectangu-lar or brick shape to the head (*see* Fig. 17.4.79). This style of beard is seen on most of the long-legged terriers and ranges from quite a lot of beard on the Airedale Terrier to just a few hairs on the end of the jaw (goatee beard) of the Irish Ter-rier.

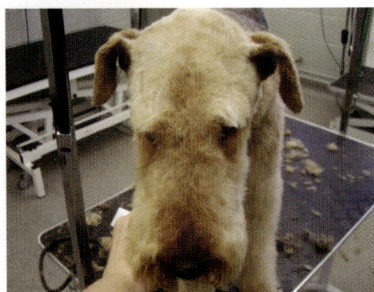

Fig. 17.4.79 *From the front aspect, the tailored beard should square off the shape of the foreface to give a 'brisk' or rectangular shape to the head.*

◆ *Full:* in this style the hair is cleared or shortened on the cheeks but left long to cover the foreface and the lips. The beard is left untrimmed unless it becomes too long, when tactful styling with blending scis-sors can shorten the length. Care should be taken never to over-trim these beards as the desired effect is supposed to preserve the natural shape. This beard is seen on Schnauzers, and to an even fuller extent on the Kerry Blue and on the Soft-Coated Wheaten Terrier.

Fig. 17.4.78 *From the side aspect, the tailored beard is shaped to a point at the front of the mouth. The sides are tapered towards the back of the beard. The tailored beard can vary in the starting position along the lip line so if you are styling for breed requirements, check with current fashion; otherwise, the most important point is to keep the shape neat.*

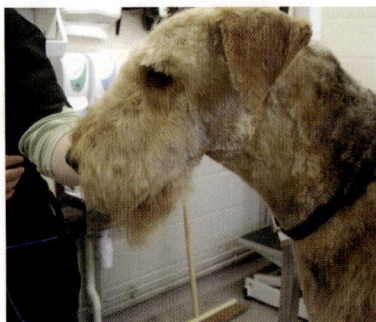

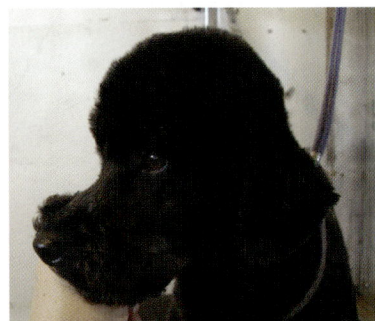

Fig. 17.4.81 *The beard is then styled into a circle around the mouth.*

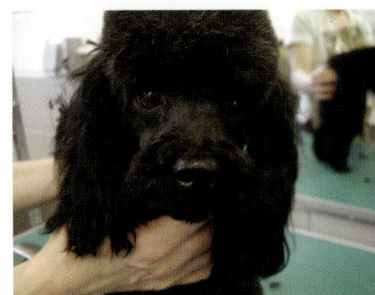

Fig. 17.4.82 *The moustache is styled by removing the hair from the bottom jaw.*

Feet

There are three basic foot styles: clipped, circular and natural.

- *Clipped* feet are usual for Poodles and Bedlington Terriers but there is no reason why it cannot be done on other breeds as well, particularly where there are medical reasons or the owner feels that the dog may benefit from having it done. Poodle feet are easy to clip because the feet are webbed and the toes splay widely apart, leaving plenty of room to work. Bedlington Terrier feet do not splay so easily but the foot is only clipped to the second joint on the two centre toes and to the first joint on the outside toes, making the job easier. If you are asked to trim the feet of other breeds, such as the Bichon Frisé, remember not to use too short a blade until the dog's skin is used to being clipped. You may also find it helpful to use a toe blade with this breed because the feet are not webbed.

- *Circular* feet (*see* 'Styling a circular foot') may be shaped to be included into a cylindrical-shaped leg, as in the Bichon Frisé or long-legged terriers, styled as on a Cocker Spaniel, where the foot should appear round and padded, or simply trimmed on long-coated breeds such as the Bearded Collie, where the long hair on the feet is shortened for convenience or tidiness. The shape is created by cutting the shape of the foot into a circle at ground level and then rounding the foot in a gentle curve upwards towards the leg. The shape of your rounded foot depends on the coat type and volume. Wool coats that have been dried to increase density will hold a very rounded pompom shape, whereas other coats that are dried straight produce a flattened circle because the coat does not have the volume to prevent it from hanging downwards. The shaping of the round foot can be improved by cutting the hair on the front of the foot back towards the toes. This shortens the length of the foot (from back to front) and stops you producing a 'boot' shape. If you do this, remember to reshape the sides of your circle so that you are not creating a 'square' or straightened front edge.

Styling a Circular Foot

Fig. 17.4.83   This foot belongs to a Bichon crossed with a Shih Tzu and the dog has a wool coat.

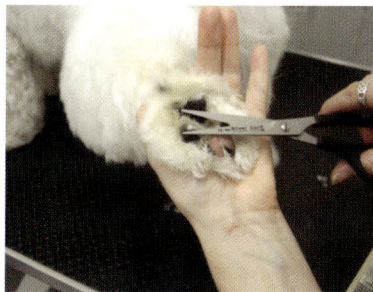

Fig. 17.4.84   Start trimming a round foot by clearing the hair from between the foot pads with your straight scissors so that the pads are visible. While working on the underside of the foot, you will be using a forehand cut.

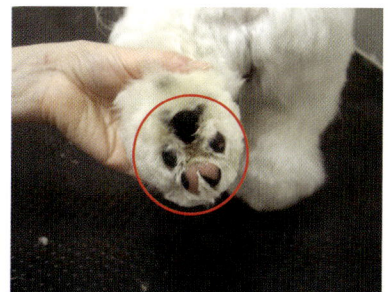

Fig. 17.4.85   Once cleared and the foot pads are visible, shape a circle around the foot.

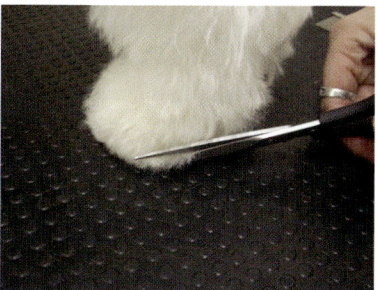

Fig. 17.4.86   Distance your circle to leave quite a length of hair on the sides of the foot so that when the foot is placed on the table, you will have plenty of hair to make adjustments to your shape.

Fig. 17.4.87   Using a backhand cut, shape and style the foot up from the table up towards the leg.

Fig. 17.4.88   Remember to continue shaping towards the inside of the leg

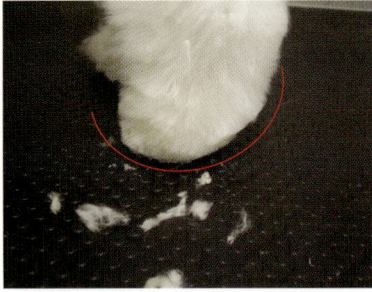

Fig. 17.4.89   You are aiming at making a gentle curve around the foot and upwards from table to form part of a sphere or pompom shape

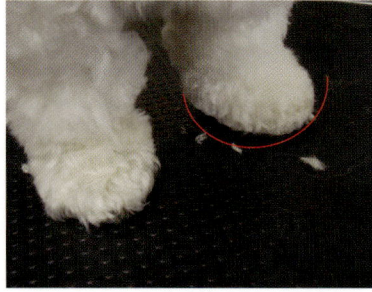

Fig. 17.4.90   When you look down from above the dog, the foot should be styled into a circle at ground level.

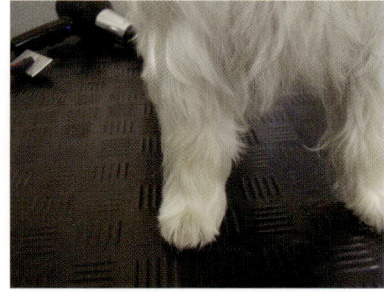

Fig. 17.4.91   This wire-coated Cairn Terrier also has a circular-shaped foot. The coat is not as dense as the Bichon X but the foot is trimmed in the same way.

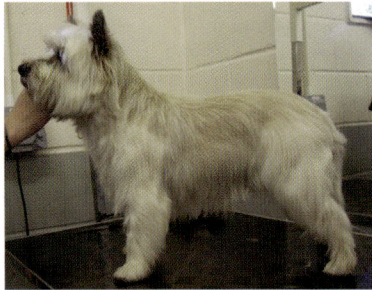

Fig. 17.4.92   The Cairn Terrier's finished feet will not look as compact as the wool coat because the coat does not have the volume but they should still be circular in shape.

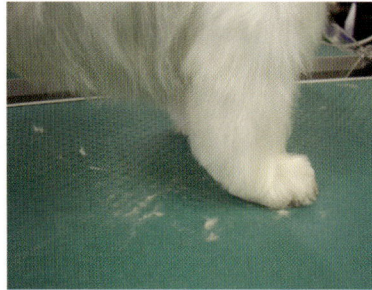

Fig. 17.4.93   This front foot belongs to a West Highland Terrier. The coat is longer and denser than that of the Cairn Terrier and not as coarse in texture so the styled shape of the foot is more obvious. Note how the feet have been curved up into the legs to accommodate the dog's country lifestyle.

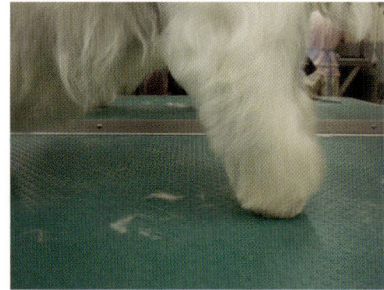

Fig. 17.4.94   At the owner's request, the leg hair on this dog has been trimmed to lift the feathering well off of the ground. Note how the circular foot shape has also been trimmed well up from ground level.

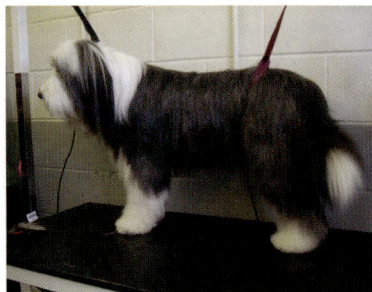

Fig. 17.4.95   The circular feet on this silk-coated Bearded Collie have not been trimmed into a compact ball because the coat will not hold the shape. Instead the foot has been shaped at table level only with just the very front and the backs of the feet being shaped up into the leg.

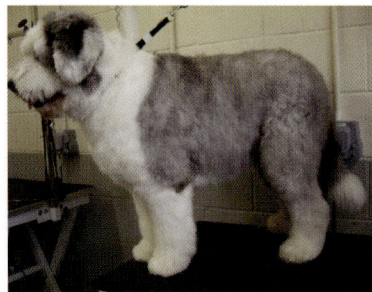

Fig. 17.4.96   The Old English Sheepdog has by contrast a much denser woollier coat and the feet can be styled into balls.

Fig. 17.4.97   This photo shows a Cockapoo that has inherited the woolly coat of the Poodle. The coat has been styled into a Long Legged Terrier trim, therefore the feet are shaped into balls. Another option for this dog would have been to clip the feet.

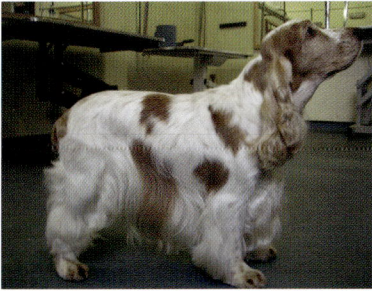

Fig. 17.4.98   The Cocker Spaniel is another breed that has circular feet. Owners of Spaniels will, however, often request that the hair is removed from between the toes to prevent knots and matts forming.

◆   *Natural* feet (*see* 'Styling a natural foot') are literally trimmed to look like feet, with the outline of the toes, pads and foot shape all clearly visible. You are aiming at producing a foot shape that resembles the foot on a smooth-coated dog. The hair on the foot should be the same length as the hair on the leg, and it gives an overall impression of being neat and tidy. Natural feet are styled onto those dogs that have body furnishings, such as Border Collies, Golden Retrievers, English Springer Spaniels and Setters, amongst many others.

Styling a Natural Foot

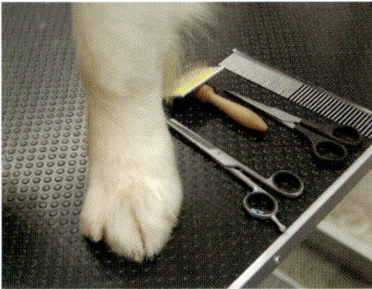

Fig. 17.4.99   To style a natural shaped foot, you need a fine slicker brush to pull up the hair, a medium and a fine comb, a pair of straight scissors and a pair of thinning scissors.

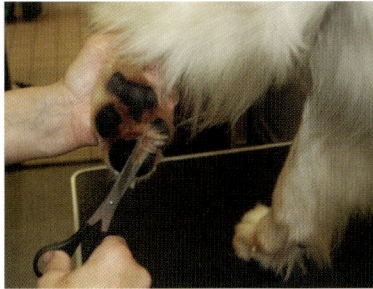

Fig.17.4.100   Use your straight scissors to remove the hair between the pads, leaving enough hair to protect the skin. Clipping the hair can and often does encourage folliculitis where the unprotected skin rubs and chaffs as the dog uses its foot, particularly when the feet are wet. If you prefer you can use bull nosed scissors.

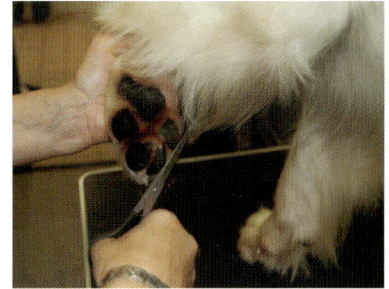

Fig.17.4.101   Use your straight scissors to take back the hair to the level of the foot pad.

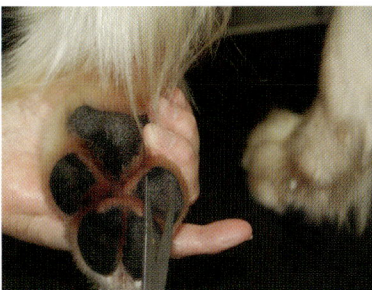

Fig.17.4.102   Removing the hair leaves the pad free to make contact with the ground as the dog walks. This in turn stimulates the blood supply to the foot and allows the nails to wear down on hard ground.

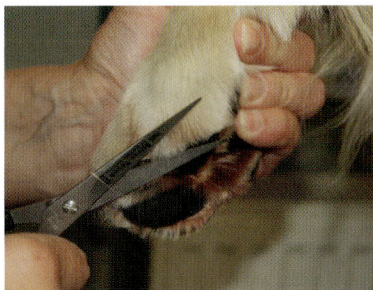

Fig.17.4.103   Remember also to trim the hair on the sides of the pads.

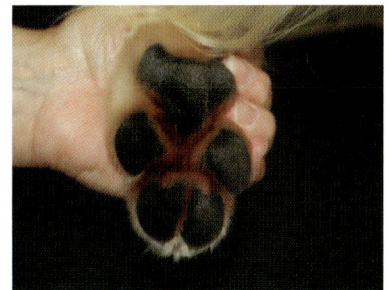

Fig.17.4.104   Once all the hair has been removed, the whole of the underside of the foot should be neat and tidy.

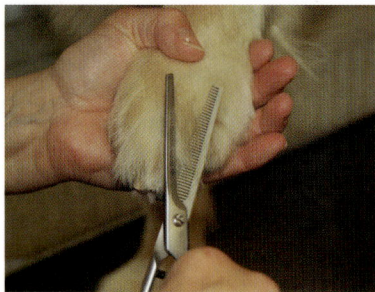

Fig.17.4.105 *Brush the hair upwards on the top of the foot and it will lift the hair from between the toes. This can then be removed with thinning or blending scissors.*

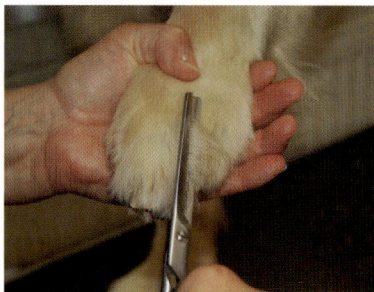

Fig.17.4.106 *Keep your hands soft and open to encourage the dog not to pull away and only cut off the hairs that are longer than the hair on the top of the foot.*

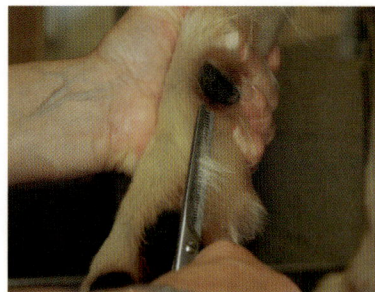

Fig.17.4.107 *The front feet on this Retriever can have the hair removed up to the stopper pad. This is done with thinning or blending scissors and the idea is to help the water to drip from the leg furnishings before it reaches the foot.*

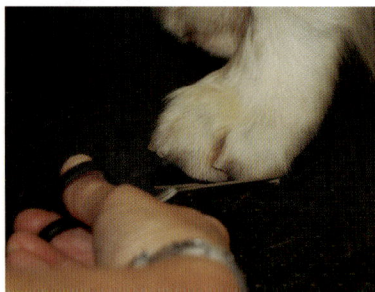

Fig.17.4.108 *With the foot on the ground, use your straight scissors to nip off any ends that spoil your shape.*

Tails

The tail balances the back end of the dog. The coat texture and coat growth pattern both have a bearing on how the tail is styled but in the UK, with the introduction of the law against tail docking, traditional ideas on tail shape are having to be revised. This is partly because tails on some breeds have been docked for many generations, and people had more or less forgotten how the breed actually carried its tail. The reintroduction of the tail has also highlighted problems with the sanitary areas of some heavily coated breeds like the Old English Sheepdog. Likewise, the traditional pompom on the Poodle that once waved cheerfully above the body of the dog is now a cylindrical shape that often lies on the dog's back, causing knotting to the tail and the body coat as it moves.

The most important thing about tails is that hygiene must take priority. The underside of the tail should be trimmed free of hair for several centimetres to clear it away from the rectum. In dogs that suffer from incontinence or stomach disorders, the tail is best trimmed to remove any excessive length of feathering that gets in the way.

Generally speaking, there are several tail shapes to choose from.

◆ A *flagged* tail is the natural shape for many silk and double coats that have furnishings but it can be styled into any coat that has enough length. It takes its description from the triangular shape of the pennant flag; it does in fact wave like a flag and is usually carried level with or lower than the dock. This is the tail shape that you see on silk-coated Setters and Spaniels, double-coated Retrievers (*see* Fig. 17.4.109) and wire-coated Dandie Dinmont Terriers (*see* Fig. 17.4.110), amongst many others. The hair is removed, or shortened, on the underside to clear the rectum and the long feathering is then shaped into either a gentle curve or a more precise pennant.

◆ Just like the tail on a squirrel, the *squirrel* tail is cylindrical in shape. It is a good alternative to the pompom on undocked Poodles (*see* Fig. 17.4.111) and really suits Shih Tzus and Lhasa Apsos in pet trim. The tail is clipped short to clear the hair from around the root, separating it from the body by enough length to clear the rectum, and it is generally trimmed into a tube so that the hair is between 2 and 6cm in length, depending on the size of the dog and the length of the hairstyle.

◆ Traditionally recognized as a Poo-

Fig. 17.4.109 *The double-coated Golden Retriever with the classic 'flagged' tail. This shape can be used on most dogs that have long tail furnishings but the shape will differ according to the coat density and length.*

Fig. 17.4.110 The Dandie Dinmont tail does not have the density, texture or length of the Retriever in the previous picture, but the tail will naturally form a 'flag' shape. (Photo: Michael Trafford)

Fig. 17.4.111 This four-month-old Poodle puppy has an undocked tail. The tail cannot be styled into a classic pompom shape so it is already being shaped into a 'squirrel' tail.

dle tail, the pompom is styled by sculpting the coat. The base of the tail is clipped to clear the rectum and the hair is then shaped up into a ball. It is difficult to suggest a size for the pompom because it will be determined to an extent by the length of the tail, but start by taking some of the hair off the end of the tail, leaving about the same length as you have on the top of the head (on the topknot). Then trim the pompom into shape, using the end of the tail as a guide. When you become better at 'balancing' your styling, this is one area where you may want to make adjustments.

◆ The *natural* tail, as the name suggests, is left as natural as possible. It ranges from the untouched tails of breeds such as the Saluki, to the Lowchen, where the base of the tail is clipped to clear the rectum, whilst leaving the tail feathering untouched, to the long silky hairs on the tail of the Japanese Chin. The hairs on the underside of the tail or the root can be shortened to clear the rectum but the feathering should be long and sleek. The tail can be trailed low from the dock or it can be tossed over the back in a

relaxed but elegant fashion. If you have to shorten these tails, hold the tail out horizontally, comb the hair down towards the table and use blending scissors to cut inverted 'V' shapes along the span of the feathers to reduce the length but take care to make only one cut on each side of the inverted 'V' and, when you reach the end of the tail, comb it and assess the length of the hair before you remove any more.

◆ *Clean* tails are left without any feathers or furnishings, and this is generally recognized as the tail style for terriers. The tail is not clipped but instead either plucked or scissored into a shape that balances the style and the morphology of the dog. That is to say, the tail should be left with a thicker covering on a dog of chunky build than on a dog that is finer in build. An example of this is the West Highland Terrier, a short-legged dog that is chunky and square so the tail is styled into a chunky 'carrot' shape to match the body. An Irish Terrier, by contrast, is smart, neat and tailored so the tail is also neat and tailored. A clean tail can be styled onto any dog where tail feathers are either not suitable

or where the dog has been clipped to remove the entire coat. It is also a popular choice for woolly coated Labradoodles (Labrador x Poodle) and, in Europe, for Poodles.

◆ *Clipped* tails are the style of choice for Bedlington Terriers (see Fig. 17.4.112), clipped Irish Water Spaniels and Curly-Coated Retrievers. The tail is clipped with a fine blade in reverse from the tip towards the base, leaving the last few centimetres of hair on the top of the tail to be scissored. The underside of the tail is clipped short up to the root so that the rectum is cleared. The tail resembles that of a rat and, whilst it is common on the breeds listed, it is not a popular style because it does leave the tail open to injury through the loss of the protective hair cover.

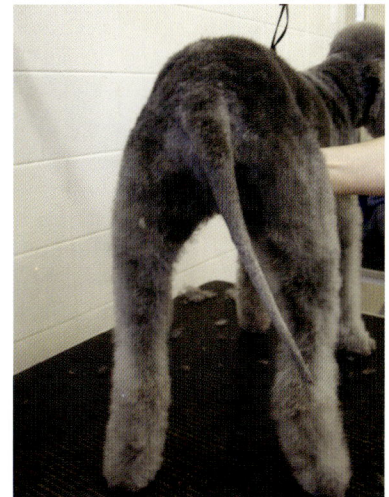

Fig. 17.4.112 The clipped 'rat' tail of the Bedlington Terrier. The root of the tail is left with a covering of hair whilst the rest of the tail is clipped with a fine blade against the coat growth.

Ears

Ear styles are very basic and it is easy to decide which one is most suitable for the dog because the shape of the ear and the way the dog holds his ears offer a good indication as to the way that you should trim them. Again, hygiene takes priority. For heavily coated dogs, it is always best to remove the hair from in front of the ear canal and, where possible, to reduce some of the weight by removing some of the hair from the inside of the pinna.

◆ A *clean ear* describes a pinna that has been plucked or clipped totally free of hair using a fine clipper blade so that it resembles that of a smooth-coated breed. Double-coated breeds like the Flat-Coated Retriever often have their ears stripped of long dead hairs by plucking, so that the ear position is improved. Wire-coated breeds, like the Dachshund and the Airedale, similarly have their ears cleaned of hair to enhance a neat tailored head shape. The ears can be cleared of hair on any breed if the need demands and the style suits.

◆ A *partly clipped ear* is one that has been partially cleared of hair by either plucking or clipping. In West Highland Terriers, approximately the top third of the ear is either clipped or plucked to show a neat tidy tip above the pompom head shape. Likewise, in English Cocker, English Springer and American Cocker Spaniels (*see* Fig. 17.4.74b) again approximately the top third of the ear is clipped to lower the position of the ear and to help it hang close to the side of the head. (There is a fold of skin on the front edge of the ear to guide you. Clear the ear to just above the bottom point of the fold.) Many spaniels also have hair on the inside of the ear, which should be removed to reduce the weight of the ear. English and Irish Setters have their ears

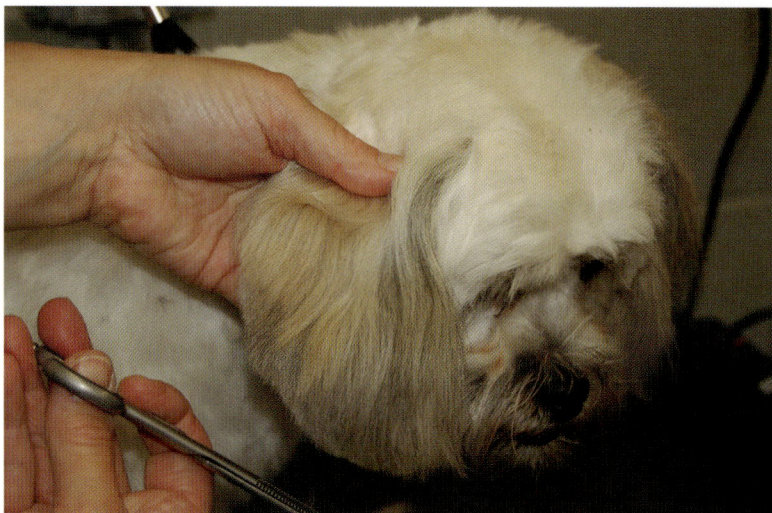

Fig. 17.4.114 *The styled ear can be any shape to compliment your work. Here the ear furnishings are being shaped into a 'bob' by shortening the hair on the back of the pinna and leaving the front edge longer to frame the face. Caution: always cut downwards from the base of the ear. If the dog flinches and you are using your scissors in the other direction, you may cut the ear. The other reason for doing this is that the coat hangs, so you will get a layered cut to the hair.*

clipped or plucked clean, leaving just a light fringe on the front edge only.

◆ *Tasselled ears:* tassels are added to the clipped ears of Bedlington Terriers (*see* Fig. 17.4.113) and Dandie Dinmont Terriers. The ear is clipped with a fine blade, leaving an inverted 'V' of hair at the bottom of the pinna, which can then be styled into a diamond-shaped tassel. Although the tassel is not generally seen on other dogs, there is no reason why it cannot be styled onto any dog with a dropped ear.

◆ *Natural ears*, as the name suggests, are ears that are left with their natural coat furnishings *in situ*. This doesn't mean, however, that the ear furnishings cannot be trimmed to tidy or shorten them. The health of the ear should be the main consideration, and if the weight or the density of the hair means that the pinna cannot lift to allow ventilation, the hair can be shortened on the ends with thinning scissors. Alternatively, some of the weight can be removed by clipping away the inside of the ear.

◆ *Styled ears* are largely up to you, but the style you choose should complement the rest of your work. You need to take into consideration the shape of the head and the length of hair that you have left on the body; you can then shape the ear to flatter the style of head shape that you have created. It may mean that you simply reduce the length of the ear, or you may shape the ear furnishings to follow the shape of the pinna. It may be that you style the ears into a neat 'bob' (*see* Fig. 17.4.114), by shaping the hair to follow the curve of the back of the pinna, leaving the front longer. The choice is yours!

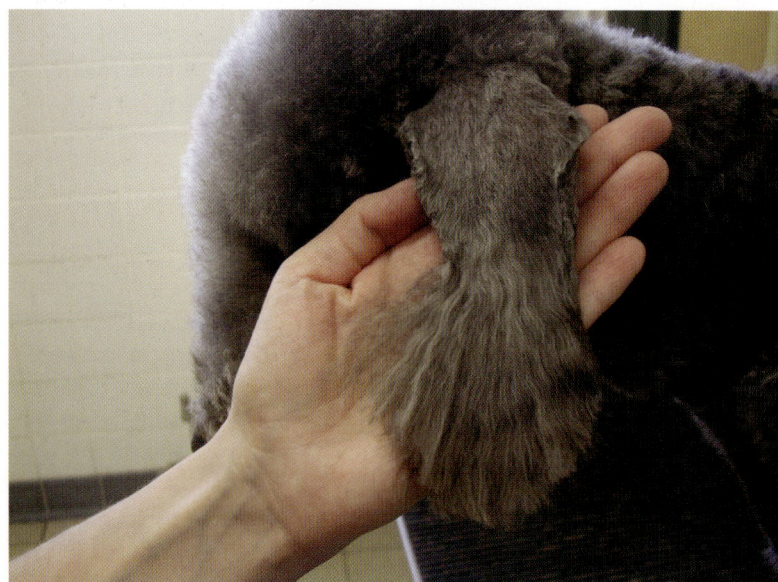

Fig. 17.4.113 *The tasselled ear of the Bedlington Terrier. The ear is clipped and an inverted 'V' is left to grace the bottom of the pinna. It is then styled into a diamond shape.*

17.5 LAYERING WITH SCISSORS

You can use your straight scissors, blending scissors or thinning scissors to reduce coat length, using a forehand cut. This method works particularly well on fine silk coats that have little undercoat, like that of Yorkshire Terriers. This is because the coat can be left with some length and naturally lies flat. The main advantage of this styling method is that you are working well away from the undercoat, so it does not alter the coat by encouraging it to take on a woolly appearance and it allows you to retain the texture and the colour of the coat. On a practical note, it is a very useful method of styling to learn, and I can think of a couple of occasions over the years when a power failure has meant that clippers could not be used, requiring me to resort to 'scissor power'! If you do not have a ready charged cordless clipper handy, you can, with this technique, carry on regardless and get the job done!

Your first attempt at this technique will take you a long time. You should therefore try to start on a small dog, such as a Shih Tzu or a Yorkshire Terrier. Once you have mastered this technique, you may find yourself working almost as fast as you would if you were clipping. And, perhaps most satisfyingly, perfecting this technique enables you to produce a much nicer effect than you can ever achieve with blade attachments.

The nature of this styling technique also means that areas needing to be a little shorter, such as eyebrows and sanitary areas, can be blended into the longer coat without obvious transitions. The entire effect is that of the dog in its natural coat but shorter, as it would have been as a puppy.

There are a few important points you need to know so that you can get this method of styling right:

◆ Your fingers are your guide to the length of hair that you are leaving (*see* Fig. 17.5.2);

◆ In all areas where you want the coat to be an even length, such as on the body and legs, the position of your fingers should remain the same so that the length of hair you are leaving stays the same (do not crumple them up!);

◆ Try to keep the side of your little finger on the dog as much as possible. With the exception of when you are working across the spine (*see* Fig. 17.5.3), keep your fingers pointing in the direction of the lie of the coat (*see* Fig. 17.5.4). This will layer the hair as you cut because every hair will be cut on a different angle depending on whether it is closest to your index finger or your little finger. If you cut the hair across the coat (*see* Fig. 17.5.5), you will get hard straight cut lines rather than soft layered cutting because all the hair will be cut on the same angle and it will not be layered;

◆ In difficult areas, such as under the throat on very small dogs, you may find it easier to turn your hand over (*see* Fig. 17.5.6) but be careful that you do not cut the coat too short or in too large a quantity;

◆ The coat is trimmed in strips that are the same width as the length of your fingers (because they are holding the hair!);

◆ If you start at the withers and work down the spine, the hair will fall either side of the centre back and this gives you a length guide when you come to work on the side;

◆ You need to work *sideways* along the body from shoulder to tail on one side and from tail to shoulder on the other. If you try to work down the coat from spine to table, you may lose your way and over-trim or under-trim some areas;

◆ Your cut lines *must* overlap. You should always have some cut hair and some uncut hair between your fingers;

◆ Use your comb to pick up the hair in *narrow* strips for you to cut – only pick up a 1cm (or less) strip at a time. This keeps your work fine. If you get lazy and use your fingers instead of the comb or pick up too much hair you will cut an unsightly mass and ruin your work (see Fig. 17.5.7);

◆ Rough cut the hairs. Try not to cut the hairs between your fingers 100 per cent even. In fact, your trim will be more natural if they aren't. If you choose to use thinning scissors or blending scissors, do not keep going until all the hairs between your fingers are perfectly even in length;

◆ Once you have cut the hair, do not drop it. Working from behind, slide the comb back in under your little finger and take up another centimetre or so of hair. You will now be holding the hairs that you have just cut and some uncut hair between your fingers. By the third cut, the shortened hairs from your original cut will start to fall from your fingers because you are working away from them; you can then start to see the effects of your work;

◆ You must learn to work so that all the hair you are cutting is being pulled upright towards the ceiling. This is so that the angle of cut on each hair tapers the ends and lies the coat down (*see* Fig. 17.5.8);

◆ Use the same technique over the whole dog, working the coat a little at a time; and

◆ **Do not rush.** Take your time until you have mastered the technique, working slowly and methodically.

Layering a Coat

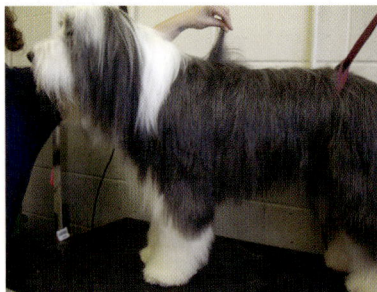

Fig. 17.5.1   The coat of the Bearded Collie represents its breed by looking long and sleek, but note how short the coat actually is.

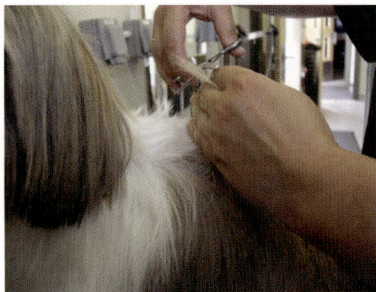

Fig. 17.5.2   With the dog facing away from you and your little finger resting on the dog, use your comb to pick up a narrow strip of hair and roughly cut it with your scissors, thinning scissors or blending scissors. Your finger depth is determining the length of hair that you are leaving.

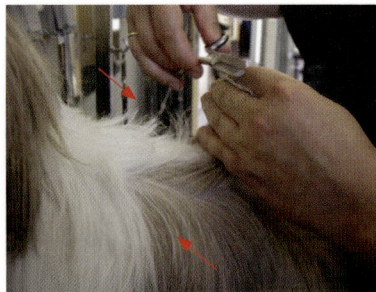

Fig. 17.5.3   Here you can see the fourth cut and how the groomer is starting to work her way down the spine. The arrows show the shortened hair that has fallen from her fingers. The hair has fallen off the centre back and will now be a guide when the groomer starts work on the sides of the dog.

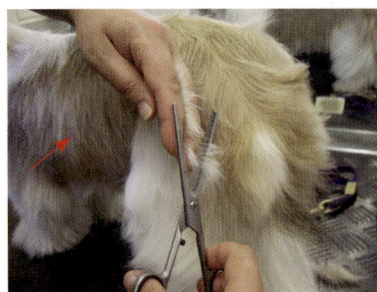

Fig. 17.5.4   The groomer has worked from the shoulder to the tail. This photo illustrates how little hair is being trimmed at any one time. The area marked by the arrow shows how the coat is falling naturally and is unmarked by the cutting process. Note how the little finger is resting on the dog.

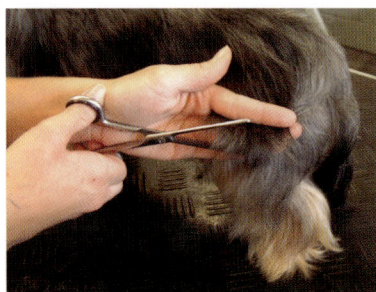

Fig. 17.5.5   If you cut across the coat, you will cut unsightly lines, even if you are using thinning scissors, because the coat will not be layered. The hair between the scissor blades will all be cut on the same angle. Once you are working on the sides of the dog, keep your little finger on the dog, and have your hand following the direction of the coat.

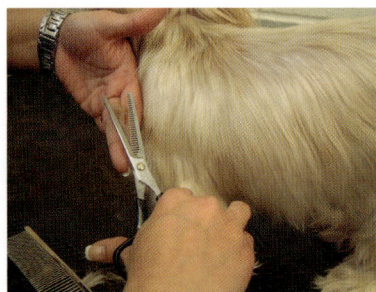

Fig. 17.5.6   In areas where it is difficult to reach, or on very small dogs like this Yorkshire Terrier, turning your hand over so that it can follow the contour of the dog can help. The chest hair on this Yorkshire Terrier is being trimmed short but will still blend in with the rest of the trim. Note how the coat is lying naturally and is unmarked on the body.

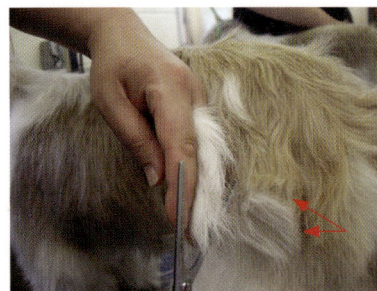

Fig. 17.5.7   This is what happens when you lose patience or work too fast. The groomer has taken up too much hair and the coat is showing hard lines and a choppy appearance.

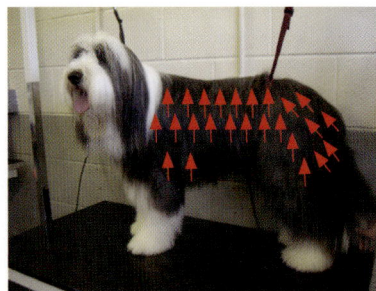

Fig. 17.5.8   Trim in strips, working along the body from the shoulder to the tail on your first side, and from the tail to the shoulder on your second. Make sure that you overlap your work and always pull the hair upwards towards the ceiling to ensure that the lowest part of the hair will not be cut shorter than the uppermost.

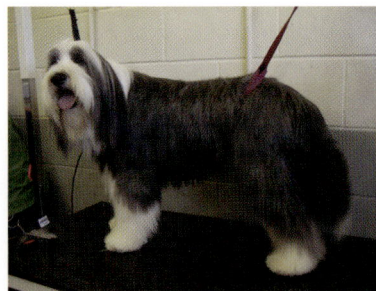

Fig. 17.5.9   To finish the trim, the groomer has rounded off the feet, taken the hair from the front of the eyes with thinning scissors and blended in the dog's shortened eyebrows.

Prepare your work by grooming out and bathing the coat and then stretch-drying it so that the hair is as straight as possible. Start by deciding how long you want to leave the coat and then use the span of your fingers as your guide. It can be anything from one to four fingers' depth and the best place to start is just above the withers.

With the dog facing away from you, use your comb to pick up a small strip of about a centimetre of hair crossing the spine from shoulder to shoulder. Hold the hair that you have picked up between the fingers of your other hand with the side of the little finger resting on the dog (*see* Fig. 17.5.2). Roughly cut the hair so that it is not too straight and severe. Then, with the help of your comb, pick up the next strip and start to work down the spine. The cut hair will start to fall away from the centre back to give you a length guide when you come to work on the sides (*see* Fig. 17.5.3).

Turn the dog sideways on. If you are left-handed, it will be easier for you to start on the right side of the dog; similarly right-handed groomers will find it easier starting on the left side of the dog. The reason for this is because it is easier, when you are learning, to work from shoulder to tail as you benefit from a better view of where you have been working and, by the time you get to the other side, you will feel more confident and be better able to tackle the more awkward side.

Work just off the spine and, starting at the shoulder, close to the withers, pick up your first strip of hair. Cut it and slide the comb under your little finger to pick up the next strip. Work in narrow strips with a few hairs at a time. If you become impatient and take up too much hair at a time, it will make your work rough and untidy (*see* Fig. 17.5.7).

In areas where you want the hair to be shorter, you can turn your hand so that the back of your hand is resting against the dog's body. This will keep your trimmed length even and makes it easier to get into difficult areas (*see* Fig. 17.5.6).

Work along the body to the tail and then go back to your starting point. This strip starts approximately four fingers' depth down from your last strip. And so it goes on until you have finished the body and the legs (*see* Fig. 17.5.8). Now turn the dog to face the other way and, using the same technique, but starting at the tail end, work your strips forwards towards the shoulder to complete this side.

Chest and tail furnishings can be shortened to whatever length is appropriate for the dog. Similarly, eyebrows can be blended shorter if desired to suit the owner's wishes. The feet will need clearing between the pads and can then be trimmed into a round shape to the length the owner has requested (*see* Fig. 17.5.9).

This method of styling is an excellent way to keep the coat looking natural and can be easily maintained by the owner who has limited time for grooming their pet.

18 Preventative Care and Procedures

Preventative care is exactly what it says: care that helps to prevent problems from occurring or worsening. For the groomer, preventative care refers to the routine healthcare checks that should be undertaken to preserve the health and well-being of the dog. The groomer is uniquely placed to keep the dog in good working order by providing regular checks and undertaking regular 'maintenance'. The groomer's role thus carries with it significant responsibilities; indeed the conscientious dog groomer will be very much aware of the duty of care they owe towards the dog.

The groomer is not there purely to make the dog pretty, they can also promote healthy functioning, prevent problems that can arise through inefficient or poor functioning, and correct problems that a dog may be predisposed to, thereby preventing any abnormal situation from worsening.

This chapter covers a number of subject areas, namely ear care, nail care, dental care, care of the anal sacs and removal of ticks. Each of these areas benefits from the care and intervention of a groomer. It is extremely important, however, that groomers should understand and respect their limitations and only provide those services that they can perform safely, competently and legally.

Whatever treatment you provide must be pain free, stress free and non-invasive, and you should never use any medically or chemically formulated product on any animal belonging to someone else, without permission from the owner and/or instructions from the dog's vet. You must also remember that in cases where medication has been provided for you to use, it is for use only on the animal it was prescribed for and must not be used on any others.

The interventions covered here are procedures that can be performed at any time. In some cases, as in ear and dental care, these procedures may even be undertaken on a daily or weekly basis. In view of this, the cooperation and involvement of the owner is to be encouraged.

The following chapter is designed to help you identify what you are looking for, when you can help and when you should leave the situation alone.

EAR CARE

Generally speaking, dogs with dropped ears or those with heavy coats that grow densely around the head are the dogs that suffer most with ear problems. All dogs, however, benefit from having their ears examined and cleaned regularly.

Irrespective of its outward appearance, the ear's anatomy lends itself to problems. The ear canal does not drain readily to the outside, allowing wax secretions to build up. In addition, whatever goes in (water, foreign bodies, etc.) can rarely get out again because there is a bend in the ear canal that makes this difficult. The ear canal itself provides a moist, warm and sheltered environment in which micro-organisms can grow.

The skin that lines the ear canal can contain hair follicles, so hair often grows within the ear canal. Woolly coated dogs in particular have hair that grows deep within the ear canal, which can usefully be removed periodically. The advantage of hairy ears is that the hair often stops debris such as grass seeds from being able to enter the ear. The major disadvantage, however, is that the ear cannot ventilate well and waxy secretions may remain trapped within the ear; this can predispose to ear infections. Dogs with pricked ears enjoy better ear ventilation; infection is therefore less likely, but without the protection of hair, debris can easily enter the canal.

Many dogs take care of their own hygiene needs but the position of the ear makes this difficult if not impossible, even if they can somehow get a toe into the ear canal! It is therefore up to someone else to worry about ear cleaning – namely you, me and dog owners everywhere! Whether you are a pet owner or a professional groomer, ear care is your responsibility.

To learn more about the ear, how it operates and the problems that affect it, please refer to Section 2.9 'The Ear, Hearing and Balance'.

18.1 EAR CARE

A healthy ear should have:

- a clean entrance to the auditory meatus;
- healthy unbroken skin lining the inside of the pinna and the canal;
- no signs of mite or insect infestation;
- no offensive smell or discharge;
- no squelching sounds that may indicate fluid at the bottom of the canal; and
- no signs of swelling, redness, pain, discomfort or injury to the pinna.

In the early stages of ear problems, the signs are very subtle. The dog may start by scratching occasionally or may rub his head along the carpet or furniture. This can often go unnoticed because, by and large, this is not abnormal behaviour for a dog. By the time the ear starts to smell, it is usually a sign that infection or mite infestation has taken hold and the ear needs treatment.

A thorough assessment of the health of the ears should be made by the groomer when the dog visits the salon. Reading the dog's records provides information on the dog's lifestyle and any previous ear problems; this can often be beneficial and will direct you to consider certain factors that may be problematic.

It is likely that a dog that either lives or is exercised in the country will be more prone to foreign objects in or around the ear, such as grass seeds, mites and ticks. Certainly look out for ticks as well as for coat discoloration at the entrance to the auditory meatus that may signify mite infestation.

One problem that is often overlooked in dogs exercised on beaches or river banks is water within the ear canal after swimming. This can cause chronic problems that progress rapidly and result in ear infections. Gently rub the base of the ear in a rotating movement and listen for squelching sounds, which may indicate that water is present in the lower part of the ear canal. Sand in the canal can also be a problem.

Town-dwelling dogs that tend to exercise at the walk rather than the run may be more likely to show signs of bacterial ear infections, particularly if they have dropped pinna. Bacteria grow rapidly in warm moist environments, and running around with the pinna flapping is a good way to ventilate, cool and dry the auditory meatus.

Owners that are able to spend time grooming their pets between trims are more likely to notice when the ears need attention and seek help. Dogs that are not groomed by their owners between salon visits are more likely to have ear infections and infestations that progress unchecked and may be beyond the help of a groomer. In these cases the groomer must know when not to interfere and to advise the owner to seek veterinary help. A past history of ear disease or infestation should alert you to look out for a recurrence of the problem.

The coat type determines the amount of hair that a groomer would expect to see in the ear. A dog with a heavy or long wool coat is likely to have a lot of hair within the auditory meatus, which is often best removed to keep the ear healthy. If such a dog presented for grooming without any hair in the ear, and the owner had not removed it, veterinary advice should be sought as this would be abnormal for this coat type.

Knotting of long hair on the pinna or behind the ear may indicate excessive scratching and should be investigated.

How to clean the ear

You need:

- fingers, forceps or bullnosed ear tweezers;
- ear powder;
- olive oil or a canine ear cleaner (or the dog's own ear cleaner if under veterinary treatment and supplied on prescription);
- cotton wool; and
- kitchen roll or a container for collecting dirty hair and used dressings.

Procedure for Cleaning Ears

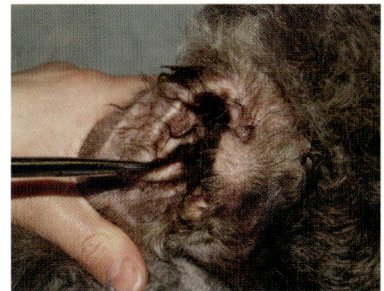

Fig. 18.1.1a-b   Woolly-coated breeds particularly have a lot of hair growing within the auditory meatus. Start cleaning the ear by removing the excess hair with either your fingers, forceps or bullnosed ear tweezers.

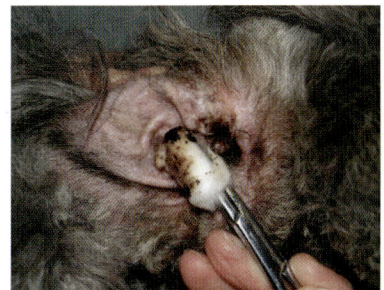

Fig. 18.1.2a-b   Once the hair is removed, use swabs of cotton wool soaked in olive oil or ear cleaner to remove the dirt. Once the ear is clean, use dry cotton wool to soak up any excess oil. Remember to sterilize your tools or use different tools for the other ear.

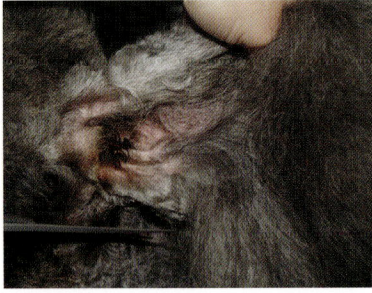

Fig. 18.1.3   You can help to keep the ear canal clean and ventilated by removing as much hair as possible from in front of the ear every time the dog is trimmed.

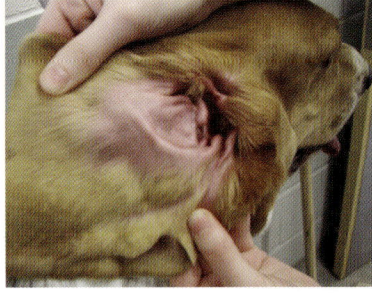

Fig. 18.1.4a-b   Even smooth-coated breeds should have their ears cleaned regularly. The ears of the Basset Hound (pictured) are vulnerable because they drag on the ground when the dog is walking. Bassets often tread on their ears, causing bruising, and because these dogs are low to the ground, grass seeds, ticks and insects can all easily enter the ear.

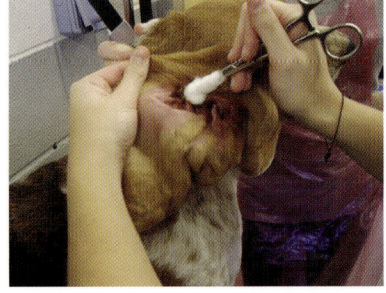

CAUTION

Ear infections are transmittable so good hygiene is essential.

◆   *Make sure that all dirty dressings are disposed of in clinical waste so that they are incinerated.*
◆   *Only insert swabs once into the ear, do not re-insert.*
◆   *Avoid cross-contamination by using either sterilized equipment or fresh equipment for each ear.*
◆   *Advise the owner to seek veterinary advice if you have seen any evidence of infection, or if the ears are unusually sore, painful or have an offensive odour.*
◆   *Clean your working area with an appropriate cleaning solution when you have finished the job.*
◆   *Wash forceps and containers in warm soapy water and sterilize after use.*
◆   *Wear disposable gloves and wash your hands thoroughly after ear cleaning has been completed.*

What is happening inside the ear

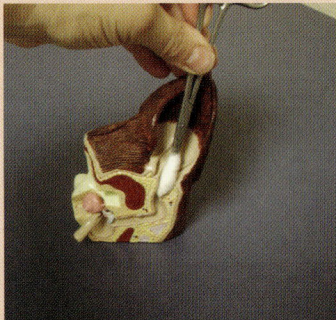

Fig. 18.1.5   This model shows the inside of a normal healthy ear. When you are cleaning the ear you should only insert your forceps as far as you can see. The model shows the cotton wool swab is well away from the bend in the auditory meatus and cannot damage the ear drum (arrowed). A cotton bud has a flexible stem that can bend around the corner and do a lot of damage to the ear drum.

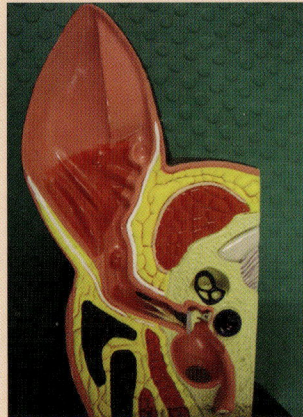

Fig. 18.1.6a-b   When a foreign body such as a grass seed enters the ear canal (left), it cannot come out again and will decompose within the ear. The model shows how the lining to the ear is becoming inflamed. Chronic inflammation of the skin (right) has closed the ear canal completely. A dog with this condition will be in a lot of pain and urgently needs veterinary help. A groomer should not attempt to clean an ear in this condition.

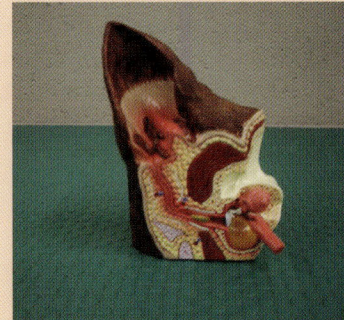

Cotton wool buds should never be used in canine ear care as the plastic rod attaching the cotton bud bends too easily. If inserted into the vertical ear canal, the rod can bend around the junction with the horizontal canal, and the tympanic membrane (ear drum) is then at risk of being ruptured. Cotton buds are also hard and may cause bruising if used aggressively.

Your fingers and thumb are excellent tools, readily available and needing little maintenance. Use them in the same movement you use for hand plucking. The disadvantage is that they should not be used on infected ears without protection from gloves, and this makes the job a little difficult as the hair is difficult to grip. Large fingers may also find the cleaning procedure difficult in little ears.

Forceps are easy to use and available in different sizes to suit all ear sizes. Ear forceps resemble a pair of scissors but they have blunt cross-ridges across the ends to hold and grip rather than cut. Forceps are suitable for use on all ears and are useful for removing hair and visible debris as they give better grip than finger and thumb. Forceps can also be used to make cotton wool swabs for ear cleaning. Forceps and bullnosed tweezers are suitable for left- and right-handed use.

Ear powder is sometimes used in the entrance of the ear to give better grip on greasy or dirty hairs. It certainly serves a purpose but it should be used with caution and care must be taken to remove all of the powder after removing the hair to prevent accumulation and blocking of the ear canal. Generally powders are not recommended for use by veterinary surgeons because of the damage that can be done if they are misused. If in doubt, you would be wise to seek advice from your own vet.

Cleaning solutions are readily available from pet shops and grooming suppliers. They are designed to be safe to use but they can cause problems if used incorrectly or with certain ear infections. Cleaning solutions are usually designed to dissolve waxy material and can help flush any build-up out from within the ear canal, bringing dirt and debris to the surface, from where it can be mopped up. Olive oil is often recommended by vets to clean the outer ear and the visible ear canal. It has a long history of use and is generally quite safe. Your vet will be able to advise on other suitable products.

Cotton wool is used to wipe out the ear and remove grease, wax and dirt. The consistency and high absorbency of cotton wool makes it ideal for wet or dry use, and it is gentle on the tender lining of the ear canal. Cotton wool is used with forceps to form a swab that is safe to use in ear care. The forceps will not bend at the junction of the vertical and horizontal canal so damage cannot be done to the tympanic membrane.

Assess the condition of the ear before you start cleaning and risk assess the dog for pain or stress anxiety aggression. Restrain him if necessary. Start by removing the hair that is visible within the ear canal. This may be done with either your finger and thumb, or with forceps. If you feel resistance when pulling, you have probably taken hold of too many hairs; this will be painful for the dog and can cause localized inflammation of the skin. Plucking a few hairs at a time is, however, usually well tolerated.

Once all the hair is removed, use a dry piece of cotton wool held by your forceps to wipe out the visible part of the inside ear. Only use the piece of cotton wool once, do not re-insert it. If the ear is not infected, or if there is very little dirt or debris to remove, repeat the cleaning process with several pieces of dry cotton wool. You may want to apply a swab soaked with olive oil or cleaning solution midway through the process to lift any stubborn dirt. If the ear is still very dirty (or indeed infected) after the initial wiping out, continue with as many pieces of cotton wool soaked in olive oil or cleaning solution as is necessary. You should aim to clean as much 'dirt' as you possibly can out of the visible part of the ear, whilst taking great care not to make the ear sore.

Use dry cotton wool swabs to mop up and remove any oil or solution from the ear. Then sterilize your forceps or use a different set to clean the other ear. When you have finished, wash your hands thoroughly. If you have found any evidence of an ear infection, you should advise the owner to seek veterinary advice.

18.2 NAIL CARE

There are basically two different actions for cutting nails: secateurs and guillotines (*see* Fig. 18.2.1). Secateurs resemble a pair of pliers (*see* Fig. 18.2.2) and are equipped with two cutting blades that cut towards each other as the blades are closed. There are several benefits to using this type of nail clip-

> *Nail care is something that some owners take care of, but commercial groomers should be offering it as part of their service. There are several designs of nail cutter available. If you are buying your first pair, handle them and make sure that you are comfortable with them in your hand.*
>
> *Make sure that you have an uninterrupted view of the nail once it is between the blades; that way, there is less chance of cutting the nail too short.*

per. They are suitable for all shapes of nail, even those that have twisted or curled around like a corkscrew, and the blades are fully open until you squeeze them together. A difficult dog, or one that refuses to settle, is thus able to remove his nail from the clipper without it being caught in any way. This reduces the chances of a nail being avulsed (pulled off) or cut too short. You can also easily see and position the cutting area when the blades are enclosed around the nail. The disadvantage is that the novice, when learning to cut nails, often has a tendency to position these clippers so that they cut the nail sideways, rather than from top to bottom. This means that the nails are pinched, which often proves uncomfortable for the dog. Failing to realize that it is the technique that is at fault, the novice will continue to clip the dog's remaining nails from side to side, hurrying because they think the dog is 'not cooperating' and failing to appreciate that they are causing further discomfort and distress.

Fig. 18.2.1   There are many designs of nail cutter available, but they all cut with either a secateur or a guillotine action.

Fig. 18.2.2   Secateur-action nail clipper, fitted with a nail guard to help prevent cutting the nail too short. (Be aware that this assumes there is enough excess nail to fill the gap; otherwise, you can still cut the nail too short.)

Fig. 18.2.3   Guillotine-action nail clipper. The nail is inserted into the circle and, as the handles are squeezed together, a blade crosses the circle and cuts the nail.

Guillotine clippers have two blades: a fixed blade that forms a complete circle, and a sectioning (cutting) blade that lies over the fixed blade and can be swept across it, to cut whatever has been placed within the circle (*see* Fig. 18.2.3). It therefore operates much as a French Revolutionary guillotine would have done, hence the name. The advantage of these clippers is that they encourage novices to place the cutting blades the correct way up for cutting the nail, so they cut the nail from top to bottom, rather than from side to side. The disadvantages, though, are significant and do need to be considered carefully. Although these clippers remain fully open until you operate the handles, the nail has to be placed within the circular blade; there is then more likelihood that if a difficult or anxious dog panics with his claw in the clipper, in the ensuing struggle the nail may get cut too short or even be pulled off completely. The other

disadvantage with this design is that they are not always suitable for unusually large, very thick, twisted, curled or otherwise deformed nails because you cannot get the circular cutters over the nail end.

Both of these designs are available in different sizes. If you are working commercially, you may require at least two different sizes.

Nail grinders

These are generally electrically or battery operated and they work by grinding down the nail in a circular motion with a hollow emery or tiny sandpaper disc fitted to the end. The grinder works in the same way as a nail file and also allows you to buff and polish nails! They certainly provide a particularly smooth and neat way to trim nails down; they are also both quick and safe to use. The disadvantages of the grinder are that some dogs object to the vibrations and noise produced, particularly if they are sensitive to their feet being handled. Dogs may also dislike this method if their first experience was not a good one, or they have reached the time of their life where change is harder to cope with.

The other disadvantage is, of course, that you need to replace the emery discs and batteries regularly so there will be further purchases to be made.

Nail files

Nail files are used to remove the rough surfaces after trimming down nails or for taking just the very tip off short nails. They resemble the sort of nail file that you would use on your own nails and they are usually made of metal, although emery board types are also suitable for the task. The disadvantage with emery board designs is that they wear out quickly and further purchases are necessary.

Coagulants

A coagulant is a preparation that stops bleeding, and in the case of nail cutting it is something you need always to have close to hand. There are several preparations available, most of which are based on a chemical called ferric (or ferrous) subsulphate; applied to a cut nail quick, this achieves haemostasis in approximately twenty seconds. In the United Kingdom this chemical is legally supplied in a powdered or crystallized form and, used correctly, is not harmful.

Apply ferric subsulphate to the nail on a piece of cotton wool or a cotton bud and hold it in place for twenty to thirty seconds. It can help to dampen the cotton first so that it picks up the powder more easily. The powder can stain skin and, although it is not carcinogenic, it will stay on the skin for several days so you may want to wear gloves when applying it!

Silver nitrate pencils are another readily available item commonly used as another means of chemically cauterizing a bleeding claw. However, these pencils can break easily if applied to the claw under pressure and they do not appear to have any significant advantages over the firm application of a cotton bud dipped in ferric subsulphate.

If you find yourself in a home situation with none of these products available, vinegar, cornflour or white pepper can be helpful in dealing with a bleeding claw.

All nail clippers, grinders and files are suitable for left- and right-handed use; those fitted with a nail guard, however, will need the guard changed (by removing a screw) to the opposite side of the cutting blades.

CAUTION

Ferric subsulphate is a chemical and should therefore be treated with respect. It is supplied in small amounts in the United Kingdom in tightly closed, lightproof containers because it is light sen-sitive.

- *It is harmful if swallowed. Whilst a dog licking a small quantity from his paw after having ferric subsulphate applied to a claw will suffer little in the way of consequences, chewing up a tub of the powder or licking up spilt product is a different matter and urgent veterinary advice should be sought.*
- *It is harmful to eyes and contact should be avoided. In the event of an accident or contamination, the eye should be washed immediately for about ten to fifteen minutes until no evidence of the powder remains and then veterinary advice should be sought.*
- *It is for external use only and should not be used inside ears or mouths.*
- *It is for use on nails only. Should you have an acci-dent and cut the dog or yourself, ferric subsulphate is not suitable for arresting bleeding. Refer to the First Aid section for further information on cuts and bleeding.*
- *If the flow of blood from the nail has not stopped after a minute, consider seeking veterinary advice as the dog may have a blood clotting problem.*
- *It is acceptable to dispose of small quantities of ferric subsulphate on cotton wool in normal clinical waste but larger quantities should be disposed of according to your local authority's hazardous waste policies. This is some-thing you should check out.*

Cutting toenails

White, unpigmented nails are easier to cut because not only can you see the pink 'quick' within the nail, you will also find that these nails tend to be a little softer. At some time or other, even the most experienced groomers and vets cut the nail 'quick' by mistake. If you do, do not panic. Have your coagulant ready and apply it firmly to the nail (20–30 seconds should suffice) to cauterize the vessels. Unless the dog has a blood clotting problem, the bleeding will stop within a few seconds. Do then take time to reassure the dog and handle his feet without doing anything to them so that you rebuild his confidence.

Technique for Cutting Nails

When you are learning how to cut nails, it is best to look first of all at the underside of the nail.

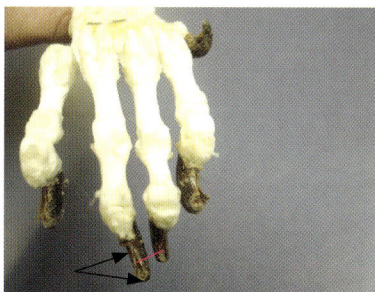

Fig. 18.2.4   The black arrows show the length of hollow nail growing beyond the 'quick'. This is similar to your nails. The red line shows where you need to cut – approximately halfway along the distance.

Fig. 18.2.5   Hold the toe securely whilst you position the nail clipper, then hold the nail between the clipper blades. Relax the hand holding the foot as you cut so that the dog does not feel his foot is trapped. These are secateurs in action.

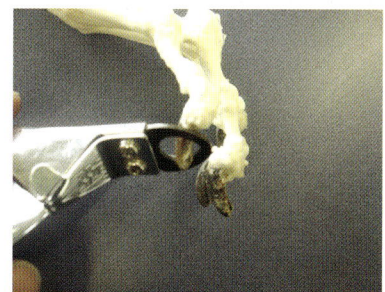

Fig. 18.2.6   To use a guillotine-action clipper, place the nail inside the circle, close the handles enough to hold the nail and relax your hand as you cut.

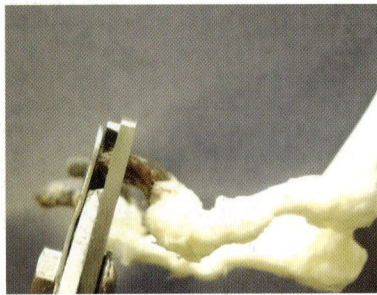

Fig. 18.2.7   *The nail guard in action.*

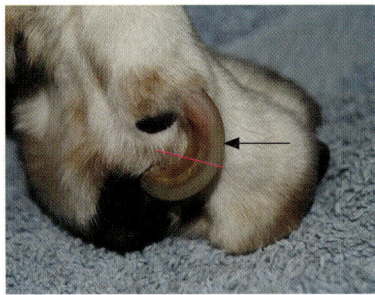

Fig. 18.2.8   *The black arrow shows where the quick ends and the red line shows where this nail will be cut. Note that the cut line is following the contour of the nail – the outside curve of the nail is longer than the inside curve. This means that there is a possibility that the quick is longer than expected because of the growth room given by the outer (longer) curve. The tighter inside curve will be putting pressure on the quick and will hinder its growth on the underside.*

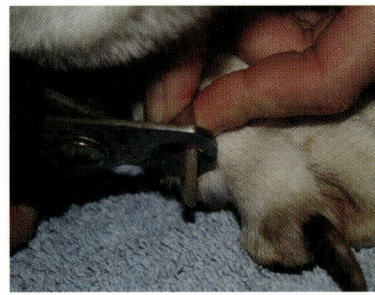

Fig. 18.2.9   *The nail being cut with secateur clippers.*

Fig. 18.2.10   *This black nail clearly shows the hollow nail. The nail will be cut at the point indicated by the red line – approximately halfway along the hollow.*

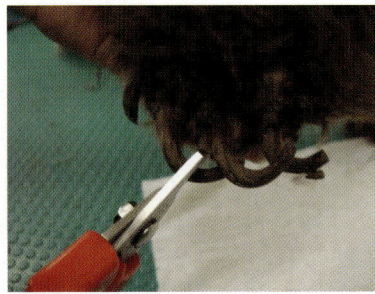

Fig. 18.2.11   *The first cut on these nails is being made at the point where the nails were sitting on the floor. This isn't a foolproof place to start, but because the weight of the dog puts pressure into the foot (and nail) there is a good chance that the quick will have receded further back than this point.*

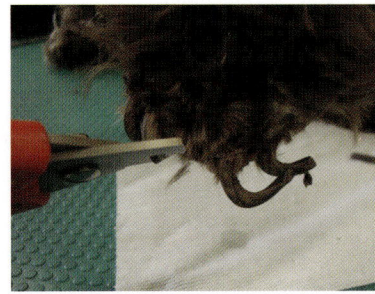

Fig. 18.2.12   *As is usual, the quick had receded so the nail is cut again by nibbling it back with the clippers until the centre of the nail is no longer hollow and starts to fill. This dog will be brought back every week until the nails are healthy and of a suitable length.*

How do you know how much to cut?

If you are new to nail cutting, start by having a look at your own nails, from the upper side of your hand. If you bite your nails or keep them very short, you will see that the 'quick' (the pink bit) has often receded away from the end of the finger. If you do not bite your nails, you will see that the quick has grown down to the end of the finger and the nail extends beyond the finger.

Turn your hand over to look at it palm side up. The nails that have been bitten do not, of course, show past the end of the finger and there will be nothing to cut. The unbitten nail will extend beyond the length of the finger

and this is of course the bit that can be cut off. It is easy to see because the nails are white and the bit of nail that you can see is thin and does not curve round to form a claw; you can see that there is no sensitive quick in it!

Now look at the finger sideways on and you can easily see where your finger ends and the empty nail extends beyond it. This profile is similar to the dog's nail. The main difference is that, because the nail grows from the end of the toe (whereas our nails grow from a point a centimetre or so from the finger tip), there is an area within the extending nail that accommodates the quick.

If you look at the dog's nail from underneath, you will see the empty bit;

if you look at the nail sideways on, you will see where the quick ends and the *empty* nail extends ready for cutting. To test the theory, introduce the tip of a biro into the *empty* bit and you will see that you can clean out the mud and dirt, much as you do when cleaning your own nails with the tip of a nail file. The hollow tube left behind is the nail.

Relax and take some deep breaths to make your hands soft, and then either stand or sit the dog facing you. Hold the paw securely but lightly as if you have a sponge full of water in your hand and you do not want to drop it or squeeze the water from it. If the dog is anxious, allow him to take his foot away once or twice so that he is assured that his leg is not trapped and he is not going to lose it! This is terribly important, particularly with puppies or nervous dogs. The natural instinct of the dog is to run from anything that may be a threat and he cannot do this if he is trapped. If he cannot move his foot, he may perceive this as being trapped – panic may set in and you may find yourself in a battle of wills. Let him see that he can move and he is not under threat.

Without changing your hand pressure, take one of the nails between the blades of the clipper and check the position of the blades before holing the nail with the blades. Relax the pressure in your supporting hand and close the handles to cut the nail.

When you are confident with the technique, you may want to use your nail clippers to remove the sharp edges of the nail before filing.

The effect of foot shape on nail growth

Sometimes the nails are excessively long. The shape of the foot has a huge bearing on this and it is wise to observe which of the following is the cause before you cut the nail. It also enables you to offer any necessary advice to the owner.

Round feet (see Fig. 18.2.13)

If the foot is in good condition, the round foot has the advantage that the nails are pointing towards the ground so the nails are naturally kept short through general wear as the dog walks. Exceptions to this are dogs that grow a long or dense coat that typically leads

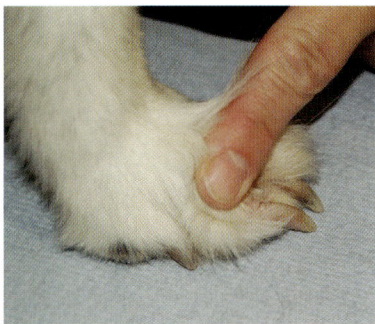

Fig. 18.2.14   In extreme cases this is what can happen if the hair is not trimmed from under the feet and the nails are not kept in check.

them to grow excessive amounts of hair between the foot pads. In these cases the hair can very often grow to such a length and depth that the nails are no longer able to reach the ground and so they do not wear down. When this happens, if the nails are not cut they can affect the dog's movement and put excess strain on hip, elbow and shoulder joints; they can also deform the foot (see Fig. 18.2.14).

Hare feet (see Fig. 18.2.15)

Some breeds, such as Greyhounds, Whippets and Bedlington Terriers, naturally have elongated feet, where the toes are long and extend along the ground. This means that the dog is not putting adequate pressure on the nail quick as he walks, which in turn allows it to continue growing in length, just like the unbitten fingernail. The shape of the foot on these breeds does not allow the nail tip to make a lot of contact with the ground surface, so the nails do not wear down with use.

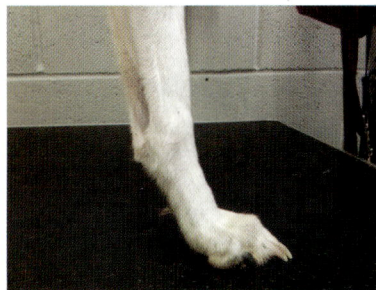

CAUTION: CLIPPING THE NAILS ON 'HARE FEET'

Be careful: the elongated quick may not be where you expect it to be, and in black nails you will not be able to see it. Use your nail clippers to nibble back the nail, a little at a time, until you see a soft centre to the nail. Stop there!

Arthritis and old age (see Fig. 18.2.16)

As dogs get older, their posture (the way they hold themselves) changes. A young dog stands upright on his front legs, with his back legs placed either underneath or behind the hips; unless the dog is hare-footed, he stands on knuckled up (bent) toes. As the dog gets older, the front legs tend to weaken at the shoulder and the back legs gradually creep forward so his hind feet are placed further towards his belly. His feet change shape because, as the position of the foot moves, the dog can no longer stand on his toes. This means that the dog gets longer in the toe as the foot muscles are not working to hold the toes in a knuckled up position, and the nails do not have the same pressure on the tips; this predisposes and encourages them to grow along the ground. Arthritis often sets in because of the altered foot shape and walking action, and this can be very painful.

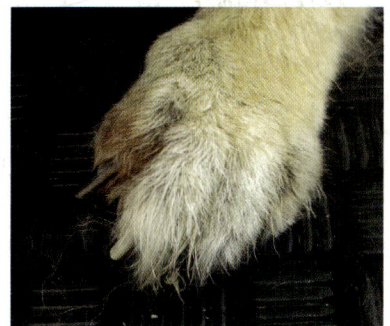

Fig. 18.2.13   A round foot, with the nails pointing towards the ground. The nails could be trimmed a little bit, but generally they are in good condition.

Fig. 18.2.15   The whippet has 'hare' feet, meaning that the nails grow along the ground to help the dog grip when running at speed. This prevents the nails from wearing down when the dog walks.

Fig. 18.2.16   The arthritic foot of an elderly German Shepherd dog. These nails are cut every week to keep them short. This helps the dog with walking and keeps the feet as comfortable as possible.

Fig. 18.2.17   Dew claws were once attached to a now non-existent digit. In the case of a round foot, the nail will be curved, as are the rest of the nails.

Dew claws (see *Fig. 18.2.17*)

These appendages are positioned on the inside of the front and sometimes the back legs at about the height of the carpal joint. Their location means that they get very little, if any, wear unless the dog uses his thumbs a lot when handling and manipulating things. It is therefore essential that the dew claws are checked and cut regularly.

The nails would once have been used on a now non-existent digit and they are generally curved in shape if the dog has round feet, along with the rest of the nails. In hare-footed dogs with straighter nails, the dew nail is also very often straighter. Curved nails in particular need to be kept in check as they can grow towards and into the leg (*see* Fig. 18.2.18). In some breeds it is not unusual to have two or more nails on the back leg (*see* Fig. 18.2.19).

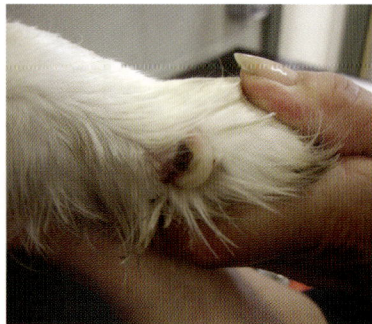

Fig. 18.2.18   If not kept trimmed, a round nail can grow into the leg.

Fig. 18.2.19   It is not unusual to have double dew claws on the hind legs.

Nail bed infections

Nail bed infections can have several causes and often present themselves as discoloration of the nail and hair at the base of the nail, or as deformed nails. Sometimes they are a secondary infection that has been passed on from the dog licking or scratching another part of his body. During grooming, it is easy for micro-organisms to be transferred as first one part of the body is licked or scratched and then another. The feet, of course, do a lot of scratching and, when used to relieve itchy ears, infectious material from the ears can be passed to the nails, where it can then develop into an infection under the skin at the nail bed.

It may surprise you to know that the lip folds and the genital areas are also at risk of secondary infection as a result of ear disease. After scratching his ears, the dog often licks his feet (and nails) clean and micro-organisms can cling to the hairs around the mouth and within the lip folds. The micro-organisms are then easily transferred by the dog to the genital areas during grooming, where the warm, damp environment can be exploited, resulting in an infection.

If a dog has an ear infection, pay particular attention to other areas and look for the possibility of secondary infections during the dog's health examination.

18.3 CARE OF THE ANAL SACS

> *The anal sacs are specialized apocrine glands situated on either side of the rectum at about 4 and 8 o'clock. They can range in size from a small pea to a large walnut, depending on the size of the dog. The sacs produce a viscous oily material that is thought to play some part in olfactory communication, and in the healthy dog they are easily and readily emptied when the dog defecates. In some cases the dog is not able to express his own anal sacs and the sacs may become diseased.*

There are three main problems with the anal sac:

◆ impaction, where the fluid becomes solidified;
◆ infection, when bacteria grow within the sac and produce yellow or bloody pus; and
◆ abscessation, when the infection builds to a hot, tender swelling that is not limited to the sac but has formed an abscess within the surrounding tissue. The abscess may rupture at the skin surface to allow the contents to drain.

The signs of anal sac disease are:

◆ scooting or dragging the bottom along the ground;
◆ excessive licking around the tail;
◆ pain or discomfort around the tail or anus;
◆ swelling on either side or both sides of the anus;
◆ a foul smell; and
◆ bloody or sticky discharge draining from the anus.

Treatment

The treatment for impaction is to firmly but gently express the sacs to empty them of the solidified matter. The treatment for infection is to express the sacs and treat the animal with antibiotics to kill the bacteria. If the sacs abscessate, they may require surgical drainage (lancing) and the dog must be treated with antibiotics.

Groomers are expected to recognize when the sacs need emptying, and whether this is within the bounds of their capabilities. They should also know when the signs suggest that the animal should be referred to a vet.

Emptying the anal sacs

The easiest place to do this, if possible, is when the dog is in the bath, because his bottom can be then washed free of discharge and odour.

Using gloves for hygiene purposes, restrain the dog's head or get someone to hold him for you. Locate the sacs, and then locate the small skin fold below the sacs (*see* Fig. 18.3.1). Hold the skin fold firmly between your thumb and index finger. Keeping your fingers in contact with each other, gently slide them up towards the anus. Try not to loosen the pressure in your fingers. They should slide behind the sacs and meet again above them.

If the sacs are healthy, they should express easily (*see* Fig. 18.3.2). If you feel that you are not capable of emptying the sacs, you should advise the owner when the dog needs attention. If you have attempted to empty the sacs but have not succeeded, tell the owner

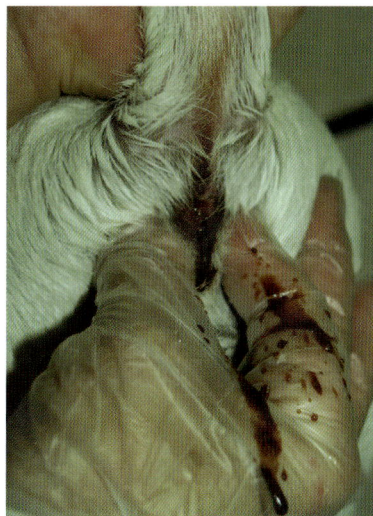

Fig 18.3.1   The anal sacs are located either side of the anus at about 4 and 8 o'clock. Palpate them gently to feel for swellings which indicate that they may need to be emptied. The best time to do this is when the dog is in the bath and the area can be washed after expressing the sac content.

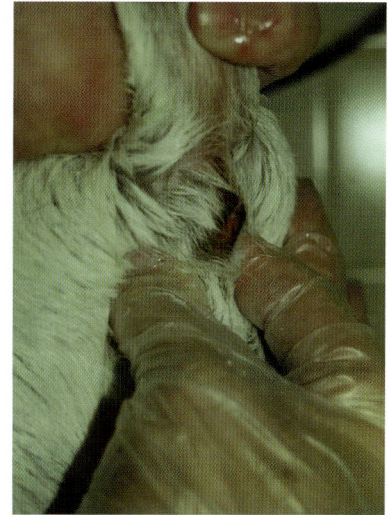

Fig 18.3.2   Squeeze firmly whilst gently pushing upwards with your fingers and the sac should empty. If the sacs do not empty after your first attempt, try once more. If it still doesn't work, advise the owner to take the dog to the vet as impaction is a possibility.

because a vet will need to complete the treatment.

The area can and does bruise very easily, so if you have not managed to express the glands by your second attempt, leave them alone and send the dog to the vet.

You can learn more about anal sac disease in Chapter 2.10.

18.4 DENTAL CARE

> *Dental care provided by a groomer is in no way a substitute for veterinary dental care. In the healthy dog a thorough dental check-up should be undertaken annually by the vet, as part of the dog's annual health assessment. In older dogs (over seven years old), or those with dental problems, it may need to be undertaken on a more regular basis. Any heavy duty cleaning or dentistry should most definitely be done at the veterinary surgery, usually under a general anaesthetic. Such interventions are indicated where the teeth and gums are diseased and require more than just a quick clean in order to re-establish a healthy mouth.*

Between veterinary interventions, there is a need for regular dental care and the groomer can play an important role here. Interim dental care is something that should be taken care of by both the owner (ideally on a daily basis) and the groomer (at the time of grooming).

Puppies should have their teeth checked as often as possible in the first few months of life. This helps them get used to having their mouths handled. As soon as adult teeth have emerged and the mouth and gums have settled down, cleaning can begin. At such a young age, this is about establishing a routine that promotes good oral hygiene and ensures that the dog learns to cope with, and becomes accepting of, regular cleaning and brushing.

Research shows that by the age of three years old as many as 80 per cent of dogs have the beginnings of dental disease. This can often be avoided if the dog has his teeth cleaned daily by the owner and a good check-up given at every grooming session.

Regular cleaning, a healthy diet and a good exercise routine all help to keep the teeth of most dogs healthy but there are some breeds, particularly the toy and brachycephalic breeds, that are particularly prone to dental problems. Man has selectively bred dogs whose faces are so distorted that they do not accommodate the teeth that would usually sit comfortably in the mouths of their ancestors. This results in over-crowding: many tiny dogs have teeth that are too big for them crammed into very small mouths. This is one of the reasons why we see so many toy dogs with bad teeth during our working day. For these dogs, and for dogs with poor dental conformation, it is particularly important that a dental care programme is put in place.

Keeping the dog's teeth clean is important not only for good oral hygiene but also for the dog's general health. Research has shown that poor dental hygiene has a major bearing on heart, lung, liver and kidney conditions and bladder infections as these organs are vulnerable to the blood-borne bacteria that cause dental disease. It is therefore very important that between the owner, the groomer and the vet, the dog's teeth are cared for properly.

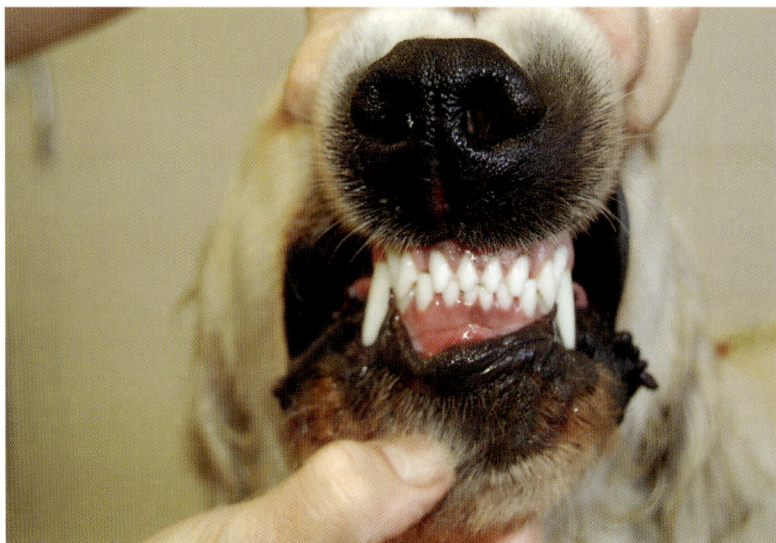

Fig. 18.4.1   The teeth on a puppy or adolescent dog should be white. Gums are not always pink but those that are should be a healthy rosy colour. Whatever the colour of the gums, they should be warm, shiny and firm.

When you are checking teeth, look first of all at the conformation of the mouth. A regular scissor bite is the least problematic, with irregular teeth formations being more troublesome. The insides of the teeth should be checked as well as the outsides.

Puppy teeth should appear white (*see* Fig. 18.4.1) and the gums should be warm, shiny and firm. Checking the capillary reflex should be done if possible, but bear in mind that this is not always possible if the puppy has black or blue gums. The mucosa inside the mouth should be warm and the breath should not smell offensive. As the dog ages, the teeth start to discolour, becoming more yellow, and the breath starts to take on a mild odour. This is normal and not a cause for concern (*see* Fig. 18.4.2). What is not normal is excessively bad smelling breath and large amounts of calculus collecting on the teeth (*see* Fig. 18.4.3).

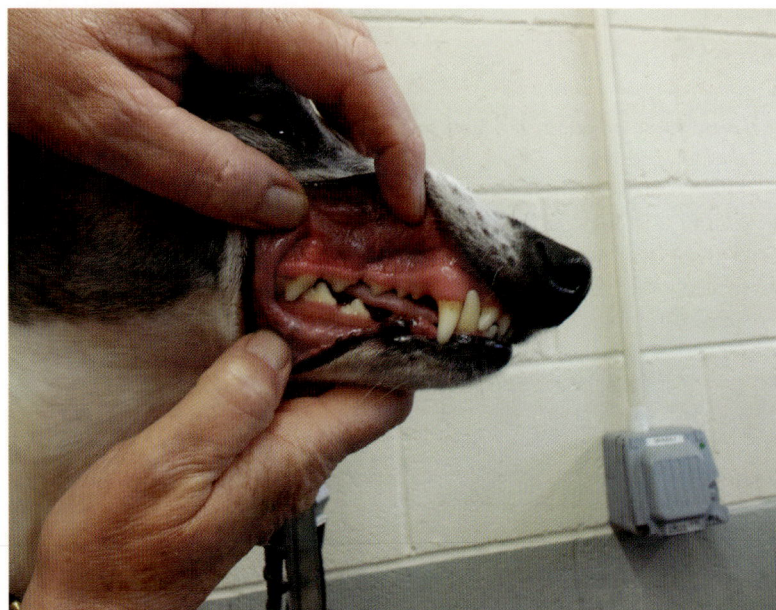

Fig. 18.4.2   This is an adult dog. The teeth formation is good but they are beginning to discolour and a little bit of calculus is starting to develop. The gums are a healthy pink so this mouth can easily be attended to.

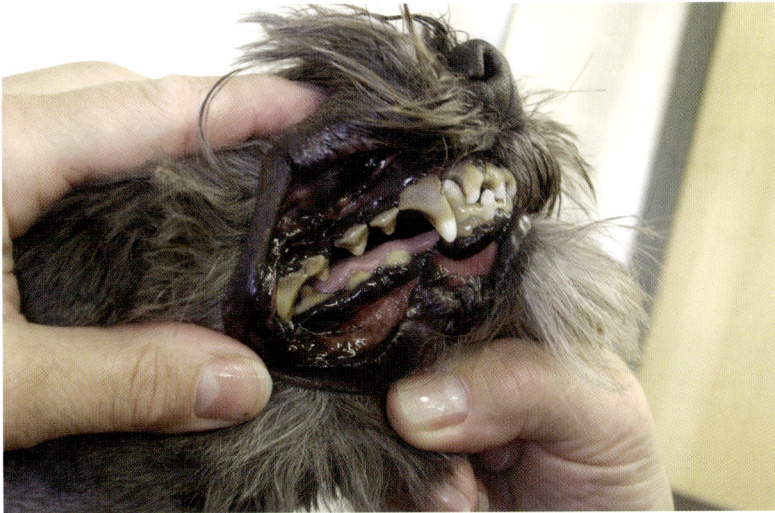

Fig. 18.4.3 *This is a very old dog. The teeth are clearly in need of treatment beyond that of the capabilities of a groomer. The gums and mucosa are black which makes checking the capillary refill difficult and the age of the dog is also a concern. This is most definitely a job for the vet.*

If the dog has had his mouth handled from an early age, a certain amount of cleaning can be undertaken without distressing the dog unduly. Usually a good brushing will suffice. This can be undertaken with a doggy toothbrush appropriate to the size of the dog's mouth, or an electronic toothbrush. The latter provides a more efficient cleaning action. In some cases minor scaling may be indicated to remove any build-up of calculus; this can halt or slow the progression of gum and dental disease. Anything beyond this should be performed by a vet.

You need:

- Either a hard toothbrush, a finger brush or an electronic toothbrush. These should be the dog's own as toothbrush heads should not be shared between dogs;
- dog toothpaste;
- a flat tooth scaler;
- a pick tooth scaler;
- and damp cotton wool to wipe the teeth when scaling.

For general cleaning and polishing, first check the dog's notes for any health conditions, and then check the mouth. If you are just polishing the teeth, use a small amount of toothpaste on a finger brush or a toothbrush (*see* Fig. 18.4.4) and remember to clean both sides of the teeth (*see* Fig. 18.4.5). Record all the details.

There are a few points to consider

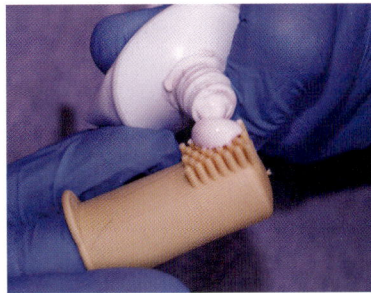

Fig. 18.4.4 *Either a finger brush like the one illustrated or a toothbrush can be used for polishing the teeth using just a small amount of toothpaste.*

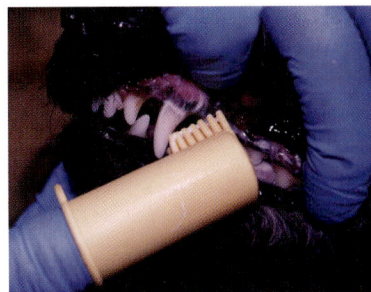

Fig. 18.4.5 *Make sure that you brush all around each tooth, including the backs.*

if you intend scaling a dog's teeth (*see* Technique for Scaling Teeth).

- Your scalers should be clean and sterilized before use.
- The mouth is not sterile and you should wear gloves.
- The mouth is full of germs so if you damage yourself with your

scaler, you should wash the wound well and record the incident in the accident book, however small the wound may appear.

- The dog is not anaesthetized so it is unlikely that you will be able to undertake a full scaling because the dog will not be relaxed enough for you to get to the less accessible parts of the mouth (inside aspects of teeth and the back of the mouth). Tell the owner what you have done and advise a veterinary check-up.
- Because the dog is not sedated, you can get bitten, particularly if the dog is not used to having his mouth handled.
- Never attempt to scale the teeth if the gums are inflamed (red) or if there is any sign of infection close to the gum line. Advise the owner to see the vet.
- Dental work can cause the gums to bleed if the calculus has extended under the gum and lifted the gum from the tooth. Check that the dog does not suffer from a clotting disorder. In some cases the owner may not be aware of the problem so you may not have it recorded, but if it is a breed known to be predisposed to clotting disorders, proceed with caution or leave the mouth alone.
- Never dig your scaler into any holes that you may find (*see* Fig. 18.4.6). This will undoubtedly cause pain and distress. Leave them alone and advise the owner to seek veterinary attention.
- Never attempt to remove any teeth, even loose ones. Leave that to someone who knows what they are doing and has the appropriate equipment to hand.

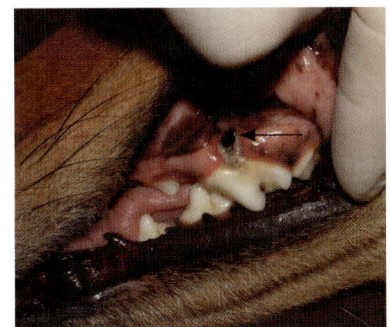

Fig. 18.4.6 *Never insert your scaler into a hole in either the tooth or the gum to clear the area. It will cause immense pain and may spread the infection.*

Technique for scaling teeth

Working from the front to the back of the mouth, start with your flat scaler and work your way around each tooth. Remember to check the back of each tooth as you get to it. Use your pick scaler to work between crevices.

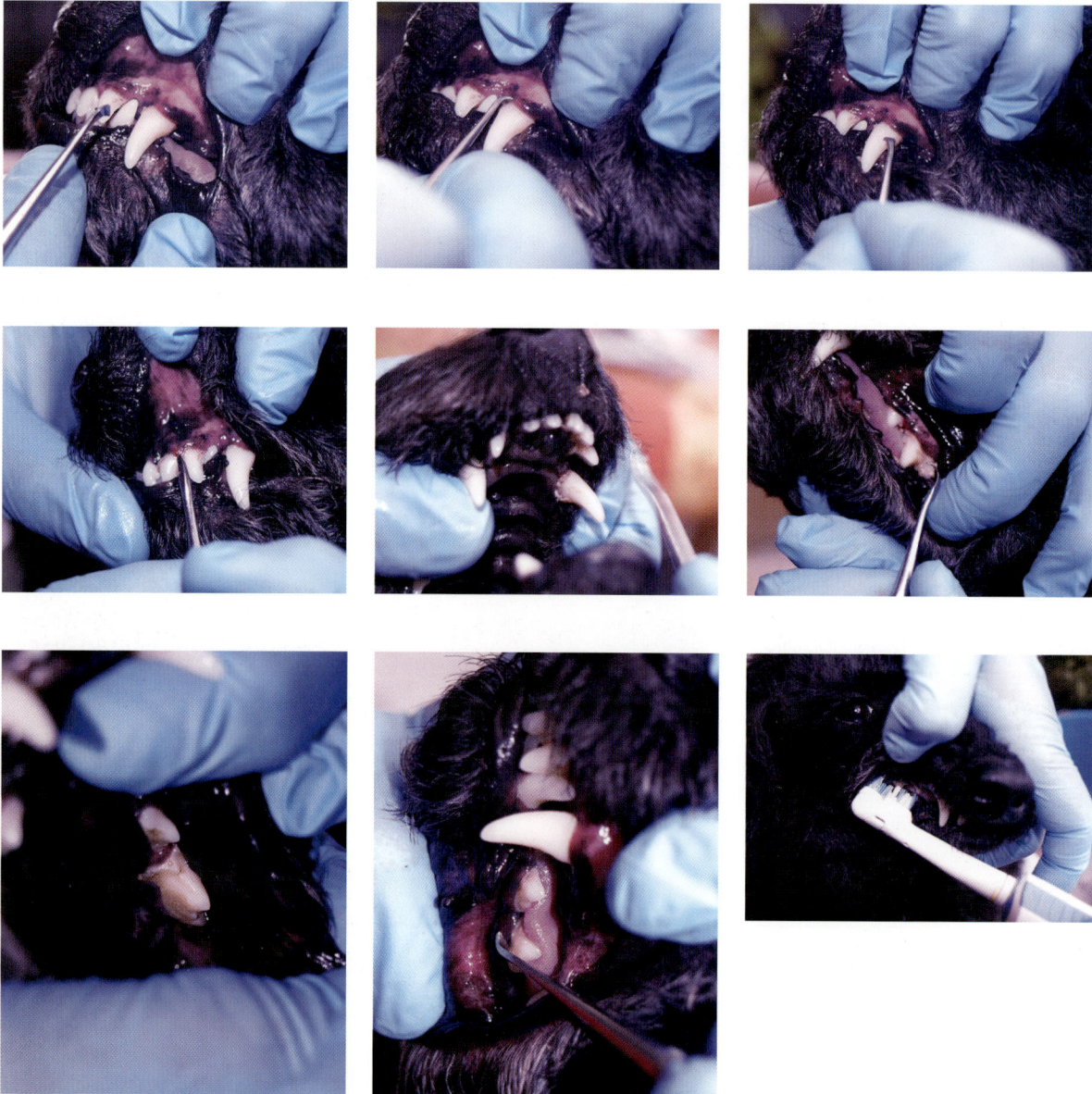

When scaling is complete, use a brush and paste to polish the teeth. This Poodle is used to clippers on her face and tolerates the vibration of a battery-operated toothbrush.

CAUTION: HUMAN TOOTHPASTE

Never use human toothpaste on dogs. Some human toothpastes contain xylitol, a sweetener that is potentially poisonous to dogs. They also contain foaming agents that can harm the stomach. You can spit toothpaste out whereas the dog swallows it, so it will go down into their stomach. Use only dog toothpaste that is designed specifically for this purpose.

18.5 REMOVING TICKS

Ticks (see Chapter 4) are parasites that live in the environment and feed from a host before returning to the environment to reproduce. Ticks are vectors of disease and can transmit disease to humans as well as to animals. Precautions should therefore be taken to prevent the spread of any such diseases.

The tick has three life stages, and for some ticks (for example, *Ixodes ricinus*) it is not unusual for each stage to feed from a different host animal with only the adults found on the dog. In others (for example, *Ixodes canisuga*) all three stages will feed on the dog. Their life-cycle lasts several months but this can be considerably longer in cooler temperatures – in the UK sometimes up to three or four years.

The tick feeds by burying its head deep into the skin of the host and gorging itself on blood, growing sometimes up to a diameter of 1cm or more. There are three important points to remember when removing ticks:

◆ if the mouth parts are left behind they can cause an abscess;
◆ if you squeeze a live tick when you remove it, it can expel the contents of its stomach into the host, increasing the risk of spreading disease; and
◆ ticks do not die easily. Once removed, they are best killed by burning or by spraying with an insecticidal chemical designed to kill ticks.

Ticks are visible to the naked eye but they can range in size from very tiny to the size of a small pea. They commonly attach themselves to the head and neck area of the host, although they can often be found on other areas of the body, where they cause irritation and blood loss.

There are several ways to remove a tick safely, so do not use your fingers to pull them off.

◆ Coating the tick with oil or Vaseline interferes with its respiration. Leaving it soaking in Vaseline for a few minutes usually causes the tick to slacken its grip; it can then be carefully removed with forceps or within a piece of cotton wool.
◆ Spray the tick with an insecticidal spray so that it loosens its grip, and then use your forceps or cotton wool.
◆ If the dog has large numbers of ticks, he can be bathed in insecticidal shampoo and the drugged ticks can then be removed.
◆ A tick remover slides under the head to release the grip of the mouth parts and remove the tick (*see* Figs 18.5.1 and 18.5.2).

Whichever method you use, remember to destroy the tick by burning or by a chemical spray formulated to kill ticks.

If you have tried to remove a tick but have not extracted the mouth parts, you should refer the dog to the vet to decide what further treatment to give.

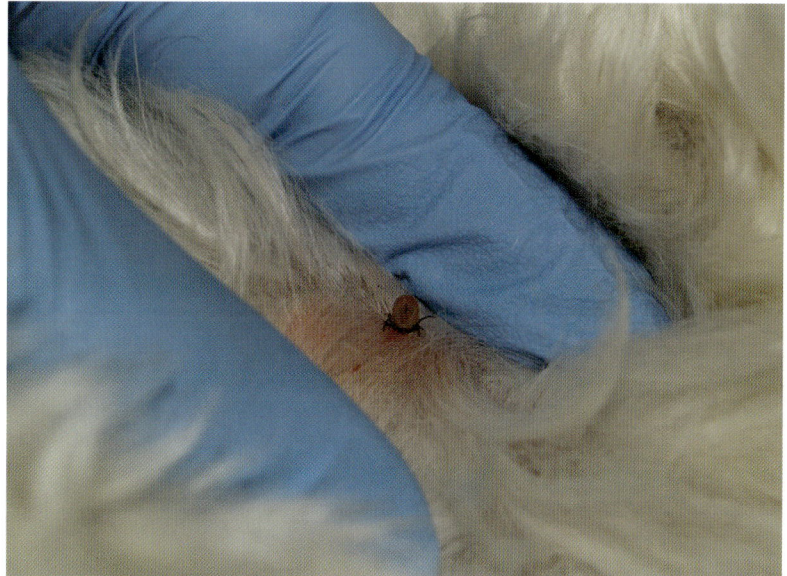

18.5.1   The tick buries its head deep into the skin so that it can feed. It is very important that you extract the complete head when you remove the tick. Any remains may cause an abscess.

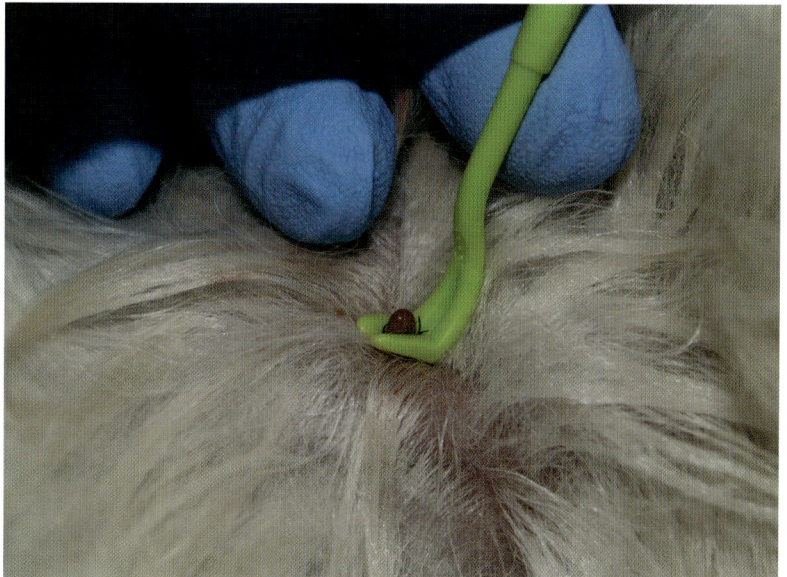

18.5.2   A tick remover slides under the head and causes the tick to release its grip. Swivel the tick remover between your fingers and the parasite will let go and come away. Dispose of the tick by burning or by spraying with insecticidal chemicals.

Tail Ends

And now, as we reach the final pages of this book, I hope that it has given you a comprehensive insight into all the subjects that underpin the professional activities, practice and role of the groomer and why they are important. I hope that, by now, it is clear to you that grooming is a vocation that requires a unique combination of science, skilled artistry and professionalism. There is far more to grooming than brushing and cutting the hair from a dog. And if your intention is to call yourself a 'professional groomer', you not only need to develop expert practical skills, you also need to acquire the knowledge, understanding, attitudes and dispositions that are recognized and expected of a 'professional' person.

Having read this book, you should now have an understanding (and, I hope, an appreciation) of how each chapter is a vast subject within its own right. Try as I might, however, I could not possibly include everything that each subject demands. What I have tried to do is provide you with the most important information and, where possible, I have included links to documented research and evidence, reliable websites and recommendations for further reading from reliable sources.

I trust that it is clear to the reader why the material covered in each chapter is there and in what ways it is relevant to your work. This understanding and appreciation may, however, only emerge as you repeatedly revisit the subject matter and start applying it to your work.

The importance and the significance of the role played by the groomer in the care and maintenance of the dog's skin and coat have been emphasized throughout this book. Your role in promoting the health of the skin and indeed of the dog should not be overlooked or underestimated.

It may be helpful to reflect back on your learning and take stock of how far you have come.

Part 1 will have developed your understanding of how the dog evolved and how, in an incredibly short period of time, man has engineered dogs to look and react as they do. Learning about breed profiles should have prepared you for what to expect, and you will know how and when the breed took on its current role in our society, what the breed should look like, what is normal for the breed and what is abnormal. Familiarity and understanding of how this influences and impacts on a dog's morphology, temperament, health and of course on the dog's skin and hair coat are essential to your work.

Your knowledge of anatomy will help you to minimize injury when handling the dog, to understand how certain malfunctions and diseases may affect the work that you do and how the physical appearance of the dog can challenge you. Similarly, your growing understanding of your role in promoting the health and wellbeing of the dog by performing a thorough and detailed health examination should encourage you to act on your findings in the knowledge that you may prevent the development of illness, minimize suffering and even save lives.

Your understanding of the importance of parasite control and of the threat of infectious diseases should encourage you actively to implement control measures in your place of work. This helps to minimize the spread of disease and allows you to manage any health risks to you and the dogs in your care.

Part 2 will have helped you to design and set up your workspace, making sure that you can work safely, hygienically, legally and with due consideration to the environment in which we all live. Accidents do happen and the onset of illness can be sudden, but the First Aid section should have prepared and equipped you for the unexpected.

You are now able to understand the dog and communicate clearly with him. You can help each dog to understand what you are expecting of him and asking him to do. You will have learnt how to handle the dog and how, when and why you may need to restrain him in order to keep yourself and your staff safe from injury.

The minefield of equipment has been explored and you will have sorted yourself out with everything that you need to do your job safely and efficiently, with your comfort, your health and your budget informing each of your decisions.

In Part 3 we discussed the art of dog grooming. My task here was not to tell you what you have to do but rather what you can do and when you can do it. You will know what your tools are used for, how they work, how to handle them and how to maintain them.

Whilst there is no doubt that you need to learn the desired presentation for many breeds, it is not necessary for me to describe each in detail, so I have not done so. Your skill in the art of grooming will come from rehearsing what you have learnt, not by trying to copy a grooming diagram, not least because the dog on the table will be very different from the dog in the diagram. Every single dog is an individual and each would need his own diagram. All you need now is to look at them, hundreds of them, and train your mind's eye to 'see' the shape that you want to achieve. Work on synchronizing your eyes and your hands to work together, so you can 'see' where you need to remove hair, or where you need to grow it longer, to carve or create the illusion that you want to achieve. Develop your confidence and dexterity by practice, practice and more practice at using your tools. And, once you have achieved that, you will be able to style whatever shape you wish.

I have explained it to you, I have shown you – but I cannot practise it for you. And nor can any other book or tutor – it is now all down to you. Go for it and enjoy your grooming!

Acknowledgements

A very special thank you to Glen, without whom this book would probably still be in the making. Thank you for your encouragement, your help, your advice, your massive input with the first editing, particularly in Parts 1 and 2, for checking references, for your guidance and for putting up with me throughout this project. Your huge contribution is greatly appreciated. Hugs and tailwags!

Thank you also to The Kennel Club of Great Britain for allowing me to use their glossary of canine terms; Bayer Animal Health for providing parasitological photographs; Paula and Graham from Groomers Ltd (www.groomers-online.com) for all your help; SARDA for photographs of rescue dogs in action; Mel for all your help with typing; Ewan for dermatology advice and for writing the Foreword; Michael, for winging photographs across the globe at lightning speed; Simon for patiently waiting, camera at the ready; everyone who has let me use their dogs and their salons; the students who have let me photograph their work; my family and friends who have patiently waited for me to finish this mammoth task – life can begin again; and an enormous thank you to the thousands of students whose willingness and enthusiasm to learn have contributed such a lot to this book and to my life in so many ways. Our journeys together have taught me so much, and without you, this book would never have happened. It has been my pleasure to teach you and I am proud of you all.

Index